Praise for
The Ruby Way, Third Edition

"Sticking to its tried and tested formula of cutting right to the techniques the modern day Rubyist needs to know, the latest edition of *The Ruby Way* keeps its strong reputation going for the latest generation of the Ruby language."

Peter Cooper
Editor of *Ruby Weekly*

"The authors' excellent work and meticulous attention to detail continues in this latest update; this book remains an outstanding reference for the beginning Ruby programmer—as well as the seasoned developer who needs a quick refresh on Ruby. Highly recommended for anyone interested in Ruby programming."

Kelvin Meeks
Enterprise Architect

Praise for Previous Editions of
The Ruby Way

"Among other things, this book excels at explaining metaprogramming, one of the most interesting aspects of Ruby. Many of the early ideas for Rails were inspired by the first edition, especially what is now Chapter 11. It puts you on a rollercoaster ride between 'How could I use this?' and 'This is so cool!' Once you get on that rollercoaster, there's no turning back."

David Heinemeier Hansson
Creator of Ruby on Rails,
Founder at Basecamp

"The appearance of the second edition of this classic book is an exciting event for Rubyists—and for lovers of superb technical writing in general. Hal Fulton brings a lively erudition and an engaging, lucid style to bear on a thorough and meticulously exact exposition of Ruby. You palpably feel the presence of a teacher who knows a tremendous amount and really wants to help you know it too."

David Alan Black
Author of *The Well-Grounded Rubyist*

THE RUBY WAY

Third Edition

Hal Fulton

with André Arko

♠ Addison-Wesley

Upper Saddle River, NJ • Boston • Indianapolis • San Francisco
New York • Toronto • Montreal • London • Munich • Paris • Madrid
Cape Town • Sydney • Tokyo • Singapore • Mexico City

Library of Congress Control Number: 2014945504

ISBN-13: 978-0-321-71463-3
ISBN-10: 0-321-71463-6

Text printed in the United States on recycled paper at RR Donnelley in Crawfordsville, Indiana
First printing: March 2015

Editor-in-Chief
Mark Taub

Executive Editor
Debra Williams-Cauley

Development Editor
Songlin Qiu

Managing Editor
Kristy Hart

Project Editor
Andy Beaster

Copy Editor
Bart Reed

Indexer
Ken Johnson

Proofreader
Sarah Kearns

Cover Designer
Chuti Prasertsith

Senior Compositor
Gloria Schurick

To my parents, without whom I would not be possible
—Hal

Contents

12 Graphical Interfaces for Ruby   443

Foreword

Foreword to the Third Edition

Yesterday I was reading an article about geek fashion in `Wired.com`. According to it, wearing a Rubyconf 2012 t-shirt these days signals to people: "I work for Oracle."

Wow. How far we've come in the last 10 years!

For quite some time, using Ruby set you apart from the mainstream. Now it seems we are the mainstream. And what a long, strange journey it has been to get there.

Ruby adoption took a long time by today's standards. I read this book in 2005, and at that point, the first edition was over four years old. Ruby had just begun its second wave of adoption thanks to DHH and the start of Rails mania. It seemed like there might be a couple hundred people in the entire (English-speaking) world that used Ruby. Amazingly, at that point, the first edition of this book was already four years old. That's how ahead of its time it was.

This new edition keeps the writing style that has made the book such a hit with experienced programmers over the years. The long first chapter covers fundamental basics of object-orientation and the Ruby language. It's a must read for anyone new to the language. But it does so in concise, fast-moving narrative that assumes you already know how to create software.

From there, the chapters follow a distinctive pattern. A bit of backstory narrative, followed by rapid-fire bits of knowledge about the Ruby language. Snippets of example code are abundant and help to illuminate the concept under discussion. You can lift code samples verbatim into your programs. Especially once you get into the more practical applications chapters later in the book.

A brief bit of personal backstory seems appropriate. I owe a huge debt of gratitude to Hal for this book and the way that he wrote it. In 2005, I started work on a manuscript for Addison Wesley about the use of Ruby on Rails in the enterprise. It was my first attempt at authoring a book, and after penning about two chapters, I got stuck. Few people were using Ruby or Rails in the enterprise at that time and I had to remind myself that I was attempting to write non-fiction.

After discussing options with my editor, we determined that the best course of action might be to ditch the idea and start on a new one. *The Rails Way* was to cover the nascent Ruby on Rails framework in the style of this book. I employed terse narrative accompanying plentiful code examples. Instead of long listings, I interspersed commentary between sprinkles of code that provided just enough samples of the framework to make sense.

Like *The Ruby Way*, I aimed for breadth of coverage rather than depth. I wanted *The Rails Way* to claim permanent real estate on the desk of the serious Rails programmer. Like *The Ruby Way*, I wanted my book to be a default go-to reference. In contrast to other Rails books, I skipped tutorial material and ignored complete beginners.

And it was a huge success! Safe to say that without Hal's book, my own book would not exist and my career would have taken a less successful trajectory.

But enough congratulatory retrospective! Let's get back to the present day and the newest edition of *The Ruby Way* that you're currently reading. The immensely talented André Arko joins Hal this time around. What a great team! They deliver a painstaking revision that brings the book up to date with the latest edition of our beloved Ruby language.

My personal highlights of this edition include the following:

- A whole chapter of in-depth coverage of the new Onigmo regular expression engine. I love its beautiful and concise explanations of concepts such as positive and negative lookahead and lookbehind.

- The Internationalization chapter tackles thorny issues around String encoding and Unicode normalization. Bloggers have covered the subject in spotty fashion over the years, but having it all presented in one place is invaluable.

- The Ruby and Web Applications chapter manages to squeeze a crash-course in Rack, Sinatra, and Rails into less than 30 pages.

---

* Want proof of André's ingenuity? See how he cuts the load time for a real Rails app down to 500ms or less at http://andre.arko.net/2014/06/27/rails-in-05-seconds/.

I predict that this edition of *The Ruby Way* will be as successful as its predecessors. It gives me great joy to make it the latest addition to our Professional Ruby Series.

Obie Fernandez
September 15, 2014

Foreword to the Second Edition

In ancient China, people, especially philosophers, thought that something was hidden behind the world and every existence. It can never be told, nor explained, nor described in concrete words. They called it *Tao* in Chinese and *Do* in Japanese. If you translate it into English, it is the word for *Way*. It is the *Do* in Judo, Kendo, Karatedo, and Aikido. They are not only martial arts, but they also include a philosophy and a way of life.

Likewise, Ruby the programming language has its philosophy and way of thinking. It enlightens people to think differently. It helps programmers have more fun in their work. It is not because Ruby is from Japan but because programming is an important part of the human being (well, at least *some* human beings), and Ruby is designed to help people have a better life.

As always, "Tao" is difficult to describe. I feel it but have never tried to explain it in words. It's just too difficult for me, even in Japanese, my native tongue. But a guy named Hal Fulton tried, and his first try (the first edition of this book) was pretty good. This second version of his trial to describe the Tao of Ruby becomes even better with help from many people in the Ruby community. As Ruby becomes more popular (partly due to Ruby on Rails), it becomes more important to understand the secret of programmers' productivity. I hope this book helps you to become an efficient programmer.

Happy Hacking.

Yukihiro "Matz" Matsumoto
August 2006, Japan
まつもと ゆきひろ

Foreword to the First Edition

Shortly after I first met with computers in the early 80s, I became interested in programming languages. Since then I have been a "language geek." I think the reason for this interest is that programming languages are ways to express human thought. They are fundamentally human-oriented.

Despite this fact, programming languages have tended to be machine-oriented. Many languages were designed for the convenience of the computer.

But as computers became more powerful and less expensive, this situation gradually changed. For example, look at structured programming. Machines do not care whether programs are structured well; they just execute them bit by bit. Structured programming is not for machines, but for humans. This is true of object-oriented programming as well.

The time for language design focusing on humans has been coming.

In 1993, I was talking with a colleague about scripting languages, about their power and future. I felt scripting to be the way future programming should be—human-oriented.

But I was not satisfied with existing languages such as Perl and Python. I wanted a language that was more powerful than Perl and more object-oriented than Python. I couldn't find the ideal language, so I decided to make my own.

Ruby is not the simplest language, but the human soul is not simple in its natural state. It loves simplicity and complexity at the same time. It can't handle too many complex things, nor too many simple things. It's a matter of balance.

So to design a human-oriented language, Ruby, I followed the Principle of Least Surprise. I consider that everything that surprises me less is good. As a result, I feel a natural feeling, even a kind of joy, when programming in Ruby. And since the first release of Ruby in 1995, many programmers worldwide have agreed with me about the joy of Ruby programming.

As always I'd like to express my greatest appreciation to the people in the Ruby community. They are the heart of Ruby's success.

I am also thankful to the author of this book, Hal E. Fulton, for declaring the Ruby Way to help people.

This book explains the philosophy behind Ruby, distilled from my brain and the Ruby community. I wonder how it can be possible for Hal to read my mind to know and reveal this secret of the Ruby Way. I have never met him face to face; I hope to meet him soon.

I hope this book and Ruby both serve to make your programming fun and happy.

Yukihiro "Matz" Matsumoto
September 2001, Japan
まつもと ゆきひろ

Acknowledgments

Acknowledgments for the Third Edition

As can be expected by now, the process of updating this book for the third edition turned out to be somewhat monumental. Ruby has changed dramatically since the days of 1.8, and being a Ruby programmer is far more popular now than it has ever been before.

Verifying, updating, and rewriting this book took quite some time longer than expected. Ruby has progressed from 1.9 through 2.0 and 2.1, and this book has progressed through at least as many edits and rewrites along the way.

Many people contributed to making this book possible. At Addison-Wesley, Debra Williams Cauley, Songlin Qiu, Andy Beaster, and Bart Reed provided the encouragement, coordination, and editing needed to complete this edition. The contributions of Russ Olsen and André Arko were *absolutely invaluable*.

This edition was technically edited by Russ Olsen and Steve Klabnik, providing feedback and suggestions that made the book more accurate and understandable. Russ also provided the Ruby libraries and scripts that compiled the latest version of the book itself. As always, any errors are mine, not theirs.

Suggestions, code samples, or simply helpful explanations were provided by Dave Thomas, David Alan Black, Eric Hodel, Chad Fowler, Brad Ediger, Sven Fuchs, Jesse Storimer, Luke Francl, and others over the years.

Special thanks go to Paul Harrison and the rest of my colleagues at Simpli.fi for their encouragement and support.

I also wish to honor the memory of Guy Decoux and more recently Jim Weirich. Jim in particular made significant contributions to this book and to our community.

Final thanks are owed, as always, to Matz himself for creating Ruby, and to you, the reader of this book. I hope it is able to teach, inform, and maybe even amuse you.

Acknowledgments for the Second Edition

Common sense says that a second edition will only require half as much work as the first edition required. Common sense is wrong.

Even though a large part of this book came directly from the first edition, even that part had to be tweaked and tuned. Every single sentence in this book had to pass through (at the very least) a filter that asked: Is what was true in 2001 still true in 2006? And that, of course, was only the beginning.

In short, I put in many hundreds of hours of work on this second edition—nearly as much time as on the first. And yet I am "only the author."

A book is possible only through the teamwork of many people. On the publisher's side, I owe thanks to Debra Williams-Cauley, Songlin Qiu, and Mandie Frank for their hard work and infinite patience. Thanks go to Geneil Breeze for her tireless copy editing and picking bits of lint from my English. There are also others I can't name because their work was completely behind the scenes, and I never talked with them.

Technical editing was done primarily by Shashank Date and Francis Hwang. They did a great job, and I appreciate it. Errors that slipped through are my responsibility, of course.

Thanks go to the people who supplied explanations, wrote sample code, and answered numerous questions for me. These include Matz himself (Yukihiro Matsumoto), Dave Thomas, Christian Neukirchen, Chad Fowler, Curt Hibbs, Daniel Berger, Armin Roehrl, Stefan Schmiedl, Jim Weirich, Ryan Davis, Jenny W., Jim Freeze, Lyle Johnson, Martin DeMello, Matt Lawrence, the infamous *why the lucky stiff*, Ron Jeffries, Tim Hunter, Chet Hendrickson, Nathaniel Talbott, and Bil Kleb.

Special thanks goes to the heavier contributors. Andrew Johnson greatly enhanced my regular expression knowledge. Paul Battley made great contributions to the internationalization chapter. Masao Mutoh added to that same chapter and also contributed material on GTK. Austin Ziegler taught me the secrets of writing PDF files. Caleb Tennis added to the Qt material. Eric Hodel added to the Rinda and Ring material, and James Britt contributed heavily to the web development chapter.

Thanks and appreciation again must go to Matz, not only for his assistance but for creating Ruby in the first place. *Domo arigato gozaimasu*!

Again I have to thank my parents. They have encouraged me without ceasing and are looking forward to seeing this book. I will make programmers of them both yet.

And once again, I have to thank all of the Ruby community for their tireless energy, productivity, and community spirit. I particularly thank the readers of this book (in both editions). I hope you find it informative, useful, and perhaps even entertaining.

Acknowledgments for the First Edition

Writing a book is truly a team effort; this is a fact I could not fully appreciate until I wrote one myself. I recommend the experience, although it is a humbling one. It is a simple truth that without the assistance of many other people, this book would not have existed.

Thanks and appreciation must first go to Matz (Yukihiro Matsumoto), who created the Ruby language in the first place. Domo arigato gozaimasu!

Thanks goes to Conrad Schneiker for conceiving the overall idea for the book and helping to create its overall structure. He also did me the service of introducing me to the Ruby language in 1999.

Several individuals have contributed material to the body of the book. The foremost of these was Guy Hurst, who wrote substantial parts of the earlier chapters as well as two of the appendices. His assistance was absolutely invaluable.

Thanks also goes to the other contributors, whom I'll name in no particular order. Kevin Smith did a great job on the GTK section of Chapter 6, saving me from a potentially steep learning curve on a tight schedule. Patrick Logan, in the same chapter, shed light on the mysteries of the FOX GUI. Chad Fowler, in Chapter 9, plumbed the depths of XML and also contributed to the CGI section.

Thanks to those who assisted in proofreading or reviewing or in other miscellaneous ways: Don Muchow, Mike Stok, Miho Ogishima, and others already mentioned. Thanks to David Eppstein, the mathematics professor, for answering questions about graph theory.

One of the great things about Ruby is the support of the community. There were many on the mailing list and the newsgroup who answered questions and gave me ideas and assistance. Again in no particular order, these are Dave Thomas, Andy Hunt, Hee-Sob Park, Mike Wilson, Avi Bryant, Yasushi Shoji ("Yashi"), Shugo Maeda, Jim Weirich, "arton," and Masaki Suketa. I'm sorry to say I have probably overlooked someone.

To state the obvious, a book would never be published without a publisher. Many people behind the scenes worked hard to produce this book; primarily I have to thank William Brown, who worked closely with me and was a constant source of encouragement; and Scott Meyer, who delved deeply into the details of putting the material together. Others I cannot even name because I have never heard of them. You know who you are.

I have to thank my parents, who watched this project from a distance, encouraged me along the way, and even bothered to learn a little bit of computer science for my sake.

A writer friend of mine once told me, "If you write a book and nobody reads it, you haven't really written a book." So, finally, I want to thank the reader. This book is for you. I hope it is of some value.

About the Authors

Hal Fulton first began using Ruby in 1999. In 2001, he started work on *The Ruby Way*, which was the second Ruby book published in English. Fulton was an attendee at the very first Ruby conference in 2001 and has presented at numerous other Ruby conferences on three continents, including the first European Ruby Conference in 2003. He holds two degrees in computer science from the University of Mississippi and taught computer science for four years. He has worked for more than 25 years with various forms of UNIX and Linux. He is now at Simpli.fi in Fort Worth, Texas, where he works primarily in Ruby.

André Arko first encountered Ruby as a student in 2004, and reading the first edition of this book helped him decide to pursue a career as a Ruby programmer. He is team lead of Bundler, the Ruby dependency manager, and has created or contributes to dozens of other open source projects. He works at Cloud City Development as a consultant providing team training and expertise on Ruby and Rails as well as developing web applications.

André enjoys sharing hard-won knowledge and experience with other developers, and has spoken at over a dozen Ruby conferences on four continents. He is a regular volunteer at RailsBridge and RailsGirls programming outreach events, and works to increase diversity and inclusiveness in both the Ruby community and technology as a field. He lives in San Francisco, California.

Introduction

The way that can be named is not the true Way.

—*Lao Tse,* Tao Te Ching

The title of this book is *The Ruby Way.* This is a title that begs for a disclaimer.

It has been my aim to align this book with the philosophy of Ruby as well as I could. That has also been the aim of the other contributors. Credit for success must be shared with these others, but the blame for any mistakes must rest solely with me.

Of course, I can't presume to tell you with exactness what the spirit of Ruby is all about. That is primarily for Matz to say, and I think even he would have difficulty communicating all of it in words.

In short, *The Ruby Way* is only a book, but the Ruby Way is the province of the language creator and the community as a whole. This is something difficult to capture in a book.

Still, I have tried in this introduction to pin down a little of the ineffable spirit of Ruby. The wise student of Ruby will not take it as totally authoritative.

About the Third Edition

Everything changes, and Ruby is no exception. There are many changes and much new material in this edition. In a larger sense, every single chapter in this book is "new." I have revised and updated every one of them, making hundreds of minor changes and dozens of major changes. I deleted items that were obsolete or of lesser importance; I changed material to fit changes in Ruby itself; I added examples and commentary to every chapter.

As the second Ruby book in the English language (after *Programming Ruby*, by Dave Thomas and Andy Hunt), *The Ruby Way was* designed to be complementary to that book rather than overlap with it; that is still true today.

There have been numerous changes between Ruby 1.8, covered in the second edition, and Ruby 2.1, covered here. It's important to realize, however, that these were made with great care, over several years. Ruby is still Ruby. Much of the beauty of Ruby is derived from the fact that it changes slowly and deliberately, crafted by the wisdom of Matz and the other developers.

Today we have a proliferation of books on Ruby and more articles published than we can bother to notice. Web-based tutorials and documentation resources abound.

New tools and libraries have appeared. The most common of these seem to be tools by developers for other developers: web frameworks, blogging tools, markup tools, and interfaces to exotic data stores. But there are many others, of course—GUIs, number-crunching, web services, image manipulation, source control, and more.

Ruby editor support is widespread and sophisticated. IDEs are available that are useful and mature (and which share some overlap with the GUI builders).

It's also undeniable that the community has grown and changed. Ruby is by no means a niche language today; it is used in government departments such as NASA and NOAA, enterprise companies such as IBM and Motorola, and well-known websites such as Wikipedia, GitHub, and Twitter. It is used for graphics work, database work, numerical analysis, web development, and more. In short—and I mean this in the positive sense—Ruby has gone mainstream.

Updating this book has been a labor of love. I hope it is useful to you.

How This Book Works

You probably won't learn Ruby from this book. There is relatively little in the way of introductóry or tutorial information. If you are totally new to Ruby, you might want start with another book.

Having said that, programmers are a tenacious bunch, and I grant that it might be possible to learn Ruby from this book. Chapter 1, "Ruby in Review," does contain a brief introduction and some tutorial information.

Chapter 1 also contains a comprehensive "gotcha" list (which has been difficult to keep up to date). The usefulness of this list in Chapter 1 will vary widely from one reader to another because we cannot all agree on what is intuitive.

This book is largely intended to answer questions of the form "How do I...?." As such, you can expect to do a lot of skipping around. I'd be honored if everyone read every page from front to back, but I don't expect that. It's more my expectation that you will browse the table of contents in search of techniques you need or things you find interesting.

As it turns out, I have talked to many people since the first edition, and they *did* in fact read it cover to cover. What's more, I have had more than one person report to me that they did learn Ruby here. So anything is possible.

Some things this book covers may seem elementary. That is because people vary in background and experience; what is obvious to one person may not be to another. I have tried to err on the side of completeness. On the other hand, I have tried to keep the book at a reasonable size (obviously a competing goal).

This book can be viewed as a sort of "inverted reference." Rather than looking up the name of a method or a class, you will look things up by function or purpose. For example, the `String` class has several methods for manipulating case: `capitalize`, `upcase`, `casecmp`, `downcase`, and `swapcase`. In a reference work, these would quite properly be listed alphabetically, but in this book they are all listed together.

Of course, in striving for completeness, I have sometimes wandered onto the turf of the reference books. In many cases, I have tried to compensate for this by offering more unusual or diverse examples than you might find in a reference.

I have tried for a high code-to-commentary ratio. Overlooking the initial chapter, I think I've achieved this. Writers may grow chatty, but programmers always want to see the code. (If not, they *should* want to.)

The examples here are sometimes contrived, for which I must apologize. To illustrate a technique or principle *in isolation from a real-world problem* can be difficult. However, the more complex or high level the task was, the more I attempted a real-world solution. Thus, if the topic is concatenating strings, you may find an unimaginative code fragment involving `"foo"` and `"bar"`, but when the topic is something like parsing XML, you will usually find a much more meaningful and realistic piece of code.

This book has two or three small quirks to which I'll confess up front. One is the avoidance of the "ugly" Perl-like global variables such as `$_` and the others. These are present in Ruby, and they work fine; they are used daily by most or all Ruby programmers. But in nearly all cases, their use can be avoided, and I have taken the liberty of omitting them in most of the examples.

Another quirk is that I avoid using standalone expressions when they don't have side effects. Ruby is expression oriented, and that is a good thing; I have tried to take advantage of that feature. But in a code fragment, I prefer to not write expressions that merely return a value that is not usable. For example, the expression `"abc" + "def"` can illustrate string concatenation, but I would write something like `str = "abc" + "def"` instead. This may seem wordy to some, but it may seem more natural to you if you are a C programmer who really notices when functions are void or nonvoid (or an old-time Pascal programmer who thinks in procedures and functions).

My third quirk is that I don't like the "pound" notation to denote instance methods. Many Rubyists will think I am being verbose in saying "instance method `crypt` of class `String`" rather than saying `String#crypt`, but I think no one will be confused. (Actually, I am slowly being converted to this usage, as it is obvious the pound notation is not going away.)

I have tried to include "pointers" to outside resources whenever appropriate. Time and space did not allow putting everything into this book that I wanted, but I hope I have partially made up for that by telling you where to find related materials. The ruby-doc.org and rdoc.info websites are probably the foremost of these sources; you will see them referenced many times in this book.

Here, at the front of the book, there is usually a gratuitous reference to the typefaces used for code, and how to tell code fragments from ordinary text. But I won't insult your intelligence; you've read computer books before.

I want to point out that roughly 10 percent of this book was written by other people. That does not even include tech editing and copy editing. You should read the acknowledgments in this (and every) book. Most readers skip them. Go read them now. They're good for you, like vegetables.

About the Book's Source Code

Every significant code fragment has been collected into an archive for the reader to download. Look for this archive on the informit.com site or at the book's own site, therubyway.io.

It is offered both as a `.tgz` file and as a `.zip` file. Code fragments that are very short or can't be run "out of context" will usually not appear in the archive.

What Is the "Ruby Way"?

> *Let us prepare to grapple with the ineffable itself, and see if we may not eff it after all.*
>
> —*Douglas Adams,* Dirk Gently's Holistic Detective Agency

What do we mean by the Ruby Way? My belief is that there are two related aspects: One is the philosophy of the design of Ruby; the other is the philosophy of its usage. It is natural that design and use should be interrelated, whether in software or hardware; why else should there be such a field as ergonomics? If I build a device and put a handle on it, it is because I expect someone to grab that handle.

Ruby has a nameless quality that makes it what it is. We see that quality present in the design of the syntax and semantics of the language, but it is also present in the programs written for that interpreter. Yet as soon as we make this distinction, we blur it.

Clearly Ruby is not just a tool for creating software, but it is a piece of software in its own right. Why should the workings of Ruby *programs* follow laws different from those that guide the workings of the *interpreter*? After all, Ruby is highly dynamic and extensible. There might be reasons that the two levels should differ here and there, probably for accommodating to the inconvenience of the real world. But in general, the thought processes can and should be the same. Ruby could be implemented in Ruby, in true Hofstadter-like fashion, though it is not at the time of this writing.

We don't often think of the etymology of the word *way*, but there are two important senses in which it is used. On the one hand, it means *a method or technique*, but it can also mean *a road or path*. Obviously these two meanings are interrelated, and I think when I say "the Ruby Way," I mean both of them.

So what we are talking about is a thought process, but it is also a path that we follow. Even the greatest software guru cannot claim to have reached perfection but only to follow the path. And there may be more than one path, but here I can only talk about one.

The conventional wisdom says that *form follows function*. And the conventional wisdom is, of course, conventionally correct. But Frank Lloyd Wright (speaking in his own field) once said, "Form follows function—that has been misunderstood. Form and function should be one, joined in a spiritual union."

What did Wright mean? I would say that this truth is not something you learn from a book, but from experience.

However, I would argue that Wright expressed this truth elsewhere in pieces easier to digest. He was a great proponent of simplicity, saying once, "An architect's most useful tools are an eraser at the drafting board and a wrecking bar at the site."

So, one of Ruby's virtues is simplicity. Shall I quote other thinkers on the subject? According to Antoine de St. Exupéry, "Perfection is achieved, not when there is nothing left to add, but when there is nothing left to take away."

But Ruby is a complex language. How can I say that it is simple?

If we understood the universe better, we might find a "law of conservation of complexity"—a fact of reality that disturbs our lives like entropy so that we cannot avoid it but can only redistribute it.

And that is the key. We can't avoid complexity, but we can push it around. We can bury it out of sight. This is the old "black box" principle at work; a black box performs a complex task, but it possesses simplicity *on the outside.*

If you haven't already lost patience with my quotations, a word from Albert Einstein is appropriate here: "Everything should be as simple as possible, but no simpler."

So in Ruby, we see simplicity embodied from the programmer's view (if not from the view of those maintaining the interpreter). Yet we also see the capacity for compromise. In the real world, we must bend a little. For example, every entity in a Ruby program should be a true object, but certain values such as integers are stored as immediate values. In a trade-off familiar to computer science students for decades, we have traded elegance of design for practicality of implementation. In effect, we have traded one kind of simplicity for another.

What Larry Wall said about Perl holds true: "When you say something in a small language, it comes out big. When you say something in a big language, it comes out small." The same is true for English. The reason that biologist Ernst Haeckel could say "Ontogeny recapitulates phylogeny" in only three words was that he had these powerful words with highly specific meanings at his disposal. We allow inner complexity of the language because it enables us to shift the complexity away from the individual utterance.

I would state this guideline this way: Don't write 200 lines of code when ten will do.

I'm taking it for granted that brevity is generally a good thing. A short program fragment will take up less space in the programmer's brain; it will be easier to grasp as a single entity. As a happy side effect, fewer bugs will be injected while the code is being written.

Of course, we must remember Einstein's warning about simplicity. If we put brevity too high on our list of priorities, we will end up with code that is hopelessly obfuscated. Information theory teaches us that compressed data is statistically similar to random noise; if you have looked at C or APL or regular expression notation—especially badly written—you have experienced this truth firsthand. "Simple, but not too simple"; that is the key. Embrace brevity, but do not sacrifice readability.

It is a truism that both brevity and readability are good. But there is an underlying reason for this—one so fundamental that we sometimes forget it. The reason is that computers exist for humans, not humans for computers.

In the old days, it was almost the opposite. Computers cost millions of dollars and ate electricity at the rate of many kilowatts. People acted as though the computer was a minor deity and the programmers were humble supplicants. An hour of the computer's time was more expensive than an hour of a person's time.

When computers became smaller and cheaper, high-level languages also became more popular. These were inefficient from the computer's point of view but efficient from the human perspective. Ruby is simply a later development in this line of thought. Some, in fact, have called it a *VHLL* (Very High-Level Language); though this term is not well-defined, I think its use is justified here.

The computer is supposed to be the servant, not the master, and, as Matz has said, a smart servant should do a complex task with a few short commands. This has been true through all the history of computer science. We started with machine languages and progressed to assembly language and then to high-level languages.

What we are talking about here is a shift from a *machine-centered* paradigm to a *human-centered* one. In my opinion, Ruby is an excellent example of human-centric programming.

I'll shift gears a little. There was a wonderful little book from the 1980s called *The Tao of Programming* (by Geoffrey James). Nearly every line is quotable, but I'll repeat only this: "A program should follow the 'Law of Least Astonishment.' What is this law? It is simply that the program should always respond to the user in the way that astonishes him least." (Of course, in the case of a language interpreter, the *user* is the programmer.)

I don't know whether James coined this term, but his book was my first introduction to the phrase. This is a principle that is well known and often cited in the Ruby community, though it is usually called the *Principle of Least Surprise*, or *POLS*. (I myself stubbornly prefer the acronym *LOLA*.)

Whatever you call it, this rule is a valid one, and it has been a guideline throughout the ongoing development of the Ruby language. It is also a useful guideline for those who develop libraries or user interfaces.

The only problem, of course, is that different people are surprised by different things; there is no universal agreement on how an object or method "ought" to behave. We can strive for consistency and strive to justify our design decisions, and each person can train his own intuition.

For the record, Matz has said that "least surprise" should refer to *him* as the designer. The more you think like him, the less Ruby will surprise you. And I assure you, imitating Matz is not a bad idea for most of us.

No matter how logically constructed a system may be, your intuition needs to be trained. Each programming language is a world unto itself, with its own set of assumptions, and human languages are the same. When I took German, I learned that all nouns were capitalized, but the word *deutsch* was not. I complained to my professor; after all, this was the *name* of the language, wasn't it? He smiled and said, "Don't fight it."

What he taught me was to *let German be German*. By extension, that is good advice for anyone coming to Ruby from some other language. Let Ruby be Ruby. Don't expect it to be Perl, because it isn't; don't expect it to be LISP or Smalltalk, either. On the other hand, Ruby has common elements with all three of these. Start by following your expectations, but when they are violated, don't fight it (unless Matz agrees it's a needed change).

Every programmer today knows the orthogonality principle (which would better be termed the *orthogonal completeness principle*). Suppose we have an imaginary pair of axes with a set of comparable language entities on one and a set of attributes or capabilities on the other. When we talk of "orthogonality," we usually mean that the space defined by these axes is as "full" as we can logically make it.

Part of the Ruby Way is to strive for this orthogonality. An array is in some ways similar to a hash, so the operations on each of them should be similar. The limit is reached when we enter the areas where they are different.

Matz has said that "naturalness" is to be valued over orthogonality. But to fully understand what is natural and what is not may take some thinking and some coding.

Ruby strives to be friendly to the programmer. For example, there are aliases or synonyms for many method names; `size` and `length` will both return the number of entries in an array. Some consider this sort of thing to be an annoyance or anti-feature, but I consider it a good design.

Ruby strives for consistency and regularity. There is nothing mysterious about this; in every aspect of life, we yearn for things to be regular and parallel. What makes it a little more tricky is learning when to violate this principle.

For instance, Ruby has the habit of appending a question mark (?) to the name of a predicate-like method. This is well and good; it clarifies the code and makes the namespace a little more manageable. But what is more controversial is the similar use of the exclamation point in marking methods that are "destructive" or "dangerous" in the sense that they modify their receivers. The controversy arises because *not all* of the destructive methods are marked in this way. Shouldn't we be consistent?

No, in fact we should not. Some of the methods by their very nature change their receiver (such as the `Array` methods `replace` and `concat`). Some of them are "writer" methods allowing assignment to a class attribute; we should *not* append an exclamation point to the attribute name or the equal sign. Some methods arguably change the state of the receiver, such as `read`; this occurs too frequently to be marked in this way. If every destructive method name ended in a !, our programs soon would look like sales brochures for a multilevel marketing firm.

Do you notice a kind of tension between opposing forces, a tendency for all rules to be violated? Let me state this as Fulton's Second Law: *Every rule has an exception, except Fulton's Second Law.* (Yes, there is a joke there, a very small one.)

What we see in Ruby is not a "foolish consistency" nor a rigid adherence to a set of simple rules. In fact, perhaps part of the Ruby Way is that it is *not* a rigid and inflexible approach. In language design, as Matz once said, you should "follow your heart."

Yet another aspect of the Ruby philosophy is, do *not fear change at runtime; do not fear what is dynamic.* The world is dynamic; why should a programming language be static? Ruby is one of the most dynamic languages in existence.

I would also argue that another aspect is, do not be a slave to performance issues. When performance is unacceptable, the issue must be addressed, but it should normally not be the first thing you think about. Prefer elegance over efficiency where efficiency is less than critical. Then again, if you are writing a library that may be used in unforeseen ways, performance may be critical from the start.

When I look at Ruby, I perceive a balance between different design goals, a complex interaction reminiscent of the *n*-body problem in physics. I can imagine it might be modeled as an Alexander Calder mobile. It is perhaps this interaction itself, the harmony, that embodies Ruby's philosophy rather than just the individual parts. Programmers know that their craft is not just science and technology but art. I hesitate to say that there is a spiritual aspect to computer science, but just between you and me, there certainly is. (If you have not read Robert Pirsig's *Zen and the Art of Motorcycle Maintenance*, I recommend that you do so.)

Ruby arose from the human urge to create things that are useful and beautiful. Programs written in Ruby should spring from the same source. That, to me, is the essence of the Ruby Way.

CHAPTER 1

Ruby in Review

Language shapes the way we think and determines what we can think about.

—*Benjamin Lee Whorf*

It is worth remembering that a new programming language is sometimes viewed as a panacea, especially by its adherents. But no one language will supplant all the others; no one tool is unarguably the best for every possible task. There are many different problem domains in the world and many possible constraints on problems within those domains.

Above all, there are different ways of *thinking* about these problems, stemming from the diverse backgrounds and personalities of the programmers themselves. For these reasons, there is no foreseeable end to the proliferation of languages. And as long as there is a multiplicity of languages, there will be a multiplicity of personalities defending and attacking them. In short, there will always be "language wars"; in this book, however, we do not intend to participate in them.

Yet in the constant quest for newer and better program notations, we have stumbled across ideas that endure, that transcend the context in which they were created. Just as Pascal borrowed from Algol, just as Java borrowed from C, so will every language borrow from its predecessors.

A language is both a toolbox and a playground; it has a practical side, but it also serves as a test bed for new ideas that may or may not be widely accepted by the computing community.

One of the most far-reaching of these ideas is the concept of object-oriented programming (OOP). Although many would argue that the overall significance of OOP is evolutionary rather than revolutionary, no one can say that it has not had an impact on the industry. Twenty-five years ago, object orientation was for the most part an academic curiosity; today it is a universally accepted paradigm.

In fact, the ubiquitous nature of OOP has led to a significant amount of "hype" in the industry. In a classic paper of the late 1980s, Roger King observed, "If you want to sell a cat to a computer scientist, you have to tell him it's object-oriented." Additionally, there are differences of opinion about what OOP really is, and even among those who are essentially in agreement, there are differences in terminology.

It is not our purpose here to contribute to the hype. We do find OOP to be a useful tool and a meaningful way of thinking about problems; we do not claim that it cures cancer.

As for the exact nature of OOP, we have our pet definitions and favorite terminology; but we make these known only to communicate effectively, not to quibble over semantics.

We mention all this because it is necessary to have a basic understanding of OOP to proceed to the bulk of this book and understand the examples and techniques. Whatever else might be said about Ruby, it is definitely an object-oriented language.

1.1   An Introduction to Object Orientation

Before talking about Ruby specifically, it is a good idea to talk about object-oriented programming in the abstract. These first few pages review those concepts with only cursory references to Ruby before we proceed to a review of the Ruby language itself.

1.1.1   What Is an Object?

In object-oriented programming, the fundamental unit is the *object*. An object is an entity that serves as a container for data and also controls access to the data. Associated with an object is a set of *attributes*, which are essentially no more than variables belonging to the object. (In this book, we will loosely use the ordinary term *variable* for an attribute.) Also associated with an object is a set of functions that provide an interface to the functionality of the object, called *methods*.

It is essential that any OOP language provide *encapsulation*. As the term is commonly used, it means first that the attributes and methods of an object are associated specifically with that object, or bundled with it; second, it means that the scope of those attributes and methods is by default the object itself (an application of the principle of *data hiding*).

An object is considered to be an instance or manifestation of an *object class* (usually simply called a *class*). The class may be thought of as the blueprint or pattern; the object itself is the thing created from that blueprint or pattern. A class is often thought of as an *abstract type*—a more complex type than, for example, an integer or character string.

When an object (an instance of a class) is created, it is said to be *instantiated*. Some languages have the notion of an explicit *constructor* and *destructor* for an object—functions that perform whatever tasks are needed to initialize an object and (respectively) to "destroy" it. We may as well mention prematurely that Ruby has what might be considered a constructor but certainly does not have any concept of a destructor (because of its well-behaved garbage collection mechanism).

Occasionally a situation arises in which a piece of data is more "global" in scope than a single object, and it is inappropriate to put a copy of the attribute into each instance of the class. For example, consider a class called MyDogs, from which three objects are created: fido, rover, and spot. For each dog, there might be such attributes as age and date of vaccination. But suppose that we want to store the owner's name (the owner of *all* the dogs). We could certainly put it in each object, but that is wasteful of memory and at the very least a misleading design. Clearly the *owner_name* attribute belongs not to any individual object but to the class itself. When it is defined that way (and the syntax varies from one language to another), it is called a class attribute (or *class variable*).

Of course, there are many situations in which a class variable might be needed. For example, suppose that we wanted to keep a count of how many objects of a certain class had been created. We could use a class variable that was initialized to zero and incremented with every instantiation; the class variable would be associated with the class and not with any particular object. In scope, this variable would be just like any other attribute, but there would only be one copy of it for the entire class and the entire set of objects created from that class.

To distinguish between class attributes and ordinary attributes, the latter are sometimes explicitly called *object attributes* (or *instance attributes*). We use the convention that any attribute is assumed to be an instance attribute unless we explicitly call it a class attribute.

Just as an object's methods are used to control access to its attributes and provide a clean interface to them, so is it sometimes appropriate or necessary to define a method associated with a class. A *class method*, not surprisingly, controls access to the class variables and also performs any tasks that might have classwide effects rather than merely objectwide. As with data attributes, methods are assumed to belong to the object rather than the class unless stated otherwise.

It is worth mentioning that there is a sense in which all methods are class methods. We should not suppose that when 100 objects are created, we actually copy the code for the methods 100 times! But the rules of scope assure us that each object method operates only on the object whose method is being called, providing us with the necessary illusion that object methods are associated strictly with their objects.

1.1.2   Inheritance

We come now to one of the real strengths of OOP, which is *inheritance*. Inheritance is a mechanism that allows us to extend a previously existing entity by adding features to create a new entity. In short, inheritance is a way of reusing code. (Easy, effective code reuse has long been the Holy Grail of computer science, resulting in the invention decades ago of parameterized subroutines and code libraries. OOP is only one of the later efforts in realizing this goal.)

Typically we think of inheritance at the class level. If we have a specific class in mind, and there is a more general case already in existence, we can define our new class to inherit the features of the old one. For example, suppose that we have a class named `Polygon` that describes convex polygons. If we then find ourselves dealing with a `Rectangle` class, we can inherit from `Polygon` so that `Rectangle` has all the attributes and methods that `Polygon` has. For example, there might be a method that calculates perimeter by iterating over all the sides and adding their lengths. Assuming that everything was implemented properly, this method would automatically work for the new class; the code would not have to be rewritten.

When a class B inherits from a class A, we say that B is a *subclass* of A, or conversely A is the *superclass* of B. In slightly different terminology, we may say that A is a *base class* or *parent class,* and B is a *derived class* or *child class.*

A derived class, as we have seen, may treat a method inherited from its base class as if it were its own. On the other hand, it may redefine that method entirely if it is necessary to provide a different implementation; this is referred to as *overriding* a method. In addition, most languages provide a way for an overridden method to call its namesake in the parent class; that is, the method `foo` in B knows how to call method `foo` in A if it wants to. (Any language that does not provide this feature is under suspicion of not being truly object oriented.) Essentially the same is true for data attributes.

The relationship between a class and its superclass is interesting and important; it is usually described as the *is-a* relationship, because a `Square` "is a" `Rectangle`, and a `Rectangle` "is a" `Polygon`, and so on. Thus, if we create an inheritance hierarchy (which tends to exist in one form or another in any OOP language), we see that the more specific entity "is a" subclass of the more general entity at any given point in the hierarchy. Note that this relationship is transitive—in the previous example, we easily see that a `Square` "is a" `Polygon`. Note also that the relationship is not commutative—we know that every `Rectangle` is a `Polygon`, but not every `Polygon` is a `Rectangle`.

This brings us to the topic of *multiple inheritance* (MI). It is conceivable that a new class could inherit from more than one class. For example, the classes `Dog` and `Cat` can both inherit from the class `Mammal`, and `Sparrow` and `Raven` can inherit from `WingedCreature`. But what if we want to define a `Bat`? It can reasonably inherit from both the classes `Mammal` and `WingedCreature`. This corresponds well with our real-life experience in which things are not members of just one category but of many non-nested categories.

MI is probably the most controversial area in OOP. One camp will point out the potential for ambiguity that must be resolved. For example, if `Mammal` and `WingedCreature` both have an attribute called `size` (or a method called `eat`), which one will be referenced when we refer to it from a `Bat` object? Another related difficulty is the *diamond inheritance problem*—so called because of the shape of its inheritance diagram, with both superclasses inheriting from a single common superclass. For example, imagine that `Mammal` and `WingedCreature` both inherit from `Organism`; the hierarchy from `Organism` to `Bat` forms a diamond. But what about the attributes that the two intermediate classes both inherit from their parent? Does `Bat` get two copies of each of them? Or are they merged back into single attributes because they come from a common ancestor in the first place?

These are both issues for the language designer rather than the programmer. Different OOP languages deal with the issues differently. Some provide rules allowing one definition of an attribute to "win out," or a way to distinguish between attributes of the same name, or even a way of aliasing or renaming the identifiers. This in itself is considered by many to be an argument against MI—the mechanisms for dealing with name clashes and the like are not universally agreed upon but are language dependent. C++ offers a minimal set of features for dealing with ambiguities; those of Eiffel are probably better, and those of Perl are different from both.

The alternative, of course, is to disallow MI altogether. This is the approach taken by such languages as Java and Ruby. This sounds like a drastic compromise; however, as we shall see later, it is not as bad as it sounds. We will look at a viable alternative to traditional MI, but we must first discuss polymorphism, yet another OOP buzzword.

1.1.3   Polymorphism

Polymorphism is the term that perhaps inspires the most semantic disagreement in the field. Everyone seems to know what it is, but everyone has a different definition. (In recent years, "What is polymorphism?" has become a popular interview question. If it is asked of you, I recommend quoting an expert such as Bertrand Meyer or Bjarne Stroustrup; that way, if the interviewer disagrees, his beef is with the expert and not with you.)

The literal meaning of polymorphism is "the ability to take on multiple forms or shapes." In its broadest sense, this refers to the ability of different objects to respond in different ways to the same message (or method invocation).

Damian Conway, in his book *Object-Oriented Perl*, distinguishes meaningfully between two kinds of polymorphism. The first, *inheritance polymorphism*, is what most programmers are referring to when they talk about polymorphism.

When a class inherits from its superclass, we know (by definition) that any method present in the superclass is also present in the subclass. Thus, a chain of inheritance represents a linear hierarchy of classes that can respond to the same set of methods. Of course, we must remember that any subclass can redefine a method; that is what gives inheritance its power. If I call a method on an object, typically it will be either the one it inherited from its superclass or a more appropriate (more specialized) method tailored for the subclass.

In statically typed languages such as C++, inheritance polymorphism establishes type compatibility down the chain of inheritance (but not in the reverse direction). For example, if B inherits from A, a pointer to an A object can also point to a B object; but the reverse is not true. This type compatibility is an essential OOP feature in such languages—indeed it almost sums up polymorphism—but polymorphism certainly exists in the absence of static typing (as in Ruby).

The second kind of polymorphism Conway identifies is *interface polymorphism*. This does not require any inheritance relationship between classes; it only requires that the interfaces of the objects have methods of a certain name. The treatment of such objects as being the same "kind" of thing is thus a kind of polymorphism (though in most writings, it is not explicitly referred to as such).

Readers familiar with Java will recognize that it implements both kinds of polymorphism. A Java class can extend another class, inheriting from it via the `extends` keyword; or it may implement an interface, acquiring a known set of methods (which

must then be overridden) via the `implements` keyword. Because of syntax requirements, the Java interpreter can determine at compile time whether a method can be
invoked on a particular object.

Ruby supports interface polymorphism but in a different way, providing *modules*
whose methods may be *mixed in* to existing classes (interfacing to user-defined methods that are expected to exist). This, however, is not the way modules are usually used.
A module consists of methods and constants that may be used as though they were
actual parts of that class or object; when a module is mixed in via the `include` statement, this is considered to be a restricted form of multiple inheritance. According to
the language designer, Yukihiro Matsumoto (often called Matz), it can be viewed as
single inheritance with implementation sharing. This is a way of preserving the benefits
of MI without suffering all the consequences.

1.1.4   A Few More Terms

In languages such as C++, there is the concept of *abstract* classes—classes that must be
inherited from and cannot be instantiated on their own. This concept does not exist
in the more dynamic Ruby language, although if the programmer really wants, it is
possible to fake this kind of behavior by forcing the methods to be overridden.
Whether this is useful is left as an exercise for the reader.

The creator of C++, Bjarne Stroustrup, also identifies the concept of a *concrete
type.* This is a class that exists only for convenience; it is not designed to be inherited
from, nor is it expected that there will ever be another class derived from it. In other
words, the benefits of OOP are basically limited to encapsulation. Ruby does not
specifically support this concept through any special syntax (nor does C++), but it is
naturally well suited for the creation of such classes.

Some languages are considered to be more "pure" OO than others. (We also use
the term *radically object oriented.*) This refers to the concept that *every* entity in the language is an object; every primitive type is represented as a full-fledged class, and variables and constants alike are recognized as object instances. This is in contrast to such
languages as Java, C++, and Eiffel. In these, the more primitive data types (especially
constants) are not first-class objects, though they may sometimes be treated that way
with "wrapper" classes. Arguably there are languages that are *more* radically object oriented than Ruby, but they are relatively few.

Most OO languages are static; the methods and attributes belonging to a class,
the global variables, and the inheritance hierarchy are all defined at compile time.
Perhaps the largest conceptual leap for a Ruby programmer is that these are all handled *dynamically* in Ruby. Definitions and even inheritance can happen at runtime—

in fact, we can truly say that every declaration or definition is actually *executed* during the running of the program. Among many other benefits, this obviates the need for conditional compilation and can produce more efficient code in many circumstances.

This sums up the whirlwind tour of OOP. Throughout the rest of the book, we have tried to make consistent use of the terms introduced here. Let's proceed now to a brief review of the Ruby language itself.

1.2   Basic Ruby Syntax and Semantics

In the previous pages, we have already seen that Ruby is a *pure, dynamic* OOP language. Let's look briefly at some other attributes before summarizing the syntax and semantics.

Ruby is an *agile* language. It is "malleable" and encourages frequent, easy (manual) refactoring.

Ruby is an *interpreted* language. Of course, there may be later implementations of a Ruby compiler for performance reasons, but we maintain that an interpreter yields great benefits not only in rapid prototyping but also in the shortening of the development cycle overall.

Ruby is an *expression-oriented* language. Why use a statement when an expression will do? This means, for instance, that code becomes more compact as the common parts are factored out and repetition is removed.

Ruby is a *very high-level language* (VHLL). One principle behind the language design is that the computer should work for the programmer rather than vice versa. The "density" of Ruby means that sophisticated and complex operations can be carried out with relative ease as compared to lower-level languages.

Let's start by examining the overall look and feel of the language and some of its terminology. We'll briefly examine the nature of a Ruby program before looking at examples.

To begin with, Ruby is essentially a line-oriented language—more so than languages such as C but not so much as antique languages such as FORTRAN. Tokens can be crowded onto a single line as long as they are separated by whitespace as needed. Statements may share a single line if they are separated by semicolons; this is the only time the terminating semicolon is really needed. A line may be continued to the next line by ending it with a backslash or by letting the parser know that the statement is not complete—for example, by ending a line with a comma.

There is no main program as such; execution proceeds in general from top to bottom. In more complex programs, there may be numerous definitions at the top, followed by the (conceptual) main program at the bottom; but even in that case, execution proceeds from the top down because definitions in Ruby are executed.

1.2.1   Keywords and Identifiers

The keywords (or reserved words) in Ruby typically cannot be used for other purposes. These are as follows:

```
BEGIN       END         alias       and         begin

break       case        class       def         defined?

do          else        elsif       end         ensure

false       for         if          in          module

next        nil         not         or          redo

rescue      retry       return      self        super

then        true        undef       unless      until

when        while       yield
```

Variables and other identifiers normally start with an alphabetic letter or a special modifier. The basic rules are as follows:

- Local variables (and pseudovariables such as `self` and `nil`) begin with a lowercase letter or an underscore.

- Global variables begin with $ (a dollar sign).

- Instance variables (within an object) begin with @ (an at sign).

- Class variables (within a class) begin with @@ (two at signs).

- Constants begin with capital letters.

- For purposes of forming identifiers, the underscore (_) may be used as a lowercase letter.

- Special variables starting with a dollar sign (such as $1 and $/) are set by the Ruby interpreter itself.

Here are some examples of each of these:

- **Local variables**   `alpha _ident some_var`

- **Pseudovariables**   `self nil __FILE__`

- **Constants**   `K9chip Length LENGTH`

- **Instance variables**   `@foobar @thx1138 @NOT_CONST`

- **Class variable**   `@@phydeaux @@my_var @@NOT_CONST`

- **Global variables**   `$beta $B12vitamin $NOT_CONST`

1.2.2   Comments and Embedded Documentation

Comments in Ruby begin with a pound sign (#) outside a string or character constant and proceed to the end of the line:

```
x = y + 5 # This is a comment.
# This is another comment.
puts "# But this isn't."
```

Comments immediately before definitions typically document the thing that is about to be defined. This embedded documentation can often be retrieved from the program text by external tools. Typical documentation comments can run to several comment lines in a row.

```
# The purpose of this class
# is to cure cancer
# and instigate world peace
class ImpressiveClass
```

Given two lines starting with =begin and =end, everything between those lines (inclusive) is treated as a comment. (These can't be preceded by whitespace.)

```
=begin
Everything on lines
inside here will be a
comment as well.
=end
```

1.2.3   Constants, Variables, and Types

In Ruby, variables do not have types, but the objects they refer to do have types. The simplest data types are character, numeric, and string.

Numeric constants are mostly intuitive, as are strings. Generally, a double-quoted string is subject to additional interpretation, and a single-quoted string is more "as is," allowing only an escaped backslash.

In double-quoted strings, we can do "interpolation" of variables and expressions, as shown here:

```
a = 3
b = 79
puts "#{a} times #{b} = #{a*b}"    #  3 times 79 = 237
```

For more information on literals (numbers, strings, regular expressions, and so on), refer to later chapters.

There is a special kind of string worth mentioning, primarily useful in small scripts used to glue together larger programs. The command output string is sent to the operating system as a command to be executed, whereupon the output of the command is substituted back into the string. The simple form of this string uses the *grave accent* (sometimes called a *back-tick* or *back-quote*) as a beginning and ending delimiter; the more complex form uses the %x notation:

```
'whoami'
'ls -l'
%x[grep -i meta *.html | wc -l]
```

Regular expressions in Ruby look similar to character strings, but they are used differently. The usual delimiter is a slash character.

For those familiar with Perl, regular expression handling is similar in Ruby. Incidentally, we'll use the abbreviation *regex* throughout the remainder of the book; many people abbreviate it as *regexp,* but that is not as pronounceable. For details on regular expressions, see Chapter 3, "Working with Regular Expressions."

Arrays in Ruby are a powerful construct; they may contain data of any type or may even mix types. As we shall see in Chapter 8, "Arrays, Hashes, and Other Enumerables," all arrays are instances of the class Array and thus have a rich set of methods that can operate on them. An array constant is delimited by brackets; the following are all valid array expressions:

```
[1, 2, 3]
[1, 2, "buckle my shoe"]
[1, 2, [3,4], 5]
["alpha", "beta", "gamma", "delta"]
```

The second example shows an array containing both integers and strings; the third example in the preceding code shows a nested array, and the fourth example shows an array of strings. As in most languages, arrays are zero based; for instance, in the last array in the preceding code, `"gamma"` is element number 2. Arrays are dynamic and do not need to have a size specified when they are created.

Because the array of strings is so common (and so inconvenient to type), a special syntax has been set aside for it, similar to what we have seen already:

```
%w[alpha beta gamma delta]
%w(Jan Feb Mar Apr May Jun Jul Aug Sep Oct Nov Dec)
%w/am is are was were be being been/
```

Such a shorthand is frequently called "syntax sugar" because it offers a more convenient alternative to another syntactic form. In this case, the quotes and commas are not needed; only whitespace separates the individual elements. In the case of an element that contains whitespace, of course, this would not work.

An array variable can use brackets to index into the array. The resulting expression can be both examined and assigned to:

```
val = myarray[0]
print stats[j]
x[i] = x[i+1]
```

Another powerful construct in Ruby is the *hash,* also known in other circles as an *associative array* or *dictionary.* A hash is a set of associations between paired pieces of data; it is typically used as a lookup table or a kind of generalized array in which the index need not be an integer. Each hash is an instance of the class `Hash`.

A hash constant is typically represented between delimiting braces, with the symbol => separating the individual keys and values. The key can be thought of as an index where the corresponding value is stored. There is no restriction on types of the keys or the corresponding values. Here are some hashes:

```
{1 => 1, 2 => 4, 3 => 9, 4 => 16, 5 => 25, 6 => 36}
{"cat" => "cats", "ox" => "oxen", "bacterium" => "bacteria"}
{"odds" => [1,3,5,7], "evens" => [2,4,6,8]}
{"foo" => 123, [4,5,6] => "my array", "867-5309" => "Jenny"}
```

Hashes also have an additional syntax that creates keys that are instances of the `Symbol` class (which is explained further in later material):

```
{hydrogen: 1, helium: 2, carbon: 12}
```

A hash variable can have its contents accessed by essentially the same bracket notation that arrays use:

```
print phone_numbers["Jenny"]
plurals["octopus"] = "octopi"
atomic_numbers[:helium] #=> 2
```

It should be stressed, however, that both arrays and hashes have many methods associated with them; these methods give them their real usefulness. The section "OOP in Ruby," later in the chapter, will expand on this a little more.

1.2.4 Operators and Precedence

Now that we have established our most common data types, let's look at Ruby's operators. They are arranged here in order from highest to lowest precedence:

`::`	Scope
`[]`	Indexing
`**`	Exponentiation
`+ - ! ~`	Unary positive/negative, not, ...
`* / %`	Multiplication, division, ...
`+ -`	Addition/subtraction
`<< >>`	Logical shifts, ...
`&`	Bitwise AND
`| ^`	Bitwise OR, XOR
`> >= < <=`	Comparison
`== === <=> != =~ !~`	Equality, inequality, ...
`&&`	Boolean AND
`||`	Boolean OR

`..  ...`	Range operators
`= (also +=, -=, ...)`	Assignment
`?:`	Ternary decision
`not`	Boolean negation
`and or`	Boolean AND, OR

Some of the preceding symbols serve more than one purpose; for example, the operator << is a bitwise left shift but is also an append operator (for arrays, strings, and so on) and a marker for a here-document. Likewise, the + is for numeric addition as well as for string concatenation. As we shall see later, many of these operators are just shortcuts for method names.

Now we have defined most of our data types and many of the possible operations on them. Before going any further, let's look at a sample program.

1.2.5   A Sample Program

In a tutorial, the first program is always `Hello, world!` But in a whirlwind tour like this one, let's start with something slightly more advanced. Here is a small interactive console-based program to convert between Fahrenheit and Celsius temperatures:

```ruby
print "Please enter a temperature and scale (C or F): "
STDOUT.flush
str = gets
exit if str.nil? || str.empty?
str.chomp!
temp, scale = str.split(" ")

abort "#{temp} is not a valid number." if temp !~ /-?\d+/

temp = temp.to_f
case scale
  when "C", "c"
    f = 1.8*temp + 32
  when "F", "f"
    c = (5.0/9.0)*(temp-32)
else
  abort "Must specify C or F."
end

if f.nil?
  puts "#{c} degrees C"
```

```
else
  puts "#{f} degrees F"
end
```

Here are some examples of running this program. These show that the program can convert from Fahrenheit to Celsius, convert from Celsius to Fahrenheit, and handle an invalid scale or an invalid number:

```
Please enter a temperature and scale (C or F): 98.6 F
37.0 degrees C

Please enter a temperature and scale (C or F): 100 C
212.0 degrees F

Please enter a temperature and scale (C or F): 92 G
Must specify C or F.

Please enter a temperature and scale (C or F): junk F
junk is not a valid number.
```

Now, as for the mechanics of the program: We begin with a `print` statement, which is actually a call to the `Kernel` method `print`, to write to standard output. This is an easy way of leaving the cursor "hanging" at the end of the line.

Following this, we call `gets` (get string from standard input), assigning the value to `str`. We then do a `chomp!` to remove the trailing newline.

Note that any apparently "free-standing" function calls such as `print` and `gets` are actually methods of `Object` (probably originating in `Kernel`). In the same way, `chomp` is a method called with `str` as a receiver. Method calls in Ruby usually can omit the parentheses; for example, `print "foo"` is the same as `print("foo")`.

The variable `str` refers to (or informally, it "holds") a character string, but there is no reason it could not hold some other type instead. In Ruby, data have types, but variables do not. A variable springs into existence as soon as the interpreter sees an assignment to that variable; there are no "variable declarations" as such.

The `exit` is a call to a method that terminates the program. On this same line there is a control structure called an *if-modifier*. This is like the `if` statement that exists in most languages, but backwards; it comes after the action, does not permit an `else`, and does not require closing. As for the condition, we are checking two things: Does `str` have a value (is it non-`nil`) and is it a non-null string? In the case of an immediate end-of-file, our first condition will hold; in the case of a newline with no preceding data, the second condition will hold.

The `||` operator has the same effect as `or`, but is preferred because it has higher precedence and produces less-confusing results. The same statement could be written this way:

```
exit if not str or not str[0]
```

The reason these tests work is that a variable can have a `nil` value, and `nil` evaluates to false in Ruby. In fact, `nil` and `false` evaluate as false, and everything else evaluates as true. Specifically, the null string `""` and the number `0` do *not* evaluate as false.

The next statement performs a `chomp!` operation on the string (to remove the trailing newline). The exclamation point as a prefix serves as a warning that the operation actually changes the value of its receiver rather than just returning a value. The exclamation point is used in many such instances to remind the programmer that a method has a side effect or is more "dangerous" than its unmarked counterpart. The method `chomp`, for example, returns the same result but does not modify its receiver.

The next statement is an example of multiple assignment. The `split` method splits the string into an array of values, using the space as a delimiter. The two assignable entities on the left-hand side will be assigned the respective values resulting on the right-hand side.

The `if` statement that follows uses a simple regex to determine whether the number is valid; if the string fails to match a pattern consisting of an optional minus sign followed by one or more digits, it is an invalid number (for our purposes), and the program exits. Note that the `if` statement is terminated by the keyword `end`; though it was not needed here, we could have had an `else` clause before the `end`. The keyword `then` is optional; we tend not to use it in this book.

The `to_f` method is used to convert the string to a floating point number. We are actually assigning this floating point value back to `temp`, which originally held a string.

The `case` statement chooses between three alternatives—the cases in which the user specified a C, specified an F, or used an invalid scale. In the first two instances, a calculation is done; in the third, we print an error and exit. When printing, the `puts` method will automatically add a newline after the string that is given.

Ruby's `case` statement, by the way, is far more general than the example shown here. There is no limitation on the data types, and the expressions used are all arbitrary and may even be ranges or regular expressions.

There is nothing mysterious about the computation. But consider the fact that the variables c and f are referenced first inside the branches of the case. There are no declarations as such in Ruby; because a variable only comes into existence when it is assigned, this means that when we fall through the case statement, only one of these variables actually has a valid value.

We use this fact to determine after the fact which branch was followed, so that we can do a slightly different output in each instance. Testing f for a nil is effectively a test of whether the variable has a meaningful value. We do this here only to show that it can be done; obviously, two different print statements could be used inside the case statement if we wanted.

The perceptive reader will notice that we used only "local" variables here. This might be confusing because their scope certainly appears to cover the entire program. What is happening here is that the variables are all local to the *top level* of the program (written *toplevel* by some). The variables appear global because there are no lower-level contexts in a program this simple; but if we declared classes and methods, these top-level variables would not be accessible within those.

1.2.6 Looping and Branching

Let's spend some time looking at control structures. We have already seen the simple if statement and the if-modifier; there are also corresponding structures based on the keyword unless (which also has an optional else), as well as expression-oriented forms of if and unless. To summarize these forms, these two statements are equivalent:

```
if x < 5
  statement1
end
```

```
unless x >= 5
  statement1
end
```

And so are these:

```
if x < 5
  statement1
else
  statement2
end
```

```
unless x < 5
  statement2
else
  statement1
end
```

And these:

```
statement1 if y == 3

statement1 unless y != 37.0
```

And these are also equivalent:

```
x = if a > 0 then b else c end

x = unless a <= 0 then c else b end
```

Note that the keyword then may always be omitted except in the final (expression-oriented) cases. Note also that the modifier form cannot have an else clause.

The case statement in Ruby is more powerful than in most languages. This multiway branch can even test for conditions other than equality—for example, a matched pattern. The test used by the case statement is called the *case equality operator* (===), and its behavior varies from one object to another. Let's look at this example:

```
case "This is a character string."
when "some value"
  puts "Branch 1"
when "some other value"
  puts "Branch 2"
when /char/
  puts "Branch 3"
else
  puts "Branch 4"
end
```

The preceding code prints Branch 3. Why? It first tries to check for equality between the tested expression and one of the strings "some value" or "some other value"; this fails, so it proceeds. The third test is for a pattern within the string; when /char/ is equivalent to if /char/ === "This is a character string.". The test succeeds, and the third `print` statement is performed. The `else` clause always handles the default case in which none of the preceding tests succeeds.

If the tested expression is an integer, the compared value can be an integer range (for example, `3..8`). In this case, the expression is tested for membership in that range. In all instances, the first successful branch will be taken.

Although the `case` statement usually behaves predictably, there are a few subtleties you should appreciate. We will look at these later.

As for looping mechanisms, Ruby has a rich set. The `while` and `until` control structures are both pretest loops, and both work as expected: One specifies a continuation condition for the loop, and the other specifies a termination condition. They also occur in "modifier" form, such as `if` and `unless`. There is also the `loop` method of the `Kernel` module (by default an infinite loop), and there are iterators associated with various classes.

The examples here assume an array called `list`, defined something like this:

```
list = %w[alpha bravo charlie delta echo]
```

They all step through the array and write out each element.

```
i = 0                        # Loop 1 (while)
while i < list.size do
  print "#{list[i]} "
  i += 1
end


i = 0                        # Loop 2 (until)
until i == list.size do
  print "#{list[i]} "
  i += 1
end

i = 0                        # Loop 3 (post-test while)
begin
  print "#{list[i]} "
  i += 1
end while i < list.size

i = 0                        # Loop 4 (post-test until)
begin
  print "#{list[i]} "
```

```ruby
    i += 1
end until i == list.size

for x in list do            # Loop 5 (for)
  print "#{x} "
end

list.each do |x|            # Loop 6 ('each' iterator)
  print "#{x} "
end

i = 0                       # Loop 7 ('loop' method)
n=list.size-1
loop do
  print "#{list[i]} "
  i += 1
  break if i > n
end

i = 0                       # Loop 8 ('loop' method)
n=list.size-1
loop do
  print "#{list[i]} "
  i += 1
  break unless i <= n
end

n=list.size                 # Loop 9 ('times' iterator)
n.times do |i|
  print "#{list[i]} "
end

n = list.size-1             # Loop 10 ('upto' iterator)
0.upto(n) do |i|
  print "#{list[i]} "
end

n = list.size-1             # Loop 11 (for)
for i in 0..n do
  print "#{list[i]} "
end

list.each_index do |x|      # Loop 12 ('each_index' iterator)
```

```
    print "#{list[x]} "
end
```

Let's examine these in detail. Loops 1 and 2 are the "standard" forms of the `while` and `until` loops; they behave essentially the same, but their conditions are negations of each other. Loops 3 and 4 are the same thing in "post-test" versions; the test is performed at the end of the loop rather than at the beginning. Note that the use of `begin` and `end` in this context is strictly a kludge or hack; what is really happening is that a `begin`/`end` block (used for exception handling) is followed by a `while` or `until` modifier. In other words, this is only an illustration. Don't code this way.

Loop 6 is arguably the "proper" way to write this loop. Note the simplicity of 5 and 6 compared with the others; there is no explicit initialization and no explicit test or increment. This is because an array "knows" its own size, and the standard iterator `each` (loop 6) handles such details automatically. Indeed, loop 3 is merely an indirect reference to this same iterator because the `for` loop works for any object having the iterator each defined. The `for` loop is only another way to call `each`.

Loops 7 and 8 both use the loop construct; as stated previously, `loop` looks like a keyword introducing a control structure, but it is really a method of the module `Kernel`, not a control structure at all.

Loops 9 and 10 take advantage of the fact that the array has a numeric index; the `times` iterator executes a specified number of times, and the `upto` iterator carries its parameter up to the specified value. Neither of these is truly suitable for this instance.

Loop 11 is a `for` loop that operates specifically on the index values, using a range, and loop 12 likewise uses the `each_index` iterator to run through the list of array indices.

In the preceding examples, we have not laid enough emphasis on the "modifier" form of the `while` and `until` loops. These are frequently useful, and they have the virtue of being concise. These two additional fragments both mean the same:

```
perform_task() until finished
```

```
perform_task() while not finished
```

Another fact is largely ignored in these examples: Loops do not always run smoothly from beginning to end, in a predictable number of iterations, or ending in a single predictable way. We need ways to control these loops further.

The first way is the `break` keyword, shown in loops 7 and 8. This is used to "break out" of a loop; in the case of nested loops, only the innermost one is halted. This will be intuitive for C programmers.

The `redo` keyword is jumps to the start of the loop body in `while` and `until` loops.

The `next` keyword effectively jumps to the end of the innermost loop and resumes execution from that point. It works for any loop or iterator.

The iterator is an important concept in Ruby, as we have already seen. What we have not seen is that the language allows user-defined iterators in addition to the predefined ones.

The default iterator for any object is called `each`. This is significant partly because it allows the `for` loop to be used. But iterators may be given different names and used for varying purposes.

It is also possible to pass parameters via `yield`, which will be substituted into the block's parameter list (between vertical bars). As a somewhat contrived example, the following iterator does nothing but generate integers from 1 to 10, and the call of the iterator generates the first ten cubes:

```
def my_sequence
  (1..10).each do |i|
    yield i
  end
end


my_sequence {|x| puts x**3 }
```

Note that `do` and `end` may be substituted for the braces that delimit a block. There are differences, but they are fairly subtle.

1.2.7 Exceptions

Ruby supports *exceptions*, which are standard means of handling unexpected errors in modern programming languages.

By using exceptions, special return codes can be avoided, as well as the nested `if else` "spaghetti logic" that results from checking them. Even better, the code that detects the error can be distinguished from the code that knows how to handle the error (because these are often separate anyway).

The `raise` statement raises an exception. Note that `raise` is not a reserved word but a method of the module `Kernel`. (There is an alias named `fail`.)

```
raise                                        # Example 1
raise "Some error message"                   # Example 2
raise ArgumentError                          # Example 3
raise ArgumentError, "Bad data"              # Example 4
raise ArgumentError.new("Bad data")          # Example 5
raise ArgumentError, "Bad data", caller[0]   # Example 6
```

In the first example in the preceding code, the last exception encountered is re-raised. In example 2, a `RuntimeError` (the default error) is created using the string `Some error message`.

In example 3, an `ArgumentError` is raised; in example 4, this same error is raised with the message "Bad data" associated with it. Example 5 behaves exactly the same as example 4. Finally, example 6 adds traceback information of the form `"filename:line"` or `"filename:line:in 'method'"` (as stored in the `caller` array).

Now, how do we handle exceptions in Ruby? The `begin-end` block is used for this purpose. The simplest form is a `begin-end` block with nothing but our code inside:

```
begin
  # Just runs our code.
  # ...
end
```

This is of no value in catching errors. The block, however, may have one or more `rescue` clauses in it. If an error occurs at any point in the code, between `begin` and `rescue`, control will be passed immediately to the appropriate `rescue` clause:

```
begin
  x = Math.sqrt(y/z)
  # ...
rescue ArgumentError
  puts "Error taking square root."
rescue ZeroDivisionError
  puts "Attempted division by zero."
end
```

Essentially the same thing can be accomplished by this fragment:

```
begin
  x = Math.sqrt(y/z)
  # ...
rescue => err
  puts err
end
```

Here, the variable `err` is used to store the value of the exception; printing it causes it to be translated to some meaningful character string. Note that because the error type is not specified, the `rescue` clause will catch any descendant of `StandardError`. The notation `rescue => variable` can be used with or without an error type before the `=>` symbol.

In the event that error types are specified, it may be that an exception does not match any of these types. For that situation, we are allowed to use an `else` clause after all the `rescue` clauses:

```
begin
  # Error-prone code...
rescue Type1
  # ...
rescue Type2
  # ...
else
  # Other exceptions...
end
```

In many cases, we want to do some kind of recovery. In that event, the keyword `retry` (within the body of a `rescue` clause) restarts the `begin` block and tries those operations again:

```
begin
  # Error-prone code...
rescue
  # Attempt recovery...
  retry  # Now try again
end
```

Finally, it is sometimes necessary to write code that "cleans up" after a `begin-end` block. In the event this is necessary, an `ensure` clause can be specified:

```
begin
  # Error-prone code...
rescue
  # Handle exceptions
ensure
  # This code is always executed
end
```

The code in an `ensure` clause is always executed before the `begin-end` block exits. This happens regardless of whether an exception occurred.

Exceptions may be caught in two other ways. First, there is a modifier form of the rescue clause:

```
x = a/b rescue puts("Division by zero!")
```

In addition, the body of a method definition is an implicit `begin-end` block; the `begin` is omitted, and the entire body of the method is subject to exception handling, ending with the `end` of the method:

```
def some_method
  # Code...
rescue
  # Recovery...
end
```

This sums up the basics of exception handling as well as the discussion of fundamental syntax and semantics.

There are numerous aspects of Ruby we have not discussed here. The rest of this chapter is devoted to the more advanced features of the language, including a collection of Ruby lore that will help the intermediate programmer learn to "think in Ruby."

1.3   OOP in Ruby

Ruby has all the elements more generally associated with OOP languages, such as objects with encapsulation and data hiding, methods with polymorphism and overriding, and classes with hierarchy and inheritance. It goes further and adds limited metaclass features, singleton methods, modules, and mixins.

Similar concepts are known by other names in other OOP languages, but concepts of the same name may have subtle differences from one language to another. This section elaborates on the Ruby understanding and usage of these elements of OOP.

1.3.1   Objects

In Ruby, all numbers, strings, arrays, regular expressions, and many other entities are actually objects. Work is done by executing the methods belonging to the object:

```
3.succ                   # 4
"abc".upcase             # "ABC"
[2,1,5,3,4].sort         # [1,2,3,4,5]
some_object.some_method  # some result
```

In Ruby, every object is an instance of some class; the class contains the implementation of the methods:

```
"abc".class        # String
"abc".class.class  # Class
```

In addition to encapsulating its own attributes and operations, an object in Ruby has an identity:

```
"abc".object_id   # 53744407
```

This object ID is usually of limited usefulness to the programmer.

1.3.2   Built-in Classes

More than 30 built-in classes are predefined in the Ruby class hierarchy. Like many other OOP languages, Ruby does not allow multiple inheritance, but that does not necessarily make it any less powerful. Modern OO languages frequently follow the single inheritance model. Ruby does support modules and mixins, which are discussed in the next section. It also implements object IDs, as we just saw, which support the implementation of persistent, distributed, and relocatable objects.

To create an object from an existing class, the new method is typically used:

```
myFile = File.new("textfile.txt","w")
myString = String.new("This is a string object")
```

This is not always explicitly required, however. When using *object literals*, you do not need to bother with calling new, as we did in the previous example:

```
your_string = "This is also a string object"
number = 5  # new not needed here, either
```

Variables are used to hold references to objects. As previously mentioned, variables themselves have no type, nor are they objects themselves; they are simply references to objects:

```
x = "abc"
```

An exception to this is that small immutable objects of some built-in classes, such as Fixnum, are copied directly into the variables that refer to them. (These objects are no bigger than pointers, and it is more efficient to deal with them in this way.) In this case, assignment makes a copy of the object, and the heap is not used.

Variable assignment causes object references to be shared:

```
y = "abc"
x = y
x           # "abc"
```

After x = y is executed, variables x and y both refer to the same object:

```
x.object_id    # 53732208
y.object_id    # 53732208
```

If the object is mutable, a modification done to one variable will be reflected in the other:

```
x.gsub!(/a/,"x")
y                  # "xbc"
```

Reassigning one of these variables has no effect on the other, however:

```
# Continuing previous example...
x = "abc"
y                  # still has value "xbc"
```

A mutable object can be made immutable using the freeze method:

```
x.freeze
x.gsub!(/b/,"y")   # Error!
```

A symbol is a little unusual; it's like an atom in Lisp. It acts like a kind of immutable string, and multiple uses of a symbol all reference the same value. A symbol can be converted to a string with the to_s method:

```
suits = [:hearts, :clubs, :diamonds, :spades]
lead = suits[1].to_s   # "clubs"
```

Similar to arrays of strings, arrays of symbols can be created using the syntax
shortcut %i:

```
suits = %i[hearts clubs diamonds spades] # an array of symbols
```

1.3.3   Modules and Mixins

Many built-in methods are available from class ancestors. Of special note are the
Kernel methods mixed-in to the Object class; because Object is the universal parent class, the methods added to it from Kernel are also universally available. These
methods form an important part of Ruby.

The terms *module* and *mixin* are nearly synonymous. A module is a collection of
methods and constants that is external to the Ruby program. It can be used simply for
namespace management, but the most common use of a module is to have its features
"mixed" into a class (by using include). In this case, it is used as a mixin.

This term was apparently borrowed most directly from Python. (It is sometimes
written as *mix-in,* but we write it as a single word.) It is worth noting that some Lisp
variants have had this feature for more than two decades.

Do not confuse this usage of the term *module* with another usage common in
computing. A Ruby module is not an external source or binary file (though it may be
stored in one of these). A Ruby module instead is an OOP abstraction similar to a
class.

An example of using a module for namespace management is the frequent use of
the Math module. To use the definition of pi, for example, it is not necessary to
include the Math module; you can simply use Math::PI as the constant.

A mixin is a way of getting some of the benefits of multiple inheritance without
dealing with all the difficulties. It can be considered a restricted form of multiple
inheritance, but the language creator Matz has called it "single inheritance with implementation sharing."

Note that include adds features of a module to the current space; the extend
method adds features of a module to an object. With include, the module's methods
become available as instance methods; with extend, they become available as class
methods.

We should mention that `load` and `require` do not relate to modules but rather to Ruby source and binary files (statically or dynamically loadable). A `load` operation reads a file and runs it in the current context so that its definitions become available at that point. A `require` operation is similar to a load, but it will not load a file if it has already been loaded.

The Ruby novice, especially from a C background, may be tripped up by `require` and `include`, which are basically unrelated to each other. You may easily find yourself doing a `require` followed by an `include` to use some externally stored module.

1.3.4 Creating Classes

Ruby has numerous built-in classes, and additional classes may be defined in a Ruby program. To define a new class, the following construct is used:

```
class ClassName
  # ...
end
```

The name of the class is itself a global constant and therefore must begin with an uppercase letter. The class definition can contain class constants, class variables, class methods, instance variables, and instance methods. Class-level information is available to all objects of the class, whereas instance-level information is available only to the one object.

By the way, classes in Ruby do not, strictly speaking, have names. The "name" of a class is just a constant that is a reference to an object of type `Class` (because, in Ruby, `Class` is a class). There can certainly be more than one constant referring to a class, and these can be assigned to variables just as we can with any other object (because, in Ruby, `Class` is an object). If all this confuses you, don't worry about it. For the sake of convenience, the novice can think of a Ruby class name as being like a C++ class name.

Here we define a simple class:

```
class Friend
  @@myname = "Fred" # a class variable

  def initialize(name, gender, phone)
    @name, @sex, @phone = name, gender, phone
    # These are instance variables
  end
```

```ruby
  def hello    # an instance method
    puts "Hi, I'm #{@name}."
  end

  def Friend.our_common_friend    # a class method
    puts "We are all friends of #{@@myname}."
  end

end

f1 = Friend.new("Susan", "female", "555-0123")
f2 = Friend.new("Tom", "male", "555-4567")

f1.hello                    # Hi, I'm Susan.
f2.hello                    # Hi, I'm Tom.
Friend.our_common_friend    # We are all friends of Fred.
```

Because class-level data is accessible throughout the class, it can be initialized at the time the class is defined. If an instance method named `initialize` is defined, it is guaranteed to be executed right after an instance is allocated. The `initialize` method is similar to the traditional concept of a constructor, but it does not have to handle memory allocation. Allocation is handled internally by `new`, and deallocation is handled transparently by the garbage collector.

Now consider this fragment, and pay attention to the `getmyvar`, `setmyvar`, and `myvar=` methods:

```ruby
class MyClass

  NAME = "Class Name" # class constant
  @@count = 0          # initialize a class variable

  def initialize       # called when object is allocated
    @@count += 1
    @myvar = 10
  end

  def self.getcount    # class method
    @@count            # class variable
  end

  def getcount         # instance returns class variable!
    @@count            # class variable
  end
```

```
  def getmyvar         # instance method
    @myvar             # instance variable
  end

  def setmyvar(val)    # instance method sets @myvar
    @myvar = val
  end

  def myvar=(val)      # Another way to set @myvar
    @myvar = val
  end
end

foo = MyClass.new  # @myvar is 10
foo.setmyvar 20    # @myvar is 20
foo.myvar = 30     # @myvar is 30
```

Instance variables are different for each object that is an instance of the class. Class variables are shared between the class itself and every instance of the class. To create a variable that belongs only to the class, use an instance variable inside a class method. This *class instance variable* will not be shared with instances and is therefore often preferred over class variables.

In the preceding code, we see that `getmyvar` returns the value of `@myvar` and that `setmyvar` sets it. (In the terminology of many programmers, these would be referred to as a *getter* and a *setter,* respectively.) These work fine, but they do not exemplify the "Ruby way" of doing things. The method `myvar=` looks like assignment overloading (though strictly speaking, it isn't); it is a better replacement for `setmyvar`, but there is a better way yet.

The class `Module` contains methods called `attr`, `attr_accessor`, `attr_reader`, and `attr_writer`. These can be used (with symbols as parameters) to automatically handle controlled access to the instance data. For example, the three methods `getmyvar`, `setmyvar`, and `myvar=` can be replaced by a single line in the class definition:

```
attr_accessor :myvar
```

This creates a method `myvar` that returns the value of `@myvar` and a method `myvar=` that enables the setting of the same variable. The methods `attr_reader` and `attr_writer` create read-only and write-only versions of an attribute, respectively.

Within the instance methods of a class, the pseudovariable `self` can be used as needed. This is only a reference to the current receiver, the object on which the instance method is invoked.

The modifying methods `private`, `protected`, and `public` can be used to control the visibility of methods in a class. (Instance variables are always private and inaccessible from outside the class, except by means of accessors.) Each of these modifiers takes a symbol like `:foo` as a parameter; if this is omitted, the modifier applies to all subsequent definitions in the class. Here is an example:

```ruby
class MyClass

  def method1
  # ...
  end

  def method2
  # ...
  end

  def method3
  # ...
  end

  private :method1
  public :method2
  protected :method3

  private

  def my_method
  # ...
  end

  def another_method
  # ...
  end

end
```

In the preceding class, `method1` will be private, `method2` will be public, and `method3` will be protected. Because of the `private` method with no parameters, both `my_method` and `another_method` will be private.

The `public` access level is self-explanatory; there are no restrictions on access or visibility. The `private` level means that the method is accessible only within the class or its subclasses, and it is callable only in "function form"—with `self`, implicit or explicit, as a receiver. The `protected` level means that a method can be called by other objects of the class or its subclasses, unlike a private method (which can only be called on `self`).

The default visibility for the methods defined in a class is `public`. The exception is the instance-initializing method `initialize`. Methods defined at the top level are also public by default; if they are private, they can be called only in function form (as, for example, the methods defined in `Object`).

Ruby classes are themselves objects, being instances of the parent class `Class`. Ruby classes are always concrete; there are no abstract classes. However, it is theoretically possible to implement abstract classes in Ruby if you really want to do so.

The class `Object` is at the root of the hierarchy. It provides all the methods defined in the built-in Kernel module. (Technically, BasicObject is the parent of Object . It acts as a kind of "blank slate" object that does not have all the baggage of a normal object.)

To create a class that inherits from another class, define it in this way:

```ruby
class MyClass < OtherClass
  # ...
end
```

In addition to using built-in methods, it is only natural to define your own and also to redefine and override existing ones. When you define a method with the same name as an existing one, the previous method is overridden. If a method needs to call the "parent" method that it overrides (a frequent occurrence), the keyword `super` can be used for this purpose.

Operator overloading is not strictly an OOP feature, but it is familiar to C++ programmers and certain others. Because most operators in Ruby are simply methods anyway, it should come as no surprise that these operators can be overridden or defined for user-defined classes. Overriding the meaning of an operator for an existing class may be rare, but it is common to want to define operators for new classes.

It is possible to create aliases or synonyms for methods. The syntax (used inside a class definition) is as follows:

```ruby
alias_method :newname, :oldname
```

The number of parameters will be the same as for the old name, and it will be called in the same way. An alias creates a copy of the method, so later changes to the original method will not be reflected in aliases created beforehand.

There is also a Ruby keyword called `alias`, which is similar; unlike the method, it can alias global variables as well as methods, and its arguments are not separated by a comma.

1.3.5   Methods and Attributes

As we've seen, methods are typically used with simple class instances and variables by separating the receiver from the method with a period (`receiver.method`). In the case of method names that are punctuation, the period is omitted. Methods can take arguments:

```
Time.mktime(2014, "Aug", 24, 16, 0)
```

Because every expression returns a value, method calls may typically be chained or stacked:

```
3.succ.to_s
/(x.z).*?(x.z).*?/.match("x1z_1a3_x2z_1b3_").to_a[1..3]
3+2.succ
```

Note that there can be problems if the cumulative expression is of a type that does not support that particular method. Specifically, some methods return `nil` under certain conditions, and this usually causes any methods tacked onto that result to fail. (Of course, `nil` is an object in its own right, but it will not have all the same methods that, for example, an array would have.)

Certain methods may have blocks passed to them. This is true of all iterators, whether built in or user defined. A block is usually passed as a `do-end` block or a brace-delimited block; it is not treated like the other parameters preceding it, if any. See especially the `File.open` example:

```
my_array.each do |x|
   x.some_action
end

File.open(filename) { |f| f.some_action }
```

Methods may take a variable number of arguments:

```
receiver.method(arg1, *more_args)
```

In this case, the method called treats `more_args` as an array that it deals with as it would any other array. In fact, an asterisk in the list of formal parameters (on the last or only parameter) can likewise "collapse" a sequence of actual parameters into an array:

```
def mymethod(a, b, *c)
  print a, b
  c.each do |x| print x end
end

mymethod(1,2,3,4,5,6,7)

# a=1, b=2, c=[3,4,5,6,7]
```

Ruby also supports *named parameters,* which are called *keyword arguments* in the Python realm; the concept dates back at least as far as the Ada language developed in the 1960s and 70s. Named parameters simultaneously set default values and allow arguments to be given in any order because they are explicitly labeled:

```
def mymethod(name: "default", options: {})
  options.merge!(name: name)
  some_action_with(options)
end
```

When a named parameter has its default omitted in the method definition, it is a required named parameter:

```
def other_method(name:, age:)
  puts "Person #{name} is aged #{age}."
  # It's an error to call this method without specifying
  # values for name and age.
end
```

Ruby has the capability to define methods on a per-object basis (rather than per class). Such methods are called *singletons,* and they belong solely to that object and have no effect on its class or superclasses. As an example, this might be useful in pro-

gramming a GUI; you can define a button action for a widget by defining a singleton
method for the button object.

Here is an example of defining a singleton method on a string object:

```
str = "Hello, world!"
str2 = "Goodbye!"

def str.spell
  self.split(/./).join("-")
end

str.spell       # "H-e-l-l-o-,- -w-o-r-l-d-!"
str2.spell      # error!
```

Be aware that the method is defined for the object itself, and not for the variable.

It is theoretically possible to create a prototype-based object system using singleton methods. This is a less traditional form of OOP without classes. The basic struc-
turing mechanism is to construct a new object using an existing object as a delegate;
the new object is exactly like the old object except for things that are overridden. This
enables you to build prototype/delegation-based systems rather than inheritance
based, and, although we do not have experience in this area, we do feel that this
demonstrates the power of Ruby.

1.4 Dynamic Aspects of Ruby

Ruby is a dynamic language in the sense that objects and classes may be altered at runtime. Ruby has the capability to construct and evaluate pieces of code in the course of
executing the existing statically coded program. It has a sophisticated reflection API
that makes it more "self-aware"; this enables the easy creation of debuggers, profilers,
and similar tools and also makes certain advanced coding techniques possible.

This is perhaps the most difficult area a programmer will encounter in learning
Ruby. In this section, we briefly examine some of the implications of Ruby's dynamic
nature.

1.4.1 Coding at Runtime

We have already discussed `load` and `require`, but it is important to realize that these
are not built-in statements or control structures or anything of that nature; they are
actual methods. Therefore, it is possible to call them with variables or expressions as

parameters or to call them conditionally. Contrast with this the `#include` directive in C or C++, which is evaluated and acted on at compile time.

Code can be constructed piecemeal and evaluated. As another contrived example, consider this `calculate` method and the code calling it:

```
def calculate(op1, operator, op2)
  string = op1.to_s + operator + op2.to_s
    # operator is assumed to be a string; make one big
    # string of it and the two operands
  eval(string)   # Evaluate and return a value
end

@alpha = 25
@beta = 12

puts calculate(2, "+", 2)        # Prints 4
puts calculate(5, "*", "@alpha") # Prints 125
puts calculate("@beta", "**", 3) # Prints 1728
```

As an even more extreme example, the following code prompts the user for a method name and a single line of code; then it actually defines the method and calls it:

```
puts "Method name: "
meth_name = gets
puts "Line of code: "
code = gets

string = %[def #{meth_name}\n #{code}\n end]   # Build a string
eval(string)                                   # Define the method
eval(meth_name)                                # Call the method
```

Frequently, programmers want to code for different platforms or circumstances and still maintain only a single code base. In such a case, a C programmer would use `#ifdef` directives, but in Ruby, definitions are executed. There is no "compile time," and everything is dynamic rather than static. So if we want to make some kind of decision like this, we can simply evaluate a flag at runtime:

```
if platform == Windows
  action1
elsif platform == Linux
```

```
    action2
else
  default_action
end
```

Of course, there is a small runtime penalty for coding in this way because the flag may be tested many times in the course of execution. But this example does essentially the same thing, enclosing the platform-dependent code in a method whose name is the same across all platforms:

```
if platform == Windows
  def my_action
    action1
  end
elsif platform == Linux
  def my_action
    action2
  end
else
  def my_action
    default_action
  end
end
```

In this way, the same result is achieved, but the flag is only evaluated once; when the user's code calls my_action, it will already have been defined appropriately.

1.4.2   Reflection

Languages such as Smalltalk, LISP, and Java implement (to varying degrees) the notion of a *reflective* programming language—one in which the active environment can query the objects that define it and extend or modify them at runtime.

Ruby allows reflection quite extensively but does not go as far as Smalltalk, which even represents control structures as objects. Ruby control structures and blocks are *not* objects. (A Proc object can be used to "objectify" a block, but control structures are never objects.)

The keyword defined? (with the question mark) may be used to determine whether an identifier name is in use:

```
if defined? some_var
  puts "some_var = #{some_var}"
```

```
else
  puts "The variable some_var is not known."
end
```

Similarly, the method `respond_to?` determines whether an object can respond to the specified method call (that is, whether that method is defined for that object). The `respond_to?` method is defined in class `Object`.

Ruby supports runtime-type information in a radical way. The type (or class) of an object can be determined at runtime using the method `class` (defined in `Object`). Similarly, `is_a?` tells whether an object is of a certain class (including the super-classes); `kind_of?` is an alias. Here is an example:

```
puts "abc".class    # Prints String
puts 345.class      # Prints Fixnum
rover = Dog.new

print rover.class   # Prints Dog

if rover.is_a? Dog
  puts "Of course he is."
end

if rover.kind_of? Dog
  puts "Yes, still a dog."
end

if rover.is_a? Animal
  puts "Yes, he's an animal, too."
end
```

It is possible to retrieve an exhaustive list of all the methods that can be invoked for a given object; this is done by using the `methods` method, defined in `Object`. There are also variations such as `instance_methods`, `private_instance_meth-ods`, and so on.

Similarly, you can determine the class variables and instance variables associated with an object. By the nature of OOP, the lists of methods and variables include the entities defined not only in the object's class but also in its superclasses. The `Module` class has a method called `constants` that is used to list the constants defined within a module.

The class `Module` has a method called `ancestors` that returns a list of modules included in the given module. This list is self-inclusive; `Mod.ancestors` will always have at least `Mod` in the list. This list comprises not only parent classes (through inheritance) but "parent" modules (through module inclusion).

The class `BasicObject` has a method called `superclass` that returns the superclass of the object or returns `nil`. Because `BasicObject` itself is the only object without a superclass, it is the only case in which `nil` will be returned.

The `ObjectSpace` module is used to access any and all "living" objects. The method `_idtoref` can be used to convert an object ID to an object reference; it can be considered the inverse of the `object_id` method. `ObjectSpace` also has an iterator called `each_object` that iterates over all the objects currently in existence, including many that you will not otherwise explicitly know about. (Remember that certain small immutable objects, such as objects of class `Fixnum`, `NilClass`, `TrueClass`, and `FalseClass`, are not kept on the stack for optimization reasons.)

1.4.3   Missing Methods

When a method is invoked (`my_object.my_method`), Ruby first searches for the named method according to this search order:

1.   Singleton methods in the receiver `my_object`

2.   Methods defined in `my_object`'s class

3.   Methods defined among `my_object`'s ancestors

If the method `my_method` is not found, Ruby searches for a method called `method_missing`. If this method is defined, it is passed the name of the missing method (as a symbol) and all the parameters that were passed to the nonexistent `mymethod`. This facility can be used for the dynamic handling of unknown messages sent at runtime.

1.4.4   Garbage Collection

Managing memory on a low level is hard and error prone, especially in a dynamic environment such as Ruby; having a garbage collection (GC) facility is a significant advantage. In languages such as C++, memory allocation and deallocation are handled by the programmer; in other languages such as Java, memory is reclaimed (when objects go out of scope) by a garbage collector.

Memory management done by the programmer is the source of two of the most common kinds of bugs. If an object is freed while still being referenced, a later access may find the memory in an inconsistent state. These so-called *dangling pointers* are difficult to track down because they often cause errors in code that is far removed from the offending statement. *Memory leaks* are caused when an object is not freed even though there are no references to it. Programs with this bug typically use up more and more memory until they crash; this kind of error is also difficult to find. Ruby has a GC facility that periodically tracks down unused objects and reclaims the storage that was allocated to them. For those who care about such things, Ruby's GC is done using a *generational mark and sweep* algorithm rather than reference counting (which can have difficulties with recursive structures).

Certain performance penalties may be associated with garbage collection. Some environment variables and methods on the GC module allow a programmer to tailor garbage collection to the needs of the individual program. We can also define an object *finalizer,* but this is an advanced topic (see Section 11.3.15, "Defining Finalizers for Objects").

1.5 Training Your Intuition: Things to Remember

It may truly be said that "everything is intuitive once you understand it." This verity is the heart of this section because Ruby has many features and personality quirks that may be different from what the traditional programmer is used to.

Some readers may feel their time is wasted by a reiteration of some of these points; if that is the case for you, you are free to skip the paragraphs that seem obvious to you. Programmers' backgrounds vary widely; an old-time C hacker and a Smalltalk guru will each approach Ruby from a different viewpoint. We hope, however, that a perusal of these following paragraphs will assist many readers in following what some call the *Ruby Way.*

1.5.1 Syntax Issues

The Ruby parser is complex and relatively forgiving. It tries to make sense out of what it finds instead of forcing the programmer into slavishly following a set of rules. However, this behavior may take some getting used to. Here is a list of things to know about Ruby syntax:

- Parentheses are usually optional with a method call. These calls are all valid:

```
foobar
foobar()
foobar(a,b,c)
foobar a, b, c
```

- Let's try to pass a hash to a method:

```
my_method {a: 1, b: 2, 5 => 25}
```

This results in a syntax error, because the left brace is seen as the start of a block. In this instance, parentheses are necessary:

```
my_method({a: 1, b: 2, 5 => 25})
```

- Now let's suppose that the hash is the *only* parameter (or the last parameter) to a method. Ruby forgivingly lets us omit the braces:

```
my_method(a: 1, b: 2, 5 => 25)
```

Some people might think that this looks like a method invocation with named parameters. Really it isn't, though it could be if the method were defined that way.

- There are other cases in which blank spaces are semi-significant. For example, these four expressions may all seem to mean the same thing:

```
x = y + z
x = y+z
x = y+ z
x = y +z
```

And in fact, the first three do mean the same thing. However, in the fourth case, the parser thinks that y is a method call and +z is a parameter passed to it! It will then give an error message for that line if there is no method named y. The moral is to use blank spaces in a reasonable way.

- Similarly, x = y * z is a multiplication of y and z, whereas x = y *z is an invocation of method y, passing an expansion of array z as a parameter.

- When parsing identifiers, the underscore is considered to be lowercase. Thus, an identifier may start with an underscore, but it will not be a constant even if the next letter is uppercase.

- In linear nested-if statements, the keyword elsif is used rather than else if or elif, as in some languages.

- Keywords in Ruby are not really reserved words. When a method is called on a receiver (or in other cases where there is no ambiguity), a keyword may be used as a method name. Do this with caution, remembering that programs should be readable by humans.

- The keyword `then` is optional (in `if` and `case` statements). Those who want to use it for readability may do so. The same is true for `do` in `while` and `until` loops.

- The question mark and exclamation point are not really part of the identifier that they modify but rather should be considered suffixes. Thus, we see that although, for example, `chomp` and `chomp!` are considered different identifiers, it is not permissible to use these characters in any other position in the word. Likewise, we use `defined?` in Ruby, but `defined` is the keyword.

- Inside a string, the pound sign (`#`) is used to signal expressions to be evaluated. This means that in some circumstances, when a pound sign occurs in a string, it has to be escaped with a backslash, but this is *only* when the next character is a `{` (left brace), `$` (dollar sign), or `@` (at sign).

- Because of the fact that the question mark may be appended to an identifier, care should be taken with spacing around the ternary operator. For example, suppose we have a variable called `my_flag`, which stores either `true` or `false`. Then the first line of code shown here will be correct, but the second will give a syntax error:

```
x = my_flag ? 23 : 45    # OK
x = my_flag? 23 : 45     # Syntax error
```

- The ending marker `=end` for embedded documentation should not be considered a token. It marks the entire line and thus any characters on the rest of that line are not considered part of the program text but belong to the embedded document.

- There are no arbitrary blocks in Ruby; that is, you can't start a block whenever you feel like it, as in C. Blocks are allowed only where they are needed—for example, attached to an iterator. The exception is the `begin-end` block, which can be used basically anywhere.

- Remember that the keywords `BEGIN` and `END` are completely different from the `begin` and `end` keywords.

- When strings bump together (static concatenation), the concatenation is of a lower precedence than a method call. Here is an example:

```
str = "First " 'second'.center(20)        # Examples 1 and 2
str = "First " + 'second'.center(20)       # are the same.
str = "First second".center(20)            # Examples 3 and 4
str = ("First " + 'second').center(20)     # are the same.
```

- Ruby has several pseudovariables, which look like local variables but really serve specialized purposes. These are `self`, `nil`, `true`, `false`, `__FILE__`, and `__LINE__`.

1.5.2   Perspectives in Programming

Presumably everyone who knows Ruby (at this point in time) has been a student or user of other languages in the past. This, of course, makes learning Ruby easy in the sense that numerous features in Ruby are just like the corresponding features in other languages. On the other hand, the programmer may be lulled into a false sense of security by some of the familiar constructs in Ruby and may draw unwarranted conclusions based on past experience—which we might term "geek baggage."

Many people have come to Ruby from Python, Java, Perl, Smalltalk, C/C++, and various other languages. Their presuppositions and expectations may all vary somewhat, but they will always be present. For this reason, we discuss here a few of the things that some programmers may "trip over" in using Ruby:

- There is no Boolean type such as many languages have. `TrueClass` and `FalseClass` are distinct classes, and their only instantiations are `true` and `false`.

- Many of Ruby's operators are similar or identical to those in C. Two notable exceptions are the increment and decrement operators (++ and –). These are not available in Ruby, neither in "pre" nor "post" forms.

- The modulus operator is known to work somewhat differently in different languages with respect to negative numbers. The two sides of this argument are beyond the scope of this book; Ruby's behavior is as follows:

```
puts (5 % 3)      # Prints 2
puts (-5 % 3)     # Prints 1
puts (5 % -3)     # Prints -1
puts (-5 % -3)    # Prints -2
```

- Some may be used to thinking that a false value may be represented as a zero, a null string, a null character, or various other things. But in Ruby, all of these are true; in fact, *everything is true* except `false` and `nil`.

- In Ruby, variables don't have classes; only values have classes.

- There are no declarations of variables in Ruby. It is good practice, however, to assign `nil` to a variable initially. This certainly does not assign a type to the variable and does not truly initialize it, but it does inform the parser that this is a variable name rather than a method name.

- `ARGV[0]` is truly the first of the command-line parameters, numbering naturally from zero; it is not the file or script name preceding the parameters, like `argv[0]` in C.

- Most of Ruby's operators are really methods; the "punctuation" form of these methods is provided for familiarity and convenience. The first exception is the set of reflexive assignment operators (`+=`, `-=`, `*=`, and so on); the second exception is the following set: `=  ..  ...  !  not  &&  and  ||  or  !=  !~`.

- As in most (though not all) modern languages, Boolean operations are always short-circuited; that is, the evaluation of a Boolean expression stops as soon as its truth value is known. In a sequence of or operations, the first true will stop evaluation; in a string of and operations, the first false will stop evaluation.

- The prefix `@@` is used for class variables (which are associated with the class rather than the instance).

- `loop` is not a keyword; it is a `Kernel` method, not a control structure.

- Some may find the syntax of `unless-else` to be slightly unintuitive. Because `unless` is the opposite of `if`, the `else` clause will be executed if the condition is *true*.

- The simpler `Fixnum` type is passed as an immediate value and therefore may not be changed from within methods. The same is true for `true`, `false`, and `nil`.

- Do not confuse the `&&` and `||` operators with the `&` and `|` operators. These are used as in C; the former are for Boolean operations, and the latter are for arithmetic or bitwise operations.

- The `and`-`or` operators have lower precedence than the `&&`-`||` operators. See the following code fragment:

```
a = true
b = false
c = true
d = true
a1 = a && b or c && d   # &&'s are done first
a2 = a && (b or c) && d # or is done first
puts a1                 # Prints false
puts a2                 # Prints true
```

- Additionally, be aware that the assignment "operator" has a *higher* precedence than the and and or operators! (This is also true for the reflexive assignment operators +=, -=, and the others.) For example, in the following code, x = y or z looks like a normal assignment statement, but it is really a freestanding expression (equivalent to (x=y) or z, in fact). The third section shows a real assignment statement, x = (y or z), which may be what the programmer really intended.

```
y = false
z = true

x = y or z    # = is done BEFORE or!
puts x        # Prints false

(x = y) or z  # Line 5: Same as previous
puts x        # Prints false

x = (y or z)  # or is done first
puts x        # Prints true
```

- Don't confuse object attributes and local variables. If you are accustomed to C++ or Java, you might forget this. The variable @my_var is an instance variable (or attribute) in the context of whatever class you are coding, but my_var, used in the same circumstance, is only a local variable within that context.

- Many languages have some kind of for loop, as does Ruby. The question sooner or later arises as to whether the index variable can be modified. Some languages do not allow the control variable to be modified at all (printing a warning or error either at compile time or runtime), and some will cheerfully allow the loop behavior to be altered in midstream by such a change. Ruby takes yet a third approach. When a variable is used as a for loop control variable, it is an ordinary variable and can be modified at will; however, such a modification does not affect the loop behavior! The `for` loop sequentially assigns the values to the variable on each iteration without regard for what may have happened to that variable inside the loop. For example, this loop will execute exactly ten times and print the values 1 through 10:

```
for var in 1..10
  puts "var = #{var}"
  if var > 5
    var = var + 2
  end
end
```

- Variable names and method names are not always distinguishable "by eye" in the immediate context. How does the parser decide whether an identifier is a variable or a method? The rule is that if the parser sees the identifier being assigned a value prior to its being used, it will be considered a variable; otherwise, it is considered to be a method name. (Note also that the assignment does not have to be *executed* but only *seen* by the interpreter.)

1.5.3   Ruby's `case` Statement

Every modern language has some kind of multiway branch, such as the `switch` statement in C, C++, and Java or the `case` statement in Pascal. These serve basically the same purpose, and function much the same in most languages.

Ruby's `case` statement is similar to these others, but on closer examination, it has some unique features. While it works somewhat intuitively in most cases, it has no preciase analogue in other well-known languages. As a result, we cover a few edge cases here for the sake of completeness.

We have already seen the syntax of this statement. We will concentrate here on its actual semantics:

- To begin with, consider the trivial `case` statement shown here. The expression shown is compared with the value, not surprisingly, and if they correspond, `some_action` is performed:

```
case expression
  when value
    some_action
end
```

Ruby uses the special operator === (called the *relationship operator*) for this. This operator is also referred to (somewhat inappropriately) as the *case equality operator*. We say "inappropriately" because it does not always denote equality.

Thus, the preceding simple statement is equivalent to this statement:

```
if value === expression
  some_action
end
```

- However, do not confuse the relationship operator with the equality operator (==). They are utterly different, although their behavior may be the same in many circumstances. The relationship operator is defined differently for different classes and, for a given class, may behave differently for different operand types passed to it.

- Do not fall into the trap of thinking that the tested expression is the receiver and the value is passed as a parameter to it. The opposite is true (as we saw previously).

- This points up the fact that x === y is not typically the same as y === x! There will be situations in which this is true, but overall the relationship operator is not commutative. (That is why we do not favor the term *case equality operator*, because equality is always commutative.) In other words, reversing our original example, the following code does not behave the same way:

```
case value
  when expression
    some_action
end
```

- As an example, consider a string str and a pattern (regular expression) pat, which matches that string. The expression str =~ pat is true, just as in Perl. Because Ruby defines the opposite meaning for =~ in Regexp, you can also say that pat =~ str is true. Following this logic further, we find that (because of how Regexp defines ===) pat === str is also true. However, note that str === pat is *not* true. This means that the code fragment:

```
case "Hello"
  when /Hell/
    puts "We matched."
else
  puts "We didn't match."
end
```

does not do the same thing as this fragment:

```
case /Hell/
  when "Hello"
    puts "We matched."
else
  puts "We didn't match."
end
```

If this confuses you, just memorize the behavior. If it does not confuse you, so much the better.

- Programmers accustomed to C may be puzzled by the absence of `break` statements in the `case` statement; such a usage of `break` in Ruby is unnecessary (and illegal). This is due to the fact that "falling through" is rarely the desired behavior in a multiway branch. There is an implicit jump from each `when`-clause (or *case limb*, as it is sometimes called) to the end of the `case` statement. In this respect, Ruby's `case` statement resembles the one in Pascal.

- The values in each case limb are essentially arbitrary. They are not limited to any certain type. They need not be constants but can be variables or complex expressions. Ranges or multiple values can be associated with each case limb.

- Case limbs may have empty actions (null statements) associated with them. The values in the limbs need not be unique but may overlap. Look at this example:

```
case x
  when 0
  when 1..5
    puts "Second branch"
  when 5..10
    puts "Third branch"
else
  puts "Fourth branch"
end
```

Here, a value of 0 for x will do nothing; a value of 5 will print `Second branch`, even though 5 is also included in the next limb.

- The fact that case limbs may overlap is a consequence of the fact that they are evaluated in sequence *and* that short-circuiting is done. In other words, if evaluation of the expressions in one limb results in success, the limbs that follow are never evaluated. Therefore, it is a bad idea for case limb expressions to have method calls that have side effects. (Of course, such calls are questionable in most circumstances anyhow.) Also, be aware that this behavior may mask runtime errors that would occur if expressions were evaluated. Here is an example:

```
case x
  when 1..10
    puts "First branch"
  when foobar()            # Possible side effects?
    puts "Second branch"
  when 5/0                 # Dividing by zero!
    puts "Third branch"
else
  puts "Fourth branch"
end
```

As long as x is between 1 and 10, foobar() will not be called, and the expression 5/0 (which would naturally result in a runtime error) will not be evaluated.

1.5.4   Rubyisms and Idioms

Much of this material overlaps conceptually with the preceding pages. Don't worry too much about why we divided it as we did; many of these tidbits were difficult to classify or organize. Our most important motivation was simply to break the information into digestible chunks.

Ruby was designed to be consistent and orthogonal. But it is also complex, and so, like every language, it has its own set of idioms and quirks. We discuss some of these in the following list:

- alias can be used to give alternate names for global variables and methods.

- The numbered global variables $1, $2, $3, and so on, cannot be aliased.

- We do not recommend the use of the "special variables," such as $_, $$, and the rest. Though they can sometimes make code more compact, they rarely make it any clearer; we use them sparingly in this book and recommend the same practice. If needed, they can be aliased to longer, readable names such as $LAST_READ_LINE or $PROCESS_ID by using require 'English'.

- Do not confuse the .. and ... range operators. The former is *inclusive* of the upper bound, and the latter is *exclusive*. For example, 5..10 includes the number 10, but 5...10 does not.

- There is a small detail relating to ranges that may cause confusion. Given the range m..n, the method end will return the endpoint of the range; its alias last will do the same thing. However, these methods will return the same value (n) for the range m...n, even though n is not included in the latter range. The method end_excluded? is provided to distinguish between these two situations.

- Do not confuse ranges with arrays. These two assignments are entirely different:

```
x = 1..5
x = [1, 2, 3, 4, 5]
```

However, there is a convenient method (to_a) for converting ranges to arrays. (Many other classes also have such a method.)

- Often we want to assign a variable a value only if it does not already have a value. Because an unassigned variable has the value nil, we can, for example, shorten x = x || 5 to x ||= 5. Beware that the value false will be overwritten just as nil will.

- In most languages, swapping two variables takes an additional temporary variable. In Ruby, multiple assignment makes this unnecessary. For example, x, y = y, x will interchange the values of x and y.

- Keep a clear distinction in your mind between *class* and *instance*. For example, a class variable such as @@foobar has a classwide scope, but an instance variable such as @foobar has a separate existence in each object of the class.

- Similarly, a class method is associated with the class in which it is defined; it does not belong to any specific object and cannot be invoked as though it did. A class method is invoked with the name of a class, and an instance method is invoked with the name of an object.

- In writing about Ruby, the *pound notation* is sometimes used to indicate an instance method—for example, we use File.chmod to denote the class method chmod of class File, and we use File#chmod to denote the instance method that has the same name. This notation is not part of Ruby syntax but only Ruby folklore. We have tried to avoid it in this book.

- In Ruby, constants are not truly constant. They cannot be changed from within instance methods, but otherwise their values can be changed.

- In writing about Ruby, the word *toplevel* is common as both an adjective and a noun. We prefer to use *top level* as a noun and *top-level* as an adjective, but our meaning is the same as everyone else's.

- The keyword `yield` comes from CLU and may be misleading to some programmers. It is used within an iterator to invoke the block with which the iterator is called. It does not mean "yield," as in producing a result or returning a value, but is more like the concept of "yielding a timeslice."

- The reflexive assignment operators `+=`, `-=`, and the rest are not methods (nor are they really operators); they are only "syntax sugar" or "shorthand" for their longer forms. Therefore, to say `x += y` is really identical to saying `x = x + y`, and if the `+` operator is overloaded, the `+=` operator is defined "automagically" as a result of this predefined shorthand.

- Because of the way the reflexive assignment operators are defined, they cannot be used to initialize variables. If the first reference to x is `x += 1`, an error will result. This will be intuitive to most programmers unless they are accustomed to a language where variables are initialized to some sort of zero or null value.

- It is actually possible in some sense to get around this behavior. One can define operators for `nil` such that the initial `nil` value of the variable produces the result we want. Here is a `nil.+` method that will allow `+=` to initialize a `String` or a `Fixnum` value, basically just returning other and thus ensuring that `nil + other` is equal to `other`:

```
def nil.+(other)
  other
end
```

  This illustrates the power of Ruby—but in general it's not useful or appropriate to code this way.

- It is wise to recall that `Class` *is an object* and `Object` *is a class*. We will try to make this clear in a later chapter; for now, simply recite it every day as a mantra.

- Some operators can't be overloaded because they are built into the language rather than implemented as methods. These are `= .. ... and or not && || ! != !~`.

  Additionally, the reflexive assignment operators (`+=`, `-=`, and so on) cannot be overloaded. These are not methods, and it can be argued they are not true operators either.

- Be aware that although assignment is not overloadable, it is still possible to write an instance method with a name such as `foo=` (allowing statements such as `x.foo = 5`). Consider the equal sign to be like a suffix.

- Recall that a "bare" scope operator has an implied `Object` before it; therefore, `::Foo` means `Object::Foo`.

- Recall that `fail` is an alias for `raise`.

- Recall that definitions in Ruby are executed. Because of the dynamic nature of the language, it is possible (for example) to define two methods completely differently based on a flag that is tested at runtime.

- Remember that the `for` construct (`for x in a`) is really calling the default iterator `each`. Any class having this iterator can be walked through with a `for` loop.

- Be aware that a method defined at the top level is added to `Kernel` and is therefore a member of `Object`.

- A *setter* method (such as `foo=`) must be called with a receiver; otherwise, it will look like a simple assignment to a local variable of that name.

- The keyword `retry` is used only in exception handling. (In older versions of Ruby, it was used in iterators as well.)

- An object's `initialize` method is always private.

- Where a block ends in a left brace (or in `end`) and results in a value, that value can be used as the receiver for further method calls. Here is an example:

```
squares = [1,2,3,4,5].collect {|x| x**2 }.reverse
# squares is now [25,16,9,4,1]
```

- The idiom `if $0 == __FILE__` is sometimes seen near the bottom of a Ruby program. This is a check to see whether the file is being run as a standalone piece of code (true) or is being used as some kind of auxiliary piece of code such as a library (false). A common use of this is to put a sort of "main program" (usually with test code in it) at the end of a library.

- Normal subclassing or inheritance is done with the < symbol:

```
class Dog < Animal
  # ...
end
```

But creation of a singleton class (an anonymous class that extends a single instance) is done with the << symbol:

```
class << platypus
  # ...
end
```

- When passing a block to an iterator, there is a slight difference between braces
  ({}) and a do-end pair. This is a precedence issue:

```
mymethod param1, foobar do ... end
# Here, do-end binds with mymethod

mymethod param1, foobar { ... }
# Here, {} binds with foobar, assumed to be a method
```

- It is somewhat traditional in Ruby to put single-line blocks in braces and multiline blocks in do-end pairs. Here are some examples:

```
my_array.each { |x| puts x }

my_array.each do |x|
  print x
  if x % 2 == 0
    puts " is even."
  else
    puts " is odd."
  end
end
```

This habit is not required, and there may be occasions where it is inappropriate
to follow this rule.

- A closure remembers the context in which it was created. One way to create a closure is by using a Proc object. As a crude example, consider the following:

```
def power(exponent)
  proc {|base| base**exponent}
end

square = power(2)
cube = power(3)

a = square.call(11)    # Result is 121
b = square.call(5)     # Result is 25
c = cube.call(6)       # Result is 216
d = cube.call(8)       # Result is 512
```

Observe that the closure "knows" the value of exponent that it was given at the
time it was created.

- However, let's assume that a closure uses a variable defined in an outer scope
  (which is perfectly legal). This property can be useful, but here we show a misuse
  of it:

```
$exponent = 0

def power
  proc {|base| base**$exponent}
end

$exponent = 2
square = power

$exponent = 3
cube = power

a = square.call(11)    # Wrong!  Result is 1331

b = square.call(5)     # Wrong!  Result is 125


# The above two results are wrong because the CURRENT
# value of $exponent is being used. This would be true
# even if it had been a local variable that had gone
# out of scope (e.g., using define_method).

c = cube.call(6) # Result is 216
d = cube.call(8) # Result is 512
```

- Finally, consider this somewhat contrived example. Inside the block of the times
  iterator, a new context is started so that x is a local variable. The variable closure
  is already defined at the top level, so it will not be defined as local to the block.

```
closure = nil        # Define closure so the name will
                       be known
1.times do            # Start a new context
  x = 5               # x is local to this block
  closure = Proc.new { puts "In closure, x = #{x}" }
end

x = 1
```

```
# Define x at top level

closure.call          # Prints: In closure, x = 5
```

Now note that the variable x that is set to 1 is a new variable, defined at the top level. It is not the same as the other variable of the same name. The closure therefore prints 5 because it remembers its creation context with the previous variable x and its previous value.

- Variables starting with a single @, defined inside a class, are generally instance variables. However, if they are defined outside any method, they are really class instance variables. (This usage is somewhat contrary to most OOP terminology in which a class instance is regarded to be the same as an instance or an object.) Here is an example:

```
class MyClass

  @x = 1          # A class instance variable
  @y = 2          # Another one

  def my_method
    @x = 3        # An instance variable
    # Note that @y is not accessible here.
  end

end
```

The class instance variable @y in the preceding code example is really an attribute of the class object MyClass, which is an instance of the class Class. (Remember, Class is an object, and Object is a class.) Class instance variables cannot be referenced from within instance methods and, in general, are not very useful.

- attr, attr_reader, attr_writer, and attr_accessor are shorthand for the actions of defining "setters" and "getters"; they take symbols as arguments (that is, instances of class Symbol).

- There is never any assignment with the scope operator; for example, the assignment Math::PI = 3.2 is illegal.

1.5.5   Expression Orientation and Other Miscellaneous Issues

In Ruby, expressions are nearly as significant as statements. If you are a C programmer, this will be somewhat familiar to you; if your background is in Pascal, it may seem utterly foreign. But Ruby carries expression orientation even further than C.

In addition, we use this section to remind you of a couple of minor issues regarding regular expressions. Consider them to be a small bonus:

- In Ruby, any kind of assignment returns the same value that was assigned. Therefore, we can sometimes take little shortcuts like the ones shown here, but be careful when you are dealing with objects! Remember that these are nearly always *references* to objects.

```
x = y = z = 0        # All are now zero.

a = b = c = []       # Danger! a, b, and c now all refer
                     # to the SAME empty array.
x = 5
y = x += 2           # Now x and y are both 7
```

However, remember that values such as `Fixnums` are actually stored as immediate values, not as object references.

- Many control structures return values—if, unless, and case. The following code is all valid; it demonstrates that the branches of a decision need not be statements but can simply be expressions:

```
a = 5
x = if a < 8 then 6 else 7 end     # x is now 6

y = if a < 8        # y is 6 also; the
  6                 # if-statement can be
else                # on a single line
  7                 # or on multiple lines.
end

# unless also works; z will be assigned 4
z = unless x == y then 3 else 4 end

t = case a          # t gets assigned
  when 0..3         # the value
    "low"           # "medium"
```

```
    when 4..6
      "medium"
  else
    "high"
  end
```

Here, we indent as though the `case` started with the assignment. This looks proper to our eyes, but you may disagree.

- Note by way of contrast that the `while` and `until` loops do not return useful values but typically return `nil`:

```
i = 0
x = while (i < 5)      # x is nil
  puts i+=1
end
```

- The ternary decision operator can be used with statements or expressions. For syntactic reasons (or parser limitations), the parentheses here are necessary:

```
x = 6
y = x == 5 ? 0 : 1                    # y is now 1
x == 5 ? puts("Hi") : puts("Bye")  # Prints Bye
```

- The `return` at the end of a method can be omitted. A method always returns the last expression evaluated in its body, regardless of where that happens.

- When an iterator is called with a block, the last expression evaluated in the block is returned as the value of the block. Therefore, if the body of an iterator has a statement such as `x = yield`, that value can be captured.

- Recall that the multiline modifier `/m` can be appended to a regex, in which case . (dot) will match a newline character.

- Beware of zero-length matches in regular expressions. If all elements of a regex are optional, then "nothingness" will match that pattern, and a match will always be found at the beginning of a string. This is a common error for regex users, particularly novices.

1.6 Ruby Jargon and Slang

You don't have to relearn English when you learn Ruby. But certain pieces of jargon and slang are commonly used in the community. Some of these may be used in slightly different ways from the rest of the computer science world. Most of these are discussed in this section.

In Ruby, the term *attribute* is used somewhat unofficially. We can think of an attribute as being an instance variable that is exposed to the outside world via one of the `attr` family of methods. This is a gray area because we could have methods such as `foo` and `foo=` that don't correspond to `@foo` as we would expect. And certainly not all instance variables are considered attributes. As always, common sense should guide your usage.

Attributes in Ruby can be broken down into readers and writers (called *getters* and *setters* in some languages—terms we don't commonly use). An *accessor* is both a reader and a writer; this is consistent with the name of the `attr_accessor` method but disagrees with common usage in other communities where an accessor is read-only.

The operator `===` is unique to Ruby (as far as I am aware). The common name for it is the *case comparison operator* because it is used implicitly by `case` statements. In this book, I often use the term *relationship operator.* I did not invent this term, but I can't find its origin, and it is not in common use today. It is sometimes also called the *threequal operator* ("three equal signs").

The `<=>` operator is probably best called the *comparison operator.* It is commonly called the *spaceship operator* because it looks like a side view of a flying saucer in an old-fashioned video game or text-based computer game.

The term *poetry mode* is used by some to indicate the omission of needless punctuation and tokens (a tongue-in-cheek reference to the punctuation habits of poets in the last six decades or so). Poetry mode is often taken to mean "omission of parentheses around method calls." Here is an example:

```
some_method(1, 2, 3)    # unneeded parentheses
some_method 1, 2, 3     # "poetry mode"
```

But I think the principle is more general than that. For example, when a hash is passed as the last or lone parameter, the braces may be omitted. At the end of a line, the semicolon may be omitted (and really always is). In most cases, the keyword `then` may be omitted, whether in `if` statements or `case` statements.

Some coders even go so far as to omit parentheses in a method definition, though most do not:

```
def my_method(a, b, c)   # Also legal:  def my_method a, b, c
  # ...
end
```

It is worth noting that in some cases, the complexity of the Ruby grammar causes the parser to be confused easily. When method calls are nested, it is better to use parentheses for clarity:

```
def alpha(x)
  x*2
end

def beta(y)
  y*3
end

gamma = 5
delta = alpha(beta(gamma))
delta = alpha beta gamma # same, but less clear
```

The term *duck typing*, as far as I can tell, originated with Dave Thomas. It refers to the old saying that if something looks like a duck, walks like a duck, and quacks like a duck, it might as well be a duck. Exactly what this term means may be open to discussion; I would say that it refers to the tendency of Ruby to be less concerned with the *class* of an object and more concerned with what methods can be called on it and what operations can be performed on it. Therefore, in Ruby we rarely use is_a? or kind_of?, but we more often use the respond_to? method. Most often of all, we simply pass an object to a method and expect that an exception will be raised if it is used inappropriately. That usually happens sooner rather than later, but the exceptions that are raised may be hard to understand and debug quickly.

The unary asterisk that is used to expand an array could be called an *array expansion operator*, but I don't think I have ever heard that. Terms such as *star* and *splat* are inevitable in casual conversation, along with derivatives such as *splatted* and *unsplatted*. David Black, author of *The Well-Grounded Rubyist*, cleverly calls this the *unary unarray* operator.

The term *singleton* is sometimes regarded as overused. It is useful to remember that this is a perfectly good English word in its own right—referring to a thing that is solitary or unique. As long as we use it as a modifier, there should be no confusion.

The *Singleton Pattern* is a well-known design pattern in which a class allows itself to be instantiated only once; the singleton library in Ruby facilitates the use of this pattern.

A *singleton class* (called an *eigenclass* by some people) is the instance of `Class` where methods are stored that are "per object" rather than "per class." It is arguably not a "true" class because it cannot be instantiated. The following is an example of opening up the singleton class for a string object and adding a method:

```ruby
str = "hello"
class << str                 # Alternatively:
  def hyphenated             # def str.hyphenated
    self.split("").join("-")
  end
end


str.hyphenated               # "h-e-l-l-o"
```

Let's go back to our previous example. Because the method `hyphenate` exists in no other object or class, it is a *singleton method* on that object. This also is unambiguous. Sometimes the object itself will be called a singleton because it is one of a kind—it is the only instance of that class.

But remember that in Ruby, a class is itself an object. Therefore, we can add a method to the singleton class *of a class*, and that method will be unique to that object, which happens to be a class. Here is an example:

```ruby
class MyClass
  class << self                # Alternatively: def self.hello
    def hello                  # or: def MyClass.hello
      puts "Hello from #{self}!"
    end
  end
end
```

So we don't have to instantiate `MyClass` to call this method:

```ruby
MyClass.hello                # Hello from MyClass!
```

However, you will notice that this is simply what we call a *class method* in Ruby. In other words, a class method is a singleton method on a class. We could also say it's a singleton method on an object that *happens to be* a class.

There are a few more terms to cover. A *class variable* is one that starts with a double-@, of course; it is perhaps a slight misnomer because of its nontrivial behavior with regard to inheritance. A *class instance variable* is a somewhat different animal. It is an ordinary instance variable where the object it belongs to happens to be a class. For more information, see Chapter 11, "OOP and Dynamic Features in Ruby."

Especially since the advent of Ruby on Rails, many have used the term "monkey-patching"; this refers to the reopening of a class (especially a system class) in order to add (or override) methods or other features. I don't use this term in this book or elsewhere because it is a disparaging term which originated outside our community. Open classes in Ruby are a feature, not a bug. They can be used properly and safely, or they can be used improperly, just like any other language feature.

1.7   Conclusion

That ends our review of object-oriented programming and our whirlwind tour of the Ruby language. Later chapters will expand on this material greatly.

Although it was not my intention to "teach Ruby" to the beginner in this chapter, it is possible that the beginner might pick it up here anyhow. (Several people have reported to me that they learned Ruby from the first or second edition of this book.) However, the later material in the book should be useful to the beginning and intermediate Rubyist alike. It is my hope that even the advanced Ruby programmer may still gain some new knowledge here and there.

CHAPTER 2
Working with Strings

Atoms were once thought to be fundamental, elementary building blocks of nature; protons were then thought to be fundamental, then quarks. Now we say the string is fundamental.

—David Gross, professor of theoretical physics, Princeton University

A computer science professor in the early 1980s started out his data structures class with a single question. He didn't introduce himself or state the name of the course; he didn't hand out a syllabus or give the name of the textbook. He walked to the front of the class and asked, "What is the most important data type?"

There were one or two guesses. Someone guessed "pointers," and he brightened but said no, that wasn't it. Then he offered his opinion: The most important data type was *character* data.

He had a valid point. Computers are supposed to be our servants, not our masters, and character data has the distinction of being human readable. (Some humans can read binary data easily, but we will ignore them.) The existence of characters (and therefore strings) enables communication between humans and computers. Every kind of information we can imagine, including natural language text, can be encoded in character strings.

A *string* is simply a sequence of characters. Like most entities in Ruby, strings are first-class objects. In everyday programming, we need to manipulate strings in many ways. We want to concatenate strings, tokenize them, analyze them, perform searches and substitutions, and more. Ruby makes most of these tasks easy.

For much of the history of Ruby, a single byte was considered a character. That is not true of special characters, emoji, and most non-Latin scripts. For a more detailed discussion of the ways that bytes and characters are often not the same, refer to Chapter 4, "Internationalization in Ruby."

2.1   Representing Ordinary Strings

A string in Ruby is composed simply of a sequence of 8-bit bytes. It is not null terminated as in C, so it may contain null characters. Strings containing bytes above 0xFF are always legal, but are only meaningful in non-ASCII encodings. Strings are assumed to use the UTF-8 encoding. Before Ruby 2.0, they were assumed to be simple ASCII. (For more information on encodings, refer to Chapter 4.)

The simplest string in Ruby is single quoted. Such a string is taken absolutely literally; the only escape sequences recognized are the single quote (\') and the escaped backslash itself (\\). Here are some examples:

```
s1 = 'This is a string'    # This is a string
s2 = 'Mrs. O\'Leary'       # Mrs. O'Leary
s3 = 'Look in C:\\TEMP'    # Look in C:\TEMP
```

A double-quoted string is more versatile. It allows many more escape sequences, such as backspace, tab, carriage return, and linefeed. It allows control characters to be embedded as octal numbers, and Unicode code points to be embedded via their hexadecimal reference number. Consider these examples:

```
s1 = "This is a tab: (\t)"
s2 = "Some backspaces: xyz\b\b\b"
s3 = "This is also a tab: \011"
s4 = "And these are both bells: \a \007"
s5 = "This is the unicode snowman: \u2603"
```

Non-ASCII characters will be shown "backslash escaped" when their string is inspected, but will print normally. Double-quoted strings also allow expressions to be embedded inside them. See Section 2.21, "Embedding Expressions within Strings."

2.2   Representing Strings with Alternate Notations

Sometimes we want to represent strings that are rich in metacharacters, such as single quotes, double quotes, and more. For these situations, we have the %q and %Q notations. Following either of these is a string within a pair of delimiters; I personally favor square brackets ([ ]).

The difference between the %q and %Q variants is that the former acts like a single-quoted string, and the latter like a double-quoted string:

```
S1 = %q[As Magritte said, "Ceci n'est pas une pipe."]
s2 = %q[This is not a tab: (\t)]  # same as: 'This is not a tab: \t'
s3 = %Q[This IS a tab: (\t)]      # same as: "This IS a tab: \t"
```

Both kinds of notation can be used with different delimiters. Besides brackets, there are other paired delimiters (parentheses, braces, and angle brackets):

```
s1 = %q(Bill said, "Bob said, 'This is a string.'")
s2 = %q{Another string.}
s3 = %q<Special characters '"[](){} in this string.>
```

There are also "nonpaired" delimiters. Basically any character may be used that is printable, but not alphanumeric, not whitespace, and not a paired character:

```
s1 = %q:"I think Mrs. O'Leary's cow did it," he said.:
s2 = %q*\r is a control-M and \n is a control-J.*
```

2.3   Using Here-Documents

If you want to represent a long string spanning multiple lines, you can certainly use a regular quoted string:

```
str = "Once upon a midnight dreary,
        While I pondered, weak and weary..."
```

However, the indentation will be part of the string.

Another way is to use a *here-document,* a string that is inherently multiline. (This concept and term are borrowed from older languages and contexts.) The syntax is the << symbol, followed by an end marker, then zero or more lines of text, and finally the same end marker on a line by itself:

```
str = <<EOF
Once upon a midnight dreary,
While I pondered weak and weary,...
EOF
```

Be careful about things such as trailing spaces on the final end marker line. Current versions of Ruby will fail to recognize the end marker in those situations.

Note that here-documents may be "stacked"; for example, here is a method call with three such strings passed to it:

```
some_method(<<STR1, <<STR2, <<STR3)
first piece
of text...
STR1
second piece...
STR2
third piece
of text.
STR3
```

By default, a here-document is like a double-quoted string—that is, its contents are subject to interpretation of escape sequences and interpolation of embedded expressions. But if the end marker is single-quoted, the here-document behaves like a single-quoted string:

```
str = <<'EOF'
This isn't a tab: \t
and this isn't a newline: \n
EOF
```

If a here-document's end marker is preceded by a hyphen, the end marker may be indented. *Only* the spaces before the end marker are deleted from the string, not those on previous lines:

```
str = <<-EOF
   Each of these lines
   starts with a pair
   of blank spaces.
   EOF
```

To delete the spaces from the beginning of each line, we need another method. The `ActiveSupport` gem (included in Rails) defines a `strip_heredoc` method that works similarly to this one:

```
class String
  def strip_heredoc
    # Find the margin whitespace on the first line
    margin = self[/\A\s*/]
    # Remove margin-sized whitespace from each line
    gsub(/\s{#{margin.size}}/,"")
  end
end
```

The amount of whitespace before the start of the first line is detected, and that amount of whitespace is then stripped off of each line. It's used in this way:

```
str = <<end.strip_heredoc
  This here-document has a "left margin"
  set by the whitespace on the first line.

  We can do inset quotations here,
    hanging indentions, and so on.
end
```

The word *end* is used naturally enough as an end marker. (This, of course, is a matter of taste. It looks like the reserved word `end` but is really just an arbitrary marker.) Many text editors use the end marker as a hint for syntax highlighting. As a result, using `<<SQL` or `<<RUBY` can make it dramatically easier to read blocks of code inside here-docs in those editors.

2.4   Finding the Length of a String

The method `length` can be used to find a string's length. A synonym is `size`:

```
str1 = "Carl"
x = str1.length     # 4
str2 = "Doyle"
x = str2.size       # 5
```

2.5   Processing a Line at a Time

A Ruby string can contain newlines. For example, a file can be read into memory and stored in a single string. Strings provide an iterator, `each_line`, to process a string one line at a time:

```
str = "Once upon\na time...\nThe End\n"
num = 0
str.each_line do |line|
  num += 1
  print "Line #{num}: #{line}"
end
```

The preceding code produces three lines of output:

```
Line 1: Once upon
Line 2: a time...
Line 3: The End
```

Iterators (such as `each_line`) can be chained together with other iterators (such as `with_index`). Connecting function outputs and inputs in a line like this is a technique sometimes called *function composition* (or *method chaining*). Instead of tracking the line number manually, `with_index` can be *composed* with `each_line` to produce the exact same output:

```
str = "Once upon\na time...\nThe End\n"
str.each_line.with_index do |line, num|
  print "Line #{num + 1}: #{line}"
end
```

2.6   Processing a Character or Byte at a Time

Ruby used to treat each byte as a character, but that is no longer the case. The bytes in a string are available as an array via the `bytes` method. To process the bytes, one at a time, use the `each_byte` iterator:

```
str = "ABC"
str.each_byte {|byte| print byte, " " }
puts
# Produces output: 65 66 67
```

A character is essentially the same as a one-character string. In multibyte encodings, a one-character string may be more than one byte:

```
str = "ABC"
str.each_char {|char| print char, " " }
puts
# Produces output: A B C
```

In any version of Ruby, you can break a string into an array of one-character strings by using scan with a simple wildcard regular expression matching a single character:

```
str = "ABC"
chars = str.scan(/./)
chars.each {|char| print char, " " }
puts
# Produces output: A B C
```

2.7 Performing Specialized String Comparisons

Ruby has built-in ideas about comparing strings; comparisons are done lexicographically, as we have come to expect (that is, based on character set order). But if we want, we can introduce rules of our own for string comparisons, and these can be of arbitrary complexity.

For example, suppose that we want to ignore the English articles *a*, *an*, and *the* at the front of a string, and we also want to ignore most common punctuation marks. We can do this by overriding the built-in method <=> (which is called for <, <=, >, and >=). Listing 2.1 shows how we do this.

Listing 2.1 Specialized String Comparisons

```
class String

  alias old_compare <=>

  def <=>(other)
    a = self.dup
    b = other.dup
    # Remove punctuation
    a.gsub!(/[\,\.\?\!\:\;]/, "")
    b.gsub!(/[\,\.\?\!\:\;]/, "")
```

```
    # Remove initial articles
    a.gsub!(/^(a |an |the )/i, "")
    b.gsub!(/^(a |an |the )/i, "")
    # Remove leading/trailing whitespace
    a.strip!
    b.strip!
    # Use the old <=>
    a.old_compare(b)
  end

end


title1 = "Calling All Cars"
title2 = "The Call of the Wild"

# Ordinarily this would print "yes"

if title1 < title2
  puts "yes"
else
  puts "no"          # But now it prints "no"
end
```

Note that we "save" the old <=> with an alias and then call it at the end. This is because if we tried to use the < method, it would call the new <=> rather than the old one, resulting in infinite recursion and a program crash.

Note also that the == operator does not call the <=> method (mixed in from Comparable). This means that if we need to check equality in some specialized way, we will have to override the == method separately. But in this case, == works as we want it to anyhow.

Suppose that we wanted to do case-insensitive string comparisons. The built-in method casecmp will do this; we just have to make sure that it is used instead of the usual comparison.

Here is one way:

```
    class String
      def <=>(other)
        casecmp(other)
      end
    end
```

But there is a slightly easier way:

```
class String
  alias <=> casecmp
end
```

However, we haven't finished. We need to redefine == so that it will behave in the same way:

```
class String
  def ==(other)
    casecmp(other) == 0
  end
end
```

Now all string comparisons will be strictly case insensitive. Any sorting operation that depends on <=> will likewise be case insensitive.

2.8   Tokenizing a String

The `split` method parses a string and returns an array of tokenized strings. It accepts two parameters: a delimiter and a field limit (which is an integer).

The delimiter defaults to whitespace. Actually, it uses `$;` or the English equivalent `$FIELD_SEPARATOR`. If the delimiter is a string, the explicit value of that string is used as a token separator:

```
s1 = "It was a dark and stormy night."
words = s1.split          # ["It", "was", "a", "dark", "and",
                          #  "stormy", "night"]
s2 = "apples, pears, and peaches"
list = s2.split(", ")     # ["apples", "pears", "and peaches"]

s3 = "lions and tigers and bears"
zoo = s3.split(/ and /)   # ["lions", "tigers", "bears"]
```

The `limit` parameter places an upper limit on the number of fields returned, according to these rules:

- If it is omitted, trailing null entries are suppressed.

- If it is a positive number, the number of entries will be limited to that number (stuffing the rest of the string into the last field as needed). Trailing null entries are retained.

- If it is a negative number, there is no limit to the number of fields, and trailing null entries are retained.

These three rules are illustrated here:

```
str = "alpha,beta,gamma,,"
list1 = str.split(",")      # ["alpha","beta","gamma"]
list2 = str.split(",",2)    # ["alpha", "beta,gamma,,"]
list3 = str.split(",",4)    # ["alpha", "beta", "gamma", ",,"]
list4 = str.split(",",8)    # ["alpha", "beta", "gamma", "", ""]
list5 = str.split(",",-1)   # ["alpha", "beta", "gamma", "", ""]
```

Similarly, the scan method can be used to match regular expressions or strings against a target string:

```
str = "I am a leaf on the wind..."

# A string is interpreted literally, not as a regex
arr = str.scan("a")    # ["a","a","a"]

# A regex will return all matches
arr = str.scan(/\w+/)
# ["I", "am", "a", "leaf", "on", "the", "wind"]

# A block will be passed each match, one at a time
str.scan(/\w+/) {|x| puts x }
```

The StringScanner class, from the standard library, is different in that it maintains state for the scan rather than doing it all at once:

```
require 'strscan'
str = "Watch how I soar!"
ss = StringScanner.new(str)
loop do
  word = ss.scan(/\w+/)     # Grab a word at a time
  break if word.nil?
  puts word
  sep = ss.scan(/\W+/)      # Grab next non-word piece
  break if sep.nil?
end
```

2.9 Formatting a String

Formatting a string is done in Ruby as it is in C: with the `sprintf` method. It takes a string and a list of expressions as parameters and returns a string. The format string contains essentially the same set of specifiers available with C's `sprintf` (or `printf`):

```
name = "Bob"
age = 28
str = sprintf("Hi, %s... I see you're %d years old.", name, age)
```

You might ask why we would use this instead of simply interpolating values into a string using the `#{expr}` notation. The answer is that `sprintf` makes it possible to do extra formatting, such as specifying a maximum width, specifying a maximum number of decimal places, adding or suppressing leading zeroes, left-justifying, right-justifying, and more:

```
str = sprintf("%-20s  %3d", name, age)
```

The `String` class has the method `%`, which does much the same thing. It takes a single value or an array of values of any type:

```
str = "%-20s  %3d" % [name, age]  # Same as previous example
```

We also have the methods `ljust`, `rjust`, and `center`; these take a length for the destination string and pad with spaces as needed:

```
str = "Moby-Dick"
s1 = str.ljust(13)        # "Moby-Dick"
s2 = str.center(13)       # "  Moby-Dick  "
s3 = str.rjust(13)        # "    Moby-Dick"
```

If a second parameter is specified, it is used as the pad string (which may possibly be truncated as needed):

```
str = "Captain Ahab"
s1 = str.ljust(20,"+")    # "Captain Ahab++++++++"
s2 = str.center(20,"-")   # "----Captain Ahab----"
s3 = str.rjust(20,"123")  # "12312312Captain Ahab"
```

2.10   Using Strings as IO Objects

Besides `sprintf` and `scanf`, there is another way to fake input/output to a string—
the `StringIO` class.

Because this is a very IO-like object, we cover it in a later chapter. See Section
10.1.24, "Treating a String as a File."

2.11   Controlling Uppercase and Lowercase

Ruby's `String` class offers a rich set of methods for controlling case. This section
offers an overview of these.

The `downcase` method converts a string to all lowercase. Likewise, `upcase` converts it to all uppercase. Here is an example each:

```
s1 = "Boston Tea Party"
s2 = s1.downcase            # "boston tea party"
s3 = s2.upcase              # "BOSTON TEA PARTY"
```

The `capitalize` method capitalizes the first character of a string while forcing
all the remaining characters to lowercase:

```
s4 = s1.capitalize          # "Boston tea party"
s5 = s2.capitalize          # "Boston tea party"
s6 = s3.capitalize          # "Boston tea party"
```

The `swapcase` method exchanges the case of each letter in a string:

```
s7 = "THIS IS AN ex-parrot."
s8 = s7.swapcase            # "this is an EX-PARROT."
```

There is also the `casecmp` method, which acts like the `<=>` method but ignores
case:

```
n1 = "abc".casecmp("xyz")   # -1
n2 = "abc".casecmp("XYZ")   # -1
n3 = "ABC".casecmp("xyz")   # -1
n4 = "ABC".casecmp("abc")   # 0
n5 = "xyz".casecmp("abc")   # 1
```

Each of these also has an in-place equivalent (`upcase!`, `downcase!`, `capitalize!`, and `swapcase!`).

There are no built-in methods for detecting case, but this is easy to do with regular expressions, as shown in the following example:

```
if string =~ /[a-z]/
  puts "string contains lowercase characters"
end

if string =~ /[A-Z]/
  puts "string contains uppercase characters"
end

if string =~ /[A-Z]/ and string =~ /a-z/
  puts "string contains mixed case"
end

if string[0..0] =~ /[A-Z]/
  puts "string starts with a capital letter"
end
```

Regular expressions of this sort will only match ASCII characters. To match Unicode uppercase or lowercase characters, use a named character class, as shown here:

```
if string =~ /\p{Upper}/
  puts "string contains uppercase Unicode characters like Ü"
end
```

For more information about regular expressions, see Chapter 3, "Working with Regular Expressions."

2.12 Accessing and Assigning Substrings

In Ruby, substrings may be accessed in several different ways. Normally the bracket notation is used, as for an array, but the brackets may contain a pair of Fixnums, a range, a regex, or a string. Each case is discussed in turn.

If a pair of Fixnum values is specified, they are treated as an offset and a length, and the corresponding substring is returned:

```
str = "Humpty Dumpty"
sub1 = str[7,4]          # "Dump"
sub2 = str[7,99]         # "Dumpty" (overrunning is OK)
sub3 = str[10,-4]        # nil (length is negative)
```

It is important to remember that these are an offset and a length (number of characters), not beginning and ending offsets.

A negative index counts backward from the end of the string. In this case, the index is one based, not zero based, but the length is still added in the forward direction:

```
str1 = "Alice"
sub1 = str1[-3,3]   # "ice"
str2 = "Through the Looking-Glass"
sub3 = str2[-13,4]  # "Look"
```

A range may be specified. In this case, the range is taken as a range of indices into the string. Ranges may have negative numbers, but the numerically lower number must still be first in the range. If the range is "backward" or if the initial value is outside the string, nil is returned, as shown here:

```
str = "Winston Churchill"
sub1 = str[8..13]      # "Church"
sub2 = str[-4..-1]     # "hill"
sub3 = str[-1..-4]     # nil
sub4 = str[25..30]     # nil
```

If a regular expression is specified, the string matching that pattern will be returned. If there is no match, nil will be returned:

```
str = "Alistair Cooke"
sub1 = str[/l..t/]   # "list"
sub2 = str[/s.*r/]   # "stair"
sub3 = str[/foo/]    # nil
```

If a string is specified, that string will be returned if it appears as a substring (or nil if it does not):

```
str = "theater"
sub1 = str["heat"]   # "heat"
sub2 = str["eat"]    # "eat"
```

```
sub3 = str["ate"]    # "ate"
sub4 = str["beat"]   # nil
sub5 = str["cheat"]  # nil
```

Finally, in the trivial case, using a **Fixnum** as the index will yield a single character (or nil if out of range):

```
str = "Aaron Burr"
ch1 = str[0]     # "A"
ch1 = str[1]     # "a"
ch3 = str[99]    # nil
```

It is important to realize that the notations described here will serve for assigning values as well as for accessing them:

```
str1 = "Humpty Dumpty"
str1[7,4] = "Moriar"     # "Humpty Moriarty"

str2 = "Alice"
str2[-3,3] = "exandra"   # "Alexandra"

str3 = "Through the Looking-Glass"
str3[-13,13]  = "Mirror" # "Through the Mirror"

str4 = "Winston Churchill"
str4[8..13] = "H"        # "Winston Hill"

str5 = "Alistair Cooke"
str5[/e$/] ="ie Monster" # "Alistair Cookie Monster"

str6 = "theater"
str6["er"] = "re"        # "theatre"

str7 = "Aaron Burr"
str7[0] = "B"            # "Baron Burr"
```

Assigning to an expression evaluating to nil will have no effect.

2.13   Substituting in Strings

We've already seen how to perform simple substitutions in strings. The sub and gsub methods provide more advanced pattern-based capabilities. There are also sub! and gsub!, their in-place counterparts.

The sub method substitutes the first occurrence of a pattern with the given substitute-string or the given block:

```
s1 = "spam, spam, and eggs"
s2 = s1.sub(/spam/,"bacon")
# "bacon, spam, and eggs"

s3 = s2.sub(/(\w+), (\w+),/,'\2, \1,')
# "spam, bacon, and eggs"

s4 = "Don't forget the spam."
s5 = s4.sub(/spam/) { |m| m.reverse }
# "Don't forget the maps."

s4.sub!(/spam/) { |m| m.reverse }
# s4 is now "Don't forget the maps."
```

As this example shows, the special symbols \1, \2, and so on may be used in a substitute string. However, special variables (such as $& or its English equivalent $MATCH) may not.

If the block form is used, the special variables may be used. However, if all you need is the matched string, it will be passed into the block as a parameter. If it is not needed at all, the parameter can of course be omitted.

The gsub method (global substitution) is essentially the same except that all matches are substituted rather than just the first:

```
s5 = "alfalfa abracadabra"
s6 = s5.gsub(/a[bl]/,"xx")      # "xxfxxfa xxracadxxra"
s5.gsub!(/[lfdbr]/) { |m| m.upcase + "-" }
# s5 is now "aL-F-aL-F-a aB-R-acaD-aB-R-a"
```

The method Regexp.last_match is essentially identical to $& or $MATCH.

2.14   Searching a String

Besides the techniques for accessing substrings, there are other ways of searching within strings. The `index` method returns the starting location of the specified substring, character, or regex. If the item is not found, the result is `nil`:

```
str = "Albert Einstein"
pos1 = str.index(?E)         # 7
pos2 = str.index("bert")     # 2
pos3 = str.index(/in/)       # 8
pos4 = str.index(?W)         # nil
pos5 = str.index("bart")     # nil
pos6 = str.index(/wein/)     # nil
```

The method `rindex` (right index) starts from the right side of the string (that is, from the end). The numbering, however, proceeds from the beginning, as usual:

```
str = "Albert Einstein"
pos1 = str.rindex(?E)        # 7
pos2 = str.rindex("bert")    # 2
pos3 = str.rindex(/in/)      # 13 (finds rightmost match)
pos4 = str.rindex(?W)        # nil
pos5 = str.rindex("bart")    # nil
pos6 = str.rindex(/wein/)    # nil
```

The `include?` method, shown next, simply tells whether the specified substring or character occurs within the string:

```
str1 = "mathematics"
flag1 = str1.include? ?e         # true
flag2 = str1.include? "math"     # true
str2 = "Daylight Saving Time"
flag3 = str2.include? ?s         # false
flag4 = str2.include? "Savings"  # false
```

The `scan` method repeatedly scans for occurrences of a pattern. If called without a block, it returns an array. If the pattern has more than one (parenthesized) group, the array will be nested:

```
str1 = "abracadabra"
sub1 = str1.scan(/a./)
# sub1 now is ["ab","ac","ad","ab"]
```

```ruby
str2 = "Acapulco, Mexico"
sub2 = str2.scan(/(.)(c.)/)
# sub2 now is [ ["A","ca"], ["l","co"], ["i","co"] ]
```

If a block is specified, the method passes the successive values to the block, as shown here:

```ruby
str3 = "Kobayashi"
str3.scan(/[^aeiou]+[aeiou]/) do |x|
  print "Syllable: #{x}\n"
end
```

This code produces the following output:

```
Syllable: Ko
Syllable: ba
Syllable: ya
Syllable: shi
```

2.15   Converting Between Characters and ASCII Codes

Single characters in Ruby are returned as one-character strings. Here is an example:

```ruby
str = "Martin"
print str[0]        # "M"
```

The `Integer` class has a method called `chr` that will convert an integer to a character. By default, integers will be interpreted as ASCII, but other encodings may be specified for values greater than 127. The `string` class has an `ord` method that is in effect an inverse:

```ruby
str = 77.chr              # "M"
s2  = 233.chr("UTF-8")    # "é"
num = "M".ord             # 77
```

2.16   Implicit and Explicit Conversion

At first glance, the `to_s` and `to_str` methods seem confusing. They both convert an object into a string representation, don't they?

There are several differences, however. First, *any* object can in principle be converted to some kind of string representation; that is why nearly every core class has a `to_s` method. But the `to_str` method is never implemented in the core.

As a rule, `to_str` is for objects that are really very much like strings—that can "masquerade" as strings. Better yet, think of the short name `to_s` as being *explicit conversion* and the longer name `to_str` as being *implicit conversion*.

You see, the core does not *define* any `to_str` methods. But core methods do *call* `to_str` sometimes (if it exists for a given class).

The first case we might think of is a *subclass* of `String`; but, in reality, any object of a subclass of `String` already "is a" `String`, so `to_str` is unnecessary there.

In real life, `to_s` and `to_str` usually return the same value, but they don't have to do so. The implicit conversion should result in the "real string value" of the object; the explicit conversion can be thought of as a "forced" conversion.

The `puts` method calls an object's `to_s` method in order to find a string representation. This behavior might be thought of as an implicit call of an explicit conversion. The same is true for string interpolation. Here's a crude example:

```
class Helium
  def to_s
    "He"
  end

  def to_str
    "helium"
  end
end

e = Helium.new
print "Element is "
puts e                      # Element is He
puts "Element is " + e      # Element is helium
puts "Element is #{e}"      # Element is He
```

So you can see how defining these appropriately in your own classes can give you a little extra flexibility. But what about honoring the definitions of the objects passed into your methods?

For example, suppose that you have a method that is "supposed" to take a `string` as a parameter. Despite our "duck typing" philosophy, this is frequently done and is often completely appropriate. For example, the first parameter of `File.new` is "expected" to be a string.

The way to handle this is simple. When you expect a string, check for the existence of to_str and call it as needed:

```ruby
def set_title(title)
  if title.respond_to? :to_str
    title = title.to_str
  end
  # ...
end
```

Now, what if an object *doesn't* respond to to_str? We could do several things. We could force a call to to_s, we could check the class to see whether it is a String or a subclass thereof, or we could simply keep going, knowing that if we apply some meaningless operation to this object, we will eventually get an ArgumentError anyway.

A shorter way to do this is

```ruby
title = title.to_str if title.respond_to?(:to_str)
```

which replaces the value of title only if it has a to_str method.

Double-quoted string interpolation will implicitly call to_s, and is usually the easiest way to turn multiple objects into strings at once:

```ruby
e = Helium.new
str = "Pi #{3.14} and element #{e}
# str is now "3.14 and element He"
```

Implicit conversion *would* allow you to make strings and numbers essentially equivalent. You could, for example, do this:

```ruby
class Fixnum
  def to_str
    self.to_s
  end
end

str = "The number is " + 345    # The number is 345
```

However, I don't recommend this sort of thing. There is such a thing as "too much magic"; Ruby, like most languages, considers strings and numbers to be different, and I believe that most conversions should be explicit for the sake of clarity.

There is nothing *magical* about the `to_str` method. It is intended to return a string, but if you code your own, it is your responsibility to see that it does.

2.17   Appending an Item onto a String

The append operator (<<) can be used to append a string onto another string. It is "stackable" in that multiple operations can be performed in sequence on a given receiver:

```
str = "A"
str << [1,2,3].to_s << " " << (3.14).to_s
# str is now "A123 3.14"
```

2.18   Removing Trailing Newlines and Other Characters

Often we want to remove extraneous characters from the end of a string. The prime example is a newline on a string read from input.

The `chop` method removes the last character of the string (typically a trailing newline character). If the character before the newline is a carriage return (\r), it will be removed also. The reason for this behavior is the discrepancy between different systems' conceptions of what a newline is. On systems such as UNIX, the newline character is represented internally as a linefeed (\n). On others, such as Windows, it is stored as a carriage return followed by a linefeed (\r\n):

```
str = gets.chop        # Read string, remove newline
s2 = "Some string\n"   # "Some string" (no newline)
s3 = s2.chop!          # s2 is now "Some string" also
s4 = "Other string\r\n"
s4.chop!               # "Other string" (again no newline)
```

Note that the "in-place" version of the method (chop!) will modify its receiver.

It is also important to note that in the absence of a trailing newline, the last character will be removed anyway:

```
str = "abcxyz"
s1 = str.chop          # "abcxy"
```

Because a newline may not always be present, the `chomp` method may be a better alternative:

```
str = "abcxyz"
str2 = "123\n"
str3 = "123\r"
str4 = "123\r\n"
s1 = str.chomp          # "abcxyz"
s2 = str2.chomp         # "123"
# With the default record separator, \r and \r\n are removed
# as well as \n
s3 = str3.chomp         # "123"
s4 = str4.chomp         # "123"
```

There is also a `chomp!` method, as we would expect.

If a parameter is specified for `chomp`, it will remove the set of characters specified from the end of the string rather than the default record separator. Note that if the record separator appears in the middle of the string, it is ignored, as shown here:

```
str1 = "abcxyz"
str2 = "abcxyz"
s1 = str1.chomp("yz")   # "abcx"
s2 = str2.chomp("x")    # "abcxyz"
```

2.19   Trimming Whitespace from a String

The `strip` method removes whitespace from the beginning and end of a string, whereas its counterpart, `strip!`, modifies the receiver in place:

```
str1 = "\t  \nabc  \t\n"
str2 = str1.strip       # "abc"
str3 = str1.strip!      # "abc"
# str1 is now "abc" also
```

Whitespace, of course, consists mostly of blanks, tabs, and end-of-line characters.

If we want to remove whitespace only from the beginning or end of a string, we can use the `lstrip` and `rstrip` methods:

```
str = "  abc  "
s2 = str.lstrip      # "abc  "
s3 = str.rstrip      # "  abc"
```

There are in-place variants (`rstrip!` and `lstrip!`) also.

2.20 Repeating Strings

In Ruby, the multiplication operator (or method) is overloaded to enable repetition of strings. If a string is multiplied by *n*, the result is *n* copies of the original string concatenated together. Here is an example:

```
etc = "Etc. "*3                         # "Etc. Etc. Etc. "
ruler = "+" + ("."*4+"5"+"."*4+"+")*3
# "+....5....+....5....+....5....+"
```

2.21 Embedding Expressions within Strings

The `#{}` notation makes embedding expressions within strings easy. We need not worry about converting, appending, and concatenating; we can interpolate a variable value or other expression at any point in a string:

```
puts "#{temp_f} Fahrenheit is #{temp_c} Celsius"
puts "The discriminant has the value #{b*b - 4*a*c}."
puts "#{word} is #{word.reverse} spelled backward."
```

Bear in mind that full statements can also be used inside the braces. The last evaluated expression will be the one returned:

```
str = "The answer is #{ def factorial(n)
                          n==0 ? 1 : n*factorial(n-1)
                        end

                        answer = factorial(3) * 7}, of course."
# The answer is 42, of course.
```

There are some shortcuts for global, class, and instance variables, in which case the braces can be dispensed with:

```
puts "$gvar = #$gvar and ivar = #@ivar."
```

Note that this technique is not applicable for single-quoted strings (because their contents are not expanded), but it does work for double-quoted here-documents and regular expressions.

2.22   Delayed Interpolation of Strings

Sometimes we might want to delay the interpolation of values into a string. There is no perfect way to do this.

A naive approach is to store a single-quoted string and then evaluate it:

```
str = '#{name} is my name, and #{nation} is my nation.'
name, nation = "Stephen Dedalus", "Ireland"
s1  = eval('"' + str + '"')
# Stephen Dedalus is my name, and Ireland is my nation.
```

However, using `eval` is almost always the worst option. Any time you use `eval`, you are opening yourself up to many problems, including extremely slow execution and unexpected security vulnerabilities, so it should be avoided if at all possible.

A much less dangerous way is to use a block:

```
str = proc do |name, nation|
  "#{name} is my name, and #{nation} is my nation."
end
s2 = str.call("Gulliver Foyle", "Terra")
# Gulliver Foyle is my name, and Terra is my nation.
```

2.23   Parsing Comma-Separated Data

The use of comma-delimited data is common in computing. It is a kind of "lowest common denominator" of data interchange used (for example) to transfer information between incompatible databases or applications that know no other common format.

We assume here that we have a mixture of strings and numbers and that all strings are enclosed in quotes. We further assume that all characters are escaped as necessary (commas and quotes inside strings, for example).

The problem becomes simple because this data format looks suspiciously like a Ruby array of mixed types. In fact, we can simply add brackets to enclose the whole expression, and we have an array of items:

```
string = gets.chop!
# Suppose we read in a string like this one:
# "Doe, John", 35, 225, "5'10\"", "555-0123"
data = eval("[" + string + "]")   # Convert to array
data.each {|x| puts "Value = #{x}"}
```

This fragment produces the following output:

```
Value = Doe, John
Value = 35
Value = 225
Value = 5' 10"
Value = 555-0123
```

For a more heavy-duty solution, refer to the CSV library (which is a standard library).

2.24 Converting Strings to Numbers (Decimal and Otherwise)

Basically there are two ways to convert strings to numbers: the `Kernel` method `Integer` and `Float` and the `to_i` and `to_f` methods of `String`. (Capitalized method names such as `Integer` are usually reserved for special data conversion functions like this.)

The simple case is trivial, and these are equivalent:

```
x = "123".to_i        # 123
y = Integer("123")    # 123
```

When a string is not a valid number, however, their behaviors differ:

```
x = "junk".to_i       # silently returns 0
y = Integer("junk")   # error
```

`to_i` stops converting when it reaches a non-numeric character, but `Integer` raises an error:

```
x = "123junk".to_i       # 123
y = Integer("123junk")   # error
```

Both allow leading and trailing whitespace:

```
x = " 123 ".to_i        # 123
y = Integer(" 123 ")    # 123
```

Floating point conversion works much the same way:

```
x = "3.1416".to_f       # 3.1416
y = Float("2.718")      # 2.718
```

Both conversion methods honor scientific notation:

```
x = Float("6.02e23")    # 6.02e23
y = "2.9979246e5".to_f # 299792.46
```

to_i and Integer also differ in how they handle different bases. The default, of course, is decimal or base ten; but we can work in other bases also. (The same is not true for floating point.)

When talking about converting between numeric bases, strings always are involved. After all, an integer is an integer, and they are all stored in binary.

Base conversion, therefore, always means converting to or from some kind of string. Here, we're looking at converting *from* a string. (For the reverse, see Section 5.18, "Performing Base Conversions," and Section 5.5, "Formatting Numbers for Output.")

When a number appears in program text as a literal numeric constant, it may have a "tag" in front of it to indicate base. These tags are 0b for binary, a simple 0 for octal, and 0x for hexadecimal.

These tags are honored by the Integer method but *not* by the to_i method, as demonstrated here:

```
x = Integer("0b111")    # binary      - returns 7
y = Integer("0111")     # octal       - returns 73
z = Integer("0x111")    # hexadecimal - returns 291

x = "0b111".to_i        # 0
y = "0111".to_i         # 0
z = "0x111".to_i        # 0
```

to_i, however, allows an optional parameter to indicate the base. Typically, the only meaningful values are 2, 8, 10 (the default), and 16. However, tags are not recognized even with the base parameter:

```
x = "111".to_i(2)        # 7
y = "111".to_i(8)        # octal       - returns 73
z = "111".to_i(16)       # hexadecimal - returns 291

x = "0b111".to_i         # 0
y = "0111".to_i          # 0
z = "0x111".to_i         # 0
```

Because of the "standard" behavior of these methods, a digit that is inappropriate for the given base will be treated differently:

```
x = "12389".to_i(8)      # 123    (8 is ignored)
y = Integer("012389")    # error  (8 is illegal)
```

Although it might be of limited usefulness, `to_i` handles bases up to 36, using all letters of the alphabet. (This may remind you of the Base64 encoding; for information on that, see Section 2.37, "Encoding and Decoding Base64 Strings.")

```
x = "123".to_i(5)        # 66
y = "ruby".to_i(36)      # 1299022
```

It's also possible to use the `scanf` standard library to convert character strings to numbers. This library adds a `scanf` method to `Kernel`, to `IO`, and to `String`:

```
str = "234 234 234"
x, y, z = str.scanf("%d %o %x")    # 234, 156, 564
```

The `scanf` methods implement all the meaningful functionality of their C counterparts: `scanf`, `sscanf`, and `fscanf`. However, `scanf` does not handle binary.

2.25   Encoding and Decoding `rot13` Text

The `rot13` method is perhaps the weakest form of encryption known to humankind. Its historical use is simply to prevent people from "accidentally" reading a piece of text. It was commonly seen in Usenet posts; for example, a joke that might be considered offensive might be encoded in `rot13`, or you could post the entire plot of *Star Wars: Episode 12* on the day before the premiere.

The encoding method consists simply of "rotating" a string through the alphabet, so that *A* becomes *N*, *B* becomes *O*, and so on. Lowercase letters are rotated in the same way; digits, punctuation, and other characters are ignored. Because 13 is half of

26 (the size of our alphabet), the function is its own inverse; applying it a second time will "decrypt" it.

The following example is an implementation as a method added to the `String` class. We present it without further comment:

```
class String

  def rot13
    self.tr("A-Ma-mN-Zn-z","N-Zn-zA-Ma-m")
  end

end


joke = "Y2K bug"
joke13 = joke.rot13     # "L2X oht"

episode2 = "Fcbvyre: Naanxva qbrfa'g trg xvyyrq."
puts episode2.rot13
```

2.26   Encrypting Strings

There are times when we don't want strings to be immediately legible. For example, passwords should not be stored in plaintext, no matter how tight the file permissions are.

The standard method `crypt` uses the standard function of the same name to DES-encrypt a string. It takes a "salt" value as a parameter (similar to the seed value for a random number generator). On non-UNIX platforms, this parameter may be different.

A trivial application for this follows, where we ask for a password that Tolkien fans should know:

```
coded = "hfCghHIE5LAM."

puts "Speak, friend, and enter!"

print "Password: "
password = gets.chop

if password.crypt("hf") == coded
  puts "Welcome!"
```

```
else
  puts "What are you, an orc?"
end
```

It is worth noting that you should never use encryption to store passwords. Instead, employ *password hashing* using a hashing algorithm designed specifically for passwords, such as bcrypt. Additionally, never rely on encryption of this nature for communications with a server-side web application. To secure web applications, use the HTTPS protocol and Secure Sockets Layer (SSL) to encrypt all traffic. Of course, you could still use encryption on the server side, but for a different reason—to protect the data as it is stored rather than during transmission.

2.27   Compressing Strings

The zlib library provides a way of compressing and decompressing strings and files.

Why might we want to compress strings in this way? Possibly to make database I/O faster, to optimize network usage, or even to obscure stored strings so that they are not easily read.

The Deflate and Inflate classes have class methods named deflate and inflate, respectively. The deflate method (which obviously compresses) has an extra parameter to specify the style of compression. The styles show a typical trade-off between compression quality and speed; BEST_COMPRESSION results in a smaller compressed string, but compression is relatively slow; BEST_SPEED compresses faster but does not compress as much. The default (DEFAULT_COMPRESSION) is typically somewhere in between in both size and speed.

```
require 'zlib'
include Zlib

long_string = ("abcde"*71 + "defghi"*79 + "ghijkl"*113)*371
# long_string has 559097 characters

s1 = Deflate.deflate(long_string,BEST_SPEED)          # 4188 chars
s2 = Deflate.deflate(long_string)                     # 3568 chars
s3 = Deflate.deflate(long_string,BEST_COMPRESSION)    # 2120 chars
```

Informal experiments suggest that the speeds vary by a factor of two, and the compression amounts vary inversely by the same amount. Speed and compression are greatly dependent on the contents of the string. Speed, of course, also is affected by hardware.

Be aware that there is a "break-even" point below which it is essentially useless to compress a string (unless you are trying to make the string unreadable). Below this point, the overhead of compression may actually result in a *longer* string.

2.28   Counting Characters in Strings

The count method counts the number of occurrences of any of a set of specified characters:

```
s1 = "abracadabra"
a  = s1.count("c")      # 1
b  = s1.count("bdr")    # 5
```

The string parameter is like a simple regular expression. If it starts with a caret, the list is negated:

```
c = s1.count("^a")      # 6
d = s1.count("^bdr")    # 6
```

A hyphen indicates a range of characters:

```
e = s1.count("a-d")     # 9
f = s1.count("^a-d")    # 2
```

2.29   Reversing a String

A string may be reversed simply by using the **reverse** method (or its in-place counterpart reverse!):

```
s1 = "Star Trek"
s2 = s1.reverse         # "kerT ratS"
s1.reverse!             # s1 is now "kerT ratS"
```

Suppose that you want to reverse the word order (rather than character order). You can use String#split, which gives you an array of words. The Array class also has a reverse method, so you can then reverse the array and join to make a new string:

```
phrase = "Now here's a sentence"
phrase.split(" ").reverse.join(" ") # "sentence a here's Now"
```

2.30 Removing Duplicate Characters

Runs of duplicate characters may be removed using the `squeeze` method. If a parameter is specified, only those characters will be squeezed.

```
s1 = "bookkeeper"
s2 = s1.squeeze          # "bokeper"
s3 = "Hello..."
s4 = s3.squeeze          # "Helo."
```

If a parameter is specified, only those characters will be squeezed.

```
s5 = s3.squeeze(".")    # "Hello."
```

This parameter follows the same rules as the one for the `count` method (see Section 2.28, "Counting Characters in Strings," earlier in this chapter); that is, it understands the hyphen and the caret.

There is also a `squeeze!` method.

2.31 Removing Specific Characters

The `delete` method removes characters from a string if they appear in the list of characters passed as a parameter:

```
s1 = "To be, or not to be"
s2 = s1.delete("b")              # "To e, or not to e"
s3 = "Veni, vidi, vici!"
s4 = s3.delete(",!")            # "Veni vidi vici"
```

This parameter follows the same rules as the one for the `count` method (see Section 2.28, "Counting Characters in Strings," earlier in this chapter); that is, it understands the hyphen and the caret.

There is also a `delete!` method.

2.32 Printing Special Characters

The `dump` method (like `inspect`) provides explicit printable representations of characters that may ordinarily be invisible or print differently. Here is an example:

```
s1 = "Listen" << "\007\007\007" # Add three ASCII BEL characters
puts s1.dump                         # Prints: Listen\007\007\007
s2 = "abc\t\tdef\tghi\n\n"
puts s2.dump                         # Prints: abc\t\tdef\tghi\n\n
s3 = "Double quote: \""
puts s3.dump                         # Prints: Double quote: \"
```

2.33   Generating Successive Strings

On rare occasions, we may want to find the "successor" value for a string; for example, the successor for "aaa" is "aab" (then "aad", "aae", and so on).

Ruby provides the method succ (successor) for this purpose:

```
droid = "R2D2"
improved  = droid.succ           # "R2D3"
pill  = "Vitamin B"
pill2 = pill.succ                # "Vitamin C"
```

We don't recommend the use of this feature unless the values are predictable and reasonable. If you start with a string that is esoteric enough, you will eventually get strange and surprising results.

There is also an upto method that applies succ repeatedly in a loop until the desired final value is reached:

```
"Files, A".upto "Files, X" do |letter|
  puts "Opening: #{letter}"
end

# Produces 24 lines of output
```

Again, we stress that this is not used frequently, and you use it at your own risk. In addition, there is no corresponding "predecessor" function.

2.34   Calculating a 32-Bit CRC

The Cyclic Redundancy Check (CRC) is a well-known way of obtaining a "signature" for a file or other collection of bytes. The CRC has the property that the chance of data being changed and keeping the same CRC is 1 in $2**N$, where N is the number of bits in the result (most often 32 bits).

The zlib library, created by Ueno Katsuhiro, enables you to do this.

The method crc32 computes a CRC given a string as a parameter:

```
require 'zlib'
include Zlib
crc = crc32("Hello")             # 4157704578
crc = crc32(" world!",crc)       # 461707669
crc = crc32("Hello world!")      # 461707669 (same as above)
```

A previous CRC can be specified as an optional second parameter; the result will be as if the strings were concatenated and a single CRC was computed. This can be used, for example, to compute the checksum of a file so large that we can only read it in chunks.

2.35   Calculating the SHA-256 Hash of a String

The `Digest::SHA256` class produces a 256-bit *hash* or *message digest* of a string of arbitrary length. This hashing function is one-way, and does not allow for the discovery of the original message from the digest. There are also `MD5`, `SHA384`, and `SHA512` classes inside `Digest` for each of those algorithms.

The most commonly used class method is `hexdigest`, but there are also `digest` and `base64digest`. They all accept a string containing the message and return the digest as a string, as shown here:

```
require 'digest'
Digest::SHA256.hexdigest("foo")[0..20]    # "2c26b46b68f"
Digest::SHA256.base64digest("foo")[0..20] # "LCa0a2j/xo/"
Digest::SHA256.digest("foo")[0..5]        # ",&\xB4kh\xFF"
```

Although the `digest` method provides a 64-byte string containing the 512-bit digest, the `hexdigest` method is actually the most useful. It provides the digest as an ASCII string of 64 hex characters representing the 64 bytes.

Instances and the `update` method allow the hash to be built incrementally, perhaps because the data is coming from a streaming source:

```
secret = Digest::SHA256.new
source.each { |chunk| secret.update(chunk) }
```

Repeated calls are equivalent to a single call with concatenated arguments:

```
# These two statements...
cryptic.update("Data...")
cryptic.update(" and more data.")

# ...are equivalent to this one.
cryptic.update("Data... and more data.")

cryptic.hexdigest[0..20] # "50605ba0a90"
```

2.36 Calculating the Levenshtein Distance Between Two Strings

The concept of distance between strings is important in inductive learning (AI), cryptography, proteins research, and in other areas.

The Levenshtein distance is the minimum number of modifications needed to change one string into another, using three basic modification operations: *del*(-etion), *ins*(-ertion), and *sub*(-stitution). A substitution is also considered to be a combination of a deletion and insertion (*indel*).

There are various approaches to this, but we will avoid getting too technical. Suffice it to say that this Ruby implementation (shown in Listing 2.2) allows you to provide optional parameters to set the cost for the three types of modification operations and defaults to a single indel cost basis (cost of insertion = cost of deletion).

Listing 2.2   The Levenshtein distance

```ruby
class String

  def levenshtein(other, ins=2, del=2, sub=1)
    # ins, del, sub are weighted costs
    return nil if self.nil?
    return nil if other.nil?
    dm = []          # distance matrix

    # Initialize first row values
    dm[0] = (0..self.length).collect { |i| i * ins }
    fill = [0] * (self.length - 1)

    # Initialize first column values
    for i in 1..other.length
      dm[i] = [i * del, fill.flatten]
    end

    # populate matrix
    for i in 1..other.length
      for j in 1..self.length
    # critical comparison
        dm[i][j] = [
            dm[i-1][j-1] +
              (self[j-1] == other[i-1] ? 0 : sub),
                dm[i][j-1] + ins,
            dm[i-1][j] + del
        ].min
      end
    end
```

```
    # The last value in matrix is the
    # Levenshtein distance between the strings
    dm[other.length][self.length]
  end

end


s1 = "ACUGAUGUGA"
s2 = "AUGGAA"
d1 = s1.levenshtein(s2)     # 9


s3 = "pennsylvania"
s4 = "pencilvaneya"
d2 = s3.levenshtein(s4)     # 7


s5 = "abcd"
s6 = "abcd"
d3 = s5.levenshtein(s6)     # 0
```

Now that we have the Levenshtein distance defined, it's conceivable that we could define a `similar?` method, giving it a threshold for similarity. Here is an example:

```
class String

  def similar?(other, thresh=2)
    self.levenshtein(other) < thresh
  end

end



if "polarity".similar?("hilarity")
  puts "Electricity is funny!"
end
```

Of course, it would also be possible to pass in the three weighted costs to the `similar?` method so that they could in turn be passed into the `levenshtein` method. We have omitted these for simplicity.

2.37   Encoding and Decoding Base64 Strings

Base64 is frequently used to convert machine-readable data into a text form with no special characters in it. For example, images and fonts stored inline inside CSS files are encoded with Base64.

The easiest way to do a Base64 encode/decode is to use the built-in `Base64` module. The `Base64` class has an `encode64` method that returns a Base64 string (with a newline appended). It also has the method `decode64`, which changes the string back to its original bytes, as shown here:

```
require "base64"
str = "\xAB\xBA\x02abdce"
encoded  = Base64.encode64(str)        # "q7oCYWJkY2U=\n"
original = Base64.decode64(encoded) # "\xAB\xBA\x02abdce"
```

2.38   Expanding and Compressing Tab Characters

Occasionally we have a string with tabs in it and we want to convert them to spaces (or vice versa). The two methods shown here do these operations:

```
class String

  def detab(ts=8)
    str = self.dup
    while (leftmost = str.index("\t")) != nil
      space = " "*(ts-(leftmost%ts))
      str[leftmost]=space
    end
    str
  end

  def entab(ts=8)
    str = self.detab
    areas = str.length/ts
    newstr = ""
    for a in 0..areas
      temp = str[a*ts..a*ts+ts-1]
      if temp.size==ts
        if temp =~ / +/
          match=Regexp.last_match[0]
```

```
          endmatch = Regexp.new(match+"$")
          if match.length>1
            temp.sub!(endmatch,"\t")
          end
        end
      end
      newstr += temp
    end
    newstr
  end

end

foo = "This       is        only    a      test.              "

puts foo
puts foo.entab(4)
puts foo.entab(4).dump
```

Note that this code is not smart enough to handle backspaces.

2.39   Wrapping Lines of Text

Occasionally we may want to take long text lines and print them within margins of
our own choosing. The code fragment shown here accomplishes this, splitting only on
word boundaries and honoring tabs (but not honoring backspaces or preserving tabs):

```
str = <<-EOF
  When in the Course of human events it becomes necessary
  for one people to dissolve the political bands which have
  connected them with another, and to assume among the powers
  of the earth the separate and equal station to which the Laws
  of Nature and of Nature's God entitle them, a decent respect
  for the opinions of mankind requires that they should declare
  the causes which impel them to the separation.
EOF

max = 20

line = 0
out = [""]
```

```
input = str.gsub(/\n/," ")
words = input.split(" ")

while input != ""
  word = words.shift
  break if not word
  if out[line].length + word.length > max
    out[line].squeeze!(" ")
    line += 1
    out[line] = ""
  end
  out[line] << word + " "
end

out.each {|line| puts line}  # Prints 24 very short lines
```

The `ActiveSupport` gem includes similar functionality in a method named word_wrap, along with many other string manipulation helpers. Search for it online.

2.40   Conclusion

In this chapter, we have seen the basics of representing strings (both single-quoted strings and double-quoted strings). We've seen how to interpolate expressions into double-quoted strings, and how the double quotes also allow certain special characters to be inserted with escape sequences. We've seen the `%q` and `%Q` forms, which permit us to choose our own delimiters for convenience. Finally, we've seen the here-document syntax, carried over from older contexts such as UNIX shells.

This chapter has demonstrated all the important operations a programmer wants to perform on a string, including concatenation, searching, extracting substrings, tokenizing, and much more. We have seen how to iterate over a string by line or by byte. We have seen how to transform a string to and from a coded form such as Base64 or compressed form.

It's time now to move on to a related topic—regular expressions. Regular expressions are a powerful tool for detecting patterns in strings. We'll cover this topic in the next chapter.

CHAPTER 3

Working with Regular Expressions

I would choose
To lead him in a maze along the patterned paths...

—*Amy Lowell, "Patterns"*

The power of regular expressions as a computing tool has often been underestimated. From their earliest theoretical beginnings in the 1940s, they found their way onto computer systems in the 1960s and from there into various tools in the UNIX operating system. In the 1990s, the popularity of Perl helped make regular expressions a household programming item rather than the esoteric domain of bearded gurus.

The beauty of regular expressions is that almost everything in our experience can be understood in terms of patterns. Where there are patterns that we can describe, we can detect matches, we can find the pieces of reality that correspond to those matches, and we can replace those pieces with others of our own choosing.

The regular expression engine used in Ruby is called *Onigmo*. Onigmo is itself a revision of another library called *Oniguruma*, which was used by Ruby 1.9. Oniguruma is commonly misspelled by non-Japanese writers; it is fortunate that Onigmo is much easier to spell.

The Onigmo engine provides several improvements to Ruby's regular expression support. Most notably, it handles internationalized strings far better, and adds some powerful features. Additional issues with internationalization and regular expressions are dealt with in Chapter 4, "Internationalization in Ruby."

3.1   Regular Expression Syntax

The typical regular expression is delimited by a pair of slashes; the `%r` form can also be used. Table 3.1 gives some simple examples.

Table 3.1   Basic Regular Expressions

Regex	Explanation
`/Ruby/`	Match the single word *Ruby*
`/[Rr]uby/`	Match *Ruby* or *ruby*
`/^abc/`	Match an *abc* at beginning of line
`%r(xyz$)`	Match an *xyz* at end of line
`%r|[0-9]*|`	Match any sequence of (zero or more) digits

It is also possible to place a modifier, consisting of a single letter, immediately after a regex. Table 3.2 shows the most common modifiers.

Table 3.2   Regular Expression Modifiers

Modifier	Meaning
`i`	Ignore case in regex
`o`	Perform expression substitution only once
`m`	Multiline mode (dot matches newline)
`x`	Extended regex (allow whitespace, comments)

Other modifiers will be covered in Chapter 4.

To complete our introduction to regular expressions, Table 3.3 lists the most common symbols and notations available.

Table 3.3 Common Notations Used in Regular Expressions

Notation	Meaning
^	Beginning of a line or string
$	End of a line or string
.	Any character except newline (unless multiline)
\w	Word character (digit, letter, or underscore)
\W	Non-word character
\s	Whitespace character (space, tab, newline, and so on)
\S	Non-whitespace character
\d	Digit (same as [0-9])
\D	Non-digit
\h	Hexadecimal digit (same as [0-9a-f])
\H	Non-hexadecimal digit
\A	Beginning of a string
\Z	End of a string or before newline at the end
\z	End of a string
\b	Word boundary (outside [] only)
\B	Non-word boundary
\b	Backspace (inside [] only)
[]	Any single character of set
*	Zero or more of previous subexpression
*?	Zero or more of previous subexpression (non-greedy)
+	One or more of previous subexpression
+?	One or more of previous subexpression (non-greedy)
{m,n}	m to n instances of previous subexpression
{m,n}?	m to n instances of previous subexpression (non-greedy)
?	Zero or one of previous regular expression
|	Alternatives
(?=)	Positive lookahead
(?!)	Negative lookahead
()	Grouping of subexpressions
(?>)	Embedded subexpression
(?:)	Noncapturing group
(?imx-imx)	Turn options on/off henceforth

(?imx-imx:expr) Turn options on/off for this expression

(?#)   Comment

Character classes in brackets can also use the && operator for combining together:

```
reg1 = /[a-z&&[^aeiou]]/ # any letter but vowels a, e, i, o, and u
reg2 = /[a-z&&[^m-p]]/   # the entire alphabet minus m through p
```

Because this can be confusing, I recommend using this feature sparingly.

An understanding of regex handling greatly benefits the modern programmer. A complete discussion of this topic is far beyond the scope of this book, but if you're interested, see the definitive work *Mastering Regular Expressions*, by Jeffrey Friedl.

3.2   Compiling Regular Expressions

Regular expressions can be compiled using the class method `Regexp.compile` (which is really only a synonym for `Regexp.new`). The first parameter is required and may be a string or a regex. (Note that if the parameter is a regex with options, the options will not carry over into the newly compiled regex.)

```
pat1 = Regexp.compile("^foo.*")  # /^foo.*/
pat2 = Regexp.compile(/bar$/i)   # /bar/ (i not propagated)
```

The second parameter, if present, is normally a bitwise OR of any of the following constants: `Regexp::EXTENDED`, `Regexp::IGNORECASE`, and `Regexp::MULTILINE`. Additionally, any non-nil value will have the result of making the regex case insensitive; we do not recommend this practice.

```
options = Regexp::MULTILINE || Regexp::IGNORECASE
pat3 = Regexp.compile("^foo", options)
pat4 = Regexp.compile(/bar/, Regexp::IGNORECASE)
```

The third parameter, if it is specified, is the language parameter, which enables multibyte character support. It can take any of four string values:

```
"N" or "n" means None
"E" or "e" means EUC
"S" or "s" means Shift-JIS
"U" or "u" means UTF-8
```

Of course, regular expression literals may be specified without calling `new` or `compile`, simply by enclosing them in slash delimiters.

```
pat1 = /^foo.*/
pat2 = /bar$/i
```

Regular expression encodings will be covered in Chapter 4.

3.3 Escaping Special Characters

The class method `Regexp.escape` escapes any characters that are special characters used in regular expressions. Such characters include the asterisk, question mark, and brackets:

```
str1 = "[*?]"
str2 = Regexp.escape(str1)  # "\[\*\?\]"
```

The method `Regexp.quote` is an alias.

3.4 Using Anchors

An *anchor* is a special expression that matches a *position* in a string rather than a character or sequence of characters. As we'll see later, this is a simple case of a *zero-width assertion,* a match that doesn't consume any of the string when it matches.

The most common anchors were already listed at the beginning of this chapter. The simplest are ^ and $, which match the beginning and end of the string.

```
string  = "abcXdefXghi"
/def/ =~ string    # 4
/abc/ =~ string    # 0
/ghi/ =~ string    # 8
/^def/ =~ string   # nil
/def$/ =~ string   # nil
/^abc/ =~ string   # 0
/ghi$/ =~ string   # 8
```

However, I've told a small lie. These anchors don't actually match the beginning and end of the string but rather *of the line.* Consider the same patterns applied to a similar string with embedded newlines:

```
string  = "abc\ndef\nghi"
/def/  =~ string      # 4
/abc/  =~ string      # 0
/ghi/  =~ string      # 8
/^def/ =~ string      # 4
/def$/ =~ string      # 4
/^abc/ =~ string      # 0
/ghi$/ =~ string      # 8
```

However, we also have the special anchors \A and \Z, which match the real beginning and end of the string itself.

```
string  = "abc\ndef\nghi"
/\Adef/ =~ string     # nil
/def\Z/ =~ string     # nil
/\Aabc/ =~ string     # 0
/ghi\Z/ =~ string     # 8
```

The \z is the same as \Z except that the latter matches *before* a terminating newline, whereas the former must match explicitly.

```
string  = "abc\ndef\nghi"
str2 << "\n"
/ghi\Z/ =~ string     # 8
/\Aabc/ =~ str2       # 8
/ghi\z/ =~ string     # 8
/ghi\z/ =~ str2       # nil
```

It's also possible to match a *word boundary* with \b, or a position that is not a word boundary with \B. These gsub examples make it clear how this works:

```
str = "this is a test"
str.gsub(/\b/,"|")      # "|this| |is| |a| |test|"
str.gsub(/\B/,"-")      # "t-h-i-s i-s a t-e-s-t"
```

There is no way to distinguish between beginning and ending word boundaries.

3.5 Using Quantifiers

A big part of regular expressions is handling optional items and repetition. An item followed by a question mark is optional; it may be present or absent, and the match depends on the rest of the regex. (It doesn't make sense to apply this to an anchor but only to a subpattern of nonzero width.)

```
pattern = /ax?b/
pat2    = /a[xy]?b/

pattern =~ "ab"      # 0
pattern =~ "acb"     # nil
pattern =~ "axb"     # 0
pat2    =~ "ayb"     # 0
pat2    =~ "acb"     # nil
```

It is common for entities to be repeated an indefinite number of times (which we can specify with the + quantifier). For example, this pattern matches any positive integer:

```
pattern = /[0-9]+/
pattern =~ "1"          # 0
pattern =~ "2345678"    # 0
```

Another common occurrence is a pattern that occurs *zero or more* times. We could do this with + and ?, of course; here we match the string Huzzah followed by zero or more exclamation points:

```
pattern = /Huzzah(!+)?/   # Parentheses are necessary here
pattern =~ "Huzzah"       # 0
pattern =~ "Huzzah!!!!"   # 0
```

However, there's a better way. The * quantifier describes this behavior:

```
pattern = /Huzzah!*/      # * applies only to !
pattern =~ "Huzzah"       # 0
pattern =~ "Huzzah!!!!"   # 0
```

What if we want to match a U.S. Social Security number? Here's a pattern for that:

```
ssn = "987-65-4320"
pattern = /\d\d\d-\d\d-\d\d\d\d/
pattern =~ ssn        # 0
```

But that's a little unclear. Let's explicitly say how many digits are in each group. A number in braces is the quantifier to use here:

```
pattern = /\d{3}-\d{2}-\d{4}/
```

This is not necessarily a shorter pattern, but it is more explicit and arguably more readable.

Comma-separated ranges can also be used. Imagine that an Elbonian phone number consists of a part with three to five digits and a part with three to seven digits. Here's a pattern for that:

```
elbonian_phone = /\d{3,5}-\d{3,7}/
```

The beginning and ending numbers are optional (though we must have one or the other):

```
/x{5}/          # Match 5 xs
/x{5,7}/        # Match 5-7 xs
/x{,8}/         # Match up to 8 xs
/x{3,}/         # Match at least 3 xs
```

Obviously, the quantifiers ?, +, and * *could* be rewritten in this way:

```
/x?/            # same as /x{0,1}/
/x*/            # same as /x{0,}
/x+/            # same as /x{1,}
```

The terminology of regular expressions is full of colorful personifying terms such as *greedy, reluctant, lazy, and possessive.* The greedy/non-greedy distinction is one of the most important.

Consider this piece of code. You might expect that this regex would match "Where the" but it matches the larger substring "Where the sea meets the" instead:

```
str = "Where the sea meets the moon-blanch'd land,"
match = /.*the/.match(str)
p match[0]   # Display the entire match:
             # "Where the sea meets the"
```

The reason is that the * operator is greedy—in matching, it consumes as much of the string as it can for the longest match possible. We can make it non-greedy by appending a question mark:

```
str = "Where the sea meets the moon-blanch'd land,"
match = /.*?the/.match(str)
p match[0]   # Display the entire match:
             # "Where the"
```

This shows us that the * operator is greedy by default unless a ? is appended. The same is true for the + and {m,n} quantifiers, and even for the ? quantifier itself.

I haven't been able to find good examples for the {m,n}? and ?? cases. If you know of any, please share them.

3.6   Positive and Negative Lookahead

Naturally, a regular expression is matched against a string in a linear fashion (with backtracking as necessary). Therefore, there is the concept of the "current location" in the string—rather like a file pointer or a cursor.

The term *lookahead* refers to a construct that matches a part of the string *ahead* of the current location. It is a zero-width assertion because even when a match succeeds, no part of the string is consumed (that is, the current location does not change).

In this next example, the string "New World" will be matched *if* it is followed by "Symphony" or "Dictionary"; however, the third word is not part of the match:

```
s1 = "New World Dictionary"
s2 = "New World Symphony"
s3 = "New World Order"

reg = /New World(?= Dictionary| Symphony)/
m1 = reg.match(s1)
m.to_a[0]            # "New World"
m2 = reg.match(s2)
m.to_a[0]            # "New World"
m3 = reg.match(s3)   # nil
```

Here is an example of negative lookahead:

```
reg2 = /New World(?! Symphony)/
m1 = reg.match(s1)
m.to_a[0]            # "New World"
m2 = reg.match(s2)
m.to_a[0]            # nil
m3 = reg.match(s3)   # "New World"
```

In this example, "New World" is matched only if it is *not* followed by "Symphony".

3.7   Positive and Negative Lookbehind

If lookahead isn't enough for you, you can use *lookbehind*—detecting whether the current location is preceded by a given pattern.

Like many areas of regular expressions, this can be difficult to understand and motivate. Thanks goes to Andrew Johnson for the following example.

Imagine that we are analyzing some genetic sequence. (The DNA molecule consists of four "base" molecules, abbreviated A, C, G, and T.) Suppose that we are scanning for all non-overlapping nucleotide sequences (of length 4) that follow a T. We couldn't just try to match a T and four characters because the T may have been the last character of the previous match.

```
gene = 'GATTACAAACTGCCTGACATACGAA'
seqs = gene.scan(/T(\w{4})/)
# seqs is: [["TACA"], ["GCCT"], ["ACGA"]]
```

But in this preceding code, we miss the GACA sequence that follows GCCT. Using a positive lookbehind (as follows), we catch them all:

```
gene = 'GATTACAAACTGCCTGACATACGAA'
seqs = gene.scan(/(?<=T)(\w{4})/)
# seqs is: [["TACA"], ["GCCT"], ["GACA"], ["ACGA"]]
```

This next example is adapted from one by K. Kosako. Suppose that we want to take a bunch of text in XML (or HTML) and shift to uppercase all the text *outside* the tags (that is, the cdata). Here is a way to do that using lookbehind:

```
text = <<-EOF
<body> <h1>This is a heading</h1>
<p> This is a paragraph with some
<i>italics</i> and some <b>boldface</b>
in it...</p>
</body>
EOF

pattern = /(?:^|             # Beginning or...
           (?<=>)      #   following a '>'
```

```
            )
            ([^<]*)          # Then all non-'<' chars (captured).
          /x

puts text.gsub(pattern) {|s| s.upcase }

# Output:
# <body> <h1>THIS IS A HEADING</h1>
# <p>THIS IS A PARAGRAPH WITH SOME
# <i>ITALICS</i> AND SOME <b>BOLDFACE</b>
# IN IT...</p>
# </body>
```

3.8   Accessing Backreferences

Each parenthesized piece of a regular expression will be a submatch of its own. These are numbered and can be referenced by these numbers in more than one way. Let's examine the more traditional "ugly" ways first.

The special global variables $1, $2, and so on, can be used to reference matches:

```
str = "a123b45c678"
if /(a\d+)(b\d+)(c\d+)/ =~ str
  puts "Matches are: '#$1', '#$2', '#$3'"
  # Prints: Matches are: 'a123', 'b45', 'c768'
end
```

Within a substitution such as sub or gsub, these variables *cannot* be used:

```
str = "a123b45c678"
str.sub(/(a\d+)(b\d+)(c\d+)/, "1st=#$1, 2nd=#$2, 3rd=#$3")
# "1st=, 2nd=, 3rd="
```

Why didn't this work? Because the arguments to sub are evaluated before sub is called. This code is equivalent:

```
str = "a123b45c678"
s2 = "1st=#$1, 2nd=#$2, 3rd=#$3"
reg = /(a\d+)(b\d+)(c\d+)/
str.sub(reg,s2)
# "1st=, 2nd=, 3rd="
```

This code, of course, makes it much clearer that the values $1 through $3 are *unrelated* to the match done inside the sub call.

In this kind of case, the special codes \1, \2, and so on, can be used:

```
str = "a123b45c678"
str.sub(/(a\d+)(b\d+)(c\d+)/, '1st=\1, 2nd=\2, 3rd=\3')
# "1st=a123, 2nd=b45, 3rd=c768"
```

Notice that we used single quotes (hard quotes) in the preceding example. If we used double quotes (soft quotes) in a straightforward way, the backslashed items would be interpreted as octal escape sequences:

```
str = "a123b45c678"
str.sub(/(a\d+)(b\d+)(c\d+)/, "1st=\1, 2nd=\2, 3rd=\3")
# "1st=\001, 2nd=\002, 3rd=\003"
```

The way around this is to double-escape:

```
str = "a123b45c678"
str.sub(/(a\d+)(b\d+)(c\d+)/, "1st=\\1, 2nd=\\2, 3rd=\\3")
# "1st=a123, 2nd=b45, 3rd=c678"
```

It's also possible to use the block form of a substitution, in which case the global variables may be used:

```
str = "a123b45c678"
str.sub(/(a\d+)(b\d+)(c\d+)/)  { "1st=#$1, 2nd=#$2, 3rd=#$3" }
# "1st=a123, 2nd=b45, 3rd=c678"
```

When using a block in this way, it is *not* possible to use the special backslashed numbers inside a double-quoted string (or even a single-quoted one). This is reasonable if you think about it.

As an aside here, I will mention the possibility of *noncapturing groups*. Sometimes you may want to regard characters as a group for purposes of crafting a regular expression, but you may not need to capture the matched value for later use. In such a case, you can use a noncapturing group, denoted by the (?:...) syntax:

```
str = "a123b45c678"
str.sub(/(a\d+)(?:b\d+)(c\d+)/, "1st=\\1, 2nd=\\2, 3rd=\\3")
# "1st=a123, 2nd=c678, 3rd="
```

In the preceding example, the second grouping was thrown away, and what was the third submatch became the *second*.

I personally don't like either the \1 or the $1 notation. They are convenient sometimes, but it isn't ever necessary to use them. We can do it in a "prettier," more object-oriented way.

The class method `Regexp.last_match` returns an object of class `MatchData` (as does the instance method match). This object has instance methods that enable the programmer to access backreferences.

The `MatchData` object is manipulated with a bracket notation as though it were an array of matches. The special element 0 contains the text of the entire matched string. Thereafter, element n refers to the nth match:

```
pat = /(.+[aiu])(.+[aiu])(.+[aiu])(.+[aiu])/i
# Four identical groups in this pattern
refs = pat.match("Fujiyama")
# refs is now: ["Fujiyama","Fu","ji","ya","ma"]
x = refs[1]
y = refs[2..3]
refs.to_a.each {|x| print "#{x}\n"}
```

Note that the object refs is not a true array. Therefore, when we want to treat it as one by using the iterator each, we must use to_a (as shown) to convert it to an array.

We may use more than one technique to locate a matched substring within the original string. The methods begin and end return the beginning and ending offsets of a match, respectively. (It is important to realize that the ending offset is really the index of the next character after the match.)

```
str = "alpha beta gamma delta epsilon"
#      0....5....0....5....0....5....
#      (for your counting convenience)

pat = /(b[^ ]+ )(g[^ ]+ )(d[^ ]+ )/
# Three words, each one a single match
refs = pat.match(str)

# "beta "
p1 = refs.begin(1)          # 6
p2 = refs.end(1)            # 11
# "gamma "
```

```
p3 = refs.begin(2)            # 11
p4 = refs.end(2)              # 17
# "delta "
p5 = refs.begin(3)            # 17
p6 = refs.end(3)              # 23
# "beta gamma delta"
p7 = refs.begin(0)            # 6
p8 = refs.end(0)              # 23
```

Similarly, the `offset` method returns an array of two numbers, which are the beginning and ending offsets of that match. To continue the previous example:

```
range0 = refs.offset(0)       # [6,23]
range1 = refs.offset(1)       # [6,11]
range2 = refs.offset(2)       # [11,17]
range3 = refs.offset(3)       # [17,23]
```

The portions of the string before and after the matched substring can be retrieved by the instance methods `pre_match` and `post_match`, respectively. To continue the previous example:

```
before = refs.pre_match      # "alpha "
after  = refs.post_match     # "epsilon"
```

3.9   Named Matches

A special form of subexpression is the *named* expression. This in effect gives a name to a pattern (rather than just a number).

The syntax is simple: `(?<name>expr)` where *name* is some name starting with a letter (like a Ruby identifier). Notice how similar this is to the non-named atomic subexpression.

What can we do with a named expression? One thing is to use it as a backreference. The following example is a simple regex that matches a doubled word (see also Section 3.15.6, "Detecting Doubled Words in Text"):

```
re1 = /\s+(\w+)\s+\1\s+/
str = "Now is the the time for all..."
re1.match(str).to_a          # ["the the","the"]
```

Note how we capture the word and then use \1 to reference it. We can use named references in much the same way. We give the name to the subexpression when we first use it, and we access the backreference by \k followed by that same name (always in angle brackets):

```
re2 = /\s+(?<anyword>\w+)\s+\k<anyword>\s+/
```

The second variant is longer but arguably more readable. (Be aware that if you use named backreferences, you *cannot* use numbered backreferences in the same regex.) Use this feature at your discretion.

Ruby has long had the capability to use backreferences in strings passed to sub and gsub; in the past, this has been limited to numbered backreferences, but in very recent versions, named matches can be used:

```
str = "I breathe when I sleep"

# Numbered matches...
r1  = /I (\w+) when I (\w+)/
s1  = str.sub(r1,'I \2 when I \1')

# Named matches...
r1  = /I (?<verb1>\w+) when I (?<verb2>\w+)/
s2  = str.sub(r2,'I \k<verb2> when I \k<verb1>')

puts s1    # I sleep when I breathe
puts s2    # I sleep when I breathe
```

Another use for named expressions is to *re-invoke* that expression. In this case, we use \g (rather than \k) preceding the name.

For example, let's define a spaces subpattern so that we can use it again. The previous regex re2 then becomes this:

```
re3 = /(?<spaces>\s+)(?<anyword>\w+)\g<spaces>\k<anyword>\g<spaces>/
```

Note how we invoke the pattern repeatedly by means of the \g marker. This feature makes more sense if the regular expression is recursive; that is the topic of the next section.

A notation such as \g<1> may also be used if there are no named subexpressions. This re-invokes a captured subexpression by referring to it by number rather than name.

One final note on the use of named matches. The name can be used (as a symbol or a string) as a `MatchData` index. Here is an example:

```
str = "My hovercraft is full of eels"
reg = /My (?<noun>\w+) is (?<predicate>.*)/
m = reg.match(str)
puts m[:noun]           # hovercraft
puts m["predicate"]     # full of eels
puts m[1]               # same as m[:noun] or m["noun"]
```

3.10   Using Character Classes

Character classes are simply a form of alternation (specification of alternative possibilities) where each submatch is a single character. In the simplest case, we list a set of characters inside square brackets:

```
/[aeiou]/     # Match any single letter a, e, i, o, u; equivalent
              # to /(a|e|i|o|u)/ except for group-capture
```

Inside a character class, escape sequences such as \n are still meaningful, but metacharacters such as . and ? do not have any special meanings:

```
/[.\n?]/      # Match any of: period, newline, question mark
```

The caret (^) has special meaning inside a character class if used at the beginning; it negates the list of characters (or refers to their complement):

```
[^aeiou]      # Any character EXCEPT a, e, i, o, u
```

The hyphen, used within a character class, indicates a range of characters (a lexicographic range, that is):

```
/[a-mA-M]/    # Any letter in the first half of the alphabet
/[^a-mA-M]/   # Any OTHER letter, or number, or non-alphanumeric
              # character
```

When a hyphen is used at the beginning or end of a character class, or a caret is used in the middle of a character class, these characters lose their special meaning and only represent themselves literally. The same is true of a left bracket, but a right bracket must obviously be escaped:

```
/[-^[\]]/        # Match a hyphen, caret, or right bracket
```

Ruby regular expressions may contain references to named character classes, which are basically named patterns (of the form `[[:name:]]`). For example, `[[:digit:]]` means the same as `[0-9]` in a pattern. In many cases, this turns out to be shorthand or is at least more readable.

Some others are `[[:print:]]` (printable characters) and `[[:alpha:]]` (alphabetic characters). Here are some examples:

```
s1 = "abc\007def"
/[[:print:]]*/.match(s1)
m1 = Regexp::last_match[0]               # "abc"

s2 = "1234def"
/[[:digit:]]*/.match(s2)
m2 = Regexp::last_match[0]               # "1234"

/[[:digit:]]+[[:alpha:]]/.match(s2)
m3 = Regexp::last_match[0]               # "1234d"
```

A caret before the character class name negates the class:

```
/[[:^alpha:]]/   # Any non-alpha character
```

Named character classes provide another non-obvious feature: they match Unicode characters. For example, the `[[:lower:]]` class matches strings such as "élan" that contain lowercase characters outside of `[a-z]`.

There are also shorthand notations for many classes. The most common ones are \d (to match a digit), \w (to match any "word" character), and \s (to match any whitespace character such as a space, tab, or newline):

```
str1 = "Wolf 359"
/\w+/.match(str1)        # matches "Wolf" (same as /[a-zA-Z_0-9]+/)
/\w+ \d+/.match(str1)    # matches "Wolf 359"
/\w+ \w+/.match(str1)    # matches "Wolf 359"
/\s+/.match(str1)        # matches " "
```

The "negated" forms are typically capitalized:

```
/\W/                    # Any non-word character
/\D/                    # Any non-digit character
/\S/                    # Any non-whitespace character
```

3.11   Extended Regular Expressions

Regular expressions are frequently cryptic, especially as they get longer. The x directive enables you to stretch out a regex across multiple lines; spaces and newlines are ignored so that you can use these for indentation and readability. This also encourages the use of comments, although comments are possible even in simple regexes.

For a contrived example of a moderately complex regular expression, let's suppose that we had a list of addresses like this:

```
addresses =
  [ "409 W Jackson Ave",          "No. 27 Grande Place",
    "16000 Pennsylvania Avenue",  "2367 St. George St.",
    "22 Rue Morgue",              "33 Rue St. Denis",
    "44 Rue Zeeday",              "55 Santa Monica Blvd.",
    "123 Main St., Apt. 234",     "123 Main St., #234",
    "345 Euneva Avenue, Suite 23", "678 Euneva Ave, Suite A"]
```

In these examples, each address consists of three parts—a number, a street name, and an optional suite or apartment number. I'm making the arbitrary rules that there can be an optional "No." on the front of the number, and the period may be omitted. Likewise, let's arbitrarily say that the street name may consist of ordinary word characters but also allows the apostrophe, hyphen, and period. Finally, if the optional suite number is used, it must be preceded by a comma and one of the following tokens: Apt., Suite, or # (number sign).

Here is the regular expression I created for this. Notice that I've commented it heavily (maybe even too heavily):

```
regex = / ^                  # Beginning of string
        ((No\.?)\s+)?         # Optional: No[.]
        \d+ \s+               # Digits and spacing
        ((\w|[.'-])+          # Street name... may be
         \s*                  #   multiple words.
        )+
```

```
(,\s*                  # Optional: Comma etc.
 (Apt\.?|Suite|\#)     # Apt[.], Suite, #
 \s+                   # Spacing
 (\d+|[A-Z])           # Numbers or single letter
)?
 $                     # End of string
/x
```

The point here is clear. When your regex reaches a certain threshold (which is a matter of opinion), make it an extended regex so that you can format it and add comments.

You may have noticed that I used ordinary Ruby comments here (# ...) instead of regex comments ((?#...)). Why did I do that? Simply because I could. The regex comments are needed only when the comment needs to be *closed* other than at the end of the line (for example, when more "meat" of the regex follows the comment on the same line).

3.12   Matching a Newline with a Dot

Ordinarily a dot matches any character except a newline. When the m (multiline) modifier is used, a newline will be matched by a dot. The same is true when the Regexp::MULTILINE option is used in creating a regex.

```
str = "Rubies are red\nAnd violets are blue.\n"
pat1 = /red./
pat2 = /red./m

str =~ pat1      # nil
str =~ pat2      # 11
```

This multiline mode has no effect on where anchors match (such as ^, $, \A, and \Z); they match in the same places. All that is affected is whether a dot matches a newline.

3.13   Using Embedded Options

The common way to specify options for a regex is to use a trailing option (such as i or m). But what if we want an option to apply only to part of a regular expression?

We can turn options on and off with a special notation. Within parentheses, a question mark followed by one or more options "turns on" those options for the remainder of the regular expression. A minus sign preceding one or more options "turns off" those options.

```
/abc(?i)def/          # Will match abcdef, abcDEF, abcDef, ...
                      #   but not ABCdef
/ab(?i)cd(?-i)ef/     # Will match abcdef, abCDef, abcDef, ...
                      #   but not ABcdef or abcdEF
/(?imx).*/            # Same as /.*/imx
/abc(?i-m).*/m        # For last part of regex, turn on case
                      #   sensitivity, turn off multiline
```

If we want, we can use a colon followed by a subexpression, and those options specified will be in effect only for that subexpression:

```
/ab(?i:cd)ef/         # Same as /ab(?i)cd(?-i)ef/
```

For technical reasons, it is not possible to treat the o option this way. The x option can be treated this way, but I don't know why anyone ever would.

3.14   Using Embedded Subexpressions

We can use the ?> notation to specify subexpressions in a regex:

```
re = /(?>abc)(?>def)/      # Same as /abcdef/
re.match("abcdef").to_a    # ["abcdef"]
```

Notice that the subexpressions themselves don't imply grouping. We *can* turn them into capturing groups with additional parentheses, of course.

Note that this notation is *possessive*—that is, it is greedy, and it does *not* allow backtracking into the subexpression.

```
str = "abccccdef"
re1 = /(abc*)cdef/
re2 = /(?>abc*)cdef/

re1 =~ str            # 0
re2 =~ str            # nil
re1.match(str).to_a   # ["abccccdef", "abccc"]
re2.match(str).to_a   # []
```

In the preceding example, re2's subexpression abc* consumes all the instances of the letter *c,* and it (possessively) won't give them back to allow backtracking.

In addition to `(?>)`, there is another way of expressing possessiveness, with the postfix + quantifier. This is distinct from the + meaning "one or more" and can in fact be combined with it. In fact, it is a "secondary" quantifier, like the ? (which gives us ??, +?, and *?).

In essence, + applied to a repeated pattern is the same as enclosing that repeated pattern in an independent subexpression. Here is an example:

```
r1 = /x*+/    # Same as:  /(?>x*)/
r2 = /x++/    # Same as:  /(?>x+)/
r3 = /x?+/    # Same as:  /(?>x?)/
```

For technical reasons, Ruby does not honor the {n,m}+ notation as possessive.

3.14.1   Recursion in Regular Expressions

The ability to re-invoke a subexpression makes it possible to craft recursive regular expressions. For example, here is one that matches any properly nested parenthesized expression. (Thanks again to Andrew Johnson.)

```
str = "a * ((b-c)/(d-e) - f) * g"

reg = /(?                     # begin named expression
       \(                     # match open paren
       (?:                    # non-capturing group
         (?>                  # possessive subexpr to match:
           \\[()]             #   either an escaped paren
           |                  # OR
           [^()]              #   a non-paren character
         )                    # end possessive
         |                    # OR
         \g                   # a nested parens group (recursive call)
       )*                     # repeat non-captured group zero or more
       \)                     # match closing paren
     )                        # end named expression
   /x
m = reg.match(str).to_a       # ["((b-c)/(d-e) - f)",
                              #  "((b-c)/(d-e) - f)"]
```

Note that *left recursion* is not allowed. This is legal:

```
str = "bbbaccc"
re1 = /(?<foo>a|b\g<foo>c)/
re1.match(str).to_a          # ["bbbaccc","bbbaccc"]
```

But this is *illegal*:

```
re2 = /(?<foo>a|\g<foo>c)/ # Syntax error!
```

This example is illegal because of the recursion at the head of each alternative. This leads, if you think about it, to an infinite regress.

3.15   A Few Sample Regular Expressions

This section presents a small list of regular expressions that might be useful either in actual use or as samples to study.

3.15.1   Matching an IP Address

Suppose that we want to determine whether a string is a valid IPv4 address. The standard form of such an address is a *dotted quad* or *dotted decimal* string. This is, in other words, four decimal numbers separated by periods, each number ranging from 0 to 255.

The pattern given here will do the trick (with a few exceptions, such as "127.1"). We break up the pattern a little just for readability. Note that the \d symbol is double-escaped so that the slash in the string gets passed on to the regex. (We'll improve on this in a minute.)

```
num = "(\\d|[01]?\\d\\d|2[0-4]\\d|25[0-5])"
pat = "^(#{num}\.){3}#{num}$"
ip_pat = Regexp.new(pat)

ip1 = "9.53.97.102"

if ip1 =~ ip_pat                       # Prints "yes"
  puts "yes"
else
  puts "no"
end
```

Note how we have an excess of backslashes when we define num in the preceding example. Let's define it as a regex instead of a string:

```
num = /(\d|[01]?\d\d|2[0-4]\d|25[0-5])/
```

When a regex is interpolated into another, to_s is called, which preserves all the information in the original regex:

```
num.to_s    # "(?-mix:(\\d|[01]?\\d\\d|2[0-4]\\d|25[0-5]))"
```

In some cases, it is more important to use a regex instead of a string for embedding. A good rule of thumb is to interpolate regexes unless there is some reason you must interpolate a string.

IPv6 addresses are not in widespread use yet, but we include them for completeness. These consist of eight colon-separated 16-bit hex numbers with zeroes suppressed:

```
num = /[0-9A-Fa-f]{0,4}/
pat = /^(#{num}:){7}#{num}$/
ipv6_pat = Regexp.new(pat)

v6ip = "abcd::1324:ea54::dead::beef"

if v6ip =~ ipv6_pat      # Prints "yes"
  puts "yes"
else
  puts "no"
end
```

3.15.2 Matching a Keyword-Value Pair

Occasionally we want to work with strings of the form "attribute=value" (as, for example, when we parse some kind of configuration file for an application).

The following code fragment extracts the keyword and the value. The assumptions are that the keyword or attribute is a single word, the value extends to the end of the line, and the equal sign may be surrounded by whitespace:

```
pat = /(\w+)\s*=\s*(.*?)$/
str = "color = blue"
```

```
matches = pat.match(str)

puts matches[1]         # "color"
puts matches[2]         # "blue"
```

3.15.3   Matching Roman Numerals

In the following example, we match against a complex pattern to determine whether a string is a valid Roman number (up to decimal 3999). As before, the pattern is broken up into parts for readability:

```
rom1 = /m{0,3}/i
rom2 = /(d?c{0,3}|c[dm])/i
rom3 = /(l?x{0,3}|x[lc])/i
rom4 = /(v?i{0,3}|i[vx])/i
roman = /^#{rom1}#{rom2}#{rom3}#{rom4}$/

year1985 = "MCMLXXXV"

if year1985 =~ roman         # Prints "yes"
  puts "yes"
else
  puts "no"
end
```

You might be tempted to put the i on the end of the whole expression and leave it off the smaller ones, like so:

```
# This doesn't work!

rom1 = /m{0,3}/
rom2 = /(d?c{0,3}|c[dm])/
rom3 = /(l?x{0,3}|x[lc])/
rom4 = /(v?i{0,3}|i[vx])/
roman = /^#{rom1}#{rom2}#{rom3}#{rom4}$/i
```

Why doesn't this work? Look at this for the answer:

```
rom1.to_s    # "(?-mix:m{0,3})"
```

Notice how the to_s captures the flags for each subexpression, and these then override the flag on the big expression.

3.15.4   Matching Numeric Constants

A simple decimal integer is the easiest number to match. It has an optional sign and consists thereafter of digits (except that Ruby allows an underscore as a digit separator). Note that the first digit should not be a zero because then it would be interpreted as an octal constant:

```
int_pat = /^[+-]?[1-9][\d_]*$/
```

Integer constants in other bases are similar. Note that the hex and binary patterns have been made case insensitive because they contain at least one letter:

```
hex_pat = /^[+-]?0x[\da-f_]+$/i
oct_pat = /^[+-]?0[0-7_]+$/
bin_pat = /^[+-]?0b[01_]+$/i
```

A normal floating point constant is a little tricky; the number sequences on each side of the decimal point are optional, but one or the other must be included:

```
float_pat = /^(\d[\d_]*)*\.[\d_]*$/
```

Finally, scientific notation builds on the ordinary floating point pattern:

```
sci_pat = /^(\d[\d_]*)?\.[\d_]*(e[+-]?)?(_*\d[\d_]*)$/i
```

These patterns can be useful if, for instance, you have a string and you want to verify its validity as a number before trying to convert it.

3.15.5   Matching a Date/Time String

Suppose that we want to match a date/time in the form mm/dd/yy hh:mm:ss. This pattern is a good first attempt:

```
datetime = /(\d\d)\/(\d\d)\/(\d\d) (\d\d):(\d\d):(\d\d)/
```

However, that will also match invalid date/times and miss valid ones. The following example is pickier. Note how we build it up by interpolating smaller regexes into larger ones:

```
mo = /(0?[1-9]|1[0-2])/        # 01 to 09 or 1 to 9 or 10-12
dd = /([0-2]?[1-9]|[1-3][01])/ # 1-9 or 01-09 or 11-19 etc.
```

```
yy = /(\d\d)/                # 00-99
hh = /([01]?[1-9]|[12][0-4])/  # 1-9 or 00-09 or...
mi = /([0-5]\d)/             # 00-59, both digits required
ss = /([0-6]\d)?/            # allows leap seconds ;-)


date = /(#{mo}\/#{dd}\/#{yy})/
time = /(#{hh}:#{mi}:#{ss})/


datetime = /(#{date} #{time})/
```

Here's how we might call it using `String#scan` to return an array of matches:

```
str="Recorded on 11/18/07 20:31:00"
str.scan(datetime)
# [["11/18/07 20:31:00", "11/18/07", "11", "18", "00",
#    "20:31:00", "20", "31", ":00"]]
```

Of course, this could all have been done as a large extended regex:

```
datetime = %r{(
   (0?[1-9]|1[0-2])/          # mo: 01 to 09 or 1 to 9 or 10-12
   ([0-2]?[1-9]|[1-3][01])/  # dd: 1-9 or 01-09 or 11-19 etc.
   (\d\d) [ ]                 # yy: 00-99
   ([01]?[1-9]|[12][0-4]):   # hh: 1-9 or 00-09 or...
   ([0-5]\d):                # mm: 00-59, both digits required
   (([0-6]\d))?              # ss: allows leap seconds ;-)
)}x
```

Note the use of the `%r{}` notation so that we don't have to escape the slashes.

3.15.6   Detecting Doubled Words in Text

In this section, we implement the famous double-word detector. Typing the same word twice in succession is a common typing error. The following code detects instances of that occurrence:

```
double_re = /\b(['A-Z]+) +\1\b/i

str="There's there's the the pattern."
str.scan(double_re)  # [["There's"],["the"]]
```

Note that the trailing `i` in the regex is for case-insensitive matching. There is an array for each grouping, hence the resulting array of arrays.

3.15.7 Matching All-Caps Words

This example is simple if we assume no numerics, underscores, and so on:

```
allcaps = /\b[A-Z]+\b/

string = "This is ALL CAPS"
string[allcaps]                 #  "ALL"
Suppose you want to extract every word in all-caps:
string.scan(allcaps)           #  ["ALL", "CAPS"]
```

If we wanted, we could extend this concept to include Ruby identifiers and similar items.

3.15.8 Matching Version Numbers

A common convention is to express a library or application version number by three dot-separated numbers. This regex matches that kind of string, with the package name and the individual numbers as submatches:

```
package = "mylib-1.8.12"
matches = package.match(/(.*)-(\d+)\.(\d+)\.(\d+)/)
name, major, minor, tiny = matches[1..-1]
```

3.15.9 A Few Other Patterns

Let's end this list with a few more "odds and ends." As usual, most of these could be done in more than one way.

Suppose that we wanted to match a two-character U.S. state postal code. The simple way is just /[A-Z]{2}/, of course. But this matches names such as XY and ZZ that look legal but are meaningless. The following regex matches all the 51 usual codes (50 states and the District of Columbia):

```
state =  /^A[LKZR] | C[AOT] | D[EC] | FL | GA | HI | I[DLNA] |
          K[SY] | LA | M[EDAINSOT] | N[EVHJMYCD] | O[HKR] |
          PA | RI | S[CD] | T[NX] | UT | V[TA] | W[AVIY]$/x
```

For clarity, I've made this an extended regex (by using the x modifier). The spaces and newlines are ignored.

In a similar vein, here is a regex to match a U.S. ZIP Code (which may be five or nine digits):

```
zip = /^\d{5}(-\d{4})?$/
```

The anchors (in this regex and others) are only to ensure that there are no extraneous characters before or after the matched string. Note that this regex will not catch all invalid codes. In that sense, it is less useful than the preceding one.

The following regex matches a phone number in the North American Numbering Plan (NANP) format; it allows three common ways of writing such a phone number:

```
phone = /^((\(\(\d{3}\) |\d{3}-)\d{3}-\d{4}|\d{3}\.\d{3}\.\d{4})$/
"(512) 555-1234"  =~ phone    # true
"512.555.1234"    =~ phone    # true
"512-555-1234"    =~ phone    # true
"(512)-555-1234"  =~ phone    # false
"512-555.1234"    =~ phone    # false
```

Matching a dollar amount with optional cents is also trivial:

```
dollar = /^\$\d+(\.\d\d)?$/
```

This one obviously requires at least one digit to the left of the decimal and disallows spaces after the dollar sign. Also note that if you only wanted to *detect* a dollar amount rather than *validate* it, the anchors would be removed and the optional cents would be unnecessary.

3.16   Conclusion

That ends our discussion of regular expressions in Ruby. Now that we have looked at both strings and regexes, let's take a look at some issues with internationalization in Ruby. This topic builds on both the string and regex material we have already seen.

CHAPTER 4

Internationalization in Ruby

Therefore, [the place] was called Babel, because there the Lord confused the language of all the earth; and from there the Lord scattered them abroad over the face of all the earth.

—Genesis 11:9

Earlier we said that character data was arguably the most important data type. But what do we mean by character data? Whose characters, whose alphabet, whose language and culture?

In the past, computing had an Anglocentric bias, perhaps going back as far as Charles Babbage. This is not necessarily a bad thing. We had to start somewhere, and it might as well be with an alphabet of 26 letters and no diacritic marks.

But computing is a much more global phenomenon now. Every country in the world now has computing hardware and access to online resources. Naturally everyone would prefer to work with web pages, email, and other data not just in English but in his own language.

Human written languages are amazingly diverse. Some are nearly phonetic; others are hardly phonetic at all. Some have true alphabets, whereas others are mostly large collections of thousands of symbols evolved from pictograms. Some languages have more than one alphabet. Some are intended to be written vertically; some are written horizontally, as most of us are used to—but from right to left, as most of us are not used to. Some alphabets are fairly plain; others are incredibly elaborate and adorned richly with diacritics. Some languages have letters that can be combined with their neighboring letters in certain circumstances; sometimes this is mandatory, sometimes optional. Some languages have the concept of upper and lowercase letters; many do not.

In 30 years or so, the computing world has managed to create a little order out of the chaos. If you deal much with programming applications that are meant to be used in linguistically diverse environments, you know the term *internationalization*. This could be defined as the enabling of software to handle more than one written language.

Related terms are *multilingualization* and *localization*. All of these are traditionally abbreviated by the curious practice of deleting the middle letters and replacing them with the number of letters deleted:

```
def shorten(str)
  (str[0] + str[1..-2].length.to_s + str[-1]).upcase
end

shorten("internationalization")  # I18N
shorten("localization")          # L10N
shorten("multilingualization")   # M17N
```

Localization involves complete support for local conventions and culture, such as currency symbols, ways of formatting dates and times, using a comma as a decimal separator, and much more. There is no universal agreement on the exact meaning of multilingualization. Many or most use this term to mean the combination of I18N and L10N; others use it as synonymous with I18N. I tend to avoid this term in this book.

In essence, internationalizing an application is a one-time process; the source needs to be modified so that it can handle multiple character sets and data in multiple languages. A program that is fully internationalized can accept strings in multiple languages, manipulate those strings, and output them.

A localized program goes beyond that, to permit selection of a language at runtime for use in prompts, error messages, and so on; this includes interpolating data in the correct places in messages and forming plurals correctly. It also includes the capability to perform correct collating (sorting), as well as formatting numbers, dates, times, and currencies.

The process of localization of course includes the translating of error messages into the target language. This process is repeated for every language the application is to support.

In this chapter, we'll examine tools and techniques that help the Ruby developer with these issues. Let's begin with a little more terminology, since this area is particularly prone to jargon.

4.1 Background and Terminology

At one time, there was a proliferation of character sets. In the early 60s, ASCII was created, and it gained widespread acceptance through the 70s and early 80s. ASCII stands for American Standard Code for Information Interchange. It was a big step forward, but the operant word here is American. It was never designed to handle even European languages, much less Asian ones.

But there were loopholes. This character set had 128 characters, being a 7-bit code). But an 8-bit byte was standard; so the natural idea was to make a superset of ASCII, using codes 128 and higher for other purposes. The trouble is, this was done many times in many different ways by IBM and others; there was no widespread agreement on what, for example, character 221 was.

The shortcomings of such an approach are obvious. Not only do the sender and receiver have to agree on the exact character set, but they are limited in what languages they can use in a single context. If you wanted to write in German but quote a couple of sources in Greek and Hebrew, you probably couldn't do it at all. This scheme didn't begin to address the complexities of Asian languages such as Chinese, Japanese, and Korean.

There were two basic kinds of solutions to this problem. One was to use a much larger character set—one with 16 bits, for example (so-called *wide characters*). The other was to use variable-length multibyte encodings.

In a variable-length scheme, some characters might be represented in a single byte, some in two bytes, and some in three or even more. Obviously, this raised many issues: For one, a string had to be uniquely decodable. The first byte of a multibyte character could be in a special class so that we could know to expect another byte, but what about the second and later bytes? Were they allowed to overlap with the set of single-byte characters? Were certain characters allowed as second or third bytes, or were they disallowed? Would we be able to jump into the middle of a string and still make sense of it? Would we be able to iterate backwards over a string if we wanted? Different encodings made different design decisions.

Eventually the idea for Unicode was born. Think of it as a "world character set." Unfortunately, nothing is ever that simple.

You may have heard it said that Unicode was (or is) limited to 65,536 characters (the number of codes representable in 16 bits). This is a common misconception; Unicode was never designed with that kind of constraint. It was understood from the beginning that in many usages, it would be a multibyte scheme. The number of characters that could be represented was essentially limitless—a good thing, because 65,000 codes would never suffice to handle all the languages of the world.

One of the first things to understand about i18n is that the interpretation of a string is not intrinsic to the string itself. That kind of old-fashioned thinking comes from the notion that there is only one way of storing strings. I can't stress this enough. Internally, a string is just a series of bytes. To emphasize this, let's imagine a single ASCII character stored in a byte of memory. If we store the letter that we call "capital A," we really are storing the number 65.

Why do we view a 65 as an A? It's because of how the data item is used (or how it is interpreted). If we take that item and add it to another number, we are using it (interpreting it) as a number; if we send it to an ASCII terminal over a serial line, we are interpreting it as an ASCII character.

Just as a single byte can be interpreted in more than one way, so, obviously, can a whole sequence of bytes. In fact, the intended interpretation scheme (or encoding) has to be known in advance for a string to make any real sense. An encoding is essentially a mapping between binary numbers and characters. And yet it still isn't quite this simple.

But before we get into these issues, let's look at some terminology. These terms are not always intuitive.

- A *byte* is simply eight bits (though in the old days, even this was not true). Traditionally, many programmers have thought of a byte as corresponding to a single character. Obviously, we can't think that way in an I18N context.

- A *codepoint* is simply a single entry in the imaginary table that represents the character set. As a half-truth, you may think of a codepoint as mapping one-to-one to a character. Nearer to the truth, it sometimes takes more than a single codepoint to uniquely specify a character.

- A *glyph* is the visual representation of a codepoint. It may seem a little unintuitive, but a character's identity is distinct from its visual representation.

- A *grapheme* is similar in concept to a glyph, but when we talk about graphemes, we are coming from the context of the language, not the context of our software. A grapheme may be the combination (naive or otherwise) of two or more glyphs. It is the way a user thinks about a character in his own native language context. The distinction is subtle enough that many programmers will simply never worry about it.

What then is a character? Even in the Unicode world, there is some fuzziness associated with this concept because different languages behave a little differently and programmers think differently from other people. Let's say that a character is an abstraction of a writing symbol that can be visually represented in one or more ways.

Let's get a little more concrete. First, let me introduce a notation to you. We habitually represent Unicode codepoints with the notation U+ followed by four or more uppercase hexadecimal digits. So what we call the letter "A" can be specified as U+0041.

Now take the letter "é" for example (lowercase e with an acute accent). This can actually be represented in two ways in Unicode. The first way is the single codepoint U+00E9 (LATIN SMALL LETTER E WITH ACUTE). The second way is two codepoints—a small e followed by an acute accent: U+0065 and U+0301 (or LATIN SMALL LETTER E followed by COMBINING ACUTE ACCENT).

Both forms are equally valid. The shorter one is referred to as the *precomposed* form. Bear in mind, though, that not every language has precomposed variants, so it isn't always possible to reduce such a character to a single codepoint.

I've referred to Unicode as an encoding, but that isn't strictly correct. Unicode maps characters to codepoints; but there are different ways to map codepoints to binary storage. In effect, Unicode is a family of encodings.

Let's take the string "Matz" as an example. This consists of four Unicode codepoints:

```
"Matz"     # U+004d U+0061 U+0074 U+007a
```

The straightforward way to store this would be as a simple sequence of bytes:

```
00 4d 00 61 00 74 00 7a
```

This is called UCS-2 (as in two bytes) or UTF-16 (as in 16 bits). Note that this encoding itself actually comes in two "flavors," a big-endian and a little-endian form. However, notice that every other byte is zero. This isn't mere coincidence; it is typical for English text, which rarely goes beyond codepoint U+00FF. It's somewhat wasteful of memory.

This brings us to the idea of UTF-8. This is a Unicode encoding where the "traditional" characters are represented as single bytes, but others may be represented as multiple bytes. Here is a UTF-8 encoding of this same string:

```
4d 61 74 7a
```

Notice that all we have done is strip off the zeroes; more importantly, note that this is the same as ordinary ASCII. This is obviously by design; "plain ASCII" can be thought as a proper subset of UTF-8. In fact, the 8-bit ISO-8859-1 (which overlaps heavily with ASCII) is also a proper subset. (Do *not* confuse ISO-8859-1, also called Latin-1, with Windows-1252.) In short, this means that UTF-8 is "backward compatible" with text encoded as ASCII or as Latin-1.

One implication of this is that when UTF-8 text is interpreted, it sometimes appears "normal" (especially if the text is mostly English). Sometimes you may find that in a browser or other application, English text is displayed correctly, but there are additional "garbage" characters. In such a case, it's likely that the application is making the wrong assumption about what encoding is being used.

So we can argue that UTF-8 saves memory (speaking from an Anglocentric point of view again, or at least ASCII-centric). When the text is primarily ASCII, memory will be conserved, but for other writing systems such as Greek or Cyrillic, the strings will actually grow in size.

It is an obvious benefit that UTF-8 is backward compatible with ASCII, still arguably the most common single-byte encoding in the world. Finally, UTF-8 also has some special features to make it convenient for programmers.

For one thing, the bytes used in multibyte characters are assigned carefully. The null character (ASCII 0) is never used as the nth byte in a sequence (where n > 1), nor are such common characters as the slash (commonly used as a pathname delimiter). As a matter of fact, no byte in the full ASCII range (0x00-0x7F) can be used as part of any other character.

The second byte in a multibyte character uniquely determines how many bytes will follow. The second byte is always in the range 0xC0 to 0xFD, and any following bytes are always in the range 0x80 to 0xBF. This ensures that the encoding scheme is stateless and allows recovery after missing or garbled bytes.

UTF-8 is one of the most flexible and common encodings in the world, in use since the early 1990s. Unless it is told otherwise, Ruby assumes that the code you write, any text input, and all text output are encoded as UTF-8. As a result, most of our attention in this chapter will be focused on working with the UTF-8 encoding in Ruby.

With respect to internationalization, there are two concepts that I consider to be fundamental, almost axiomatic. First, a string has no intrinsic interpretation. It must be interpreted according to some external standard. Second, a byte does not correspond to a character; a character may be one or more bytes. There are other lessons to be learned, but these two come first.

4.2   Working with Character Encodings

Even if you as a programmer only use English, there is a strong chance that users of your program will want to enter non-English text. Personal names, place names, and many other such pieces of text often contain characters from other languages.

Handling those languages can be an extremely challenging task. Different languages sort words completely differently: in Slovak, "ch" comes after "h," whereas in Swedish, "Å" comes after "Z." In Russian, there are two different plural word endings, one for numbers ending in 2, 3, or 4, and one for numbers ending in 5, 6, 7, 8, 9, or 0. Modern programs, especially those written for the Web, should be prepared to accept multilingual text even if they will never be localized into other languages.

Programs that are fully multinationalized should be able to take input in multiple languages and express output in multiple languages, including correctly-formed plurals. They need to format numbers, dates, and currencies correctly for the current language, and they must be able to sort strings correctly as well.

Let's investigate the various tools available to the Ruby programmer that allow us to do I18N and L10N. We need to understand how Ruby stores character strings.

As I said, UTF-8 is now the default for Ruby. Unless the interpreter is told otherwise, it assumes that the code you write, any text input, and all text output are encoded as UTF-8.

The letter "e" with an acute accent has the codepoint U+00E9. In Ruby, Unicode characters can also be written in the form u plus the hexadecimal codepoint. As a result, these strings are equal:

```
"épée" == "\u00E9p\u00E9e"  # true
# The French word "épée" refers to a kind of sword
```

In Ruby, strings are always a series of codepoints, but some codepoints are encoded as more than one byte. The interpreter permits us to access the underlying series of bytes. Let's look at some examples:

```
sword = "épée"
sword.length        # 4
sword.bytes         # [195, 169, 112, 195, 169, 101]
sword.bytes.length  # 6
```

The string contains four characters, but encoding those four characters requires 6 bytes. The character é is represented in UTF-8 as the bytes 195 and 169, in that order.

```
cp = sword.codepoints    # [233, 112, 233, 101]
cp.map {|c| c.to_s(16) } # ["e9", "70", "e9", "65"]
sword.scan(/./)          # ["é", "p", "é", "e"]
```

Using the `String#unpack` function allows us to see the Unicode codepoint numbers. We can convert those numbers to hexadecimal to see that the codepoint for "é" is in fact `U+00E9`.

Also in the previous example, note that regular expressions are fully Unicode-aware. They match characters rather than bytes.

4.2.1   Normalization

Many characters are conceptually made up of two other existing characters, such as the letter e and the acute accent combining to create the letter é. In addition to LATIN SMALL LETTER E WITH ACUTE ACCENT, Unicode contains separate codepoints for LATIN SMALL LETTER E (`U+0065`) and COMBINING ACUTE ACCENT (`U+0301`) for the e and the acute accent, respectively.

Combining codepoints is called *composition,* and separating them is *decomposition.* In order to compare a sequence of codepoints to see if they include the same characters, any program that deals with Unicode must first compose (or decompose) the codepoints using the same set of rules. This process is called *normalization.* Once a sequence of codepoints has been normalized, it can be accurately compared with others that have been normalized the same way.

Up until now, we've been using precomposed characters—ones in which the base character and diacritic are combined into a single entity and a single Unicode codepoint. In general, though, Unicode supports the separate encoding of base characters and their diacritics.

Why is this separation supported? It provides flexibility and allows us to apply diacritic marks to any character, not just the combinations considered by the encoding designer. In fact, fonts will typically include glyphs for common combinations of character and diacritic, but the display of an entity is separate from its encoding. Table 4.1 clarifies this a little.

Table 4.1 Precomposed and Decomposed Forms

Precomposed Form of "é"

Character Name	Glyph	Codepoint	UTF-8 Bytes	Comments
LATIN SMALL LETTER E WITH ACUTE	é	U+00E9	0xC3 0xA9	One character, one codepoint, two UTF-8 bytes

Decomposed Form of "é"

Character Name	Glyph	Codepoint	UTF-8 Bytes	Comments
LATIN SMALL LETTER E	e	U+0065	0x65	One character, two codepoints (two "programmer's characters"), three UTF-8 bytes
COMBINING ACUTE ACCENT	´	U+0301	0xCC 0x81	

Unicode has numerous design considerations such as efficiency and round-trip compatibility with existing national encodings. Sometimes these constraints may introduce some redundancy; for example, not only does Unicode include codepoints for decomposed forms but also for many of the precomposed forms already in use. This means that there is also a codepoint for LATIN SMALL LETTER E WITH ACUTE ACCENT, as well as for things such as the double-f ligature.

For example, let's consider the German word "öffnen" (to open). Without even considering case, there are four ways to encode it:

1. o + COMBINING DIAERESIS (U+0308) + f + f + n + e + n
2. LATIN SMALL LETTER O WITH DIAERESIS (U+00F6) + f + f + n + e + n
3. o + COMBINING DIAERESIS + DOUBLE-F LIGATURE (U+FB00) + n + e + n
4. LATIN SMALL LETTER O WITH DIAERESIS + DOUBLE-F LIGATURE + n + e + n

The *diaeresis* (also spelled *dieresis*) is simply a pair of dots over a character. In German, it is called an *umlaut*.

Normalizing is the process of standardizing the character representations used. After normalizing, we can be sure that a given character is encoded in a particular way. Exactly what those forms are depends on what we are trying to achieve. Annex 15 of the Unicode Standard lists four normalization forms:

1. D (Canonical Decomposition)
2. C (Canonical Decomposition followed by Canonical Composition)
3. KD (Compatibility Decomposition)
4. KC (Compatibility Decomposition followed by Canonical Composition)

You may see these written as NFKC (Normalization Form KC) and so on.

The precise rules set out in the standard are complex and cover the difference between "canonical equivalence" and "compatibility equivalence." (Korean and Japanese require particular attention, but we won't address these here.) Table 4.2 summarizes the effects of each normalization form on the strings we started with previously.

Table 4.2 Normalized Unicode Forms

Original	NFD	NFC	NFKD	NFKC
o+¨+f+f+n+e+n	o+¨+f+f+n+e+n	ö+f+f+n+e+n	o+¨+f+f+n+e+n	ö+f+f+n+e+n
ö+f+f+n+e+n	o+¨+f+f+n+e+n	ö+f+f+n+e+n	o+¨+f+f+n+e+n	ö+f+f+n+e+n
o+¨+ff+n+e+n	o+¨+ff+n+e+n	ö+ff+n+e+n	o+¨+f+f+n+e+n	ö+f+f+n+e+n
ö+ff+n+e+n	o+¨+ff+n+e+n	ö+ff+n+e+n	o+¨+f+f+n+e+n	ö+f+f+n+e+n

Which form is most appropriate depends on the application at hand. C and D are simply "fully composed" and "fully decomposed" forms, respectively; these forms are reversible. KC and KD are the "compatibility" forms; they require conversions such as the ligature "ffi" being separated into its three component letters (making these forms irreversible). Therefore the compatibility forms are preferred for storage, especially if the text will be compared with other texts during tasks such as search and validation.

The `activesupport` gem provides the `ActiveSupport::MultiByte::Chars` class, which wraps the `String` class. It allows manipulation of Unicode codepoints in ways that the String class does not. Perhaps the most unexpected Unicode functionality neglected by the `String` class is that of changing case:

```
require 'active_support'

chars = ActiveSupport::Multibyte::Chars.new("épée")
"épée".upcase              # "éPéE"
chars.upcase.to_s          # "ÉPÉE"
"épée".capitalize          # "épée"
chars.capitalize.to_s      # "Épée"
```

This feature provided by `activesupport` is "neglected" in Ruby by design. This is because many languages do not have the concept of upper and lower case characters. In such languages, these operations are meaningless and are therefore meaningless in the general case. Only perform this kind of transformation if you are certain of the behavior with respect to all the languages you plan to support.

The gem also provides useful methods for truncation, codepoint composition and decomposition, and finally normalization to all four forms.

```
sword_kc = chars.normalize(:kc)
sword_kd = chars.normalize(:kd)
sword_kc.bytes       # [195, 169, 112, 195, 169, 101]
sword_kd.bytes       # [101, 204, 129, 112, 101, 204, 129, 101]
sword_kc.scan(/./)   # ["é", "p", "é", "e"]
sword_kd.scan(/./)   # ["e", "´'", "p", "e", "´", "e"]
```

4.2.2   Encoding Conversions

Each `String` in Ruby has an encoding that determines how the bytes in the string are interpreted as characters. This allows input to be provided using different encodings and used together in the same program, but it can cause unexpected problems. Trying to combine strings with incompatible encodings will cause an `Encoding::CompatibilityError` exception. Fortunately, the `encode` method allows strings to be converted from one character encoding to another. Using the `encode` method, we can convert strings into the same encoding before we try to combine them:

```
sword = "épée"
sword_mac = sword.encode("macRoman")
sword.bytes          # [195, 169, 112, 195, 169, 101]
sword_mac.bytes      # [142, 112, 142, 101]

str = sword + sword_mac
# incompatible character encodings: UTF-8 and macRoman

str = sword + sword_mac.encode("UTF-8")
# "épée"
```

In a similar way, receiving input in an unexpected encoding can easily cause an exception later on when that input is processed:

```ruby
File.write("sword.txt", sword.encode("macRoman"))
invalid_sword = File.read("sword.txt")   # "\x8Ep\x8Ee"
invalid_sword.encoding                    # #<Encoding:UTF-8>
invalid_sword.valid_encoding?             # false

strings = invalid_sword.split("p")
# invalid byte sequence in UTF-8 error
```

One fix is to use the `force_encoding` method to correct the encoding of the bytes that have already been read:

```ruby
forced_sword = invalid_sword.force_encoding("macRoman")
forced_sword.encoding           # #<Encoding:macRoman>
forced_sword.valid_encoding?    # true
forced_sword.split("p")         # ["\x8E", "\x8Ee"]
```

The other way to handle invalid byte sequences is to tell Ruby what the encoding of the file is, so it can be read correctly:

```ruby
read_sword = File.read("sword.txt", :encoding => "macRoman")
read_sword.encoding    # #<Encoding:macRoman>
read_sword.split("p")  # ["\x8E", "\x8Ee"]

open_sword = File.open("sword.txt", "r:macRoman:UTF-8") do |f|
  f.read
end
open_sword.encoding    # #<Encoding:UTF-8>
open_sword.split("p")  # ["é", "ée"]
```

In the second example, we used the `IO.open` API to tell Ruby to read in one encoding, but translate the result into another encoding before returning it.

However, sometimes the encoding of some text is simply unknown, or the data is so garbled that there is no possible valid encoding. In that case, it is still possible to avoid an encoding exception, by replacing invalid bytes with valid ones.

```ruby
bad_sword = "\x8Ep\x8Ee"
bad_sword.encode!("UTF-8", :invalid => :replace,
                          :undef => :replace)
bad_sword                 # "�p�e"
bad_sword.valid_encoding? # true
```

Using the `:replace` option means that any bytes that cannot be decoded will be replaced with ◆, the Unicode replacement character. If desired, unreadable bytes can be replaced by any string of your choosing, including an empty string.

4.2.3 Transliteration

A completely different way of converting between encodings is called *transliteration*. This is the process of taking characters from one alphabet and converting them to characters in another alphabet. In the context of I18N, transliteration almost always means simplifying alphabets into their closest equivalent in basic ASCII.

Examples include converting "épée" into "epee," "dziękuję" into "dziekuje," and "εὐδαιμονία" into "eudaimonia." In transliterations from other writing systems, there can even be multiple ways to transliterate the same thing. Although transliteration can be useful for signage or names that are readable in another alphabet, it can often cause some information to be lost. For these reasons, transliteration does not provide a true encoding option, and should be avoided when possible.

4.2.4 Collation

In computing, *collation* refers to the process of arranging text according to a particular order. Generally, but not always, this implies some kind of alphabetical or similar order. Collation often depends on normalization to be done correctly, because most languages group letters with and without accents together when sorting.

For example, let's consider an array of strings that we want to collate. Note the presence of both composed and decomposed characters. What happens when we use the `Array#sort` method?

```
eacute = [0x00E9].pack('U')
acute  = [0x0301].pack('U')
array  = ["epicurean", "#{eacute}p#{eacute}e", "e#{acute}lan"]
array.sort  # ["epicurean", "élan", "épée"]
```

That's not what we want. But let's try to understand why it happens. Let's look at the first two characters of each string and the bytes into which they're encoded:

```
array.map {|word| {word[0,2] => word[0,2].bytes} }
# [{"ep"=>[101, 112]},
#  {"é"=>[101, 204, 129]},
#  {"ép"=>[195, 169, 112]}]
```

In the first word, the 2 bytes encode two characters. In the second, 3 bytes encode two codepoints that compose into just one character. The third word has a 2-byte and then 1-byte character. By examining the values of the bytes, we can see that the words are sorted based on the bytes that comprise them.

The "e" has a lower value than the first byte of the "é," so it is sorted first. In UTF-8, ASCII characters have the lowest possible values, so non-ASCII characters will always be sorted last. The middle "é" will always be sorted after "e" but before "f" due to the accent's high first byte.

Bear in mind that this type of sorting problem is something of an issue even with plain ASCII. For example, uppercase characters all have lower byte values than their lowercase equivalents, so they don't sort together. We might expect "pyre" and "PyrE" to be adjacent after sorting, but "Pyramus" would come between them. Basically this just means that lexicographic sorting is *not* alphabetic sorting, and it certainly does not follow any complex rules such as we see in a dictionary or phone book.

Each language has its own set of rules, so let's start with a simple one. We'll sort according to the English alphabet and ignore accents. To do that, we can simply decompose each string and then remove any diacritical marks. The Unicode range for combining diacritical marks is from U+0300 to U+036F.

Let's assume that we are processing our list according to English rules and that we are going to ignore accents. The first step is to define our transformation method. We'll normalize our strings to decomposed forms and then elide the diacritics, leaving just the base characters, and sort by the result. For reference, the Unicode range for combining diacritical marks runs from U+0300 to U+036F.

```
Chars = ActiveSupport::Multibyte::Chars  # for convenience

def english_sort(str)
   kd = Chars.new(str).downcase.normalize(:kd)
   cp = kd.codepoints.select {|c| c < 0x0300 || c > 0x036F }
   cp.pack("U*")
 end


array.map{|s| english_sort(s) }
# ["epicurean", "epee", "elan"]

array.sort_by{|s| english_sort(s) }
# ["élan", "épée", "epicurean"]
```

That's better. Although we have addressed capitalization (by using the Unicode-aware downcase method), we haven't addressed character equivalents yet. Let's look at German as an example.

In fact, there is more than one collation for German; we'll use the DIN-2 collation (or phone book collation) for this exercise, in which the German character "ß" is equivalent to "ss," and the umlaut is equivalent to a letter "e." So "ö" is equivalent to "oe", and so on.

Our transformation method should address this. Once again, we will start by normalizing our string to a decomposed form. For reference, the combining diaeresis (or umlaut) is U+0308. We'll also use Ruby's case conversion, but we need to augment it a little. Here, then, is a basic transformation method:

```ruby
def sort_german(str)
  mb = ActiveSupport::Multibyte::Chars.new(str)
  kd = mb.downcase.normalize(:kd)
  kd.gsub('ß', 'ss').gsub("\u0308", 'e').to_s
end

["Straße", "öffnen"].map {|x| sort_german(x) }
# ["strasse", "oeffnen"]
```

Real-world collation algorithms are more complex than the examples we have seen here, and employ multiple levels. Usually, the first level tests the character only (ignoring accents and case), the second level orders by accents, the third level takes case into consideration, and so on. Each level is only used if the previous level was inconclusive.

Even with multiple levels, sorting is still extremely difficult, and often requires detailed knowledge of the language. Some languages sort multiple-character sequences as a single semantic unit (for example, "lj" in Croatian is placed between "l" and "m").

In Danish, "aa" (or "å") is sorted after "z," but only for Danish words. For foreign words, "aa" is just sorted with the other "a" words. That rule means that the city of Aachen comes before Atlanta, but Aalborg comes after Zurich.

Ultimately, it's not possible to devise a truly generic collation algorithm that works for all languages, because many languages have directly contradictory sorting requirements. Keep this in mind when sorting lists for other languages.

4.3   Translations

Lojban is culturally fully neutral. Its vocabulary was built algorithmically using today's six most widely spoken languages: Chinese, Hindi, English, Russian, Spanish, and Arabic.

—*Nick Nicholas and John Cowan, from "What Is Lojban?"*

Now that we have covered how to handle program input and output in any alphabet, we turn to handling input and output in any *language*. Translating a program into other languages is a lot of work, but makes your program usable by many additional people.

Fully localizing your program means translating all of the text, including instructions, error messages, and output. It also means formatting all numbers correctly, including currencies, numbers, dates, and times. We're going to start with the basics of translation, then work our way up through more complex examples, including pluralization and formatting numerical data.

By using the i18n gem, we can use translations from an external file or files, which can be written and edited by translators. The files are formatted in a human-readable format called YAML (Yet Another Markup Language), and each message can be looked up by a key. The I18n.translate method (which is aliased to I18n.t for brevity) accepts a key, and it returns the message that corresponds to that key.

Let's look at an example. First, we'll require the i18n gem (you can install it with gem install i18n if needed), and then we'll supply some translations.

```
require 'i18n'
I18n.backend.store_translations(:en,
   greeting: { hello: "Hello there!" })
I18n.backend.store_translations(:ja,
   greeting: { hello: "こんにちは" })
```

The two-letter abbreviations each refer to a language, and they come from the ISO 639 international standard. Many programming languages, including C, Java, PHP, Perl, and Python, also use these same codes.

The second part of the translation sets *keys* that allow the lookup of *messages*. Beneath the language codes, messages can be organized in any arbitrary hierarchy of keys.

The `translate` method (or `t` for short) takes a key and looks up the message stored under that key in the current locale. The locale defaults to `:en`, but can be changed at any time.

```
I18n.locale              # :en
I18n.t "greeting.hello" # "Hello there!"

I18n.locale = :ja        # :ja
I18n.t "greeting.hello" # "こんにちは"
```

Each period in the key passed to `I18n.t` indicates a level of hierarchy. Each key segment after that indicates a key in the hash of translations.

In large programs, translations are typically stored in dedicated Ruby or YAML files in a `locale/` directory. When multiple files are used, all their keys and messages will be combined, so files are normally separated by language or by type of message.

Let's create a small program that surveys the user and then prints the results of the survey. We'll ask for the user's name, home city, and number of children, using the i18n gem to provide translations for the program output.

First, we need to require the i18n gem, tell it where we will store our translation files, and set the locale. On UNIX systems, the locale is traditionally provided in the LANG environment variable in a form like en_US.UTF-8, so we'll use that.

```
# survey.rb
require 'i18n'
I18n.load_path = Dir["locale/*"]
I18n.enforce_available_locales = true
I18n.locale = ENV["LANG"].split("_").first || :en

puts I18n.t("ask.name")
name = gets.chomp
puts I18n.t("ask.location")
place = gets.chomp
puts I18n.t("ask.children")
childnum = gets.chomp.to_i
puts I18n.t("ask.thanks")

puts name, place, childnum
```

If you run the code at this point, however, you'll simply see an `I18n::InvalidLocale` exception. That's because we haven't supplied English translations yet. Let's create files containing translations in English and Japanese:

```
# locale/en.yml
en:
  ask:
    name: "What is your name?"
    location: "Where do you live?"
    children: "How many children do you have?"
    thanks: "Thank you!"


# locale/ja.yml
ja:
  ask:
    name: "お名前は？"
    location: "どこに住んでいますか。"
    children: "何人子供がいますか。"
    thanks: "ありがとうございます。"
```

Now, our program can ask questions in either English or Japanese, based on the `LANG` environment variable:

```
$ ruby survey.rb
What is your name?
[…]
$ LANG=ja ruby survey.rb
お名前は？
[?]
```

4.3.1 Defaults

Translating your program into many languages can make it usable by a much larger audience, but this comes with some dangers of its own. The `translate` method expects every language to have a translation for every key. Missing keys don't raise errors, but can cause a program to be unusable. If we add an empty Russian translation file, we can run our survey in Russian and see the missing translation message:

```
$ echo "ru:\n  ask:" > locale/ru.yml
$ LANG=ru ruby survey.rb
translation missing: ru.ask.name
```

As you might expect, this can interfere with using your program successfully. There are two strategies to handle this type of problem: One option is to raise an exception when a translation is missing. This reveals the problem early, and can be especially useful while running automated tests. To raise an error on missing translations, set an `I18n.exception_handler` like this one:

```
I18n.exception_handler = -> (problem, locale, key, options) {
  raise problem.to_exception
}
```

In production, it's probably a bad idea to raise an error whenever a translation is missing. By enabling fallbacks, it is possible to provide a different translation that does actually exist. The simplest way to enable fallbacks is to include the `Fallback` backend extension and set a default locale:

```
require "i18n/backend/fallback"
I18n::Backend::Simple.send(:include, I18n::Backend::Fallback)
I18n.default_locale = :en
```

After a default locale of `:en` has been set, locales with missing translations will use the English translation instead:

```
$ LANG=ru ruby survey.rb
What is your name?
[...]
```

Note that setting both a default locale and an exception handler means that keys in both the current locale and the default locale will be tried before the exception is raised.

4.3.2 Namespaces

As you may have noticed earlier, every translation key for a survey question starts with `ask`. Using the `namespace` argument to the `translate` method, it is possible to create a helper method that only requires the name of the question.

```
def ask(key)
  I18n.translate(key, namespace: "ask")
end

puts ask("name")
name = gets.chomp
```

It is good practice to use named helper methods or to define a common translation method that supplies the correct namespace when it is used in different contexts. This makes it easier to manage complex sets of translations.

4.3.3   Interpolation

Without translations, inserting variables into strings is very straightforward. To generate a greeting given a `name` variable, you can simply write the string `"Hello, #{name}!"`.

With translated strings, that isn't possible. In other languages, variables might need to be inserted before, or after, or even in between other words. Deciding where to interpolate needs to be done by translators, not developers.

To handle this problem, translation strings have their own interpolation format, using the percent sign and curly braces. Developers can supply named variables when asking for a translation, and translators can insert those named variables at the appropriate location.

Using interpolation, we can add another message to our translations, and another line of code that prints out the survey results in a much clearer way:

```
# survey.rb
puts I18n.t("result.lives_in", name: name,
  place: place, childnum: childnum)

# locale/en.yml
en:
  result:
    lives_in: >
      %{name} lives in %{place},
      and has %{childnum} child(ren).

# locale/ja.yml
ja:
  result:
    lives_in: >
      %{name}は%{place}に住んでいて、
      そして%{childnum}人子供がいます。
```

Now the results are printed out as a complete sentence in both English and Japanese:

```
John Smith lives in San Francisco, and has 4 child(ren).
John SmithはSan Franciscoに住んでいて、そして 4人子供がいます。
```

There's one place where our "new and improved" output looks quite awkward, though. We have to say "child(ren)" because there might be one child, but there might be zero (or several) children. In Japanese, it's even worse: We might end up saying "zero children exist," which doesn't even make sense.

4.3.4 Pluralization

Counting things in multiple languages is even harder than just translating. A single translation might have to be completely different depending on how many things are being talked about.

In English, pluralization isn't too bad. Nouns have singular and plural forms (such as "child" and "children"), or a single word that works for both (like "sheep" or "deer"). Japanese is even easier—nouns are the same whether there is one or many.

Other languages can be far more complex. Russian has three forms: one singular, one plural for numbers ending in 2, 3, or 4, and one for all other numbers. Russian isn't even alone: Polish and others have similar patterns for plural words.

In order to pluralize and translate at the same time, pluralized translations need to contain separate keys for each plural form. In English, that means "zero," "one," and "other." Here's what the English locale file looks like with pluralizations:

```
# locale/en.yml
en:
  result:
    lives_in: "%{name} lives in %{place}, and has "
    children:
      zero: "no children."
      one: "a single child."
      other: "%{count} children."
```

With pluralized translations, just call the `translate` method and pass it a `count` parameter. The correct pluralization form will be added to the key automatically:

```
# survey.rb
puts I18n.t("result.lives_in", name: name, place: place) +
  " " + I18n.t("result.children", count: childnum)
```

In order to pluralize in Japanese, we'll need to require the `Pluralization` backend and start using it:

```ruby
# survey.rb
require "i18n/backend/pluralization"
I18n::Backend::Simple.send(:include,
  I18n::Backend::Pluralization)
```

Next, we add a pluralization rule, written in Ruby, to a new locale file for pluralization rules:

```ruby
# locale/plurals.rb
{ ja: { 18n: { plural: {
  keys: [:other],
  rule: -> (n) { n.zero? ? :zero : :other }
}}}}
```

Then, we can add keys for just "zero" and "other" because Japanese doesn't treat one object differently from two or more objects:

```yaml
# locale/ja.yml
ja:
  result:
    lives_in: "%{name}は%{place}に住んでいて、そして"
    children:
      zero: "子供がいません。"
      other: "%{count}人子供がいます。"
```

Pluralization rules for other languages, both more and less complicated, can be implemented in a very similar way. Rather than rediscover pluralization rules for every language separately, developers from many countries have cooperated together and created fairly exhaustive lists of pluralization and other formatting rules.

The Unicode Consortium hosts a large set of rules at the Common Locale Data Repository, online at cldr.unicode.org. Twitter has released a version of that data, usable directly in Ruby, as the `twitter_cldr` gem.

4.4   Localized Formatting

As hinted at in our discussion of pluralization, there are other formatting rules beyond count-based noun forms. Every language has their own standards for how to represent dates, times, numbers, and currency.

The bare i18n gem includes support for formatting dates and times, but doesn't supply any translations. The twitter_cldr gem is the easiest way to format dates, times, numbers, and currencies for the current locale. We'll use it in the following examples, but keep in mind that it hard-codes the CLDR formats and cannot be customized as easily as editing a .yml file.

4.4.1   Dates and Times

The CLDR defines four date and time formats for every language: full, long, medium, and short. Other formats may be available for some languages, so check the documentation for the gem if you'd like to learn more about the options. Formatting dates and times into a format that you create (using strftime) is covered in Section 7.21, "Formatting and Printing Time Values."

Before using any of the localize methods, install the twitter_cldr gem by running gem install twitter_cldr and then require it in your Ruby script:

```
require 'twitter_cldr'
```

To format dates and times together into a single localized string, use DateTime#localize:

```
date = DateTime.parse("2014-12-15")
date.localize(:en).to_short_s     # "12/15/14, 12:00 AM"
date.localize(:fr).to_short_s     # "15/12/2014 00:00"
```

To convert times, there is a similar Time#localize method:

```
time = Time.parse("9:00 PM GMT")
time.localize(:en).to_short_s     # "9:00 PM"
time.localize(:fr).to_short_s     # "21:00"
```

Printing dates is the odd case out, because localized DateTime objects must be converted to dates before they can be formatted. There is no Date#localize method.

```
date = DateTime.parse("2014-12-15")
date.localize(:en).to_date.to_short_s  # "12/15/14"
date.localize(:fr).to_date.to_short_s  # "15/12/2014"
```

Predictably, there are also methods named to_medium_s, to_long_s, and to_full_s that format dates into strings that spell out month names and weekdays:

```
date.localize(:en).to_medium_s
# "Dec 15, 2014, 12:00:00 AM"

date.localize(:en).to_long_s
# "December 15, 2014 'at' 12:00:00 AM UTC"

date.localize(:en).to_full_s
# "Monday, December 15, 2014 'at' 12:00:00 AM UTC +00:00"
```

4.4.2   Numbers

Formatting numbers is similarly straightforward because every number gains a localize method:

```
num = 1_337
num.localize(:en).to_s  # "1,337"
num.localize(:fr).to_s  # "1 337"
```

Formatting decimals is as simple as localizing a Float or calling to_decimal on the localized number:

```
1337.00.localize(:en).to_s(precision: 2)         # "1,337.00"
num.localize(:fr).to_decimal.to_s(precision: 2)  # "1 337,00"
```

Finally, localized numbers can be formatted as percentages using the to_percent method, which also takes a precision parameter:

```
num.localize(:en).to_percent.to_s               # "1,337%"
num.localize(:fr).to_percent.to_s(precision: 2)  # "1 337,00 %"
```

4.4.3 Currencies

Currency formatting defaults to USD (American dollars), but can easily be set using three-letter currency codes, as shown here:

```
num.localize(:en).to_currency.to_s
# "$1,337.00"
num.localize(:fr).to_currency.to_s(currency:"EUR")
# "1 337,00 €"
```

4.5 Conclusion

In this chapter, we've looked at the issues faced by programmers as they internationalize and localize their applications. I18N and L10N are regarded as passionately important by many users and developers, and when well done can greatly multiply the reach and user base of any application.

As part of I18N, we examined character encodings and how the Unicode standard provides a way to encode almost any character that exists. Next, we reviewed L10N and how to implement a localized application with fully translated output, including pluralization. Finally, we looked at how to format numbers, dates, times, and currencies according to the rules of a particular locale.

Finally, we saw how to use the i18n gem in conjunction with other gems to translate and pluralize strings as well as format numbers correctly for any locale.

At this point, we'll take a short break from strings and formatting. In the next chapter, we'll look at how to represent numbers in Ruby and perform calculations with them.

CHAPTER 5

Performing Numerical Calculations

On two occasions I have been asked [by members of Parliament], "Pray, Mr.
Babbage, if you put into the machine wrong figures, will the right answers
come out?" I am not able rightly to apprehend the kind of confusion of ideas
that could provoke such a question.

—Charles Babbage

Numeric data is the original data type, the native language of the computer. We would
be hard-pressed to find areas of our experience where numbers are not applicable. It
doesn't matter whether you're an accountant or an aeronautical engineer; you can't sur-
vive without numbers. We present in this chapter a few ways to process, manipulate,
convert, and analyze numeric data.

Like all modern languages, Ruby works well with both integers and floating point
numbers. It has the full range of standard mathematical operators and functions that
you would expect, but it also has a few pleasant surprises such as the `Bignum`,
`BigDecimal`, and `Rational` classes.

Besides covering all of the numeric features in the core and standard libraries, a
little domain-specific material has been added (in such areas as trigonometry, calculus,
and statistics). These examples serve not only as informative examples in math, but as
examples of Ruby code that illustrates principles from the rest of this book.

5.1 Representing Numbers in Ruby

If you know any other language, the representation of numbers in Ruby is mostly intuitive. A `Fixnum` may be signed or unsigned:

```
237     # unsigned (positive) number
+237    # same as above
-237    # negative number
```

When numbers have many digits, we can insert underscores at will (between any two digits). This is purely cosmetic and does not affect the value of the constant. Typically, we would insert them at the same places where accountants might insert commas:

```
1048576     # a simple number
1_048_576   # the same value
```

It's also possible to represent integers in the most common alternative bases (bases 2, 8, and 16). These are "tagged" with the prefixes `0b`, `0`, and `0x`, respectively:

```
0b10010110     # binary
0b1211         # error!
01234          # octal (base 8)
01823          # error!
0xdeadbeef     # hexadecimal (base 16)
0xDEADBEEF     # same
0xdeadpork     # error!
```

Floating point numbers have to have a decimal point and may optionally have a signed exponent:

```
3.14           # pi to two digits
-0.628         # -2*pi over 10, to two digits
6.02e23        # Avogadro's number
6.626068e-34   # Planck's constant
```

Certain constants in the `Float` class help define limits for floating point numbers. These are machine dependent. Some of the more important follow:

```
Float::MIN       # 2.2250738585072e-308 (on this machine)
Float::MAX       # 1.79769313486232e+308
Float::EPSILON   # 2.22044604925031e-16
```

5.2   Basic Operations on Numbers

The normal operations of addition, subtraction, multiplication, and division are implemented in Ruby, much as in the typical programming language with the operators +, –, *, and /. Most of the operators are actually methods (and therefore can be overridden).

Exponentiation (raising to a power) is done with the ** operator, as in older languages such as BASIC and FORTRAN. The operator obeys the "normal" mathematical laws of exponentiation:

```
a = 64**2    # 4096
b = 64**0.5  # 8.0
c = 64**0    # 1
d = 64**-1   # 0.015625
```

Division of one integer by another results in a truncated integer. This is a feature, not a bug. If you need a floating point number, make sure that at least one operand is a floating point:

```
3 / 3        # 3
5 / 3        # 1
3 / 4        # 0
3.0 / 4      # 0.75
3 / 4.0      # 0.75
3.0 / 4.0    # 0.75
```

If you are using variables and are in doubt about the division, `Float` or `to_f` will ensure that an operand is a floating point number:

```
z = x.to_f / y
z = Float(x) / y
```

See also Section 5.17, "Performing Bit-Level Operations on Numbers," later in this chapter.

5.3   Rounding Floating Point Values

Kirk: What would you say the odds are on our getting out of here?

Spock: It is difficult to be precise, Captain. I should say approximately 7824.7 to one.

—Star Trek, "Errand of Mercy"

If you want to round a floating point value to an integer, the method `round` will do the trick:

```
pi = 3.14159
new_pi = pi.round    # 3
temp = -47.6
temp2 = temp.round   # -48
```

Sometimes we want to round not to an integer but to a specific number of decimal places. In this case, we would pass the desired number of digits after the decimal to round:

```
pi = 3.1415926535
pi6 = pi.round(6)  # 3.141593
pi5 = pi.round(5)  # 3.14159
pi4 = pi.round(4)  # 3.1416
```

Occasionally we follow a different rule in rounding to integers. The tradition of rounding n+0.5 upward results in slight inaccuracies at times; after all, n+0.5 is no closer to n+1 than it is to n. So there is an alternative tradition that rounds to the nearest even number in the case of 0.5 as a fractional part. If we wanted to do this, we might extend the `Float` class with a method of our own called `round_down`, as shown here:

```
class Float

  def round_down
    whole = self.floor
    fraction = self - whole
    if fraction == 0.5
```

```
      if (whole % 2) == 0
        whole
      else
        whole+1
      end
    else
      self.round
    end
  end

end
```

```
a = (33.4).round_down  # 33
b = (33.5).round_down  # 34
c = (33.6).round_down  # 34
d = (34.4).round_down  # 34
e = (34.5).round_down  # 34
f = (34.6).round_down  # 35
```

Obviously, `round_down` differs from `round` only when the fractional part is exactly `0.5`; note that `0.5` can be represented perfectly in binary, by the way. What is less obvious is that this method works fine for negative numbers also. (Try it.) Also note that the parentheses used here are not actually necessary but are used for readability.

As an aside, it should be obvious that adding a method to a system class is something that should be done with caution and awareness. Though there are times and places where this practice is appropriate, it is easy to overdo. These examples are shown primarily for ease of illustration, not as a suggestion that this sort of code should be written frequently.

Now, what if we wanted to round to a number of decimal places, but we wanted to use the "even rounding" method? In this case, we could add a parameter to `round_down`:

```
class Float

  def roundf_down(places = 0)
    shift = 10 ** places
    num = (self * shift).round_down / shift.to_f
    num.round(places)
  end
```

```
end

a = 6.125
b = 6.135
x = a.roundf_down(2)    # 6.12
y = b.roundf_down(2)    # 6.14
z = b.roundf_down       # 6
```

The `roundf_down` method has certain limitations. Large floating point numbers might overflow when multiplied by a large power of ten. For these occurrences, error-checking should be added.

5.4   Comparing Floating Point Numbers

It is a sad fact of life that computers do not represent floating point values exactly. The following code fragment, in a perfect world, would print "yes"; on every architecture we have tried, it will print "no" instead:

```
x = 1000001.0/0.003
y = 0.003*x
if y == 1000001.0
  puts "yes"
else
  puts "no"
end
```

The reason, of course, is that a floating point number is stored in some finite number of bits, and no finite number of bits is adequate to store a repeating decimal with an infinite number of digits.

Because of this inherent inaccuracy in floating point comparisons, we may find ourselves in situations (like the one we just saw) where the values we are comparing are the same for all practical purposes, but the hardware stubbornly thinks they are different.

The following code is a simple way to ensure that floating point comparisons are done "with a fudge factor"—that is, the comparisons will be done within any tolerance specified by the programmer:

```
class Float

  EPSILON = 1e-6    # 0.000001
```

```
  def ==(x)
    (self-x).abs < EPSILON
  end

end


x = 1000001.0/0.003
y = 0.003*x
if y == 1.0          # Using the new ==
  puts "yes"         # Now we output "yes"
else
  puts "no"
end
```

We may find that we want different tolerances for different situations. For this case, we define a new method, `nearly_equal?`, as a member of `Float`. (This name avoids confusion with the standard methods `equal?` and `eql?`; the latter in particular should not be overridden.)

```
class Float

  EPSILON = 1e-6

  def nearly_equal?(x, tolerance=EPSILON)
    (self-x).abs < tolerance
  end

end
```

```
flag1 = (3.1416).nearly_equal? Math::PI          # false
flag2 = (3.1416).nearly_equal?(Math::PI, 0.001)  # true
```

We could also use a different operator entirely to represent approximate equality; the =~ operator might be a good choice.

Bear in mind that this sort of thing is not a real solution. As successive computations are performed, error is compounded. If you must use floating point math, be prepared for the inaccuracies. If the inaccuracies are not acceptable, use `BigDecimal` or some other solution. (See Section 5.8, "Using `BigDecimal`," and Section 5.9, "Working with Rational Values," later in the chapter.)

5.5   Formatting Numbers for Output

To output numbers in a specific format, you can use the `printf` method in the `Kernel` module. It is virtually identical to its C counterpart. For more information, see the documentation for the `printf` method:

```
x = 345.6789
i = 123
printf("x = %6.2f\n", x)      # x = 345.68
printf("x = %9.2e\n", x)      # x = 3.457e+02
printf("i = %5d\n", i)        # i =   123
printf("i = %05d\n", i)       # i = 00123
printf("i = %-5d\n", i)       # i = 123
```

To store a result in a string rather than printing it immediately, `sprintf` can be used in much the same way. The following method returns a string:

```
str = sprintf("%5.1f",x)     # "345.7"
```

Finally, the `String` class has the `%` method, which performs this same task. The `%` method has a format string as a receiver; it takes a single argument (or an array of values) and returns a string:

```
# Usage is 'format % value'
str = "%5.1f" % x               # "345.7"
str = "%6.2f, %05d" % [x,i]   # "345.68, 00123"
```

5.6   Formatting Numbers with Commas

There may be better ways to format numbers with commas, but this one works. We reverse the string to make it easier to do global substitution and then reverse it again at the end:

```
def commas(x)
  str = x.to_s.reverse
  str.gsub!(/([0-9]{3})/,"\\1,")
  str.gsub(/,$/,"").reverse
end

puts commas(123)          # "123"
```

```
puts commas(1234)        # "1,234"
puts commas(12345)       # "12,435"
puts commas(123456)      # "123,456"
puts commas(1234567)     # "1,234,567"
```

5.7   Working with Very Large Integers

The control of large numbers is possible, and like unto that of small numbers, if we subdivide them.

—*Sun Tze*

In the event it becomes necessary, Ruby programmers can work with integers of arbitrary size. The transition from a `Fixnum` to a `Bignum` is handled automatically and transparently. In this following piece of code, notice how a result that is large enough is promoted from `Fixnum` to `Bignum`:

```
num1 = 1000000          # One million (10**6)
num2 = num1*num1        # One trillion (10**12)
puts num1               # 1000000
puts num1.class         # Fixnum
puts num2               # 1000000000000
puts num2.class         # Bignum
```

The size of a `Fixnum` varies from one architecture to another. Calculations with `Bignum`s are limited only by memory and processor speed. They take more memory and are obviously somewhat slower, but number-crunching with very large integers (hundreds of digits) is still reasonably practical.

5.8   Using `BigDecimal`

The `Bigdecimal` standard library enables us to work with large numbers of significant digits in fractional numbers. In effect, it stores numbers as arrays of digits rather than converting to a binary floating point representation. This allows arbitrary precision, though of course at the cost of speed.

To motivate ourselves, look at the following simple piece of code using floating
point numbers:

```
if (3.2 - 2.0) == 1.2
  puts "equal"
else
  puts "not equal"     # prints "not equal"!
end
```

This is the sort of situation that BigDecimal helps with. However, note that with
infinitely repeating decimals, we still will have problems. For yet another approach,
see Section 5.9, "Working with Rational Values."

A BigDecimal is initialized with a string. (A Float would not suffice because the
error would creep in before we could construct the BigDecimal object.) The method
BigDecimal is equivalent to BigDecimal.new; this is another special case where a
method name starts with a capital letter. The usual mathematical operations such as +
and * are supported. Note that the to_s method can take a parameter to specify its
format. For more details, see the BigDecimal documentation.

```
require 'bigdecimal'

x = BigDecimal("3.2")
y = BigDecimal("2.0")
z = BigDecimal("1.2")

if (x - y) == z
  puts "equal"           # prints "equal"!
else
  puts "not equal"
end

a = x*y*z
a.to_s                   # "0.768E1" (default: engineering notation)
a.to_s("F")              # "7.68"    (ordinary floating point)
```

We can specify the number of significant digits if we want. The precs method
retrieves this information as an array of two numbers: the number of bytes used and
the maximum number of significant digits.

```
x = BigDecimal("1.234",10)
y = BigDecimal("1.234",15)
```

```
x.precs                  # [8, 16]
y.precs                  # [8, 20]
```

The bytes currently used may be less than the maximum. The maximum may also be greater than what you requested (because `BigDecimal` tries to optimize its internal storage).

The common operations (addition, subtraction, multiplication, and division) have counterparts that take a number of digits as an extra parameter. If the resulting significant digits are more than that parameter specifies, the result will be rounded to that number of digits.

```
a = BigDecimal("1.23456")
b = BigDecimal("2.45678")

# In these comments, "BigDecimal:objectid" is omitted
c  = a+b          # <'0.369134E1',12(20)>
c2 = a.add(b,4)   # <'0.3691E1',8(20)>

d  = a-b          # <'-0.122222E1',12(20)>
d2 = a.sub(b,4)   # <'-0.1222E1',8(20)>

e  = a*b          # <'0.3033042316 8E1',16(36)>
e2 = a.mult(b,4)  # <'0.3033E1',8(36)>

f  = a/b          # <'0.5025114173 8372992290 7221E0',24(32)>
f2 = a.div(b,4)   # <'0.5025E0',4(16)>
```

The `BigDecimal` class defines many other functions, such as `floor`, `abs`, and others. There are operators such as `%` and `**`, as you would expect, along with relational operators such as `<`. The `==` operator is not intelligent enough to round off its operands; that is still the programmer's responsibility.

The `BigMath` module defines constants `E` and `PI` to arbitrary precision. (They are really methods, not constants.) It also defines functions such as `sin`, `cos`, `exp`, and others, all taking a digits parameter.

The following sublibraries are all made to work with `BigDecimal`:

- `bigdecimal/math`—The `BigMath` module.

- `bigdecimal/jacobian`—Methods for finding a Jacobian matrix.

- `bigdecimal/ludcmp`—The `LUSolve` module, for LU decomposition.

- `bigdecimal/newton`—Provides `nlsolve` and `norm`.

These sublibraries are not documented in this chapter. For more information, consult the ruby-doc.org site or any detailed reference.

5.9   Working with Rational Values

The Rational class enables us (in many cases) to work with fractional values with "infinite" precision. It helps us only when the values involved are true rational numbers (the quotient of two integers). It won't help with irrational numbers such as pi, e, or the square root of 2.

To create a rational number, we use the special method Rational (which is one of our rare capitalized method names, usually used for data conversion or initialization):

```
r = Rational(1,2)    # 1/2 or 0.5
s = Rational(1,3)    # 1/3 or 0.3333...
t = Rational(1,7)    # 1/7 or 0.14...
u = Rational(6,2)    # "same as" 3.0
z = Rational(1,0)    # error!
```

An operation on two rationals will typically be another rational:

```
r+t        #  Rational(9, 14)
r-t        #  Rational(5, 14)
r*s        #  Rational(1, 6)
r/s        #  Rational(3, 2)
```

Let's look once again at our floating point inaccuracy example (see Section 5.4, "Comparing Floating Point Numbers"). In the following example, we do the same thing with rationals rather than reals, and we get the "mathematically expected" results instead:

```
x = Rational(1000001,1)/Rational(3,1000)
y = Rational(3,1000)*x
if y == 1000001.0
  puts "yes"          # Now we get "yes"!
else
  puts "no"
end
```

Some operations, of course, don't always give us rationals back:

```
x = Rational(9,16)     #  Rational(9, 16)
Math.sqrt(x)           #  0.75
x**0.5                 #  0.75
x**Rational(1,2)       #  0.75
```

However, the `mathn` library changes some of this behavior. See Section 5.12, "Using `mathn`," later in this chapter.

5.10   Matrix Manipulation

If you want to deal with numerical matrices, the standard library `matrix` is for you. This actually defines two separate classes: `Matrix` and `Vector`.

You should also be aware of the excellent `NArray` library by Masahiro Tanaka (available as a gem from rubygems.org). This is not a standard library but is well known and very useful. If you have speed requirements, if you have specific data representation needs, or if you need capabilities such as Fast Fourier Transform, you should definitely look into this package. For most general purposes, however, the standard `matrix` library should suffice, and that is what we cover here.

To create a matrix, we naturally use a class-level method. There are multiple ways to do this. One way is simply to call `Matrix.[]` and list the rows as arrays. In the following example, we do this in multiple lines, though of course that isn't necessary:

```
m = Matrix[[1,2,3],
           [4,5,6],
           [7,8,9]]
```

A similar method is to call `rows`, passing in an array of arrays (so that the "extra" brackets are necessary). The optional `copy` parameter, which defaults to `true`, determines whether the individual arrays are copied or simply stored. Therefore, let this parameter be `true` to protect the original arrays, or `false` if you want to save a little memory, and you are not concerned about this issue.

```
row1 = [2,3]
row2 = [4,5]
m1 = Matrix.rows([row1,row2])         # copy=true
m2 = Matrix.rows([row1,row2],false)   # don't copy
row1[1] = 99                          # Now change row1
p m1                                  # Matrix[[2, 3], [4, 5]]
p m2                                  # Matrix[[2, 99], [4, 5]]
```

Matrices can similarly be specified in column order with the `columns` method. It does not accept the `copy` parameter because the arrays are split up anyway to be stored internally in row-major order:

```
m1 = Matrix.rows([[1,2],[3,4]])
m2 = Matrix.columns([[1,3],[2,4]])  # m1 == m2
```

Matrices are assumed to be rectangular. If you assign a matrix with rows or columns that are shorter or longer than the others, you will immediately get an error informing you that your matrix input was not rectangular.

Certain special matrices, especially square ones, are easily constructed. The "identity" matrix can be constructed with the `identity` method (or its aliases `I` and `unit`):

```
im1 = Matrix.identity(3)   # Matrix[[1,0,0],[0,1,0],[0,0,1]]
im2 = Matrix.I(3)          # same
im3 = Matrix.unit(3)       # same
```

A more general form is `scalar`, which assigns some value other than 1 to the diagonal:

```
sm = Matrix.scalar(3,8)  # Matrix[[8,0,0],[0,8,0],[0,0,8]]
```

Still more general is `diagonal`, which assigns an arbitrary sequence of values to the diagonal. (Obviously, it does not need the dimension parameter.)

```
dm = Matrix.diagonal(2,3,7)  # Matrix[[2,0,0],[0,3,0],[0,0,7]]
```

The `zero` method creates a special matrix of the specified dimension, full of zero values:

```
zm = Matrix.zero(3)  # Matrix[[0,0,0],[0,0,0],[0,0,0]]
```

Obviously, the `identity`, `scalar`, `diagonal`, and `zero` methods all construct square matrices.

To create a 1×N or an N×1 matrix, you can use the `row_vector` or `column_vector` shortcut methods, respectively:

```
a = Matrix.row_vector(2,4,6,8)     # Matrix[[2,4,6,8]]
b = Matrix.column_vector(6,7,8,9)  # Matrix[[6],[7],[8],[9]]
```

Individual matrix elements can naturally be accessed with the bracket notation (with both indices specified in a single pair of brackets). Note that there is no `[ ]=` method. This is for much the same reason that `Fixnum` lacks that method: Matrices are immutable objects (evidently a design decision by the library author).

```
m = Matrix[[1,2,3],[4,5,6]]
puts m[1,2]    # 6
```

Be aware that indexing is from zero, as with Ruby arrays; this may contradict your mathematical expectation, but there is no option for one-based rows and columns unless you implement it yourself.

```
# Naive approach... don't do this!

class Matrix
  alias bracket []

  def [](i,j)
    bracket(i-1,j-1)
  end
end

m = Matrix[[1,2,3],[4,5,6],[7,8,9]]
p m[2,2]       # 5
```

The preceding code does seem to work. Many or most matrix operations still behave as expected with the alternate indexing. Why might it fail? Because we don't know all the internal implementation details of the `Matrix` class. If it always uses its own `[ ]` method to access the matrix values, it should always be consistent. But if it ever accesses some internal array directly or uses some kind of shortcut, it might fail. Therefore, if you use this kind of trick at all, it should be with caution and testing.

In reality, you would have to change the `row` and `vector` methods as well. These methods use indices that number from zero without going through the `[ ]` method. I haven't checked to see what else might be required.

Sometimes we need to discover the dimensions or shape of a matrix. There are various methods for this purpose, such as `row_size` and `column_size`, which return the number of rows and columns in the matrix, respectively.

To retrieve a section or piece of a matrix, several methods are available. The `row_vectors` method returns an array of `Vector` objects representing the rows of the matrix. (See the following discussion of the `Vector` class.) The `column_vectors` method works similarly. Finally, the `minor` method returns a smaller matrix from the larger one; its parameters are either four numbers (lower and upper bounds for the rows and columns) or two ranges.

```
m = Matrix[[1,2,3,4],[5,6,7,8],[6,7,8,9]]


rows = m.row_vectors        # three Vector objects
cols = m.column_vectors     # four Vector objects
m2 = m.minor(1,2,1,2)       # Matrix[[6,7,],[7,8]]
m3 = m.minor(0..1,1..3)     # Matrix[[[2,3,4],[6,7,8]]
```

The usual matrix operations can be applied: addition, subtraction, multiplication, and division. Some of these make certain assumptions about the dimensions of the matrices and may raise exceptions if the operands are incompatible (for example, trying to multiply a 3×3 matrix with a 4×4 matrix).

Ordinary transformations, such as `inverse`, `transpose`, and `determinant`, are supported. For matrices of integers, the determinant will usually be better behaved if the `mathn` library is used (see the Section 5.12, "Using `mathn`").

A `Vector` is in effect a special one-dimensional matrix. It can be created with the `[]` or `elements` method; the first takes an expanded array, and the latter takes an unexpanded array and an optional `copy` parameter (which defaults to `true`).

```
arr = [2,3,4,5]
v1 = Vector[*arr]                 # Vector[2,3,4,5]
v2 = Vector.elements(arr)         # Vector[2,3,4,5]
v3 = Vector.elements(arr,false)   # Vector[2,3,4,5]
arr[2] = 7                        # v3 is now Vector[2,3,7,5]
```

The `covector` method converts a vector of length N to an N×1 (effectively transposed) matrix.

```
v = Vector[2,3,4]
m = v.covector    # Matrix[[2,3,4]]
```

Addition and subtraction of similar vectors are supported. A vector may be multiplied by a matrix or by a scalar. All these operations are subject to normal mathematical rules.

```
v1 = Vector[2,3,4]
v2 = Vector[4,5,6]
v3 = v1 + v2             # Vector[6,8,10]
```

```
v4 = v1*v2.covector   # Matrix[[8,10,12],[12,15,18],[16,20,24]]
v5 = v1*5             # Vector[10,15,20]
```

There is an `inner_product` method:

```
v1 = Vector[2,3,4]
v2 = Vector[4,5,6]
x  = v1.inner_product(v2)   # 47
```

For additional information on the `Matrix` and `Vector` classes, see the class documentation online or via the `ri` command.

5.11 Working with Complex Numbers

The standard library `complex` enables us to handle imaginary and complex numbers in Ruby. Much of it is self-explanatory.

Complex values can be created with this slightly unusual notation:

```
z = Complex(3,5)      # 3+5i
```

What is unusual about this is that we have a method name that is the same as the class name. In this case, the presence of the parentheses indicates a method call rather than a reference to a constant. In general, method names do not look like constants, and I don't recommend the practice of capitalizing method names except in special cases like this. (Note that there are also methods called `Integer` and `Float`; in general, the capitalized method names are for data conversion or something similar.)

The `im` method converts a number to its imaginary counterpart (effectively multiplying it by i). Therefore, we can represent imaginary and complex numbers with a more convenient notation:

```
a = 3.im        # 3i
b = 5 - 2.im    # 5-2i
```

If we're more concerned with polar coordinates, we can also call the `polar` class method:

```
z = Complex.polar(5,Math::PI/2.0)   # radius, angle
```

The `Complex` class also gives us the constant `I`, which of course represents i, the square root of negative one:

```
z1 = Complex(3,5)
z2 = 3 + 5*Complex::I    # z2 == z1
```

If you choose to require the `complex` library, certain common math functions have their behavior changed. Trig functions such as `sin`, `sinh`, `tan`, and `tanh` (along with others such as `exp` and `log`) accept complex arguments in addition to their normal behavior. In some cases, such as `sqrt`, they are "smart" enough to return complex results also.

```
x = Math.sqrt(Complex(3,5))  # roughly: Complex(2.1013, 1.1897)
y = Math.sqrt(-1)            # Complex(0,1)
```

For more information, refer the `Complex` class documentation.

5.12   Using `mathn`

For math-intensive programs, you will want to know about the `mathn` library created by Keiju Ishitsuka. It provides a few convenience methods and classes, and replaces many methods in Ruby's numeric classes so that they "play well" together.

The easiest way to "use" this library is simply to require it and forget it. Because it requires the `complex`, `rational`, and `matrix` libraries (in that order), there is no need to do separate `requires` of those if you are using them. In general, the `mathn` library tries to produce "sensible" results from computations—for example, the square root of a `Rational` will be returned when possible as another `Rational` rather than a `Float`. Table 5.1 shows some typical effects of loading this library.

Table 5.1   Computation with and without the `mathn` Library

Expression	Without **mathn**	With **mathn**
1/2	0	Rational(1,2)
Math.sqrt(64/25)	1.4142...	Rational(8,5)
Rational(1,10).inspect	Rational(1,10)	1/10
Math.sqrt(Rational(9,16))	0.75	Rational(3,4)
Matrix.identity(3)/3	Matrix[[0,0,0], [0,0,0], [0,0,0]]	Matrix[[0,1/3,0], [0,1/3,0], [0,0,1/3]]

The `mathn` library adds the `**` and `power2` methods to `Rational`. It changes the behavior of `Math.sqrt` and adds the rational-aware function `Math.rsqrt`.

See also Section 5.13, "Finding Prime Factorization, GCD, and LCM," and Section 5.14, "Working with Prime Numbers."

5.13   Finding Prime Factorization, GCD, and LCM

The `mathn` library also defines some new methods on the `Integer` class. One is `gcd2`, which finds the greatest common divisor of the receiver and the other specified number:

```
n = 36.gcd2(120)     # 12
k = 237.gcd2(79)     # 79
```

The `prime_division` method performs a prime factorization of its receiver. The result returned is an array of arrays where each smaller array consists of a prime number and its exponent:

```
factors = 126.prime_division  # [[2,1], [3,2], [7,1]]
                              # i.e. 2**1 * 3**2 * 7**1
```

There is also the class method `Integer.from_prime_division`, which reverses that factorization. It is a class method because it is like a "constructor" for an integer.

```
factors = [[2,1],[3,1],[7,1]]
num = Integer.from_prime_division(factors)    # 42
```

The following code is an example of using prime factorization to find the least common multiple (LCM) of a pair of numbers:

```
require 'mathn'

class Integer
  def lcm(other)
    pf1 = self.prime_division.flatten
    pf2 = other.prime_division.flatten
    h1 = Hash[*pf1]
    h2 = Hash[*pf2]
    hash = h2.merge(h1) {|key,old,new| [old,new].max }
    Integer.from_prime_division(hash.to_a)
  end
```

```
end

p 15.lcm(150)      # 150
p 2.lcm(3)         # 6
p 4.lcm(12)        # 12
p 200.lcm(30)      # 600
```

5.14 Working with Prime Numbers

The `mathn` library defines a class for generating prime numbers. The iterator `each` generates these in succession in an infinite loop. The `succ` method naturally generates the next prime number.

For example, here are two ways to list the first 100 primes:

```
require 'mathn'

list = []
gen = Prime.new
gen.each do |prime|
  list << prime
  break if list.size == 100
end

# or alternatively:

list = []
gen = Prime.new
100.times { list << gen.succ }
```

The following code tests the primality of a number. With large enough numbers, this may take a moment to complete:

```
require 'mathn'

class Integer
  def prime?
    max = Math.sqrt(self).ceil
    max -= 1 if max % 2 == 0
    pgen = Prime.new
    pgen.each do |factor|
      return false if self % factor == 0
```

```
        return true if factor > max
    end
  end
end


31.prime?              # true
237.prime?             # false
1500450271.prime?      # true
```

5.15   Implicit and Explicit Numeric Conversion

The new Rubyist is often confused that there are methods named `to_i` and `to_int` (and by analogy, `to_f` and `to_flt`, as well as others). In general, explicit conversion is done using the "short name" and implicit conversion using the "long name."

What does this mean? First, most classes define explicit convertors but not implicit.

Second, your own classes will tend to define implicit convertors, but you will not usually call them manually (unless you are writing "client" code or library-oriented code that tries to play well with the outside world).

The following code is a contrived example. The class `MyClass` as defined in this example returns constants from `to_i` and `to_int`. This is nonsensical behavior, but it illustrates a point:

```
class MyClass

  def to_i
    3
  end

  def to_int
    5
  end

end
```

If we want to convert a `MyClass` object explicitly to an integer, we can call `to_i`:

```
m = MyClass.new
x = m.to_i        # 3
```

But the `to_int` method gets called implicitly ("behind our backs") when we pass in a `MyClass` object to something that expects an integer. For example, suppose that we want to create an array with an initial number of values; `Array.new` can take an integer, but what happens if we give it a `MyClass` object instead?

```
m = MyClass.new
a = Array.new(m)    # [nil,nil,nil,nil,nil]
```

As we see, the `new` method was smart enough to call `to_int` and thus create an array with five entries.

For more explanation in a different context (strings), see Section 2.16, "Implicit and Explicit Conversion." See also the following section, 5.16, "Coercing Numeric Values."

5.16   Coercing Numeric Values

Coercion can be thought of as another form of implicit conversion. When a method (+ for example) is passed an argument it doesn't understand, it tries to coerce the receiver and the argument to compatible types and then do the addition based on those types. The pattern for using `coerce` in a class you write is straightforward:

```
class MyNumberSystem

def +(other)
   if other.kind_of?(MyNumberSystem)
     result = some_calculation_between_self_and_other
     MyNumberSystem.new(result)
   else
     n1, n2 = other.coerce(self)
     n1 + n2
   end
  end

end
```

The value returned by `coerce` is a two-element array containing its argument and its receiver converted to compatible types.

In this example, we're relying on the type of our argument to perform some kind of coercion for us. If we want to be good citizens, we also need to implement coercion in our class, allowing other types of numbers to work with us. To do this, we need to know the specific types that we can work with directly and convert to those types when appropriate. When we can't do that, we fall back on asking our parent class:

```
def coerce(other)
  if other.kind_of?(Float)
    return other, self.to_f
  elsif other.kind_of?(Integer)
    return other, self.to_i
  else
    super
  end
end
```

Of course, for this to work, our object must implement `to_i` and `to_f`.

You can use `coerce` as part of the solution for implementing a Perl-like auto-conversion of strings to numbers:

```
class String

  def coerce(n)
    if self['.']
      [n, Float(self)]
    else
      [n, Integer(self)]
    end
  end

end

x = 1 + "23"        # 24
y = 23 * "1.23"     # 28.29
```

This can cause many unexpected results, so we recommend against ever doing this. But we do recommend that you automatically coerce other number types whenever you are creating some kind of numeric class.

5.17 Performing Bit-Level Operations on Numbers

Occasionally we may need to operate on a `Fixnum` as a binary entity. This is less common in application-level programming, but the need still arises.

Ruby has a relatively full set of capabilities in this area. For convenience, numeric constants may be expressed in binary, octal, or hexadecimal. The usual operators AND, OR, XOR, and NOT are expressed by the Ruby operators &, |, ^, and ~, respectively.

```
x = 0377              # Octal   (decimal 255)
y = 0b00100110        # Binary (decimal   38)
z = 0xBEEF            # Hex     (decimal 48879)

a = x | z            # 48895 (bitwise OR)
b = x & z            #   239 (bitwise AND)
c = x ^ z            # 48656 (bitwise XOR)
d = ~ y              #   -39 (negation or 1's complement)
```

The instance method `size` can be used to determine the word size of the specific architecture on which the program is running:

```
bytes = 1.size    # Returns 4 for one particular machine
```

There are left-shift and right-shift operators (<< and >>, respectively). These are logical shift operations; they do not disturb the sign bit (though >> does propagate it).

```
x = 8
y = -8

a = x >> 2        # 2
b = y >> 2        # -2
c = x << 2        # 32
d = y << 2        # -32
```

Of course, anything shifted far enough to result in a zero value will lose the sign bit because -0 is merely 0.

Brackets can be used to treat numbers as arrays of bits. The 0th bit is the least significant bit, regardless of the bit order (endianness) of the architecture.

```
x = 5                 # Same as 0b0101
a = x[0]              # 1
b = x[1]              # 0
c = x[2]              # 1
d = x[3]              # 0
# Etc.                # 0
```

It is not possible to assign bits using this notation (because a `Fixnum` is stored as an immediate value rather than an object reference). However, you can always fake it by left-shifting a 1 to the specified bit position and then doing an OR or AND operation.

```
# We can't do x[3] = 1
# but we can do:
x |= (1<<3)
# We can't do x[4] = 0
# but we can do:
x &= ~(1<<4)
```

5.18   Performing Base Conversions

Obviously all integers are representable in any base, because they are all stored internally in binary. Further, we know that Ruby can deal with integer constants in any of the four commonly used bases. This means that if we are concerned about base conversions, we must be concerned with strings in some fashion.

If you are concerned with converting a string to an integer, that is covered in Section 2.24, "Converting Strings to Numbers (Decimal and Otherwise)."

If you are concerned with converting numbers to strings, the simplest way is to use the `to_s` method with the optional base parameter. This naturally defaults to 10, but it does handle bases up to 36 (using all letters of the alphabet).

```
237.to_s(2)         # "11101101"
237.to_s(5)         # "1422"
237.to_s(8)         # "355"
237.to_s            # "237"
237.to_s(16)        # "ed"
237.to_s(30)        # "7r"
```

Another way is to use the `%` method of the `String` class:

```
hex = "%x" % 1234   # "4d2"
oct = "%o" % 1234   # "2322"
bin = "%b" % 1234   # "10011010010"
```

The `sprintf` method also works:

```
str = sprintf(str,"Nietzsche is %x\n",57005)
# str is now: "Nietzsche is dead\n"
```

Obviously, `printf` will also suffice if you want to print out the value as you convert it.

5.19   Finding Cube Roots, Fourth Roots, and So On

Ruby has a built-in square root function (`Math.sqrt`) because that function is so commonly used. But what if you need higher-level roots? If you remember your math, this is easy.

One way is to use logarithms. Recall that e to the x is the inverse of the natural log of x, and that when we multiply numbers, that is equivalent to adding their logarithms:

```
x = 531441
cuberoot = Math.exp(Math.log(x)/3.0)      # 81.0
fourthroot = Math.exp(Math.log(x)/4.0)    # 27.0
```

However, it is just as easy and perhaps clearer simply to use fractions with an exponentiation operator (which can take any integer or floating point value):

```
include Math

y = 4096
cuberoot = y**(1.0/3.0)        # 16.0
fourthroot = y**(1.0/4.0)      # 8.0
fourthroot = sqrt(sqrt(y))     # 8.0 (same thing)
twelfthroot = y**(1.0/12.0)    # 2.0
```

Note that in all these examples, we have used floating point numbers when dividing (to avoid truncation to an integer).

5.20   Determining the Architecture's Byte Order

It is an interesting fact of the computing world that we cannot all agree on the order in which binary data ought to be stored. Is the most significant bit stored at the higher-numbered address or the lower? When we shove a message over a wire, do we send the most significant bit first, or the least significant?

Believe it or not, it's not entirely arbitrary. There are good arguments on both sides (which we will not delve into here).

For more than 30 years, the terms little-endian and big-endian have been applied to the two extreme opposites. These apparently were first used by Danny Cohen; refer to his classic article "On Holy Wars and a Plea for Peace" (IEEE Computer, October 1981). The actual terms are derived from the novel *Gulliver's Travels* by Jonathan Swift.

Most of the time, we don't care what byte order our architecture uses. But what if we do need to know?

The following method determines this for us. It returns a string that is LITTLE, BIG, or OTHER. It depends on the fact that the l directive packs in native mode, and the N directive unpacks in network order (or big-endian):

```
def endianness
  num=0x12345678
  little = "78563412"
  big    = "12345678"
  native = [num].pack('l')
  netunpack = native.unpack('N')[0]
  str = "%8x" % netunpack
  case str
    when little
      "LITTLE"
    when big
      "BIG"
    else
      "OTHER"
  end
end


puts endianness   # In this case, prints "LITTLE"
```

This technique might come in handy if, for example, you are working with binary data (such as scanned image data) imported from another architecture.

5.21   Numerical Computation of a Definite Integral

I'm very good at integral and differential calculus....

—*W. S. Gilbert, The Pirates of Penzance, Act 1*

If you want to estimate the value of a definite integral, there is a time-tested technique for doing so. This is what the calculus student will remember as a Riemann sum.

The `integrate` method shown here takes beginning and ending values for the dependent variable as well as an increment. The fourth parameter (which is not really a parameter) is a block. This block should evaluate a function based on the value of the dependent variable passed into that block. (Here we are using "variable" in the mathematical sense, not in the computing sense.) It is not necessary to define a function to call in this block, but we do so here for clarity:

```
def integrate(x0, x1, dx=(x1-x0)/1000.0)
  x = x0
  sum = 0
  loop do
    y = yield(x)
    sum += dx * y
    x += dx
    break if x > x1
  end
  sum
end


def f(x)
  x**2
end


z = integrate(0.0,5.0) {|x| f(x) }

puts z                    # 41.72918749999876
```

Note that in the preceding example, we are relying on the fact that a block returns a value that `yield` can retrieve. We also make certain assumptions here. First, we assume that x0 is less than x1 (otherwise, an infinite loop results); the reader can easily improve the code in details such as this one. Second, we assume that the function can be evaluated at arbitrary points in the specified domain. If at any time we try to evaluate the function at such a point, chaos will ensue. (Such functions are generally not integrable anyway, at least over that set of x values. Consider the function `f(x)=x/(x-3)` when x is 3.)

Drawing on our faded memories of calculus, we might compute the result here to be `41.666` or thereabout (5 cubed divided by 3). Why is the answer not as exact as we might like? It is because of the size of the "slice" in the Riemann sum; a smaller value for `dx` will result in greater accuracy (at the expense of an increase in runtime).

Finally, I will point out that a function like this is more useful when we have a variety of functions of arbitrary complexity, not just a simple function such as `f(x) = x**2`.

5.22 Trigonometry in Degrees, Radians, and Grads

When it comes to measuring arc, the mathematical or "natural" unit is the radian, defined in such a way that an angle of one radian corresponds to an arc length equal to the radius of the circle. A little thought will show that there are 2π radians in a circle.

The degree of arc, which we use in everyday life, is a holdover from ancient Babylonian base-60 units; this system divides the circle into 360 degrees. The less-familiar grad is a pseudo-metric unit defined in such a way that there are 100 grads in a right angle (or 400 in a circle).

Programming languages often default to the radian when calculating trigonometric functions, and Ruby is no exception. But we show here how to do these calculations in degrees or grads, in the event that any of our readers are engineers or ancient Babylonians.

Because the number of units in a circle is a simple constant, it follows that there are simple conversion factors between all these units. We define these here and simply use the constant names in subsequent code. As a matter of convenience, we'll stick them in the Math module:

```
module Math

  RAD2DEG  = 360.0/(2.0*PI)  # Radians to degrees
  RAD2GRAD = 400.0/(2.0*PI)  # Radians to grads

end
```

Now we can define new trig functions if we want. Because we are converting to radians in each case, we will divide by the conversion factor we calculated previously. We could place these in the Math module if we wanted, though we don't show it here:

```ruby
def sin_d(theta)
  Math.sin (theta/Math::RAD2DEG)
end

def sin_g(theta)
  Math.sin (theta/Math::RAD2GRAD)
end
```

Of course, the corresponding cos and tan functions may be similarly defined.

The atan2 function is a little different. It takes two arguments (the opposite and adjacent legs of a right triangle) and returns an angle. Therefore, we convert the result, not the argument, handling it this way:

```ruby
def atan2_d(y,x)
  Math.atan2(y,x)/Math::RAD2DEG
end

def atan2_g(y,x)
  Math.atan2(y,x)/Math::RAD2GRAD
end
```

5.23   Finding Logarithms with Arbitrary Bases

When working with logarithms, we frequently use the natural logarithms (or base e, sometimes written ln); we may also use the common or base 10 logarithms. These are defined in Ruby as Math.log and Math.log10, respectively.

In computer science, specifically in such areas as coding and information theory, a base 2 log is not unusual. For example, this will tell the minimum number of bits needed to store a number. We define this function here as log2:

```ruby
def log2(x)
  Math.log(x)/Math.log(2)
end
```

The inverse is obviously `2**x`, just as the inverse of `log x` is `Math::E**x` or `Math.exp(x)`.

Furthermore, this same technique can be extended to any base. In the unlikely event that you ever need a base 7 logarithm, this will do the trick:

```
def log7(x)
  Math.log(x)/Math.log(7)
end
```

In practice, the denominator should be calculated once and kept around as a constant.

5.24   Finding the Mean, Median, and Mode of a Data Set

Given an array, x, let's find the mean of all the values in that array. Actually, there are three common kinds of mean. The ordinary or arithmetic mean is what we call the **average** in everyday life. The harmonic mean is the number of terms divided by the sum of all their reciprocals. And finally, the geometric mean is the nth root of the product of the n values. We show each of these in the following example:

```
def mean(x)
  sum = 0
  x.each {|v| sum += v}
  sum/x.size
end

def hmean(x)
  sum = 0
  x.each {|v| sum += (1.0/v)}
  x.size/sum
end

def gmean(x)
  prod = 1.0
  x.each {|v| prod *= v}
  prod**(1.0/x.size)
end

data = [1.1, 2.3, 3.3, 1.2, 4.5, 2.1, 6.6]
```

```
am = mean(data)    # 3.014285714285714
hm = hmean(data)   # 2.1019979464765117
gm = gmean(data)   # 2.5084114744285384
```

The median value of a data set is the value that occurs approximately in the middle of the (sorted) set. (The following code fragment computes a median.) For this value, half the numbers in the set should be less, and half should be greater. Obviously, this statistic will be more appropriate and meaningful for some data sets than others. See the following code:

```ruby
def median(x)
  sorted = x.sort
  mid = x.size/2
  sorted[mid]
end

data = [7,7,7,4,4,5,4,5,7,2,2,3,3,7,3,4]
puts median(data) # 4
```

The mode of a data set is the value that occurs most frequently. If there is only one such value, the set is unimodal; otherwise, it is multimodal. A multimodal data set is a more complex case that we do not consider here. The interested reader can extend and improve the code we show here:

```ruby
def mode(x)
  f = {}       # frequency table
  fmax = 0     # maximum frequency
  m = nil      # mode
  x.each do |v|
    f[v] ||= 0
    f[v] += 1
    fmax,m = f[v], v if f[v] > fmax
  end
  return m
end

data = [7,7,7,4,4,5,4,5,7,2,2,3,3,7,3,4]
puts mode(data) # 7
```

5.25 Variance and Standard Deviation

The variance of a set of data is a measure of how "spread out" the values are. (Here we do not distinguish between biased and unbiased estimates.) The standard deviation, usually represented by a sigma (σ), is simply the square root of the variance:

```
data = [2, 3, 2, 2, 3, 4, 5, 5, 4, 3, 4, 1, 2]

def variance(x)
  m = mean(x)
  sum = 0.0
  x.each {|v| sum += (v-m)**2 }
  sum/x.size
end

def sigma(x)
  Math.sqrt(variance(x))
end

puts variance(data)   # 1.4615384615384615
puts sigma(data)      # 1.2089410496539776
```

Note that the `variance` function in the preceding code uses the `mean` function defined earlier.

5.26 Finding a Correlation Coefficient

The correlation coefficient is one of the simplest and most universally useful statistical measures. It is a measure of the "linearity" of a set of x-y pairs, ranging from `-1.0` (complete negative correlation) to `+1.0` (complete positive correlation).

We compute this using the mean and sigma (standard deviation) functions defined previously in Section 5.25, "Variance and Standard Deviation." For a detailed explanation of this tool, consult a statistics reference such as The Elements of Statistical Learning, available online.

The following version assumes two arrays of numbers (of the same size):

```
def correlate(x,y)
  sum = 0.0
  x.each_index do |i|
    sum += x[i]*y[i]
  end
```

```
    xymean = sum/x.size.to_f
    xmean  = mean(x)
    ymean  = mean(y)
   sx = sigma(x)
   sy = sigma(y)
   (xymean-(xmean*ymean))/(sx*sy)
 end


 a = [3, 6, 9, 12, 15, 18, 21]
 b = [1.1, 2.1, 3.4, 4.8, 5.6]
 c = [1.9, 1.0, 3.9, 3.1, 6.9]


 c1 = correlate(a,a)              # 1.0
 c2 = correlate(a,a.reverse)  # -1.0
 c3 = correlate(b,c)              # 0.8221970227633335
```

The following version is similar, but it operates on a single array, each element of which is an array containing an x-y pair:

```
def correlate2(v)
  sum = 0.0
  v.each do |a|
    sum += a[0]*a[1]
  end
  xymean = sum/v.size.to_f
  x = v.collect {|a| a[0]}
  y = v.collect {|a| a[1]}
  xmean  = mean(x)
  ymean  = mean(y)
  sx = sigma(x)
  sy = sigma(y)
  (xymean-(xmean*ymean))/(sx*sy)
end


d = [[1,6.1], [2.1,3.1], [3.9,5.0], [4.8,6.2]]


c4 = correlate2(d)            # 0.22778224915306602
```

Finally, the following version assumes that the x-y pairs are stored in a hash. It simply builds on the previous example:

```
def correlate_h(h)
  correlate2(h.to_a)
```

```
end

e = { 1 => 6.1, 2.1 => 3.1, 3.9 => 5.0, 4.8 => 6.2}

c5 = correlate_h(e)          # 0.22778224915306602
```

5.27 Generating Random Numbers

If a pseudorandom number is good enough for you, you're in luck. This is what most language implementations supply you with, and Ruby is no exception.

The `Kernel` method `rand` returns a pseudorandom floating point number, `x`, such that `x>=0.0` and `x<1.0`. Here is an example (note that yours will vary):

```
a = rand     # 0.6279091137
```

If it is called with the integer parameter `max`, it returns an integer in the range `0...max` (noninclusive of the upper bound). Here is an example (note that yours will vary):

```
n = rand(10)  # 7
```

If we want to seed the random number generator, we can do so with the `Kernel` method `srand`, which takes a single numeric parameter. If we pass no value to it, it will construct its own using (among other things) the time of day. If we pass a number to it, it will use that number as the seed. This can be useful in testing, when we want a repeatable sequence of pseudorandom numbers from one script invocation to the next:

```
srand(5)
i, j, k = rand(100), rand(100), rand(100)
# 26, 45, 56

srand(5)
l, m, n = rand(100), rand(100), rand(100)
# 26, 45, 56
```

5.28   Caching Functions with Memoization

Suppose you have a computationally expensive mathematical function that will be called repeatedly in the course of execution. If speed is critical and you can afford to sacrifice a little memory, it may be effective to store the function results in a table and look them up. This makes the implicit assumption that the function will likely be called more than once with the same parameters; we are simply avoiding "throwing away" an expensive calculation only to redo it later on. This technique is sometimes called *memoizing*.

The following example defines a complex function called `zeta`. (This solves a simple problem in population genetics, but we won't explain it here.)

```ruby
def zeta(x, y, z)
  lim = 0.0001
  gen = 0
  loop do
    gen += 1
    p,q = x + y/2.0, z + y/2.0
    x1, y1, z1 =  p*p*1.0, 2*p*q*1.0, q*q*0.9
    sum = x1 + y1 + z1
    x1 /= sum
    y1 /= sum
    z1 /= sum
    delta = [[x1, x], [y1, y], [z1, z]]
    break if delta.all? { |a,b| (a-b).abs < lim }
    x,y,z = x1,y1,z1
  end

  gen
end

g1 = zeta(0.8, 0.1, 0.1)
```

Once the function has been defined, it is possible to write another method that stores the results of the calculation for each set of arguments. These methods could have been combined into a single method, but are separated here to illustrate the memoization technique in isolation:

```ruby
def memoized_zeta(x, y, z)
  @results ||= {}
  @results[[x, y, z]] ||= zeta(x, y, z)
```

```
end

g2 = memoized_zeta(0.8, 0.1, 0.1)
g3 = memoized_zeta(0.8, 0.1, 0.1)
```

In this example, the value of `g3` will not be calculated. The `||=` operator checks to see if a value is already present (that is, not `nil` or `false`). If there is already a "truthy" value assigned to the variable, the value is returned and the right side is not even evaluated.

Although the improvement in speed will of course depend entirely on the speed of the calculation being memoized, the difference can be quite dramatic. To achieve this speed, the tradeoff is made to use additional memory and store all previous results.

One more thing should be noted here: Memoization is not just a technique for mathematical functions. It can be used for any computationally expensive method.

5.29   Conclusion

In this chapter, we have looked at various representations for numbers, including integers (in different bases) and floats. We've seen problems with floating point math, and how working with rational values can help avoid these problems. We've looked at implicit and explicit numeric conversion and coercion.

We've seen numerous ways to manipulate numbers, vectors, and matrices. We've had a good overview of most of the number-related standard libraries—in particular, the `mathn` library.

Let's move on. In the next chapter, we discuss two very Rubyish data types: symbols and ranges.

CHAPTER 6

Symbols and Ranges

I hear, and I forget. I see, and I remember. I do, and I understand.

—Confucius

Two fairly Rubyesque objects are symbols and ranges. They are covered together in this chapter not because they are related but because there is not so much to say about them.

The Ruby concept of a symbol is sometimes difficult to grasp. If you are familiar with the concept of "atoms" in LISP, you can think of Ruby symbols as being similar. But rather than give a lengthy and abstruse definition, I will concentrate on what can be done with a symbol and how it can be used. After all, the question "What is a number?" could have a complex answer, but we all understand how to use and manipulate numbers.

Ranges are simpler. A *range* is simply a representation of a group or collection delimited by its endpoints. Similar constructs exist in Pascal, PHP, and even SQL.

Let's look at symbols and ranges in greater detail, and see how we can use them in everyday Ruby code.

6.1 Symbols

A *symbol* in Ruby is an instance of the class `Symbol`. The syntax is simple in the typical case: a colon followed by an identifier.

A symbol is like a string in that it corresponds to a sequence of characters. It is *unlike* a string in that each symbol has only one instance (just as a `Fixnum` works). Therefore, there is a memory or performance issue to be aware of. For example, in the following code, the string `"foo"` is stored as three separate objects in memory, but the symbol `:foo` is stored as a single object (referenced more than once):

```
array = ["foo", "foo", "foo", :foo, :foo, :foo]
```

Some people are confused by the leading colon on a symbol name. There is no need for confusion; it's a simple matter of syntax. Strings, arrays, and hashes have both beginning and ending delimiters; a symbol has only a beginning delimiter. Think of it as a *unary* delimiter rather than a *binary* one. You may consider the syntax strange at first, but there is no mystery. Internally, Ruby represents each symbol with a number, instead of the symbol's characters. The number can be retrieved with `to_i`, but there is little need for it.

According to Jim Weirich, a symbol is "an object that has a name." Austin Ziegler prefers to say "an object that *is* a name." In any case, there is a one-to-one correspondence between symbols and names. What kinds of things do we need to apply names to? Such things as variables, methods, and arbitrary constants.

One common use of symbols is to represent the name of a variable or method. For example, we know that if we want to add a read/write attribute to a class, we can do it this way:

```
class SomeClass
  attr_accessor :whatever
end
```

This is equivalent to the following:

```
class SomeClass
  def whatever
    @whatever
  end
  def whatever=(val)
    @whatever = val
  end
end
```

In other words, the symbol `:whatever` tells the `attr_accessor` method that the "getter" and "setter" (as well as the instance variable) will all be given names corresponding to that symbol.

You might well ask why we couldn't use a string instead. As it happens, we could. Many or most core methods that expect symbols are content to get strings instead:

```
attr_reader :alpha
attr_reader "beta"   # This is also legal
```

In fact, a symbol is "like" a string in that it corresponds to a sequence of characters. This leads some people to say that "a symbol is just an immutable string." However, the Symbol class does *not* inherit from String, and the typical operations we might apply to a string are not necessarily applicable to symbols.

Another misunderstanding is to think that symbols necessarily correspond directly to identifiers. This leads some people to talk of "the symbol table" (as they would in referring to an assembled object program). But this is not really a useful concept; although symbols are certainly stored in a kind of table internally, Ruby does not expose the table as an entity we can access, and we as programmers don't care that it is there.

What is more, symbols need not even look like identifiers. Typically they do, whatever that means; but they can also contain punctuation if they are enclosed in quotes. These are also valid Ruby symbols:

```
sym1 = :"This is a symbol"
sym2 = :"This is, too!"
sym3 = :")(*&^%$"          # and even this
```

You could even use such symbols to define instance variables and methods, but then you would need such techniques as send and instance_variable_get to reference them. In general, such a thing is not recommended.

6.1.1 Symbols as Enumerations

Languages such as Pascal and later versions of C have the concept of an enumerated type. Ruby doesn't have type checking, but symbols are frequently useful for their mnemonic value; we might represent directions as :north, :south, :east, and :west. If we're going to refer to those values repeatedly, we could store them in a constant:

```
Directions = [:north, :south, :east, :west]
```

If these were strings rather than symbols, storing them in a constant would save memory, but each symbol exists only once in object space anyhow. (Symbols, like Fixnums, are stored as immediate values.)

6.1.2   Symbols as Metavalues

Frequently, we use exceptions as a way of avoiding return codes. But if you prefer to use return codes, you can. The fact that Ruby's methods are not limited to a single return type makes it possible to pass back "out-of-band" values.

We frequently have need for such values. At one time, the ASCII NUL character was considered to be not a character at all. C has the idea of the NULL pointer, Pascal has the nil pointer, SQL has NULL, and so on. Ruby, of course, has nil.

The trouble with such metavalues is that they keep getting absorbed into the set of valid values. Everyone today considers NUL a true ASCII character. And in Ruby, nil isn't really a non-object; it can be stored and manipulated. Thus, we have minor annoyances such as hash[key] returning nil; did it return nil because the key was not found or because the key is really associated with a nil?

The point here is that symbols can sometimes be used as good metavalues. Imagine a method that somehow grabs a string from the network (perhaps via HTTP or something similar). If we want, we can return non-string values to indicate exceptional occurrences:

```
str = get_string
case str
  when String
    # Proceed normally
  when :eof
    # end of file, socket closed, whatever
  when :error
    # I/O or network error
  when :timeout
    # didn't get a reply
end
```

Is this really "better" or clearer than using exceptions? Not necessarily. But it is a technique to keep in mind, especially when you want to deal with conditions that may be "edge cases" but not necessarily errors.

6.1.3   Symbols, Variables, and Methods

Probably the best known use of symbols is in defining attributes on a class:

```
class MyClass
  attr_reader :alpha, :beta
  attr_writer :gamma, :delta
  attr_accessor :epsilon
  # ...
end
```

Bear in mind that there is some code at work here. For example, `attr_acces-sor` uses the symbol name to determine the name of the instance variable and the reader and writer methods. That does *not* mean that there is always an exact correspondence between that symbol and that instance variable name. For example, if we use `instance_variable_set`, we have to specify the exact name of the variable, including the at sign:

```
instance_variable_set(:@foo, "str")  # Works
instance_variable_set(:foo, "str")   # error
```

In short, a symbol passed into the `attr` family of methods is just an argument, and these methods create instance variables and methods as needed, *based on* the value of that symbol. (The writer has an equal sign appended to the end, and the instance variable name has an at sign added to the front.) In other cases, the symbol must exactly correspond to the identifier it is referencing.

In most if not all cases, methods that expect symbols can also take strings. The reverse is not necessarily true.

6.1.4   Converting to/from Symbols

Strings and symbols can be freely interconverted with the `to_str` and `to_sym` methods:

```
a = "foobar"
b = :foobar
a == b.to_str    # true
b == a.to_sym    # true
```

If you're doing metaprogramming, the following method might prove useful sometimes while experimenting:

```
class Symbol
  def +(other)
    (self.to_s + other.to_s).to_sym
  end
end
```

The preceding method allows us to concatenate symbols (or append a string onto a symbol). It's generally bad form to change the behavior of core classes in code that others will use, but it can be a powerful tool for understanding by experimentation.

The following is an example that uses it; this trivial piece of code accepts a symbol and tries to tell us whether it represents an accessor (that is, a reader and writer both exist):

```
class Object
  def accessor?(sym)
    return self.respond_to?(sym) and self.respond_to?(sym+"=")
  end
end
```

There is a clever usage of symbols that I'll mention here. When we do a map operation, sometimes a complex block may be attached. But in many cases, we are simply calling a method on each element of the array or collection:

```
list = words.map {|x| x.capitalize }
```

In such a case, it may seem we are doing a little too much punctuation for the benefit we're getting. The Symbol class defines a to_proc method. This ensures that any symbol can be coerced into a proc object. A proc is effectively a method that can be manipulated like an object: assigned to variables, or called at will. On a Symbol, the proc returned by the method will simply call the method named by the symbol— in other words, it will send the symbol itself as a message to the object. The method might be defined like this:

```
def to_proc
  proc {|obj, *args| obj.send(self, *args) }
end
```

With this method in place, we can rewrite our original code fragment:

```
list = words.map(&:capitalize)
```

It's worth spending a minute understanding how this works. The `map` method ordinarily takes only a block (no other parameters). The ampersand notation allows us to pass a `proc` instead of an explicit attached block if we want. Because we use the ampersand on an object that isn't a `proc`, the interpreter tries to call `to_proc` on that object. The resulting `proc` takes the place of an explicit block so that `map` will call it repeatedly, once for each element in the array. Now, why does `self` make sense as the thing passed as a message to the array element? It's because a `proc` is a *closure* and therefore remembers the context in which it was created. At the time it was created, `self` referred to the symbol on which the `to_proc` was called.

Next, we look at ranges, which are straightforward but surprisingly handy.

6.2 Ranges

Ranges are fairly intuitive, but they do have a few confusing uses and qualities. A numeric range is one of the simplest:

```
digits = 0..9
scale1 = 0..10
scale2 = 0...10
```

The `..` operator is *inclusive* of its endpoint, and the `...` operator is *exclusive* of its endpoint. (This may seem unintuitive to you; if so, just memorize this fact.) Therefore, `digits` and `scale2`, shown in the preceding example, are effectively the same.

But ranges are not limited to integers or numbers. The beginning and end of a range may be any Ruby object. However, not all ranges are meaningful or useful, as we shall see.

The primary operations you might want to do on a range are to iterate over it, convert it to an array, or determine whether it includes a given object. Let's look at all the ramifications of these and other operations.

6.2.1 Open and Closed Ranges

We call a range "closed" if it includes its end, and "open" if it does not:

```
r1 = 3..6      # a closed range
r2 = 3...6     # an open range
a1 = r1.to_a   # [3,4,5,6]
a2 = r2.to_a   # [3,4,5]
```

There is no way to construct a range that excludes its beginning point. This is arguably a limitation of the language.

6.2.2   Finding Endpoints

The `first` and `last` methods return the left and right endpoints of a range. Synonyms are `begin` and `end` (which are normally keywords but may be called as methods when there is an explicit receiver).

```
r1 = 3..6
r2 = 3...6
r1a, r1b = r1.first, r1.last    # 3, 6
r1c, r1d = r1.begin, r1.end     # 3, 6
r2a, r2b = r1.begin, r1.end     # 3, 6
```

The `exclude_end?` method tells us whether the endpoint is excluded:

```
r1.exclude_end?    # false
r2.exclude_end?    # true
```

6.2.3   Iterating Over Ranges

Typically, it's possible to iterate over a range. For this to work, the class of the endpoints must define a meaningful `succ` method:

```
(3..6).each {|x| puts x }  # prints four lines
                           # (parens are necessary)
```

So far, so good. But be *very cautious* when dealing with `string` ranges! It is possible to iterate over ranges of strings because the `string` class defines a `succ` operator, but it is of limited usefulness. You should use this kind of feature only in well-known, isolated circumstances because the `succ` method for strings is not defined with exceptional rigor. (It is "intuitive" rather than lexicographic; therefore, some strings have a successor that is surprising or meaningless.)

```
r1 = "7".."9"
r2 = "7".."10"
r1.each {|x| puts x }   # Prints three lines
r2.each {|x| puts x }   # Prints no output!
```

The preceding examples look similar but work differently. The reason lies partly in the fact that in the second range, the endpoints are strings of different length. To our eyes, we expect this range to cover the strings `"7"`, `"8"`, `"9"`, and `"10"`, but what really happens?

When we try to iterate over `r2`, we start with a value of `"7"` and enter a loop that terminates when the current value is greater than the endpoint on the right. But because `"7"` and `"10"` are strings, not numbers, they are compared as such. In other words, they are compared lexicographically, and we find that the left endpoint is *greater* than the right endpoint. Therefore, we don't loop at all.

What about floating point ranges? We can construct them, and we can certainly test membership in them, which makes them useful. But we can't iterate over them because there is no `succ` method. Here is an example:

```
fr = 2.0..2.2
fr.each {|x| puts x }    # error!
```

Why isn't there a floating point `succ` method? It would be theoretically possible to increment the floating point number by *epsilon* each time. But this would be highly architecture dependent, it would result in a frighteningly high number of iterations for even "small" ranges, and it would be of limited usefulness.

6.2.4   Testing Range Membership

Ranges are not much good if we can't determine whether an item lies within a given range. As it turns out, the `include?` method makes this easy:

```
r1 = 23456..34567
x = 14142
y = 31416
r1.include?(x)       # false
r1.include?(y)       # true
```

The method `member?` is an alias.

But how does this work internally? How does the interpreter determine whether an item is in a given range? Actually, it makes this determination simply by comparing the item with the endpoints (so that range membership is dependent on the existence of a meaningful `<=>` operator).

Therefore, to say `(a..b).include?(x)` is equivalent to saying `x >= a` and `x <= b`.

Once again, beware of string ranges:

```
s1 = "2".."5"
str = "28"
s1.include?(str)    # true (misleading!)
```

6.2.5   Converting to Arrays

When we convert a range to an array, the interpreter simply applies succ repeatedly until the end is reached, appending each item onto an array that is returned:

```
r = 3..12
arr = r.to_a    # [3,4,5,6,7,8,9,10,11,12]
```

This naturally won't work with Float ranges. It may sometimes work with String ranges, but this should be avoided because the results will not always be obvious or meaningful.

6.2.6   Backward Ranges

Does a *backward* range make any sense? Yes and no. For example, this is a perfectly valid range:

```
r = 6..3
x = r.begin              # 6
y = r.end                # 3
flag = r.end_excluded?   # false
```

As you see, we can determine its starting and ending points and whether the end is included in the range. However, that is nearly *all* we can do with such a range.

```
arr = r.to_a       # []
r.each {|x| p x}   # No iterations
y = 5
r.include?(y)      # false (for any value of y)
```

Does that mean that backward ranges are necessarily "evil" or useless? Not at all. It is still useful, in some cases, to have the endpoints encapsulated in a single object.

In fact, arrays and strings frequently take "backward ranges" because these are zero-indexed from the left but "minus one"-indexed from the right. Therefore, we can use expressions like these:

```
string = "flowery"
str1   = string[0..-2]    # "flower"
str2   = string[1..-2]    # "lower"
str3   = string[-5..-3]   # "owe" (actually a forward range)
```

6.2.7   The Flip-Flop Operator

When the range operator is used in a condition, it is treated specially. This usage of .. is called the *flip-flop operator* because it is essentially a toggle that keeps its own state rather than a true range.

This trick, apparently originating with Perl, is useful. But understanding how it works takes a little effort.

Imagine we had a Ruby source file with embedded docs between =begin and =end tags. How would we extract and output only those sections? (Our state toggles between "inside" a section and "outside" a section, hence the flip-flop concept.) The following piece of code, while perhaps unintuitive, will work:

```
file.each_line do |line|
  puts line if (line=~/=begin/)..(line=~/=end/)
end
```

How can this work? The magic all happens in the flip-flop operator.

First, realize that this "range" is preserving a state internally, but this fact is hidden. When the left endpoint becomes true, the range itself returns true; it then remains true until the right endpoint becomes true, and the range toggles to false.

This kind of feature might be used in some cases, such as parsing section-oriented config files, selecting ranges of items from lists, and so on.

However, I personally don't like the syntax, and others are also dissatisfied with it. Removing it has been discussed publicly at bugs.ruby-lang.org/issues/5400, and Matz himself has said that it will eventually be removed.

So what's wrong with the flip-flop? Here is my opinion.

First, in the preceding example, take a line with the value =begin. As a reminder, the =~ operator does not return true or false as we might expect; it returns the position of the match (a Fixnum) or nil if there was no match. So then the expressions in the range evaluate to 0 and nil, respectively.

However, if we try to construct a range from 0 to `nil`, it gives us an error because it is nonsensical:

```
range = 0..nil    # error!
```

Furthermore, bear in mind that in Ruby, only `false` and `nil` evaluate to false; everything else evaluates as `true`. Then a range ordinarily would not evaluate as `false`.

```
puts "hello" if x..y
# Prints "hello" for any valid range x..y
```

And again, suppose we stored these values in variables and then used the variables to construct the range. This doesn't work because the test is always true:

```
file.each_line do |line|
  start = line=~/=begin/
  stop = line=~/=end/
  puts line if start..stop
end
```

What if we put the range itself in a variable? This doesn't work either because, once again, the test is always true:

```
file.each_line do |line|
  range = (line=~/=begin/)..(line=~/=end/)
  puts line if range
end
```

To understand this, we have to understand that the entire range (with both end-points) is reevaluated each time the loop is run, but the internal state is also factored in. The flip-flop operator is therefore not a true range at all. The fact that it looks like a range but is not is considered a bad thing by some.

Finally, think of the endpoints of the flip-flop. They are reevaluated every time, but this reevaluation cannot be captured in a variable that can be substituted. In effect, the flip-flop's endpoints are like `procs`. They are not values; they are code. The fact that something that looks like an ordinary expression is really a `proc` is also undesirable.

Having said all that, the functionality is still useful. Can we write a class that encapsulates this function without being so cryptic and magical? As it turns out, this is not difficult. Listing 6.1 introduces a simple class called `Transition` that mimics the behavior of the flip-flop.

Listing 6.1   The `Transition` Class

```ruby
class Transition
  A, B = :A, :B
  T, F = true, false

          # state,p1,p2  => newstate, result
  Table = {[A,F,F]=>[A,F], [B,F,F]=>[B,T],
           [A,T,F]=>[B,T], [B,T,F]=>[B,T],
           [A,F,T]=>[A,F], [B,F,T]=>[A,T],
           [A,T,T]=>[A,T], [B,T,T]=>[A,T]}

  def initialize(proc1, proc2)
    @state = A
    @proc1, @proc2 = proc1, proc2
  end

  def check?
    p1 = @proc1.call ? T : F
    p2 = @proc2.call ? T : F
    @state, result = *Table[[@state,p1,p2]]
    return result
  end
end
```

In the `Transition` class, we use a simple state machine to manage transitions. We initialize it with a pair of `procs` (the same ones used in the flip-flop). We do lose a little convenience in that any variables (such as `line`) used in the `procs` must already be in scope. But we now have a solution with no "magic" in it, where all expressions behave as they do any other place in Ruby.

Here's a slight variant on the same solution. Let's change the `initialize` method to take two arbitrary expressions:

```ruby
def initialize(flag1, flag2)
  @state = A
  @flag1, @flag2 = flag1, flag2
end

def check?(item)
```

```
   p1 = (@flag1 === item) ? T : F
   p2 = (@flag2 === item) ? T : F
   @state, result = *Table[[@state, p1, p2]]
   return result
 end
```

The case equality operator is used to check the relationship of the starting and ending flags with the variable.

Here is how we use the new version:

```
trans = Transition.new(/=begin/, /=end/)
file.each_line do |line|
  puts line if trans.check?(line)
end
```

I do recommend an approach like this, which is more explicit and less magical.

6.2.8   Custom Ranges

Let's look at an example of a range made up of some arbitrary object. Listing 6.2 shows a simple class to handle Roman numerals.

Listing 6.2   A Roman Numeral Class

```
class Roman
  include Comparable

  I,IV,V,IX,X,XL,L,XC,C,CD,D,CM,M =
    1, 4, 5, 9, 10, 40, 50, 90, 100, 400, 500, 900, 1000

  Values = %w[M CM D CD C XC L XL X IX V IV I]

  def Roman.encode(value)
    return "" if self == 0
    str = ""
    Values.each do |letters|
      rnum = const_get(letters)
      if value >= rnum
        return(letters + str=encode(value-rnum))
      end
    end
    str
  end

  def Roman.decode(rvalue)
    sum = 0
```

```
    letters = rvalue.split('')
    letters.each_with_index do |letter,i|
      this = const_get(letter)
      that = const_get(letters[i+1]) rescue 0
      op = that > this ? :- : :+
      sum = sum.send(op,this)
    end
    sum
  end

  def initialize(value)
    case value
      when String
        @roman = value
        @decimal = Roman.decode(@roman)
      when Symbol
        @roman = value.to_s
        @decimal = Roman.decode(@roman)
      when Numeric
        @decimal = value
        @roman = Roman.encode(@decimal)
    end
  end

  def to_i
    @decimal
  end

  def to_s
    @roman
  end

  def succ
    Roman.new(@decimal+1)
  end

  def <=>(other)
    self.to_i <=> other.to_i
  end
end

def Roman(val)
  Roman.new(val)
end
```

I'll cover a few highlights of this class first. It can be constructed using a string or a symbol (representing a Roman numeral) or a Fixnum (representing an ordinary Hindu-Arabic decimal number). Internally, conversion is performed, and both forms are stored. There is a "convenience method" called Roman, which simply is a shortcut to calling the `Roman.new` method. The class-level methods `encode` and `decode` handle conversion to and from Roman form, respectively.

For simplicity, I haven't done any error checking. I also assume that the Roman letters are uppercase.

The `to_i` method naturally returns the decimal value, and the `to_s` method predictably returns the Roman form. We define `succ` to be the next Roman number—for example, `Roman(:IV).succ` would be `Roman(:V)`.

We implement the comparison operator by comparing the decimal equivalents in a straightforward way. We do an `include` of the `Comparable` module so that we can get the less-than and greater-than operators (which depend on the existence of the comparison method `<=>`).

Notice the gratuitous use of symbols in this fragment:

```
op = that > this ? :- : :+
sum = sum.send(op,this)
```

In the preceding fragment, we're actually choosing which operation (denoted by a symbol) to perform—addition or subtraction. This code fragment is just a short way of saying the following:

```
if that > this
  sum -= this
else
  sum += this
end
```

The second fragment is longer but arguably clearer.

Because this class has both a `succ` method and a full set of relational operators, we can use it in a range. The following sample code demonstrates this:

```
require 'roman'

y1 = Roman(:MCMLXVI)
y2 = Roman(:MMIX)
range = y1..y2                  # 1966..2009
range.each {|x| puts x}         # 44 lines of output

epoch = Roman(:MCMLXX)
range.include?(epoch)           # true
```

```
doomsday = Roman(2038)
range.include?(doomsday)        # false

Roman(:V) == Roman(:IV).succ  # true
Roman(:MCM) < Roman(:MM)       # true
```

6.3   Conclusion

In this chapter, we've seen what symbols are in Ruby and how they are used. We've seen both standard and user-defined uses of symbols.

We've also looked at ranges in depth. We've seen how to convert them to arrays, how to use them as array or string indices, how to iterate over them, and other such operations. We've looked in detail at the flip-flop operator (and an alternative to the existing syntax). Finally, we've seen in detail how to construct a class so that it works well with range operators.

That ends our discussion of symbols and ranges. However, because they are commonly used in Ruby (and are extremely useful), you'll see more of them in incidental code throughout the rest of the book.

CHAPTER 7

Working with Times and Dates

Does anybody really know what time it is?

—Chicago, *Chicago IV*

One of the most complex and confusing areas of human life is that of measuring time. To come to a complete understanding of the subject, you would need to study physics, astronomy, history, law, business, and religion. Astronomers know (as most of us don't!) that solar time and sidereal time are not quite the same thing, and why a "leap second" is occasionally added to the end of the year. Historians know that the calendar skipped several days in October 1582, when Italy converted from the Julian calendar to the Gregorian. Few people know the difference between astronomical Easter and ecclesiastical Easter (which are almost always the same). Many people don't know that century years not divisible by 400 (such as the year 1900) are not leap years.

Performing calculations with times and dates is common in computing but has traditionally been somewhat tedious in most programming languages. It is tedious in Ruby, too, because of the nature of the data. However, Ruby has taken some incremental steps toward making these operations easier.

As a courtesy to the reader, we'll go over a few terms that may not be familiar to everyone. Most of these come from standard usage or from other programming languages.

Greenwich Mean Time (GMT) is an old term not really in official use anymore. The new global standard is Coordinated Universal Time (or UTC, from the French version of the name). GMT and UTC are virtually the same thing; over a period of years, the difference will be on the order of seconds. Much of the software in the industry does not distinguish between the two at all (nor does Ruby).

Daylight Saving Time is a semiannual shift in the official time, amounting to a difference of one hour. Thus, the U.S., time zones change every year from ending in ST (Standard Time) to DT (Daylight Time) and back again. This annoying trick is used in most (though not all) of the United States and in many other countries.

The *epoch* is a term borrowed from UNIX lore. In this realm, a time is typically stored internally as a number of seconds from a specific point in time (called the epoch). In UNIX, the epoch was midnight January 1, 1970, GMT. (Note that in U.S. time zones, this will actually be the preceding December 31.) An *epoch time* is one measured by the distance in time from that point.

The `Time` class is used for most operations. The `Date` and `DateTime` classes provide some extra flexibility. Let's look at some common uses of these.

7.1   Determining the Current Time

The most fundamental problem in time/date manipulation is to answer the question: "What are the time and date right now?" In Ruby, when we create a `Time` object with no parameters, it is set to the current date and time:

```
t0 = Time.new
```

`Time.now` is a synonym:

```
t0 = Time.now
```

Note that the resolution of system clocks varies from one architecture to another. It often includes microseconds, and two `Time` objects created immediately in succession will almost always record different times.

7.2   Working with Specific Times (Post-Epoch)

Most software only needs to work with dates in the future or in the recent past. For these circumstances, the `Time` class is adequate. The relevant class methods are `mktime`, `local`, `gm`, and `utc`.

The `mktime` method creates a new `Time` object based on the parameters passed to it. These time units are given in reverse, from longest to shortest: year, month, day, hours, minutes, seconds, microseconds. All but the year are optional; they default to the lowest possible value. The microseconds may be ignored on many architectures. The hours must be between 0 and 23 (that is, a 24-hour clock).

```
t1 = Time.mktime(2014)                 # January 1, 2014 at 0:00:00
t2 = Time.mktime(2014,3)
t3 = Time.mktime(2014,3,15)
t4 = Time.mktime(2014,3,15,21)
t5 = Time.mktime(2014,3,15,21,30)
t6 = Time.mktime(2014,3,15,21,30,15)   # March 15, 2014 9:30:15 pm
```

Note that `mktime` assumes the local time zone. In fact, `Time.local` is a synonym for it:

```
t7 = Time.local(2014,3,15,21,30,15)    # March 15, 2014 9:30:15 pm
```

The `Time.gm` method is basically the same, except that it assumes GMT (or UTC). Because the authors are in the U.S. Pacific time zone, we would see an eight-hour difference here:

```
t8 = Time.gm(2014,3,15,21,30,15)       # March 15, 2014 9:30:15 pm
# This is only 2:30:15 pm in Pacific time!
```

The `Time.utc` method is a synonym:

```
t9 = Time.utc(2014,3,15,21,30,15)      # March 15, 2014 9:30:15 pm
# Again, 2:30:15 pm Pacific time.
```

There is one more important item to note. All these methods can take an alternate set of parameters. The instance method `to_a` (which converts a time to an array of relevant values) returns a set of values in this order: seconds, minutes, hours, day, month, year, day of week (`0..6`), day of year (`1..366`), daylight saving (`true` or `false`), and time zone (as a string).

Thus, these are also valid calls:

```
t0 = Time.local(0,15,3,20,11,1979,2,324,false,"GMT-7:00")
t1 = Time.gm(*Time.now.to_a)
```

However, in the first example, do not fall into the trap of thinking that you can change the computable parameters such as the day of the week (in this case, 2 meaning Tuesday). A change like this simply contradicts the way our calendar works, and it will have no effect on the time object created. November 20, 1979 was a Tuesday regardless of how we might write our code.

Finally, note that there are obviously many ways to attempt coding incorrect times, such as a 13th month or a 35th day of the month. In cases like these, an `ArgumentError` will be raised.

7.3 Determining the Day of the Week

There are several ways to determine the day of the week. First, the instance method `to_a` returns an array of time information. You can access the seventh element, which is a number from 0 to 6 (0 meaning Sunday and 6 meaning Saturday).

```
time = Time.now
day = time.to_a[6]              # 2 (meaning Tuesday)
```

It's better to use the instance method `wday`, as shown here:

```
day = time.wday                 # 2 (meaning Tuesday)
```

But both these techniques are a little cumbersome. Sometimes we want the value coded as a number, but more often we don't. To get the actual name of the weekday as a string, we can use the `strftime` method. This name will be familiar to C programmers. There are nearly two dozen different specifiers that it recognizes, enabling us to format dates and times more or less as we want (see Section 7.21, "Formatting and Printing Time Values").

```
name = time.strftime("%A")      # "Tuesday"
```

It's also possible to obtain an abbreviated name:

```
tln = time.strftime("%a")    # "Tue"
```

7.4 Determining the Date of Easter

Traditionally, this holiday is one of the most difficult to compute because it is tied to the lunar cycle. The lunar month does not go evenly into the solar year, and thus anything based on the moon can be expected to vary from year to year.

The algorithm we present here is a well-known one that has made the rounds. We have seen it coded in BASIC, Pascal, and C. We now present it to you in Ruby:

```
def easter(year)
  c = year/100
  n = year - 19*(year/19)
  k = (c-17)/25
  i = c - c/4 - (c-k)/3 + 19*n + 15
  i = i - 30*(i/30)
  i = i - (i/28)*(1 -(i/28)*(29/(i+1))*((21-n)/11))
  j = year + year/4 + i + 2 - c + c/4
  j = j - 7*(j/7)
  l = i - j
  month = 3 + (l+40)/44
  day = l + 28 - 31*(month/4)
  [month, day]
end

date = easter 2014          # Find month/day for 2001
t = Time.local 2014, *date  # Pass parameters to Time.local
puts t                      # 2014-04-20 00:00:00 -0700
```

One reader on seeing this section on Easter asked, "Ecclesiastical or astronomical?" Truthfully, I don't know. If you find out, let us all know.

I'd love to explain this algorithm to you, but I don't understand it myself. Some things must be taken on faith, and in the case of Easter, this may be especially appropriate.

7.5 Finding the Nth Weekday in a Month

Sometimes for a given month and year, we want to find the date of the third Monday in the month, or the second Tuesday, and so on. The code in Listing 7.1 makes that calculation simple.

If we are looking for the *n*th occurrence of a certain weekday, we pass n as the first parameter. The second parameter is the number of that weekday (0 meaning Sunday,

1 meaning Monday, and so on). The third and fourth parameters are the month and year, respectively.

Listing 7.1   Finding the *N*th Weekday

```
def nth_wday(n, wday, month, year)
  if (!n.between? 1,5) or
     (!wday.between? 0,6) or
     (!month.between? 1,12)
    raise ArgumentError, "Invalid day or date"
  end
  t = Time.local year, month, 1
  first = t.wday
  if first == wday
    fwd = 1
  elsif first < wday
    fwd = wday - first + 1
  elsif first > wday
    fwd = (wday+7) - first + 1
  end
  target = fwd + (n-1)*7
  begin
    t2 = Time.local year, month, target
  rescue ArgumentError
    return nil
  end
  if t2.mday == target
    t2
  else
    nil
  end
end
```

The peculiar-looking code near the end of the method is put there to counteract a long-standing tradition in the underlying time-handling routines. You might expect that trying to create a date of November 31 would result in an error of some kind. You would be mistaken. Most systems would happily (and silently) convert this to December 1. If you are an old-time UNIX hacker, you may think this is a feature; otherwise, you may consider it a bug.

We will not venture an opinion here as to what the underlying library code ought to do or whether Ruby ought to change that behavior. But we don't want to have this routine perpetuate the tradition. If you are looking for the date of, say, the fifth Friday in November 2014, you will get a `nil` value back (rather than December 5, 2014).

7.6 Converting Between Seconds and Larger Units

Sometimes we want to take a number of seconds and convert to days, hours, minutes, and seconds. This following routine will do just that:

```
def sec2dhms(secs)
  time = secs.round          # Get rid of microseconds
  sec = time % 60            # Extract seconds
  time /= 60                 # Get rid of seconds
  mins = time % 60           # Extract minutes
  time /= 60                 # Get rid of minutes
  hrs = time % 24            # Extract hours
  time /= 24                 # Get rid of hours
  days = time                # Days (final remainder)
  [days, hrs, mins, sec]     # Return array [d,h,m,s]
end


t = sec2dhms(1000000)        # A million seconds is...

puts "#{t[0]} days,"         # 11 days,
puts "#{t[1]} hours,"        # 13 hours,
puts "#{t[2]} minutes,"      # 46 minutes,
puts " and #{t[3]} seconds." # and 40 seconds.
```

We could, of course, go up to higher units. However, a week is not an overly useful unit, a month is not a well-defined term, and a year is far from being an integral number of days.

We also present here the inverse of that function:

```
def dhms2sec(days,hrs=0,min=0,sec=0)
  days*86400 + hrs*3600 + min*60 + sec
end
```

7.7 Converting to and from the Epoch

For various reasons, we may want to convert back and forth between the internal (or traditional) measure and the standard date form. Internally, dates are stored as a number of seconds since the epoch.

The `Time.at` class method creates a new time given the number of seconds since the epoch:

```
epoch = Time.at(0)              # Find the epoch (1 Jan 1970 GMT)
newmil = Time.at(978307200) # Happy New Millennium! (1 Jan 2001)
```

The inverse is the instance method `to_i` which converts to an integer:

```
now = Time.now                  # 2014-07-23 17:24:26 -0700
sec = now.to_i                  # 1406161466
```

If you need microseconds, you can use `to_f` to convert to a floating point number.

7.8   Working with Leap Seconds: Don't!

Ah, but my calculations, people say,
Reduced the year to better reckoning? Nay,
'Twas only striking from the calendar
Unborn Tomorrow and dead Yesterday.

—Omar Khayyam, *The Rubaiyat* (trans. Fitzgerald)

You want to work with leap seconds? Our advice: Don't.

Leap seconds are very real. One was added to the year 2012, when June 30's final minute had 61 seconds rather than the usual 60. Although the library routines have for years allowed for the possibility of a 61-second minute, our experience has been that most systems do not keep track of leap seconds. When we say "most," we mean all the ones we've ever checked.

```
t0 = Time.gm(2012, 6, 30, 23, 59, 59)
puts t0 + 1  # 2012-07-01 00:00:00 UTC
```

It is (barely) conceivable that Ruby could add a layer of intelligence to correct for this. At the time of this writing, however, there are no plans to add such functionality.

7.9   Finding the Day of the Year

The day number within the year is sometimes called the Julian date; this is not directly related to the Julian calendar, which has gone out of style. Other people insist that this usage is not correct, so we won't use it from here on.

No matter what you call it, there will be times you want to know what day of the year it is, from 1 to 366. This is easy in Ruby; we use the `yday` method:

```
t = Time.now
day = t.yday       # 315
```

7.10   Validating a Date or Time

As we saw in Section 7.5 "Finding the *N*th Weekday in a Month," the standard date/time functions do not check the validity of a date, but "roll it over" as needed. For example, November 31 is translated to December 1.

At times, this may be the behavior you want. If it is not, you will be happy to know that the standard library `Date` does not regard such a date as valid. We can use this fact to perform validation of a date as we instantiate it:

```
class Time

  def Time.validate(year, month=1, day=1,
                    hour=0, min=0, sec=0, usec=0)
    require "date"

    begin
      d = Date.new(year,month,day)
    rescue
      return nil
    end
    Time.local(year,month,day,hour,min,sec,usec)
  end

end

t1 = Time.validate(2014,11,30)  # Instantiates a valid object
t2 = Time.validate(2014,11,31)  # Returns nil
```

Here, we have taken the lazy way out; we simply set the return value to `nil` if the parameters passed in do not form a valid date (as determined by the `Date` class). We have made this method a class method of `Time` by analogy with the other methods that instantiate objects.

Note that the `Date` class can work with dates prior to the epoch. This means that passing in a date such as 31 May 1961 will succeed as far as the `Date` class is concerned. But when these values are passed into the `Time` class, an `ArgumentError` will result. We don't attempt to catch that exception here because we think it's appropriate to let it be caught at the same level as (for example) `Time.local`, in the user code.

Speaking of `Time.local`, we used that method here; but if we wanted GMT instead, we could have called the `gmt` method. It would be a good idea to implement both flavors.

7.11   Finding the Week of the Year

The definition of "week number" is not absolute and fixed. Various businesses, coalitions, government agencies, and standards bodies have differing concepts of what it means. This stems, of course, from the fact that the year can start on any day of the week; we may or may not want to count partial weeks, and we may start on Sunday or Monday.

We offer only three alternatives in this section. The first two are made available by the `Time` method `strftime`. The `%U` specifier numbers the weeks starting from Sunday, and the `%W` specifier starts with Monday.

The third possibility comes from the `Date` class. It has an accessor called `cweek`, which returns the week number based on the ISO 8601 definition (which says that week 1 is the week containing the first Thursday of the year).

If none of these three suits you, you may have to "roll your own." We present these three in a single code fragment:

```
require "date"

# Let's look at May 1 in the years
# 2005 and 2015.

t1 = Time.local(2005,5,1)
d1 = Date.new(2005,5,1)

week1a = t1.strftime("%U").to_i   # 18
week1b = t1.strftime("%W").to_i   # 17
week1c = d1.cweek                 # 17
```

```
t2 = Time.local(2015,5,1)
d2 = Date.new(2015,5,1)

week2a = t2.strftime("%U").to_i   # 17
week2b = t2.strftime("%W").to_i   # 17
week2c = d2.cweek                 # 18
```

7.12 Detecting Leap Years

The Date class has two class methods: julian_leap? and gregorian_leap?. Only the latter is of use in recent years. It also has a method called leap?, which is an alias for the gregorian_leap? method.

```
require "date"
flag1 = Date.julian_leap? 1700      # true
flag2 = Date.gregorian_leap? 1700   # false
flag3 = Date.leap? 1700             # false
```

Every child knows the first rule for leap years: The year number must be divisible by four. Fewer people know the second rule, that the year number must not be divisible by 100; and fewer still know the exception, that the year can be divisible by 400. In other words, a century year is a leap year only if it is divisible by 400; therefore, 1900 was not a leap year, but 2000 was. (This adjustment is necessary because a year is not exactly 365.25 days, but a little less, approximately 365.2422 days.)

The Time class does not have a method like this, but if we needed one, it would be simple to create:

```
class Time

  def Time.leap? year
    if year % 400 == 0
      true
    elsif year % 100 == 0
      false
    elsif year % 4 == 0
      true
    else
      false
  end

end
```

I've written this to make the algorithm explicit; an easier implementation, of course, would be simply to call the `Date.leap?` method from this one. I implement this as a class method by analogy with the `Date` class methods. It could also be implemented as an instance method.

7.13   Obtaining the Time Zone

The accessor `zone` in the `Time` class returns a `String` representation of the time zone name:

```
z1 = Time.gm(2000,11,10,22,5,0).zone      # "UTC"
z2 = Time.local(2000,11,10,22,5,0).zone   # "PST"
```

Unfortunately, times are stored relative to the current time zone, not the one with which the object was created. If necessary, you can do a little arithmetic here.

7.14   Working with Hours and Minutes Only

We may want to work with times of day as strings. Once again, `strftime` comes to our aid.

We can print the time with hours, minutes, and seconds if we want:

```
t = Time.now
puts t.strftime("%H:%M:%S")    # 22:07:45
```

We can print hours and minutes only (and, using the trick of adding 30 seconds to the time, we can even round to the nearest minute):

```
puts t.strftime("%H:%M")       # 22:07
puts (t+30).strftime("%H:%M")  # 22:08
```

Finally, if we don't like the standard 24-hour (or military) clock, we can switch to the 12-hour clock. It's appropriate to add a meridian indicator then (AM/PM):

```
puts t.strftime("%I:%M %p")    # 10:07 PM
```

There are other possibilities, of course. Use your imagination.

7.15 Comparing Time Values

The `Time` class conveniently mixes in the `Comparable` module so that dates and times may be compared in a straightforward way:

```
t0 = Time.local(2014,11,10,22,15)    # 10 Nov 2014 at 22:15
t1 = Time.local(2014,11,9,23,45)     #  9 Nov 2014 at 23:45
t2 = Time.local(2014,11,12,8,10)     # 12 Nov 2014 at  8:10
t3 = Time.local(2014,11,11,10,25)    # 11 Nov 2014 at 10:25

if t0 > t1 then puts "t0 > t1" end
if t1 != t2 then puts "t1 != t2" end
if t1 <= t2 then puts "t1 <= t2" end
if t3.between?(t1,t2)
  puts "t3 is between t1 and t2"
end

# All four if statements test true
```

7.16 Adding Intervals to Time Values

We can obtain a new time by adding an interval to a specified time; the number is interpreted as a number of seconds:

```
t0 = Time.now
t1 = t0 + 60       # Exactly one minute past t0
t2 = t0 + 3600     # Exactly one hour past t0
t3 = t0 + 86400    # Exactly one day past t0
```

The function `dhms2sec` (defined in Section 7.6, "Converting Between Seconds and Larger Units," earlier in the chapter) might be helpful here (recall that the hours, minutes, and seconds all default to 0):

```
t4 = t0 + dhms2sec(5,10)       # Ahead 5 days, 10 hours
t5 = t0 + dhms2sec(22,18,15)   # Ahead 22 days, 18 hrs, 15 min
t6 = t0 - dhms2sec(7)          # Exactly one week ago
```

Don't forget that we can move backward in time by subtracting, as seen with `t6` in the preceding code example.

7.17   Computing the Difference in Two Time Values

We can find the interval of time between two points in time. Subtracting one `Time` object from another gives us a number of seconds:

```
today = Time.local(2014,11,10)
yesterday = Time.local(2014,11,9)
diff = today - yesterday              # 86400 seconds
```

Once again, the function `sec2dhms` comes in handy (this is defined in Section 7.6, "Converting Between Seconds and Larger Units"):

```
past = Time.local(2012,9,13,4,15)
now = Time.local(2014,11,10,22,42)
diff = now - past                     # 68153220.0
unit = sec2dhms(diff)
puts "#{unit[0]} days,"               # 788 days,
puts "#{unit[1]} hours,"              # 19 hours,
puts "#{unit[2]} minutes,"            # 27 minutes,
puts "and #{unit[3]} seconds."        # and 0 seconds.
```

7.18   Working with Specific Dates (Pre-Epoch)

The standard library `Date` provides a class of the same name for working with dates that precede midnight GMT, January 1, 1970.

Although there is some overlap in functionality with the `Time` class, there are significant differences. Most notably, the `Date` class does not handle the time of day at all. Its resolution is a single day. Also, the `Date` class performs more rigorous error-checking than the `Time` class; if you attempt to refer to a date such as June 31 (or even February 29 in a non-leap year), you will get an error. The code is smart enough to know the different cutoff dates for Italy and England switching to the Gregorian calendar (in 1582 and 1752, respectively), and it can detect "nonexistent" dates that are a result of this switchover. This standard library is a tangle of interesting and arcane code. We do not have space to document it further here.

7.19 Time, Date, and DateTime

Ruby has three basic classes dealing with dates and times: `Time`, `Date`, and `DateTime`.

- The `Time` class is mostly a wrapper for the underlying time functions in the C library. These are typically based on the UNIX epoch and therefore cannot represent times before 1970.

- The `Date` class was created to address this shortcoming of the `Time` class. It can easily deal with older dates, such as Leonardo da Vinci's birthday (April 15, 1452), and it is intelligent about the dates of calendar reform. But it has its own shortcoming; for example, it can't deal with the time of day that Leonardo was born. It deals strictly with dates.

- The `DateTime` class inherits from `Date` and tries to be the best of both worlds. It can represent dates as well as `Date` can, and times as well as `Time` can. This is often the "right" way to represent a date-time value. The tradeoff made is one of speed, and `DateTime` can be vastly slower if used extensively for calculations.

  But don't be fooled into thinking that a `DateTime` is just a `Date` with an embedded `Time`. There are, in fact, `Time` methods missing from `DateTime`, such as `nsec`, `dst?`, `utc`, and others.

Both the `Date` and `DateTime` classes are part of the standard library, and must be loaded with `require "date"` before they can be used. Once the `Date` library is loaded, conversions are provided by methods with the highly predictable `to_time`, `to_date`, and `to_datetime` methods.

7.20 Parsing a Date or Time String

A date and time can be formatted as a string in many different ways because of abbreviations, varying punctuation, different orderings, and so on. Because of the various ways of formatting, writing code to decipher such a character string can be daunting. Consider these examples:

```
s1 = "9/13/14 2:15am"
s2 = "1961-05-31"
s3 = "11 July 1924"
s4 = "April 17, 1929"
s5 = "20 July 1969 16:17 EDT"  # That's one small step...
s6 = "Mon Nov 13 2000"
```

```
s7 = "August 24, 79"              # Destruction of Pompeii
s8 = "8/24/79"
```

The `Time` and `Date` libraries provide minimal parsing via the `parse` class method. Unfortunately, those methods assume that two-digit years are in a recent century, thus misplacing the destruction of Pompeii by 1900 years. They also cannot interpret American-style dates, such as those in the preceding `s1` and `s8` examples.

To solve the century issue, use the second argument to `Date.parse`. When it is set to `false`, the century will no longer be guessed:

```
Date.parse("August 24, 79", false) # 0079-08-24
```

Keep in mind that the default is to guess the century, which may or may not be the one you intend. Two-digit years up to 69 are interpreted as 20XX, whereas years 70 and above are rendered 19XX.

To parse American-style dates, and in fact a huge range of more exotic formats, use the `Chronic` gem (installed with `gem install chronic`). Although it shares the `Time` limits on two-digit years, it provides fairly exhaustive time parsing.

```
Chronic.parse "next tuesday"
Chronic.parse "3 weeks ago monday at 5pm"
Chronic.parse "time to go home" # Well, not every possible time
```

If `Chronic` can't understand a time, it will simply return `nil` instead of raising an exception.

When parsing times, be careful of time zones. CST, for example, has at least five different meanings around the world. See Section 7.22, "Time Zone Conversions," for more information about how to handle times in multiple time zones.

7.21 Formatting and Printing Time Values

You can obtain the canonical representation of the date and time by calling the `to_s` method. This is the same as the result you would get if doing a simple `puts` of a time value.

Similarly, a traditional UNIX format that includes the day of the week is available via the `asctime` method ("ASCII time"); it has an alias called `ctime`, for those who already know it by that name.

The `strftime` method of class `Time` formats a date and time in almost any form you can think of. Other examples in this chapter have shown the use of the directives `%a`, `%A`, `%U`, `%W`, `%H`, `%M`, `%S`, `%I`, and `%p`; we list here all the remaining directives that `strftime` recognizes:

```
%b    Abbreviated month name ("Jan")
%B    Full month name ("January")
%c    Preferred local date/time representation
%d    Day of the month (1..31)
%j    Day of the year (1..366); so-called "Julian date"
%m    Month as a number (1..12)
%w    Day of the week as a number (0..6)
%x    Preferred representation for date (no time)
%y    Two-digit year (no century)
%Y    Four-digit year
%Z    Time zone name
%%    A literal "%" character
```

For more information, consult a Ruby reference.

7.22   Time Zone Conversions

In plain Ruby, it is only possible to work with two time zones: UTC (or GMT) is one, and the other is whatever time zone you happen to be in.

The `utc` method converts a time to UTC (changing the receiver in place). There is also an alias named `gmtime`.

You might expect that it would be possible to convert a time to an array, tweak the time zone, and convert it back. The trouble with this is that all the class methods that create a `Time` object, such as `local` and `gm` (or their aliases `mktime` and `utc`), use either your local time zone or UTC.

There is a workaround to get time zone conversions. This does require that you know the time difference in advance. See the following code fragment:

```
mississippi = Time.local(2014,11,13,9,35) # 9:35 am CST
california  = mississippi - 2*3600         # Minus two hours

time1 = mississippi.strftime("%X CST")     # 09:35:00 CST
time2 = california.strftime("%X PST")      # 07:35:00 PST
```

The %X directive to strftime that we see here simply uses the hh:mm:ss format as shown.

This kind of conversion is not usable around the world, however, because some zone abbreviations are used by multiple countries in different zones.

If you will be converting between time zones frequently, or simply need to accept and manipulate times that include many time zones, the ActiveSupport gem supplies extensions to Time that add thorough time zone support.

```
require 'active_support/time'
Time.zone = -8
Time.zone.name       # "Pacific Time (US & Canada)"
Time.zone.now        # Wed, 25 Jun 2014 12:20:35 PDT -07:00
Time.zone.now.in_time_zone("Hawaii") # 09:20:36 HST -10:00
```

For more information on how to use ActiveSupport to handle the full range of worldwide time zones, see the gem documentation online, especially the TimeWithZone class.

7.23   Determining the Number of Days in a Month

Although there is no built-in function to do this, it is provided by the days_in_month method added to Time by the ActiveSupport gem. Without ActiveSupport, you can easily write a simple method for this:

```
require 'date'
def month_days(month,year=Date.today.year)
  mdays = [nil,31,28,31,30,31,30,31,31,30,31,30,31]
  mdays[2] = 29 if Date.leap?(year)
  mdays[month]
end

days = month_days(5)          # 31 (May)
days = month_days(2,2000)     # 29 (February 2000)
days = month_days(2,2100)     # 28 (February 2100)
```

7.24   Dividing a Month into Weeks

Imagine that you wanted to divide a month into weeks—for example, to print a calendar. The following code does that. The array returned is made up of subarrays, each of size seven (7); Sunday corresponds to the first element of each inner array. Leading entries for the first week and trailing entries for the last week may be `nil`:

```
def calendar(month,year)
  days = month_days(month,year)
  t = Time.mktime(year,month,1)
  first = t.wday
  list = *1..days
  weeks = [[]]
  week1 = 7 - first
  week1.times { weeks[0] << list.shift }
  nweeks = list.size/7 + 1
  nweeks.times do |i|
    weeks[i+1] ||= []
    7.times do
      break if list.empty?
      weeks[i+1] << list.shift
    end
  end
  pad_first = 7-weeks[0].size
  pad_first.times { weeks[0].unshift(nil) }
  pad_last = 7-weeks[0].size
  pad_last.times { weeks[-1].unshift(nil) }
  weeks
end
```

```
arr = calendar(12,2008)    # [[nil, 1, 2, 3, 4, 5, 6],
                           #  [7, 8, 9, 10, 11, 12, 13],
                           #  [14, 15, 16, 17, 18, 19, 20],
                           #  [21, 22, 23, 24, 25, 26, 27],
                           #  [28, 29, 30, 31, nil, nil, nil]]
```

To illustrate it a little better, the following method prints out this array of arrays:

```
def print_calendar(month,year)
  weeks = calendar(month,year)
  weeks.each do |wk|
    wk.each do |d|
      item = d.nil? ? " "*4 : " %2d " % d
```

```
        print item
      end
      puts
    end
    puts
end

# Output:
#        1    2    3    4    5    6
#   7    8    9   10   11   12   13
#  14   15   16   17   18   19   20
#  21   22   23   24   25   26   27
#  28   29   30   31
```

7.25   Conclusion

In this chapter, we have looked at how the `Time` class works as a wrapper for the underlying C-based functions. We've seen its features and its limitations.

We've seen the motivation for the `Date` and `DateTime` classes and the functionality they provide. We've looked at how to convert between these three kinds of objects, and we've added a few useful methods of our own.

That ends our discussion of times and dates. Let's move on to look at arrays, hashes, and other enumerable data structures in Ruby.

CHAPTER 8

Arrays, Hashes, and Other Enumerables

All parts should go together without forcing. You must remember that the parts you are reassembling were disassembled by you. Therefore, if you can't get them together again, there must be a reason. By all means, do not use a hammer.

—*IBM maintenance manual (1925)*

Simple variables are not adequate for real-life programming. Every modern language supports more complex forms of structured data and also provides mechanisms for creating new abstract data types.

Historically, *arrays* are the earliest known and most widespread of the complex data structures. Long ago, in FORTRAN, they were called *subscripted variables*. Today, they have changed somewhat, but the basic idea is the same in all languages.

In the last few decades, the *hash* has also become an extremely popular programming tool. Like the array, it is an indexed collection of data items; unlike the array, it may be indexed by any arbitrary object. (In Ruby, as in most languages, array elements are accessed by a numerical index.)

Finally, we'll take a more general look at the `Enumerable` module itself and how it works. Arrays and hashes both mix in this module, as can any other class for which this functionality makes sense.

But let's not get ahead of ourselves. We will begin with arrays.

8.1   Working with Arrays

Arrays in Ruby are indexed by integers and are zero-based, just like C arrays. There the resemblance ends, however.

A Ruby array is dynamic. It is possible (but not necessary) to specify its size when you create it. After creation, it can grow as needed without any intervention by the programmer.

A Ruby array is *heterogeneous* in the sense that it can store multiple data types rather than just one type. Actually, it stores object references rather than the objects themselves, except in the case of immediate values such as `Fixnums`.

An array keeps track of its own length so that we don't have to waste our time calculating it or keeping an external variable in sync with the array. Iterators also are defined so that, in practice, we rarely need to know the array length anyway.

Finally, the `Array` class in Ruby provides arrays with many useful functions for accessing, searching, concatenating, and otherwise manipulating arrays. We'll spend the remainder of this section exploring the built-in functionality and expanding on it.

8.1.1   Creating and Initializing an Array

The `[ ]` syntax or the class method `[ ]` is used to create an array; the data items listed in the brackets are used to populate the array. The three ways of creating an array are shown in the following lines (note that arrays `a`, `b`, and `c` will all be populated identically):

```
a = Array.[](1,2,3,4)
b = Array[1,2,3,4]
c = [1,2,3,4]
```

There is also a class method called `new` that can take zero, one, or two parameters. The first parameter is the initial size of the array (number of elements). The second parameter is the initial value of each of the elements. Here is an example:

```
d = Array.new            # Create an empty array
e = Array.new(3)         # [nil, nil, nil]
f = Array.new(3, "blah") # ["blah", "blah", "blah"]
```

Look carefully at the last line of the preceding example. A common error is to think that the objects in the array are distinct. Actually, they are three references to the same object. Therefore, if you change that object (as opposed to replacing it with another object), you will change all elements of the array. To avoid this behavior, use a block. Then that block is evaluated once for each element, and all elements are different objects:

```
f[0].upcase!              # f is now: ["BLAH", "BLAH", "BLAH"]
g = Array.new(3) { "blah" } # ["blah", "blah", "blah"]
g[0].upcase!              # g is now: ["BLAH", "blah", "blah"]
```

Finally, the Array() method takes one argument and wraps it in an array if necessary. This is often useful when a variable might be an array or might be a single item because it converts single values into one-element arrays:

```
h = Array(1)      # [1]    non-arrays are wrapped in an array
i = Array([1])    # [1]    arrays stay arrays
i = Array(nil)    # []     nil is ignored
j = Array([nil])  # [nil]  arrays containing nil are left alone
```

8.1.2 Accessing and Assigning Array Elements

Element reference and assignment are done using the instance methods [] and []=, respectively. Each can take an integer parameter, a pair of integers (start and length), or a range. A negative index counts backward from the end of the array, starting at -1.

The special instance method at works like the simple case of element reference. Because it can take only a single-integer parameter, it is slightly faster:

```
a = [1, 2, 3, 4, 5, 6]
b = a[0]                  # 1
c = a.at(0)               # 1
d = a[-2]                 # 5
e = a.at(-2)              # 5
f = a[9]                  # nil
g = a.at(9)               # nil
h = a[3, 3]               # [4, 5, 6]
i = a[2..4]               # [3, 4, 5]
j = a[2...4]              # [3, 4]

a[1] = 8                  # [1, 8, 3, 4, 5, 6]
a[1,3] = [10, 20, 30]     # [1, 10, 20, 30, 5, 6]
a[0..3] = [2, 4, 6, 8]    # [2, 4, 6, 8, 5, 6]
a[-1] = 12                # [2, 4, 6, 8, 5, 12]
```

Note in the following example how a reference beyond the end of the array causes the array to grow. Note also that a subarray can be replaced with more elements than were originally there, also causing the array to grow:

```
k = [2, 4, 6, 8, 10]
k[1..2] = [3, 3, 3]      # [2, 3, 3, 3, 8, 10]
k[7] = 99                # [2, 3, 3, 3, 8, 10, nil, 99]
```

Finally, we should mention that an array assigned to a single element actually inserts that element as a nested array (unlike an assignment to a range):

```
m = [1, 3, 5, 7, 9]
m[2] = [20, 30]          # [1, 3, [20, 30], 7, 9]

# On the other hand...
m = [1, 3, 5, 7, 9]
m[2..2] = [20, 30]       # [1, 3, 20, 30, 7, 9]
```

The method `slice` is simply an alias for the `[]` method:

```
x = [0, 2, 4, 6, 8, 10, 12]
a = x.slice(2)               # 4
b = x.slice(2, 4)            # [4, 6, 8, 10]
c = x.slice(2..4)            # [4, 6, 8]
```

The special methods `first` and `last` return the first and last elements of an array, respectively, and they return `nil` if the array is empty:

```
x = %w[alpha beta gamma delta epsilon]
a = x.first      # "alpha"
b = x.last       # "epsilon"
```

We have seen that some of the element-referencing techniques actually can return an entire subarray. There are other ways to access multiple elements, which we'll look at now.

The method `values_at` takes a list of indices and returns an array consisting of only those elements. It can be used where a range cannot (when the elements are not all contiguous):

```
x = [10, 20, 30, 40, 50, 60]
y = x.values_at(0, 1, 4)         # [10, 20, 50]
z = x.values_at(0..2, 5)         # [10, 20, 30, 60]
```

8.1.3 Finding an Array's Size

The method `length` or its alias `size` gives the number of elements in an array. (As always, this is one greater than the index of the last item.)

```
x = ["a", "b", "c", "d"]
a = x.length              # 4
b = x.size                # 4
```

8.1.4 Comparing Arrays

Comparing arrays is tricky. If you do it at all, do it with caution.

The instance method `<=>`, also called the *spaceship operator*, is used to compare arrays. It works the same as in the other contexts in which it is used, returning either –1 (meaning "less than"), 0 (meaning "equal"), or 1 (meaning "greater than"). The methods `==` and `!=` depend on this method.

Arrays are compared in an "elementwise" manner; the first two elements that are not equal determine the inequality for the whole comparison. (Thus, preference is given to the leftmost elements, just as if we were comparing two long integers "by eye," looking at one digit at a time.)

```
a = [1, 2, 3, 9, 9]
b = [1, 2, 4, 1, 1]
c = a <=> b               # -1 (meaning a < b)
```

If all elements are equal, the arrays are equal. If one array is longer than another, and they are equal up to the length of the shorter array, the longer array is considered to be greater:

```
d = [1, 2, 3]
e = [1, 2, 3, 4]
f = [1, 2, 3]
if d < e                  # false
  puts "d is less than e"
end
if d == f
  puts "d equals f"       # Prints "d equals f"
end
```

Because the `Array` class does not mix in the `Comparable` module, the usual operators <, >, <=, and >= are not defined for arrays. But we can easily define them ourselves if we choose:

```
class Array

  def <(other)
    (self <=> other) == -1
  end

  def <=(other)
    (self < other) or (self == other)
  end

  def >(other)
    (self <=> other) == 1
  end

  def >=(other)
    (self > other) or (self == other)
  end

end
```

However, it would be easier simply to include `Comparable` ourselves:

```
class Array
  include Comparable
end
```

Having defined these new operators, we can use them as you would expect:

```
if a < b
  print "a < b"        # Prints "a < b"
else
  print "a >= b"
end
if d < e
  puts "d < e"         # Prints "d < e"
end
```

It is conceivable that comparing arrays will result in the comparison of two elements for which <=> is undefined or meaningless. The following code results in an ArgumentError because the comparison 3 <=> "x" is problematic:

```
g = [1, 2, 3]
h = [1, 2, "x"]
if g < h             # Error!
  puts "g < h"       # No output
end
```

However, in case you are still not confused, equal and not-equal will still work in this case. This is because two objects of different types are naturally considered to be unequal, even though we can't say which is greater or less than the other:

```
if g != h            # No problem here.
  puts "g != h"      # Prints "g != h"
end
```

Finally, it is conceivable that two arrays containing mismatched data types will still compare with < and > operators. In the case shown here, we get a result before we stumble across the incomparable elements:

```
i = [1, 2, 3]
j = [1, 2, 3, "x"]
if i < j             # No problem here.
  puts "i < j"       # Prints "i < j"
end
```

8.1.5   Sorting an Array

The easiest way to sort an array is to use the built-in sort method, as follows:

```
words = %w(the quick brown fox)
list = words.sort  # ["brown", "fox", "quick", "the"]
# Or sort in place:
words.sort!        # ["brown", "fox", "quick", "the"]
```

This method assumes that all the elements in the array are comparable with each other. Sorting a mixed array such as [1, 2, "three", 4] gives an error.

In a case like this one, you can use the block form of the same method call. The following example assumes that there is at least a `to_s` method for each element (to convert it to a string):

```
a = [1, 2, "three", "four", 5, 6]
b = a.sort {|x,y| x.to_s <=> y.to_s}
# b is now [1, 2, 5, 6, "four", "three"]
```

Of course, such an ordering (in this case, depending on ASCII) may not be meaningful. If you have such a heterogeneous array, you may want to ask yourself why you are sorting it in the first place or why you are storing different types of objects.

This technique works because the block returns an integer (-1, 0, or 1) on each invocation. When a -1 is returned, meaning that x is less than y, the two elements are swapped. Therefore, to sort in descending order, we could simply swap the order of the comparison:

```
x = [1, 4, 3, 5, 2]
y = x.sort {|a,b| b <=> a}     # [5, 4, 3, 2, 1]
```

The block style can also be used for more complex sorting. Let's suppose that we want to sort a list of book and movie titles in a certain way: We ignore case, we ignore spaces entirely, and we want to ignore certain kinds of embedded punctuation. Here, we present a simple example. (Both English teachers and computer programmers will be equally confused by this kind of alphabetizing.)

```
titles = ["Starship Troopers",
          "A Star is Born",
          "Star Wars",
          "Star 69",
          "The Starr Report"]
sorted = titles.sort do |x,y|
  # Delete leading articles
  a = x.sub(/^(a |an |the )/i, "")
  b = y.sub(/^(a |an |the )/i, "")
  # Delete spaces and punctuation
  a.delete!(" .,-?!")
  b.delete!(" .,-?!")
  # Convert to uppercase
  a.upcase!
  b.upcase!
  # Compare a and b
```

```
    a <=> b
end

# sorted is now:
# [ "Star 69", "A Star is Born", "The Starr Report"
#   "Starship Troopers", "Star Wars"]
```

This example is not overly useful, and it could certainly be written more compactly. The point is that any arbitrarily complex set of operations can be performed on two operands to compare them in a specialized way. (Note, however, that we left the original operands untouched by manipulating copies of them.) This general technique can be useful in many situations—for example, sorting on multiple keys or sorting on keys that are computed at runtime.

The `Enumerable` module also has a `sort_by` method (which of course is mixed into `Array`). This is important to understand.

The `sort_by` method employs what Perl people call a *Schwartzian transform* (after Randal Schwartz). Rather than sort based on the array elements themselves, we apply a function to the values and sort based on the results.

For a contrived example, imagine that we had a list of files and wanted to sort them by size. A straightforward way would be as follows:

```
files = files.sort {|x,y| File.size(x) <=> File.size(y) }
```

However, there are two problems here. First, this seems slightly verbose. We should be able to condense it a little.

Second, this results in multiple disk accesses, each of which is a fairly expensive operation (compared to simple in-memory operations). To make it worse, we are doing many of these operations more than once.

Using `sort_by` addresses both these issues. Here is the "right" way to do it:

```
files = files.sort_by {|x| File.size(x) }
```

In the preceding example, each key is computed only once and is then stored internally as part of a key/data tuple. Then the items in the array are sorted based on the stored values returned by the block. For smaller arrays, this may actually *decrease* efficiency, but might be worth it for more readable code.

There is no `sort_by!` method. However, you could always write your own.

What about a multikey sort? Imagine that we had an array of objects and needed to sort them based on three of their attributes: name, age, and height. The fact that arrays are comparable means that this technique will work:

```
list = list.sort_by {|x| [x.name, x.age, x.height] }
```

Of course, you're not limited to simple array elements like these. Any arbitrary expression could be an array element.

8.1.6   Selecting from an Array by Criteria

Sometimes we want to locate an item or items in an array much as though we were querying a table in a database. There are several ways to do this; the ones we outline here are all mixed in from the `Enumerable` module.

The `detect` method will find at most a single element. It takes a block (into which the elements are passed sequentially) and returns the first element for which the block evaluates to a value that tests true:

```
x = [5, 8, 12, 9, 4, 30]
# Find the first multiple of 6
x.detect {|e| e % 6 == 0 }          # 12
# Find the first multiple of 7
x.detect {|e| e % 7 == 0 }          # nil
```

Of course, the objects in the array can be of arbitrary complexity, as can the test in the block.

The `find` method is a synonym for `detect`; the method `find_all` is a variant that returns multiple elements as opposed to a single element. Finally, the method `select` is a synonym for `find_all`:

```
# Continuing the above example...
x.find {|e| e % 2 == 0}          # 8
x.find_all {|e| e % 2 == 0}      # [8, 12, 4, 30]
x.select {|e| e % 2 == 0}        # [8, 12, 4, 30]
```

The `grep` method invokes the relationship operator (that is, the case equality operator) to match each element against the pattern specified. In its simplest form, it returns an array containing the matched elements. Because the relationship operator (`===`) is used, the so-called pattern need not be a regular expression. (The name *grep*, of course, comes from the UNIX command, historically related to the old editor command `g/re/p`.)

```
a = %w[January February March April May]
a.grep(/ary/)      # ["January, "February"]
b = [1, 20, 5, 7, 13, 33, 15, 28]
b.grep(12..24)     # [20, 13, 15]
```

There is a block form that effectively transforms each result before storing it in the array; the resulting array contains the return values of the block rather than the values passed into the block:

```
# Continuing above example...
# Let's store the string lengths
a.grep(/ary/) {|m| m.length}     # [7, 8]
# Let's square each value
b.grep(12..24) {|n| n*n}         # {400, 169, 225}
```

The reject method is complementary to select. It excludes each element for which the block evaluates to true. The in-place mutator reject! is also defined:

```
c = [5, 8, 12, 9, 4, 30]
d = c.reject {|e| e % 2 == 0}    # [5, 9]
c.reject! {|e| e % 3 == 0}
# c is now [5, 8, 4]
```

The min and max methods may be used to find the minimum and maximum values, respectively, in an array. There are two forms of each of these; the first form uses the "default" comparison, whatever that may be in the current situation (as defined by the <=> method). The second form uses a block to do a customized comparison:

```
a = %w[Elrond Galadriel Aragorn Saruman Legolas]
b = a.min                                # "Aragorn"
c = a.max                                # "Saruman"
d = a.min {|x,y| x.reverse <=> y.reverse} # "Elrond"
e = a.max {|x,y| x.reverse <=> y.reverse} # "Legolas"
```

Suppose we wanted to find the *index* of the minimum or maximum element (assuming it is unique). We could use the index method for tasks such as this:

```
# Continuing above example...
i = a.index a.min    # 2
j = a.index a.max    # 3
```

This same technique can be used in other similar situations. However, if the element is not unique, the first one in the array will naturally be the one found.

8.1.7   Using Specialized Indexing Functions

The internals of a language handle the mapping of array indices to array elements through an *indexing function*. Because the methods that access array elements can be overridden, we can in effect index an array in any way we want.

For example, in the following code, we implement a one-based array rather than a zero-based array:

```
class Array1 < Array

  def [](index)
    if index > 0
      super(index - 1)
    else
      raise IndexError
    end
  end

  def []=(index, obj)
    if index > 0
      super(index - 1, obj)
    else
      raise IndexError
    end
  end

end

x = Array1.new

x[1]=5
x[2]=3
x[0]=1  # Error
x[-1]=1 # Error
```

Note that the negative indexing (from the end of an array) is disallowed here. And be aware that if this were a real-life solution, there would be other changes to make, such as the `slice` method and others. But this gives the general idea.

A similar approach can be used to implement multidimensional arrays (as we will see in Section 8.1.11, "Using Multidimensional Arrays").

It is also possible to implement something like a triangular matrix, as shown here. This is like a special case of a two-dimensional array in which element x,y is always the same as element y,x (so that only one need be stored). This is sometimes useful, for example, in storing an undirected graph (as we will see toward the end of this chapter).

```ruby
class TriMatrix

  def initialize
    @store = []
  end

  def [](x, y)
    if x > y
      index = (x * x + x)/2 + y
      @store[index]
    else
      raise IndexError
    end
  end

  def []=(x, y, v)
    if x > y
      index = (x * x + x)/2 + y
      @store[index] = v
    else
      raise IndexError
    end
  end

end


t = TriMatrix.new

t[3, 2] = 1
puts t[3, 2]   # 1
puts t[2, 3]   # IndexError
```

In the preceding example, we chose to implement the matrix so that the row number must be greater than or equal to the column number; we also could have coded it so that the same pair of indices simply mapped to the same element. These design decisions will depend on your use of the matrix.

It would have been possible to inherit from `Array`, but we thought this solution was easier to understand. The indexing formula is a little complex, but 10 minutes with pencil and paper should convince anyone it is correct. Enhancements probably could be made to this class to make it truly useful, but we will leave that to you.

Also, it is possible to implement a triangular matrix as an array containing arrays that increase in size as the row number gets higher. This is similar to what we do in Section 8.1.11, "Using Multidimensional Arrays." The only tricky part would be to make sure that a row does not accidentally grow past its proper size.

8.1.8   Implementing a Sparse Matrix

Sometimes we need an array that has very few elements defined; the rest of its elements can be undefined (or more often zero). This so-called *sparse matrix* has historically been a waster of memory that led people to seek indirect ways of implementing it.

Of course, in most cases, a Ruby array will suffice because modern architectures typically have large amounts of memory. An unassigned element will have the value `nil`, which takes only a few bytes to store.

But on the other hand, assigning an array element beyond the previous bounds of the array also creates all the `nil` elements in between. For example, if elements `0` through `9` are defined, and we suddenly assign to element `1000`, we have in effect caused elements `10` through `999` to spring into being as `nil` values. If this is unacceptable, you might consider another alternative.

The alternative we have to suggest, however, does not involve arrays at all. If we really need a sparse matrix, a hash might be the best solution. See Section 8.2.14, "Using a Hash as a Sparse Matrix."

8.1.9   Using Arrays as Mathematical Sets

Most languages do not directly implement sets (Pascal being one exception). But Ruby arrays have some features that make them usable as sets. We'll present these here and add a few of our own.

For more serious needs, however, consider using the `set` class from the standard library rather than actual arrays. These are covered in Chapter 9, "More Advanced Data Structures."

An array isn't a perfect fit for representing a set because an array can have duplicate entries. If you specifically want to treat the array as a set, you can remove these (using `uniq` or `uniq!`).

The two most basic operations performed on sets are union and intersection. These are accomplished by the `|` (or) and `&` (and) operators, respectively. In accordance with the idea that a set does not contain duplicates, any duplicates will be removed. (This may be contrary to your expectations if you are used to array union and intersection operations in some other language.)

```
a = [1, 2, 3, 4, 5]
b = [3, 4, 5, 6, 7]
c = a | b              # [1, 2, 3, 4, 5, 6, 7]
d = a & b              # [3, 4, 5]

# Duplicates are removed...
e = [1, 2, 2, 3, 4]
f = [2, 2, 3, 4, 5]
g = e & f              # [2, 3, 4]
```

The concatenation operator (+) can be used for set union, but it does *not* remove duplicates.

The − method is a "set difference" operator that produces a set with all the members of the first set except the ones appearing in the second set (see Section 8.1.12, "Finding Elements in One Array But Not Another").

```
a = [1, 2, 3, 4, 5]
b = [4, 5, 6, 7]
c = a - b              # [1, 2, 3]
# Note that the extra items 6 and 7 are irrelevant.
```

To "accumulate" sets, it is possible to use the `|=` operator; as expected, `a |= b` simply means `a = a | b`. Likewise `&=` can progressively "narrow down" the elements of a set.

There is no exclusive-or defined for arrays, but we can make our own easily. In set terms, this corresponds to elements that are in the union of two sets but *not* in the intersection:

```ruby
class Array

  def ^(other)
    (self | other) - (self & other)
  end

end

x = [1, 2, 3, 4, 5]
y = [3, 4, 5, 6, 7]
z = x ^ y                # [1, 2, 6, 7]
```

To check for the presence of an element in a set, we can use the method
include? (or member?, which is essentially an alias mixed in from Comparable):

```ruby
x = [1, 2, 3]
puts "yes" if x.include?(2) # Prints "yes"
```

Of course, this is a little backward from what we are used to in mathematics,
where the operator resembling a Greek epsilon denotes set membership. It is backward
in the sense that the set is on the left rather than on the right; we are not asking "Is
this element in this set?" but rather "Does this set contain this element?"

Many people will not be bothered by this at all. But if you are used to Pascal or
Python (or you have ingrained mathematical inclinations), you may want a different
way. We present an option in the following code:

```ruby
class Object

  def in(other)
    other.include? self
  end

end

x = [1, 2, 3]
if 2.in x
  puts "yes"      # Prints "yes"
else
  puts "no"
end
```

I personally have championed an `in` operator for Ruby. This would be similar to the operator in Pascal or Python or even SQL. The idea has its advantages (and `in` is already a reserved word), but it has been received with mixed popularity. It may or may not ever be part of Ruby. (The Elixr language, which is heavily inspired by Ruby, does implement it.)

Now let's look at subsets and supersets. How do we tell whether a set is a subset or a superset of another? There are no built-in methods, but we can do it this way:

```ruby
class Array

  def subset?(other)
    self.each  do |x|
      return false if !(other.include? x)
    end
    true
  end

  def superset?(other)
    other.subset?(self)
  end

end

a = [1, 2, 3, 4]
b = [2, 3]
c = [2, 3, 4, 5]

flag1 = c.subset? a      # false
flag2 = b.subset? a      # true
flag3 = c.superset? b    # true
```

Note that we've chosen the "natural" ordering—that is, `x.subset? y` means "Is x a subset of y?" rather than vice versa.

To detect the null set (or empty set), we simply detect the empty array. The `empty?` method does this.

The concept of set negation (or complement) depends on the concept of a *universal set*. Because in practical terms this varies from one application or situation to another, the best way is the simplest: Define the universe; then do a set difference.

```ruby
universe = [1, 2, 3, 4, 5, 6]
a = [2, 3]
```

```
b = universe - a   # complement of a = [1, 4, 5, 6]
```

Of course, if you really felt the need, you could define a unary operator (such as – or ~) to do this.

You can iterate through a set just by iterating through the array. The only difference is that the elements will come out in order, which you may not want. To iterate randomly, see Section 8.1.18, "Iterating over an Array."

Finally, we may sometimes want to compute the powerset of a set. This is simply the set of all possible subsets (including the null set and the original set itself). Ruby provides an array method that returns each combination of array elements with length n. The powerset is comprised of the results for every n, from zero to the length of the array:

```
class Array

  def powerset
    (0..length).flat_map{|n| combination(n).to_a }
  end

end

x = [1, 2, 3]
y = x.powerset
# y is now:
#    [[], [1], [2], [3], [1,2], [1,3], [2,3], [1,2,3]]
```

The `flat_map` method uses `map` to get arrays of combinations for each length n, and then combines each result array into a single array that is returned.

8.1.10   Randomizing an Array

Sometimes we want to scramble an array into a random order. The first example that might come to mind is a card game, but there are other circumstances such as presenting a list of questions to a user in a random order.

To accomplish this task, we can use the `shuffle` method:

```
x = [1, 2, 3, 4, 5]
y = x.shuffle      # [3, 2, 4, 1 ,5]
x.shuffle!         # x is now [3, 5, 4, 1, 2]
```

If we wanted simply to pick an array element at random (without disallowing duplicates), we could use `sample`:

```
x = [1, 2, 3, 4, 5]
x.sample    # 4
x.sample(2) # [5, 1]
```

Finally, we should remember that we can generate a predictable sequence (for example, in unit testing) simply by seeding with a known seed using `srand` (see Section 5.27, "Generating Random Numbers").

8.1.11 Using Multidimensional Arrays

For very simple cases, it can be possible to simply nest arrays to create additional dimensions. The following example presents a way of handling multidimensional arrays by overloading the `[ ]` and `[ ]=` methods to map elements onto a nested array. The class `Array3` presented here handles three-dimensional arrays in a rudimentary fashion, but it is far from complete:

```ruby
class Array3

  def initialize
    @store = [[[]]]
  end

  def [](a,b,c)
    if @store[a]==nil ||
       @store[a][b]==nil ||
       @store[a][b][c]==nil
      return nil
    else
      return @store[a][b][c]
    end
  end

  def []=(a,b,c,x)
    @store[a] = [[]] if @store[a]==nil
    @store[a][b] = [] if @store[a][b]==nil
    @store[a][b][c] = x
  end

end
```

```
x = Array3.new
x[0,0,0] = 5
x[0,0,1] = 6
x[1,2,3] = 99

puts x[1,2,3]
```

Note that all we really gain here is the convenience of a "comma" notation [x,y,z] instead of the more C-like [x][y][z]. If the C-style notation is acceptable to you, you can just use nested arrays in Ruby. Another minor benefit is the prevention of the situation in which nil is the receiver for the bracket method.

For more complex multidimensional arrays, there is a Matrix standard library, as mentioned in Section 5.10, "Matrix Manipulation." However, the performance of the standard library is likely insufficient for serious numerical work. Instead, use the nmatrix gem, an optimized multidimensional array library created by the SciRuby project. For more information, see SciRuby.com.

8.1.12   Finding Elements in One Array But Not Another

Finding elements in one array but not another is simpler in Ruby than in many languages. It is a simple "set difference" problem:

```
text = %w[the magic words are squeamish ossifrage]
dictionary = %w[an are magic the them these words]
# Find potential misspellings
unknown = text - dictionary   # ["squeamish", "ossifrage"]
```

8.1.13   Transforming or Mapping Arrays

The collect method (part of Enumerable) is a useful tool that proves to be a time and labor saver in many circumstances. If you are a Smalltalk programmer, this may be more intuitive than if you come from a C background.

This method simply operates on each element of an array in some arbitrary way to produce a new array. In other words, it "maps" an array onto another array (hence the synonym map):

```
x = %w[alpha bravo charlie delta echo foxtrot]
# Get the initial letters
```

```
a = x.collect {|w| w[0..0]}          # %w[a b c d e f]
# Get the string lengths
b = x.collect {|w| w.length}         # [5, 5, 7, 5, 4, 7]
# map is a shorter alias
c = x.map {|w| w.length}             # [5, 5, 7, 5, 4, 7]
```

The in-place variant collect! (or map!) is also defined:

```
x.collect! {|w| w.upcase }
# x is now %w[ALPHA BRAVO CHARLIE DELTA ECHO FOXTROT]
x.map! {|w| w.reverse }
# x is now %w[AHPLA OVARB EILRAHC ATLED OHCE TORTXOF]
```

8.1.14 Removing **nil** Values from an Array

The compact method (or its in-place version compact!) removes nil values from an array, leaving the rest untouched:

```
a = [1, 2, nil, 3, nil, 4, 5]
b = a.compact      # [1, 2, 3, 4, 5]
a.compact!         # a is now [1, 2, 3, 4, 5]
```

8.1.15 Removing Specific Array Elements

It is easy to delete elements from a Ruby array, and there are many ways to do it. If you want to delete one specific element by index, delete_at is a good way:

```
a = [10, 12, 14, 16, 18]
a.delete_at(3)              # Returns 16
# a is now [10, 12, 14, 18]
a.delete_at(9)              # Returns nil (out of range)
```

If you want to delete all instances of a certain piece of data, delete will do the job. It returns the value of the objects deleted or nil if it was not found:

```
b = %w(spam spam bacon spam eggs ham spam)
b.delete("spam")           # Returns "spam"
# b is now ["bacon", "eggs", "ham"]
b.delete("caviar")         # Returns nil
```

The `delete` method also accepts a block. This may be a little counterintuitive; all that happens is that the block is evaluated (potentially performing a wide range of operations) if the object is not found, and the value of the block is returned:

```
c = ["alpha", "beta", "gamma", "delta"]
c.delete("delta") { "Nonexistent" }
# Returns "delta" (block is never evaluated)
c.delete("omega") { "Nonexistent" }
# Returns "Nonexistent"
```

The `delete_if` passes every element into the supplied block and deletes the elements for which the block evaluates to `true`. It behaves similarly to `reject!`, except that the latter can return `nil` when the array remains unchanged:

```
email = ["job offers", "greetings", "spam", "news items"]
# Delete four-letter words
email.delete_if {|x| x.length==4 }
# email is now ["job offers", "greetings", "news items"]
```

The `slice!` method accesses the same elements as `slice` but deletes them from the array as it returns their values:

```
x = [0, 2, 4, 6, 8, 10, 12, 14, 16]
a = x.slice!(2)                        # 4
# x is now [0, 2, 6, 8, 10, 12, 14, 16]
b = x.slice!(2,3)                      # [6, 8, 10]
# x is now [0, 2, 12, 14, 16]
c = x.slice!(2..3)                     # [12, 14]
# x is now [0, 2, 16]
```

The `shift` and `pop` methods can be used for deleting array elements (for more about their intended uses, see Section 9.2, "Working with Stacks and Queues"):

```
x = [1, 2, 3, 4, 5]
x.pop                  # Delete the last element
# x is now [1, 2, 3, 4]
x.shift                # Delete the first element
# x is now [2, 3, 4]
```

The `reject` method takes a block and produces a new array *without* the elements for which the block returns `true`:

```
arr = [1,2,3,4,5,6,7,8]
odd = arr.reject {|x| x % 2 == 0 }      # [1,3,5,7]
```

Finally, the `clear` method deletes all the elements in an array. It is equivalent to assigning an empty array to the variable but is marginally more efficient.

```
x = [1, 2, 3]
x.clear
# x is now []
```

8.1.16   Concatenating and Appending onto Arrays

Frequently we want to append an element or another array onto an array. You can do this in many ways with a Ruby array.

The "append" operator (<<) appends an object onto an array; the return value is the array itself, so that these operations can be "chained."

```
x = [1, 5, 9]
x << 13         # x is now [1, 5, 9, 13]
x << 17 << 21   # x is now [1, 5, 9, 13, 17, 21]
```

Similar to the append operator are the `unshift` and `push` methods, which add to the beginning and end of an array, respectively (see Section 8.1.17, "Using an Array as a Stack or Queue"):

```
x = [1, 5, 9]
x.push *[2, 6, 10]    # x is now [1, 5, 9, 2, 6, 10]
x.unshift 3           # x is now [3, 1, 5, 9, 2, 6, 10]
```

Arrays may be concatenated with the `concat` method or by using the + and += operators:

```
x = [1,2]
y = [3,4]
z = [5,6]
b = y + z         # [3,4,5,6]
b += x            # [3,4,5,6,1,2]
z.concat y        # z is now [5,6,3,4]
```

Bear in mind that +, concat, and even += always create a new array object. Also bear in mind that while << adds to the existing array, it appends a new array element (which may itself be an array):

```
a = [1,2]
b = [3,4]
a += b              # [1,2,3,4]

a = [1,2]
b = [3,4]
a << b              # [1,2,[3,4]]

a = [1,2]
b = [3,4]
a = a.concat(b)  # [1,2,3,4]
```

8.1.17   Using an Array as a Stack or Queue

The basic stack operations are push and pop, which add and remove items at the end of an array, respectively. The basic queue operations are shift (which removes an item from the beginning of an array) and unshift (which adds an element to the beginning). The append operator << can also be used to add an item to the end of an array (basically a synonym for push).

Don't get confused. The shift and unshift methods work on the *beginning* of an array; the push, pop, and << methods work on the *end*.

For a better discussion of this topic, see Section 9.2, "Working with Stacks and Queues."

8.1.18   Iterating over an Array

The Array class has the standard iterator each, as is to be expected. However, it also has other useful iterators.

The reverse_each method iterates in reverse order. It is equivalent to using reverse and then each, but it is faster:

```
words = %w(Son I am able she said)
str = ""
words.reverse_each { |w| str += "#{w} "}
# str is now "said she able am I Son "
```

If we only want to iterate over the indices, we can use `each_index`. Saying `x.each_index` is equivalent to saying `(0..(x.size-1)).each` (that is, iterating over the range of indices).

The chainable iterator `with_index` (mixed in from `Enumerable`) adds the element index to an existing iterator:

```
x = ["alpha", "beta", "gamma"]
x.each.with_index do |x, i|
  puts "Element #{i} is #{x}"
end
# Produces three lines of output
```

Suppose that we wanted to iterate over an array in random order. We show here the iterator `random_each` (which simply uses the `shuffle` method):

```
class Array

  def random_each
    self.shuffle.each {|x| yield x}
  end

end

dwarves = %w(Sleepy Dopey Happy Sneezy Grumpy Bashful Doc)
list = ""
dwarves.random_each {|x| list += "#{x} "}
# list is now: "Bashful Dopey Sleepy Happy Grumpy Doc Sneezy "
# (Your mileage may vary.)
```

8.1.19 Interposing Delimiters to Form a String

Frequently we will want to insert delimiters in between array elements in a "fencepost" fashion; that is, we want to put delimiters between the elements but not before the first one or after the last one. The method `join` will do this, as will the `*` operator:

```
been_there = ["Veni", "vidi", "vici."]
journal = been_there.join(", ") # "Veni, vidi, vici."

letters = ["Phi", "Mu", "Alpha"]
musicians = letters.join(" ")   # "Phi Mu Alpha"
```

```
people = ["Bob", "Carol", "Ted", "Alice"]
movie = people * " and "          # "Bob and Carol and Ted and Alice"
```

Note that if we really need to treat the last element differently, perhaps by inserting the word *and*, we can do it manually:

```
list = %w[A B C D E F]
with_commas = list[0..-2] * ", " + ", and " + list[-1]
# with_commas is now "A, B, C, D, E, and F"
```

8.1.20   Reversing an Array

To reverse the order of an array, use the `reverse` or `reverse!` method:

```
inputs = ["red", "green", "blue"]
outputs = inputs.reverse         # ["green","blue","red"]
priorities = %w(eat sleep code)
priorities.reverse!              # ["code","sleep","eat"]
```

8.1.21   Removing Duplicate Elements from an Array

If you want to remove duplicate elements from an array, the `uniq` method (or its in-place mutator `uniq!`) will do the job:

```
breakfast = %w[spam spam eggs ham eggs spam]
lunch = breakfast.uniq   # ["spam","eggs","ham"]
breakfast.uniq!          # breakfast has changed now
```

8.1.22   Interleaving Arrays

Suppose that we wanted to take two arrays and "interleave" them so that the new array contains an array of paired elements for each of the two original ones. That's what the `zip` method in `Enumerable` does:

```
a = [1, 2, 3, 4]
b = ["a", "b", "c", "d"]
c = a.zip(b)
# c is now [[1,"a"], [2,"b"], [3,"c"], [4,"d"]]
# Use flatten if you want to eliminate the nesting
```

```
d = c.flatten
# d is now [1, "a", 2, "b", 3, "c", 4, "d"]
```

If a block is specified, the output subarrays will be passed successively into the block:

```
a.zip(b) {|x1, x2| puts x2 + "-" + x1.to_s  }
# Prints: a-1
#         b-2
#         c-3
#         d-4
# and returns nil
```

8.1.23   Counting Frequency of Values in an Array

Strings have a count method to discover how many times certain letters are used in the string, but arrays have no similar method. Therefore, here is a method that counts the occurrences of each data item in an Array:

```
class Array

  def counts
    each_with_object(Hash.new(0)){|x,h| h[x] += 1 }
  end

end

meal = %w[spam spam eggs ham eggs spam]
items = meal.counts
# items is {"ham" => 1, "spam" => 3, "eggs" => 2}
spams = items["spam"]   # 3
```

Note that a hash is returned. No pun intended.

8.1.24   Inverting an Array to Form a Hash

An array is used to associate an integer index with a piece of data. But what if you want to invert that association—that is, associate the data with the index, producing a hash? The following method will do just that:

```
class Array

  def invert
    each_with_object({}).with_index{|(x,h),i| h[x] = i }
  end

end

a = ["red","yellow","orange"]
h = a.invert      # {"orange"=>2, "yellow"=>1, "red"=>0}
```

8.1.25 Synchronized Sorting of Multiple Arrays

Suppose we wanted to sort an array, but we had other arrays that corresponded with this one on an element-for-element basis. In other words, we don't want to get them out of sync.

The solution presented here sorts an array and gathers the resulting set of indices. The list of indices (itself an array) can be applied to any other array to put its elements in the same order:

```
class Array

  def sort_index
    d=[]
    each.with_index{|x,i| d[i] = [x,i] }
    if block_given?
      d.sort{|x,y| yield x[0], y[0] }.collect{|x| x[1] }
    else
      d.sort.collect{|x| x[1] }
    end
  end

  def sort_with(ord = [])
    return nil if self.length != ord.length
    values_at(*ord)
  end

end


a = [21, 33, 11, 34, 36, 24, 14]
```

```
b = a.sort_index
a2 = a.sort_with(b)
c = a.sort_index {|x,y| x%2 <=> y%2 }
a3 = a.sort_with(c)

p a        # [21, 33, 11, 34, 36, 24, 14]
p b        # [2, 6, 0, 5, 1, 3, 4]
p a2       # [11, 14, 21, 24, 33, 34, 36]
p c        # [6, 5, 4, 3, 2, 1, 0]
p a3       # [14, 24, 36, 34, 11, 33, 21]
```

8.1.26 Establishing a Default Value for New Array Elements

When an array grows and new (unassigned) elements are created, these default to nil values:

```
a = Array.new
a[0]="x"
a[3]="y"
# a is now ["x", nil, nil, "y"]
```

What if we want to set those new elements to some other value? As a specific instance of a general principle, we offer the ZeroArray class, which defaults new unassigned elements to 0:

```
class ZeroArray < Array

  def [](x)
    if x > size
      (size+1..x).each{|i| self[i] = 0 }
    end
    v = super(x)
  end

  def []=(x, v)
    max = size
    super(x, v)
    if size - max > 1
      (max..size-2).each{|i| self[i] = 0 }
    end
  end
```

```
end
```

```
num = ZeroArray.new
num[1] = 1
num[2] = 4
num[5] = 25
# num is now [0, 1, 4, 0, 0, 25]
```

8.2   Working with Hashes

Hashes are known in some circles as associative arrays, dictionaries, hash maps, and various other names. Python, Java, and Perl programmers in particular will already be familiar with this data structure.

Think of an array as an entity that creates an association between an index x and a data item y. A hash creates a similar association with at least two exceptions. First, for an array, x is always an integer; for a hash, it need not be. Second, an array is an ordered data structure; we typically think of a hash as having no ordering. (That said, Ruby started tracking the ordering of hashes in version 1.9.)

A hash key can be of any arbitrary type. As a side effect, this makes a hash intrinsically a nonsequential data structure. In an array, we know that element 4 follows element 3; but in a hash, the key may be of a type that does not define a real predecessor or successor. However, hashes "remember" their insertion order since Ruby 1.9, in effect making a hash a kind of ordered data structure.

You may think of a hash as an array with a specialized index, or as a database "synonym table" with two fields stored in memory. Regardless of how you perceive it, a hash is a powerful and useful programming construct.

8.2.1   Creating a New Hash

As with `Array`, the special class method `[ ]` is used to create a hash. The data items listed in the brackets are used to form the mapping of the hash.

Six ways of calling this method are shown here (hashes `a1` through `c2` will all be populated identically):

```
a1 = Hash.[]("flat", 3, "curved", 2)
a2 = Hash.[]("flat" => 3,"curved" => 2)
b1 = Hash["flat", 3, "curved", 2]
```

```
b2 = Hash["flat" => 3,"curved" => 2]
c1 = {"flat", 3, "curved", 2}
c2 = {"flat" => 3,"curved" => 2}
# For a1, b1, and c1: There must be
# an even number of elements.
```

There is an alternate "convenience" syntax for a hash literal in the special case where the keys are symbols, added in Ruby 1.9. The preceding colon is omitted and the "arrow" is replaced with a colon:

```
h1 = {:alpha => 123, :beta => 456}
h2 = {alpha: 123, beta: 456}
h1 == h2 # true
```

There is also a class method called new that can take a parameter specifying a *default* value. Note that this default value is not actually part of the hash; it is simply a value returned in place of nil:

```
d = Hash.new           # Create an empty hash
e = Hash.new(99)       # Create an empty hash
f = Hash.new("a" => 3) # Create an empty hash
e["angled"]            # 99
e.inspect              # {}
f["b"]                 # {"a" => 3} (default value is
                       #   actually a hash itself)
f.inspect              # {}
```

Finally, there is a to_h method available on Array. It converts any array of two-element arrays into a hash of keys and values:

```
g = [["a", 1]].to_h  # {"a" => 1}
```

8.2.2   Specifying a Default Value for a Hash

The default value of a hash is an object referenced in place of nil in the case of a missing key. This is useful if you plan to use methods with the hash value that are not defined for nil. It can be assigned upon creation of the hash or at a later time using the default= method.

All missing keys point to the same default value object, so changing the default value has a side effect:

```
a = Hash.new("missing")    # default value object is "missing"
a["hello"]                 # "missing"
a.default = "nothing"
a["hello"]                 # "nothing"
a["good"] << "bye"         # "nothingbye"
a.default                  # "nothingbye"
```

In contrast to `default`, a block can allow each missing key to have its own default. A common idiom is a hash where the default value is an array, so that items can be added without having to explicitly check for a value and create an empty array:

```
a = Hash.new{|h, key| h[key] = [] } # default value is a new []
a["hello"]                 # []
a["good"] << "bye"         # {"good" => ["bye"]}
```

There is also an instance method called `fetch` that raises an `IndexError` exception if the key does not exist in the `Hash` object. It takes a second parameter that serves as a default value. Also, `fetch` optionally accepts a block to produce a default value in case the key is not found. This is similar to default values created by a block:

```
a = {"flat" => 3, "curved" => 2, "angled" => 5}
a.fetch("pointed")                 # IndexError
a.fetch("curved", "na")            # 2
a.fetch("x", "na")                 # "na"
a.fetch("flat") {|x| x.upcase }    # 3
a.fetch("pointed") {|x| x.upcase } # "POINTED"
```

8.2.3   Accessing and Adding Key-Value Pairs

`Hash` has class methods `[ ]` and `[ ]=`, just as `Array` has; they are used much the same way, except that they accept only one parameter. The parameter can be any object, not just a string (although string objects are commonly used):

```
a = {}
a["flat"] = 3          # {"flat" => 3}
a.[]=("curved", 2)     # {"flat" => 3, "curved" => 2}
a.store("angled", 5)   # {"flat" => 3, "curved" => 2, "angled" => 5}
```

The method `store` is simply an alias for the `[ ]=` method, both of which take two arguments, as shown in the preceding example.

The `[ ]` method is similar to the `fetch` method, except that it does not raise an `IndexError` on missing keys, and returns `nil` instead:

```
a.fetch("flat")   # 3
a.[]("flat")      # 3
a["flat"]         # 3
a["bent"]         # nil
```

Suppose that we are not sure whether the `Hash` object exists, and we want to avoid clearing an existing hash. One way is to check whether the hash is defined:

```
a = {} unless defined? a
a["flat"] = 3
```

But a more idiomatic way is as follows:

```
a ||= {}
a["flat"] = 3
# Or even:
(a ||= {})["flat"] = 3
```

The same problem can be applied to individual keys, where you want to assign a value only if the key does not exist:

```
a = Hash.new(99)
a[2]              # 99
a                 # {}
a[2] ||= 5        # 99
a                 # {}
b = Hash.new
b                 # {}
b[2]              # nil
b[2] ||= 5        # 5
b                 # {2 => 5}
```

Note that `nil` may be used as either a key or an associated value:

```
b = {}
b[2]        # nil
b[3] = nil
b           # {3 => nil}
b[2].nil?   # true
```

```
b[3].nil?  # true
b[nil] = 5
b              # {3 => nil, nil => 5}
b[nil]     # 5
b[b[3]]    # 5
```

8.2.4   Deleting Key-Value Pairs

Key-value pairs of a Hash object can be deleted using clear, delete, delete_if, reject, reject!, and shift.

Use clear to remove all key-value pairs. This is essentially the same as assigning a new empty hash but marginally faster.

Use shift to remove an unspecified key-value pair. This method returns the pair as a two-element array, or nil if no keys are left:

```
a = {1 => 2, 3 => 4}
b = a.shift # [1, 2]
# a is now {3 => 4}
```

Use delete to remove a specific key-value pair. It accepts a key and returns the value associated with the key removed (if found). If not found, the default value is returned. It also accepts a block to produce a unique default value rather than just a reused object reference:

```
a = {1 => 1, 2 => 4, 3 => 9, 4 => 16}
a.delete(3)                     # 9
# a is now {1 => 1, 2 => 4, 4 => 16}
a.delete(5)                     # nil in this case
a.delete(6) { "not found" }     # "not found"
```

Use delete_if, reject, or reject! in conjunction with the required block to delete all keys for which the block evaluates to true. The method reject uses a copy of the hash, and reject! returns nil if no changes were made.

8.2.5   Iterating Over a Hash

The Hash class has the standard iterator each, as is to be expected. It also has each_key, each_pair, and each_value (each is an alias for each_pair).

```
{"a" => 3,"b" => 2}.each do |key, val|
  print val, " from ", key, "; "    # 3 from a; 2 from b;
end
```

The other two provide only one or the other of key or value to the block:

```
{"a" => 3,"b" => 2}.each_key do |key|
  print "key = #{key};"       # Prints: key = a; key = b;
end
```

```
{"a" => 3, "b" => 2}.each_value do |value|
  print "val = #{value};"    # Prints: val = 3; val = 2;
end
```

As of Ruby 1.9, iteration order is the same as insertion order.

8.2.6   Inverting a Hash

Inverting a hash in Ruby is trivial with the `invert` method:

```
a = {"fred" => "555-1122", "jane" => "555-7779"}
b = a.invert
b["555-7779"]     # "jane"
```

Because hashes have unique keys, there is potential for data loss when doing this: Duplicate associated values will be converted to a unique key using only one of the associated keys as its value. There is no predictable way to tell which one will be used.

8.2.7   Detecting Keys and Values in a Hash

Determining whether a key has been assigned can be done with `has_key?` or any one of its aliases: `include?`, `key?`, and `member?`.

```
a = {"a" => 1, "b" => 2}
a.has_key? "c"   # false
a.include? "a"   # true
a.key? 2         # false
a.member? "b"    # true
```

You can also use `empty?` to see whether any keys at all are left in the hash. Likewise, `length` or its alias `size` can be used to determine how many there are:

```
a.empty?   # false
a.length   # 2
```

Alternatively, you can test for the existence of an associated value using `has_value?` or `value?`:

```
a.has_value? 2   # true
a.value? 99      # false
```

8.2.8   Extracting Hashes into Arrays

To convert the entire hash into an array, use the `to_a` method. The resulting array will contain two-element arrays of key and value pairs:

```
h = {"a" => 1, "b" => 2}
h.to_a   # [["a", 1], ["b", 2]]
```

It is also possible to convert only the keys or only the values of the hash into an array:

```
h.keys     # ["a","b"]
h.values   # [1,2]
```

Finally, you can extract an array of values selectively based on a list of keys, using the method. This works for hashes much as the method of the same name works for arrays. (Also, as for arrays, `values_at` replaces the obsolete methods `indices` and `indexes`.)

```
h = {1 => "one", 2 => "two", 3 => "three",
     4 => "four", "cinco" => "five"}
h.values_at(3, "cinco", 4)   # ["three","five","four"]
h.values_at(1,3)             # ["one","three"]
```

8.2.9   Selecting Key-Value Pairs by Criteria

The `Hash` class mixes in the `Enumerable` module, so you can use `detect` (`find`), `select` (`find_all`), `grep`, `min`, `max`, and `reject` as with arrays.

The `detect` method (alias `find`) finds a single key-value pair. It takes a block (into which the pairs are passed one at a time) and returns the first pair for which the block evaluates to `true`:

```
names = {"fred" => "jones", "jane" => "tucker",
         "joe" => "tucker", "mary" => "SMITH"}
# Find a tucker
names.detect {|k,v| v == "tucker" }  # ["joe","tucker"]
# Find a capitalized surname
names.find {|k,v| v == v.upcase }    # ["mary", "SMITH"]
```

Of course, the objects in the hash can be of arbitrary complexity, as can the test in the block, but comparisons between differing types can cause problems.

The `select` method (alias `find_all`) returns multiple matches as opposed to a single match:

```
names.select {|k,v| v == "tucker" }
# [["joe", "tucker"], ["jane", "tucker"]]
names.find_all {|k,v| k.count("r")>0}
# [["mary", "SMITH"], ["fred", "jones"]]
```

8.2.10 Sorting a Hash

Hashes are by their nature not ordered according to the value of their keys or associated values. In performing a sort on a hash, Ruby converts the hash to an array and then sorts that array. The result is naturally an array:

```
names = {"Jack" => "Ruby", "Monty" => "Python",
         "Blaise" => "Pascal", "Minnie" => "Perl"}
list = names.sort
# list is now:
# [["Blaise", "Pascal"], ["Jack", "Ruby"],
#  ["Minnie","Perl"], ["Monty","Python"]]
```

Here is how to convert such an array back to a hash:

```
list_hash = list.to_h
```

See also Section 8.2.12, "Creating a Hash from an Array."

8.2.11   Merging Two Hashes

Merging hashes may be useful sometimes. Ruby's merge method merges the entries of two hashes, forming a third hash and overwriting any previous duplicates:

```
dict = {"base" => "foundation", "pedestal" => "base"}
added = {"base" => "non-acid", "salt" => "NaCl"}
new_dict = dict.merge(added)
# {"base" => "non-acid", "pedestal" => "base", "salt" => "NaCl"}
```

An alias for merge is update.

If a block is specified, it can contain logic to deal with collisions. For example, here we assume that if we have two keys colliding, we use the value that is *less* than the other (alphabetically, numerically, or however):

```
dict = {"base" => "foundation", "pedestal" => "base"}
added = {"base" => "non-acid", "salt" => "NaCl"}
new_dict = dict.merge(added) {|key,old,new| old < new ? old : new }
# {"salt" => "NaCl", "pedestal" => "base", "base" => "foundation"}
```

The second result using the block is thus different from the previous example. Also be aware that the mutator methods merge! and update! will change the receiver in place.

8.2.12   Creating a Hash from an Array

The easiest way to create a hash from an array is with the to_h method on an array of two-element arrays. It's also possible to use the bracket method on the Hash class, with either two-element arrays or a single array with an even number of elements:

```
pairs = [[2, 3], [4, 5], [6, 7]]
array = [2, 3, 4, 5, 6, 7]
h1 = pairs.to_h      # {2 => 3, 4 => 5, 6 => 7}
h2 = Hash[pairs]     # {2 => 3, 4 => 5, 6 => 7}
h3 = Hash[*array]    # {2 => 3, 4 => 5, 6 => 7}
```

8.2.13   Finding Difference or Intersection of Hash Keys

Because the keys of a hash can be extracted as a separate array, the extracted arrays of different hashes can be manipulated using the Array class methods & and - to produce the intersection and difference of the keys. The matching values can be generated with the each method performed on a third hash representing the merge of the two hashes (to ensure all keys can be found in one place):

```
a = {"a" => 1,"b" => 2,"z" => 3}
b = {"x" => 99,"y" => 88,"z" => 77}
intersection = a.keys & b.keys
difference = a.keys - b.keys
c = a.merge(b)
inter = {}
intersection.each {|k| inter[k] = c[k] }
# inter is {"z" => 77}
diff={}
difference.each {|k| diff[k] = c[k] }
# diff is {"a" => 1, "b" => 2}
```

8.2.14 Using a Hash as a Sparse Matrix

Often we want to use an array or matrix that is nearly empty. We could store it in the conventional way, but this is often wasteful of memory. A hash provides a way to store only the values that actually exist.

In the following example, we assume that the nonexistent values should default to zero:

```
values = Hash.new(0)
values[1001] = 5
values[2010] = 7
values[9237] = 9
x = values[9237]  # 9
y = values[5005]  # 0
```

Obviously, in the preceding example, an array would have created more than 9,000 unused elements. This may not be acceptable.

What if we want to implement a sparse matrix of two or more dimensions? All we need do is use arrays as the hash keys:

```
cube = Hash.new(0)
cube[[2000,2000,2000]] = 2
z = cube[[36,24,36]]       # 0
```

In this case, we see that literally *billions* of array elements would need to be created if this three-dimensional matrix were to be complete.

8.2.15   Implementing a Hash with Duplicate Keys

Purists would likely say that if a hash has duplicate keys, it isn't really a hash. We don't want to argue. Call it what you will; there might be occasions where you want a data structure that offers the flexibility and convenience of a hash but allows duplicate key values.

We offer a partial solution in Listing 8.1. It is partial for two reasons: First, we have not bothered to implement all the functionality that could be desired but only a good representative subset. Second, the inner workings of Ruby are such that a hash literal is always an instance of the `Hash` class, and even if we were to inherit from `Hash`, a hash literal would not be allowed to contain duplicates.

Listing 8.1   Hash with Duplicate Keys

```ruby
class HashDup

  def initialize(*all)
    all.flatten!
    raise IndexError if all.size % 2 != 0
    @store = {}
    all.each do |key, val|
      self.store(key, val)
    end
  end

  def store(k, v)
    if @store.has_key?(k)
      @store[k] += [v]
    else
      @store[k] = [v]
    end
  end

  def [](key)
    @store[key]
  end

  def []=(key,value)
    self.store(key,value)
  end

  def to_s
    @store.to_s
  end

  def to_a
    @store.to_a
  end
```

```ruby
def inspect
  @store.inspect
end

def keys
  result=[]
  @store.each do |k,v|
    result += ([k]*v.size)
  end
  result
end

def values
  @store.values.flatten
end

def each
  @store.each {|k,v| v.each {|y| yield k, y }}
end

alias each_pair each

def each_key
  self.keys.each {|k| yield k }
end

def each_value
  self.values.each {|v| yield v }
end

def has_key? k
  self.keys.include? k
end

def has_value? v
  self.values.include? v
end

def length
  self.values.size
end

alias size length

def delete(k)
  val = @store[k]
  @store.delete k
  val
end

def delete(k,v)
  @store[k] -= [v] if @store[k]
```

```
      v
   end

   # Other methods omitted here...

end


# This won't work... dup key will ignore
# first occurrence.
h = {1 => 1, 2 => 4, 3 => 9, 4 => 16, 2 => 0}

# This will work...
h = HashDup.new(1,1, 2,4, 3,9, 4,16, 2,0)

k = h.keys         # [4, 1, 2, 2, 3]
v = h.values       # [16, 1, 4, 0, 9]

n = h.size         # 5

h.each {|k,v| puts "#{k} => #{v}"}
# Prints:
# 4 => 16
# 1 => 1
# 2 => 4
# 2 => 0
# 3 => 9
```

As long as you stay away from the hash-literal notation, this problem is doable. In Listing 8.1, we implement a class that has a "store" (`@store`), which is a simple hash; each value in the hash is an array. We control access to the hash in such a way that when we find ourselves adding a key that already exists, we add the value to the existing array of items associated with that key.

What should `size` return? Obviously the "real" number of key-value pairs *including* duplicates. Likewise, the `keys` method returns a value potentially containing duplicates. The iterators behave as expected; as with a normal hash, there is no predicting the order in which the pairs will be visited.

Besides the usual `delete`, we have implemented a `delete_pair` method. The former deletes *all* values associated with a key; the latter deletes only the specified key-value pair. (Note that it would have been difficult to make a single method like `delete(k,v=nil)` because `nil` is a valid value for any hash.)

For brevity, we have not implemented the entire class, and, frankly, some of the methods such as `invert` would require some design decisions as to what their behavior should be. The interested reader can flesh out the rest as needed.

8.2.16   Other Hash Operations

Hashes normally are indexed based on the *value* of the key. If we want to, we can alter the hash to store by the object identity instead. The method `compare_by_identity` will force the hash to this special state, and `compare_by_identity?` will tell which state a hash is in:

```
h1 =  { "alpha" => 1, :echo => 2, 35 => 3 }
h2 = h1.dup.compare_by_identity

h1.compare_by_identity?                      # false
h2.compare_by_identity?                      # true

a1 = h1.values_at("alpha", :echo, 35)        # [1, 2, 3]
a2 = h2.values_at("alpha", :echo, 35)        # [nil, 2, 3]
```

The reason for the preceding behavior, of course, is that symbols and integers are immediate values in Ruby (as are `true`, `false`, and `nil`). Two quoted strings, however, will create different objects with different object IDs.

8.3   Enumerables in General

What makes a collection *enumerable?* Largely it is just the fact of being a collection. The module `Enumerable` has the requirement that the default iterator `each` should be defined. Sequence as such is not an issue because even an unordered collection can have an iterator.

Additionally, if the methods `min`, `max`, and `sort` are to be used, the collection must have a comparison method (`<=>`). This is fairly obvious.

So an enumerable is just a collection that can be traversed, and thus searched, and then possibly sorted. As a rule of thumb, any user-defined collection that does not subclass an existing core class should probably mix in the `Enumerable` module.

Bear in mind that what we say about one enumerable applies in effect to all of them. The actual data structure could be an array, a hash, or a tree, to name a few.

There are, of course, some nuances of behavior. An array is a collection of individual items, whereas a hash is a collection of paired key-value associations. Naturally there will be differences in their behavior.

Many of the methods we looked at for arrays and/or hashes (such as `map` and `find`) really originate here in the `Enumerable` module. In many cases, it was difficult to determine how to cover this material. Any confusion or inaccuracy should be considered my fault.

The array is the most common and representative collection that mixes in this module. Therefore, by default, I will use it as an example.

8.3.1   The `inject` Method

The `inject` method comes to Ruby via Smalltalk. Its behavior is interesting, if a little difficult to grasp at first sight.

This method relies on the fact that frequently we will iterate through a list and "accumulate" a result that changes as we iterate. The most common example might be finding the sum of a list of numbers. Whatever the operation, there is usually an "accumulator" of some kind (for which we supply an initial value) and a function or operation we apply (represented in Ruby as a block).

For a trivial example or two, suppose that we have this array of numbers and we want to find the sum of all of them:

```
nums = [3,5,7,9,11,13]
sum = nums.inject(0) {|x,n| x+n }
```

Note how we start with an accumulator of 0 (the "addition identity"). Then the block gets the current accumulated value and the current value from the list passed in. In each case, the block takes the previous sum and adds the current item to it.

Obviously, this is equivalent to the following piece of code:

```
sum = 0
nums.each {|n| sum += n }
```

So the abstraction level is only slightly higher. If `inject` never fits nicely in your brain, don't use it. But if you get over the initial confusion, you might find yourself inventing new and elegant ways to use it.

The accumulator value is optional. If it is omitted, the first item is used as the accumulator and is then omitted from iteration:

```
sum = nums.inject {|x,n| x+n }

# Means the same as:

sum = nums[0]
nums[1..-1].each {|n| sum += n }
```

A similar example is finding the product of the numbers. Note that the accumulator, if given, must be 1 because that is the "multiplication identity."

```
prod = nums.inject(1) {|x,n| x*n }

# or:

prod = nums.inject {|x,n| x*n }
```

The following slightly more complex example takes a list of words and finds the longest word in the list:

```
words = %w[ alpha beta gamma delta epsilon eta theta ]
longest_word = words.inject do |best,w|
  w.length > best.length ? w : best
end
# return value is "epsilon"
```

8.3.2 Using Quantifiers

The quantifiers `any?` and `all?` make it easier to test the nature of a collection. Each of these takes a block (which of course tests true or false).

```
nums = [1,3,5,8,9]

# Are any of these numbers even?
flag1 = nums.any? {|x| x % 2 == 0 }    # true

# Are all of these numbers even?
flag2 = nums.all? {|x| x % 2 == 0 }    # false
```

In the absence of a block, these simply test the truth value of each element. That is, a block `{|x|  x  }` is added implicitly.

```
flag1 = list.all?   # list contains no falses or nils
flag1 = list.any?   # list contains at least one true value (non-nil
                    #   or non-false)
```

Bear in mind that the `all?` quantifier works in the true mathematical sense. That is, an empty collection will return a true value (because there is no element for which the block is evaluated).

8.3.3   The partition Method

As the saying goes, "There are two kinds of people in the world—those who divide people into two kinds, and those who don't." The partition method doesn't deal with people (unless we can encode them as Ruby objects), but it does divide a collection into two parts.

When partition is called and passed a block, the block is evaluated for each element in the collection. The truth value of each result is then evaluated, and a pair of arrays (inside another array) is returned. All the elements resulting in true go in the first array; the others go in the second:

```
nums = [1, 2, 3, 4, 5, 6, 7, 8, 9]

odd_even = nums.partition {|x| x % 2 == 1 }
# [[1,3,5,7,9],[2,3,4,6,8]]

under5 = nums.partition {|x| x < 5 }
# [[1,2,3,4],[5,6,7,8,9]]

squares = nums.partition {|x| Math.sqrt(x).to_i**2 == x }
# [[1,4,9],[2,3,5,6,7,8]]
```

If we wanted to partition into more than two groups, we could use group_by, which returns a hash, with one key for each result of the given block:

```
nums = [1,2,3,4,5,6,7,8,9]
mod3 = nums.group_by {|x| x % 3 }
# { 0 => [3,6,9], 1 => [1,4,7], 2 => [2,5,8] }


words = %w[ area arboreal brick estrous clear
            donor ether filial patina ]
vowels = words.group_by {|x| x.count("aeiou") } # How many vowels?
# {1 => ["brick"], 2 => ["clear", "donor", "ether"],
#  3 => ["area", "estrous", "filial", "patina"], 4 => ["arboreal"]}

initials = words.group_by {|x| x[0..0] } # By first letter
# {"a" => ["area", "arboreal"], "b" => ["brick"],
#  "c" => ["clear"], "d" => ["donor"], "f" => ["filial"],
#  "p" => ["patina"], "e" =>["estrous", "ether"]}
```

8.3.4 Iterating by Groups

In every case we've seen so far, we iterate over a list a single item at a time. However, there might be times when we want to grab these in pairs or triples or some other quantity.

The iterator `each_slice` takes a parameter, n, and iterates over that many elements at a time. If there are not enough items left to form a slice, the last slice will be smaller in size.

```ruby
arr = [1,2,3,4,5,6,7,8,9,10]
arr.each_slice(3) do |triple|
  puts triple.join(",")
end

# Output:
# 1,2,3
# 4,5,6
# 7,8,9
# 10
```

There is also the possibility of iterating with a "sliding window" of the given size with the `each_cons` iterator. (If this name seems unintuitive, it is part of the heritage of LISP. Think of it as meaning *consecutive*.) In this case, the slices will always be the same size.

```ruby
arr = [1,2,3,4,5,6,7,8,9,10]
arr.each_cons(3) do |triple|
  puts triple.join(",")
end

# Output:
# 1,2,3
# 2,3,4
# 3,4,5
# 4,5,6
# 5,6,7
# 6,7,8
# 7,8,9
# 8,9,10
```

8.3.5   Converting to Arrays or Sets

Every enumerable can in theory be converted trivially to an array (by using to_a). For example, a hash results in a nested array of pairs:

```
hash = {1 => 2, 3 => 4, 5 => 6}
arr  =  hash.to_a           #  [[5, 6], [1, 2], [3, 4]]
```

The method entries is an alias for the to_a method.

If the set library has been required, you can use the to_set method, which works as expected. See Section 9.1, "Working with Sets," for a discussion of sets.

```
require 'set'
hash = {1 => 2, 3 => 4, 5 => 6}
set = hash.to_set          # #<Set: {[1, 2], [3, 4], [5, 6]}>
```

8.3.6   Using Enumerator Objects

An enumerator is basically an object that can be used for external or internal iteration. In internal iteration, we simply iterate over each item in the collection and execute the block for each item in sequence; external iteration means that the code can grab the next item in sequence "on demand."

To understand external versus internal iteration, think of getline as providing an external iterator onto an IO object. You call it at will, and it provides you with data. Contrast that with the internal iterator each_line, which simply passes each line in succession into the code block.

Sometimes internal iterators are not appropriate to the problem at hand. There is always a valid solution, but it may not always be convenient. Sometimes an external iterator is more convenient.

The iterator method each does not require a block. If one is not specified, the method returns an enumerator object:

```
items = [1,2,3,4]
enum = items.each
enum.each {|x| puts x }    # Prints numbers one per line
```

Obviously, in the preceding code fragment, converting to an enumerator is a waste of effort. However, here is an example of external iteration. Imagine we have an array of numbers and names. Each number tells how many words (separate array

elements) are in the next name. We want to extract the names and print them. With
internal iteration, this is inconvenient; but in this example, it is easy:

```ruby
people = [2, "George ", "Washington",
          3, "Edgar ", "Allan ", "Poe",
          2, "John ", "Glenn",
          4, "Little ", "Red ", "Riding ", "Hood",
          1, "Sting"]
enum = people.each
loop do
  count = enum.next      # Grab next item from array
  count.times { print enum.next }
  puts
end
```

Notice that we extract an item from the array with the `next` method. For simplicity, I embedded spaces in the names, and there is no error checking here.

You may be wondering how an apparently infinite loop ever terminates. The
"magic" here is that when we try to take an item that isn't there, we get a `nil` value,
but something else happens. The enumerator raises a `StopIteration` exception,
which is implicitly caught. If this happens other than in a loop, it should be caught
explicitly. Otherwise, the program will terminate with that exception.

The methods `each_slice` and `each_cons` also return enumerator objects:

```ruby
deck = (1..52).sort_by { rand }      # shuffle
dealer = deck.each_slice(5)
hands = []
4.times do |i|
  hands << dealer.next } # not actually how a human deals
end

sequence = %w[In Xanadu did Kublai Khan
              a stately pleasure dome decree]
search_term = %w[stately pleasure dome]
enum = sequence.each_cons(search_term.length)
index = 0

loop do
  triplet = enum.next
  break if triplet == search_term
  index += 1
end
```

```
if index < sequence.length - 1
  puts "Search term found at position #{index}"
else
  puts "Search term not found"
end
```

There is a rewind method that "resets" the internal state to the beginning of the enumerable sequence:

```
list = [10, 20, 30, 40, 50]
enum = list.each
puts enum.next      # 10
puts enum.next      # 20
puts enum.next      # 30
enum.rewind
puts enum.next      # 10
```

The with_index method is a simple (internal) iterator. It can be used with another enumerator, and it returns an iterator itself:

```
list = [10, 20, 30, 40, 50]
list.each.with_index {|x,i| puts "list[#{i}] = #{x}"] }
# or...
enum = list.each.with_index
loop { x, i = enum2.next; puts "list[#{i}] = #{x}" }  # Same result
```

8.4   More on Enumerables

There are many other methods on Enumerable, and I cover most of them here. For convenience, I've divided them a little arbitrarily into four areas: searching and selecting, counting and comparing, iterating, and (finally) extracting and converting.

8.4.1   Searching and Selecting

In addition to other methods I've covered, such as select and reject, there is a method called find_index, which is the "generic" equivalent of an index on an array (in fact, for an array, both these methods will return the same result). This method will do a search for the first object equal to the one passed as a parameter and return the (zero-based) index for that object. Here is an example:

```
array = [10, 20, 30, 40, 50, 30, 20]
location = array.find_index(30)        # result is 2
```

Not every enumerable will necessarily be able to return a meaningful result (for example, a set, which is unordered). In this case, nil will be returned.

The methods first and last will return the first or last n items of the collection (defaulting to 1):

```
array = [14, 17, 23, 25, 29, 35]
head = array.first         # 14
tail = array.last          # 35
front = array.first(2)     # [14, 17]
back = array.last(3)       # [25, 29, 35]
```

There are also two quantifiers: one? and none?. The one? method is easy to understand; the code block must evaluate to true exactly once for it to return true:

```
array = [1, 3, 7, 10, 15, 17, 21]
array.one? {|x| x % 2 == 0 }    # true (one even number)
array.one? {|x| x > 16 }        # false
[].one? {|x| true }             # empty array always returns false
```

But none? might be a little less intuitive. The rule is, it returns true if the block *never* evaluates to true.

```
array = [1, 3, 7, 10, 15, 17, 21]
array.none? {|x| x > 50 } # true (block was false for all elements)
array.none? {|x| x == 1 } # false
[].none? {|x| true }      # true (block is not run on empty array)
```

If the code block is omitted, every item in the collection is tested for truth or falsehood, and they must all test false for none? to return true.

8.4.2 Counting and Comparing

The count method is easy to understand. It may take a parameter, a code block, or neither. In the degenerate case, it simply returns the size of the collection. If an object is specified as a parameter, the number of instances of that object will be counted (using ==). Given a block, it counts the number of items in the collection for which the block returns true.

```
days = %w[Sunday Monday Tuesday Wednesday Thursday Friday Saturday]
days.count                        # 7 in all
days.count("Saturday")            # 1 (there's only one Saturday!)
days.count {|x| x.length == 6 }   # 3 are six letters long
```

We have already seen the min and max methods. These depend on the existence of the spaceship comparison method <=> (or the inclusion of the module Comparable). There is also a method called minmax that returns both at once in an array:

```
days = %w[Sunday Monday Tuesday Wednesday Thursday Friday Saturday]
days.minmax    # ["Friday", "Wednesday"]
```

If we want to compare items by some complex metric rather than a straightforward comparison, the variants min_by, max_by, and minmax_by will take an arbitrary code block (by analogy with sort_by, which we saw earlier in this chapter):

```
days = %w[Sunday Monday Tuesday Wednesday Thursday Friday Saturday]
days.min_by {|x| x.length }    # "Sunday" (though there are others)
days.max_by {|x| x.length }    # "Wednesday"
days.minmax_by {|x| x.reverse } # ["Friday", "Thursday"]
```

The final result contains the first and last elements of the array after it has been sorted in reverse alphabetical order.

8.4.3 Iterating

We've seen almost every form of iteration already. But one that we have missed is cycle, which can iterate over the collection more than once or even "infinitely." The parameter specifies the number of cycles, defaulting to infinity.

```
months = %w[Jan Feb Mar Apr May Jun Jul Aug Sep Oct Nov Dec]
months.cycle(2) {|m| puts m }    # loops 24 times in all
months.cycle {|m| puts m }       # a true infinite loop
```

The each_with_object method works similarly to inject, but it conveniently returns the same object passed into it. This avoids the situation in which you must explicitly return the accumulator at the end of the block, which is ugly. (This example comes from David Alan Black.)

```
h = Hash.new(0)
result = [1,2,3,4].inject(h) {|acc,n| acc[n] += 1; acc } # Ugly

h = Hash.new(0)
result = [1,2,3,4].each_with_object(h) do |n, acc|
  acc[n] += 1 } # Better
end
```

8.4.4   Extracting and Converting

Any enumerable collection can be extracted into an array by using to_a or entries, as we have already seen. There are also ways of intelligently extracting certain parts of the collection into an array.

An example is take and its companion take_while. These methods return a list of items from the front of a collection. In this example, we start with a hash; each "item" in the collection is a key-value pair, returned as a subarray. For another example, we do these same operations on arrays:

```
hash = {1 => 2, 3 => 6, 4 => 8, 5 => 10, 7 => 14}
arr1 = hash.take(2)                   # [[1,2], [3,6]]
arr2 = hash.take_while {|k,v| v <= 8 } # [[1,2], [3,6], [4,8]]
arr3 = arr1.take(1)                   # [[1,2]]
arr4 = arr2.take_while {|x| x[0] < 4 } # [[1,2], [3,6]]
```

The drop method is complementary to take. It ignores (drops) items on the front of the collection and returns the remaining items. There is a drop_while also.

```
hash = {1 => 2, 3 => 6, 4 => 8, 5 => 10, 7 => 14}
arr1 = hash.drop(2)                   # [[4,8], [5,10], [7 => 14]]
arr2 = hash.take_while {|k,v| v <= 8 } # [[5,10], [7 => 14]]
```

The reduce method is also similar in spirit to inject. It applies a binary operation (specified by a symbol) to each pair of items in the collection, or it may take a block instead. If an initial value is specified for the accumulator, it will be used; otherwise, the first value in the collection will be used. So the basic variations are these:

```
range = 3..6
# symbol
range.reduce(:*)                      # 3*4*5*6 = 360
# initial value, symbol
range.reduce(2, :*)                   # 2*3*4*5*6 = 720
```

```
# initial value, block
range.reduce(10) {|acc, item| acc += item }   # 10+3+4+5+6 = 28
# block
range.reduce {|acc, item| acc += item }       # 3+4+5+6 = 28
```

Note that it's impossible to specify both a binary operator symbol and a block together.

Enumerables can also be converted to JSON format (if the `json` library is required) or to a set (if the `set` library is required):

```
require 'set'
require 'json'

array = [3,4,5,6]
p array.to_set  # #<Set: {3, 4, 5, 6}>
p array.to_json # "[3,4,5,6]"
```

8.4.5   Lazy Enumerators

Each `Enumerable` covered in this chapter (and others, such as `Range`) also allows its iteration methods to be called without a block. In that case, an instance of `Enumerator` is returned. That `Enumerator` can be iterated on later or combined with other `Enumerator`s, such as `with_index`, for additional functionality (as we saw in Section 8.1.18, "Iterating over an Array").

More than just combining, though, the `Enumerable` method `lazy` returns a special type of `Enumerator` that calculates the next item only when it is requested. This makes it possible to iterate over groups that are too big to store, like every odd number between 1 and infinity:

```
enum = (1..Float::INFINITY).each  # an Enumerator
lazy = enum.lazy                  # a LazyEnumerator of integers
odds = lazy.select(&:odd?)        # a LazyEnumerator of odd integers

odds.first(5)   # [1, 3, 5, 7, 9]
odds.next       # 1
odds.next       # 3
```

Lazy enumerators provide some new ways to save memory and time while iterating over big groups, so I encourage you to read the `LazyEnumerator` class documentation.

8.5   Conclusion

We've taken a good look here at arrays, hashes, and enumerables in general. We've seen some similarities between arrays and hashes—most of which are due to the fact that both mix in `Enumerable`—as well as some differences. We've looked at converting between arrays and hashes, and we've seen some interesting ways of extending their standard behavior.

We've examined common methods of iteration, such as `each_slice` and `each_cons`. We've also seen how enumerator objects work.

In Chapter 9, we again look at high-level data structures. But these will be slightly higher level and may not necessarily be provided as part of the Ruby core or standard libraries. These include sets, stacks, queues, trees, and graphs.

CHAPTER 9

More Advanced Data Structures

A graphic representation of data abstracted from the banks of every computer in the human system. Unthinkable complexity. Lines of light ranged in the non-space of the mind, clusters and constellations of data. Like city lights, receding.

—*William Gibson*

There are, of course, more complex and interesting data structures than arrays, hashes, and their cousins. Some of the ones we'll look at here have direct or indirect support in Ruby; others are "roll-your-own" for the most part. Fortunately, Ruby simplifies the construction of custom data structures.

The mathematical set can be dealt with by means of arrays, as we've already seen. But recent versions of Ruby have a `Set` class that serves this purpose well.

Stacks and queues are two common data structures in computer science. I have outlined a few of their general uses here. For more detail, there are many first-year computer science books with extensive explanations.

Trees are useful from the perspective of sorting, searching, and simply representing hierarchical data. We cover binary trees here, with a few notes about multiway trees.

The generalization of a tree is a *graph,* which is simply a collection of nodes joined by edges that may have weights or directions associated with them. These are useful in many different areas of problem solving, such as networking and knowledge engineering.

Since sets are the easiest topic, we'll look at them first.

9.1 Working with Sets

We've already seen how certain methods of the `Array` class let it serve as an acceptable representation of a mathematical set. But for a little more rigor and a little tighter coding, Ruby has a `Set` class that hides more of the detail from the programmer.

A simple `require` makes the `Set` class available:

```
require 'set'
```

This also adds a `to_set` method to `Enumerable` so that any enumerable object can be converted to a set.

Creating a new set is easy. The `[ ]` method works much as it does for hashes. The `new` method takes an optional enumerable object and an optional block. If the block is specified, it is used as a kind of "preprocessor" for the list (like a `map` operation):

```
s1 = Set[3,4,5]                  # {3,4,5} in math notation
arr = [3,4,5]
s2 = Set.new(arr)               # same
s3 = Set.new(arr) {|x| x.to_s } # set of strings, not numbers
```

9.1.1 Simple Set Operations

Union is accomplished by the `union` method (aliases are `|` and `+`):

```
x = Set[1,2,3]
y = Set[3,4,5]

a = x.union(y)     # Set[1,2,3,4,5]
b = x | y          # same
c = x + y          # same
```

Intersection is done by `intersection` (aliased as `&`):

```
x = Set[1,2,3]
y = Set[3,4,5]
```

```
a = x.intersection(y)     # Set[3]
b = x & y                 # same
```

The binary set operators don't have to have a set on the right side. Any enumerable will work, producing a set as a result.

The unary minus is set difference, as we saw in the array discussion (refer to Section 8.1.9, "Using Arrays as Mathematical Sets"):

```
diff = Set[1,2,3] - Set[3,4,5]    # Set[1,2]
```

Membership is tested with `member?` or `include?`, as with arrays. Remember the operands are "backwards" from mathematics.

```
Set[1,2,3].include?(2)    # true
Set[1,2,3].include?(4)    # false
Set[1,2,3].member?(4)     # false
```

We can test for the null or empty set with `empty?`, as we would an array. The `clear` method will empty a set regardless of its current contents.

```
s = Set[1,2,3,4,5,6]
s.empty?                # false
s.clear
s.empty?                # true
```

We can test the relationship of two sets: Is the receiver a subset of the other set? Is it a proper subset? Is it a superset?

```
x = Set[3,4,5]
y = Set[3,4]

x.subset?(y)            # false
y.subset?(x)            # true
y.proper_subset?(x)     # true
x.subset?(x)            # true
x.proper_subset?(x)     # false
x.superset?(y)          # true
```

The `add` method (alias `<<`) adds a single item to a set, normally returning its own value; `add?` returns `nil` if the item was already there. The `merge` method is useful for adding several items at once. All these potentially modify the receiver, of course. The `replace` method acts as it does for a string or array.

Finally, two sets can be tested for equality in an intuitive way:

```
Set[3,4,5] == Set[5,4,3]    # true
```

9.1.2   More Advanced Set Operations

It's possible, of course, to iterate over a set, but (as with hashes) do not expect a sensible ordering because sets are inherently unordered, and Ruby does not guarantee a sequence. (You may even get consistent, unsurprising results at times, but it is unwise to depend on that fact.)

```
s = Set[1,2,3,4,5]
puts s.each.first  # may output any set member
```

The `classify` method is like a multiway `partition` method; in other words, it is the rough equivalent of the `Enumerable` method called `group_by`.

```
files = Set.new(Dir["*"])
hash = files.classify do |f|
  if File.size(f) <= 10_000
    :small
  elsif File.size(f) <= 10_000_000
    :medium
  else
    :large
  end
end

big_files = hash[:large]   # big_files is a Set
```

The `divide` method is similar, but it calls the block to determine "commonality" of items, and it results in a set of sets.

If the arity of the block is 1, it will perform calls of the form `block.call(a) == block.call(b)` to determine whether a and b belong together in a subset. If the arity is 2, it will perform calls of the form `block.call(a,b)` to determine whether these two items belong together.

For example, the following block (with arity 1) divides the set into two sets, one containing the even numbers and one containing the odd ones:

```
require 'set'
```

```
numbers = Set[1,2,3,4,5,6,7,8,9,0]
set = numbers.divide{|i| i % 2}
p set #  #<Set: {#<Set: {1, 3, 5, 7, 9}>, #<Set: {2, 4, 6, 8, 0}>}>
```

Here's another contrived example. Twin primes are prime numbers that differ by 2 (such as 11 and 13); singleton primes are the others (such as 23). The following example separates these two groups, putting pairs of twin primes in the same set with each other. This example uses a block with arity 2:

```
primes = Set[2, 3, 5, 7, 11, 13, 17, 19, 23, 29, 31]
set = primes.divide{|i,j| (i-j).abs == 2}
# set is #<Set: { #<Set: {2}>, #<Set: {3, 5, 7}>, #<Set: {11, 13}>,
#  #<Set: {17, 19}>, #<Set: {23}>, #<Set: {29, 31}> }>
```

As I said in the previous section, it's important to realize that the `Set` class doesn't always insist that a parameter or operand has to be another set. (Refer to the discussion of *duck typing* in Chapter 1, "Ruby in Review," if this confuses you.) In fact, most of these methods will take *any enumerable object* as an operand. Consider this a feature.

Other incidental methods can be applied to sets (including all methods in `Enumerable`). I choose not to cover things such as `flatten` here; for more information, consult ruby-doc.org or any other Ruby API reference.

9.2 Working with Stacks and Queues

Stacks and queues are the first entities we have discussed that are not strictly built in to Ruby. By this we mean that Ruby does not have `Stack` and `Queue` classes as it does `Array` and `Hash` classes (except for the `Queue` class in `thread.rb`, which we'll examine later).

And yet, in a way, they are built in to Ruby after all. In fact, the `Array` class implements all the functionality we need to treat an array as a stack or a queue. We'll see this in detail shortly.

Although it is possible to use an `Array` as a stack or a queue, the `Array` class in Ruby is not *thread-safe*. This means that any array is vulnerable to multiple threads modifying it simultaneously and thus corrupting its data. When sharing objects between threads, be sure to use the `Queue` class, immutable data objects, or some other thread-safe data structure.

A *stack* is a last-in, first-out (LIFO) data structure. The traditional everyday example is a stack of cafeteria trays on its spring-loaded platform; trays are added at the top and also taken away from the top.

A limited set of operations can be performed on a stack. These include *push* and *pop* (to add and remove items) at the very least; usually there is a way to test for an empty stack, and there may be a way to examine the top element without removing it. A stack implementation never provides a way to examine an item in the middle of the stack.

You might ask how an array can implement a stack given that array elements may be accessed randomly, and stack elements may not. The answer is simple. A stack sits at a higher level of abstraction than an array; it is a stack only so long as you treat it as one. The moment you access an element illegally, it ceases to be a stack.

Of course, you can easily define a `Stack` class so that elements can only be accessed legally. We will show how this is done.

It is worth noting that many algorithms that use a stack also have elegant recursive solutions. The reason for this becomes clear with a moment's reflection. Function or method calls result in data being pushed onto the system stack, and this data is popped upon return. Thus, a recursive algorithm simply trades an explicit user-defined stack for the implicit system-level stack. Which is better? That depends on how you value readability, efficiency, and other considerations.

A *queue* is a first-in, first-out (FIFO) data structure. It is analogous to a group of people standing in line at (for example) a movie theater. Newcomers go to the end of the line, while those who have waited the longest are the next served. In most areas of programming, queues are probably used less often than stacks.

Queues are useful in more real-time environments where entities are processed as they are presented to the system. They are useful in producer-consumer situations (especially where threads or multitasking are involved). A printer queue is a good example; print jobs are added to one end of the queue, and they "stand in line" until they are removed at the other end.

The two basic queue operations are usually called *enqueue* and *dequeue* in the literature. The corresponding instance methods in the `Array` class are called `unpush` and `shift`, respectively.

Note that `unshift` could serve as a companion for `shift` in implementing a stack, not a queue, because `unshift` adds to the same end from which `shift` removes. Various combinations of these methods could implement stacks and queues, but we will not concern ourselves with all the variations.

That ends our introductory discussion of stacks and queues. Now let's look at some examples.

9.2.1   Implementing a Stricter Stack

We promised earlier to show how a stack could be made "idiot proof" against illegal access. We may as well do that now. Here is a simple class that has an internal array and manages access to that array. (There are other ways of doing this—by delegating, for example—but what we show here is simple and works fine.)

```
class Stack

  def initialize
    @store = []
  end

  def push(x)
    @store.push x
  end

  def pop
    @store.pop
  end

  def peek
    @store.last
  end

  def empty?
    @store.empty?
  end

end
```

We have added one more operation that is not defined for arrays; peek simply examines the top of the stack and returns a result without disturbing the stack.

Some of the rest of our examples assume this class definition.

9.2.2   Detecting Unbalanced Punctuation in Expressions

Because of the nature of grouped expressions such as parentheses and brackets, their validity can be checked using a stack. For every level of nesting in the expression, the stack will grow one level higher; when we find closing symbols, we can pop the corresponding symbol off the stack. If the symbol does not correspond as expected, or if there are symbols left on the stack at the end, we know the expression is not well formed.

```ruby
def paren_match(str)
  stack = Stack.new
  lsym = "{[(<"
  rsym = "}])>"
  str.each_char do |sym|
    if lsym.include? sym
      stack.push(sym)
    elsif rsym.include? sym
      top = stack.peek
      if lsym.index(top) != rsym.index(sym)
        return false
      else
        stack.pop
      end
      # Ignore non-grouped characters...
    end
  end
  # Ensure stack is empty...
  return stack.empty?
end

str1 = "(((a+b))*((c-d)-(e*f))"
str2 = "[[(a-(b-c))], [[x,y]]]"

paren_match str1        # false
paren_match str2        # true
```

The nested nature of this problem makes it natural for a stack-oriented solution. A slightly more complex example would be the detection of unbalanced tags in HTML and XML. The tokens are multiple characters rather than single characters, but the structure and logic of the problem remain exactly the same. Some other common stack-oriented problems are conversion of infix expressions to postfix form (or vice versa), evaluation of a postfix expression (as is done in Java VMs and many other interpreters), and in general any problem that has a recursive solution. In the next section, we'll take a short look at the relationship between stacks and recursion.

9.2.3   Understanding Stacks and Recursion

As an example of the isomorphism between stack-oriented algorithms and recursive algorithms, we will take a look at the classic "Towers of Hanoi" problem.

According to legend, there is an ancient temple somewhere in the Far East, where monks have the sole task of moving disks from one pole to another while obeying certain rules about the moves they can make. There were originally 64 disks on the first pole; when they finish, the world will come to an end.

As an aside, we like to dispel myths when we can. It seems that in reality, this puzzle originated with the French mathematician Edouard Lucas in 1883 and has no actual basis in eastern culture. What's more, Lucas himself named the puzzle the "Tower of Hanoi" (in the singular).

So if you were worried about the world ending... don't worry on that account. And anyway, 64 disks would take $2^{64}-1$ moves. A few minutes with a calculator reveals that those monks would be busy for millions of years.

But on to the rules of the game. (Probably every first-year computer science student in the world has seen this puzzle.) We have a pole with a certain number of disks stacked on it; call this the *source* pole. We want to move all of these to the *destination* pole, using a third (auxiliary) pole as an intermediate resting place. The catch is that you can only move one disk at a time, and you cannot ever place a larger disk onto a smaller one.

The following example uses a stack to solve the problem. We use only three disks because 64 would occupy a computer for centuries:

```
def towers(list)
  while !list.empty?
    n, src, dst, aux = list.pop
    if n == 1
      puts "Move disk from #{src} to #{dst}"
    else
      list.push [n-1, aux, dst, src]
      list.push [1, src, dst, aux]
      list.push [n-1, src, aux, dst]
    end
  end
end
```

```
end
```

```
list = []
list.push([3, "a", "c", "b"])

towers(list)
```

The output produced is shown here:

```
Move disk from a to c
Move disk from a to b
Move disk from c to b
Move disk from a to c
Move disk from b to a
Move disk from b to c
Move disk from a to c
```

Of course, the classic solution to this problem is recursive. And as we already pointed out, the close relationship between the two algorithms is no surprise because recursion implies the use of an invisible system-level stack.

```
def towers(n, src, dst, aux)
  if n==1
    puts "Move disk from #{src} to #{dst}"
  else
    towers(n-1, src, aux, dst)
    towers(1, src, dst, aux)
    towers(n-1, aux, dst, src)
  end
end

towers(3, "a", "c", "b")
```

The output produced here is the same. And it may interest you to know that we tried commenting out the output statements and comparing the runtimes of these two methods. Don't tell anyone, but the recursive version is five times as fast.

9.2.4 Implementing a Stricter Queue

We define a queue here in much the same way we defined a stack earlier. If you want to protect yourself from accessing such a data structure in an illegal way, we recommend this practice.

```ruby
class Queue

  def initialize
    @store = []
  end

  def enqueue(x)
    @store << x
  end

  def dequeue
    @store.shift
  end

  def peek
    @store.first
  end

  def length
    @store.length
  end

  def empty?
    @store.empty?
  end

end
```

As mentioned, the Queue class in the thread library is needed in threaded code. It is accompanied by a SizedQueue variant that is also thread-safe.

Those queues use the method names enq and deq rather than the longer names shown in the preceding example. They also allow the names *push* and *pop*, which seems misleading to me. The data structure is FIFO, not LIFO; that is, it is a true queue and not a stack.

If you need a thread-safe stack class, I recommend you take the Queue class as a starting point. It should be a relatively quick and easy class to create.

9.3   Working with Trees

I think that I shall never see
A poem as lovely as a tree...

—*"Trees," [Alfred] Joyce Kilmer*

Trees in computer science are a relatively intuitive concept (except that they are usually drawn with the "root" at the top and the "leaves" at the bottom). This is because we are familiar with so many kinds of hierarchical data in everyday life—from the family tree, to the corporate organization chart, to the directory structures on our hard drives.

The terminology of trees is rich but easy to understand. Any item in a tree is a *node*; the first or topmost node is the *root*. A node may have *descendants* that are below it, and the immediate descendants are called *children*. Conversely, a node may also have a *parent* (only one) and *ancestors*. A node with no child nodes is called a *leaf*. A *subtree* consists of a node and all its descendants. To travel through a tree (for example, to print it out) is called *traversing* the tree.

We will look mostly at binary trees, though in practice a node can have any number of children. We will discuss how to create a tree, populate it, and traverse it; and we will look at a few real-life tasks that use trees.

We should mention here that in many languages, such as C and Pascal, trees are implemented using true address pointers. But in Ruby (as in Java, for instance), we don't use pointers; object references work just as well or better.

9.3.1   Implementing a Binary Tree

There is more than one way to implement a binary tree in Ruby. For example, we could use an array to store the values. Here, we use a more traditional approach, coding much as we would in C, except that pointers are replaced with object references.

What is required to describe a binary tree? Well, each node needs an attribute of some kind for storing a piece of data. Each node also needs a pair of attributes for referring to the left and right subtrees under that node.

We also need a way to insert into the tree and a way of getting information out of the tree. A pair of methods will serve these purposes.

The first tree we'll look at implements these methods in a slightly unorthodox way. Then we will expand on the `Tree` class in later examples.

A tree is in a sense defined by its insertion algorithm and by how it is traversed. In this first example, shown in Listing 9.1, we define an `insert` method that inserts in a *breadth-first* fashion—that is, top to bottom and left to right. This guarantees that the tree grows in depth relatively slowly and that the tree is always balanced. Corresponding to the *insert* method, the `traverse` iterator will iterate over the tree in the same breadth-first order.

Listing 9.1   Breadth-First Insertion and Traversal in a Tree

```ruby
class Tree

attr_accessor :left
attr_accessor :right
attr_accessor :data

def initialize(x=nil)
  @left = nil
  @right = nil
  @data = x
end

def insert(x)
  list = []
  if @data == nil
    @data = x
  elsif @left == nil
    @left = Tree.new(x)
  elsif @right == nil
    @right = Tree.new(x)
  else
    list << @left
    list << @right
    loop do
      node = list.shift
      if node.left == nil
        node.insert(x)
        break
      else
        list << node.left
      end
      if node.right == nil
        node.insert(x)
        break
      else
        list << node.right
      end
```

```ruby
      end
    end
  end

  def traverse()
    list = []
    yield @data
    list << @left if @left != nil
    list << @right if @right != nil
    loop do
      break if list.empty?
      node = list.shift
      yield node.data
      list << node.left if node.left != nil
      list << node.right if node.right != nil
    end
  end

end


items = [1, 2, 3, 4, 5, 6, 7]

tree = Tree.new

items.each {|x| tree.insert(x)}

tree.traverse {|x| print "#{x} "}
puts

# Prints "1 2 3 4 5 6 7 "
```

This kind of tree, as defined by its insertion and traversal algorithms, is not especially interesting. It does, however, serve as an introduction and something on which we can build.

9.3.2   Sorting Using a Binary Tree

For random data, a binary tree is a good way to sort. (Although in the case of already sorted data, it degenerates into a simple linked list.) The reason, of course, is that with each comparison, we are eliminating half the remaining alternatives as to where we should place a new node.

Although it might be fairly rare to implement this nowadays, it can't hurt to know how to do it. The code in Listing 9.2 builds on the previous example.

Listing 9.2   Sorting with a Binary Tree

```ruby
class Tree

  # Assumes definitions from
  # previous example...

  def insert(x)
    if @data == nil
      @data = x
    elsif x <= @data
      if @left == nil
        @left = Tree.new x
      else
        @left.insert x
      end
    else
      if @right == nil
        @right = Tree.new x
      else
        @right.insert x
      end
    end
  end

  def inorder()
    @left.inorder {|y| yield y} if @left != nil
    yield @data
    @right.inorder {|y| yield y} if @right != nil
  end

  def preorder()
    yield @data
    @left.preorder {|y| yield y} if @left != nil
    @right.preorder {|y| yield y} if @right != nil
  end

  def postorder()
    @left.postorder {|y| yield y} if @left != nil
    @right.postorder {|y| yield y} if @right != nil
    yield @data
  end

end

items = [50, 20, 80, 10, 30, 70, 90, 5, 14,
         28, 41, 66, 75, 88, 96]

tree = Tree.new

items.each {|x| tree.insert(x)}
```

```
tree.inorder {|x| print x, " "}
puts
tree.preorder {|x| print x, " "}
puts
tree.postorder {|x| print x, " "}
puts

# Output:
# 5 10 14 20 28 30 41 50 66 70 75 80 88 90 96
# 50 20 10 5 14 30 28 41 80 70 66 75 90 88 96
# 5 14 10 28 41 30 20 66 75 70 88 96 90 80 50
```

9.3.3   Using a Binary Tree as a Lookup Table

Suppose we have a tree already sorted. Traditionally this has made a good lookup table; for example, a balanced tree of a million items would take no more than 20 comparisons (the depth of the tree or log base 2 of the number of nodes) to find a specific node. For this to be useful, we assume that the data for each node is not just a single value but has a key value and other information associated with it.

In most if not all situations, a hash or even an external database table will be preferable. But we can implement such a search very simply:

```
class Tree

  # Assumes definitions
  # from previous example...

  def search(x)
    if self.data == x
      return self
    elsif x < self.data
      return left ? left.search(x) : nil
    else
      return right ? right.search(x) : nil
    end
  end

end

keys = [50, 20, 80, 10, 30, 70, 90, 5, 14,
        28, 41, 66, 75, 88, 96]
```

```
tree = Tree.new

keys.each {|x| tree.insert(x)}

s1 = tree.search(75)    # Returns a reference to the node
                        # containing 75...

s2 = tree.search(100)   # Returns nil (not found)
```

9.3.4   Converting a Tree to a String or Array

The same old tricks that allow us to traverse a tree will allow us to convert it to a string or array if we want. Here we assume an *in-order* traversal, though any other kind could be used:

```
class Tree

  # Assumes definitions from
  # previous example...

  def to_s
    str = "["
    str << left.to_s << ", " if left
    str << data.inspect
    str << ", " << right.to_s if right
    str << "]"
  end

  def to_a
    array = []
    array << left.to_a if left
    array << data
    array << right.to_a if right
    array
  end

end

items = %w[bongo grimace monoid jewel plover nexus synergy]

tree = Tree.new
items.each {|x| tree.insert x}
```

```
tree.to_a * ", "
# "bongo, grimace, jewel, monoid, nexus, plover, synergy"
tree.to_a
# ["bongo", ["grimace", [["jewel"], "monoid", [["nexus"],
#   "plover", ["synergy"]]]]]
```

Note that the resulting array is as deeply nested as the depth of the tree from which it came. You can, of course, use `flatten` to produce a non-nested array.

9.4   Working with Graphs

A *graph* is a collection of nodes that interconnect with each other arbitrarily. (A tree is a special case of a graph.) We will not delve deeply into the subject of graphs because the theory and terminology can have a steep learning curve. Before long, we would find ourselves wandering out of the field of computer science entirely and into the province of mathematicians.

Yet, graphs do have many practical applications. Consider any ordinary highway map with highways connecting cities, or consider a circuit diagram. These are both best represented as graphs. A computer network can be thought of in terms of graph theory, whether it is a LAN of a dozen systems or the Internet itself with its countless millions of nodes.

When we say *graph,* we usually mean an *undirected graph*. In naive terms, this is a graph in which the connecting lines don't have arrows; two nodes are either connected or they are not. By contrast, a *directed graph* or *digraph* can have "one-way streets"; just because node *x* is connected to node *y* doesn't mean that the reverse is true. (A node is also commonly called a *vertex.*) Finally, a *weighted graph* has connections (or edges) that have weights associated with them; these weights may express, for instance, the "distance" between two nodes. We won't go beyond these basic kinds of graphs; the interested reader can refer to numerous references in computer science and mathematics.

In Ruby, as in most languages, a graph can be represented in multiple ways—for example, as a true network of interconnected objects or as a matrix storing the set of edges in the graph. We will look at both of these as we review a few practical examples of manipulating graphs.

9.4.1   Implementing a Graph as an Adjacency Matrix

The example here builds on two previous examples. In Listing 9.3, we implement an undirected graph as an adjacency matrix, using the `ZeroArray` class (see Section

8.1.26, "Establishing a Default Value for New Array Elements") to make sure that new elements are zero. Also, we inherit from the TriMatrix (see Section 8.1.7, "Using Specialized Indexing Functions") to get a *lower triangular matrix* form.

Listing 9.3   Adjacency Matrix

```
class LowerMatrix < TriMatrix

  def initialize
    @store = ZeroArray.new
  end

end


class Graph

  def initialize(*edges)
    @store = LowerMatrix.new
    @max = 0
    edges.each do |e|
      e[0], e[1] = e[1], e[0] if e[1] > e[0]
      @store[e[0], e[1]] = 1
      @max = [@max, e[0], e[1]].max
    end
  end

  def [](x, y)
    if x > y
      @store[x, y]
    elsif x < y
      @store[y, x]
    else
      0
    end
  end

  def []=(x, y, v)
    if x > y
      @store[x, y]=v
    elsif x < y
      @store[y, x]=v
    else
      0
    end
  end

  def edge?(x, y)
    x, y = y, x if x < y
    @store[x, y]==1
```

```ruby
    end

    def add(x, y)
      @store[x,y] = 1
    end

    def remove(x, y)
      x, y = y, x if x < y
      @store[x, y] = 0
      if (degree @max) == 0
        @max -= 1
      end
    end

    def vmax
      @max
    end

    def degree(x)
      (0..@max).inject(0){|sum, i| sum + self[x,i] }
    end

    def each_vertex
      (0..@max).each {|v| yield v }
    end

    def each_edge
      (0..@max).each do |v0|
        (0..v0-1).each do |v1|
          yield v0, v1 if edge?(v0, v1)
        end
      end
    end

end


mygraph = Graph.new([1,0],[0,3],[2,1],[3,1],[3,2])

# Print the degrees of all the vertices: 2 3 2 3
mygraph.each_vertex {|v| puts mygraph.degree(v)}

# Print the list of edges
mygraph.each_edge do |a,b|
  puts "(#{a},#{b})"
end

# Remove a single edge
mygraph.remove 1,3

# Print the degrees of all the vertices: 2 2 2 2
mygraph.each_vertex {|v| puts mygraph.degree(v) }
```

Note that in the kind of graph we are implementing here, a node cannot be connected to itself, and two nodes can be connected by only one edge.

We provide a way to specify edges initially by passing pairs into the constructor. We also provide a way to add and remove edges and detect the presence of edges. The vmax method returns the highest-numbered vertex in the graph. The `degree` method finds the *degree* of the specified vertex—that is, the number of edges that connect to it.

Finally, we provide two iterators: `each_vertex` and `each_edge`. These iterate over edges and vertices, respectively.

9.4.2 Determining Whether a Graph Is Fully Connected

Not all graphs are fully connected. That is, sometimes "you can't get there from here"; there may be vertices that are unreachable from other vertices no matter what path you try. Connectivity is an important property of a graph to be able to assess, telling whether the graph is "of one piece." If it is, every node is ultimately reachable from every other node.

We won't explain the algorithm in detail here because it is covered in any introductory discrete math text; however, we do offer the Ruby method in Listing 9.4.

Listing 9.4 Determining Whether a Graph Is Fully Connected

```
class Graph

  def connected?
    x = vmax
    k = [x]
    l = [x]
    for i in 0..@max
      l << i if self[x,i]==1
    end
    while !k.empty?
      y = k.shift
      # Now find all edges (y,z)
      self.each_edge do |a,b|
        if a==y || b==y
          z = a==y ? b : a
          if !l.include? z
            l << z
            k << z
          end
        end
      end
    end
    if l.size < @max
      false
```

```
    else
       true
    end
  end

end
```

```
mygraph = Graph.new([0,1], [1,2], [2,3], [3,0], [1,3])

puts mygraph.connected?      # true
puts mygraph.euler_path?     # true

mygraph.remove 1,2
mygraph.remove 0,3
mygraph.remove 1,3

puts mygraph.connected?      # false
puts mygraph.euler_path?     # false
```

I've referenced a method here (euler_path?) that you haven't seen yet. It is defined in Section 9.4.4, "Determining Whether a Graph Has an Euler Path."

A refinement of this algorithm could be used to determine the set of all connected components (or *cliques*) in a graph that is not overall fully connected. I won't cover this here.

9.4.3   Determining Whether a Graph Has an Euler Circuit

There is no branch of mathematics, however abstract, which may not some day be applied to phenomena of the real world.

—*Nikolai Lobachevsky*

Sometimes we want to know whether a graph has an Euler circuit. This term (pronounced *oiler circuit*) comes from the mathematician Leonhard Euler, who essentially founded the field of topology by dealing with a particular instance of this question. (A graph of this nature is sometimes called a *unicursive* graph because it can be drawn without lifting the pen from the paper or retracing.)

In the German town of Königsberg, there was an island in the middle of the river (near where the river split into two parts). Seven bridges crisscrossed at various places between opposite shores and the island. The townspeople wondered whether it was possible to make a walking tour of the city in such a way that you would cross each bridge exactly once and return to your starting place. In 1735, Euler proved that it was impossible. This, then, is not just a classic problem, but the *original* graph theory problem.

And, as with many things in life, when you discover the answer, it is easy. It turns out that for a graph to have an Euler circuit, it must possess only vertices with *even degree*. Here we add a little method to check that property:

```
class Graph

  def euler_circuit?
    return false if !connected?
    (0..@max).each do |i|
      return false if degree(i) % 2 != 0
    end
    true
  end

end

mygraph = Graph.new([1,0],[0,3],[2,1],[3,1],[3,2])
mygraph.euler_circuit?    # false

mygraph.remove 1,3
mygraph.euler_circuit?    # true
```

9.4.4 Determining Whether a Graph Has an Euler Path

An *Euler path* is not quite the same as an Euler circuit. The word *circuit* implies that you must return to your starting point; with a *path*, we are really only concerned with visiting each edge exactly once. The following code fragment illustrates the difference:

```
class Graph

  def euler_path?
    return false if !connected?
    odd=0
    each_vertex do |x|
      if degree(x) % 2 == 1
        odd += 1
      end
```

```
      end
      odd <= 2
  end

end

mygraph = Graph.new([0,1],[1,2],[1,3],[2,3],[3,0])
mygraph.euler_circuit?    # false
mygraph.euler_path?       # true
```

9.4.5   Graph Tools in Ruby

A few graphing libraries are available for Rubyists. The most popular are intended to create graphs on websites using JavaScript, but several can also create images. The most popular pure-Ruby graphing gems are `gruff`, `gnuplot`, and `rubyvis`. Another option is to use the `ruby-graphviz` gem to create a document, and then use GraphViz to render those documents as images or printable Postscript.

In short, there may be a need for more tools of this sort. If you need more than what is already available, I urge you to write your own—or better, join an existing project. If working with graphs becomes easy enough, it may become one of those techniques we wonder how we did without.

9.5   Conclusion

We've taken a look here at the `Set` class in Ruby as well as a few examples of "home-grown" data structures. Where more advanced data structures are concerned, we've seen examples of inheriting from an existing class and examples of limited delegation by encapsulating an instance of another class. We've seen ways to store data creatively, ways to use various data structures, and how to create iterators for these classes.

We've looked at stacks and queues in general, and how they might be used in problem solving. We've also taken a cursory look at trees and graphs.

In the next chapter, we are again looking at the manipulation of data. But where we have so far been concerned with objects stored in memory, we will now be looking at secondary storage—working with files (and I/O in general), databases, and persistent objects.

CHAPTER 10

I/O and Data Storage

On a clean disk, you can seek forever.

—Thomas B. Steel, Jr.

Computers are good at computing. This tautology is more profound than it appears. If we only had to sit and chew up the CPU cycles and reference RAM as needed, life would be easy.

A computer that only sits and thinks to itself is of little use, however. Sooner or later we have to get information into it and out of it, and that is where life becomes more difficult.

Several things make I/O complicated. First, input and output are rather different things, but we naturally lump them together. Second, the varieties of I/O operations (and their usages) are as diverse as species of insects.

History has seen such devices as drums, paper tapes, magnetic tapes, punched cards, and teletypes. Some operated with a mechanical component; others were purely electromagnetic. Some were read-only; others were write-only or read-write. Some writable media were erasable, and others were not. Some devices were inherently sequential; others were random access. Some media were permanent; others were transient or volatile. Some devices depended on human intervention; others did not. Some were character oriented; others were block oriented. Some block devices were fixed length; others were variable length. Some devices were polled; others were interrupt-driven. Interrupts could be implemented in hardware or software or both. We have both buffered and non-buffered I/O. There has been memory-mapped I/O and channel-oriented I/O, and with the advent of operating systems such as UNIX, we have seen I/O devices mapped to files in a filesystem. We have done I/O in machine language, in assembly language, and in high-level languages. Some languages have the I/O capabilities firmly hardwired in place; others leave it out of the language specification completely. We have done I/O with and without suitable device drivers or layers of abstraction.

If this seems like a confusing mess, that is because it is. Part of the complexity is inherent in the concept of input/output, part of it is the result of design trade-offs, and part of it is the result of legacies or traditions in computer science and the quirks of various languages and operating systems.

Ruby's I/O is complex because I/O in general is complex. But we have tried here to make it understandable and present a good overview of how and when to use various techniques.

The core of all Ruby I/O is the IO class, which defines behavior for every kind of input/output operation. Closely allied to IO (and inheriting from it) is the File class. A nested class within File, called Stat, encapsulates various details about a file that we might want to examine (such as its permissions and time stamps). The methods stat and lstat return objects of type File::Stat.

The module FileTest also has methods that allow us to test much the same set of properties. These methods also appear in the File class as class methods. Finally, there are I/O methods in the Kernel module that are mixed into Object (the ancestor of all objects, including classes). These are the simple I/O routines that we have used all along without worrying about what their receiver was. These naturally default to standard input and standard output.

The beginner may find these classes to be a confused jumble of overlapping functionality. The good news is that you need only use small pieces of this framework at any given time.

On a higher level, Ruby offers features to make object persistence possible. The Marshal, YAML, and JSON libraries allow simple serialization of objects, while CSV and SQLite persist data to files on disk.

On the highest level of all, external data stores such as PostgreSQL, MySQL, and Redis provide a way to share a single data store across many Ruby processes. External data stores are complex enough that they have their own books. We will provide only a brief overview to get the programmer started. In some cases, we provide only a pointer to online documentation.

10.1   Working with Files and Directories

When we say *file*, we usually mean a disk file, though not always. We do use the concept of a file as a meaningful abstraction in Ruby as in other programming languages. When we say *directory*, we mean a directory in the normal Windows or UNIX sense.

The `File` class is closely related to the `IO` class from which it inherits. The `Dir` class is not so closely related, but we chose to discuss files and directories together because they are still conceptually related.

10.1.1   Opening and Closing Files

The class method `File.new` instantiates a `File` object and opens the file. The first parameter is naturally the filename.

The optional second parameter is called the *mode string* and tells how to open the file, whether for reading, writing, and so on. (The mode string has nothing to do with the mode as in permissions.) This defaults to `"r"` for reading. The following code demonstrates opening files for reading and writing:

```
file1 = File.new("one")        # Open for reading
file2 = File.new("two", "w")   # Open for writing
```

Another form for `new` takes three parameters. In this case, the second parameter specifies the original permissions for the file (usually as an octal constant), and the third is a set of flags ORed together. The flags are constants such as `File::CREAT` (create the file when it is opened if it doesn't already exist) and `File::RDONLY` (open for reading only). This form will rarely be used.

```
file = File.new("three", 0755, File::CREAT|File::WRONLY)
```

As a courtesy to the operating system and the runtime environment, always close a file that you open. In the case of a file open for writing, this is more than mere politeness and can actually prevent lost data. Not surprisingly, the `close` method serves this purpose:

```
out = File.new("captains.log", "w")
# Process as needed...
out.close
```

There is also an open method. In its simplest form, it is merely a synonym for new, as we see here:

```
trans = File.open("transactions","w")
```

But open can also take a block; this is the form that is more interesting. When a block is specified, the open file is passed in as a parameter to the block. The file remains open throughout the scope of the block and is closed automatically at the end. Here is an example:

```
File.open("somefile","w") do |file|
  file.puts "Line 1"
  file.puts "Line 2"
  file.puts "Third and final line"
end
# The file is now closed
```

This is obviously an elegant way of ensuring that a file is closed when we've finished with it. In addition, the code that handles the file is grouped visually into a unit.

The reopen method will associate a new stream with its receiver. In this example, we turn off output to standard error, and later we turn it back on:

```
save = STDERR.dup
STDERR.reopen("/dev/null")
# Quiet now...
STDERR.reopen(save)
```

10.1.2   Updating a File

Suppose that we want to open a file for reading and writing. This is done simply by adding a plus sign (+) in the file mode when we open the file (see Section 10.1.1, "Opening and Closing Files"):

```
f1 = File.new("file1", "r+")
# Read/write, starting at beginning of file.

f2 = File.new("file2", "w+")
# Read/write; truncate existing file or create a new one.

f3 = File.new("file3", "a+")
# Read/write; start at end of existing file or create a
# new one.
```

10.1.3   Appending to a File

Suppose that we want to append information onto an existing file. This is done simply by using `"a"` in the file mode when we open the file (see Section 10.1.1, "Opening and Closing Files"):

```
logfile = File.open("captains_log", "a")
# Add a line at the end, then close.
logfile.puts "Stardate 47824.1: Our show has been canceled."
logfile.close
```

10.1.4   Random Access to Files

If you want to read a file randomly rather than sequentially, you can use the method seek, which File inherits from IO. The simplest usage is to seek to a specific byte position. The position is relative to the beginning of the file, where the first byte is numbered 0.

```
# myfile contains only: abcdefghi
file = File.new("myfile")
file.seek(5)
str = file.gets                   # "fghi"
```

If you took care to ensure that each line was a fixed length, you could seek to a specific line, as in the following example:

```
# Assume 20 bytes per line.
# Line N starts at byte (N-1)*20
file = File.new("fixedlines")
file.seek(5*20)                   # Sixth line!
# Elegance is left as an exercise.
```

If you want to do a relative seek, you can use a second parameter. The constant IO::SEEK_CUR assumes that the offset is relative to the current position (which may be negative):

```
file = File.new("somefile")
file.seek(55)                   # Position is 55
file.seek(-22, IO::SEEK_CUR)    # Position is 33
file.seek(47, IO::SEEK_CUR)     # Position is 80
```

You can also seek relative to the end of the file. Only a negative offset makes sense here:

```
file.seek(-20, IO::SEEK_END)   # twenty bytes from eof
```

There is also a third constant, IO::SEEK_SET, but it is the default value (seek relative to beginning of file).

The method tell reports the file position; pos is an alias:

```
file.seek(20)
pos1 = file.tell              # 20
file.seek(50, IO::SEEK_CUR)
pos2 = file.pos               # 70
```

The rewind method can also be used to reposition the file pointer at the beginning. This terminology comes from the use of magnetic tapes.

If you are performing random access on a file, you may want to open it for update (reading and writing). Updating a file is done by specifying a plus sign (+) in the mode string. See Section 10.1.2, "Updating a File."

10.1.5   Working with Binary Files

Although every file is ultimately binary code, *binary* is colloquially used to mean data that is not readable as text. It may be compressed, encrypted, or contain audio or video data.

To tell Ruby it will read binary data, add the "b" character to the mode string when opening a file. The resulting string will always have the encoding ASCII-8BIT, which is a string of bytes without any encoding.

Binary mode allows reading and manipulating bytes that are invalid in an encoding:

```
File.write("invalid", "\xFC\x80\x80 \x80\x80\xAF")
File.read("invalid", mode: "r").split(" ")
# invalid byte sequence in UTF-8
File.read("invalid", mode: "rb").split(" ")
# ["\xFC\x80", "\x80\xAF"]
```

On Windows, binary mode also means that each line break is not translated into a single \n linefeed but is kept as the \r\n carriage-return/linefeed pair.

Another important difference is that Ctrl+Z is treated as end-of-file in non-binary mode, as shown here:

```
# myfile contains "12345\0326789\r".
# Note the embedded octal 032 (^Z)
File.open("myfile","rb") {|f| str = f.sysread(15) }.size  # 11
File.open("myfile","r")  {|f| str = f.sysread(15) }.size  # 5
```

The following code fragment shows that carriage returns remain untranslated in binary mode on Windows:

```
# Input file contains a single line: Line 1.
file = File.open("data")
line = file.readline              # "Line 1.\n"
puts "#{line.size} characters."   # 8 characters
file.close

file = File.open("data","rb")
line = file.readline              # "Line 1.\r\n"
puts "#{line.size} characters."   # 9 characters
file.close
```

Note that the `binmode` method, shown in the following code example, can switch a stream to binary mode. Once switched, it cannot be switched back.

```
file = File.open("data")
file.binmode
line = file.readline              # "Line 1.\r\n"
puts "#{line.size} characters."   # 9 characters
file.close
```

If you really want to do low-level input/output, you can use the `sysread` and `syswrite` methods. The former takes a number of bytes as a parameter; the latter takes a string and returns the actual number of bytes written. (You should *not* use other methods to read from the same stream; the results may be unpredictable.)

```
input = File.new("infile")
output = File.new("outfile")
instr = input.sysread(10);
bytes = output.syswrite("This is a test.")
```

Note that `sysread` raises `EOFError` if it is invoked at end-of-file (though not if it encounters end-of-file during a successful read). Either of these methods will raise `SystemCallError` when an error occurs.

The `Array` method `pack` and the `String` method `unpack` can be useful in dealing with binary data.

10.1.6   Locking Files

On operating systems where it is supported, the `flock` method of `File` will lock or unlock a file. The second parameter is one of these constants: `File::LOCK_EX`, `File::LOCK_NB`, `File::LOCK_SH`, `File::LOCK_UN`, or a logical-OR of two or more of these. Note, of course, that many of these combinations will be nonsensical; the nonblocking flag is the one most frequently used:

```
file = File.new("somefile")

file.flock(File::LOCK_EX)    # Lock exclusively; no other process
                             # may use this file.
file.flock(File::LOCK_UN)    # Now unlock it.

file.flock(File::LOCK_SH)    # Lock file with a shared lock
                             # (other processes may do the same).
file.flock(File::LOCK_UN)    # Now unlock it.

locked = file.flock(File::LOCK_EX | File::LOCK_NB)
# Try to lock the file, but don't block if we can't; in that
# case, locked will be false.
```

This function is not available on the Windows family of operating systems.

10.1.7   Performing Simple I/O

You are already familiar with some of the I/O routines in the `Kernel` module; these are the ones we have called all along without specifying a receiver for the methods. Calls such as `gets` and `puts` originate here; others are `print`, `printf`, and `p` (which calls the object's `inspect` method to display it in some way readable to humans).

There are some others that we should mention for completeness, though. The `putc` method outputs a single character. (The corresponding method `getc` is *not* implemented in `Kernel` for technical reasons; it can be found in any `IO` object, however.) If a `String` is specified, the first character of the string will be taken.

```
putc(?\n)    # Output a newline
putc("X")    # Output the letter X
```

A reasonable question is, where does output go when we use these methods without a receiver? Well, to begin with, three constants are defined in the Ruby environment, corresponding to the three standard I/O streams we are accustomed to on UNIX. These are STDIN, STDOUT, and STDERR. All are global constants of the type IO.

There is also a global variable called $stdout, which is the destination of all the output coming from Kernel methods. This is initialized (indirectly) to the value of STDOUT so that this output all gets written to standard output as we expect. The variable $stdout can be reassigned to refer to some other IO object at any time.

```
diskfile = File.new("foofile","w")
puts "Hello..."       # prints to stdout
$stdout = diskfile
puts "Goodbye!"       # prints to "foofile"
diskfile.close
$stdout = STDOUT      # reassign to default
puts "That's all."    # prints to stdout
```

Beside gets, Kernel also has the methods readline and readlines for input. The former is equivalent to gets, except that it raises EOFError at the end of a file instead of just returning a nil value. The latter is equivalent to the IO.readlines method (that is, it reads an entire file into memory).

Where does input come from? Well, there is also the standard input stream $stdin, which defaults to STDIN. In the same way, there is a standard error stream ($stderr, which defaults to STDERR).

There is also an interesting global object called ARGF, which represents the concatenation of all the files named on the command line. It is not really a File object, though it resembles one. Default input is connected to this object in the event files are named on the command line.

```
# cat.rb
# Read all files, then output again
puts ARGF.read
# Or more memory-efficient:
puts ARGF.readline until ARGF.eof?
# Example usage:  ruby cat.rb file1 file2 file3
```

Reading from standard input (STDIN) will bypass the `Kernel` methods. That way, you can bypass ARGF (or not), as shown here:

```
# Read a line from standard input
str1 = STDIN.gets
# Read a line from ARGF
str2 = ARGF.gets
# Now read again from standard input
str3 = STDIN.gets
```

It is possible to read at the character and byte levels as well. In a single-byte encoding, these will be essentially the same, except that a byte is a `Fixnum`, and character is a single-character string:

```
c = input.getc
b = input.getbyte
input.ungetc          # These two operations are not
input.ungetbyte       #   always possible.
b = input.readbyte    # Like getbyte, but can raise EOFError
```

10.1.8   Performing Buffered and Unbuffered I/O

Ruby does its own internal buffering in some cases. Consider this fragment:

```
print "Hello... "
sleep 5
print "Goodbye!\n"
```

If you run this, you will notice that the hello and goodbye messages both appear at the same time, *after* the sleep. The first output is not terminated by a newline.

This can be fixed by calling `flush` to flush the output buffer. In this case, we use the stream $defout (the default stream for all `Kernel` method output) as the receiver. It then behaves as we probably wanted, with the first message appearing earlier than the second one:

```
print "Hello... "
STDOUT.flush
sleep 10
print "Goodbye!\n"
```

This buffering can be turned off (or on) with the `sync=` method; the `sync` method lets us know the status:

```
buf_flag = $defout.sync      # true
STDOUT.sync = false
buf_flag = STDOUT.sync       # false
```

There is also at least one lower level of buffering going on behind the scenes. Just as the `getc` method returns a character and moves the file or stream pointer, `ungetc` will push a character back onto the stream:

```
ch = mystream.getc      # ?A
mystream.ungetc(?C)
ch = mystream.getc      # ?C
```

You should be aware of three things. First, the buffering we speak of here is unrelated to the buffering mentioned earlier in this section; in other words, `sync=false` won't turn it off. Second, only one character can be pushed back; if you attempt more than one, only the last one will actually be pushed back onto the input stream. Finally, the `ungetc` method will not work for inherently unbuffered read operations (such as `sysread`).

10.1.9   Manipulating File Ownership and Permissions

The issue of file ownership and permissions is highly platform dependent. Typically, UNIX provides a superset of the functionality; for other platforms, many features may be unimplemented.

To determine the owner and group of a file (which are integers), `File::Stat` has a pair of instance methods, `uid` and `gid`, as shown here:

```
data = File.stat("somefile")
owner_id = data.uid
group_id = data.gid
```

Class `File::Stat` has an instance method called `mode` that returns the mode (or permissions) of the file:

```
perms = File.stat("somefile").mode
```

File has class and instance methods named chown to change the owner and group IDs of a file. The class method accepts an arbitrary number of filenames. Where an ID is not to be changed, nil or -1 can be used:

```
uid = 201
gid = 10
File.chown(uid, gid, "alpha", "beta")
f1 = File.new("delta")
f1.chown(uid, gid)
f2 = File.new("gamma")
f2.chown(nil, gid)        # Keep original owner id
```

Likewise, the permissions can be changed by chmod (also implemented both as class and instance methods). The permissions are traditionally represented in octal, though they need not be:

```
File.chmod(0644, "epsilon", "theta")
f = File.new("eta")
f.chmod(0444)
```

A process always runs under the identity of some user (possibly root); as such, there is a user ID associated with it. (Here, we are talking about the *effective* user ID.) We frequently need to know whether that user has permission to read, write, or execute a given file. There are instance methods in File::Stat to make this determination:

```
info = File.stat("/tmp/secrets")
rflag = info.readable?
wflag = info.writable?
xflag = info.executable?
```

Sometimes we need to distinguish between the effective user ID and the real user ID. The appropriate instance methods are readable_real?, writable_real?, and executable_real?, respectively.

```
info = File.stat("/tmp/secrets")
rflag2 = info.readable_real?
wflag2 = info.writable_real?
xflag2 = info.executable_real?
```

We can test the ownership of the file as compared with the effective user ID (and group ID) of the current process. The class `File::Stat` has the instance methods `owned?` and `grpowned?` to accomplish this.

Note that many of these methods can also be found in the module `FileTest`:

```
rflag = FileTest::readable?("pentagon_files")
# Other methods are: writable? executable?
#   readable_real? writable_real?
# executable_real? owned? grpowned?
# Not found here: uid gid mode
```

The `umask` associated with a process determines the initial permissions of new files created. The standard mode 0777 is logically ANDed with the negation of the `umask` so that the bits set in the `umask` are "masked" or cleared. If you prefer, you can think of this as a simple subtraction (without borrowing). Thus, a `umask` of 022 results in files being created with a mode of 0755.

The `umask` can be retrieved or set with the class method `umask` of class `File`. If a parameter is specified, the `umask` will be set to that value (and the previous value will be returned).

```
File.umask(0237)              # Set the umask
current_umask = File.umask    # 0237
```

Some file mode bits (such as the *sticky bit*) are not strictly related to permissions. For a discussion of these, see Section 10.1.12, "Checking Special File Characteristics."

10.1.10   Retrieving and Setting Timestamp Information

Each disk file has multiple timestamps associated with it (though there are some variations between operating systems). The three timestamps that Ruby understands are the modification time (the last time the file contents were changed), the access time (the last time the file was read), and the change time (the last time the file's directory information was changed).

These three pieces of information can be accessed in three different ways. Each of these fortunately gives the same result.

The `File` class methods `mtime`, `atime`, and `ctime` return the times without the file being opened or any `File` object being instantiated.

```
t1 = File.mtime("somefile")
```

```
# Thu Jan 04 09:03:10 GMT-6:00 2001
t2 = File.atime("somefile")
# Tue Jan 09 10:03:34 GMT-6:00 2001
t3 = File.ctime("somefile")
# Sun Nov 26 23:48:32 GMT-6:00 2000
```

If there happens to be a `File` instance already created, the instance method can be used:

```
myfile = File.new("somefile")
t1 = myfile.mtime
t2 = myfile.atime
t3 = myfile.ctime
```

And if there happens to be a `File::Stat` instance already created, it has instance methods to do the same thing:

```
myfile = File.new("somefile")
info = myfile.stat
t1 = info.mtime
t2 = info.atime
t3 = info.ctime
```

Note that a `File::Stat` is returned by `File`'s class (or instance) method `stat`. The class method `lstat` (or the instance method of the same name) is identical except that it reports on the status of the link itself instead of following the link to the actual file. In the case of links to links, all links are followed but the last one.

File access and modification times may be changed using the `utime` method. It will change the times on one or more files specified. The times may be given either as `Time` objects or a number of seconds since the epoch:

```
today = Time.now
yesterday = today - 86400
File.utime(today, today, "alpha")
File.utime(today, yesterday, "beta", "gamma")
```

Because both times are changed together, if you want to leave one of them unchanged, you have to save it off first:

```
mtime = File.mtime("delta")
File.utime(Time.now, mtime, "delta")
```

10.1.11 Checking File Existence and Size

One fundamental question we sometimes want to know is whether a file of a given name exists. The `exist?` method in the `File` class provides a way to find out:

```
flag = File.exist?("LochNessMonster")
flag = File.exists?("UFO")
# exists? is a synonym for exist?
```

Related to the question of a file's existence is the question of whether it has any contents. After all, a file may exist but have zero length (which is the next best thing to not existing).

If we are only interested in this yes/no question, `File` has two instance methods that are useful. The method `zero?` returns `true` if the file is zero length and `false` otherwise:

```
flag = File.zero?("somefile")
```

Conversely, the method `size?` returns either the size of the file in bytes if it is nonzero length, or the value `nil` if it is zero length. It may not be immediately obvious why `nil` is returned rather than `0`. The answer is that the method is primarily intended for use as a predicate, and `0` is true in Ruby, whereas `nil` tests as false.

```
if File.size?("myfile")
  puts "The file has contents."
else
  puts "The file is empty."
end
```

This leads naturally to the question, how big is this file? We've already seen that in the case of a nonempty file, `size?` returns the length; but if we're not using it as a predicate, the `nil` value would confuse us.

The `File` class has both class and instance methods to give us this answer:

```
size1 = File.size("filename")  # returns 0 if filename is empty
```

If we want the file size in blocks rather than bytes, we can use the instance method `blocks` in `File::Stat`. This is certainly dependent on the operating system. (The method `blksize` also reports on the operating system's idea of how big a block is.)

```
info = File.stat("somefile")
total_bytes = info.blocks * info.blksize
```

10.1.12   Checking Special File Characteristics

There are numerous aspects of a file that we can test. We summarize here the relevant built-in methods that we don't discuss elsewhere. Most, though not all, are predicates.

Bear in mind two facts throughout this section (and most of this chapter). First, any test that can be done by invoking the class method may also be called as an instance method of any file object. Second, remember that there is a high degree of overlap between `File` and the `File::Stat` object returned by `stat` (or `lstat`). In some cases, there will be different ways to call what is essentially the same method. We won't necessarily show this every time.

Some operating systems have the concept of block-oriented devices as opposed to character-oriented devices. A file may refer to either but not both. The methods `blockdev?` and `chardev?` in the `FileTest` module tests for this:

```
flag1 = File.chardev?("/dev/hdisk0")  # false
flag2 = File.blockdev?("/dev/hdisk0") # true
```

Sometimes we want to know whether the stream is associated with a terminal. The `IO` class method `tty?` tests for this (as does the synonym `isatty`):

```
flag1 = STDIN.tty?                     # true
flag2 = File.new("diskfile").isatty   # false
```

A stream can be a pipe or a socket. There are corresponding `FileTest` methods to test for these cases:

```
flag1 = File.pipe?(myfile)
flag2 = File.socket?(myfile)
```

Recall that a directory is really just a special case of a file. Therefore, we need to be able to distinguish between directories and ordinary files, which a pair of methods enable us to do:

```
file1 = File.new("/tmp")
file2 = File.new("/tmp/myfile")
test1 = file1.directory?        # true
test2 = file1.file?             # false
test3 = file2.directory?        # false
test4 = file2.file?             # true
```

There is also a `File` class method named `ftype`, which tells us what kind of thing a stream is; it can also be found as an instance method in the `File::Stat` class. This method returns a string that has one of the following values: `file`, `directory`, `blockSpecial`, `characterSpecial`, `fifo`, `link`, or `socket`. (The string `fifo` refers to a pipe.)

```
this_kind = File.ftype("/dev/hdisk0")      # "blockSpecial"
that_kind = File.new("/tmp").stat.ftype    # "directory"
```

Certain special bits may be set or cleared in the permissions of a file. These are not strictly related to the other bits that we discuss in Section 10.1.9, "Manipulating File Ownership and Permissions." These are the *set-group-id bit*, the *set-user-id bit*, and the *sticky bit*. There are methods for each of these:

```
file = File.new("somefile")
sticky_flag = file.sticky?
setgid_flag = file.setgid?
setuid_flag = file.setuid?
```

A disk file may have symbolic or hard links that refer to it (on operating systems supporting these features). To test whether a file is actually a symbolic link to some other file, use the `symlink?` method. To count the number of hard links associated with a file, use the `nlink` method (found only in `File::Stat`). A hard link is virtually indistinguishable from an ordinary file; in fact, it *is* an ordinary file that happens to have multiple names and directory entries.

```
File.symlink("yourfile","myfile")          # Make a link
is_sym = File.symlink?("myfile")           # true
hard_count = File.new("myfile").stat.nlink # 0
```

Incidentally, note that in the previous example, we used the `File` class method `symlink` to create a symbolic link.

In rare cases, you may want even lower-level information about a file. The `File::Stat` class has three more instance methods that give you the gory details. The method `dev` gives you an integer identifying the device on which the file resides, `rdev` returns an integer specifying the kind of device, and for disk files, `ino` gives you the starting *inode* number for the file.

```
file = File.new("diskfile")
info = file.stat
```

```
device = info.dev
devtype = info.rdev
inode = info.ino
```

10.1.13   Working with Pipes

There are various ways of reading and writing pipes in Ruby. The class method
IO.popen opens a pipe and hooks the process's standard input and standard output
into the IO object returned. Frequently we will have different threads handling each
end of the pipe; here, we just show a single thread writing and then reading:

```
check = IO.popen("spell","r+")
check.puts("'T was brillig, and the slithy toves")
check.puts("Did gyre and gimble in the wabe.")
check.close_write
list = check.readlines
list.collect! { |x| x.chomp }
# list is now %w[brillig gimble gyre slithy toves wabe]
```

Note that the close_write call is necessary. If it were not issued, we would not
be able to reach the end-of-file when we read the pipe.

There is a block form that works as follows:

```
File.popen("/usr/games/fortune") do |pipe|
  quote = pipe.gets
  puts quote
  # On a clean disk, you can seek forever. - Thomas Steel
end
```

If the string "-" is specified, a new Ruby instance is started. If a block is specified
with this, the block is run as two separate processes, rather like a fork: The child gets
nil passed into the block, and the parent gets an IO object with the child's standard
input and/or output connected to it.

```
IO.popen("-") do |mypipe|
  if mypipe
    puts "I'm the parent: pid = #{Process.pid}"
    listen = mypipe.gets
    puts listen
  else
```

```
      puts "I'm the child: pid = #{Process.pid}"
   end
 end

 # Prints:
 #   I'm the parent: pid = 10580
 #   I'm the child: pid = 10582
```

A pipe method also returns a pair of pipe ends connected to each other. In the following code example, we create a pair of threads and let one pass a message to the other (the first message that Samuel Morse sent over the telegraph). Refer to Chapter 13, "Threads and Concurrency," for more information.

```
pipe = IO.pipe
reader = pipe[0]
writer = pipe[1]

str = nil
thread1 = Thread.new(reader,writer) do |reader,writer|
  # writer.close_write
  str = reader.gets
  reader.close
end

thread2 = Thread.new(reader,writer) do |reader,writer|
  # reader.close_read
  writer.puts("What hath God wrought?")
  writer.close
end

thread1.join
thread2.join

puts str         # What hath God wrought?
```

10.1.14   Performing Special I/O Operations

It is possible to do lower-level I/O in Ruby. We will only mention the existence of these methods; if you need to use them, some of them will be highly machine-specific anyway (varying even between different versions of UNIX).

The `ioctl` method ("I/O control") accepts two arguments. The first is an integer specifying the operation to be done. The second is either an integer or a string representing a binary number.

The `fcntl` method is also for low-level control of file-oriented streams in a system-dependent manner. It takes the same kinds of parameters as `ioctl`.

The `select` method (in the `Kernel` module) accepts up to four parameters; the first is the *read-array*, and the last three are optional (*write-array*, *error-array*, and the *timeout* value). This method allows a process to wait for an I/O opportunity. When input is available from one or more devices in the read-array, or when one or more devices in the write-array are ready, the call returns an array of three elements representing the respective arrays of devices that are ready for I/O.

The `Kernel` method `syscall` takes at least one integer parameter (and up to nine string or integer parameters in all). The first parameter specifies the I/O operation to be done.

The `fileno` method returns an old-fashioned file descriptor associated with an I/O stream. This is the least system-dependent of all the methods mentioned here:

```
desc = $stderr.fileno      # 2
```

10.1.15   Using Nonblocking I/O

Ruby makes a concerted effort "behind the scenes" to ensure that I/O does not block. For this reason, it is possible in most cases to use Ruby threads to manage I/O—a single thread may block on an I/O operation while another thread goes on processing.

However, those who want to turn off nonblocking I/O can do so using `read_nonblock` and `write_nonblock`. The former uses the internal `read(2)` system call; for this reason, it may raise exceptions corresponding to the usual set of errors, such as `Errno::EWOULDBLOCK` and others. It is equivalent to `readpartial` with the nonblocking flag set (see Section 10.1.16, "Using `readpartial`").

```
string = input.read(64)       # read 64 bytes
buffer = ""
input.read(64, buffer)        # optional buffer
```

When end-of-file is reached, `EOFError` is raised. When `EWOULDBLOCK` is raised, you should avoid calling the method again until input is available. Here is an example:

```
begin
  data = input.read_nonblock(256)
rescue Errno::EWOULDBOCK
  IO.select([input])
  retry
end
```

Likewise, `write_nonblock` invokes the `write(2)` system call (and can raise corresponding exceptions). It takes a string as an argument and returns the number of bytes written (which may be smaller than the length of the string). The EWOULDBLOCK exception can be handled the same as with the `read_nonblock` shown previously.

10.1.16 Using `readpartial`

The `readpartial` method makes I/O easier with streams, such as a socket.

The "max length" parameter is required. If the buffer parameter is specified, it should refer to a string where the data will be stored.

```
data = sock.readpartial(128)  # Read at most 128 bytes
```

The `readpartial` method doesn't honor the nonblocking flag. It will sometimes block, but only when three conditions are true: The IO object's buffer is empty, the stream content is empty, and the stream has not yet reached an end-of-file condition.

So in effect, if there is data in the stream, `readpartial` will *not* block. It will read up to the maximum number of bytes specified, but if there are fewer bytes available, it will grab those and continue.

If the stream has no data, but it is at end-of-file, `readpartial` will immediately raise an EOFError.

If the call blocks, it waits until either it receives data or it detects an EOF condition. If it receives data, it simply returns that data. If it detects EOF, it raises an EOFError.

When `sysread` is called in blocking mode, its behavior is similar to that of `readpartial`. If the buffer is empty, their behavior is identical.

10.1.17 Manipulating Pathnames

In manipulating pathnames, the first things to be aware of are the class methods `File.dirname` and `File.basename`; these work like the UNIX commands of the

same name and return the directory name and the filename, respectively. If an extension is specified as a second parameter to basename, that extension will be removed.

```
str = "/home/dave/podbay.rb"
dir = File.dirname(str)          # "/home/dave"
file1 = File.basename(str)       # "podbay.rb"
file2 = File.basename(str,".rb") # "podbay"
```

Note that although these are methods of File, they are really simply doing string
manipulation.

A comparable method is File.split, which returns these two components
(directory and filename) in a two-element array:

```
info = File.split(str)         # ["/home/dave","podbay.rb"]
```

The expand_path class method expands a relative pathname, converting to an
absolute path. If the operating system understands such idioms as ~ and ~user, these
will be expanded also. The optional second argument serves as a path to expand from,
and is often used with the current file path, __FILE__.

```
Dir.chdir("/home/poole/personal/docs")
abs = File.expand_path("../../misc")          # "/home/poole/misc"
abs = File.expand_path("misc", "/home/poole") # "/home/poole/misc"
```

Given an open file, the path instance method returns the pathname used to open
the file:

```
File.new("../../foobar").path  # "../../foobar"
```

The constant File::Separator gives the character used to separate pathname
components (typically backslash for Windows, slash for UNIX). An alias is
File::SEPARATOR.

The class method join uses this separator to produce a path from a list of directory components:

```
path = File.join("usr","local","bin","someprog")
# path is "usr/local/bin/someprog"
# Note that it doesn't put a separator on the front!
```

Don't fall into the trap of thinking that File.join and File.split are somehow inverses. They're not.

10.1.18   Using the `Pathname` Class

You should also be aware of the standard library `pathname`, which gives us the `Pathname` class. This is essentially a wrapper for `Dir`, `File`, and `FileUtils`; as such, it has much of the functionality of these, unified in a way that is supposed to be logical and intuitive.

```
path = Pathname.new("/home/hal")
file = Pathname.new("file.txt")
p2 = path + file


path.directory?      # true
path.file?           # false
p2.directory?        # false
p2.file?             # true


parts = path2.split  # [Pathname:/home/hal, Pathname:file.txt]
ext = path2.extname  # .txt
```

There are also a number of convenience methods, as you would expect. The `root?` method attempts to detect whether a path refers to the root directory; it can be "fooled" because it merely analyzes the string and does not access the filesystem. The `parent?` method returns the pathname of this path's parent. The `children` method returns a list of the next-level children below this path; it includes both files and directories but is not recursive:

```
p1 = Pathname.new("//")           # odd but legal
p1.root?                          # true
p2 = Pathname.new("/home/poole")
p3 = p2.parent                    # Pathname:/home
items = p2.children               # array of Pathnames (all files
                                  # and dirs directly inside poole)
```

As you would expect, `relative` and `absolute` try to determine whether a path is relative (by looking for a leading slash):

```
p1 = Pathname.new("/home/dave")
p1.absolute?                      # true
p1.relative?                      # false
```

Many methods, such as `size`, `unlink`, and others, are actually delegated to `File` and `FileUtils`; the functionality is not reimplemented.

For more details on `Pathname`, consult ruby-doc.org or any good reference.

10.1.19 Command-Level File Manipulation

Often we need to manipulate files in a manner similar to the way we would at a command line. That is, we need to copy, delete, rename, and so on.

Many of these capabilities are built-in methods; a few are in the `FileUtils` module in the `fileutils` library. Be aware that `FileUtils` used to mix functionality directly into the `File` class by reopening it; now these methods stay in their own module.

To delete a file, we can use `File.delete` or its synonym, `File.unlink`:

```
File.delete("history")
File.unlink("toast")
```

To rename a file, we can use `File.rename`, as follows:

```
File.rename("Ceylon", "Sri Lanka")
```

File links (hard and symbolic) can be created using `File.link` and `File.symlink`, respectively:

```
File.link("/etc/hosts", "/etc/hostfile")    # hard link
File.symlink("/etc/hosts", "/tmp/hosts")    # symbolic link
```

We can truncate a file to zero bytes (or any other specified number) by using the `truncate` instance method:

```
File.truncate("myfile",1000)    # Now at most 1000 bytes
```

Two files may be compared by means of the `compare_file` method. There is an alias named `cmp` (and there is also `compare_stream`):

```
require "fileutils"

same = FileUtils.compare_file("alpha","beta")  # true
```

The `copy` method will copy a file to a new name or location. It has an optional flag parameter to write error messages to standard error. The UNIX-like name `cp` is an alias:

```
require "fileutils"

# Copy epsilon to theta and log any errors.
FileUtils.copy("epsilon","theta", true)
```

A file may be moved with the `move` method (alias `mv`). Like `copy`, it also has an optional verbose flag:

```
require "fileutils"

FileUtils.move("/tmp/names","/etc")      # Move to new directory
FileUtils.move("colours","colors")       # Just a rename
```

The `safe_unlink` method deletes the specified file or files, first trying to make the files writable so as to avoid errors. If the last parameter is `true` or `false`, that value will be taken as the verbose flag:

```
require "fileutils"

FileUtils.safe_unlink("alpha","beta","gamma")
# Log errors on the next two files
FileUtils.safe_unlink("delta","epsilon",true)
```

Finally, the `install` method basically does a `syscopy`, except that it first checks that the file either does not exist or has different content.

```
require "fileutils"

FileUtils.install("foo.so","/usr/lib")
# Existing foo.so will not be overwritten
# if it is the same as the new one.
```

For more on `FileUtils`, consult ruby-doc.org or any other reference.

10.1.20   Grabbing Characters from the Keyboard

Here we use the term *grabbing* because we sometimes want to process a character as soon as it is pressed rather than buffer it and wait for a newline to be entered.

This can be done in both UNIX variants and Windows variants. Unfortunately, the two methods are completely unrelated to each other.

The UNIX version is straightforward. We use the well-known technique of putting the terminal in raw mode (and we usually turn off echoing at the same time):

```
def getchar
  system("stty raw -echo")   # Raw mode, no echo
  char = STDIN.getc
  system("stty -raw echo")   # Reset terminal mode
  char
end
```

In the Windows world, we would need to write a C extension for this. An alternative is to use a small feature of the `Win32API` library:

```
require 'Win32API'

def getchar
  char = Win32API.new("crtdll", "_getch", [], 'L').Call
end
```

In either case, the behavior is effectively the same.

10.1.21   Reading an Entire File into Memory

To read an entire file into an array, you need not even open the file. The method `IO.readlines` will do this, opening and closing the file on its own:

```
arr = IO.readlines("myfile")
lines = arr.size
puts "myfile has #{lines} lines in it."

longest = arr.collect {|x| x.length}.max
puts "The longest line in it has #{longest} characters."
```

We can also use `IO.read` (which returns a single large string rather than an array of lines):

```
str = IO.read("myfile")
bytes = arr.size
puts "myfile has #{bytes} bytes in it."

longest = str.collect {|x| x.length}.max  # strings are enumerable!
puts "The longest line in it has #{longest} characters."
```

Obviously because IO is an ancestor of File, we can say File.readlines and File.read just as easily.

10.1.22   Iterating Over a File by Lines

To iterate over a file a line at a time, we can use the class method IO.foreach or the instance method each. In the former case, the file need not be opened in our code:

```
# Print all lines containing the word "target"
IO.foreach("somefile") do |line|
  puts line if line =~ /target/
end

# Another way...
File.new("somefile").each do |line|
  puts line if line =~ /target/
end
```

Note that each_line is an alias for each. It can also be used to get an enumerator:

```
lines = File.new("somefile").each_line
lines.find{|line| line =~ /target/ }  # Treat as any enumerator
```

10.1.23   Iterating Over a File by Byte or Character

To iterate a byte at a time, use the each_byte instance method. It feeds a byte (that is, a Fixnum in the range 0..255) into the block:

```
a_count = 0
File.new("myfile").each_byte do |byte|
  a_count += 1 if byte == 97     # lowercase a in ASCII
end
```

You can also iterate by character (where a character is really a one-character string). Depending on what encoding you are using, a character may be a single byte (as in ASCII) or multiple bytes.

```
a_count = 0
File.new("myfile").each_char do |char|
  a_count += 1 if char == "a"
end
```

The `each_char` method also returns an ordinary enumerator.

10.1.24   Treating a String As a File

Sometimes people want to know how to treat a string as though it were a file. The answer depends on the exact meaning of the question.

An object is defined mostly in terms of its methods. The following code shows an iterator applied to an object called `source`; with each iteration, a line of output is produced. Can you tell the type of `source` by reading this fragment?

```
source.each_line do |line|
  puts line
end
```

Actually, `source` could be a file, or it could be a string containing embedded newlines. Therefore, in cases like these, a string can trivially be treated as a file.

The `StringIO` class provides many of the methods of the `IO` class that a regular string lacks. It also has a `string` accessor that refers to the contents of the string itself:

```
require 'stringio'

ios = StringIO.new("abcdefghijkl\nABC\n123")

ios.seek(5)
ios.puts("xyz")
puts ios.tell             # 9
puts ios.string.inspect   # "abcdexyz\njkl\nABC\n123"

puts ios.getc            # j
ios.ungetc(?w)
puts ios.string.inspect   # "abcdexyz\nwkl\nABC\n123"
```

```
s1 = ios.gets            # "wk1\n"
s2 = ios.gets            # "ABC"
```

10.1.25   Copying a Stream

Use the class method `copy_stream` for copying a stream. All the data will be dumped from the source to the destination. The source and destination may be IO objects or filenames. The third (optional) parameter is the number of bytes to be copied (defaulting, of course, to the entire source). The fourth parameter is a beginning offset (in bytes) for the source:

```
src = File.new("garbage.in")
dst = File.new("garbage.out")
IO.copy_stream(src, dst)

IO.copy_stream("garbage.in","garbage.out", 1000, 80)
# Copy 1000 bytes to output starting at offset 80
```

10.1.26   Working with Character Encodings

For this topic, refer to Chapter 4, "Internationalization in Ruby." Using and manipulating character encodings for `String` and IO objects is covered there.

10.1.27   Reading Data Embedded in a Program

In days gone by, children learned BASIC by copying programs out of magazines. One convenient feature of this language (if any of it was convenient) was the DATA statement. The information was embedded in the program, but it could be read as if it originated outside.

Should you ever want to, you can do much the same thing in Ruby. The directive `__END__` at the end of a Ruby program signals that embedded data follows. This can be read using the global constant DATA, which is an IO object like any other. (Note that the `__END__` marker must be at the beginning of the line on which it appears.)

```
# Print each line backwards...
DATA.each_line do |line|
  puts line.reverse
end
__END__
```

```
A man, a plan, a canal... Panama!
Madam, I'm Adam.
,siht gnidaer er'uoy fI
.evisserpmi si noitacided ruoy
```

10.1.28   Reading Program Source

Suppose you wanted to access the source of your own program. This can be done using a variation on a trick we used earlier (see Section 10.1.27, "Reading Data Embedded in a Program").

The global constant DATA is an IO object that refers to the data following the __END__ directive. But if you do a rewind operation, it resets the file pointer to the beginning of the program source.

The following program prints itself with line numbers:

```
DATA.rewind
DATA.each_line.with_index do |line, i|
  puts "#{'%03d' % (i + 1)}  #{line.chomp}"
end
__END__
```

Note that the __END__ directive *is* necessary; without it, DATA cannot be accessed at all.

Another way to read the source of the current file is by using the special variable __FILE__. It contains the full path of the file itself, and can be read:

```
puts File.read(__FILE__)
```

10.1.29   Working with Temporary Files

There are many circumstances in which we need to work with files that are all but anonymous. We don't want to trouble with naming them or making sure there is no name conflict, and we don't want to bother with deleting them.

All these issues are addressed in the Tempfile library. The new method (alias open) takes an arbitrary name as a *seed* and concatenates it with the process ID and a unique sequence number. The optional second parameter is the directory to be used; it defaults to the value of environment variable TMPDIR, TMP, or TEMP, and finally the value "/tmp".

The resulting IO object may be opened and closed many times during the execution of the program. Upon termination of the program, the temporary file will be deleted.

The close method has an optional flag; if set to true, the file will be deleted immediately after it is closed (instead of waiting until program termination). The path method returns the actual pathname of the file, should you need it.

```ruby
require "tempfile"

temp = Tempfile.new("stuff")
name = temp.path              # "/tmp/stuff17060.0"
temp.puts "Kilroy was here"
temp.close

# Later...
temp.open
str = temp.gets               # "Kilroy was here"
temp.close(true)              # Delete it NOW
```

10.1.30 Changing and Setting the Current Directory

The current directory may be determined by the use of Dir.pwd or its alias Dir.getwd; these abbreviations historically stand for *print working directory* and *get working directory*, respectively.

The method Dir.chdir may be used to change the current directory. On Windows, the logged drive may appear at the front of the string:

```ruby
Dir.chdir("/var/tmp")
puts Dir.pwd          # "/var/tmp"
puts Dir.getwd        # "/var/tmp"
```

This method also takes a block parameter. If a block is specified, the current directory is changed only while the block is executed (and restored afterward):

```ruby
Dir.chdir("/home")
Dir.chdir("/tmp") do
  puts Dir.pwd        # /tmp
end
puts Dir.pwd          # /home
```

10.1.31   Changing the Current Root

On most UNIX variants, it is possible to change the current process's idea of where root or "slash" is. This is typically done to prevent code that runs later from being able to reach the entire filesystem. The `chroot` method sets the new root to the specified directory:

```
Dir.chdir("/home/guy/sandbox/tmp")
Dir.chroot("/home/guy/sandbox")
puts Dir.pwd                    # "/tmp"
```

10.1.32   Iterating Over Directory Entries

The class method `foreach` is an iterator that successively passes each directory entry into the block. The instance method `each` behaves the same way.

```
Dir.foreach("/tmp") { |entry| puts entry }

dir = Dir.new("/tmp")
dir.each   { |entry| puts entry }
```

Both of these code fragments print the same output (the names of all files and subdirectories in /tmp).

10.1.33   Getting a List of Directory Entries

The class method `Dir.entries` returns an array of all the entries in the specified directory:

```
list = Dir.entries("/tmp")  # %w[. .. alpha.txt beta.doc]
```

As shown in the preceding code, the current and parent directories are included. If you don't want these, you'll have to remove them manually.

10.1.34   Creating a Chain of Directories

Sometimes we want to create a chain of directories where the intermediate directories themselves don't necessarily exist yet. At the UNIX command line, we would use `mkdir -p` for this.

In Ruby code, we can do this by using the `FileUtils.makedirs` method:

```
require "fileutils"
FileUtils.mkpath("/tmp/these/dirs/need/not/exist")
```

10.1.35 Deleting a Directory Recursively

In the UNIX world, we can type `rm -rf dir` at the command line, and the entire subtree starting with `dir` will be deleted. Obviously, we should exercise caution in doing this.

`Pathname` has a method called `rmtree` that will accomplish this:

```
require 'pathname'
dir = Pathname.new("/home/poole")
dir.rmtree
```

There is also a method called `rm_r` in `FileUtils` that will do the same:

```
require 'fileutils'
FileUtils.rm_r("/home/poole")
```

10.1.36 Finding Files and Directories

The `Dir` class provides the `glob` method (aliased as `[]`), which returns an array of files that match the given shell glob. In simple cases, this is often enough to find a specific file inside a given directory:

```
Dir.glob("*.rb")        # all ruby files in the current directory
Dir["spec/**/*_spec.rb"] # all files ending _spec.rb inside spec/
```

For more complicated cases, the standard library `find` allows us to iterate over every file in a directory and all its subdirectories. Here is a method that finds files in a given directory by either filename (that is, a string) or regular expression:

```
require "find"

def findfiles(dir, name)
  list = []
  Find.find(dir) do |path|
```

```
      Find.prune if [".",".."].include? path
      case name
      when String
        list << path if File.basename(path) == name
      when Regexp
        list << path if File.basename(path) =~ name
      else
        raise ArgumentError
      end
    end
    list
  end


findfiles "/home/hal", "toc.txt"
# ["/home/hal/docs/toc.txt", "/home/hal/misc/toc.txt"]

findfiles "/home", /^[a-z]+.doc/
# ["/home/hal/docs/alpha.doc", "/home/guy/guide.doc",
#  "/home/bill/help/readme.doc"]
```

Contrary to its name, the `find` library can be used to do any task that requires
traversing a directory and its children, such as adding up the total space taken by all
files in a directory.

10.2   Higher-Level Data Access

Frequently, we want to store some specific data for later, rather than simply write bytes
to a file. In order to do this, we convert data from objects into bytes and back again,
a process called *serialization*. There are many ways to serialize data, so we will examine only the simplest and most common formats.

The `Marshal` module offers simple object persistence, and the `PStore` library
builds on that functionality. The YAML format (and Ruby library) provides another
way to marshal objects, but using plaintext that is easily human readable.

JSON can only persist numbers, strings, arrays, and hashes, but can be written
and read by any language. CSV files can be used to exchange tabular data with many
applications, including spreadsheets such as Excel.

External databases, with a socket interface to the database server process, will be
examined in the next section.

10.2.1   Simple Marshaling

The simplest way to save an object for later use is by *marshaling* it. The `Marshal` module enables programs to *serialize* and *unserialize* Ruby objects into strings, and therefore also files.

```
# array of elements [composer, work, minutes]
works = [["Leonard Bernstein", "Overture to Candide", 11],
  ["Aaron Copland", "Symphony No. 3", 45],
  ["Jean Sibelius", "Finlandia", 20]]


# We want to keep this for later...
File.write "store", Marshal.dump("works")

# Much later...
works = Marshal.load File.read("store")
```

Storing data in this way can be extremely convenient, but can potentially be very dangerous. Loading marshaled data can potentially be exploited to execute *any* code, rather than the code of your program.

Never unmarshal data that was supplied by any external source, including users of your program. Instead, use the YAML and JSON libraries to safely read and write data provided by untrusted sources, as shown later this section.

Marshaling also has limits: Not all objects can be dumped. Objects of system-specific classes cannot be dumped, including `IO`, `Thread`, and `Binding`. Anonymous and singleton classes also cannot be serialized.

Data produced by `Marshal.dump` includes two bytes at the beginning, a major and minor version number:

```
Marshal.dump("foo").bytes[0..1]  # [4, 8]
```

Ruby will only load marshaled data with the same major version and the same or lower minor version. When the "verbose" flag is set, the versions must match exactly. The version number is incremented when the marshal format changes, but it has been stable for many years at this point.

10.2.2 "Deep Copying" with `Marshal`

Ruby has no "deep copy" operation. For example, using `dup` or `clone` on a hash will not copy the keys and values that the hash references. With enough nested object references, a copy operation turns into a game of Pick-Up-Sticks.

We offer here a way to handle a restricted deep copy. It is restricted because it is still based on `Marshal` and has the same inherent limitations:

```
def deep_copy(obj)
  Marshal.load Marshal.dump(obj)
end


a = deep_copy(b)
```

10.2.3 More Complex Marshaling

Sometimes we want to customize our marshaling to some extent. Creating `marshal_load` and `marshal_dump` methods make this possible. If they exist, these hooks are called when marshaling is done so that you are handling your own conversion to and from a string.

In the following example, a person has been earning 5% interest on his beginning balance since he was born. We don't store the age and the current balance because they are a function of time:

```
class Person

  attr_reader :balance, :name

  def initialize(name, birthdate, deposit)
    @name = name
    @birthdate = birthdate
    @deposit = deposit
    @age = (Time.now - @birthdate) / (365*86400)
    @balance = @deposit * (1.05 ** @age)
  end

  def age
    @age.floor
  end

  def marshal_dump
```

```
        {name: @name, birthdate: @birthdate, deposit: @deposit}
    end

    def marshal_load(data)
        initialize(data[:name], data[:birthdate], data[:deposit])
    end
end

p1 = Person.new("Rudy", Time.now - (14 * 365 * 86400), 100)
[p1.name, p1.age, p1.balance]  # ["Rudy", 14, 197.9931599439417]

p2 = Marshal.load Marshal.dump(p1)
[p2.name, p2.age, p2.balance]  # ["Rudy", 14, 197.9931599440351]
```

When an object of this type is saved, the age and current balance will not be
stored; when the object is "reconstituted," they will be computed. Notice how the
marshal_load method assumes an existing object; this is one of the few times you
might want to call initialize explicitly (just as new calls it).

10.2.4   Marshaling with YAML

YAML stands for "YAML Ain't Markup Language," and it was created to serve as a
flexible, human-readable format that allows data to be exchanged between programs
and across programming languages.

When using the yaml library, we can use the YAML.dump and YAML.load methods almost identically to those of Marshal. It is instructive to dump a few objects to
see how YAML deals with them:

```
require 'yaml'

Person = Struct.new(:name)

puts YAML.dump("Hello, world.")
puts YAML.dump({this: "is a hash",
    with: "symbol keys and string values"})
puts YAML.dump([1, 2, 3])
puts YAML.dump Person.new("Alice")

# Output:
# --- Hello, world.
# ...
# ---
```

```
# :this: is a hash
# :with: symbol keys and string values
# ---
# - 1
# - 2
# - 3
# --- !ruby/struct:Person
# name: Alice
```

Each YAML document begins with "---" and then contains the object(s) being serialized, converted into a human-readable text format.

Using `YAML.load` to load a string is similarly straightforward. In fact, `YAML.load_file` takes it one step further and allows us to simply supply the name of the file we want to load. Assume that we have a file named `data.yml`, as shown here:

```
---
- "Hello, world"
- 237
-
  - Jan
  - Feb
  - Mar
  - Apr
-
  just a: hash.
  This: is
```

This is the same as the four data items we just looked at, except they are collected into a single array. If we now load this file, we get the array back:

```
require 'yaml'
p YAML.load_file("data.yaml")
# Output:
# ["Hello, world", 237, ["Jan", "Feb", "Mar", "Apr"],
#  {"just a"=>"hash.", "This"=>"is"}]
```

In general, YAML is just a way to marshal objects. At a higher level, it can be used for many purposes. For example, the fact that it is human readable also makes it human editable, and it becomes a natural format for configuration files and such things.

Because YAML can marshal Ruby objects, the dangers of marshaled data apply to YAML as well. Never load YAML files that come from an external source. However, the `YAML.safe_load` method limits the classes that can be unmarshaled, and it can be used to load data from untrusted sources.

There is more to YAML than shown here. For further information, consult the Ruby `stdlib` documentation, or the official website at yaml.org.

10.2.5   Persisting Data with `JSON`

JSON, despite being an acronym for JavaScript Object Notation, allows basic data types to be serialized in a human-readable format containing a few basic data types shared by almost every programing language.

Because it is so simple, readable, and widespread, it has become the preferred data format for transmitting data between programs on the Internet.

Using the JSON standard library is nearly identical to YAML, with the caveat that only hashes, arrays, numbers, strings, `true`, `false`, and `nil` can be dumped. Any object that is not one of those classes will be converted to a string when it is serialized:

```
require 'json'

data = {
  string: "Hi there",
  array: [1, 2, 3],
  boolean: true,
  object: Object.new
}

puts JSON.dump(data)
# Output: {"string":"Hi there","array":[1,2,3],
#         "boolean":true,"object":"#<Object:0x007fd61b890320>"}
```

Converting Ruby objects into JSON and back requires writing code similar to the `marshal_dump` and `marshal_load` methods seen earlier. There is a convention, started in Ruby on Rails, of implementing an `as_json` method to convert an object into the data types supported by JSON.

Here is how to implement `as_json` and convert a `Person` (from Section 10.2.3, "More Complex Marshaling") into JSON and back:

```
require 'json'
require 'time'
```

```
class Person
  # other methods as before...

  def as_json
    {name: @name, birthdate: @birthdate.iso8601, deposit: @deposit}
  end

  def self.from_json(json)
    data = JSON.parse(json)
    birthdate = Time.parse(data["birthdate"])
    new(data["name"], birthdate, data["deposit"])
  end
end

p1 = Person.new("Rudy", Time.now - (14 * 365 * 86400), 100)
p1.as_json # {:name=>"Rudy", :deposit=>100,
           #  :birthdate=>"2000-07-23T23:25:02-07:00"}

p2 = Person.from_json JSON.dump(p1.as_json)
[p2.name, p2.age, p2.balance] # ["Rudy", 14, 197.9931600356966]
```

Because JSON cannot contain `Time` objects, we convert to a string using the `iso8601` method, and then parse the string back into a `Time` when creating a new `Person` object.

As we've just illustrated, JSON cannot serialize Ruby objects, unlike `Marshal` and YAML. This means there is no danger in calling `JSON.load` on untrusted JSON documents, and makes JSON suitable for exchanging data with systems that are not under your control.

10.2.6   Working with CSV Data

CSV (comma-separated values) format is something you may have had to deal with if you have ever worked with spreadsheets or databases. Fortunately, Ruby includes the CSV library, written by James Edward Gray III.

The CSV library can parse or generate data in CSV format. There is no universal agreement on the exact format of CSV data, but there are some common conventions. The defaults used by the CSV library are as follows:

- The record separator is CR + LF.

- The field separator is a comma (,).

- Quote data with double quotes if it contains a CR, LF, or comma.

- Quote a double quote by prefixing it with another double quote (" -> "").

- An empty field with quotes means an empty string (*data,"",data*).

- An empty field without quotes means nil (*data,,data*).

These conventions can be adjusted.

Let's start by creating a file. To write out comma-separated data, we can simply open a file for writing; the open method will pass a writer object into the attached block. We then use the append operator to append arrays of data (which are converted to comma-separated format upon writing). The first line will be a header:

```
require 'csv'

CSV.open("data.csv","w") do |wr|
  wr << ["name", "age", "salary"]
  wr << ["mark", "29", "34500"]
  wr << ["joe", "42", "32000"]
  wr << ["fred", "22", "22000"]
  wr << ["jake", "25", "24000"]
  wr << ["don", "32", "52000"]
end
```

The preceding code gives us a data file called data.csv:

```
"name","age","salary"
"mark",29,34500
"joe",42,32000
"fred",22,22000
"jake",25,24000
"don",32,52000
```

Another program can read this file:

```
require 'csv'

CSV.open('data.csv', 'r') do |row|
  p row
end
```

```
# Output:
# ["name", "age", "salary"]
# ["mark", "29", "34500"]
# ["joe", "42", "32000"]
# ["fred", "22", "22000"]
# ["jake", "25", "24000"]
# ["don", "32", "52000"]
```

The preceding code could also be written *without* a block; then the open call would return a reader object. We could then invoke shift on the reader (as though it were an array) to retrieve the next row. However, the block-oriented way seems more straightforward.

Regardless of the method used to create the CSV files, they can then be read and modified by Excel and other spreadsheet programs.

10.2.7 SQLite3 for SQL Data Storage

SQLite3 is a data store for those who appreciate *zero configuration* software. It is a small self-contained executable, written in C, that can handle a complete database in a single file. Although it is usually used for small databases, it can deal with data up to hundreds of gigabytes.

The biggest advantage of using SQLite3 is that it provides the same query interface as other full-sized databases such as MySQL and PostgreSQL. This makes it possible to start a project using SQLite3 and then migrate to an external database server without having to rewrite the database code.

The Ruby bindings for SQLite3 are relatively straightforward. The SQLite::Database class allows you to open a database file and execute SQL queries against it. Here is a brief piece of sample code:

```
require "sqlite3"

# Open a new database
db = SQLite::Database.new("library.db")

# Create a table to store books
db.execute "create table books (
  title varchar(1024), author varchar(256) );"

# Insert records into the table
{
  "Robert Zubrin" => "The Case for Mars",
```

```
    "Alexis de Tocqueville" => "Democracy in America"
}.each do |author, title|
  db.execute "insert into books values (?, ?)", [title, author]
end

# Read records from the table using a block
db.execute("select title,author from books") do |row|
  p row
end

# Close the open database
db.close

# Output:
# ["The Case for Mars", "Robert Zubrin"]
# ["Democracy in America", "Alexis de Tocqueville"]
```

If a block is not specified, execute returns an array of arrays, and each row can be iterated over:

```
rs = db.execute("select title,author from books")
rs.each {|row| p row }      # Same results as before
```

Several different exceptions may be raised by this library. All are subclasses of SQLite::Exception, so it is easy to catch any or all of them.

Although the sqlite library is fairly full featured, SQLite itself does not *completely* implement the SQL92 standard. Use PostgreSQL or MySQL (examined in the next section) if you need the features of a full SQL database.

For more information on SQLite3, see sqlite.org. For more information on the Ruby bindings, see the project's online documentation at github.com/sparklemotion/sqlite3-ruby.

10.3   Connecting to External Data Stores

External data stores run in their own process, and they accept connections from clients over a socket. The clients send queries over this connection, and the data stores reply with results.

Data stores are able to hold only basic data types, but can provide advantages in flexibility, shared access, and speed. Libraries exist to connect to almost any data store that exists, including SQL databases, key-value stores, and document stores.

In this section, we will look at the Ruby libraries for the three most widely used data stores: MySQL, PostgreSQL, and Redis.

10.3.1   Connecting to MySQL Databases

Ruby's MySQL interface is among the most stable and fully functional of its database interfaces. After installing both Ruby and MySQL, install the `mysql2` gem using either `gem install` or `bundle install`.

There are three steps to using the gem after you have it installed. First, load the gem in your script; then connect to the database; finally, work with your tables. Connecting requires the usual parameters of `host`, `username`, `password`, `database`, and so on.

The module is composed of two classes (`Mysql2::Client` and `Mysql2::Result`), as described in the README. We summarize some useful methods here, but you can always find more information in the actual documentation.

The class method `Mysql2::Client.new` takes several string parameters, all defaulting to `nil`, and returns a client object. The most useful parameters are `host`, `username`, `password`, `port`, and `database`. Use the `query` method on the client object to interact with the database:

```
require 'mysql2'

client = Mysql2::Client.new(
  :host => "localhost",
  :username => "root"
)

# Create a database
client.query("CREATE DATABASE mailing_list")

# Use the database
client.query("USE mailing_list")
```

If the database already exists, you can skip the `USE` statement by providing the `database` parameter:

```
# Create a table to hold names and email addresses
client.query("CREATE TABLE members (
  name varchar(1024), email varchar(1024))")
```

```
# Insert two mailing list member rows
client.query <<-SQL
  INSERT INTO members VALUES
  ('John Doe', 'jdoe@rubynewbie.com'),
  ('Fred Smith', 'smithf@rubyexpert.com')
SQL
```

When inserting data, keep in mind that values are not escaped! Malicious users might provide data specifically crafted to delete your database or even grant administrator access. Use the escape method on data before you insert it to prevent this.

```
escaped = ["Bob Howard", "bofh@laundry.gov.uk"].map do |value|
  "'#{client.escape(value)}'"
end
client.query("INSERT INTO members VALUES (#{escaped.join(",")})")
```

Queries that yield results will return a Mysql2::Result instance that mixes in Enumerable. The result rows can then be iterated over with each or any other Enumerable method.

```
# Query for the data and return each row as a hash
client.query("SELECT * from members").each do |member|
  puts "Name: #{member["name"]}, Email: #{member["email"]}"
end
# Output:
# Name: John Doe, Email: jdoe@rubynewbie.com
# Name: Fred Smith, Email: smithf@rubyexpert.com
# Name: Bob Howard, Email: bofh@laundry.gov.uk
```

MySQL data types are fully supported, and strings, numbers, times, and other types are automatically converted into instances of the corresponding Ruby classes.

The Result yields each result row as a hash. Each hash has string keys by default, but can have symbol keys if the query method is passed the option :symbolize_keys => true.

Other useful Result methods include count (the number of rows returned) and fields (an array of column names in the results). The each method can also yield each result row as an array of values if the :as => :array option is passed.

```
# Query for the data and return each row as an array
result = client.query("SELECT * FROM members")
puts "#{result.count} records"
```

```
puts result.fields.join(" - ")
result.each(:as => :array){|m| puts m.join(" - ") }
# Output:
# 3 records
# name - email
# John Doe - jdoe@rubynewbie.com
# Fred Smith - smithf@rubyexpert.com
# Bob Howard - bofh@laundry.gov.uk
```

The names of existing databases can be found using the MySQL-specific query SHOW DATABASES, like so:

```
client.query("SHOW DATABASES").to_a(:as => :array).flatten
# ["information_schema", "mailing_list", "mysql",
#   "performance_schema", "test"]
```

Finally, the connection to the database can be closed via the close method:

```
# Close the connection to the database
client.close
```

As usual, we have only covered a fraction of what is possible. For more information, see the MySQL website at mysql.com, and the mysql2 gem website at github.com/brianmario/mysql2.

10.3.2   Connecting to PostgreSQL Databases

The pg gem provides an interface to connect to PostgreSQL databases, and it can be installed with gem install or bundle install after PostgreSQL and Ruby have been installed.

As in other database adapters, load the module, connect to the database, and then do your work with the tables. The PG class provides the connect method to obtain a connection to the database.

The connection provides the exec method (aliased as query) to run SQL queries against the database:

```
require 'pg'

# Create the database
PG.connect.exec("CREATE DATABASE pets")
```

```
# Open a connection to the created database
conn = PG.connect(dbname: "pets")
```

Note that, unlike MySQL, changing databases requires creating an entirely new connection, rather than executing a query.

Sending a query using the pg gem is very similar to any other SQL library:

```
# Create a table and insert some data
conn.exec("CREATE TABLE pets (name varchar(255),
  species varchar(255), birthday date)")
conn.exec <<-SQL
  INSERT INTO pets VALUES
    ('Spooky', 'cat', '2008-10-03'),
    ('Spot', 'dog', '2004-06-10')
SQL
```

Escaping values as they are inserted is greatly simplified by the exec_params method, which can escape values as they are provided:

```
# Escape data as it is inserted
require 'date'
conn.exec_params("INSERT INTO pets VALUES ($1, $2, $3)",
  ['Maru', 'cat', Date.today.to_s])
```

Unlike the mysql2 gem, however, the pg gem does not convert query results into their corresponding Ruby classes. All results are provided as strings and must be converted if necessary. Here, we use Date.parse on each result's date field:

```
# Query for the data
res = conn.query("SELECT * FROM pets")
puts "There are #{res.count} pets."
res.each do |pet|
  name = pet["name"]
  age = (Date.today - Date.parse(pet["birthday"]))/365
  species = pet["species"]
  puts "#{name} is a #{age.floor}-year-old #{species}."
end

# Output:
# There are 3 pets.
# Spooky is a 5-year-old cat.
# Spot is a 10-year-old dog.
# Maru is a 0-year-old cat.
```

Whereas the `each` method always yields result rows as hashes with string keys, the `PG::Result` instance returned by the query also provides values for an array of rows as arrays. Additional useful methods include `count` for the number of result rows and `fields` for an array of field names.

As always, see the PostgreSQL website at postgresql.org and the pg gem's website at bitbucket.org/ged/ruby-pg for further details and documentation.

10.3.3   Object-Relational Mappers (ORMs)

The traditional relational database is good at what it does. It handles queries in an efficient way without foreknowledge of the nature of those *ad hoc* queries. But this model is not very object oriented, especially in cases where all result fields are returned as strings.

The ubiquity of both these models (RDBMS and OOP) and the "impedance mismatch" between them has led many people to try to bridge this gap. The software bridge that accomplishes this is called an *Object-Relational Mapper* (*ORM*).

There are many ways of approaching this problem. All have their advantages and disadvantages. Here, we'll take a short look at `ActiveRecord`, probably the best known of these.

The `ActiveRecord` library for Ruby is named after Martin Fowler's "Active Record" design pattern. In the pattern, an Active Record "wraps a row in a database table or view, encapsulates the database access, and adds domain logic on that data" (see *Patterns of Enterprise Application Architecture* by Martin Fowler, Addison-Wesley, 2003).

The `activerecord` gem does this with a Ruby class for each database table. It can make some queries without SQL, it represents each row as an instance of the class, and it allows domain logic to be added to each class. Classes are named after tables and descend from the `ActiveRecord::Base` class. Only one database connection is required for all classes.

Here is a short example of how it all works:

```
require 'active_record'

class Pet < ActiveRecord::Base
end

ActiveRecord::Base.establish_connection(
  :adapter => "postgresql", :database => "pets")

snoopy = Pet.new(name: "Snoopy", species: "dog")
snoopy.birthday = Date.new(1950, 10, 4)
```

```
snoopy.save
```

```
p Pet.all.map {|pet| pet.birthday.to_s }
```

As you can see, it can infer table names, provide attribute accessors based on column names, and execute queries in an object-oriented manner. It also provides the same API, including data type conversion, with any underlying SQL database.

The `activerecord` API is rich and complex, and entire books have been written about how to use it. For more information, consult any reference.

10.3.4   Connecting to Redis Data Stores

Although it is not a database (SQL or otherwise), the Redis data store has become extremely popular in recent years. It provides key-value storage, and allows values to contain strings, hashes, arrays, sets, and sorted sets.

Although Redis makes a bad permanent data store, it makes an excellent place to cache data. It can be an excellent way to handle the results of expensive calculations that can be derived from permanently stored data.

Connecting to a Redis server using the `redis` gem is extremely easy. When the Redis server is running on the same machine, no parameters are required.

```
require 'redis'
r = Redis.new
```

One useful storage type is the set. Redis can take the difference, intersection, and union of multiple sets quickly, and either return the result or store the result in another key.

```
# Store pet names in a set
r.sadd("pets", "spooky")
# Get the members of a set
r.smembers("pets") # ["spooky"]
```

The hash type allow multiple fields to be read and written beneath a single key, either one at a time or all at once.

```
# Use pet name as key for a hash of other attributes
r.hset("spooky", "species", "cat")
r.hset("spooky", "birthday", "2008-10-03")
```

```
# Get a single hash value
r.hget("spooky", "species") # "cat"
# Get the entire hash
r.hgetall("spooky") # {"species"=>"cat", "birthday"=>"2008-10-03"}
```

The sorted set associates a score with each value, and it provides specific instructions to increment and decrement scores, as well as retrieve values sorted by score.

```
# Use a sorted set to store pets by weight
r.zadd("pet_weights", 6,  "spooky")
r.zadd("pet_weights", 12, "spot")
r.zadd("pet_weights", 2,  "maru")

# Retrieve the first value from the set sorted highest to lowest
r.zrevrange("pet_weights", 0, 0) # => ["spot"]
```

Many more complex and optimized uses can be made of Redis by leveraging the various data types it provides. See the Redis website at redis.io for thorough documentation of every data type and command available.

10.4 Conclusion

This chapter provided an overview of I/O in Ruby. We've looked at the IO class itself and its descendant File, along with other related classes such as Dir and Pathname. We've seen some useful tricks for manipulating IO objects and files.

We've also looked at data storage at a slightly higher level—storing data externally as marshaled and serialized objects. Finally, we've had a short overview of the true database solutions available in Ruby, along with some OOP techniques for interacting with them in easier ways.

Later, we will look at I/O again from the perspective of sockets and network programming. But before getting too deep into that, let's examine some other topics.

Chapter 11

OOP and Dynamic Features in Ruby

Of his quick objects hath the mind no part,
Nor his own vision holds what it doth catch...

—*William Shakespeare, "Sonnet 113"*

This is an unusual chapter. Whereas many of the chapters in this book deal with a specific problem subdomain such as strings or files, this one doesn't. If the "problem space" is viewed as stretching out on one axis of a graph, this chapter extends out on the other axis, encompassing a slice of each of the other areas. This is because object-oriented programming and dynamicity aren't problem domains themselves but are paradigms that can be applied to any problem, whether it be system administration, low-level networking, or web development.

For this reason, much of this chapter's information should already be familiar to a programmer who knows Ruby. In fact, the rest of the book wouldn't make sense without some of the fundamental knowledge here. Any Ruby programmer knows how to create a subclass, for instance.

This raises the question of what to include and what to exclude. Does every Ruby programmer know about the `extend` method? What about the `instance_eval` method? What is obvious to one person might be big news to another.

We have decided to err on the side of completeness. We include in this chapter some of the more esoteric tasks you might want to do with dynamic OOP in Ruby, but we also include the more routine tasks in case anyone is unfamiliar with them. We go right down to the simplest level because people won't agree on where the "middle" level ends. And we have tried to offer a little extra information even on the most basic of topics to justify their inclusion here. On the other hand, topics that are fully covered elsewhere in the book are omitted here.

We'll also make two other comments. First, there is nothing magical about dynamic OOP. Ruby's object orientation and its dynamic nature do interact with each other, but they aren't inherently interrelated; we put them in a single chapter largely for convenience. Second, some language features might be mentioned here that aren't strictly related to either topic. Consider this to be cheating, if you will. We wanted to put them somewhere.

11.1 Everyday OOP Tasks

If you don't already understand OOP, you won't learn it here. And if you don't already understand OOP in Ruby, you probably won't learn it here either. If you're rusty on those concepts, you can scan Chapter 1, "Ruby in Review," where we cover it rapidly (or you can go to another book).

On the other hand, much of this current chapter is tutorial oriented and fairly elementary. Therefore, it will be of some value to the beginner and perhaps less value to the intermediate Ruby programmer. We maintain that a book is a random access storage device, so you can easily skip the parts that don't interest you.

11.1.1 Using Multiple Constructors

There is no real "constructor" in Ruby as there is in C++ or Java. The concept is certainly there because objects have to be instantiated and initialized, but the behavior is somewhat different.

In Ruby, a class has a class method called `new`, which is used to instantiate new objects. The `new` method calls the user-defined special method `initialize`, which then initializes the attributes of the object appropriately, and `new` returns a reference to the new object.

But what if we want to have multiple constructors for an object? How should we handle that?

There is nothing to prevent the creation of additional class methods that return new objects. Listing 11.1 shows a contrived example in which a rectangle can have two side lengths and three color values. We create additional class methods that assume certain defaults for some of the parameters. (For example, a square is a rectangle with all sides the same length.)

Listing 11.1   Multiple Constructors

```
class ColoredRectangle

  def initialize(r, g, b, s1, s2)
    @r, @g, @b, @s1, @s2 = r, g, b, s1, s2
  end

  def self.white_rect(s1, s2)
    new(0xff, 0xff, 0xff, s1, s2)
  end

  def self.gray_rect(s1, s2)
    new(0x88, 0x88, 0x88, s1, s2)
  end

  def self.colored_square(r, g, b, s)
    new(r, g, b, s, s)
  end

  def self.red_square(s)
    new(0xff, 0, 0, s, s)
  end

  def inspect
    "#@r #@g #@b #@s1 #@s2"
  end
end

a = ColoredRectangle.new(0x88, 0xaa, 0xff, 20, 30)
b = ColoredRectangle.white_rect(15,25)
c = ColoredRectangle.red_square(40)
```

So, we can define any number of methods that create objects according to various specifications. Whether the term *constructor* is appropriate here is a question that we will leave to the language lawyers.

11.1.2 Creating Instance Attributes

An instance attribute in Ruby is always prefixed by an @ sign. It is like an ordinary variable in that it springs into existence when it is first assigned.

In OO languages, we frequently create methods that access attributes to avoid issues of data hiding. We want to have control over how the internals of an object are accessed from the outside. Typically we use setter and getter methods for this purpose (although in Ruby we don't typically use these terms). These are simply methods used to assign (set) a value or retrieve (get) a value, respectively.

Of course, it is possible to create these functions "by hand," as shown here:

```ruby
class Person

  def name
    @name
  end

  def name=(x)
    @name = x
  end

  def age
    @age
  end

  # ...

end
```

However, Ruby gives us a shorthand for creating these methods. The `attr` method takes a symbol as a parameter and creates the associated attribute. It also creates a getter of the same name, and if the optional second parameter is `true`, it creates a setter as well:

```ruby
class Person
  attr :name, true  # Create @name, name, name=
  attr :age         # Create @age, age
end
```

The related methods `attr_reader`, `attr_writer`, and `attr_accessor` take any number of symbols as parameters. The first creates only "read" methods (to get the value of an attribute); the second creates only "write" methods (to set values); the third creates both. Here is an example:

```
class SomeClass
  attr_reader :a1, :a2    # Creates @a1, a1, @a2, a2
  attr_writer :b1, :b2    # Creates @b1, b1=, @b2, b2=
  attr_accessor :c1, :c2  # Creates @c1, c1, c1=, @c2, c2, c2=
  # ...

  def initialize
    @a1 = 237
    @a2 = nil
  end

end
```

Recall that assignment to a writer of this form can only be done with a receiver, so within a method, the receiver `self` must be used:

```
def update_ones(a1, b1, c1)
  self.a1 = a1
  self.b1 = b1
  self.c1 = c1
end
```

Without invoking the method on `self`, Ruby will instead simply create a local variable inside the method with that name, which is not at all what we want in this case.

There is a special method to determine whether an instance variable is already defined:

```
obj = SomeClass.new
obj.instance_variable_defined?(:b2)    # true
obj.instance_variable_defined?(:d2)    # true
```

In accordance with our desire to use `eval` only when necessary, Ruby also has methods that can retrieve or assign instance variable values given the variable name as a string:

```ruby
class MyClass
  attr_reader :alpha, :beta

  def initialize(a, b, g)
    @alpha, @beta, @gamma = a, b, g
  end
end

x = MyClass.new(10, 11, 12)

x.instance_variable_set("@alpha", 234)
p x.alpha                                # 234

x.instance_variable_set("@gamma", 345)   # 345
v = x.instance_variable_get("@gamma")    # 345
```

Note first of all that we do have to use the at-sign on the variable name; not to do so is an error. If this is unintuitive, remember that methods such as `attr_accessor` actually take a symbol used to name the methods, which is why they omit the at-sign.

You may wonder whether the existence of these methods is a violation of encapsulation. The answer is no.

It's true these methods are powerful and potentially dangerous. They should be used cautiously, not casually. But it's impossible to say whether encapsulation is violated without looking at how these tools are used.

If they are used intentionally as part of a good design, then all is well. If they are used to violate the design, or to circumvent a bad design, then all is not well. Ruby intentionally grants access to the interiors of objects for people who really need it; the mark of the responsible programmer is not to abuse that freedom.

11.1.3   Using More Elaborate Constructors

As objects grow more complex, they accumulate more attributes that must be initialized when an object is created. The corresponding constructor can be long and cumbersome, forcing us to count parameters and wrap the line past the margin.

One way to deal with this complexity is to pass in a block that accepts the new object to the `initialize` method (see Listing 11.2). We can then evaluate the block to initialize the object.

Listing 11.2 A "Fancy" Constructor

```ruby
class PersonalComputer
  attr_accessor :manufacturer,
                :model, :processor, :clock,
                :ram, :disk, :monitor,
                :colors, :vres, :hres, :net

  def initialize
    yield self if block_given?
  end

  # Other methods...
end

desktop = PersonalComputer.new do |pc|
  pc.manufacturer = "Acme"
  pc.model = "THX-1138"
  pc.processor = "Z1"
  pc.clock = 9.6          # GHz
  pc.ram = 512            # Gb
  pc.disk = 20            # Tb
  pc.monitor = 30         # inches
  pc.colors = 16777216
  pc.vres = 1600
  pc.hres = 2000
  pc.net = "OC-768"
end

p desktop
```

Note that we're using accessors for our attributes so that we can assign values to them. Additionally, we could perform any arbitrary logic we wanted inside the body of this block. For example, we could derive certain fields from others by computation.

What if you didn't really want an object to have accessors for each of the attributes? In that case, we could use `instance_eval` instead and make the setter methods `protected`. This could prevent "accidental" assignment of an attribute from outside the object:

```ruby
class Library
  attr_reader :shelves

  def initialize(&block)
    instance_eval(&block)
  end

  protected
```

```
    attr_writer :shelves

end

branch = Library.new do
  self.shelves = 10
end

branch.shelves = 20
# NoMethodError: protected method `shelves=' called
branch.shelves       # 10
```

Even when you are using `instance_eval`, explicit calls to setters on `self` are still required. A setter method always takes an explicit receiver to distinguish the method call from an ordinary assignment to a local variable.

11.1.4   Creating Class-Level Attributes and Methods

A method or attribute isn't always associated with a specific instance of a class; it can be associated with the class itself. The typical example of a class method is the `new` method; it is always invoked in this way because it is called to create a new instance (and therefore can't belong to any particular instance).

We can define class methods of our own. You have already seen this in Section 11.1.1, "Using Multiple Constructors." However, their functionality certainly isn't limited to constructors; they can be used for any general-purpose task that makes sense at the class level.

In this next highly incomplete fragment, we assume that we are creating a class to play sound files. The `play` method can reasonably be implemented as an instance method; we can instantiate many objects referring to many different sound files. However, the `detect_hardware` method has a larger context, and depending on our implementation, it might not even make sense to create new objects if this method fails. Its context is that of the whole sound-playing environment rather than any particular sound file:

```
class SoundPlayer
  MAX_SAMPLE = 192

  def self.detect_hardware
    # ...
  end
```

```
   def play
     # ...
   end
end
```

Notice that there is another way to declare this class method. The following fragment is essentially the same:

```
class SoundPlayer
  MAX_SAMPLE = 192

  def play
    # ...
  end

end

def SoundPlayer.detect_hardware
  # ...
end
```

The only difference relates to constants declared in the class. When the class method is declared outside its class declaration, these constants aren't in scope. For example, `detect_hardware` in the first fragment can refer directly to `MAX_SAMPLE` if it needs to; in the second fragment, the notation `SoundPlayer::MAX_SAMPLE` would have to be used instead.

Not surprisingly, there are class variables as well as class methods. These begin with a double @ sign, and their scope is the class rather than any instance of the class.

The traditional example of using class variables is counting instances of the class as they are created. But they can actually be used for any purpose in which the information is meaningful in the context of the class rather than the object. For a different example, see Listing 11.3.

Listing 11.3   Class Variables and Methods

```
class Metal
  @@current_temp = 70

  attr_accessor :atomic_number

  def self.current_temp=(x)
    @@current_temp = x
```

```ruby
  end

  def self.current_temp
    @@current_temp
  end

  def liquid?
    @@current_temp >= @melting
  end

  def initialize(atnum, melt)
    @atomic_number = atnum
    @melting = melt
  end

end


aluminum = Metal.new(13, 1236)
copper = Metal.new(29, 1982)
gold = Metal.new(79, 1948)

Metal.current_temp = 1600

puts aluminum.liquid?        # true
puts copper.liquid?          # false
puts gold.liquid?            # false

Metal.current_temp = 2100

puts aluminum.liquid?        # true
puts copper.liquid?          # true
puts gold.liquid?            # true
```

Note here that the class variable is initialized at the class level before it is used in a class method. Note also that we can access a class variable from an instance method, but we can't access an instance variable from a class method. After a moment of thought, this makes sense.

But what happens if we try? What if we try to print the attribute @atomic_number from within the Metal.current_temp method? We find that it seems to exist—it doesn't cause an error—but it has the value nil. What is happening here?

The answer is that we're not actually accessing the instance variable of class Metal at all. We're accessing an instance variable of class Class instead. (Remember that in Ruby, Class is a class!)

Such a thing is called a *class instance variable* (a term that comes from Smalltalk). For more comments on this, see Section 11.2.4, "Creating Parametric Classes." Listing 11.4 summarizes the situation.

Listing 11.4 Class and Instance Data

```ruby
class MyClass

  SOME_CONST = "alpha"          # A class-level constant

  @@var = "beta"                # A class variable
  @var = "gamma"                # A class instance variable

  def initialize
    @var = "delta"              # An instance variable
  end

  def mymethod
    puts SOME_CONST             # (the class constant)
    puts @@var                  # (the class variable)
    puts @var                   # (the instance variable)
  end

  def self.classmeth1
    puts SOME_CONST             # (the class constant)
    puts @@var                  # (the class variable)
    puts @var                   # (the class instance variable)
  end

end

def MyClass.classmeth2
  puts MyClass::SOME_CONST      # (the class constant)
  # puts @@var                  # error - out of scope
  puts @var                     # (the class instance variable)
end


myobj = MyClass.new
MyClass.classmeth1              # alpha, beta, gamma
MyClass.classmeth2              # alpha, gamma
myobj.mymethod                  # alpha, beta, delta
```

We should mention that a class method can be made private with the method `private_class_method`. This works the same way `private` works at the instance level.

11.1.5   Inheriting from a Superclass

We can inherit from a class by using the < symbol:

```
class Boojum < Snark
  # ...
end
```

Given this declaration, we can say that the class `Boojum` is a subclass of the class `Snark`, or in the same way, `Snark` is a superclass of `Boojum`. As we all know, every boojum is a snark, but not every snark is a boojum.

The purpose of inheritance, of course, is to add or enhance functionality. We are going from the more general to the more specific.

As an aside, many languages such as C++ implement multiple inheritance (MI). Ruby (like Java and some others) doesn't allow MI, but the mixin facility can compensate for this; see Section 11.1.12, "Working with Modules."

Let's look at a (slightly) more realistic example. Suppose that we have a `Person` class and want to create a `Student` class that derives from it.

We'll define `Person` this way:

```
class Person
  attr_accessor :name, :age, :sex

  def initialize(name, age, sex)
    @name, @age, @sex = name, age, sex
  end

  # ...
end
```

And we'll then define `Student` this way:

```
class Student < Person
      attr_accessor :id_number, :hours

      def initialize(name, age, sex, id_number, hours)
        super(name, age, sex)
```

```
      @id_number = id_number
      @hours = hours
    end

    # ...

  end


  # Create two objects
  a = Person.new("Dave Bowman", 37, "m")
  b = Student.new("Franklin Poole", 36, "m", "000-13-5031", 24)
```

Now let's look at what we've done here. What is this `super` that we see called from `Student`'s `initialize` method? It is simply a call to the corresponding method in the parent class. As such, we give it three parameters (whereas our own `initialize` method takes five).

It's not always necessary to use `super` in such a way, but it is often convenient. After all, the attributes of a class form a superset of the attributes of the parent class, so why not use the parent's constructor to initialize them?

Concerning what inheritance really means, it definitely represents the "is-a" relationship. A Student is a Person, just as we expect. Here are three other observations:

- Every attribute (and method) of the parent is reflected in the child. If `Person` had a `height` attribute, `Student` would inherit it, and if the parent had a method named `say_hello`, the child would inherit that, too.

- The child can have additional attributes and methods, as you have already seen. That is why the creation of a subclass is often referred to as "extending a superclass."

- The child can override or redefine any of the attributes and methods of its parent.

This last point brings up the question of how a method call is resolved. How do you know whether you're calling the method of this particular class or its superclass?

The short answer is, you don't know, and you don't care. If we invoke a method on a `Student` object, the method for that class will be called if it exists. If it doesn't, the method in the superclass will be called, and so on.

We say "and so on" because every class (except `BasicObject`) has a superclass. As an aside, `BasicObject` is a "blank slate" type of object that has even fewer methods than `Object` does.

What if we specifically want to call a superclass method, but we don't happen to be in the corresponding method? We can always create an alias in the subclass before we do anything with it:

```
class Student    # reopening class
  # Assuming Person has a say_hello method...
  alias :say_hi :say_hello

  def say_hello
    puts "Hi, there."
  end

  def formal_greeting
    # Say hello the way my superclass would.
    say_hi
  end
end
```

There are various subtleties relating to inheritance that we don't discuss here, but this is essentially how it works. Be sure to refer to the next section.

11.1.6   Testing Classes of Objects

Frequently we will want to know the answer to a question such as: What kind of object is this? Or how does it relate to this class? There are many ways of making this kind of determination.

First, the `class` method (that is, the instance method named `class`) always returns the class of an object:

```
s = "Hello"
n = 237
sc = s.class     # String
nc = n.class     # Fixnum
```

Don't be misled into thinking that the thing returned by `class` or `type` is a string representing the class. It is an actual instance of the class `Class`! Therefore, if we wanted, we could call a class method of the target type as though it were an instance method of Class (which it is):

```
s2 = "some string"
var = s2.class             # String
my_str = var.new("Hi...")  # A new string
```

We could compare such a variable with a constant class name to see whether they are equal; we could even use a variable as the superclass from which to define a subclass! Confused? Just remember that in Ruby, Class is an object, and Object is a class.

Sometimes we want to compare an object with a class to see whether the object belongs to that class. The method instance_of? will accomplish this. Here is an example:

```
puts 5.instance_of?(Fixnum)        # true
puts "XYZZY".instance_of?(Fixnum)  # false
puts "PLUGH".instance_of?(String)  # true
```

But what if we want to take inheritance relationships into account? The kind_of? method (similar to instance_of?) takes this issue into account. A synonym is is_a?, naturally enough, because what we are describing is the classic is-a relationship:

```
n = 9876543210
flag1 = n.instance_of? Bignum    # true
flag2 = n.kind_of? Bignum        # true
flag3 = n.is_a? Bignum           # true
flag3 = n.is_a? Integer          # true
flag4 = n.is_a? Numeric          # true
flag5 = n.is_a? Object           # true
flag6 = n.is_a? String           # false
flag7 = n.is_a? Array            # false
```

Obviously kind_of? or is_a? is more generalized than the instance_of? relationship. For an example from everyday life, every dog is a mammal, but not every mammal is a dog.

There is one surprise here for the Ruby neophyte. Any module that is mixed in by a class maintains the is-a relationship with the instances. For example, the Array class mixes in Enumerable; this means that any array is a kind of enumerable entity:

```
x = [1, 2, 3]
flag8 = x.kind_of? Enumerable      # true
flag9 = x.is_a? Enumerable         # true
```

We can also use the numeric relational operators in a fairly intuitive way to compare one class to another. We say "intuitive" because the less-than operator is used to denote inheritance from a superclass:

```
flag1 = Integer < Numeric          # true
flag2 = Integer < Object           # true
flag3 = Object == Array            # false
flag4 = IO >= File                 # true
flag5 = Float < Integer            # nil
```

Every class has the operator === (sometimes called the "threequal" operator) defined. The expression class === instance will be true if the instance belongs to the class. The relationship operator is usually known as the case equality operator because it is used implicitly in a case statement. This is therefore a way to act on the class of an expression.

For more information on this operator, see Section 11.1.7, "Testing Equality of Objects."

We should also mention the respond_to? method. This is used when we don't really care what the class is but just want to know whether it implements a certain method. This, of course, is a rudimentary kind of type information. (In fact, we might say this is the most important type information of all.) The method is passed a symbol and an optional flag (indicating whether to include private methods in the search):

```
# Search public methods
if wumpus.respond_to?(:bite)
  puts "It's got teeth!"
else
  puts "Go ahead and taunt it."
end

# Optional second parameter will search
# private and protected methods as well.

if woozle.respond_to?(:bite, true)
  puts "Woozles bite!"
else
  puts "Ah, the non-biting woozle."
end
```

Sometimes we want to know what class is the immediate parent of an object or class. The instance method `superclass` of class `Class` can be used for this:

```
array_parent = Array.superclass          # Object
fn_parent = 237.class.superclass         # Integer
obj_parent = Object.superclass           # BasicObject
basic_parent = BasicObject.superclass    # nil
```

Every class except `BasicObject` will have a superclass.

11.1.7 Testing Equality of Objects

All animals are equal, but some are more equal than others.

—*George Orwell,* Animal Farm

When you write classes, it's convenient if the semantics for common operations are the same as for Ruby's built-in classes. For example, if your classes implement objects that may be ranked, it makes sense to implement the method <=> and mix in the `Comparable` module. Doing so means that all the normal comparison operators work with objects of your class.

However, the picture is less clear when it comes to dealing with object equality. Ruby objects implement five different methods that test for equality. Your classes might well end up implementing some of these, so let's look at each in turn.

The most basic comparison is the `equal?` method (which comes from `BasicObject`). It returns `true` if its receiver and parameter have the same object ID. This is a fundamental part of the semantics of objects and shouldn't be overridden in your classes.

The most common test for equality uses our old friend ==, which tests the values of its receiver with its argument. This is probably the most intuitive test for equality.

Next on the scale of abstraction is the method `eql?`, which is part of `Object`. (Actually, `eql?` is implemented in the `Kernel` module, which is mixed into `Object`.) Like the == operator, `eql?` compares its receiver and its argument, but it is slightly stricter. For example, different numeric objects will be coerced into a common type when compared using ==, but objects of different types will never test equal using `eql?`:

```
flag1 = (1 == 1.0)     # true
flag2 = 1.eql?(1.0)    # false
```

The `eql?` method exists for one reason: It is used to compare the values of hash keys. If you want to override Ruby's default behavior when using your objects as hash keys, you'll need to override the methods `eql?` and `hash` for those objects.

Two more equality tests are implemented by every object. The `===` method is used to compare the target in a case statement against each of the selectors, using selector `===` target. Although apparently complex, this rule allows Ruby case statements to be intuitive in practice. For example, you can switch based on the class of an object:

```
case an_object
when String
  puts "It's a string."
when Numeric
  puts "It's a number."
else
  puts "It's something else entirely."
end
```

This works because class `Module` implements `===` to test whether its parameter is an instance of its receiver (or the receiver's parents). Therefore, if `an_object` is the string "cat", the expression `String === an_object` would be true, and the first clause in the case statement would fire.

Finally, Ruby implements the match operator `=~`. Conventionally, this is used by strings and regular expressions to implement pattern matching. However, if you find a use for it in other classes, you're free to overload it.

The equality tests `==` and `=~` also have negated forms, `!=` and `!~`, respectively. These are implemented internally by reversing the sense of the non-negated form. This means that if you implement, say, the method `==`, you also get the method `!=` for free.

11.1.8   Controlling Access to Methods

In Ruby, an object is pretty much defined by the interface it provides: the methods it makes available to others. However, when writing a class, you often need to write other helper methods that are used within your class but dangerous if available externally. That is where the `private` method of class `Module` comes in handy.

You can use `private` in two different ways. If in the body of a class or method definition you call `private` with no parameters, subsequent methods will be made private to that class or module. Alternatively, you can pass a list of method names (as symbols) to `private`, and these named methods will be made private. Listing 11.5 shows both forms.

Listing 11.5   Private Methods

```
class Bank
  def open_safe
    # ...
  end

  def close_safe
    # ...
  end

  private :open_safe, :close_safe

  def make_withdrawal(amount)
    if access_allowed
      open_safe
      get_cash(amount)
      close_safe
    end
  end

  # make the rest private
private

  def get_cash
    # ...
  end

  def access_allowed
    # ...
  end
end
```

Because the `attr` family of statements effectively just defines methods, attributes are affected by access control statements such as `private`.

The implementation of `private` might seem strange but is actually clever. Private methods cannot be called with an explicit receiver: They are always called with an implicit receiver of `self`. This means that you can never invoke a private method in another object: There is no way to specify that other object as the receiver of the method call. It also means that private methods are available to subclasses of the class that defines them but again only in the same object.

The `protected` access modifier is less restrictive. Protected methods can be accessed only by instances of the defining class and its subclasses. As you saw in Section 11.1.3, "Using More Elaborate Constructors," this allows calling setters on `self` (which is not allowed by `private`).

Protected methods can be invoked on other objects (as long as they are objects of the same class as the sender). A common use for protected methods is defining accessors to allow two objects of the same type to cooperate with each other. In the following example, objects of class `Person` can be compared based on the person's age, but that age is not accessible outside the `Person` class. The private attribute `pay_scale` may be read from inside the class, but not from outside the class, even by other objects of the same class:

```ruby
class Person
  attr_reader :name, :age, :pay_scale
  protected   :age
  private     :pay_scale

  def initialize(name, age, pay_scale)
    @name, @age, @pay_scale = name, age, pay_scale
  end

  def <=>(other)
    age <=> other.age    # allowed by protected
  end

  def same_rank?(other)
    pay_scale == other.pay_scale   # not allowed by private
  end

  def rank
    case pay_scale
    when 1..3
      "lower"
    when 4..6
      "middle"
    when 7..9
      "high"
    end
  end
```

```
    end


p1 = Person.new("Fred", 31, 5)
p2 = Person.new("Agnes", 43, 7)


x = p1.age              # NoMethodError: protected method 'age'
compare = (p1 <=> p2)   # -1
r = p1.rank             # "middle"
x = p2.same_rank?(p1)   # NoMethodError: private method 'pay_scale'
```

To complete the picture, the access modifier `public` is used to make methods public. This shouldn't be a surprise.

As a final twist, normal methods defined outside a class or module definition (that is, the methods defined at the top level) are made private by default. Because they are defined in class `Object`, they are globally available, but they cannot be called with a receiver.

11.1.9   Copying an Object

The Ruby built-in methods `Object#clone` and `#dup` produce copies of their receiver. They differ in the amount of context about the object that they copy. The `dup` method copies just the object's content, whereas `clone` also preserves things such as singleton classes associated with the object:

```
s1 = "cat"

def s1.upcase
  "CaT"
end

s1_dup   = s1.dup
s1_clone = s1.clone
s1                      #=> "cat"
s1_dup.upcase           #=> "CAT"   (singleton method not copied)
s1_clone.upcase         #=> "CaT"   (uses singleton method)
```

Both `dup` and `clone` are shallow copies: They copy the immediate contents of their receiver only. If the receiver contains references to other objects, those objects aren't in turn copied; the duplicate simply holds references to them. The following example illustrates this. The object `arr2` is a copy of `arr1`, so changing entire elements such as `arr2[2]` has no effect on `arr1`. However, both the original array and the duplicate contain a reference to the same `String` object, so changing its contents via `arr2` also affects the value referenced by `arr1`:

```
arr1 = [ 1, "flipper", 3 ]
arr2 = arr1.dup

arr2[2] = 99
arr2[1][2] = 'a'

arr1              # [1, "flapper", 3]
arr2              # [1, "flapper", 99]
```

Sometimes you want a deep copy, where the entire object tree rooted in one object is copied to create the second object. This way, there is guaranteed to be no interaction between the two. Ruby provides no built-in method to perform a deep copy, but there are a couple of techniques you can use to implement one.

The pure way to do it is to have your classes implement a `deep_copy` method. As part of its processing, this method calls `deep_copy` recursively on all the objects referenced by the receiver. You then add a `deep_copy` method to all the Ruby built-in classes that you use.

Fortunately, there's a quicker (albeit hackier) way using the `Marshal` module. If you use marshaling to dump an object into a string and then load it back into a new object, that new object will be a deep copy of the original:

```
arr1 = [ 1, "flipper", 3 ]
arr2 = Marshal.load(Marshal.dump(arr1))

arr2[2] = 99
arr2[1][2] = 'a'

arr1              # [1, "flipper", 3]
arr2              # [1, "flapper", 99]
```

In this case, notice how changing the string via `arr2` doesn't affect the string referenced by `arr1`.

11.1.10 Using `initialize_copy`

When you copy an object with dup or clone, the constructor is bypassed. All the state information is copied.

But what if you don't want this to happen? Consider this example:

```ruby
class Document
  attr_accessor :title, :text
  attr_reader   :timestamp

  def initialize(title, text)
    @title, @text = title, text
    @timestamp = Time.now
  end
end


doc1 = Document.new("Random Stuff",File.read("somefile"))
sleep 300                        # Wait awhile...
doc2 = doc1.clone

doc1.timestamp == doc2.timestamp  # true
# Oops... the timestamps are the same!
```

When a Document is created, it is given a timestamp. If we copy that object, we copy the timestamp also. But what if we wanted instead to capture the time that the copy operation happened?

Defining an `initialize_copy` makes this possible. This method is called when an object is copied. It is analogous to `initialize`, giving us complete control over the object's state.

```ruby
class Document      # Reopen the class
  def initialize_copy(other)
    @timestamp = Time.now
  end
end

doc3 = Document.new("More Stuff", File.read("otherfile"))
sleep 300                        # Wait awhile...
doc4 = doc3.clone

doc3.timestamp == doc4.timestamp   # false
# Timestamps are now accurate.
```

Note that the `initialize_copy` is called after the information is copied. That is why we omitted this line:

```
@title, @text = other.title, other.text
```

As a matter of fact, an empty `initialize_copy` would behave just as if the method were not there at all.

11.1.11   Understanding `allocate`

In rare circumstances, you might want to create an object without calling its constructor (bypassing `initialize`). For example, maybe you have an object whose state is determined entirely by its accessors; then it isn't necessary to call `new` (which calls `initialize`) unless you really want to. Imagine you are gathering data a piece at a time to fill in the state of an object; you might want to start with an "empty" object rather than gathering all the data up front and calling the constructor.

The `allocate` makes this easier. It returns a "blank" object of the proper class, yet uninitialized:

```ruby
class Person
  attr_accessor :name, :age, :phone

  def initialize(n, a, p)
    @name, @age, @phone = n, a, p
  end
end

p1 = Person.new("John Smith", 29, "555-1234")
p2 = Person.allocate

p p1.age    # 29
p p2.age    # nil
```

11.1.12   Working with Modules

There are two basic reasons to use modules in Ruby. The first is simply namespace management; we'll have fewer name collisions if we store constants and methods in modules. A method stored in this way (a module method) is called with the module name, analogous to the way a class method is called. If we see calls such as

`File.ctime` and `FileTest.exist?`, we can't tell just from context that `File` is a class and `FileTest` is a module.

The second reason is more interesting: We can use a module as a mixin. A mixin is like a specialized implementation of multiple inheritance in which only the interface portion is inherited.

We've talked about module methods, but what about instance methods? A module isn't a class, so it can't have instances, and an instance method can't be called without a receiver.

As it turns out, a module can have instance methods. These become part of whatever class does the `include` of the module:

```ruby
module MyMod

  def method_1
    puts "This is method 1"
  end

end


class MyClass
  include MyMod
end

x = MyClass.new
x.method_1          # This is method 1
```

Here, `MyMod` is mixed into `MyClass`, and the instance method `method_1` is inherited. You have also seen an `include` done at the top level; in that case, the module is mixed into `Object` as you might expect.

But what happens to our module methods, if there are any? You might think they would be included as class methods, but Ruby doesn't behave that way. The module methods aren't mixed in.

However, we have a trick we can use if we want that behavior. There is a hook called `included` that we can override. It is called with a parameter, which is the "destination" class or module (into which this module is being included). For an example of its use, see Listing 11.6.

Listing 11.6   Including a Module with `included`

```
module MyMod

  def self.included(klass)
    def klass.module_method
      puts "Module (class) method"
    end
  end

  def method_1
    puts "Method 1"
  end

end


class MyClass

  include MyMod

  def self.class_method
    puts "Class method"
  end

  def method_2
    puts "Method 2"
  end

end


x = MyClass.new

                           # Output:
MyClass.class_method       #  Class method
x.method_1                 #  Method 1
MyClass.module_method      #  Module (class) method
x.method_2                 #  Method 2
```

This example is worth examining in detail. First, we should understand that `included` is a hook that is called when an `include` happens. If we really wanted to, we could implement our own `include` method by defining `append_features`, but that is far less common (if it is ever desired at all).

Also note that within the `included` method definition there is yet another definition. This looks unusual, but it works because the inner method definition is a singleton method (class level or module level). An attempt to define an instance method in the same way would result in a `Nested method` error.

Conceivably a module might want to determine the initiator of a mixin. The `included` method can also be used for this because the class is passed in as a parameter.

It is also possible to mix in the instance methods of a module as class methods using `include` or `extend`. Listing 11.7 shows an example.

Listing 11.7   Module Instance Methods Becoming Class Methods

```
module MyMod

  def meth3
    puts "Module instance method meth3"
    puts "can become a class method."
  end

end

class MyClass

  class << self      # Here, self is MyClass
    include MyMod
  end

end


MyClass.meth3

# Output:
#    Module instance method meth3
#    can become a class method.
```

The `extend` method is useful here. This example simply becomes the following:

```
class MyClass
  extend MyMod
end
```

We've been talking about methods. What about instance variables? Although it is certainly possible for modules to have their own instance data, it usually isn't done. However, if you find a need for this capability, there is nothing stopping you from using it.

It is possible to mix a module into an object rather than a class (for example, with the `extend` method). See Section 11.2.2, "Specializing an Individual Object."

It's important to understand one more fact about modules. It is possible to define methods in your class that will be called by the mixin. This is a powerful technique that will seem familiar to those who have used Java interfaces.

The classic example is mixing in the `Comparable` module and defining a `<=>` method. Because the mixed-in methods can call the comparison method, we now have such operators as <, >, <=, and so on.

Another example is mixing in the `Enumerable` module and defining `<=>` and the iterator `each`. This gives us numerous useful methods such as `collect`, `sort`, `min`, `max`, and `select`.

You can also define modules of your own to be used in the same way. The principal limitation is the programmer's imagination.

11.1.13   Transforming or Converting Objects

Sometimes an object comes in exactly the right form at the right time, but sometimes we need to convert it to something else or pretend it's something it isn't. A good example is the heavily used `to_s` method.

Every object can be converted to a string representation in some fashion. But not every object can successfully masquerade as a string. That in essence is the difference between the `to_s` and `to_str` methods. Let's elaborate on that.

Methods such as `puts` and contexts such as `#{…}` interpolation in strings all expect to receive a `String` as a parameter. If they don't, they ask the object they did receive to convert itself to a `String` by sending it a `to_s` message. This is where you can specify how your object will appear when displayed; simply implement a `to_s` method in your class that returns an appropriate `String`:

```
class Pet

  def initialize(name)
    @name = name
  end

  # ...

  def to_s
    "Pet: #@name"
  end

end
```

Other methods (such as the `String` concatenation operator +) are more picky; they expect you to pass in something that is really pretty close to a `String`. In this case, Matz decided not to have the interpreter call `to_s` to convert non-string arguments because he felt this would lead to too many errors. Instead, the interpreter invokes a stricter method, `to_str`. Of the built-in classes, only `String` and `Exception` implement `to_str`, and only `String`, `Regexp`, and `Marshal` call it. Typically when you see the runtime error `TypeError: Failed to convert xyz into String`, you know that the interpreter tried to invoke `to_str` and failed.

You can implement `to_str` yourself. For example, you might want to allow numbers to be concatenated to strings:

```
class Numeric

  def to_str
    to_s
  end

end

label = "Number " + 9      # "Number 9"
```

An analogous situation holds for arrays. The method `to_a` is called to convert an object to an array representation, and `to_ary` is called when an array is expected.

An example of when `to_ary` is called is with multiple assignment. Suppose we have a statement of this form:

```
a, b, c = x
```

Assuming that x is an array of three elements, this would behave in the expected way. But if it isn't an array, the interpreter will try to call `to_ary` to convert it to one. For what it's worth, the method we define can be a singleton (belonging to a specific object). The conversion can be completely arbitrary; here we show an (unrealistic) example in which a string is converted to an array of strings:

```
class String

  def to_ary
    return self.split("")
  end
```

```
end

str = "UFO"
a, b, c = str      # ["U", "F", "O"]
```

The inspect method implements another convention. Debuggers, utilities such as irb, and the debug print method p use the inspect method to convert an object to a printable representation. If you want classes to reveal internal details when being debugged, you should override inspect.

Numeric coercion is another example of transforming or converting an object. Refer to Section 5.16, "Coercing Numeric Values."

11.1.14   Creating Data-Only Classes (Structs)

Sometimes you need to group together a bunch of related data. Initially, it can be easy to simply use an array or a hash. That approach is brittle, and makes changes or adding accessor methods difficult. You could solve the problem by defining a class:

```
class Address

  attr_accessor :street, :city, :state

  def initialize(street, city, state)
    @street, @city, @state = street, city, state
  end

end

books = Address.new("411 Elm St", "Dallas", "TX")
```

This works, but it's tedious, and a fair amount of repetition is in there. That's why the built-in class Struct comes in handy. In the same way that convenience methods such as attr_accessor define methods to access attributes, class Struct defines classes that contain attributes. These classes are structure templates:

```
Address = Struct.new("Address", :street, :city, :state)
books = Address.new("411 Elm St", "Dallas", "TX")
```

So, why do we pass the name of the structure to be created in as the first parameter of the constructor and also assign the result to a constant (Address in this case)?

When we create a new structure template by calling `Struct.new`, we may pass a string with the class name as the first argument. If we do, a new class is created within class `Struct` itself, with the name passed in as the first parameter and the attributes given as the rest of the parameters. This means that if we wanted, we could access this newly created class within the namespace of class `Struct`:

```
Struct.new("Address", :street, :city, :state)
books = Struct::Address.new("411 Elm St", "Dallas", "TX")
```

If the first argument to `Struct.new` is a symbol, all of the arguments are taken to be attribute names, and a class inside the `Struct` namespace will not be created.

When creating a `Struct` class, additional methods can be defined for the class by simply providing a block to `Struct.new`. The block will be evaluated as if it were the class body, much like any other class definition.

After you've created a structure template, you call its `new` method to create new instances of that particular structure. You don't have to assign values to all the attributes in the constructor: Those that you omit will be initialized to `nil`. Once it is created, you can access the structure's attributes using normal syntax or by indexing the structure object as if it were a `Hash`. For more information, look up class `Struct` in any reference (such as `rdoc.info` online).

By the way, we advise against the creation of a `Struct` named `Tms`. There is already a predefined `Struct::Tms` class.

11.1.15 Freezing Objects

Sometimes we want to prevent an object from being changed. The `freeze` method (in `Object`) allows us to do this, effectively turning an object into a constant.

After we freeze an object, an attempt to modify it results in a `TypeError`. Listing 11.8 shows a pair of examples.

Listing 11.8 Freezing an Object

```
str = "This is a test. "
str.freeze

begin
  str << " Don't be alarmed."    # Attempting to modify
rescue => err
  puts "#{err.class} #{err}"
end

arr = [1, 2, 3]
```

```
arr.freeze

begin
  arr << 4                      # Attempting to modify
rescue => err
  puts "#{err.class} #{err}"
end

# Output:
#   TypeError: can't modify frozen string
#   TypeError: can't modify frozen array
```

Freezing strings is handled as a special case: The interpreter will create a single frozen string object and return it for every instance of the frozen string. This can reduce memory usage if, for example, a particular string will be returned from a method that is called many times:

```
str1 = "Woozle".freeze
str2 = "Woozle".freeze

str1.object_id == str2.object_id  # true
```

Although freezing prevents modification, bear in mind that `freeze` operates on an object reference, not on a variable! This means that any operation resulting in a new object will work. Sometimes this isn't intuitive. In the following example, we might expect that the += operation would fail—but it acts normally. This is because assignment is not a method call. It acts on variables, not objects, and it creates a new object as needed. The old object is indeed still frozen, but it is no longer referenced by that variable name:

```
str = "counter-"
str.freeze
str += "intuitive"   # "counter-intuitive"

arr = [8, 6, 7]
arr.freeze
arr += [5, 3, 0, 9]  # [8, 6, 7, 5, 3, 0, 9]
```

Why does this happen? The statement a += x is semantically equivalent to a = a + x. The expression a + x is evaluated to a new object, which is then assigned to a! The object isn't changed, but the variable now refers to a new object. All the reflexive assignment operators exhibit this behavior, as do some other methods. Always ask yourself whether you are creating a new object or modifying an existing one; then freeze will not surprise you.

There is a method called frozen? that will tell you whether an object is frozen:

```
hash = { 1 => 1, 2 => 4, 3 => 9 }
hash.freeze
arr = hash.to_a
puts hash.frozen?    # true
puts arr.frozen?     # false
hash2 = hash
puts hash2.frozen?   # true
```

As you can see here (with hash2), the object, not the variable, is frozen.

11.1.16   Using tap in Method Chaining

The tap method runs a block with access to the value of an expression in the middle of other operations. (Think "tap" as in tapping a phone, or as in using the tap in the kitchen.)

One use of tap can be to print intermediate values while they are being processed, because the block is passed the object that tap is called on:

```
a = [1, 5, 1, 4, 2, 3, 4, 3, 2, 5, 2, 1]
p a.sort.uniq.tap{|x| p x }.map {|x| x**2 + 2*x + 7 }
# [1, 2, 3, 4, 5]
# [10, 15, 22, 31, 42]
```

Providing this sort of access can be helpful, but the real power of tap comes from its ability to change the object inside the block. This allows code to alter an object and still return the original object, rather than the result of the last operation:

```
def feed(woozle)
  woozle.tap do |w|
    w.stomach << Steak.new
  end
end
```

Without tap, our feed method would return the stomach that now contains a steak. Instead, it returns the newly fed (and presumably happy) woozle.

This technique is highly useful inside class methods that construct an object, call methods on the object, and then return the object. It is also handy when implementing methods that are intended to be chained together.

11.2   More Advanced Techniques

Not everything in Ruby OOP is straightforward. Some techniques are more complex than others, and some are rarely used. The dividing line will be different for each programmer. We've tried to put items in this part of the chapter that were slightly more involved or slightly more rare in terms of usage.

From time to time, you might ask yourself whether it's possible to do some task or other in Ruby. The short answer is that Ruby is a rich dynamic OOP language with a good set of reasonably orthogonal features, and if you want to do something that you're used to in another language, you can probably do it in Ruby.

As a matter of fact, all Turing-complete languages are pretty much the same from a theoretical standpoint. The whole field of language design is the search for a meaningful, convenient notation. The reader who doubts the importance of a convenient notation should try writing a LISP interpreter in COBOL or doing long division with Roman numerals.

Of course, we won't say that every language task is elegant or natural in Ruby. Someone would quickly prove us wrong if we made that assertion.

This section also touches on the use of Ruby in various advanced programming styles such as functional programming and aspect-oriented programming. We don't claim expertise in these areas; we are only reporting what other people are saying. Take it all with a grain of salt.

11.2.1   Sending an Explicit Message to an Object

In a static language, you take it for granted that when you call a function, that function name is hard-coded into the program; it is part of the program source. In a dynamic language, we have more flexibility than that.

Every time you invoke a method, you're sending a message to an object. Most of the time, these messages are hard-coded as in a static language, but they need not always be. We can write code that determines at runtime which method to call. The `send` method will allow us to use a `Symbol` to represent a method name.

For an example, suppose that we had an array of objects, and we wanted to get another array that contained an attribute on each object. That's not a problem; we can easily write customized map blocks. But suppose that we wanted to be a little more elegant and write only a single routine that could return whatever attribute we specified. Listing 11.9 shows an example.

Listing 11.9   Using a Method Named by a Parameter

```
class Person
  attr_reader :name, :age, :height

  def initialize(name, age, height)
    @name, @age, @height = name, age, height
  end

  def inspect
    "#@name #@age #@height"
  end
end


class Array
  def map_by(sym)
    self.map {|x| x.send(sym) }
  end
end


people = []
people << Person.new("Hansel", 35, 69)
people << Person.new("Gretel", 32, 64)
people << Person.new("Ted", 36, 68)
people << Person.new("Alice", 33, 63)

p1 = people.map_by(:name)     # Hansel, Gretel, Ted, Alice
p2 = people.map_by(:age)      # 35, 32, 36, 33
p3 = people.map_by(:height)   # 69, 64, 68, 63
```

This particular code is not really necessary because we can simply call `map(&:name)` and get the same result, but it illustrates the send method well. We'll look at this option more carefully in Section 11.2.7, "Using Symbols as Blocks."

We'll also mention the alias `__send__`, which does exactly the same thing. It is given this peculiar name, of course, because send is a name that might be used (purposefully or accidentally) as a user-defined method name.

One issue that some coders have with send is that it allows circumvention of Ruby's privacy model (in the sense that private methods may be called indirectly by sending the object a string or symbol). This was intended more as a feature than a design flaw; however, if you are more comfortable "protecting yourself" against doing this accidentally, you can use the `public_send` method instead.

11.2.2   Specializing an Individual Object

I'm a Solipsist, and I must say I'm surprised there aren't more of us.

—Letter received by Bertrand Russell

In most object-oriented languages, all objects of a particular class share the same behavior. The class acts as a template, producing an object with the same interface each time the constructor is called.

Although Ruby acts the same way, that isn't the end of the story. Once you have a Ruby object, you can change its behavior "on the fly." Effectively, you're giving that object a private, anonymous subclass: All the methods of the original class are available, but you've added additional behavior for just that object. Because this behavior is private to the associated object, it can only occur once. A thing occurring only once is called a "singleton," so we sometimes refer to singleton methods and singleton classes (also called metaclasses).

The word "singleton" can be confusing because it is also used in a different sense—as the name of a well-known design pattern for a class that can only be instantiated once. For this usage, refer to the `singleton` library.

In the following example, we see a pair of objects, both of which are strings. For the second one, we will add a method called `upcase` that will override the existing method of that name:

```
a = "hello"
b = "goodbye"

def b.upcase  # create single method
  gsub(/(.)(.)/) { $1.upcase + $2 }
end

puts a.upcase    # HELLO
puts b.upcase    # GoOdBye
```

Adding a singleton method to an object creates a singleton class for that object if one doesn't already exist. This singleton class's parent will be the object's original class. (This could be considered an anonymous subclass of the original class.) If you want to add multiple methods to an object, you can create the singleton class directly:

```
b = "goodbye"

class << b

  def upcase        # create single method
    gsub(/(.)(.)/) { $1.upcase + $2 }
  end

  def upcase!
    gsub!(/(.)(.)/) { $1.upcase + $2 }
  end

end

puts b.upcase   # GoOdBye
puts b          # goodbye
b.upcase!
puts b          # GoOdBye
```

As an aside, note that the more "primitive" objects (such as a `Fixnum`) cannot have singleton methods added. This is because an object of this nature is stored as an immediate value rather than as an object reference. However, this functionality is planned for a future revision of Ruby (though the values will still be immediate).

If you read some of the library code, you're bound to come across an idiomatic use of singleton classes. Within class definitions, you might see something like this:

```
class SomeClass

  # Stuff...

  class << self
    # more stuff...
  end

  # ... and so on.

end
```

Within the body of a class definition, `self` is the class you're defining, so creating a singleton based on it modifies the class's class. At the simplest level, this means that instance methods in the singleton class are class methods externally:

```
class TheClass
  class << self
    def hello
      puts "hi"
    end
  end
end


# invoke a class method
TheClass.hello              # hi
```

Another common use of this technique is to define class-level helper functions, which we can then access in the rest of the class definition. As an example, we want to define several accessor functions that always convert their results to a string. We could do this by coding each individually. A neater way might be to define a class-level function `accessor_string` that generates these functions for us (as shown in Listing 11.10).

Listing 11.10   A Class-Level Method `accessor_string`

```
class MyClass

  class << self

    def accessor_string(*names)
      names.each do |name|
        class_eval <<-EOF
          def #{name}
            @#{name}.to_s
          end
        EOF
      end
    end

  end

  def initialize
    @a = [1, 2, 3]
    @b = Time.now
  end

  accessor_string :a, :b

end
```

```
o = MyClass.new
puts o.a        # 123
puts o.b        # 2014-07-26 00:45:12 -0700
```

More imaginative examples are left up to you.

It is also possible to use the `extend` method to mix a module into a single object. The instance methods from the module become instance methods for the object. Let's look at Listing 11.11.

Listing 11.11   Using `extend`

```
module Quantifier
  def two?
    2 == self.select { |x| yield x }.size
  end

  def four?
    4 == self.select { |x| yield x }.size
  end

end


list = [1, 2, 3, 4, 5]
list.extend(Quantifier)

flag1 = list.two? {|x| x > 3 }          # => true
flag2 = list.two? {|x| x >= 3 }         # => false
flag3 = list.four? {|x| x <= 4 }        # => true
flag4 = list.four? {|x| x % 2 == 0 }    # => false
```

In this example, the `two?` and `four?` methods are mixed into the `list` array.

11.2.3   Nesting Classes and Modules

It's possible to nest classes and modules arbitrarily. The programmer new to Ruby might not know this.

Mostly this is for namespace management. Note that the `File` class has a `Stat` class embedded inside it. This helps to "encapsulate" the `Stat` class inside a class of related functionality and also allows for a future class named `Stat`, which won't conflict with that one (perhaps a statistics class, for instance).

The `Struct::Tms` class is a similar example. Any new `Struct` is placed in this namespace so as not to pollute the one above it, and `Tms` is really just another `Struct`.

It's also conceivable that you might want to create a nested class simply because the outside world doesn't need that class or shouldn't access it. In other words, you can create classes that are subject to the principle of "data hiding," just as the instance variables and methods are subject to the same principle at a lower level.

```
class BugTrackingSystem

  class Bug
    #...
  end

  #...

end

# Nothing out here knows about Bug.
```

You can nest a class within a module, a module within a class, and so on.

11.2.4   Creating Parametric Classes

Learn the rules; then break them.

—Basho

Suppose we wanted to create multiple classes that differed only in the initial values of the class-level variables. Recall that a class variable is typically initialized as a part of the class definition:

```
class Terran

  @@home_planet = "Earth"

  def Terran.home_planet
    @@home_planet
  end

  def Terran.home_planet=(x)
    @@home_planet = x
```

```
  end

  #...

end
```

That is all fine, but suppose we had a number of similar classes to define. The novice will think, "Ah, I'll just define a superclass" (see Listing 11.12).

Listing 11.12   Parametric Classes: The Wrong Way

```
class IntelligentLife    # Wrong way to do this!

  @@home_planet = nil

  def IntelligentLife.home_planet
    @@home_planet
  end

  def IntelligentLife.home_planet=(x)
    @@home_planet = x
  end

  #...
end

class Terran < IntelligentLife
  @@home_planet = "Earth"
  #...
end

class Martian < IntelligentLife
  @@home_planet = "Mars"
  #...
end
```

However, this won't work. If we call `Terran.home_planet`, we expect a result of "Earth"—but we get "Mars"!

Why would this happen? The answer is that class variables aren't truly class variables; they belong not to the class but to the entire inheritance hierarchy. The class variables aren't copied from the parent class but are shared with the parent (and thus with the "sibling" classes).

We could eliminate the definition of the class variable in the base class, but then the class methods we define no longer work!

We could fix this by moving these definitions to the child classes, but now we've defeated our whole purpose. We're declaring separate classes without any "parameterization."

We'll offer a different solution. We'll defer the evaluation of the class variable until runtime by using the `class_eval` method. Listing 11.13 shows a complete solution.

Listing 11.13   Parametric Classes: A Better Way

```
class IntelligentLife

  def IntelligentLife.home_planet
    class_eval("@@home_planet")
  end

  def IntelligentLife.home_planet=(x)
    class_eval("@@home_planet = #{x}")
  end

  #...
end

class Terran < IntelligentLife
  @@home_planet = "Earth"
  #...
end

class Martian < IntelligentLife
  @@home_planet = "Mars"
  #...
end


puts Terran.home_planet                # Earth
puts Martian.home_planet               # Mars
```

It goes without saying that inheritance still operates normally here. Any instance methods or instance variables defined within `IntelligentLife` will be inherited by `Terran` and `Martian`, just as you would expect.

Listing 11.14 is perhaps the best solution. In this case, we don't use class variables at all but class instance variables.

Listing 11.14   Parametric Classes: The Best Way

```
class IntelligentLife
  class << self
    attr_accessor :home_planet
```

```
    end

    #...
  end

class Terran < IntelligentLife
  self.home_planet = "Earth"
  #...
end

class Martian < IntelligentLife
  self.home_planet = "Mars"
  #...
end


puts Terran.home_planet          # Earth
puts Martian.home_planet         # Mars
```

Here, we open up the singleton class and define an accessor called `home_planet`. The two child classes call their own accessors and set the variable. These accessors work strictly on a per-class basis now.

As a small enhancement, let's also add a `private` call in the singleton class:

```
private :home_planet=
```

Making the writer private will prevent any code outside the hierarchy from changing this value. As always, using `private` is an "advisory" protection and is easily bypassed by the programmer who wants to. Making a method private at least tells us we are not meant to call that method in this particular context.

I should mention that there are other ways of implementing these techniques. Use your creativity.

11.2.5 Storing Code as `Proc` Objects

Not surprisingly, Ruby gives you several alternatives when it comes to storing a chunk of code in the form of an object. We'll take a look at `Proc` objects and lambdas here.

The built-in class `Proc` represents a Ruby block as an object. `Proc` objects, like blocks, are closures and therefore carry around the context where they were defined. The `proc` method is a shorthand alias for `Proc.new`.

```
local = 12
myproc = Proc.new {|a| puts "Param is #{a}, local is #{local}" }
myproc.call(99)  # Param is 99, local is 12
```

`Proc` objects are also created automatically by Ruby when a method defined with a trailing `&` parameter is called with a block:

```
def take_block(x, &block)
  puts block.class
  x.times {|i| block[i, i*i] }
end
```

```
take_block(3) { |n,s| puts "#{n} squared is #{s}" }
```

This example also shows the use of brackets (`[]`) as an alias for the `call` method. The output is shown here:

```
Proc
0 squared is 0
1 squared is 1
2 squared is 4
```

If you have a `Proc` object, you can pass it to a method that's expecting a block, preceding its name with an `&`, as shown here:

```
myproc = proc { |n| print n, "... " }
(1..3).each(&myproc)                      # 1... 2... 3...
```

Although it can certainly be useful to pass a `Proc` to a method, calling `return` from inside the `Proc` returns from the entire method. A special type of `Proc` object, called a *lamdba*, returns only from the block:

```
def greet(&block)
  block.call
  "Good morning, everyone."
end
```

```
philippe_proc = Proc.new { return "Too soon, Philippe!" }
philippe_lambda = lambda { return "Too soon, Philippe!" }
```

```
p greet(philippe_proc)    # Too soon, Philippe!
p greet(philippe_lambda)  # Good morning, everyone.
```

In addition to the keyword `lambda`, the `->` notation also creates lambdas. Just keep in mind that `->` (sometimes called "stabby proc" or "stabby lambda") puts block arguments outside the curly braces:

```
non_stabby_lambda = lambda {|king| greet(king) }
stabby_lambda     = -> (king) { stab(king) }
```

11.2.6 Storing Code as `Method` Objects

Ruby also lets you turn a method into an object directly using `Object#method`. The `method` method returns a `Method` object, which is a closure that is bound to the object it was created from:

```
str = "cat"
meth = str.method(:length)

a = meth.call              #  3   (length of "cat")
str << "erpillar"
b = meth.call              # 11   (length of "caterpillar")

str = "dog"
c = meth.call              # 11   (length of "caterpillar")
```

Note the final `call`! The variable `str` refers to a new object (`"dog"`) now, but `meth` is still bound to the old object.

A call to `public_method` works the same way, but as the name implies, it only searches public methods on the receiver.

To get a method that can be used with any instance of a particular class, you can use `instance_method` to create `UnboundMethod` objects. Before calling an `UnboundMethod` object, you must first bind it to a particular object. This act of binding produces a `Method` object, which you call normally:

```
umeth = String.instance_method(:length)

m1 = umeth.bind("cat")
m1.call                    # 3

m2 = umeth.bind("caterpillar")
m2.call                    # 11
```

Binding a method to the wrong class can cause an error, but allowing binding to other objects makes `UnboundMethod` a little more intuitive than `Method`.

11.2.7 Using Symbols as Blocks

When a parameter is prefixed with an ampersand, it is treated by Ruby as a block parameter. As shown earlier, it is possible to create a `Proc` object, assign it to a variable, and then use that `Proc` as the block for a method that takes a block.

However, as mentioned in Section 11.2.1, "Sending an Explicit Message to an Object," it is possible to call methods that require blocks but only pass them a symbol prefixed by an ampersand. Why is that possible? The answer lies in the to_proc method.

A non-obvious side effect of providing a block parameter as an argument is that if the argument is not a `Proc`, Ruby will attempt to convert it into one by calling to_proc on it.

Some clever Ruby developers realized that this could be leveraged to simplify their calls to map, and they defined the to_proc method on the `Symbol` class. The implementation looks something like this:

```
class Symbol
  def to_proc
    Proc.new {|obj| obj.send(self) }
  end
end

# Which allows map to be invoked like this:
%w[A B C].map(&:chr)    # [65, 66, 67]
```

This shortcut proved to be so popular that it was added to Ruby itself, and can now be used anywhere.

11.2.8 How Module Inclusion Works

When a module is included into a class, Ruby in effect creates a proxy class as the immediate ancestor of that class. You may or may not find this intuitive. Any methods in an included module are "masked" by any methods that appear in the class:

```
module MyMod
  def meth
    "from module"
```

```
    end
  end

class ParentClass
  def meth
    "from parent"
  end
end

class ChildClass < ParentClass
  def meth
    "from child"
  end
  include MyMod
end

x = ChildClass.new
p x.meth              # from child
```

This is just like a regular inheritance relationship: Anything the child redefines is the new current definition. This is true regardless of whether the `include` is done before or after the redefinition.

Here's a similar example, where the child method invokes `super` instead of returning a simple string. What do you expect it to return?

```
# MyMod and ParentClass unchanged
class ChildClass < ParentClass
  include MyMod
  def meth
    "from child: super = " + super
  end
end

x = ChildClass.new
p x.meth              # from child: super = from module
```

As you can see, `MyMod` is really the new parent of `ChildClass`. What if we also let the module invoke `super` in the same way?

```
module MyMod
  def meth
    "from module: super " + super
  end
```

```
end

# ParentClass is unchanged

class ChildClass < ParentClass
  include MyMod
  def meth
    "from child: super " + super
  end
end


x = ChildClass.new
p x.meth        # from child: super from module: super from parent
```

Modules have one more trick up their sleeve, though, in the form of the `prepend` method. It allows a module method to be inserted beneath the method of the including class:

```
# MyMod and ParentClass unchanged

class ChildClass < ParentClass
  prepend MyMod
  def meth
    "from child: super " + super
  end
end

x = ChildClass.new
p x.meth        # from module: super from child: super from parent
```

This feature of Ruby allows modules to alter the behavior of methods even when the method in the child class does not call `super`.

Whether included or prepended, the `meth` from `MyMod` can call `super` only because there actually is a `meth` in the superclass (that is, in at least one ancestor). What would happen if we called this in another circumstance?

```
module MyMod
  def meth
    "from module: super = " + super
  end
end


class Foo
```

```
    include MyMod
end


x = Foo.new
x.meth
```

This code would result in a `NoMethodError` (or a call to `method_missing`, if it had been defined).

11.2.9   Detecting Default Parameters

The following question was once asked by Ian Macdonald on the Ruby mailing list: "How can I detect whether a parameter was specified by the caller, or the default was taken?" This is an interesting question; not something you would use every day, but still interesting.

At least three solutions were suggested. By far the simplest and best was by Nobu Nakada, which is shown in the following code:

```
def meth(a, b=(flag=true; 345))
  puts "b is #{b} and flag is #{flag.inspect}"
end

meth(123)      # b is 345 and flag is true
meth(123,345)  # b is 345 and flag is nil
meth(123,456)  # b is 456 and flag is nil
```

As the preceding example shows, this trick works even if the caller explicitly supplies what happens to be the default value. The trick is obvious when you see it: The parenthesized expression sets a local variable called `flag` but then returns the default value 345. This solution is a tribute to the power of Ruby.

11.2.10   Delegating or Forwarding

Ruby has two libraries that offer solutions for delegating or forwarding method calls from the receiver to another object. These are `delegate` and `forwardable`; we'll look at them in that order.

The `delegate` library gives you three ways of solving this problem.

The `SimpleDelegator` class can be useful when the object delegated to can change over the lifespan of the receiving object. The `__setobj__` method is used to select the object to which you're delegating.

However, I find the `SimpleDelegator` technique to be a little too simple. Because I am not convinced it offers a significant improvement over doing the same thing by hand, I won't cover it here.

The `DelegateClass` top-level method takes a class (to be delegated to) as a parameter. It then creates a new class from which we can inherit. Here's an example of creating our own `Queue` class that delegates to an `Array` object:

```ruby
require 'delegate'
class MyQueue < DelegateClass(Array)

  def initialize(arg=[])
    super(arg)
  end

  alias_method :enqueue, :push
  alias_method :dequeue, :shift
end

mq = MyQueue.new

mq.enqueue(123)
mq.enqueue(234)

p mq.dequeue       # 123
p mq.dequeue       # 234
```

It's also possible to inherit from `Delegator` and implement a `__getobj__` method; this is the way `SimpleDelegator` is implemented, and it offers more control over the delegation.

However, if you want more control, you should probably be doing per-method delegation rather than per-class anyway. The `forwardable` library enables you to do this. Let's revisit the queue example:

```ruby
require 'forwardable'

class MyQueue
  extend Forwardable

  def initialize(obj=[])
    @queue = obj     # delegate to this object
  end
```

```
    def_delegator :@queue, :push,  :enqueue
    def_delegator :@queue, :shift, :dequeue

    def_delegators :@queue, :clear, :empty?, :length, :size, :<<

    # Any additional stuff...
  end
```

This example shows that the `def_delegator` method associates a method call (for example, `enqueue`) with a delegated object `@queue` and the correct method to call on that object (`push`). In other words, when we call `enqueue` on a `MyQueue` object, we delegate that by making a `push` call on our object `@queue` (which is usually an array).

Notice that we say `:@queue` rather than `:queue` or `@queue`; this is simply because of the way the `Forwardable` class is written. It could have been done differently.

Sometimes we want to pass methods through to the delegate object by using the same method name. The `def_delegators` method allows us to specify an unlimited number of these. For example, as shown in the preceding code example, invoking `length` on a `MyQueue` object will in turn call `length` on `@queue`.

Unlike the first example in this chapter, the other methods on the delegate object are simply not supported. This can be a good thing. For example, you don't want to invoke `[]` or `[]=` on a queue; if you do, you're not using it as a queue anymore.

Also notice that the previous code allows the caller to pass an object into the constructor (to be used as the delegate object). In the spirit of duck-typing, this means that we can choose the kind of object we want to delegate to—as long as it supports the set of methods that we reference in the code.

For example, the following calls are all valid (note that the last two assume that we've done a `require 'thread'` previously):

```
    q1 = MyQueue.new                  # use an array
    q2 = MyQueue.new(my_array)        # use one specific array
    q3 = MyQueue.new(Queue.new)       # use a Queue (thread.rb)
    q4 = MyQueue.new(SizedQueue.new)  # use a SizedQueue (thread.rb)
```

So, for example, q3 and q4 in the preceding examples are now magically thread-safe because they delegate to an object that is thread-safe. (That's unless any customized code not shown here violates that.)

There is also a `SingleForwardable` class that operates on an instance rather than on an entire class. This is useful if you want just one instance of a class to delegate to another object, while all other instances continue to not delegate, as before.

One final option is manual delegation. Ruby makes it extremely straightforward to simply wrap one object in another, which is another way to implement our queue:

```ruby
class MyQueue
  def initialize(obj=[])
    @queue = obj    # delegate to this object
  end

  def enqueue(arg)
    @queue.push(arg)
  end

  def dequeue(arg)
    @queue.shift(arg)
  end

  %i[clear empty? length size <<].each do |name|
    define_method(name){|*args| @queue.send(name, *args) }
  end

  # Any additional stuff…
end
```

As you can see, in some cases, it may not be a noticeable advantage to use a library for delegation instead of writing some simple code.

You might ask, "Is delegation better than inheritance?" But that's the wrong question in a sense. Sometimes the situation calls for delegation rather than inheritance; for example, suppose that a class already has a parent class. We can still use delegation (in some form), but we can't inherit from an additional parent (because Ruby doesn't allow multiple inheritance).

11.2.11   Defining Class-Level Readers and Writers

We have seen the methods `attr_reader`, `attr_writer`, and `attr_accessor`, which make it a little easier to define readers and writers (getters and setters) for instance attributes. But what about class-level attributes?

Ruby has no similar facility for creating these automatically. However, we could create something similar on our own very simply. Just open the singleton class and use the ordinary `attr` family of methods.

The resulting instance variables in the singleton class will be class instance variables. These are often better for our purposes than class variables because they are strictly "per class" and are not shared up and down the hierarchy.

```ruby
class MyClass
  @alpha = 123                   # Initialize @alpha

  class << self
    attr_reader :alpha           # MyClass.alpha()
    attr_writer :beta            # MyClass.beta=()
    attr_accessor :gamma         # MyClass.gamma() and MyClass.gamma=()
  end

  def MyClass.look
    puts "#@alpha, #@beta, #@gamma"
  end

  #...
end


puts MyClass.alpha               # 123
MyClass.beta = 456
MyClass.gamma = 789
puts MyClass.gamma               # 789

MyClass.look                     # 123, 456, 789
```

Most classes are no good without instance level data as well, but we've omitted it here for clarity.

11.2.12   Working in Advanced Programming Disciplines

Brother, can you paradigm?

—Graffiti seen at IBM Austin, 1989

Many philosophies of programming are popular in various circles. These are often difficult to characterize in relation to object-oriented or dynamic techniques, and some of these styles can actually be independent of whether a language is dynamic or object oriented.

Because we are far from experts in these matters, we are relying mostly on hearsay. So take these next paragraphs with a grain of sodium chloride.

Some programmers prefer a flavor of OOP known as prototype-based OOP (or classless OOP). In this world, an object isn't described as a member of a class; it is built from the ground up, and other objects are created based on the prototype. Ruby has at least rudimentary support for this programming style because it allows singleton methods for individual objects, and the `clone` method will clone these singletons. Interested readers should also look at the simple `OpenStruct` class for building Python-like objects; you should also be aware of how `method_missing` works.

One or two limitations in Ruby hamper classless OOP. Certain objects such as `Fixnums` are stored not as references but as immediate values so that they can't have singleton methods. This is supposed to change in the future, but at the time of this writing, it's impossible to project when it will happen.

In functional programming (FP), emphasis is placed on the evaluation of expressions rather than the execution of commands. An FP language is one that encourages and supports functional programming, and as such, there is a natural gray area. Nearly all would agree that Haskell is a pure functional language, whereas Ruby certainly isn't one.

But Ruby has at least some minimal support for FP; it has a fairly rich set of methods for operating on arrays (lists), and it has `Proc` objects so that code can be encapsulated and called over and over. Ruby allows the method chaining that is so common in FP. There have been some initial efforts at creating a library that would serve as a kind of FP "compatibility layer," borrowing certain ideas from Haskell. At the time of this writing, these efforts aren't complete.

The concept of aspect-oriented programming (AOP) is an interesting one. In AOP, programmers to deal with programming issues that crosscut the modular structure of the program. In other words, some activities or features of a system will be scattered across the system in code fragments here and there, rather than being gathered into one tidy location. AOP can modularize things that are difficult to modularize using traditional OOP or procedural techniques. It works at right angles to the usual way of thinking.

Ruby certainly wasn't created specifically with AOP in mind. However, it was designed to be a flexible and dynamic language, and it is conceivable that these techniques can be facilitated by a library. The `Module#prepend` method and the `aspector` gem both provide some amount of AOP within Ruby.

The concept of design by contract (DBC) is well known to Eiffel devotees, although it is certainly known outside those circles also. The general idea is that a piece of code (a method or class) implements a contract; certain preconditions must be true if the code is going to do its job, and the code guarantees that certain post-conditions are true afterward. The robustness of a system can be greatly enhanced by the ability to specify this contract explicitly and have it automatically checked at runtime. The usefulness of the technique is expanded by the inheritance of contract information as classes are extended.

The Eiffel language had DBC explicitly built in; Ruby does not. There are usable implementations of DBC libraries, however, and they are worth investigating.

Design patterns have inspired much discussion over the last few years. These, of course, are highly language independent and can be implemented well in many languages. But again, Ruby's unusual flexibility makes them perhaps more practical than in some other environments. Well-known examples of these are given elsewhere; the Visitor pattern is essentially implemented in Ruby's default iterator `each`, and other patterns are part of Ruby's standard distribution (such as the standard libraries `delegator` and `singleton`).

We don't use the term "Extreme Programming" (XP) anymore, but many of its principles are ingrained in our culture by now. This methodology encourages (among other things) early testing and refactoring on the fly.

The "culture of testing" isn't language specific, although it might be easier in some languages than others. Certainly we maintain that Ruby makes (manual) refactoring easier than many languages would, although that is a highly subjective claim. However, the existence of the `RSpec` library (and others) makes for a real blending of Ruby and XP. This library facilitates unit testing; it is powerful, easy to use, and has proven useful in developing much other Ruby software in current use. We highly recommend the practice of testing early and often, and we recommend `RSpec` for those who want to do this in Ruby. (`Minitest` is another excellent gem, for those who prefer the `Test::Unit` style.)

By the time you read this, many of the issues we talk about in this section will have been fleshed out more. As always, your best resources for the latest information are online. It's difficult to list online resources in print because they are in constant flux. In this case, the search engine is your friend.

11.3   Working with Dynamic Features

Skynet became self-aware at 2:14 a.m. EDT August 29, 1997.

—Terminator 2: Judgment Day

Some of you may come from the background of a static language such as C. To those readers, we will address this rhetorical question: Can you imagine writing a C function that will take a string, treat it as a variable name, and return the value of the variable? No? Then can you imagine removing or replacing the definition of a function? Can you imagine trapping calls to nonexistent functions?

Ruby makes this sort of thing possible. These capabilities take getting used to, and they are easy to abuse. However, the concepts have been around for many years (they are at least as old as LISP) and are regarded as "tried and true" in the Scheme and Smalltalk communities as well. Python has many dynamic features, and even Java has some dynamic features, so we expect this way of thinking to continue to increase in popularity over time.

11.3.1   Evaluating Code Dynamically

The global function `eval` compiles and executes a string that contains a fragment of Ruby code. This is a powerful (albeit extremely dangerous) mechanism, because it allows you to build up code to be executed at runtime. For example, the following code reads in lines of the form "name = expression." It then evaluates each expression and stores the result in a hash indexed by the corresponding variable name:

```
parameters = {}

ARGF.each do |line|
  name, expr = line.split(/\s*=\s*/, 2)
  parameters[name] = eval expr
end
```

Suppose the input contained these lines:

```
a = 1
b = 2 + 3
c = `date`
```

Then the hash parameters would end up with the value `{"a"=>1, "b"=>5,` `"c"=>"Sat Jul 26 00:51:48 PDT 2014\n"}`. This example also illustrates the danger of `eval`ing strings when you don't control their contents; a malicious user could put `d=`rm *`` in the input and ruin your day.

Ruby has three other methods that evaluate code "on the fly": `class_eval`, `module_eval`, and `instance_eval`. The first two are synonyms, and all three do effectively the same thing; they evaluate a string or a block, but while doing so they change the value of `self` to their own receiver. Perhaps the most common use of `class_eval` allows you to add methods to a class when all you have is a reference to that class.

We use this in the `hook_method` code in the `Trace` example in Section 11.4.3, "Tracking Changes to a Class or Object Definition." You'll find other examples in the more dynamic library modules, such as the standard library `delegate.rb`.

The `eval` method also makes it possible to evaluate local variables in a context outside their scope. We don't advise doing this lightly, but it's nice to have the capability.

Ruby associates local variables with blocks, with high-level definition constructs (class, module, and method definitions), and with the top-level of your program (the code outside any definition constructs). Associated with each of these scopes is the binding of variables, along with other housekeeping details.

Probably the ultimate user of bindings is `pry`, an interactive Ruby console. It not only uses bindings to keep the variables in the program that you type in separate from its own, but adds the `Binding#pry` method to open a new interactive console within that binding. We'll look more closely at `pry` in Chapter 16, "Testing and Debugging."

You can encapsulate the current binding in an object using the method `Kernel#binding`. Having done that, you can pass the binding as the second parameter to `eval`, setting the execution context for the code being evaluated.

```
def some_method
  a = "local variable"
  return binding
end

the_binding = some_method
eval "a", the_binding   # "local variable"
```

Interestingly, the presence of a block associated with a method is stored as part of the binding, enabling tricks such as this:

```
def some_method
  return binding
end

the_binding = some_method { puts "hello" }
eval "yield", the_binding                 # hello
```

11.3.2   Retrieving a Constant by Name

The `const_get` method retrieves the value of a constant (by name) from the module or class to which it belongs:

```
str = "PI"
Math.const_get(str)     # Evaluates to Math::PI
```

This is a way of avoiding the use of `eval`, which is both dangerous and considered inelegant. This type of solution is better code, it's computationally cheaper, and it's safer. Other similar methods are `instance_variable_set`, `instance_variable_get`, and `define_method`.

It's true that `const_get` is faster than `eval`. In informal tests, `const_get` was roughly 350% as fast; your results will vary. But is this really significant? The fact is, the test code ran a loop 10 million times to get good results and still finished in under 30 seconds.

The usefulness of `const_get` is that it is easier to read, more specific, and more self-documenting. This is the real reason to use it. In fact, even if it did not exist, to make it a synonym for `eval` might still be a step forward.

See also the next section (11.3.3, "Retrieving a Class by Name") for another trick.

11.3.3   Retrieving a Class by Name

We have seen this question more than once. Given a string containing the name of a class, how can we create an instance of that class?

Classes in Ruby are normally named as constants in the "global" namespace—that is, members of `Object`. That means the proper way is with `const_get`, which we just saw:

```
classname = "Array"
klass = Object.const_get(classname)
x = klass.new(4, 1)  # [1, 1, 1, 1]
```

If the constant is inside a namespace, just provide a string that with namespaces delimited by two colons (as if you were writing Ruby directly):

```
class Alpha
  class Beta
    class Gamma
      FOOBAR = 237
    end
  end
end

str = "Alpha::Beta::Gamma::FOOBAR"
val = Object.const_get(str)          # 237
```

11.3.4 Using `define_method`

Other than `def`, `define_method` is the only normal way to add a method to a class or object; the latter, however, enables you to do it at runtime.

Of course, essentially everything in Ruby happens at runtime. If you surround a method definition with `puts` calls, as in the following example, you can see that:

```
class MyClass
  puts "before"

  def meth
    #...
  end

  puts "after"
end
```

However, within a method body or similar place, we can't just reopen a class (unless it's a singleton class). In such a case, we use `define_method`. It takes a symbol (for the name of the method) and a block (for the body of the method):

```
if today =~ /Saturday|Sunday/
  define_method(:activity)  { puts "Playing!" }
else
  define_method(:activity)  { puts "Working!" }
end


activity
```

Note, however, that `define_method` is private. This means that calling it from inside a class definition or method will work just fine, as shown here:

```
class MyClass
  define_method(:body_method) { puts "The class body." }

  def self.new_method(name, &block)
    define_method(name, &block)
  end
end

MyClass.new_method(:class_method) { puts "A class method." }

x = MyClass.new
x.body_method      # Prints "The class body."
x.class_method     # Prints "A class method."
```

We can even create an instance method that dynamically defines other instance methods:

```
class MyClass
  def new_method(name, &block)
    self.class.send(:define_method, name, &block)
  end
end

x = MyClass.new
x.new_method(:instance_method) { puts "An instance method." }
x.mymeth  # Prints "An instance method."
```

Here, we're still defining an instance method dynamically. Only the means of invoking `new_method` has changed. Note the `send` trick that we use to circumvent the privacy of `define_method`. This works because `send` always allows you to call private methods. (This is another "loophole," as some would call it, that has to be used responsibly.)

It's important to realize another fact about `define_method`: It takes a block, and a block in Ruby is a closure. This means that, unlike an ordinary method definition, we are capturing context when we define the method. The following example is useless, but it illustrates the point:

```ruby
class MyClass
  def self.new_method(name, &block)
    define_method(name, &block)
  end
end

a, b = 3, 79
MyClass.new_method(:compute) { a*b }

x = MyClass.new
puts x.compute            # 237

a, b = 23, 24
puts x.compute            # 552
```

The point is that the new method can access variables in the original scope of the block, even if that scope "goes away" and is otherwise inaccessible. This will be useful at times, perhaps in a metaprogramming situation or with a GUI toolkit that allows defining methods for event callbacks.

Note that the closure only has access to variables with the same names. On rare occasions, this can be tricky. Here, we use `define` to expose a class variable (not really the way we should do it, but it illustrates the point):

```ruby
class SomeClass
  @@var = 999

  define_method(:peek) { @@var }
end

x = SomeClass.new
p x.peek            # 999
```

Now let's try this with a class instance variable:

```
class SomeClass
  @var = 999

  define_method(:peek) { @var }
end

x = SomeClass.new
p x.peek                # prints nil
```

We expect 999 but get nil instead. Observe, on the other hand, that the following works fine:

```
class SomeClass
  @var = 999
  x = @var

  define_method(:peek) { x }
end

x = SomeClass.new
p x.peek        # 999
```

So what is happening? Well, it is true that a closure captures the variables from its context. But even though a closure knows the variables from its scope, the method context is the context of the instance, not the class itself.

Because @var in the instance context would refer to an instance variable of the object, the class instance variable is hidden by the object's instance variable—even though it has never been used and technically doesn't exist.

When working with individual objects, define_singleton_method is a convenient alternative to opening the singleton class and defining a method. It works analogously to define_method.

Although you can define methods at runtime by calling eval, avoid doing this. Instead, define_method can and should be used in all these circumstances. Minor subtleties like those just mentioned shouldn't deter you.

11.3.5 Obtaining Lists of Defined Entities

The reflection API of Ruby enables us to examine the classes and objects in our environment at runtime. We'll look at methods defined in `Module`, `Class`, and `Object`.

The `Module` module has a method named `constants` that returns an array of all the constants in the system (including class and module names). The `nesting` method returns an array of all the modules nested at the current location in the code.

The instance method `Module#ancestors` returns an array of all the ancestors of the specified class or module:

```
list = Array.ancestors  # [Array, Enumerable, Object,
                             Kernel, BasicObject]
```

The `constants` method lists all the constants accessible in the specified module. Any ancestor modules are included:

```
list = Math.constants   # [:DomainError, :PI, :E]
```

The `class_variables` method returns a list of all class variables in the given class and its superclasses. The `included_modules` method lists the modules included in a class:

```
class Parent
  @@var1 = nil
end

class Child < Parent
  @@var2 = nil
end

list1 = Parent.class_variables   # [:@@var1]
list2 = Array.included_modules   # [Enumerable, Kernel]
```

The `Class` methods `instance_methods` and `public_instance_methods` are synonyms; they return a list of the public instance methods for a class. The methods `private_instance_methods` and `protected_instance_methods` behave as expected. Any of these can take a Boolean parameter, which defaults to `true`; if it is set to `false`, superclasses will not be searched, thus resulting in a smaller list:

```
n1 = Array.instance_methods.size          # 174
n2 = Array.public_instance_methods.size   # 174
```

```
n3 = Array.public_instance_methods(false).size    # 90
n4 = Array.private_instance_methods.size          # 84
n5 = Array.protected_instance_methods.size        # 0
```

The `Object` class has a number of similar methods that operate on instances (see Listing 11.15). Calling `methods` will return a list of all methods that can be invoked on that object. Calling `public_methods` will return a list of publicly accessible methods; this takes a parameter, defaulting to `true`, to choose whether methods from superclasses are included. The methods `private_methods`, `protected_methods`, and `singleton_methods` all take a similar parameter, and they return the methods you would expect them to return.

Listing 11.15 Reflection and Instance Variables

```
class SomeClass

  def initialize
    @a = 1
    @b = 2
  end

  def mymeth
    #...
  end

  protected :mymeth

end


x = SomeClass.new

def x.newmeth
  # ...
end

iv = x.instance_variables     # [:@a, :@b]


x.methods.size                # 61

x.public_methods.size         # 60
x.public_methods(false).size  # 1

x.private_methods.size        # 85
x.private_methods(false).size # 1
```

```
x.protected_methods.size          # 1
x.singleton_methods.size          # 1
```

11.3.6 Removing Definitions

The dynamic nature of Ruby means that pretty much anything that can be defined can also be undefined. One conceivable reason to do this is to decouple pieces of code that are in the same scope by getting rid of variables after they have been used; another reason might be to specifically disallow certain dangerous method calls. Whatever your reason for removing a definition, it should naturally be done with caution because it can conceivably lead to debugging problems.

The radical way to undefine something is with the `undef` keyword (not surprisingly the opposite of `def`). You can `undef` methods, local variables, and constants at the top level. Although a class name is a constant, you cannot remove a class definition this way:

```
def asbestos
  puts "Now fireproof"
end

tax = 0.08

PI = 3

asbestos
puts "PI=#{PI}, tax=#{tax}"

undef asbestos
undef tax
undef PI

# Any reference to the above three
# would now give an error.
```

Within a class definition, a method or constant can be undefined in the same context in which it was defined. You can't `undef` within a method definition or `undef` an instance variable.

The `remove_method` and `undef_method` methods also are available (defined in `Module`). The difference is subtle: `remove_method` will remove the current (or nearest) definition of the method; `undef_method` will literally cause the method to be undefined (removing it from superclasses as well). Listing 11.16 is an illustration of this.

Listing 11.16   Removing and Undefining Methods

```
class Parent

  def alpha
    puts "parent alpha"
  end

  def beta
    puts "parent beta"
  end

end

class Child < Parent

  def alpha
    puts "child alpha"
  end

  def beta
    puts "child beta"
  end

  remove_method :alpha    # Remove "this" alpha
  undef_method :beta      # Remove every beta

end


x = Child.new

x.alpha            # parent alpha
x.beta             # Error!
```

The `remove_const` method will remove a constant:

```
module Math
   remove_const :PI
end


# No PI anymore!
```

Note that it is possible to remove access to a class definition in this way (because a class identifier is simply a constant). The following code demonstrates this:

```
class BriefCandle
  #...
end

out_out = BriefCandle.new

class Object
  remove_const :BriefCandle
end

BriefCandle.new      # NameError: uninitialized constant BriefCandle
out_out.class.new    # Another BriefCandle instance
```

Note that methods such as `remove_const` and `remove_method` are (naturally enough) private methods. That is why we show these being called from inside a class or module definition rather than outside.

11.3.7 Handling References to Nonexistent Constants

The `const_missing` method is called when you try to reference a constant that isn't known. A symbol referring to the constant is passed in. It is analogous to the `method_missing` method, which we will examine in Section 11.3.8, "Handling Calls to Nonexistent Methods."

To capture a constant globally, define this method within `Module` itself. (Remember that `Module` is the parent of `Class`.)

```
class Module
  def const_missing(x)
    "from Module"
  end
end

class X
end

p X::BAR      # "from Module"
p BAR         # "from Module"
p Array::BAR  # "from Module"
```

You can, of course, do anything you want to give the constant a fake value, compute its value, or whatever. Remember the Roman class from Chapter 6, "Symbols and Ranges"? Here we use it to ensure that arbitrary uppercase Roman numeral constants are treated as such:

```ruby
class Module
  def const_missing(name)
    Roman.decode(name)
  end
end


year1 = MCMLCCIV  # 1974
year2 = MMXIV     # 2014
```

If you want something less global, define the method as a class method on a class. That class and all its children will call that version of the method as needed:

```ruby
class Alpha
  def self.const_missing(sym)
    "Alpha has no #{sym}"
  end
end

class Beta
  def self.const_missing(sym)
    "Beta has no #{sym}"
  end
end

class A < Alpha
end

class B < Beta
end

p Alpha::FOO      # "Alpha has no FOO"
p Beta::FOO       # "Beta has no FOO"
p A::FOO          # "Alpha has no FOO"
p B::FOO          # "Beta has no FOO"
```

11.3.8   Handling Calls to Nonexistent Methods

Sometimes it's useful to be able to write classes that respond to arbitrary method calls. For example, you might want to wrap calls to external programs in a class, providing access to each program as a method call. You can't know ahead of time the names of all these programs, so you can't create the methods as you write the class.

That's okay, though. Here come `Object#method_missing` and `respond_to_missing?` to the rescue. Whenever a Ruby object receives a message for a method that isn't implemented in the receiver, it invokes the `method_missing` method instead. You can use that to catch what would otherwise be an error, treating it as a normal method call. Let's implement an operating system command wrapper class:

```ruby
class CommandWrapper

  def method_missing(method, *args)
    system(method.to_s, *args)
  end

end

cw = CommandWrapper.new
cw.date                       # Sat Jul 26 02:08:06 PDT 2014
cw.du '-s', '/tmp'            # 166749  /tmp
```

The first parameter to `method_missing` is the name of the method that was called (and that couldn't be found). Whatever was passed in that method call is then given as the remaining parameters.

If your `method_missing` handler decides that it doesn't want to handle a particular call, it should call `super` rather than raising an exception. That allows `method_missing` handlers in superclasses to have a shot at dealing with the situation. Eventually, the `method_missing` method defined in class `Object` will be invoked, and that will raise an exception.

In order to safely use `method_missing`, always also define the `respond_to_missing?` method. By doing this, it is possible for Ruby to provide results for both the `respond_to?` method and `method` method. Here is an example of this technique:

```
class CommandWrapper # reopen previous class

  def respond_to_missing?(method, include_all)
    system("which #{method} > /dev/null")
  end

end

cw = CommandWrapper.new
cw.respond_to?(:foo)       # false
cw.method(:echo)           # #<Method: CommandWrapper#echo>
cw.respond_to?(:echo)      # true
```

The second parameter (`include_all`) allows the method definition to know whether to include private and protected methods in the respond check. In this example, we do not add any private or protected methods, and can ignore it.

Although the `respond_to_missing?` method is complementary to `method_missing`, there is no enforcement of this. Each method can be written alone, albeit with highly confusing behavior unless the other is also present.

11.3.9   Improved Security with `taint`

The dynamic nature of Ruby means that there are potential "security holes" in some Ruby code. As a trivial example, consider the `eval` method; if the string it is passed originates in the outside world, it is possible for a malicious user to cause arbitrary code to be executed—such as the ever-popular `system("nohup rm -rf / &")` string. Even without malice, it's possible for an outside input to cause significant problems.

The first feature of Ruby that defends against these kinds of attacks is the *safe level*. The safe level is stored in a thread-local global variable and defaults to 0. Assigning a number to `$SAFE` sets the safe level, which can never be decreased.

When the safe level is 1 or higher, Ruby starts blocking certain dangerous actions using tainted objects. Every object has a tainted or non-tainted status flag. If an object has its origin in the "outside world" (for example, a string on the command line or a URL parameter), it is automatically tainted. This taint is passed on to objects that are derived from such an object.

Many core methods (notably `eval`) behave differently or raise an exception when passed tainted data as the safe level increases. Let's look at this using strings:

```
str1 = "puts 'The answer is: '"
str2 = ARGV.first.dup  # "3*79" (duped to unfreeze)
```

```
str1.tainted?          # false
str2.tainted?          # true

str1.taint             # If we want to, we can
str2.untaint           #   change the taint status

eval(str1)             # Prints: The answer is:
puts eval(str2)        # Prints: 237

$SAFE = 1

eval(str1)             # Raises SecurityError: Insecure operation
puts eval(str2)        # Prints: 237
```

For a full summary of the interaction between taint levels and $SAFE values, see
Table 11.1.

Table 11.1   Understanding $SAFE Levels

	0	1	2	3
$RUBYLIB and $RUBYOPT are not honored.		x	x	x
Current directory is not added to path.		x	x	x
Disallows command-line options: -e -i -l -s -x -S.		x	x	x
Disallows $PATH if any directory in it is world-writable.		x	x	x
Disallows manipulation of a directory named by a tainted string.		x	x	x
chroot will not accept a tainted string.		x	x	x
load/require will not accept a tainted string (unless wrapped).		x	x	x
Cannot manipulate file or pipe named by tainted string.		x	x	x
system and exec will not accept a tainted string.		x	x	x
glob, eval, and trap will not accept a tainted string.		x	x	x
Cannot manipulate directories or use chroot.			x	x
Cannot load a file from a world-writable directory.			x	x
Cannot load a file whose name is tainted string starting with ~.		x	x	
Cannot use File methods: chmod chown lstat truncate flock.			x	x
Cannot use File class methods: stat umask.			x	x
Cannot use IO methods: ioctl stat.			x	x
Cannot use Object methods: fork syscall trap.			x	x

	0	1	2	3
Cannot use Process class methods: setpgid setsid.		x	x	
Cannot use Process class methods: setpriority egid=.		x	x	
Cannot use trap to handle signals.			x	x
All objects are created tainted.				x
Objects cannot be untainted.				x

11.3.10   Defining Finalizers for Objects

Ruby classes have constructors (the methods new and initialize) but don't have
destructors (methods that delete objects). That's because Ruby uses garbage collection
to remove unreferenced objects; a destructor would make no sense.

However, people coming to Ruby from languages such as C++ seem to miss the
facility and often ask how they can write code to handle the finalization of objects.
The simple answer is that there is no real way to do it reliably. However, you can
arrange to have code called when an object is garbage collected:

```
a = "hello"
puts "The string 'hello' has an object id #{a.object_id}"
ObjectSpace.define_finalizer(a) { |id| puts "Destroying #{id}" }
puts "Nothing to tidy"
GC.start
a = nil
puts "The original string is now a candidate for collection"
GC.start
```

This produces the following output:

```
The string 'hello' has an object id 537684890
Nothing to tidy
The original string is now a candidate for collection
Destroying 537684890
```

Note that by the time the finalizer is called, the object has basically been destroyed
already. An attempt to convert the ID you receive back into an object reference using
ObjectSpace._id2ref will raise a RangeError, complaining that you are attempting to use a recycled object.

Also, be aware that Ruby uses a "conservative" GC mechanism. There is no guarantee that an object will undergo garbage collection before the program terminates.

However, all this might be moot. There's a style of programming in Ruby that uses blocks to encapsulate the use of a resource. At the end of the block, the resource is deleted, and life carries on merrily, all without the use of finalizers. For example, consider the block form of `File.open`:

```
File.open("myfile.txt") do |file|
  line = file.gets
  # ...
end
```

Here, the `File` object is passed into the block, and when the block exits, the file is closed, all under control of the `open` method. Whereas `File.open` is written in C for efficiency, writing it in Ruby might look something like this:

```
def File.open(name, mode = "r")
  f = os_file_open(name, mode)
  if block_given?
    begin
      yield f
    ensure
      f.close
    end
    return nil
  else
    return f
  end
end
```

First, check for the presence of a block. If found, invoke that block, passing in the open file. The block is called inside a `begin-ensure-end` section, ensuring that the file will be closed after the block terminates, even if an exception is thrown.

11.4 Program Introspection

The runtime flexibility of Ruby extends even beyond the dynamic features we have seen so far. Code in Ruby is able to accomplish things during program execution that are astonishing when compared to programs in C.

Among other things, it is possible to determine the name of the calling function and automatically list every user-defined element (objects, classes, or functions). This runtime flexibility, by allowing the programmer to examine and change program elements at runtime, makes many problems easier.

In this section, we'll look at a few runtime tricks Ruby allows. We'll look at some of the libraries built on top of these tricks later, in Chapter 16.

11.4.1   Traversing the Object Space

The Ruby runtime system needs to keep track of all known objects (if for no other reason than to be able to garbage collect those that are no longer referenced). This information is made accessible via the `ObjectSpace.each_object` method. If you specify a class or module as a parameter to `each_object`, only objects of that type will be returned:

```
ObjectSpace.each_object(Bignum) do |obj|
  printf "%20s: %s\n", obj.class, obj.inspect
end

# Prints:
#    Bignum: 1341682904165828065463660688519097 66153
#    Bignum: 9223372036854775807
```

If all you're after is a count of each type of object that has been created, the `count_objects` method will return a hash with object types and counts:

```
require 'pp'
p ObjectSpace.count_objects
# {:TOTAL=>33013, :FREE=>284, :T_OBJECT=>2145, :T_CLASS=>901,
    :T_MODULE=>32, :T_FLOAT=>4, :T_STRING=>18999, :T_REGEXP=>167,
    :T_ARRAY=>4715, :T_HASH=>325, :T_STRUCT=>2, :T_BIGNUM=>4,
    :T_FILE=>8, :T_DATA=>1518, :T_MATCH=>205, :T_COMPLEX=>1,

    :T_NODE=>3663, :T_ICLASS=>40}
```

The `ObjectSpace` module is also useful in defining object finalizers (see Section 11.3.10, "Defining Finalizers for Objects").

11.4.2   Examining the Call Stack

And you may ask yourself: Well, how did I get here?

—Talking Heads, "Once in a Lifetime"

Sometimes we want to know who our caller was. This could be useful information if, for example, we had a fatal exception. The `caller` method, defined in `Kernel`, makes this possible. It returns an array of strings in which the first element represents the caller, the next element represents the caller's caller, and so on:

```
def func1
  puts caller[0]
end

def func2
  func1
end

func2   # somefile.rb:6:in 'func2'
```

Each string in the caller array takes the form `file:line: in method`.

11.4.3   Tracking Changes to a Class or Object Definition

Perhaps we should start this section by asking: Who cares? Why are we interested in tracking changes to classes?

One possible reason is that we're trying to keep track of the state of the Ruby program being run. Perhaps we're implementing some kind of GUI-based debugger, and we need to refresh a list of methods if our user adds one on the fly.

Another reason might be that we're doing clever things to other classes. For example, say that we wanted to write a module that could be included in any class. From then on, any changes in that class would be traced. We could implement this module as shown in Listing 11.17.

Listing 11.17 Tracing Module

```ruby
module Tracing

  def self.hook_method(const, meth)
    const.class_eval do
      alias_method "untraced_#{meth}", "#{meth}"
      define_method(meth) do |*args|
        puts "#{meth} called with params (#{args.join(', ')})"
        send("untraced_#{meth}",*args)
      end
    end
  end

  def self.included(const)
    const.instance_methods(false).each do |m|
      hook_method(const, m)
    end

    def const.method_added(name)
      return if @disable_method_added
      puts "The method #{name} was added to class #{self}"
      @disable_method_added = true
      Tracing.hook_method(self, name)
      @disable_method_added = false
    end

    if const.is_a?(Class)
      def const.inherited(name)
        puts "The class #{name} inherited from #{self}"
      end
    end

    if const.is_a?(Module)
      def const.extended(name)
        puts "The class #{name} extended itself with #{self}"
      end

      def const.included(name)
        puts "The class #{name} included #{self} into itself"
      end
    end

    def const.singleton_method_added(name, *args)
      return if @disable_singleton_method_added
      return if name == :singleton_method_added

      puts "The class method #{name} was added to class #{self}"
      @disable_singleton_method_added = true
      singleton_class = (class << self; self; end)
      Tracing.hook_method(singleton_class, name)
```

```
      @disable_singleton_method_added = false
    end
  end

end
```

This module has two main methods. The first, `trace_method`, is pretty straightforward: When a method is added, it is immediately aliased to the name `untraced_`*name*. The original method is then replaced by our tracing code, which dumps out the method name and parameters before invoking the original method.

Note the use of `alias_method` here. It works much like `alias`, except that it works only on methods (and it itself is a method, not a keyword). It can accept method names as symbols or strings.

The second method, `included`, is the callback invoked when our module is inserted into a class. It does a few things to track method calls and changes to the class that happen in the future.

First, it calls `trace_method` for every method that already exists the target class. That lets us trace methods that were defined before the `Tracing` module was even included. Then it defines a `method_added` class method, so any subsequently added method will both be logged and traced:

```ruby
class MyClass
  def first_meth
  end
end

class MyClass
  include Tracing

  def second_meth(x, y)
  end
  # Output: The method second_meth was added to class MyClass
end

m = MyClass.new
m.first_meth
# Output: first_meth called with params ()
m.second_meth(1, 'cat')
# Output: second_meth called with params (1, 'cat')
```

Next, it does some conditional things we'll come back to in a moment. Finally, it detects the addition of new singleton methods by defining the `singleton_method_added` hook on the tracing target. (Recall that a singleton method in this sense is what we usually refer to as a class method—because `Class` is an object.)

```ruby
class MyClass
  def self.a_class_method(options)
  end
end

MyClass.a_class_method(green: "super")

# Output:
# The class method a_class_method was added to class MyClass
# a_class_method called with params ({:green=>"super"})
```

The `singleton_method_added` callback is defined last so that the other class methods added by the `Tracing` module will not be printed. Also, note that (perhaps contrary to expectation) it can track its own addition to the class; therefore, we must explicitly exclude it from tracing.

Inside the first conditional, the `inherited` method is defined for every `Class` target. It is then called whenever our target class is subclassed by another:

```ruby
class MySubClass < MyClass
end

# Output: The class MySubClass inherited from MyClass
```

Finally, in the conditional for `Module` targets, we define the included and extended callbacks, so we can trace when a class includes or extends the target:

```ruby
module MyModule
  include Tracing
end

class MyClass
  include MyModule
  extend MyModule
end

# Output:
```

```
# The class MyClass included MyModule into itself
# The class MyClass extended itself with MyModule
```

11.4.4   Monitoring Program Execution

A Ruby program can introspect or examine its own execution. There are many applications for such a capability; most provide some type of profiling or debugging functionality, and will be examined in Chapter 16.

In some cases, those libraries may not be needed at all, because it is possible to do any amount of introspection purely in Ruby. It has a significant performance penalty (making it unsuitable for production), but the TracePoint class allows us to invoke our own code whenever an event that interests us occurs. Here is an example that traces method calls and returns, indenting the output to show nested function calls:

```ruby
def factorial(n)
  (1..n).inject(:*) || 1
end

@call_depth = 0

TracePoint.trace(:a_call) do |tp|
  @call_depth += 1
  print "#{tp.path}:#{sprintf("%-4d", tp.lineno)} #{"  " * @depth}"
  puts  "#{tp.defined_class}##{tp.method_id}"
end

TracePoint.trace(:a_return) do |tp|
  print "#{tp.path}:#{sprintf("%-4d", tp.lineno)} #{"  " * @depth}"
  puts  "#{tp.defined_class}##{tp.method_id} => #{tp.return_value}"
  @call_depth -= 1
end

factorial(4)
```

Here, we use TracePoint.trace, which is a shorthand for calling new and then enable. It is also possible to trace a single block of code by passing the block to TracePoint#enable. Executing our code produces the following output:

```
factorial.rb:12    #<Class:TracePoint>#trace
factorial.rb:12    #<Class:TracePoint>#trace =>
                       #<TracePoint:0x007ffe8a893f10>
factorial.rb:1     Object#factorial
factorial.rb:2       Enumerable#inject
factorial.rb:2         Range#each
factorial.rb:2           Fixnum#*
factorial.rb:2           Fixnum#* => 2
factorial.rb:2           Fixnum#*
factorial.rb:2           Fixnum#* => 6
factorial.rb:2           Fixnum#*
factorial.rb:2           Fixnum#* => 24
factorial.rb:2         Range#each => 1..4
factorial.rb:2       Enumerable#inject => 24
factorial.rb:3     Object#factorial => 24
```

Another related method is Kernel#trace_var, which invokes a block whenever a global variable is assigned a value.

If you simply want to trace everything, rather than write your own specific tracers, you can just require the tracer standard library. Here is a program called factorial.rb:

```
def factorial(n)
  (1..n).inject(:*) || 1
end


factorial(4)
```

Given this program, you can simply load tracer from the command line:

```
$ ruby —disable-gems —r tracer factorial.rb
#0:factorial.rb:1::-: def factorial(n)
#0:factorial.rb:5::-: factorial(4)
#0:factorial.rb:1:Object:>: def factorial(n)
#0:factorial.rb:2:Object:-:    (1..n).inject(:*) || 1
#0:factorial.rb:2:Object:-:    (1..n).inject(:*) || 1
#0:factorial.rb:3:Object:<: end
```

The lines output by `tracer` show the thread number, the filename and line number, the class being used, the event type, and the line from the source file being executed. The event types include `'-'` when a source line is executed, `'>'` for a call, `'<'` for a return, `'C'` for a class, and `'E'` for an end. (If you do not disable Rubygems, or if you require some other library, you will see many other lines of output as well.)

These techniques can be used to build quite sophisticated debugging and instrumentation tools. We'll examine how to use some tools that have already been written, such as `pry`, `rbtrace`, and `ruby-prof`, in Chapter 16. In the meantime, we encourage reading documentation, experimentation, and investigation as an excellent way to learn more.

11.5   Conclusion

In this chapter, we've seen a few of the more esoteric or advanced techniques in OOP, as well as some of the more everyday usages. We've seen some of the design patterns implemented (and some that don't need to be). We've also looked at Ruby's reflection API, some interesting consequences of Ruby's dynamic nature, and various neat tricks that can be done in a dynamic language.

It's time now to rejoin the real world. After all, OOP is not an end in itself but rather a means to an end; the end is to write applications that are effective, bug free, and maintainable.

In modern computing, these applications sometimes need a graphical interface. In Chapter 12, "Graphical Interfaces for Ruby," we discuss creating graphical interfaces in Ruby.

CHAPTER 12

Graphical Interfaces for Ruby

There is nothing worse than a sharp image of a fuzzy concept.

—Ansel Adams

There is no denying that we are in the age of the graphical user interface (GUI). For as far into the future as we can see, some form of graphical interface is going to be the preferred way to interact with a computer.

I don't see the command line going away anytime soon; it definitely has its place in the world. But even the old-time hackers (who would rather use `cp -R` than a mouse) still enjoy a GUI when it is appropriate.

However, there are new difficulties when it comes to programming graphically. The first problem, of course, is designing a meaningful, usable "front end" for a program. In interface design, a picture is *not* always worth a thousand words. This book can't address these issues; our topic here is not ergonomics, aesthetics, or psychology.

The second problem is that graphical programming is more complex. We have to worry about the sizes, shapes, locations, and behaviors of all the controls that can be displayed and manipulated with mouse, keyboard, or finger.

The third difficulty is that various computing subcultures have differing ideas of what a windowing system is and how it should be implemented. The disparity between these systems has to be experienced to be fully appreciated; many a programmer has attempted to produce a cross-platform tool only to find that the impedance mismatch between the GUIs was the hardest part to deal with.

This chapter can't help much with these problems. The most I can do is give a gentle introduction to a few popular GUI systems (as they relate to Ruby) and offer a few hints and observations.

The bulk of this chapter is devoted to Shoes, Tk, GTK, and Qt. Whatever your background, there is a good chance you are asking, "Why wasn't *(insert name of favorite GUI)* included here?"

There could be several reasons. One reason is limited space, because this book is not primarily about graphical interfaces. Another reason might be that your favorite system doesn't have a mature set of Ruby bindings yet (in which case you are encouraged to create them). Finally, not all GUI systems are created equal. This chapter tries to cover the most mature and widely used options, and give the rest a passing mention.

12.1   Shoes 4

Shoes is a uniquely "Rubyesque" GUI system—and at present the most widely used way to create graphical programs in Ruby. Shoes provides an extremely simple and straightforward graphics API, and has been used for both teaching and building applications. It was originally created by _why the lucky stiff_ for his teaching tool Hackety Hack, and after _why disappeared, the project was adopted by Steve Klabnik.

The latest version of Shoes runs on JRuby, which is a Ruby interpreter written in Java. It allows Ruby programs to run on the Java Virtual Machine (JVM) with easy access to any Java library. Although it has not always been true, JRuby today is stable, mature, and sometimes even faster than MRI (the main Ruby interpreter).

Today, the team of volunteers working on Shoes 4 is led by Tobias Pfeiffer and Jason R. Clark. They are working to complete _why's original vision of making it easy for children to create graphical and interactive programs using Ruby.

12.1.1   Starting Out with Shoes

Installing JRuby for Shoes is probably the hardest part of using it. You'll need to install JRuby, following whatever instructions are appropriate for your current platform. For detailed instructions, see the JRuby website at jruby.org. Another option is to use a Ruby version manager, which is discussed in Section 21.6, "Ruby Version Managers," of Chapter 21, "Ruby Development Tools."

Once JRuby is installed and running, installing Shoes is just one command:

```
gem install shoes -v "~> 4.0.pre"
```

The version requirement `~> 4.0` tells Rubygems to install Shoes 4.0 or greater, but less than 5.0, whereas the `.pre` allows prerelease versions.

With the gem installed, Shoes programs can be run with the `shoes` command. To run a Shoes program saved into the file `program.rb`, you would run the command `shoes program.rb`.

The simplest possible Shoes program just creates an empty window when launched:

```
Shoes.app
```

The size of the window can be changed by passing `height:` and `width:` arguments to the `app` method. Elements inside the application window are created by passing a block to the app method that declares those elements. There are ten basic elements, and they can be used to create GUI programs containing buttons, text, graphics, text, forms, and links.

12.1.2   An Interactive Button

Buttons in shoes are extremely straightforward to create: Call the `button` method, and supply the text of the button as the first argument. If a block is passed, it will be run whenever the button is clicked. Here is a small application with a button that will display an alert when clicked:

```
Shoes.app(height: 30, width: 125) do
  button "Declaim poem" do
    alert "O freddled gruntbuggly thy micturations " \
      "are to me\n As plurdled gabbleblotchits on a " \
      "lurgid bee."
  end
end
```

The `alert` method simply takes a string and displays it in a modal dialog box with an "OK" button. Figure 12.1 displays the application window and the alert that appears when the button is clicked.

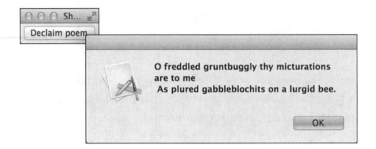

Figure 12.1   Shoes application with alert dialog box

12.1.3   Text and Input

Text can be inserted into the window by passing a string to the `para` method. After the string, options can be given, including `size` and `stroke` (which changes the color of the text). Additional methods are provided as shortcuts for certain sets of options. Larger text can be inserted using `banner`, `title`, `subtitle`, and other methods, whereas styled text can be added with the `em`, `strong`, and `code`, among others.

By saving a reference to a text element, it becomes possible to update the contents of that element later. Here, we create a title element as well as a button that, when clicked, changes the text of that title element, as shown in Figure 12.2.

```
Shoes.app(height: 75, width: 225) do
  @book = title "The Urby Way"
  button "Correct spelling" do
    @book.text = "The Ruby Way"
  end
end
```

Figure 12.2   Styled title text in Shoes

The `title` element is saved as `@book` so that the contents of the title can be updated later, when the button is clicked. Notice that the instance variable `@book` is available inside both the `Shoes.app` block and the `button` block. Each block is run using `instance_eval` on the instance of the `App` class that is currently running. This provides the same set of instance variables to every block, no matter which method the block was given to.

Text input is supplied by the `edit_line` and `edit_box` methods, which create single-line and multiple-line text entry areas, respectively. If a block is given, it will be called when the field is changed and then passed the field as an argument. Here, we take any string that is entered into the field and display it in reverse, as shown in Figure 12.3.

```
Shoes.app do
  edit_line do |line|
    @name.text = line.text.reverse
  end
  @name = para "", margin: 10
end
```

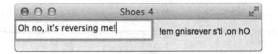

Figure 12.3   Edit line with reversed text

The `para` containing the reversed text starts out empty (like the `edit_field`)
but updates as each letter is typed into the field.

12.1.4 Layout

As you probably noticed in the last example (especially if you typed a lot of text into
the `edit_field`), new elements fill up the available space left to right and then top
to bottom, just like text in a paragraph. In Shoes, this kind of layout is called a *flow*,
and the main `Shoes.app` block provides a flow for you. The other type of layout is
called a *stack*. Inside a stack, each new element is added underneath the previous element.

Predictably, stacks and flows are created by passing blocks to the methods `stack`
and `flow`. By combining them together, it is easy to create screens with elements laid
out naturally, even with multiple columns. In this example, we create a form with
columns containing text, fields, and buttons:

```
Shoes.app width: 500, height: 240 do
  stack width: 220, margin: 10 do
    caption "Name"
    @name = edit_line

    caption "Nation"
    @nation = edit_line

    caption "Home"
    @home = edit_line

    caption "Destination"
    @destination = edit_line

    button "Compose", margin_top: 10 do
```

```
      @result.clear
      @result.append do
        caption "#{@name.text} is my name,"
        caption "and #{@nation.text} is my nation."
        caption "#{@home.text} is my dwelling place,"
        caption "#{@destination.text} my destination."
      end
    end
  end

  @result = stack width: -220, margin: 20
end
```

The first stack has a fixed width of 220 pixels. The negative width on the second stack indicates that it should fill the entire width except 220 pixels. Because the main app block creates a flow, the two stacks are placed next to one another to create two columns.

Rather than use the `edit_line` blocks to create a live-updating result, we create a button that removes all elements (if any) from the right column and adds several text elements. Because the right column is also a stack, each element is stacked onto a new line.

The ultimate effect is one of a form on the left and text on the right, created when the button is clicked. Figure 12.4 shows what using the program might look like.

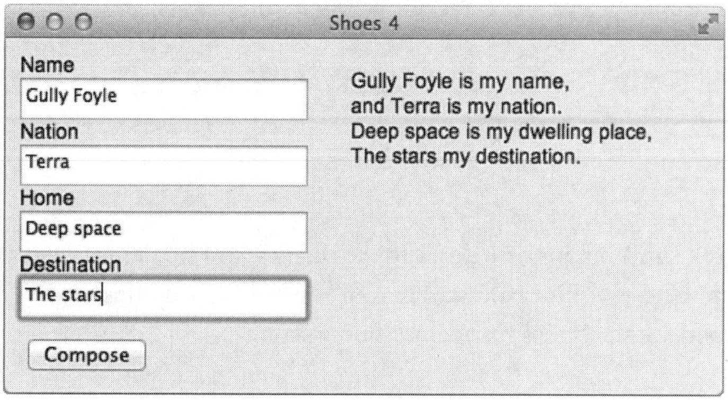

Figure 12.4 Quatrain generator

12.1.5 Images and Shapes

Shoes also provides straightforward graphical elements. Adding images to a Shoes window is as simple as calling the `image` method with the path to an image. The path can point to a local file or to an image hosted on the internet.

Graphics can be constructed using the basic `arc`, `line`, `oval`, and `rect` methods. Arbitrary shapes can be constructed as well, using the `shape` method. Colors can be set by calling `stroke` to set the outline color and `fill` to set the interior color before creating the shape. In this example, we simply draw a green oval and then a black rectangle at a 30-degree angle. The result is shown in Figure 12.5.

```
Shoes.app width: 250, height: 125 do
  fill green
  nostroke
  oval top: 25, left: 125, width: 45, height: 65

  rotate 30
  rect top: 30, left: 30, width: 60, height: 40
end
```

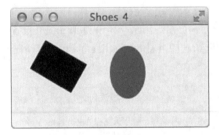

Figure 12.5 Shapes

The stroke and fill are be cleared by `nostroke` and `nofill`, whereas the stroke thickness can be set with `strokewidth`. For more details about drawing and manipulating shapes, see the Shoes manual at shoesrb.com.

12.1.6 Events

We've already seen how clicking buttons and changing text fields can cause blocks to run. Shoes provides a few other events that can also be given blocks:

- **keypress**—Calls the given block with each key pushed while your app is running.

- **motion**—Runs when the mouse moves, and passes the left and top location of the mouse.

- **hover**—Runs when the mouse enters a stack or flow.

- **click**—Runs when the mouse clicks the element.

- **release**—Runs when the mouse is released after having clicked the element.

- **leave**—Runs when the mouse exits the stack or flow.

Note that `keypress` always applies to the entire Shoes app, whereas the other events apply only to the stack or flow that contains them. Using events, we can move shapes whenever someone interacts with our program:

```
Shoes.app do
  @circle = oval top: 5, left: 5, radius: 30

  motion do |left, top|
    if @track
      @circle.left, @circle.top = left - 15, top - 15
    else
      @circle.left = (width - left)
      @circle.top = (height - top)
    end
  end

  click { @track = true }
  release { @track = false }
end
```

In this program, a circle will react to mouse movement, moving to the opposite side of the window. While the mouse is held down, however, the circle will follow the cursor exactly. A screenshot is simply unable to capture the experience, so I encourage you to try it out for yourself.

12.1.7 Other Notes

Any program written in Shoes can be packaged into a standalone executable that can be distributed and run on Windows, Mac OS X, and Linux computers. Work is ongoing on different backends, allowing Shoes to run inside Qt and GTK, which are both examined later in this chapter.

Although Shoes is not very much like other GUI toolkits, its extreme simplicity and its focus on being easy to use with Ruby make it the most popular way to create GUI Ruby applications today. For the latest news and more documentation, including a hand-drawn manual and API reference, see the Shoes website at shoesrb.com.

12.2   Ruby/Tk

The roots of Tk go back as far as 1988, if you count prerelease versions. It has a long association with the Tcl programming language, but now has bindings for many other languages, including Perl and Ruby.

In 2001, Tk was probably the most common GUI in use with Ruby. It was the first one made available and has long been part of the standard Ruby installation. Though it is not as popular as it was then, it is still in use.

Although Ruby/Tk is included in the Ruby standard library, most would say that Tk is showing its age; for those who like clean, object-oriented interfaces, it may be something of a disappointment. However, it still has the advantages of being well known, portable, and stable. The examples shown in this section will work with Ruby on Windows, Mac OS X, and Linux.

12.2.1   Overview

Any Ruby/Tk application must use `require` to load the `tk` extension. Following that, the application's interface is built up piecemeal, starting with some kind of container and the controls that populate it. Finally, a call to `Tk.mainloop` is made; this method captures all the events, such as mouse movements and button presses, and acts on them accordingly.

```
require "tk"
# Launch the app...
Tk.mainloop
```

As with most or all windowing systems, Tk graphical controls are called *widgets*, and these widgets are typically grouped together in containers. The top-level container is called the *root*. Although it is not always necessary to specify an explicit root, doing so is a good idea.

Every widget class is named according to its name in the Tk world (by appending `Tk` to the front). Thus, the `Frame` widget corresponds to the `TkFrame` class.

Widgets are naturally instantiated using the `new` method. The first parameter specifies the container into which the widget is placed; if it is omitted, the root is assumed.

The options used to instantiate a widget may be specified in two ways. The first way is to pass in a hash of attributes and values. (Recall that it is a quirk of Ruby syntax that a hash passed in as the last or only parameter may have its braces omitted.)

```
my_widget = TkSomewidget.new(borderwidth: 2,
  height: 40, justify: "center")
```

The other way is to pass a block to the constructor that will be evaluated with `instance_eval`. Within this block, we can call methods to set the attributes of the widget (using methods that are named the same as the attributes). Bear in mind that the code block is evaluated *in the context of the object, not the caller.* This means, for instance, that the caller's instance variables cannot be referenced inside this block. This code will create a widget with the exact same settings as the previous example will:

```
my_widget = TkSomewidget.new do
  borderwidth 2
  height 40
  justify "center"
end
```

Three geometry managers are available with Tk; they all serve the purpose of controlling the relative size and placement of the widgets as they appear onscreen. The first (and most commonly used) is `pack`; the other two are `grid` and `place`. The `grid` manager is sophisticated but somewhat prone to bugs; the `place` manager is the most simpleminded of all because it requires absolute values for the positioning of widgets. We will only use `pack` in our examples.

12.2.2 A Simple Windowed Application

Here, we'll demonstrate the simplest possible application—a simple calendar app that displays the current date. For good form, we'll begin by explicitly creating a `root` and placing a `Label` widget inside it:

```
require "tk"

root = TkRoot.new() { title "Today's Date" }
str = Time.now.strftime("Today is \n%B %d, %Y")
lab = TkLabel.new(root) do
  text str
  pack("padx" => 15, "pady" => 10,
  "side" => "top")
end
Tk.mainloop
```

After creating the root itself, we create a string containing the date. Then, while creating the label, we set the text to be the value of `str` and call `pack` to arrange everything neatly. We tell `pack` to use a padding of 15 pixels horizontally and 10 pixels vertically, and we ask that the text be centered on the label.

Figure 12.6 shows what the application looks like.

Figure 12.6   A simple Tk application

As we mentioned, the creation of the label could also be done in this way:

```
lab = TkLabel.new(root) do
  text str
  pack(padx: 15, pady: 10, side: "top")
end
```

The units for screen measurement (as used in this example for `padx` and `pady`) are in pixels by default. We can also work in another unit by appending a suffix onto the number; the value now becomes a string, of course, but because Ruby/Tk doesn't care about that, we don't care either. The available units are centimeters (`c`), millimeters (`m`), inches (`i`), and points (`p`). All of these are valid `padx` calls:

```
pack(padx: "80m")
pack(padx: "8c")
pack(padx: "3i")
pack(padx: "12p")
```

The `side` attribute doesn't actually contribute anything in this case because we have set it to its default. If you resize the application window, you will notice that the text "sticks" to the top part of the area in which it lives. Other possible values are `right`, `left`, and `bottom`, as you might expect.

The `pack` method has other options that govern the placement of widgets onscreen. We'll look at just a few.

The `fill` option specifies whether a widget fills its allocation rectangle (in the horizontal and/or vertical directions). Possible values are `x`, `y`, `both`, and `none` (the default being `none`).

The `anchor` option will anchor the widget inside its allocation rectangle using a "compass point" notation; the default is `center`, and the other possible values are `n`, `s`, `e`, `w`, `ne`, `nw`, `se`, and `sw`.

The `in` option will pack the widget with respect to some container other than its parent. The default, of course, is the parent.

The `before` and `after` options can be used to change the packing order of the widgets in any way desired. This is useful because widgets may not be created in any particular order as compared to their locations onscreen.

All in all, Tk is fairly flexible about placing widgets onscreen. Search the documentation and try things out.

12.2.3 Working with Buttons

One of the most common widgets in any GUI is the *pushbutton* (or simply *button*). As you would expect, the `TkButton` class enables the use of buttons in Ruby/Tk applications.

In any nontrivial application, we usually create frames to contain the various widgets we'll be placing onscreen. Button widgets can be placed in these containers.

A button will ordinarily have at least three attributes set:

• The text of the button

• The command associated with the button (to be executed when it is clicked)

• The packing of the button within its container

Here is a little example of a button:

```
btn_ok = TkButton.new do
  text "OK"
  command { puts "The user says OK." }
  pack(side: "left")
end
```

Here we create a new button and assign the new object to the `btn_OK` variable; we pass in a block to the constructor, although we could use a hash if we chose. In this case, we use the multiline form (which we prefer), though in practice you can cram as much code onto a single line as you want. Recall, by the way, that the block is executed using `instance_eval` so that it is evaluated in the context of the object (in this case, the new `TkButton` object).

The text specified as a parameter to the `text` method will simply be placed on the button. It can be multiple words or even multiple lines.

The `pack` method we have already seen. It is nothing interesting, though it is essential if the widget is going to be visible at all.

The interesting part here is the `command` method, which takes a block and runs the block when the button is clicked.

The action we're performing here is rather silly. When the user clicks the button, a (nongraphical) `puts` will be done; the output will go to the command-line window from which the program was started or perhaps an auxiliary console window.

We now offer a better example. Listing 12.1 is a fake thermostat application that will increment and decrement the displayed temperature (giving us at least the illusion that we are controlling the heating or cooling and making ourselves more comfortable). An explanation follows the code.

Listing 12.1 A Simulated Thermostat

```
require 'tk'

# Common packing options...
top  = { side: 'top', padx: 5, pady: 5 }
left = { side: 'left', padx: 5, pady: 5 }
bottom = { side: 'bottom', padx: 5, pady: 5 }

# Starting temperature...
temp = 74

root = TkRoot.new { title "Thermostat" }
tframe = TkFrame.new(root) { background "#606060" }
```

```
bframe = TkFrame.new(root)

tlab = TkLabel.new(tframe) do
  text temp.to_s
  font "{Helvetica} 54 {bold}"
  foreground "green"
  background "#606060"
  pack left
end

# the "degree" symbol
TkLabel.new(tframe) do
  text "o"
  font "{Helvetica} 14 {bold}"
  foreground "green"
  background "#606060"
  # Anchor-north above text like a degree symbol
  pack left.update(anchor: 'n')
end

TkButton.new(bframe) do
  text " Up "
  pack left
  command do
    temp += 1
    tlab.configure(text: temp.to_s)
  end
end

TkButton.new(bframe) do
  text "Down"
  pack left
  command do
    temp -= 1
    tlab.configure(text: temp.to_s)
  end
end

tframe.pack top
bframe.pack bottom

Tk.mainloop
```

We create two frames here. The upper one holds only a display. We display the temperature in Fahrenheit in a large font for realism (using a small, strategically placed letter *o* for a degree mark). The bottom frame holds the "up" and "down" buttons.

Notice that we are using some new attributes for the `TkLabel` object. The `font` method specifies the typeface and size of the text in the label. The string value is platform dependent; the one shown here is valid on a Mac OS X or Windows system. On a UNIX system, it would typically be a full X-style font name, long and unwieldy (something like `-Adobe-Helvetica-Bold-R-Normal-*-120-*-*-*-*-*-*`).

The `foreground` method sets the color of the text itself. Here, we pass in the string `"green"` (which has a predefined meaning in the internals of Tk). If you wonder whether a color is predefined in Tk, an easy way to find out is simply to try it.

Likewise, the `background` method sets the color of the background against which the text appears. In this case, we pass it a different kind of string as a parameter, a color in typical red-green-blue hex format, as you would see in HTML or in various other situations. (The string `"#606060"`, for example, represents a nice gray color.)

Notice that we haven't added any kind of "exit" button here (to avoid cluttering a nice, simple design). As always, you can close the app by clicking the Close button in the upper right (or upper left) of the window frame.

Note that the `configure` method is used in the commands for the buttons; this changes the text of the top label as it increments or decrements the current temperature. As mentioned earlier, basically any attribute can be changed at runtime in this way, and the change will be reflected onscreen immediately.

We'll mention two other tricks you can do with text buttons. The `justify` method will accept a parameter (`"left"`, `"right"`, or `"center"`) to specify how the text will be placed on the button (`"center"` is the default). We already mentioned that multiple lines could be displayed; the `wraplength` method will specify the column at which word wrapping should occur.

The button's style may be changed with the `relief` method, giving it a slight three-dimensional appearance. The parameter to this method must be one of these strings: `"flat"`, `"groove"`, `"raised"`, `"ridge"` (the default), `"sunken"`, or `"solid"`. The `width` and `height` methods will control the size of the button explicitly, and methods such as `borderwidth` also are available. For a full list of options (which are numerous), check the API documentation.

Let's look at an additional example of using a button. This new button will have an image on it rather than just text.

I created a pair of GIF images composed of an upward-pointing arrow and a downward-pointing arrow (`up.gif` and `down.gif`). We can use the `TkPhotoImage` class to get references to each of these. Then we can use these references when we instantiate the buttons:

```
TkButton.new(bframe) do
  image TkPhotoImage.new(file: "up.gif")
  pack left
  command do
    temp += 1
    tlab.configure(text: temp.to_s)
  end
end

TkButton.new(bframe) do
  image TkPhotoImage.new(file: "down.gif")
  pack left
  command do
    temp -= 1
    tlab.configure(text: temp.to_s)
  end
end
```

This button code simply replaces the corresponding lines in our first thermostat example. Except for the appearance of the buttons, the behavior is the same. Figure 12.7 shows the graphical buttons in the thermostat application.

Figure 12.7   Thermostat simulation (with graphical buttons)

12.2.4   Working with Text Fields

A text entry field can be displayed and manipulated using the `TkEntry` widget. As you would expect, numerous options are available for governing the size, color, and behavior of this widget; we will offer one sizable example that illustrates a few of these.

An entry field is only useful if there is some way to retrieve the value typed into it. Typically the field will be bound to a variable (actually a `TkVariable`, as you'll see), though the `get` method can also be used.

For our code fragment, let's assume that we're writing a telnet client that will accept four pieces of information: the host machine, the port number (defaulting to 23), the user ID, and the password. We'll add a couple of buttons just for looks, for the "sign on" and "cancel" operations.

As we've written it, this code fragment also does some little tricks with frames to make things line up and look better, though a real Tk guru would probably disdain our approach. But just for your information, we've documented this "quick and dirty" approach to screen layout.

The screenshot is shown in Figure 12.8, and the code in Listing 12.2.

Figure 12.8   A simulated telnet client

Listing 12.2   A Simulated Telnet Client

```
require "tk"

def packing(padx, pady, side = "left", anchor = "n")
  { padx: padx, pady: pady, side: side, anchor: anchor }
end

root = TkRoot.new() { title "Telnet session" }
top  = TkFrame.new(root)
fr1  = TkFrame.new(top)
```

```ruby
fr1a    = TkFrame.new(fr1)
fr1b    = TkFrame.new(fr1)
fr2     = TkFrame.new(top)
fr3     = TkFrame.new(top)
fr4     = TkFrame.new(top)

LabelPack   = packing(5, 5, "top", "w")
EntryPack   = packing(5, 2, "top")
ButtonPack  = packing(15, 5, "left", "center")
FramePack   = packing(2, 2, "top")
Frame1Pack  = packing(2, 2, "left")

var_host = TkVariable.new
var_port = TkVariable.new
var_user = TkVariable.new
var_pass = TkVariable.new

lab_host = TkLabel.new(fr1a) do
  text "Host name"
  pack LabelPack
end

ent_host = TkEntry.new(fr1a) do
  textvariable var_host
  font "{Helvetica} 10"
  pack EntryPack
end

lab_port = TkLabel.new(fr1b) do
  text "Port"
  pack LabelPack
end

ent_port = TkEntry.new(fr1b) do
  width 4
  textvariable var_port
  font "{Helvetica} 10"
  pack EntryPack
end

lab_user = TkLabel.new(fr2) do
  text "User name"
  pack LabelPack
end

ent_user = TkEntry.new(fr2) do
  width 21
  font "{Helvetica} 12"
  textvariable var_user
  pack EntryPack
end
```

```
lab_pass = TkLabel.new(fr3) do
  text "Password"
  pack LabelPack
end

ent_pass = TkEntry.new(fr3) do
  width 21
  show "*"
  textvariable var_pass
  font "{Helvetica} 12"
  pack EntryPack
end

btn_signon = TkButton.new(fr4) do
  text "Sign on"
  command {}          # Does nothing!
  pack ButtonPack
end

btn_cancel = TkButton.new(fr4) do
  text "Cancel"
  command { exit }  # Just exits
  pack ButtonPack
end

top.pack FramePack
fr1.pack FramePack
fr2.pack FramePack
fr3.pack FramePack
fr4.pack FramePack
fr1a.pack Frame1Pack
fr1b.pack Frame1Pack

var_host.value = "addison-wesley.com"
var_user.value = "debra"
var_port.value = 23

ent_pass.focus
foo = ent_user.font

Tk.mainloop
```

Let's get the layout issues out of the way. Note that we begin by creating some frames that will stack vertically from top to bottom. The topmost frame will have two smaller ones inside it, placed onscreen from left to right.

Listing 12.2 also has a method called packing, which exists only to make the code a tiny bit cleaner. It returns a hash with the specified values set for the padx, pady, side, and anchor options.

We use the `TkVariable` objects just to associate the entry fields with variables. A `TkVariable` has a `value` accessor that will allow these values to be set and retrieved.

When we create a `TkEntry` such as `ent_host`, we use the `textvariable` option to associate it with its corresponding `TkVariable` object. In some cases, we use `width` to set the horizontal width of the field; if it is omitted, a reasonable default will be picked, usually based on the width of the current value stored in the field. Often it's acceptable to pick these widths by trial and error.

Fonts work for entry fields as they do for labels; so do colors, which aren't addressed in this example. If a font is proportional, two fields that are given the same width may not appear equally sized onscreen.

As always, `pack` must be called. We've simplified these calls a little with constants.

The Password field has a call to the `show` method because it is the one field whose value is kept secret from people reading over our shoulders. The character specified as a parameter to `show` (here an asterisk) will be displayed in place of each of the user's keystrokes.

As I said, the buttons are there for show. The Sign on button does nothing at all, and the Cancel button exits the program.

There are other options for manipulating entry fields. We can change the value under program control rather than having the user change it; we can specify the font and the foreground/background colors; we can change the characteristics of the insertion cursor and move it where we want; and much more. For all the details, see the documentation.

Because the topic is entering text, it's appropriate to mention the related `Text` widget. It is related to the entry widget in the same way a two-seater plane is related to the space shuttle. It is specifically designed to handle large pieces of multiline text and, in effect, forms the basis for a full-fledged editor. Although it's too complex to cover here, be sure to investigate it if you plan to provide text editing with Tk.

12.2.5   Working with Other Widgets

Many other widgets are available for Tk. We'll mention a few here.

A check box is commonly used for a toggled value, such as a simple true/false or on/off field. The Tk terminology is *check button*, and `TkCheckButton` is the class name for the widget.

The example shown in Listing 12.3 is a completely bare-bones code fragment because it does not even have any buttons. It displays check boxes for three areas in

which you might take coursework (computer science, music, and literature). It prints
a message to the console when you select (or deselect) one of these.

Listing 12.3   Tk Check Boxes

```
require "tk"

root = TkRoot.new { title "Checkbutton demo" }
top = TkFrame.new(root)

pack_opts  = { side: "top", anchor: "w" }

cb1var = TkVariable.new
cb2var = TkVariable.new
cb3var = TkVariable.new

cb1 = TkCheckButton.new(top) do
  variable cb1var
  text "Computer science"
  command { puts "Button 1 = #{cb1var.value}" }
  pack pack_opts
end

cb2 = TkCheckButton.new(top) do
  variable cb2var
  text "Music"
  command { puts "Button 2 = #{cb2var.value}" }
  pack pack_opts
end

cb3 = TkCheckButton.new(top) do
  variable cb3var
  text "Literature"
  command { puts "Button 3 = #{cb3var.value}" }
  pack pack_opts
end

top.pack pack_opts

Tk.mainloop
```

Note that the variable associated with a check box receives the value 1 when the
box is selected and 0 when it is deselected. These default values can be changed with
the `onvalue` and `offvalue` methods. Furthermore, the variable can be set prior to
the creation of the check box to establish its initial on/off status.

If for some reason we want a check box to be grayed out, we can use the `state` method to set its state to `disabled`. The other states are `active` and `normal`; the latter is the default.

Let's alter the example in Listing 12.3. Suppose we are representing not just areas of potential but actual university majors. Ignoring double majors, it's not appropriate for more than one option to be selected at a time. In this case, of course, we need *radio buttons* (implemented by the `TkRadioButton` class).

The example in Listing 12.4 is nearly the same as the example in Listing 12.3. Obviously the class name is different. Another critical difference is that the radio buttons all share the *same variable*. In fact, this is how Tk knows that these buttons all belong to the same group. It is possible to have more than one group of radio buttons, but each group must share one variable among its buttons.

Listing 12.4   Tk Radio Buttons

```
require "tk"

root = TkRoot.new { title "Radiobutton demo" }
top = TkFrame.new(root)

pack_opts = { side: "top", anchor: "w" }

major = TkVariable.new

b1 = TkRadioButton.new(top) do
  variable major
  text "Computer science"
  value 1
  command { puts "Major = #{major.value}" }
  pack pack_opts
end

b2 = TkRadioButton.new(top) do
  variable major
  text "Music"
  value 2
  command { puts "Major = #{major.value}" }
  pack pack_opts
end

b3 = TkRadioButton.new(top) do
  variable major
  text "Literature"
  value 3
  command { puts "Major = #{major.value}" }
  pack pack_opts
```

```
end

top.pack pack_opts

Tk.mainloop
```

The `value` method is used here to associate a specific value with each of the buttons. It's important to realize that *any* values can be used here (strings, for example). We didn't use strings simply because we wanted to emphasize that there is no direct relationship between the text of the widget and the value that is returned.

Numerous options are available to customize the appearance and behavior of both check boxes and radio button groups. The `image` method, for example, allows you to display an image rather than a text string. Most of the usual options for formatting and displaying widgets also apply; consult a reference for complete details.

If this book (or even this chapter) were fully devoted to Tk, we would have more to say. However, it's not possible to cover these topics in detail; they are mentioned only to make you aware of their existence.

The list box (`TkListBox`) widget allows you to specify a list of values in a pull-down format so that the user can select from these. The selection mode (governed by the `selectmode` method) makes it possible to select these in `single`, `extended`, or `browse` mode. The first two modes simply determine whether the user can select only one or more than one item at a time. Browse mode is like single mode, except that the selection can be moved around as the mouse button is held down. List boxes can be made fully scrollable and can hold an arbitrary number of items.

Tk has advanced menuing capabilities, including pull-down menus, tear-off menus, cascade submenus, keyboard shortcut facilities, radio button menu items, and much more. Investigate the classes `TkMenu`, `TkMenubar`, and `TkMenuButton`.

Perhaps the sexiest of the widgets is `TkCanvas`, which enables the programmer to manipulate images more or less at the pixel level. It has facilities for drawing lines and shapes, manipulating colors, and loading images in various graphics formats. If your application involves advanced graphics or user-controlled drawing, this widget will be of interest to you.

The scrollbar widget handles customized scrolling, both horizontal and vertical (for example, synchronized scrolling of two separate windows). The scale widget is basically a slider that represents a numeric value; it can be placed horizontally or vertically and can be used as input or output. An exhaustive list is available in the Tk API documentation.

12.2.6   Other Notes

Although the future of Tk is uncertain (like any software system), it is not going away anytime soon. Tk (along with the Tcl language) continues to be actively developed. At the time of this writing, Ruby/Tk is based on the most recent release, Tk 8.5.

I should also say a few words about operating systems. In theory, Tk is completely platform independent, and the practice is close to the theory. That said, some users have reported that the Windows version is not as stable as the UNIX and Mac OS X versions. All the Tk examples in this chapter have been tested on Windows and are known to work as expected.

12.3   Ruby/GTK3

The GTK library is a byproduct of the GIMP (GNU Image Manipulation Program); the name actually means *The GIMP Toolkit*. Like UNIX and LSD, GTK comes to us from the University of California at Berkeley.

For those familiar with X/Motif, GTK has a similar look and feel but is more lightweight. GTK originates in the UNIX world and forms the underlying basis for GNOME (an entire UI for Linux users), but it is relatively cross-platform.

12.3.1   Overview

Ruby/GTK3 is a library that allows Ruby applications to use the GTK+ library. It is a product of the Ruby-GNOME2 project, which also provides bindings for GTK2 and many other components of GTK+. GTK+ is open source and is released under the GNU LGPL license, so it may be used freely in commercial applications.

Like most GUI toolkits, GTK+ has such concepts as frames, windows, dialog boxes, and layout managers. It has a rich set of widgets; it includes all the most basic ones, such as labels, buttons, and text edit boxes, as well as advanced widgets, such as tree controls and multicolumn lists.

Although GTK+ was written in C, it was designed with a strong object-oriented flavor. Ruby/GTK3 thus presents an object-oriented API, while also staying close to the underlying C. In addition, Ruby/GTK3 is implemented carefully by hand, not by using a code generator. As a result, the API is very "Ruby like," using blocks, optional arguments, and so on. The API reference is available at ruby-gnome2.sourceforge.jp.

GTK+ is a conglomerate of projects, built on top of libraries including GLib, Pango, ATK, Cairo, and GDK. It supports nongraphical functions (GLib), layout and rendering of internationalized text using UTF-8 (Pango), accessibility (ATK), graphics (Cairo), low-level graphical objects (GDK), and many widgets and high-level graphical objects (GTK).

The `gtk3` gem works with Ruby on Linux, Windows, and Mac OS X, as long as GTK+ 3 is installed. On Mac OS X, it only works inside XQuartz, which is a port of the X Window System to OS X. Although there is an ongoing port to the native Mac OS X UI, it is currently not stable.

GTK+ is object oriented and has a logical widget hierarchy. The concepts of `Gtk::Bin` and `Gtk::Container` are powerful, and the combination of the `Gtk::Box` and `Gtk::Table` layout managers is simple yet flexible. The Ruby/GTK3 mechanism for setting up signal handlers is also convenient.

Some of the GTK+ widgets include menus, toolbars, tooltips, trees, progress bars, sliders, and calendars. However, one current weakness of GTK+ is that it does not yet provide a good selection of standard dialog boxes, and it is difficult to set them up modally. In addition, the standard multiline text editor widget has some weaknesses.

All strings you pass to Ruby/GTK3 methods must be in UTF-8. Ensure that your programs are configured to convert input into UTF-8 before using them as arguments. For more information about string encodings and conversion, see Chapter 4, "Internationalization in Ruby."

12.3.2   A Simple Windowed Application

Any program using Ruby/GTK3 must `require 'gtk3'`. Ruby/GTK3 provides its functionality through the `Gtk` and `Gdk` modules, meaning that GTK+ classes are typically prefixed with `Gtk::` (or `Gdk::`).

Normally we call `Gtk.init` to initialize Ruby/GTK3 and then create a top-level window and a handler for the **destroy** signal (which results when a window is closed by the user). A call to **show_all** makes the window (and its children) visible, and a call to `Gtk.main` initiates the event loop.

We'll expand on this a little after looking at an example. The following code fragment is similar to the one for Tk, which displays the current date:

```
require "gtk3"
Gtk.init

window = Gtk::Window.new("Today's Date")
window.signal_connect("destroy") { Gtk.main_quit }
str = Time.now.strftime("Today is \n%B %d, %Y")
window.add(Gtk::Label.new(str))
```

```
window.set_default_size(200, 100)
window.show_all
Gtk.main
```

The `Gtk.init` call initializes Ruby/GTK3. The main window (of type `Gtk::Window`) is created as a "top-level" window with the text that will appear in the title bar. Top-level windows have a standard title bar and generally behave as you would expect the main window of an application to behave.

Next, a handler is created for the `destroy` signal, which is generated after the main window is closed. This handler (here, a single block) simply exits the main event loop. The Ruby/GTK3 documentation lists all the signals that each widget might receive. (Be sure to look at superclasses, too.) These are typically triggered by mouse or keyboard input, timers, changes in window state, and so on.

The next line of code adds a text label widget directly to the main window. The default size of the label will be calculated automatically based on the size of the text.

By default, GTK+ parent widgets are automatically sized according to the sizes of their children. In this case, the size of the string in the default font will determine the size of the label widget, and the main window would become just large enough to hold the label. That's pretty small, so `set_default_size` is used to indicate that the initial size of the main window is 200 pixels wide and 100 pixels tall.

After that, `show_all` is used to make the main window and all its children visible. By default, the main window is hidden, so it is necessary to invoke this method for the main window of most applications.

The call to `Gtk.main` starts the GTK+ event loop. This method will not return until GTK+ is terminated. In this application, the `destroy` event handler will trigger when the window is closed. This will in turn cause `Gtk.main` to exit, at which point the app will terminate.

12.3.3 Working with Buttons

To create a pushbutton in Ruby/GTK3, we define it using the `Gtk::Button` class. In the simple case, we set up a handler for the `clicked` event that is generated when a user clicks the button.

Listing 12.5 will accept a simple line of text in a text entry field and (when the All Caps! button is clicked) will convert the string to uppercase. Figure 12.9 shows the text entry field before the button is clicked.

Listing 12.5 Buttons in GTK

```ruby
require "gtk3"

class SampleWindow < Gtk::Window

  def initialize
    super("Ruby/GTK3 Sample")
    signal_connect("destroy") { Gtk.main_quit }

    entry = Gtk::Entry.new

    button = Gtk::Button.new("All Caps!    ")
    button.signal_connect("clicked") {
      entry.text = entry.text.upcase
    }

    box = Gtk::HBox.new
    box.add(Gtk::Label.new("Text:"))
    box.add(entry)
    box.add(button)

    add(box)
    show_all
  end
end

Gtk.init
SampleWindow.new
Gtk.main
```

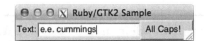

Figure 12.9   A simple GTK pushbutton example

In Listing 12.5, a `SampleWindow` class is defined; this is a cleaner approach because it allows the class to control its own look and behavior (rather than requiring the caller to configure the window). This main window is derived from `Gtk::Window`.

As with the "Today's Date" example, a signal handler for `destroy` exits the GTK+ event loop when the main window is closed.

This class creates a single-line text entry field using the `Gtk::Entry` class and a `Gtk::Button` with the text label `All Caps!`. The signal handler for the button's `clicked` event calls the signal handler. (The `clicked` event is generated after the user *clicks and releases* the button.)

The `Gtk::Window` class is a `Gtk::Bin`, so it can only contain a single child widget. To put our two child widgets in the window, we place those widgets in a box and add the box to the main window. As widgets are added to a `Gtk::Box`, they are positioned at the right edge of the box (by default). To stack multiple widgets, pass the symbol `:vertical` to get a vertically stacking box.

As with the earlier example, `show_all` is necessary to make the main window (and all its children) visible.

The signal handler of `clicked` is invoked whenever the button is clicked. It gets the current text out of the entry field, converts it to uppercase, and sets it back into the entry field.

The actual application code is below the `SampleWindow` class definition. It simply creates the main window and runs the GTK+ event loop.

12.3.4   Working with Text Fields

GTK+ provides the `Gtk::Entry` class for single-line input, as shown in the previous example. It also has a `Gtk::TextView` class, which is a powerful multiline editor that we will describe here.

Listing 12.6 creates a multiline edit box and inserts some text into it. As the contents change, the current length of the text is reflected in a label at the bottom of the window (see Figure 12.10).

Listing 12.6   A GTK Text Editor

```
require "gtk3"

class TextWindow < Gtk::Window

  def initialize
    super("Text Sample")
    signal_connect("destroy") { Gtk.main_quit }
    set_default_size(200, 50)

    @text = Gtk::TextView.new
    @text.wrap_mode = :word

    @buffer = @text.buffer
    @buffer.signal_connect("changed") {
      @status.text = "Length: " + @buffer.char_count.to_s
    }
```

```
    @buffer.create_tag('notice',
                        'font' => "Times Bold Italic 18",
                        'foreground' => "red")

    @status = Gtk::Label.new

    scroller = Gtk::ScrolledWindow.new
    scroller.set_policy(:automatic, :never)
    scroller.add(@text)

    box = Gtk::Box.new(:vertical)
    box.add(scroller)
    box.add(@status)
    add(box)

    iter = @buffer.start_iter
    @buffer.insert(iter, "This is an editor")
    iter.offset = 5
    @buffer.insert(iter, "really ", "notice")

    show_all
  end
end

Gtk.init
TextWindow.new
Gtk.main
```

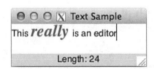

Figure 12.10   A small GTK text editor

The basic structure of the code is similar to the button example: Initialize
Ruby/GTK2, define a window class with an event handler to terminate the app
cleanly, and set the initial size of the main window. At the end of `initialize`,
`show_all` is used to make the window visible. The last two lines actually create the
window and run the GTK+ event loop.

We create an editor widget named `@text`. Word wrap is enabled here; the default
is to wrap lines regardless of word breaks.

The variable `@buffer` is the text buffer of `@text`. We give it a signal handler for
the `changed` event; any time text is inserted, deleted, or modified, this signal will fire,

and the signal handler will be called. The signal handler uses `char_count` to determine the length of the current text in the text editor and creates a message string; that message is displayed by setting `@status.text = text`.

Next we want to configure the `@text` widget to display its text in a different style. Create a "notice" tag using `create_tag`. This tag has the font "Times Bold Italic 18" and a foreground color of red. In a similar way, you can define tags with various other properties using `Gtk::TextTag`.

In this case, we attempt to use a font from the Times family, which on a Windows platform is likely to bring up some variant of Times Roman. On a Linux/UNIX platform, the parameter would be a standard X Window System font string. The system will return whatever font is the closest match available.

The `@status` label is initially empty. We will change its text later.

GTK+ provides two ways to add scrollbars to an application. You can directly create `Gtk::ScrollBar` objects and use signals to synchronize them with the content widget(s). However, in most cases, it is simpler to use the `Gtk::ScrolledWindow` widget instead.

The `Gtk::ScrolledWindow` widget is a `Gtk::Bin`, meaning it can only contain a single child widget. Of course, that child widget could be a `Gtk::Box` or other container that allows multiple children. Several GTK+ widgets, including `Gtk::TextView`, automatically interact with a `Gtk::ScrolledWindow`, requiring almost no additional code.

In this example, we create a `Gtk::ScrolledWindow` named `scroller` and configure it using `set_policy`. We choose never to display a horizontal scrollbar and to automatically display a vertical scrollbar only when the editor has more lines than can be seen at once. We add the text editor directly to `scroller`.

We now set up a `Gtk::Box` that will stack our widgets vertically. The scrolling window that contains the text field is added first, so it will appear at the top of the main window. The `@status` text will appear at the bottom. The box is then added to our main window.

The next four lines insert text into the text editor. The first line gets the `Gtk::TextIter` of the beginning of the text (`offset = 0`) and then inserts a string there. Because there was no text, zero is the only reasonable place to insert. We then insert some additional text at offset five. The result is a text editor containing the string `This really is an editor`.

Because we already configured the handler for the `changed` event, it will be triggered by our calls to `insert`. This means the status will already display correctly, even before the user makes any changes to the text.

12.3.5   Working with Other Widgets

Even a relatively simple GUI may need more than text fields and buttons. Often we
find a need for radio buttons, check boxes, and similar widgets. This next example
illustrates a few of these.

Listing 12.7 assumes that the user is making an airline reservation. The
`Gtk::TreeView`, `Gtk::ListStore`, and `Gtk::TreeViewColumn` classes (representing a multicolumn list) are used for the destination city. A check box (actually called
a `Gtk::CheckButton`) determines whether the ticket is round trip, and a set of radio
buttons (class `Gtk::RadioButton`) is used for the seating. A Purchase button completes the interface (see Figure 12.11).

Listing 12.7   Airline Ticket Example

```
require "gtk3"

class TicketWindow < Gtk::Window

  def initialize
    super("Purchase Ticket")
    signal_connect("destroy") { Gtk.main_quit }

    dest_model = Gtk::ListStore.new(String, String)
    dest_view = Gtk::TreeView.new(dest_model)
    dest_column = Gtk::TreeViewColumn.new("Destination",
                      Gtk::CellRendererText.new,
                      :text => 0)
    dest_view.append_column(dest_column)
    country_column = Gtk::TreeViewColumn.new("Country",
                        Gtk::CellRendererText.new,
                        :text => 1)
    dest_view.append_column(country_column)
    dest_view.selection.set_mode(:single)

    [["Cairo", "Egypt"], ["New York", "USA"],
      ["Tokyo", "Japan"]].each do |destination, country|
      iter = dest_model.append
      iter[0] = destination
      iter[1] = country
    end
    dest_view.selection.signal_connect("changed") do
      @city = dest_view.selection.selected[0]
    end
```

```ruby
    @round_trip = Gtk::CheckButton.new("Round Trip")

    purchase = Gtk::Button.new(label: "Purchase")
    purchase.signal_connect("clicked") { cmd_purchase }

    @result = Gtk::Label.new

    @coach = Gtk::RadioButton.new("Coach class")
    @business = Gtk::RadioButton.new(@coach, "Business class")
    @first = Gtk::RadioButton.new(@coach, "First class")

    flight_box = Gtk::Box.new(:vertical)
    flight_box.add(dest_view).add(@round_trip)

    seat_box = Gtk::Box.new(:vertical)
    seat_box.add(@coach).add(@business).add(@first)

    top_box = Gtk::Box.new(:horizontal)
    top_box.add(flight_box).add(seat_box)

    main_box = Gtk::Box.new(:vertical)
    main_box.add(top_box).add(purchase).add(@result)

    add(main_box)
    show_all
  end

  def cmd_purchase
    text = @city
    if @first.active?
      text += ": first class"
    elsif @business.active?
      text += ": business class"
    elsif @coach.active?
      text += ": coach"
    end
    text += ", round trip " if @round_trip.active?
    @result.text = text
  end

end

Gtk.init
TicketWindow.new
Gtk.main
```

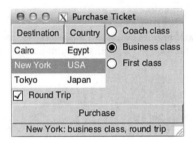

Figure 12.11   Various GTK widgets

This application creates a main window with a signal handler as before. Next, a multicolumn list box widget is created with two columns. This list box is designed around a Model-View-Controller (MVC) design; Gtk::ListStore (the model class) has two String columns.

Then Gtk::TreeView is created. Gtk::TreeViewColumn configures the column. The title of first column is "Destination" and the cell renderer is Gtk::CellRendererText. The first column (column number zero) of the model (Gtk::ListStore) is used as the text property value. In this way, cell renderers are used to draw the data in the tree model. Several cell renderers come with GTK+ 2.x, including the Gtk::CellRendererText, Gtk::CellRendererPixbuf, and the Gtk:: CellRendererToggle. Then three rows of data are added to the list, and a signal handler is created for the "changed" event. This will be invoked whenever the user selects a different row. The handler will update the @city member variable to contain the text from the first column (column number zero) of the newly selected row.

A simple check box (Gtk::CheckButton) and pushbutton (Gtk::Button) are created. The signal handler for the pushbutton will execute the cmd_purchase method whenever the button is clicked. The label named @result is initially blank but later will be set to a string indicating what type of ticket was purchased.

Three radio buttons are created as a group, meaning that only one of them can be selected at a time. When the user clicks any of these radio buttons, any previously selected button will automatically be deselected. The first parameter to the radio button constructor is the previous radio button within the same group. Therefore, the first radio button doesn't have the group as an argument, and the rest of the buttons pass the first radio button.

The widgets need to be arranged in a way that will make sense to the user, so a combination of Gtk::Boxes is used. The list box will appear above the check box. The three radio buttons will appear in a vertical stack to the right of the list box. Finally, the purchase pushbutton will appear below all the other widgets.

The cmd_purchase method is straightforward: It builds a string that reflects all the current widget states when the Purchase button is clicked. Radio buttons and check boxes have a method named active? that returns true if the button is selected. The text is then placed in the @result label so it will appear on the screen.

Most applications use menus as a key part of their user interface. This next example demonstrates how to set up menus using Ruby/GTK3. It also shows how easy it is to add tooltips, a nice touch for any program.

Listing 12.8 creates a main window that has a File menu, along with two other dummy items on the menu bar. The File menu contains an Exit item that exits the application. Both the File and Exit items have tooltips.

Listing 12.8   GTK Menu Example

```ruby
require "gtk3"

class MenuWindow < Gtk::Window

  def initialize
    super("Ruby/GTK2 Menu Sample")
    signal_connect("destroy") { Gtk.main_quit }

    file_exit_item = Gtk::MenuItem.new("_Exit")
    file_exit_item.signal_connect("activate") { Gtk.main_quit }

    file_menu = Gtk::Menu.new
    file_menu.add(file_exit_item)

    file_menu_item = Gtk::MenuItem.new("_File")
    file_menu_item.submenu = file_menu

    menubar = Gtk::MenuBar.new
    menubar.append(file_menu_item)
    menubar.append(Gtk::MenuItem.new("_Nothing"))
    menubar.append(Gtk::MenuItem.new("_Useless"))

    file_exit_item.set_tooltip_text "Exit the app"

    box = Gtk::Box.new(:vertical)
    box.pack_start(menubar, expand: false, fill: false, padding: 0)
    box.add(Gtk::Label.new("Try the menu and tooltips!"))

    add(box)
    set_default_size(400, 100)
    show_all
```

```
    end
end

Gtk.init
MenuWindow.new
Gtk.main
```

Again, the basic structure is like the other examples. In this case, we create a
`Gtk::MenuItem` named `Exit` and create a signal handler so it will actually exit the
program. The signal is `activate`, and it will be generated when a user actually
invokes this item on the menu.

The `File` menu is created, and the `Exit` item is added to it. This is all that is
required to create a pop-up menu. Next, the `File` menu item is created—this is what
will actually appear on the menu bar. We call `submenu=` to connect the `File` menu
item with the `File` menu itself.

We create the `Gtk::MenuBar` and add its three items: `File`, `Nothing`, and
`Useless`. Only the first item is actually functional—the other two are just for show.

Tooltips are fully integrated into all widgets, including menu items. To create a
tooltip, call `set_tooltip_tip`, passing the tooltip text.

A `Gtk::Box` is used to place the menu bar at the top of the main window, above
any other widgets. In this case, instead of using `add` to place the menu bar in the box,
we use `pack_start` to gain more control over the exact look and placement of the
widget.

The first parameter to `pack_start` is the widget we are placing. The `expand`
option is a Boolean indicating whether this widget should take up all the available
space. Note that it won't make the widget actually grow; instead, it will typically center the widget. In this case, we want the menu bar at the top of the screen, so we pass
`false`.

The `fill` option is a Boolean for whether this widget should grow to fill all the
available space. Because we just want a small menu bar, we pass `false` for this as well.
The `padding` option is used to create additional space all around the widget. We don't
want any, so we pass zero.

A text label will be in the main window. Finally, we force the initial size of the
window to be 400 pixels wide by 100 pixels tall.

12.3.6 Other Notes

Ruby/GTK3 is a part of the Ruby-GNOME2 project. GNOME is a higher-level package that depends on GTK+, and Ruby-GNOME2 has bindings for all GNOME libraries.

The `gtk3` gem includes these libraries:

- **Ruby/GLib**—GLib is the low-level core library that forms the lowest-level infrastructure. It provides data structure handling for C, portability wrappers, Unicode support, and interfaces for such runtime functionality as an event loop, threads, dynamic loading, and an object system. Ruby/GLib is a wrapper for the GLib library. Because Ruby already has good string and list classes, some GLib functions are not implemented. On the other hand, it does provide some important functions to convert C and Ruby objects. This library is required from all other Ruby/GTK libraries.

- **Ruby/GIO**—This library provides an API for interacting with volumes, drives, files, streams, icons, and DNS.

- **Ruby/ATK**—This provides a set of interfaces for accessibility. By supporting the ATK interfaces, an application or toolkit can be used with such tools as screen readers, magnifiers, and alternative input devices.

- **Ruby/Pango**—A library for layout and rendering of text, with an emphasis on internationalization using UTF-8. It forms the core of text and font handling for GTK+ (2.0).

- **Ruby/GdkPixbuf**—An image loading and manipulation library. It supports numerous image formats such as JPEG, PNG, GIF, and others.

- **Ruby/GDK**—An intermediate layer that isolates GTK+ from the details of the windowing system.

- **Ruby/GTK**—This comprises the main GUI widgets.

Along with the core libraries, the Ruby-GNOME2 project provides additional libraries, including additional widgets, configuration, structured graphics, audio, video, OpenGL 3D rendering, HTML, XML, PDF, SVG, and terminal emulation.

The official Ruby-GNOME2 home page is at http://ruby-gnome2.sourceforge.jp/. You can find released files, the install guide, API references, tutorials, and sample code. The official GNOME home page is www.gnome.org, and the GTK+ home page is www.gtk.org.

12.4   QtRuby

Qt is a GUI toolkit created and distributed by Trolltech. The main focus of Qt is to be a multiplatform toolkit that provides the same programmatic interface for the Windows, Mac, and UNIX operating systems. Developers need only write the code once; it compiles on each of the three platforms without modification.

Qt is distributed via dual license—either the GPL or a purchased commercial license for proprietary work. This dual license scenario is also used by other companies such as MySQL. It allows the toolkit to be used by open source projects that may benefit from many of the offered features. It also allows Trolltech a revenue stream from the sale of commercial licenses for customers who may want to use a less restrictive license than the GPL.

12.4.1   Overview

The Qt bindings for Ruby are the result of the work of many people, most notably Arno Rehn and Richard Dale. They are distributed as a gem named `qtbindings`, which provides not only a large set of GUI-related classes but also a whole suite of application add-ons that are often needed by programmers (such as XML and SQL libraries). The entire Qt toolkit is supported.

A key aspect of Qt, and thus QtRuby, is the concept of signals and slots. Signals are asynchronous events that occur when something spontaneous happens, such as a mouse button press or a user entering some text into a field. A slot is simply a reacting method that will be called when a certain signal happens. We take advantage of them by using the `connect` method to associate signals with slots.

To take advantage of signals and slots, as well as many other QtRuby features, all of our classes use the `Qt::Object` class. Furthermore, any GUI classes we may create will inherit from the base class `Qt::Widget`, which itself inherits from `Qt::Object`.

12.4.2   A Simple Windowed Application

A QtRuby program must first do a `require` of the Qt library. QtRuby provides its functionality through the `Qt` module (meaning that Qt classes are prefixed with `Qt::`). Because all Qt classes start with the letter *Q*, this Q is dropped during the conversion from Qt to QtRuby. So, for example, the Qt-based `QWidget` class becomes `Qt::Widget` in QtRuby.

```
require 'Qt'
```

```
app = Qt::Application.new(ARGV)
str = Time.now.strftime("Today is %B %d, %Y")
label = Qt::Label.new(str)
label.show
app.exec
```

Let's look at the preceding code in detail. The initial call to
`Qt::Application.new` is performed to start up a Qt-based application; it initializes
the window system and gets it ready for us to create the widgets we will be using.

Then we create a `Qt::Label`, which is a simple way of presenting text to the user.
In this case, the text is initialized to the string created in the previous line. The next
line tells the label to display itself on the screen.

Finally, the application event loop is started with a call to `app.exec`. This
method does not return until the application is told to terminate, generally by the user
clicking the close button on the window.

12.4.3   Working with Buttons

Creating a pushbutton with QtRuby is as easy as creating a new instance of
`Qt::PushButton` (see Listing 12.9 and Figure 12.12). Most likely, we will want to
perform some event when the button is clicked. This is handled via QtRuby's signal
and slots.

Listing 12.9   Buttons in Qt

```
require 'Qt'

class MyWidget < Qt::Widget
  slots 'buttonClickedSlot()'

  def initialize(parent = nil)
    super(parent)

    setWindowTitle("QtRuby example");

    @lineedit = Qt::LineEdit.new(self)
    @button = Qt::PushButton.new("All Caps!",self)

    connect(@button, SIGNAL('clicked()'),
            self, SLOT('buttonClickedSlot()'))

    box = Qt::HBoxLayout.new
    box.addWidget(Qt::Label.new("Text:"))
    box.addWidget(@lineedit)
```

```
    box.addWidget(@button)

    setLayout(box)
  end

  def buttonClickedSlot
    @lineedit.setText(@lineedit.text.upcase)
  end

end

app = Qt::Application.new(ARGV)
widget = MyWidget.new
widget.show
app.exec
```

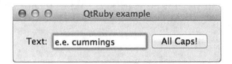

Figure 12.12   Buttons in Qt

In this example, we create our own widget class named `MyWidget`; this inherits from the generic `Qt::Widget` class that we use for all custom widget classes.

Before the initializer, we establish a list of the slots we will be defining in this class. Slots are ordinary Ruby class methods, but we must specify them by name so that the QtRuby runtime is aware that we want to be able to use them as slots. The call to the class method `slots` takes a list of strings, as shown here:

```
slots 'slot1()', 'slot2()'
```

The initializer for this class takes an argument named `parent`; almost all widget classes in the Qt world take such an argument. The parent argument simply specifies a widget that will take ownership of the widget being created. Passing `nil` as the parent means that it is a "top-level widget" and that no other widget owns it. The "ownership" concept probably makes more sense in the C++ world; parents take ownership of their child widgets, so that when parents are destroyed or removed, their children are removed as well.

The class creates a `Qt::LineEdit` to allow a user to enter text and a `Qt::PushButton` with the text `All Caps!` on it. Note that we pass `self` as the parent argument to each of these widgets. This means that when a `MyWidget` instance is created, it "adopts" these widgets.

Next, we use a key part of the Qt toolkit—the capability to connect signals and slots together. The `Qt::Pushbutton` class defines a `clicked` signal that is *emitted* whenever the button is clicked. We can connect that to a slot, which in this case is the ordinary method `buttonClickedSlot`. The name of the slot we connect to is not important; we sometimes use the suffix `slot` for emphasis.

Finally, we create an instance of the `Qt::HBoxLayout` class. This class provides a nice way to have an automatically resizing layout by simply adding widgets to it. It handles the rest for us.

12.4.4   Working with Text Fields

As shown in Listing 12.9, QtRuby provides the `Qt::LineEdit` class for simple single-line input. The `Qt::TextEdit` class is for multiline editing.

In Listing 12.10, we see a multiline edit box. As the contents change, the current length of the text is reflected in a label at the bottom of the window, as shown in Figure 12.13.

Listing 12.10   A Simple Qt Editor

```
require 'Qt'

class MyTextWindow < Qt::Widget
  slots 'theTextChanged()'

  def initialize(parent = nil)
    super(parent)

    @textedit = Qt::TextEdit.new(self)
    @textedit.setWordWrapMode(Qt::TextOption::WordWrap)

    @textedit.setFont( Qt::Font.new("Times", 24) )

    @status = Qt::Label.new(self)

    box = Qt::VBoxLayout.new
    box.addWidget(@textedit)
    box.addWidget(@status)
    setLayout(box)
```

```
    @textedit.insertPlainText("This really is an editor")

    connect(@textedit, SIGNAL('textChanged()'),
            self, SLOT('theTextChanged()'))
  end

  def theTextChanged
    text = "Length: " + @textedit.toPlainText.length.to_s
    @status.setText(text)
  end

end

app = Qt::Application.new(ARGV)
widget = MyTextWindow.new
widget.setWindowTitle("QtRuby Text Editor")
widget.show
app.exec
```

Figure 12.13 A simple Qt editor

We create our own custom widget, much like the earlier button example. In this case, we create an instance of Qt::TextEdit and a Qt::Label used for status updates.

The first interesting thing of note is that we set the font of the @textedit to an instance of a 24-point Times font. Each class inheriting from Qt:Widget (including Qt::TextEdit) has a font property that we can both retrieve and set.

Next, we create a vertical box layout (Qt::VBoxLayout) that holds the child widgets, inserts some text into the @textedit widget, and then performs the connection of the editor widget's `textChanged` signal to our custom `theTextChanged` slot.

Within the slot `theTextChanged`, we grab the text from the editor and query its length. Then we update the `@status` label to reflect this length.

Note that all the signal and slot action happens asynchronously. After the application enters into the event loop (`app.exec`), the GUI event loop takes over. This is why signals and slots are so important. We define the actions that can happen (signals) and the actions we want to take when they do (slots).

12.4.5   Working with Other Widgets

Qt provides many more GUI widgets for general consumption, such as radio buttons, check boxes, and other display widgets. Listing 12.11 shows some more of these, and Figure 12.14 provides a screenshot.

Listing 12.11   Other Qt Widgets

```
require 'Qt'

class MyWindow < Qt::Widget
  slots 'somethingClicked(QAbstractButton *)'

  def initialize(parent = nil)
    super(parent)

    groupbox = Qt::GroupBox.new("Some Radio Button",self)

    radio1 = Qt::RadioButton.new("Radio Button 1", groupbox)
    radio2 = Qt::RadioButton.new("Radio Button 2", groupbox)
    check1 = Qt::CheckBox.new("Check Box 1", groupbox)

    vbox = Qt::VBoxLayout.new
    vbox.addWidget(radio1)
    vbox.addWidget(radio2)
    vbox.addWidget(check1)
    groupbox.setLayout(vbox)

    bg = Qt::ButtonGroup.new(self)
    bg.addButton(radio1)
    bg.addButton(radio2)
    bg.addButton(check1)

    connect(bg, SIGNAL('buttonClicked(QAbstractButton *)'),
            self, SLOT('somethingClicked(QAbstractButton *)') )
```

```ruby
    @label = Qt::Label.new(self)

    vbox = Qt::VBoxLayout.new
    vbox.addWidget(groupbox)
    vbox.addWidget(@label)
    setLayout(vbox)
  end

  def somethingClicked(who)
    @label.setText("You clicked on a " + who.className)
  end

end

app = Qt::Application.new(ARGV)
widget = MyWindow.new
widget.show
app.exec
```

Figure 12.14   Other Qt widgets

In this new class, we first create a `Qt::GroupBox`, which is a box with a frame and an optional title that can hold other widgets. We then create two `Qt::RadioButtons` and a `Qt::CheckBox`, setting the group box as their parent.

Next, we create a `Qt::VBoxLayout` that holds the radio buttons and check box. Then we set that layout on the group box.

The next important thing is to create a `Qt::ButtonGroup` and add our check box and radio buttons to it. A `Qt::ButtonGroup` is a logical grouping of buttons, check boxes, and radio buttons. It has no impact on the visual layout of these widgets; instead, it allows us to group them together logically to provide things such as *exclusion* (unclicking certain widgets when certain others are clicked). In this case, we use the button group as a source of the `buttonClicked` signal, which is emitted when one of the buttons in that group becomes clicked.

The emission of this signal is a bit different from what we've previously seen, because this signal also emits an argument. In this case, it emits the object that was clicked. Note the C++ style syntax, namely in the use of the `QAbstractButton  *` argument. Remember that Qt is a C++ toolkit, so some use of the C++ notation for certain parameter types is currently unavoidable (though it perhaps may be fixed in future versions).

The final result of the `connect` statement is that any time a button is clicked, that button is passed into the `somethingClicked` slot. Finally, we create a `Qt::Label` and a `Qt::VBoxLayout` and bring the whole thing together.

In the `somethingClicked` slot definition, we modify the text of the label every time a button is clicked. In this case, we display the class name of the object that caused the signal to be emitted and the slot to be invoked.

When using built-in widgets is not enough, Qt provides a powerful painting system for creation of your own custom widgets. Listing 12.12 shows a small example to highlight some of those features.

Listing 12.12   A Custom TimerClock Widget

```ruby
require 'Qt'

class TimerClock < Qt::Widget

  def initialize(parent = nil)
    super(parent)

    @timer = Qt::Timer.new(self)
    connect(@timer, SIGNAL('timeout()'), self, SLOT('update()'))
    @timer.start(25)

    setWindowTitle('Stop Watch')
    resize(200, 200)
  end

  def paintEvent(e)
    fastHand = Qt::Polygon.new([Qt::Point.new(7, 8),
                                Qt::Point.new(-7, 8),
                                Qt::Point.new(0, -80)])

    secondHand = Qt::Polygon.new([Qt::Point.new(7, 8),
                                  Qt::Point.new(-7, 8),
                                  Qt::Point.new(0, -65)])

    secondColor = Qt::Color.new(100, 0, 100)
    fastColor = Qt::Color.new(0, 150, 150, 150)
```

```ruby
    side = [width, height].min
    time = Qt::Time.currentTime

    painter = Qt::Painter.new(self)
    painter.renderHint = Qt::Painter::Antialiasing
    painter.translate(width() / 2, height() / 2)
    painter.scale(side / 200.0, side / 200.0)

    painter.pen = Qt::NoPen
    painter.brush = Qt::Brush.new(secondColor)

    painter.save
    painter.rotate(6.0 * time.second)
    painter.drawConvexPolygon(secondHand)
    painter.restore

    painter.pen = secondColor
    (0...12).each do |i|
        painter.drawLine(88, 0, 96, 0)
        painter.rotate(30.0)
    end

    painter.pen = Qt::NoPen
    painter.brush = Qt::Brush.new(fastColor)

    painter.save
    painter.rotate(36.0 * (time.msec / 100.0) )
    painter.drawConvexPolygon(fastHand)
    painter.restore

    painter.pen = fastColor
    (0...60).each do |j|
      if (j % 5) != 0
        painter.drawLine(92, 0, 96, 0)
      end
      painter.rotate(6.0)
    end

    painter.end
  end
end

app = Qt::Application.new(ARGV)
wid = TimerClock.new
wid.show
app.exec
```

In this example, we again create a custom widget, this time called `TimerClock`. In its initializer, we create an instance of `Qt::Timer`, which we can set up to emit a signal periodically. In this case, we connect its `timeout` signal to the `update` slot of the `TimerClock`. The `update` slot is built in; it causes the widget to repaint itself.

The timer is started through a call to the `start` method. Its argument specifies that it is to time out every 25 milliseconds (and emit a `timeout` signal). This means that the widget's `update` slot will also get executed every 25 milliseconds.

Next, we create the `paintEvent` method. This method is an override of the method provided by `Qt::Widget`. When a widget wants to repaint itself (as this one will every time the `Qt::Timer` expires), this method gets called. Overriding this method allows us to customize how the widget draws itself on the screen. Within this method, the code is responsible for handling the primitive drawing routines for the widget.

From here, it's all about geometry. We create some `Qt::Polygons` that represent the hands on the clock we are about to draw. Note that the orientation of the polygons doesn't matter because we will be able to manipulate them later.

We set up a few properties we will want to use. We define two `Qt::Colors` for the two hands that will be on the timer. The arguments to the `Qt::Color` initializer are "RGB" values followed by an optional alpha transparency value.

Because the timer we're drawing is laid out in a square, it is possible that the window could be rectangular, making our widget an odd shape. We use the `side` variable to store whichever is smaller between the width and the height of the widget as it will be drawn on the screen. We also grab the current time using `Qt::Time.currentTime`.

Next, we create a `Qt::Painter` and use it to begin executing drawing routines.

We set up antialiasing during drawing to make edges look smooth. We also move the painter's starting coordinate to the middle of the drawing area by the call to `painter.translate(width/2, height/2)`. The painter is also rescaled to a 200:200 frame of reference. This means that all our drawing commands can rely on the fact that the drawing will be 200:200 units. If it gets resized bigger or smaller, the scaling automatically adjusts for us.

From here, we perform a series of drawing operations. In some places where there are transformations such as rotations, they are enveloped inside a call to `painter.save` and `painter.restore`. The `save` operation stores the current painter properties on a stack so that they can easily be restored.

The code draws the two hands after rotating them to the proper angle to represent the time. Also we tell the painter to draw some tick marks at certain intervals along the outer edge of the clock face.

Finally, we tell the painter we've finished (with a call to `painter.end`). We tie up our final loose ends with the four lines of code that create the `Qt::Application` and our timer clock widget and then start the event loop. Figure 12.15 shows the final result.

Figure 12.15   The `TimerClock` widget

12.4.6   Other Notes

Because Qt is a C++ toolkit, some idioms are used in the toolkit that are necessary due to constraints in the language. Sometimes the translation to Ruby isn't 100% natural because the Ruby way of doing the same thing may be slightly different. So, in some places, there are overrides that let you do some things in QtRuby in a Rubyish way.

For example, the camel-case naming of Qt methods can also be written as underscored names. The following two are equivalent:

```
Qt::Widget::minimumSizeHint
Qt::Widget::minimum_size_hint
```

All Qt setters begin with the word `set`, such as `Qt::Widget::setMinimumSize`. This can be overridden in Ruby by dropping the `set` and using assignment. This means the following three statements are equivalent:

```
widget.setMinimumSize(50)
widget.minimumSize = 50    # same
widget.minimum_size = 50   # same
```

Similarly, some Boolean methods in Qt begin with `is` or `has`, such as `Qt::Widget:: isVisible`. Again, QtRuby gives us a more Rubyish way of calling this method:

```
a.isVisible
a.visible?      # same
```

12.5 Swing

In the Java world, Swing is the GUI of choice. Through the magic of JRuby, it is possible to use Swing directly from Ruby. It is mature and stable, and runs well anywhere Java runs.

A full discussion of Swing is far beyond the scope of this chapter or this book, but the examples here should give you a taste of how it works.

This example will display a single, simple window:

```ruby
include Java

import javax.swing.JFrame

class SimpleWindow < JFrame

  def initialize
    super "Just another window..."
    init_gui
  end

  def init_gui
    set_size 400, 300
    self.default_close_operation = JFrame::EXIT_ON_CLOSE
    self.location_relative_to = nil
    self.visible = true
  end

end

SimpleWindow.new
```

We start by including the Java module and doing an import (which in JRuby, of course, is a method call). Our `SimpleWindow` class inherits from `JFrame`; we initialize it by calling the parent's initializing method and then calling our custom code (here `init_gui`) to create the window according to the parameters we want.

Java programmers are used to names such as `setSize` and `setDefaultClose Operation`, and these still work fine. But in order to be more Rubylike, we also allow underscore-separated lowercase names as synonyms (`set_size` and `set_default_close_operation`). In most cases, a method named, for example, `setWhatever(value)` can be written as `set_whatever(value)` but also as `self.whatever = value`. In the third case, note the use of `self` to distinguish from a local variable.

Here is a slightly more interesting example involving buttons:

```ruby
include Java

import javax.swing.JFrame
import javax.swing.JButton
import javax.swing.JPanel

class ButtonWindow < JFrame
  def initialize
    super "Button example..."
    init_gui
  end

  def init_gui
    win = self
    panel = JPanel.new
    self.content_pane.add panel
    panel.layout = nil
    eat = JButton.new "Eat Me"
    eat.set_bounds 50, 60, 80, 30
    eat.add_action_listener {|event| win.set_size 600, 400 }

    drink = JButton.new "Drink Me"
    drink.set_bounds 50, 90, 80, 30
    drink.add_action_listener {|event| win.set_size 200, 150 }

    panel.add eat
    panel.add drink
```

```
      self.default_close_operation = JFrame::EXIT_ON_CLOSE
      set_size 300, 200
      self.location_relative_to = nil
      self.visible = true
    end
  end


ButtonWindow.new
```

Note that we now use a `JPanel` as a container to hold two `JButton` objects. Each button has a code block associated with it, and this block will be executed when the button is clicked. Other than that, this is much the same as the previous example.

Countless books and tutorials (both online and print) cover Swing. We suggest you look at any of these for more information.

12.6   Other GUI Toolkits

As already mentioned, your favorite GUI may not be covered here. We'll use the remaining space in this chapter to mention some other alternatives.

12.6.1   UNIX and X11

The *X Window System* is colloquially (though not correctly) referred to as X Windows. It is perhaps not the grandfather of all GUI systems, but it is certainly the ancestor of many of them.

UNIX users of all breeds have long been familiar with X (as users, even if not as developers). The advantages of X are that it is widely known, portable, and has a rich feature set. The disadvantages are that it is complex and difficult to use.

Not surprisingly, there are libraries for using X with Ruby. They aren't documented here because of their complexity.

We refer you instead to the Ruby Application Archive, where you can find Xlib by Kazuhiro Yoshida (also known as moriq) and Ruby/X11 by Mathieu Bouchard (also known as matju). Either can be used to create X client applications.

12.6.2   FXRuby (FOX)

FOX (Free Objects for X) isn't as widespread as Tk or GTK+, but was once popular among Ruby programmers. Part of the reason for this was the excellent Ruby binding called FXRuby, the work of Lyle Johnson. Since he left the project in 2010, this library is not maintained as actively as it used to be, but it should still work. Lyle's excellent book *FXRuby: Create Lean and Mean GUIs with Ruby* is still available.

12.6.3   RubyMotion for iOS and Mac OS X

RubyMotion allows Ruby programs to directly use the native GUI of iOS and Mac OS X. It is effectively a Ruby runtime written in Objective-C, the native language of iOS and Mac OS X. It also includes a compiler and toolchain for packaging and shipping Ruby applications as machine code binaries for iOS and Mac OS X. The creator of RubyMotion, Laurent Sansonetti, previously created the defunct MacRuby project, a Ruby interpreter written in (and tightly integrated with) Objective-C.

As of this writing, a RubyMotion toolchain and compiler for Android has been announced, but not yet released. Also note that RubyMotion is a commercial tool, sold for $199.

12.6.4   The Windows Win32API

In Ruby, it is possible to access the entire Windows API directly via the `WIN32API` library. We show one example of this in Chapter 14, "Scripting and System Administration." This (at least theoretically) allows a Ruby program to create and manipulate native Windows applications and widgets. I don't necessarily recommend the practice, but you should be aware of the possibility.

12.7   Conclusion

This chapter provided a good overview of the GUI toolkits available for Ruby. We've looked at general concepts such as event loops, messages and signals, and more. We've looked at widgets of various kinds, including pushbuttons, check boxes, radio buttons, text fields, and more.

We've looked at the implementations of these concepts in Tk, GTK, Qt, and Shoes. We've also seen some of the special terminology and minor changes in paradigm from one toolkit to another and looked at some of the special features and benefits that each toolkit offers.

Now let's move on to a different topic entirely. Chapter 13, "Threads and Concurrency," will discuss how to manipulate threads in Ruby.

CHAPTER 13
Threads and Concurrency

He draweth out the thread of his argument finer than the staple of his verbosity.

—*William Shakespeare,*
Love's Labours Lost, *Act V, Sc. 1*

One of the wonders of modern computers is that they appear to be able to do more than one thing at a time. Even back in the days of single-core processes, the lone CPU could switch between its various jobs quickly enough that it appeared to be doing many things at once. With the advent of inexpensive computers with multiple CPUs, that illusion has become reality. Thus, we take it for granted that we can simultaneously download a gem while we surf the Internet and print a document. This concurrency is exposed to programmers in two fundamental forms: processes and threads. In general, a process is a fairly self-sufficient entity, with its own flow of control and its own address space, safely out of reach of other processes (with important exceptions—an operating system must not only protect processes from each other but also provide mechanisms for sharing memory).

Threads are sometimes called *lightweight processes.* They are a way to achieve concurrency without all the overhead of switching tasks at the operating system level. Although the computing community is not in perfect agreement about the definition of threads, we'll use the most common definition here.

A *thread* generally lives inside a process, sharing its address space and open files. The good news about threads is that because they do share so much with their parent process, they are relatively cheap to create. The bad news about threads is that because they share so much with their parent process—and any other threads within that process—they have a tendency to interfere with each other.

Threads are useful in circumstances where separate pieces of code naturally function independently of each other. They are also useful when an application spends much of its time waiting for an event. Often while one thread is waiting, another can be doing useful processing. On the other hand, there are some potential disadvantages in the use of threads. Switching between threads can reduce the speed at which each individual task runs. In some cases, access to a resource is inherently serialized so that threading doesn't help. Sometimes, the overhead of synchronizing access to resources exceeds the savings due to multithreading.

Threads always incur some kind of performance hit, both in memory and in execution time; it is easy to pass the point of diminishing returns. For these and other reasons, some authorities claim that threaded programming is to be avoided. Indeed, concurrent code can be complex, error prone, and difficult to debug. But with so many CPU cores available in modern computers, the increase in speed for concurrent tasks can be enormous. We leave it to the reader to decide when it is worthwhile to use these techniques.

The difficulties associated with unsynchronized threads are well known. A data structure can be corrupted by threads attempting simultaneous access to the data. *Race conditions* may occur wherein one thread makes some assumption about what another has done already; these commonly result in "nondeterministic" code that may run differently with each execution. Finally, there is the danger of deadlock, wherein no thread can continue because it is waiting for a resource held by some other thread, which is also blocked. Code written to avoid these problems is referred to as *thread-safe* code.

Using threads in Ruby presents some additional challenges. The main version of Ruby (MRI, Matz's Ruby Interpreter) creates threads in the usual way. But—and this is a huge *but*—it still contains legacy code that is not thread-safe. As a result, it only allows one thread to run at a time. The result is low overhead, but very low concurrency. Multiple threads are only useful in MRI when a program will spend time waiting for I/O.

The story is different if you happen to be using the Rubinius or JRuby interpreters. JRuby is the implementation of Ruby for the Java Virtual Machine, while Rubinius is an experimental interpreter that attempts to implement Ruby using as

much Ruby as possible. JRuby's threads rely on the threading supplied by the underlying Java platform, while Rubinius uses operating system level threads like MRI does.
Unlike MRI, both Rubinius and JRuby do not artificially synchronize their threads.
This means that in Ruby interpreters other than MRI, threads *can* run at the same
time, using all of the processors available on the machine.

A big part of understanding threads is knowing the synchronization methods that
allow you to control access to variables and resources, protect critical sections of code,
and avoid deadlock. We will examine each of these techniques and illustrate them with
code.

13.1   Creating and Manipulating Threads

The most basic operations on threads include creating a thread, passing information
in and out, waiting for a thread, and stopping a thread. We can also obtain lists of
threads, check the state of a thread, and check various other information.

13.1.1   Creating Threads

Every program you have ever run had at least one thread associated with it—the initial flow of control that we call the "main" thread. Multithreading happens when we
start other threads.

Creating a thread in Ruby is easy. Simply call the new method and attach a block
that will be the body of the thread:

```
thread = Thread.new do
  # Statements comprising
  # the thread...
end
```

The method `fork` is an alias for new, so we could have created our thread by calling `Thread.fork` instead of `Thread.new`. No matter which name you use, the value
returned is an instance of `Thread`. You can use the `Thread` instance to control the
thread.

If you want to pass parameters into your thread, you can do so by passing them
into `Thread.new`:

```
thread2 = Thread.new(99, 100) do |a, b|
  # a is a parameter that starts out equal to 99
  # b is also a parameter which starts out at 100
end
```

Thus, the thread block in the preceding example takes two parameters, a and b, which start out as 99 and 100, respectively.

Because threads are built around ordinary code blocks, they can also access variables from the scope in which they were created. Therefore, the following thread can change the values of x and y because those two variables were in scope when we created the block associated with the thread:

```
x = 1
y = 2

thread3 = Thread.new(99, 100) do |a, b|
  # x and y are visible and can be changed!
  x = 10
  y = 11
end

puts x, y
```

The danger in doing this sort of thing lies in the question of *when*. When exactly do the values of x and y change? We can say that they will change sometime after thread3 starts, but that is pretty much all we can say. Once a thread starts, it takes on a life of its own, and unless you do something to synchronize with it, you will have no idea of how fast it will run. Because of this unpredictability, it's hard to say what the last example will print out. If thread3 finishes very rapidly, we might well see 10 and 11 printed. Conversely, if thread3 is slow off the mark, we might see 1 and 2 printed. There is even a small chance that we might see a 1 followed by an 11 printed if the race between thread3 and the main thread is very close. In real programs, this is exactly the kind of random behavior we would like to avoid.

13.1.2   Accessing Thread-Local Variables

So how do you go about building threads that can share results with the rest of the program without stepping all over variables from outside their scope? Fortunately, Ruby provides us with a special mechanism for this purpose. The trick is that you can treat a thread instance like a hash, setting and getting values by key. This thread-local data can be accessed from both inside *and* outside of the thread and provide a convenient sharing mechanism between the two. Here is an example of thread-local data in action:

```
thread = Thread.new do
  t = Thread.current
  t[:var1] = "This is a string"
  t[:var2] = 365
end

sleep 1                 # Let the thread spin up

# Access the thread-local data from outside...

x = thread[:var1]                # "This is a string"
y = thread[:var2]                # 365

has_var2 = thread.key?(:var2)  # true
has_var3 = thread.key?(:var3)  # false
```

As you can see from the code, a thread can set its own local data by calling
`Thread.current` to get its own `Thread` instance and then treating that object like a
hash. `Thread` instances also have a convenient `key?` instance method that will tell you
if a particular key is set. One other nice thing about thread-local data is that it hangs
around even after the thread has expired.

Note that thread-local data is *not* the same as the local variables inside the thread
block. The local variable `var3` and `thread[:var3]` may look somewhat alike, but
they are definitely not the same:

```
thread = Thread.new do
  t = Thread.current
  t["var3"] = "thread local!!"
  var3 = "a regular local"
end

sleep 1                 # Let the thread spin up

a = thread[:var3]       # "thread local!!"
```

You should also keep in mind that although threads with their thread-local data
do act a bit like hashes, they are definitely *not* the real thing: Threads lack most of the
familiar `Enumerable` methods such as `each` and `find`. More significantly, threads are
picky about the keys you are allowed to use for the thread-local data. Besides symbols,
your only other choice for a thread local key is a string, and if you do use a string, it
will get silently converted to a symbol. We can see all of this going on here:

```
thread = Thread.new do
  t = Thread.current
  t["started_as_a_string"] = 100
  t[:started_as_a_symbol] = 101
end

sleep 1                    # Let the thread spin up

a = thread[:started_as_a_string]    # 100
b = thread["started_as_a_symbol"]   # 101
```

It's important to note that while thread-local data can help solve the *where* problem by giving you a thread-specific *place* to put data, thread-local data alone doesn't help with the *when* problem: Absent some kind of synchronization, you will have no idea when a thread will get around to doing something with its thread-local data. The common case is to "return" thread-local data as the thread finishes executing. No synchronization is needed then because the thread has terminated.

13.1.3   Querying and Changing Thread Status

The `Thread` class sports a number of useful class methods for managing threads. For example, the `list` method returns an array of all living threads, whereas the `main` method returns a reference to the main thread, the one that kicks everything off. And as you have seen, there is also a `current` method that allows a thread to find its own identity.

```
t1 = Thread.new { sleep 100 }

t2 = Thread.new do
  if Thread.current == Thread.main
    puts "This is the main thread."   # Does NOT print
  end
  1.upto(1000) { sleep 0.1 }
end

count = Thread.list.size             # 3

if Thread.list.include?(Thread.main)
  puts "Main thread is alive."       # Always prints!
end
```

```
if Thread.current == Thread.main
  puts "I'm the main thread."        # Prints here...
end
```

The `exit`, `pass`, `start`, `stop`, and `kill` methods are used to control the execution of threads, either from inside or outside:

```
# In the main thread...
Thread.kill(t1)          # Kill thread t1 from the previous example
Thread.pass              # Give up my timeslice
t3 = Thread.new do
  sleep 20
  Thread.exit            # Exit the current thread
  puts "Can't happen!"   # Never reached
end

Thread.kill(t2)          # Now kill t2

# Now exit the main thread (killing any others)
Thread.exit
```

Note that there is no instance method `stop`, so a thread can stop itself but not another thread.

There are also various methods for checking the state of a thread. The instance method `alive?` will tell whether the thread is still "living" (not exited), and `stop?` will return `true` if the thread is either dead or sleeping. Note that `alive?` and `stop?` are not really opposites: Both will return `true` if the thread is sleeping because a sleeping thread is a) still alive and b) not doing anything at the moment:

```
count = 0
t1 = Thread.new { loop { count += 1 } }
t2 = Thread.new { Thread.stop }

sleep 1                  # Let the threads spin up

flags = [t1.alive?,      # true
         t1.stop?,       # false
         t2.alive?,      # true
         t2.stop?]       # true
```

To get a complete picture of where a thread is in its life cycle, use the `status` method. The possible return values of `status` are something of a hodgepodge: If the thread is currently running, `status` will return the string `"run"`; you will get `"sleep"` if the thread is stopped, sleeping, or waiting on I/O. If the thread terminated normally, you will get `false` back from `status`. Alternatively, `status` will return `nil` if the thread died horribly with an exception. You can see all of this in the next example:

```
t1 = Thread.new { loop {} }
t2 = Thread.new { sleep 5 }
t3 = Thread.new { Thread.stop }
t4 = Thread.new { Thread.exit }
t5 = Thread.new { raise "exception" }

sleep 1              # Let the threads spin up

s1 = t1.status       # "run"
s2 = t2.status       # "sleep"
s3 = t3.status       # "sleep"
s4 = t4.status       # false
s5 = t5.status       # nil
```

Threads are also aware of the `$SAFE` global variable; but when it comes to threads, `$SAFE` is not quite as global as it seems because each thread effectively has its own. This does seem inconsistent, but we probably shouldn't complain; this allows us to have threads run with different levels of safety. Because `$SAFE` isn't terribly global when it comes to threads, `Thread` instances have a `safe_level` method that returns the safe level for that particular thread:

```
t1 = Thread.new { $SAFE = 1; sleep 5 }
t2 = Thread.new { $SAFE = 3; sleep 5 }
sleep 1
level0 = Thread.main.safe_level      # 0
level1 = t1.safe_level               # 1
level2 = t2.safe_level               # 3
```

Ruby threads also have a numeric priority: Threads with a higher priority will be scheduled more often. You can look at and change the priority of a thread with the `priority` accessor:

```
t1 = Thread.new { loop { sleep 1 } }
t2 = Thread.new { loop { sleep 1 } }
t2.priority = 3     # Set t2 at priority 3
p1 = t1.priority   # 0
p2 = t2.priority   # 3
```

The special method `pass` is used when a thread wants to yield control to the scheduler. A thread that calls `pass` merely yields its current timeslice; it doesn't actually stop or go to sleep:

```
t1 = Thread.new do
  Thread.pass
  puts "First thread"
end

t2 = Thread.new do
  puts "Second thread"
end

sleep 3     # Give the threads a change to run.
```

In this contrived example, we are more likely to get see the second thread print before the first. If we take out the call to `pass`, we are a bit more likely to see the first thread—which started first—win the race. Of course, when it comes to unsynchronized threads, there are simply no guarantees. The `pass` method and thread priorities are there to provide *hints* to the scheduler, not to keep your threads synchronized.

A thread that is stopped may be awakened by use of the `run` or `wakeup` method:

```
t1 = Thread.new do
  Thread.stop
  puts "There is an emerald here."
end

t2 = Thread.new do
  Thread.stop
  puts "You're at Y2."
end

sleep 0.5     # Let the threads start
```

```
t1.wakeup
t2.run

sleep 0.5      # Give t2 a chance to run
```

The difference between these is subtle. The wakeup call will change the state of the thread so that it is runnable but will not schedule it to be run; on the other hand, run will wake up the thread and schedule it for immediate running. When we ran this code, we got the following output:

```
You're at Y2.
There is an emerald here.
```

Again, depending on the exact timing and the whims of the thread scheduler, the output could have been reversed. In particular, you should not rely on stop, wakeup, and run to synchronize your threads.

The raise instance method will raise an exception in the thread specified as the receiver. The call does not have to originate within the thread:

```
factorial1000 = Thread.new do
  begin
    prod = 1
    1.upto(1000) {|n| prod *= n }
    puts "1000! = #{prod}"
  rescue
    # Do nothing...
  end
end

sleep 0.01                    # Your mileage may vary.
if factorial1000.alive?
  factorial1000.raise("Stop!")
  puts "Calculation was interrupted!"
else
  puts "Calculation was successful."
end
```

The thread spawned in the preceding example tries to calculate the factorial of 1,000; if it doesn't succeed within a hundredth of a second, the main thread will get impatient and kill it. Thus, on a relatively slow machine, this code fragment will print the message Calculation was interrupted!.

13.1.4   Achieving a Rendezvous (and Capturing a Return Value)

Sometimes one thread wants to wait for another thread to finish. The instance method join will accomplish this:

```
t1 = Thread.new { do_something_long }

do_something_brief
t1.join                 # Don't continue until t1 is done
```

A very common mistake when doing thread programming is to start some threads and then let the main thread exit. The trouble is that the main thread is special: Ruby terminates the entire process. For example, the following code fragment would never give us its final answer without the join at the end:

```
meaning_of_life = Thread.new do
  puts "The answer is..."
  sleep 2
  puts 42
end

meaning_of_life.join  # Wait for the thread to finish
```

Another useful little join idiom is to wait for all the other living threads to finish:

```
Thread.list.each { |t| t.join if t != Thread.current }
```

Note that we have to check that the thread is not the current thread before calling join: It is an error for any thread, even the main thread, to call join on itself.

If two threads try to join the other at the same time, Ruby will detect this deadlock situation and raise an exception:

```
thr = Thread.new { sleep 1; Thread.main.join }

thr.join                # Deadlock results!
```

As you have seen, every thread has an associated block. Elementary Ruby knowledge tells us that a block can have a return value. This implies that a thread can return a value. The value method will implicitly perform a join operation and wait for the thread to complete; then it will return the value of the last evaluated expression in the thread:

```
max = 10000
t = Thread.new do
  sleep 0.2      # Simulate some deep thought time
  42
end

puts "The secret is #{t.value}"
```

13.1.5   Dealing with Exceptions

What happens if an exception occurs within a thread? Under normal circumstances, an exception inside a thread will not raise in the main thread. Here is an example of a thread raising an exception:

```
t1 = Thread.new do
  puts "Hello"
  sleep 1
  raise "some exception"
end

t2 = Thread.new do
  sleep 2
  puts "Hello from the other thread"
end

sleep 3
puts "The End"
```

That example says hello from both threads, and the main thread announces the end.

Exceptions inside threads are not raised until the `join` or `value` method is called on that thread. It is up to some other thread to check on the thread that failed and report the failure. Here is an example of catching an exception raised inside a thread in a safe manner:

```
t1 = Thread.new do
  raise "Oh no!"
```

```
    puts "This will never print"
  end

  begin
    t1.status # nil, indicating an exception occurred
    t1.join
  rescue => e
    puts "Thread raised #{e.class}: #{e.message}"
  end
```

The example will print the text "Thread raised RuntimeError: Oh no!" It is important to raise errors from threads at a known point so that they can be rescued or re-raised without interrupting critical sections of other threads.

While debugging threaded code, it can sometimes be helpful to use the abort_on_exception flag. When it is set to true (for a single thread or globally on the Thread class), uncaught exceptions will terminate *all* running threads.

Let's try that initial example again with abort_on_exception set to true on thread t1:

```
t1 = Thread.new do
  puts "Hello"
  sleep 1
  raise "some exception"
end

t1.abort_on_exception = true   # Watch the fireworks!

t2 = Thread.new do
  sleep 2
  puts "Hello from the other thread"
end

sleep 3
puts "The End"
```

In this case, the only output you will see is a single Hello because the uncaught exception in thread t1 will abort both the main thread and t2.

Whereas t1.abort_on_exception only affects the behavior of the one thread, the class-level Thread.abort_on_exception will take down all the threads if *any* of them raises an uncaught exception.

Note that this option is only suitable for development or debugging because it is equivalent to `Thread.list.each(&:kill)`. The `kill` method is (ironically) not thread-safe. Only use `kill` or `abort_on_exception` for debugging or to terminate threads that are definitely safe to abruptly kill. Aborted threads can hold a lock or be prevented from running clean-up code in an `ensure` block, which can leave your program in an unrecoverable state.

13.1.6   Using a Thread Group

A thread group is a way of managing threads that are logically related to each other. Normally all threads belong to the `Default` thread group (which is a class constant). However, you can create thread groups of your own and add threads to them. A thread can only be in one thread group at a time so that when a thread is added to a thread group, it is automatically removed from whatever group it was in previously.

The `ThreadGroup.new` class method will create a new thread group, and the `add` instance method will add a thread to the group:

```
t1 = Thread.new("file1") { sleep(1) }
t2 = Thread.new("file2") { sleep(2) }

threads = ThreadGroup.new
threads.add t1
threads.add t2
```

The instance method `list` will return an array of all the threads in the thread group:

```
# Count living threads in this_group
count = 0
this_group.list.each {|x| count += 1 if x.alive? }
if count < this_group.list.size
  puts "Some threads in this_group are not living."
else
  puts "All threads in this_group are alive."
end
```

`ThreadGroup` instances also feature the oddly named `enclose` method, which mostly prevents new threads from being added to the group:

```
tg = ThreadGroup.new
tg.enclose                    # Enclose the group
tg.add Thread.new {sleep 1}   # Boom!
```

We say "mostly" because any new threads started from a thread already in an enclosed group will still be added to the group. Thread groups also have an `enclosed?` instance method that will return `true` if the group has in fact been enclosed.

There is plenty of room for useful methods to be added to `ThreadGroup`. The following example shows methods to wake up every thread in a group, to wait for all threads to catch up (via `join`), and to kill all threads in a group:

```
class ThreadGroup

  def wakeup
    list.each { |t| t.wakeup }
  end

  def join
    list.each { |t| t.join if t != Thread.current }
  end

  def kill
    list.each { |t| t.kill }
  end

end
```

One thing to keep in mind about thread groups is that as threads die, they are silently removed from their group. So just because you stick threads in a group does not mean they will all be there ten minutes or ten seconds from now.

13.2 Synchronizing Threads

Why is synchronization necessary? It is because the "interleaving" of operations causes variables and other entities to be accessed in ways that are not obvious from reading the code of the individual threads. Two or more threads accessing the same variable may interact with each other in ways that are unforeseen and difficult to debug.

Let's take this simple piece of code as an example:

```
def new_value(i)
  i + 1
end


x = 0

t1 = Thread.new do
  1.upto(1000000) { x = new_value(x) }
end

t2 = Thread.new do
  1.upto(1000000) { x = new_value(x) }
end

t1.join
t2.join
puts x
```

In the example, we start by setting the variable x to zero. Then we start two threads; each thread increments x a million times using the new_value method. Finally, we print out the value of x. Logic tells us that x should be two million when it is printed out. However, sometimes running this code only results in one million!

When this is run on JRuby, the results are even more unexpected: 1143345 on one run, followed by 1077403 on the next and 1158422 on a third. Is this a terrible bug in Ruby?

Not really. Our code assumes that the incrementing of an integer is an atomic (or indivisible) operation. But it isn't. Consider the logic flow in the following code example. We put thread t1 on the left side and t2 on the right. We put each separate timeslice on a separate line and assume that when we enter this piece of logic, x has the value 123:

```
t1                              t2

_____       _____


Retrieve value of x (123)
                                Retrieve value of x (123)

Add one to value (124)
                                Add one to value (124)

Store 124 back in x
                                Store 124 back in x
```

It should be clear that each thread is doing a simple increment from its own point of view. But it can also been seen that, in this case, x is still 124 after having been incremented by *both* threads. We deliberately made things worse in our example by introducing the call to new_value, which increases the interval between retrieving the value of x and storing the incremented value. Even the relatively minuscule delay of a single function call is enough to dramatically decrease the number of times the value is incremented correctly.

MRI's ability to sometimes produce the correct result might lead a casual observer to think this code is thread-safe. The problem is hidden as a side effect of MRI's GIL, or Global Interpreter Lock, which ensures that only one thread can run at a time. As you just saw, even with the GIL, MRI suffers from the same synchronization problem and can still produce the wrong result.

The worse news is that this is only the simplest of synchronization problems. Complex multithreaded programs can be full of subtle "works most of the time" bugs, and the best way to handle these issues is still a hot topic of study by computer scientists and mathematicians.

13.2.1 Performing Simple Synchronization

The simplest form of synchronization is to use `Thread.exclusive`. The `Thread.exclusive` method defines a *critical section* of code: Whenever one thread is in a critical section, no other threads will run.

Using `Thread.exclusive` is easy: You simply pass in a block. Ruby will ensure that no other thread is running while the code in the block is executed. In the following code, we revisit the previous example and use the `Thread.exclusive` method to define the critical section and protect the sensitive parts of the code:

```
def new_value(i)
  i + 1
end


x = 0

t1 = Thread.new do
  1.upto(1000000) do
    Thread.exclusive { x = new_value(x) }
  end
end
```

```
t2 = Thread.new do
  1.upto(1000000) do
    Thread.exclusive { x = new_value(x) }
  end
end

t1.join
t2.join
puts x
```

Although we haven't changed the actual code very much, we have changed the flow of execution quite a bit. The calls to `Thread.exclusive` prevent our threads from stepping all over each other:

```
t1                                      t2
_____               _____


Retrieve value of x (123)
Add one to value (124)
Store 124 back in x
                                        Retrieve value of x (124)
                                        Add one to value (125)
                                        Store 125 back in x
```

In practice, using `Thread.exclusive` presents a number of problems, the key one being just how expansive its effects are. Using `Thread.exclusive` means that you are blocking *almost all* other threads, including innocent ones that will never touch any of your precious data.

The *almost* touches on another problem: Although `Thread.exclusive` is expansive, it is not completely airtight. There are circumstances under which another thread can run even while a `Thread.exclusive` block is under way. For example, if you start a second thread inside your exclusive block, *that thread will run.*

For these reasons, `Thread.exclusive` is at its best in simple examples like the one in this section. Fortunately, Ruby has a number of other, more flexible and easily targeted thread-synchronization tools.

13.2.2   Synchronizing Access with a Mutex

One such tool is the mutex (short for *mutual exclusion*). To see Ruby's mutex in action, let's rework our last counting example to use one:

```
require 'thread'

def new_value(i)
  i + 1
end

x = 0
mutex = Mutex.new

t1 = Thread.new do
  1.upto(1000000) do
    mutex.lock
    x = new_value(x)
    mutex.unlock
  end
end

t2 = Thread.new do
  1.upto(1000000) do
    mutex.lock
    x = new_value(x)
    mutex.unlock
  end
end

t1.join
t2.join
puts x
```

Instances of the `Mutex` class provide a sort of privately scoped synchronization: `Mutex` ensures that only one thread at a time can call `lock`. If two threads happen to call `lock` at about the same time, one of the threads will be suspended until the lucky thread—the one that got the lock—calls `unlock`. Because any given mutex instance only affects the threads that are trying to call `lock` for that instance, we can have our synchronization without making all but one of our threads come to a halt.

In addition to `lock`, the `Mutex` class also has a `try_lock` method. The `try_lock` method behaves just like `lock`, except that it doesn't block: If another thread already has the lock, `try_lock` will return `false` immediately:

```
require 'thread'

mutex = Mutex.new
```

```ruby
t1 = Thread.new do
  mutex.lock
  sleep 10
end

sleep 1

t2 = Thread.new do
  if mutex.try_lock
    puts "Locked it"
  else
    puts "Could not lock"    # Prints immediately
  end
end
```

This feature is useful any time a thread doesn't want to be blocked. Mutex instances also have a `synchronize` method that takes a block:

```ruby
x = 0
mutex = Mutex.new

t1 = Thread.new do
  1.upto(1000000) do
    mutex.synchronize { x = new_value(x) }
  end
end
```

Finally, there is also a `mutex_m` library defining a `Mutex_m` module, which can be mixed into a class (or used to extend an object). Any such extended object has the mutex methods so that the object itself can be treated as a mutex:

```ruby
require 'mutex_m'

class MyClass
  include Mutex_m

  # Now any MyClass object can call
  # lock, unlock, synchronize, ...
  # or external objects can invoke
  # these methods on a MyClass object.
end
```

13.2.3 Using the Built-in Queue Classes

The thread library `thread.rb` has a couple of queueing classes that will be useful from time to time. The class `Queue` is a thread-aware queue that synchronizes access to the ends of the queue; that is, different threads can share the same queue without interfering with each other. The class `SizedQueue` is essentially the same, except that it allows a limit to be placed on the number of elements a given queue instance can hold.

`Queue` and `SizedQueue` have much the same set of methods available because `SizedQueue` actually inherits from `Queue`. The `SizedQueue` class also has the accessor `max`, used to get or set the maximum size of the queue:

```
buff = SizedQueue.new(25)
upper1 = buff.max        # 25
# Now raise it...
buff.max = 50
upper2 = buff.max        # 50
```

Listing 13.1 is a simple producer-consumer illustration. The consumer is delayed slightly longer on average (through a longer sleep) so that the items will "pile up" a little.

Listing 13.1 The Producer-Consumer Problem

```
require 'thread'

buffer = SizedQueue.new(2)

producer = Thread.new do
  item = 0
  loop do
    sleep(rand * 0.1)
    puts "Producer makes #{item}"
    buffer.enq item
    item += 1
  end
end

consumer = Thread.new do
  loop do
    sleep((rand 0.1) + 0.09)
    item = buffer.deq
    puts "Consumer retrieves #{item}"
    puts "  waiting = #{buffer.num_waiting}"
```

```
  end
end

sleep 10   # Run a 10 secs, then die and kill threads
```

The methods `enq` and `deq` are the recommended way to get items into and out of the queue. We can also use `push` to add to the queue and `pop` or `shift` to remove items, but these names have somewhat less mnemonic value when we are explicitly using a queue.

The method `empty?` will test for an empty queue, and `clear` will remove all items from a queue. The method `size` (or its alias `length`) will return the actual number of items in the queue:

```
require 'thread'

# Assume no other threads interfering...
buff = Queue.new
buff.enq "one"
buff.enq "two"
buff.enq "three"
n1 = buff.size       # 3
flag1 = buff.empty?  # false
buff.clear
n2 = buff.size       # 0
flag2 = buff.empty?  # true
```

The `num_waiting` method is the number of threads waiting to access the queue. In a plain-old `Queue` instance, this is the number of threads waiting to remove elements; with a `SizedQueue`, `num_waiting` also includes the threads waiting to add elements to the queue.

An optional parameter, `non_block`, defaults to `false` for the `deq` method in the `Queue` class. If it is true, an empty queue will give a `ThreadError` rather than block the thread.

13.2.4 Using Condition Variables

And he called for his fiddlers three.

—"Old King Cole" (traditional folk tune)

A condition variable is really just a queue of threads. It is used in conjunction with a mutex to provide a higher level of control when synchronizing threads. A condition variable allows you to relinquish control of the mutex until a certain condition has been met. Imagine a situation in which a thread has a mutex locked but cannot continue because the circumstances aren't right. It can sleep on the condition variable and wait to be awakened when the condition is met.

It is important to understand that while a thread is waiting on a condition variable, the mutex is released so that other threads can gain access. It is also important to realize that when another thread does a signal operation (to awaken the waiting thread), the waiting thread reacquires the lock on the mutex.

Let's look at a slightly tongue-in-cheek example in the tradition of the Dining Philosophers. Imagine a table where three violinists are seated, all of whom want to take turns playing. However, there are only two violins and only one bow. Obviously a violinist can play only if he has one of the violins and the lone bow at the same time.

We keep a count of the violins and bows available. When a player wants a violin or a bow, he must wait for it. In our code, we protect the test with a mutex and do separate waits for the violin and the bow, both associated with that mutex. If a violin or a bow is not available, the thread sleeps. It loses the mutex until it is awakened by another thread signaling that the resource is available, whereupon the original thread wakes up and once again owns the lock on the mutex. Listing 13.2 shows the code.

Listing 13.2 The Three Violinists

```
require 'thread'

@music  = Mutex.new
@violin = ConditionVariable.new
@bow    = ConditionVariable.new

@violins_free = 2
@bows_free    = 1

def musician(n)
  3.times do
```

```
    sleep rand
    @music.synchronize do
      @violin.wait(@music) while @violins_free == 0
      @violins_free -= 1
      puts "#{n} has a violin"
      puts "violins #@violins_free, bows #@bows_free"

      @bow.wait(@music) while @bows_free == 0
      @bows_free -= 1
      puts "#{n} has a bow"
      puts "violins #@violins_free, bows #@bows_free"
    end

    sleep rand
    puts "#{n}:  (...playing...)"
    sleep rand
    puts "#{n}: Now I've finished."

    @music.synchronize do
      @violins_free += 1
      @violin.signal if @violins_free == 1
      @bows_free += 1
      @bow.signal if @bows_free == 1
    end
  end
end

threads = []
3.times {|i| threads << Thread.new { musician(i) } }

threads.each {|t| t.join }
```

We believe that this solution will never deadlock, though we've found it difficult
to prove. However, it is interesting to note that this algorithm is not necessarily a fair
one. In our tests, the first player always got to play more often than the other two, and
the second more often than the third. The cause and cure for this behavior are left, as
they say, as an exercise for the reader.

13.2.5   Other Synchronization Techniques

Yet another synchronization mechanism is the monitor, implemented in Ruby in the
form of monitor.rb. This technique is somewhat more advanced than the mutex;
notably you can nest monitor locks.

Like the Spanish Inquisition, nested locks are mostly unexpected. No one, for
example, would ever write the following:

```ruby
@mutex = Mutex.new

@mutex.synchronize do
  @mutex.synchronize do
    #...
  end
end
```

But that doesn't mean that a nested lock can't happen. What if the call to syn-chronized lives in a recursive method? Or suppose one method grabs the mutex and then innocently calls another method:

```ruby
def some_method
  @mutex = Mutex.new

  @mutex.synchronize do
    #...
    some_other_method
  end
end

def some_other_method
  @mutex.synchronize do        # Deadlock!
    #...
  end
end
```

The answer—at least when you are using a mutex—is deadlock followed by an ugly exception. Because monitors do allow nested locks, this code will run happily:

```ruby
def some_method
  @monitor = Monitor.new

  @monitor.synchronize do
    #...
    some_other_method
  end
end

def some_other_method
  @monitor.synchronize do      # No problem!!
```

```
    #...
  end
end
```

Like the mutex, Ruby's monitors come in two flavors: the class version, `Monitor`, which you have just met, and the very pedantically named `MonitorMixin` module. `MonitorMixin` allows you to use instances of any class as a monitor:

```
class MyMonitor
  include MonitorMixin
end
```

The `monitor.rb` file also improves on the `ConditionVariable` class that comes with the standard thread. The `monitor.rb` version adds the `wait_until` and `wait_while` methods, which will block a thread based on a condition. It also allows a timeout while waiting because the `wait` method has a timeout parameter, which is a number of seconds (defaulting to `nil`).

Because we are rapidly running out of thread examples, Listing 13.3 presents a rewrite of the `Queue` and `SizedQueue` classes using the monitor technique. The code is based on Shugo Maeda's work, used with permission.

Listing 13.3   Implementing a Queue with a Monitor

```ruby
# Slightly modified version of code by Shugo Maeda.

require 'monitor'

class OurQueue
  def initialize
    @que = []
    @monitor = Monitor.new
    @empty_cond = @monitor.new_cond
  end

  def enq(obj)
    @monitor.synchronize do
      @que.push(obj)
      @empty_cond.signal
    end
  end

  def deq
    @monitor.synchronize do
      while @que.empty?
        @empty_cond.wait
```

```
        end
        return @que.shift
      end
  end

  def size
    @que.size
  end
end

class OurSizedQueue < OurQueue
  attr :max

  def initialize(max)
    super()
    @max = max
    @full_cond = @monitor.new_cond
  end

  def enq(obj)
    @monitor.synchronize do
      while @que.length >= @max
        @full_cond.wait
      end
      super(obj)
    end
  end

  def deq
    @monitor.synchronize do
      obj = super
      if @que.length < @max
        @full_cond.signal
      end
      return obj
    end
  end

  def max=(max)
    @monitor.synchronize do
      @max = max
      @full_cond.broadcast
    end
  end
end
```

The sync.rb library is one more way of performing thread synchronization (using a two-phase lock with a counter). It defines a Sync_m module used in an include or an extend (much like Mutex_m). This module makes available methods such as `sync_locked?`, `sync_shared?`, `sync_exclusive?`, `sync_lock`, `sync_unlock`, and `sync_try_lock`.

13.2.6   Setting a Timeout for an Operation

Sometimes we want to set a maximum length of time for some code to run. This is most useful when interacting with remote computers over a network, as network requests may or may not ever complete.

The `timeout` library is a thread-based solution to this problem (see Listing 13.4). The `timeout` method executes the block associated with the method call; when the specified number of seconds has elapsed, it throws a `Timeout::Error`, which can be caught with a `rescue` clause.

Listing 13.4   A Timeout Example

```
require 'timeout'

flag = false
answer = nil

begin
  timeout(5) do
    puts "I want a cookie!"
    answer = gets.chomp
    flag = true
  end
rescue TimeoutError
  flag = false
end

if flag
  if answer == "cookie"
    puts "Thank you! Chomp, chomp, ..."
  else
    puts "That's not a cookie!"
    exit
  end
else
  puts "Hey, too slow!"
  exit
end

puts "Bye now..."
```

Timeouts in Ruby come with two important caveats, however. First, they are not thread-safe. The underlying mechanism of timeouts is to create a new thread, monitor that thread for completion, and forcibly kill the thread if it has not completed within the timeout specified. As mentioned in Section 13.1.5, "Dealing with Exceptions," killing threads may not be a thread-safe operation, because it can leave your program in an unrecoverable state.

To create a timeout-like effect safely, write the processing thread such that it will periodically check if it needs to abort. This allows the thread to do any required cleanup while terminating in a controlled way. Here is an example that calculates as many prime numbers as possible in 5 seconds, without requiring an external thread to forcibly abort the computation:

```
require 'prime'
primes = []
generator = Prime.each
start = Time.now

while Time.now < (start + 5)
  10.times { primes << generator.next }
end


puts "Ran for #{Time.now - start} seconds."
puts "Found #{primes.size} primes, ending in #{primes.last}"
```

In testing, this code printed "Ran for 5.005569 seconds. Found 2124010 primes, ending in 34603729." Although your results may vary, this example demonstrates how to monitor for a timeout without having to forcibly kill an executing thread.

Second, keep in mind that the `Timeout::Error` exception will not be caught by a simple `rescue` with no arguments. Calling `rescue` with no arguments will automatically rescue any instance of `StandardError` and its subclasses, but `Timeout::Error` is not a subclass of `StandardError`.

If you are in any situation that might raise a timeout error, be sure to rescue both types of errors. Note that this includes any usage of the `Net::HTTP` library, which uses the `Timeout` library to time out requests that take too long.

13.2.7 Waiting for an Event

In many situations, we might want to have one or more threads monitoring the "outside world" while other threads are doing other things. The examples here are all rather contrived, but they do illustrate the general principle.

In the following example, we see three threads doing the "work" of an application. Another thread simply wakes up every second, checks the global variable $flag, and wakes up two other threads when it sees the flag set. This saves the three worker threads from interacting directly with the two other threads and possibly making multiple attempts to awaken them:

```ruby
$flag = false
work1 = Thread.new { job1() }
work2 = Thread.new { job2() }
work3 = Thread.new { job3() }

thread4 = Thread.new { Thread.stop; job4() }
thread5 = Thread.new { Thread.stop; job5() }

watcher = Thread.new do
  loop do
    sleep 1
    if $flag
      thread4.wakeup
      thread5.wakeup
      Thread.exit
    end
  end
end
```

If at any point during the execution of the job methods the variable $flag becomes true, thread4 and thread5 are guaranteed to start within a second. After that, the watcher thread terminates.

In this next example, we are waiting for a file to be created. We check every second for it, and start another thread if we see it; meanwhile, other threads can be doing anything at all. Actually, we are watching for three separate files here:

```ruby
def process_file(filename)
  puts "processing file #{filename}"
end
```

```
def waitfor(filename)
  loop do
    if File.exist? filename
      puts "found #{filename}"
      file_processor = Thread.new { process_file(filename) }
      Thread.exit
    else
      sleep 1
    end
  end
end
waiter1 = Thread.new { waitfor("Godot") }
waiter2 = Thread.new { waitfor("Guffman") }
headwaiter = Thread.new { waitfor("head") }

# Main thread goes off to do other things...
```

There are many other situations in which a thread might wait for an outside event, such as a networked application where the server at the other end of a socket is slow or unreliable.

13.2.8 Collection Searching in Parallel

Threads also make it straightforward to work on a number of alternative solutions simultaneously. To see how this might work, let's write some code to find the biggest number in a bunch of arrays in a limited amount of time. Our `threaded_max` method takes a time limit argument, as well as an array containing the arrays of numbers that are to be searched. It returns the biggest number it can find within the given time limit.

To get the most out of a limited time, our code doesn't just search through all of the arrays one after another. Instead, it starts a bunch of threads, one for each array:

```
require 'thread'

def threaded_max(interval, collections)
  threads = []

  collections.each do |col|
    threads << Thread.new do
      me = Thread.current
      me[:result] = col.first
      col.each do |n|
```

```
        me[:result] = n if n > me[:result]
      end
    end
  end

  sleep(interval)

  threads.each {|t| t.kill }
  results = threads.map {|t| t[:result]}

  results.compact.max     # Max be nil
end

collections = [
  [ 1, 25, 3, 7, 42, 64, 55 ],
  [ 3, 77, 1, 2, 3, 5, 7, 9, 11, 13, 102, 67, 2, 1],
  [ 3, 33, 7, 44, 77, 92, 10, 11]]

biggest = threaded_max(0.5, collections)
```

A few of things to note about this code: First, to keep things simple, the code assumes that there is actually something in each array.

Second, the threads report their results back in a thread local value called `:result`. The threads update `:result` every step of the way because the main bit of the `threaded_max` method will only wait so long before it kills off all of the threads and returns the biggest value found so far. Finally, `threaded_max` can conceivably actually return `nil`: No matter how long we wait, it is possible that the threads will not have done anything before `threaded_max` runs out of patience. (Not very likely, but possible.)

Does using a bunch of threads actually make things faster? It's hard to say. The answer probably depends on your operating system as well as on the number of arrays you are searching.

13.2.9   Recursive Deletion in Parallel

Just for fun, let's write some code to delete an entire directory tree, and let's make it concurrent. The trick to this example is that each time we come across a directory, we start a new thread to delete that directory and its contents.

As we go along, we keep track of the threads we've created in an array called `threads`; because this is a local variable, each thread will have its own copy of the array. It can be accessed by only one thread at a time, and there is no need to synchronize access to it.

Note also that we pass `fullname` into the thread block so that we don't have to worry about the thread accessing a variable that is changing. The thread uses `fn` as a local copy of the same variable.

When we have traversed an entire directory, we want to wait on the threads we have created before deleting the directory we've just finished working on:

```
def delete_all(dir)
  threads = []
  Dir.foreach(dir) do |e|
    next if [".",".."].include? e       # Skip . and ..
    fullname = dir + "/" + e
    if FileTest.directory?(fullname)
      threads << Thread.new(fullname) {|fn| delete_all(fn) }
    else
      File.delete(fullname)
      puts "delete: #{fullname}"
    end
  end
  threads.each { |t| t.join }
  Dir.delete(dir)
  puts "deleting dir #{dir}"
end

delete_all("/tmp/stuff")
```

Is this actually faster than the non-threaded version? We've found that the answer is not consistent. It probably depends on your operating system as well as on the actual directory structure being deleted—that is, its depth, size of files, and so on.

13.3 Fibers and Cooperative Multitasking

Along with full operating system threads, Ruby also provides *fibers*, which can be described as cut-down threads or as code blocks with superpowers.

Fibers do not create an OS thread, but they can contain a block of code that maintains its state, can be paused and resumed, and can yield results. To see what this means, let's start by creating one with a call to `Fiber.new`:

```
fiber = Fiber.new do
  x = 2
  Fiber.yield x
  x = x * 2
  Fiber.yield x
  x * 2
end
```

`Fiber.new` doesn't actually cause any of the code in the fiber's block to execute. To get things going, you need to call the `resume` method. Calling `resume` will cause the code inside of the block to run until it either hits the end of the block or `Fiber.yield` is called. Because our fiber has a `Fiber.yield` on the second line of the block, the initial call to `resume` will run until that second line. The call to `resume` returns whatever is passed to `Fiber.yield` so that our call to `resume` will return 2:

```
answer1 = fiber.resume    # answer1 will be 2
```

So far this is all very lambda-like, but now things get interesting. If we call `resume` a second or third time, the fiber will pick up where it left off:

```
answer2 = fiber.resume    # should be 4
answer3 = fiber.resume    # should be 8
```

Note that if the execution hits the end of the block, fibers will do the usual block thing and return the last value computed in the block.

Given all this, you can look at a fiber as a restartable code block: Each time a fiber hits a `Fiber.yield`, the fiber remembers where it is and lets you restart from that point. You can keep restarting a fiber until it finishes running the code block; call `resume` after that and you will raise a `FiberError`.

As we say, a fiber is a sort of restartable code block. However, you can also look at a fiber as a sort of thread, a thread that you schedule by hand. Instead of running more or less continuously in the background, fibers run in the thread that calls `resume`, hanging onto it only until the fiber finishes or hits the next `Fiber.yield`. In other words, whereas threads implement preemptive multitasking, fibers implement cooperative multitasking.

Along with the basic `Fiber.new` and `yield`, you can get at some bonus fiber methods if you require the `'fiber'` library. Doing so will give you access to `Fiber.current`, which returns the currently executing fiber instance. You also get the `alive?` instance method, which will tell you if a fiber is still alive. Finally, the `fiber` library will give every fiber instance the `transfer` instance method, which allows fibers to transfer control from one to the other (making fibers truly cooperative).

To fill out our look at fibers, here is the multiple-array-searching example rewritten to use fibers:

```ruby
require 'fiber'

class MaxFiber < Fiber
  attr_accessor :result
end
```

```ruby
def max_by_fiber(interval, collections)
  fibers = []
  collections.each_with_index do |numbers|
    fibers << MaxFiber.new do
      me = Fiber.current
      me.result = numbers[0]
      numbers.each_with_index do |n, i|
        me.result = n if n > me.result
        Fiber.yield me.result if (i+1) % 3 == 0
      end
      me.result
    end
  end

  start_time = Time.now
  while fibers.any? &:alive?
    break if Time.now - start_time > interval
    fibers.each {|f| puts f.resume if f.alive? }
  end

  values = fibers.map &:result
  values.compact.max || 0
end

collections = [
  [ 1, 25, 3, 7, 42, 64, 55 ],
  [ 3, 77],
  [ 3, 33, 7, 44, 77, 102, 92, 10, 11],
  [1, 2, 3, 4, 5, 6, 7, 8, 9, 77, 2, 3 ]]

biggest = max_by_fiber(0.5, collections)
```

Because we are using fibers instead of threads, there is no real parallelism going on here. Instead, the fibers just give us a nice way of keeping track of where we are as we do a round-robin search through the various arrays.

The power that fibers provide, of pausing execution until a later time, is most useful when it is useful to wait before calculating the next item in a succession. As you may have noticed, this is very similar to how Ruby's `Enumerator` objects work. Perhaps unsurprisingly, every enumerator is in fact implemented using fibers. The `next`, `take`, and every other enumerator method simply calls `resume` on its fiber as many times as is needed to produce the requested results.

13.4 Conclusion

As you have seen in this chapter, Ruby provides support for threading via native OS threads. However, the GIL ensures only one thread can run at a time in MRI, whereas JRuby and Rubinius allow multiple threads to run at once.

This chapter gave you a hint of just how difficult multithreaded programming can be and how to use Ruby's synchronization primitives, such as mutexes, monitors, condition variables, and queues, to keep your threads coordinated. Finally, we had a quick look at fibers, Ruby's "almost-not-quite threads."

In Chapter 14, "Scripting and System Administration," we move away from a discussion of programming technique in itself to a more task-oriented topic. We'll be discussing the use of Ruby for everyday scripting and system administration tasks.

CHAPTER 14

Scripting and System Administration

Thus spake the master programmer: "Though a program be but three lines long, someday it will have to be maintained."

—*Geoffrey James,* The Tao of Programming

Programmers often need to "glue" programs together with little scripts that talk to the operating system at a fairly high level and run external programs. This is especially true in the UNIX world, which daily relies on shell scripts for countless tasks.

For programmers already proficient in Ruby, it can be an extremely convenient way to create small, useful scripts. In fact, one of Matz's original motivations when creating Ruby, inspired by Perl, was to make it easier to create small scripts to accomplish useful tasks.

In many cases, you might just as well use one of the more traditional languages for this purpose. The advantage that Ruby has, of course, is that it really is a general-purpose, full-featured language and one that's truly object oriented. Because some people want to use Ruby to talk to the OS at this level, we present here a few tricks that might prove useful.

Much of what *could* be covered in this chapter is actually dealt with in other chapters entirely. Refer in particular to Chapter 10, "I/O and Data Storage," which covers file I/O and attributes of files; these features are frequently used in scripts of the kind discussed in the present chapter.

14.1   Running External Programs

A language can't be a glue language unless it can run external programs. Ruby offers more than one way to do this.

I can't resist mentioning here that if you are going to run an external program, make sure that you know what that program does. I'm thinking about viruses and other potentially destructive programs. Don't just run any old command string, especially if it came from a source outside the program. This is true regardless of whether the application is web based.

14.1.1   Using system and exec

The `system` method (in `Kernel`) is equivalent to the C call of the same name. It will execute the given command in a subshell:

```
system("date")
# Output goes to stdout as usual...
```

Note that additional parameters, if present, will be used as a list of arguments; in most cases, the arguments can also be specified as part of the command string with the same effect. The only difference is that filename expansion is done on the first string but not on the others:

```
system("rm", "/tmp/file1")
system("rm /tmp/file2")
# Both the above work fine.

# However, below, there's a difference...
system("echo *")     # Print list of all files
system("echo", "*") # Print an asterisk (no filename
                     # expansion done)

# More complex command lines also work.
system("ls -l | head -n 1")
```

Note that if you want to capture the output (for example, in a variable), `system` isn't the right way. See the next section.

I'll also mention `exec` here. The `exec` method behaves much the same as `system`, except that the new process actually replaces the current one. Thus, any code following the `exec` won't be executed:

```
puts "Here's a directory listing:"
exec("ls", "-l")

puts "This line is never reached!"
```

14.1.2 Capturing Command Output

The simplest way to capture command output is to use the *backtick* (also called *backquote* or *grave accent*) to delimit the command. Here are a couple of examples:

```
listing = 'ls -l'   # Multiple lines in one string
now = 'date'        # "Mon Mar 12 16:50:11 CST 2001"
```

The generalized delimiter `%x` calls the backquote operator (which is really a `kernel` method). It works essentially the same way:

```
listing = %x(ls -l)
now = %x(date)
```

The `%x` form is often useful when the string to be executed contains characters such as single and double quotes.

Because the backquote method really is (in some sense) a method, it is possible to override it. Here, we change the functionality so that we return an array of lines rather than a single string (of course, we have to save an alias to the old method so that we can call it):

```
alias old_execute '

def '(cmd)
  out = old_execute(cmd)  # Call the old backtick method
  out.split("\n")         # Return an array of strings!
end
```

```
entries = 'ls -1 /tmp'
num = entries.size                          # 95

first3lines = %x(ls -1 | head -n 3)
how_many = first3lines.size                 # 3
```

Note that, as shown here, the functionality of %x is affected when we perform this redefinition.

In the following example, we append a "shellism" to the end of the command to ensure that standard error is mixed with standard output:

```
alias old_execute '

def '(cmd)
  old_execute(cmd + " 2>&1")
end

entries = 'ls -1 /tmp/foobar'
# "/tmp/foobar: No such file or directory\n"
```

Of course, most of the time it is more useful to create a method of our own that implements desired behaviors rather than overwrite the backquote method itself.

14.1.3   Manipulating Processes

We discuss process manipulation in this section, even though a new process might not involve calling an external program. The principal way to create a new process is the fork method, which takes its name from the UNIX tradition's idea of a fork in the path of execution, like a fork in the road. (Note, however, that Ruby does not support the fork method on Windows platforms.)

The fork method in Kernel (also found in the Process module) shouldn't, of course, be confused with the Thread instance method of the same name.

There are two ways to invoke the fork method. The first is the more UNIX-like way: Simply call it and test its return value. If that value is nil, we are in the child process; otherwise, we execute the parent code. The value returned to the parent is actually the process ID (or *pid*) of the child:

```
pid = fork
if (pid == nil)
  puts "Ah, I must be the child."
```

```
    puts "I guess I'll speak as a child."
  else
    puts "I'm the parent."
    puts "Time to put away childish things."
  end
```

In this unrealistic example, the output might be interleaved, or the parent's output might appear first. For the purposes of this example, it's irrelevant.

We should also note that the child process might outlive the parent. We've seen that this isn't the case with Ruby threads, but system-level processes are entirely different.

The second form of `fork` takes a block. The code in the block comprises the child process. The previous example could thus be rewritten in this simpler way:

```
fork do
  puts "Ah, I must be the child."
  puts "I guess I'll speak as a child."
end

puts "I'm the parent."
puts "Time to put away childish things."
```

The pid is still returned, of course. We just don't show it in the example.

When we want to wait for a process to finish, we can call the `wait` method in the `Process` module. It waits for any child to exit and returns the process ID of that child. The `wait2` method behaves similarly except that it returns a two-value array consisting of the pid and a `Process::Status` object with the pid and exit status code:

```
pid1 = fork { sleep 2; exit 3 }
pid2 = fork { sleep 1; exit 3 }

pid2_again = Process.wait        # Returns pid2
pid1_and_status = Process.wait2  # Returns [pid1, #<Process::Status
exit 3>]
```

To wait for a specific child, use `waitpid` and `waitpid2`, respectively:

```
pid3 = fork { sleep 2; exit 3 }
pid4 = fork { sleep 1; exit 3 }
```

```
sleep 3   # Give the child processes time to finish

pid4_again = Process.waitpid(pid4, Process::WNOHANG)
pid3_array = Process.waitpid2(pid3, Process::WNOHANG)
# pid3_array is now [pid3, #<Process::Status exit 3>]
```

If the second parameter is unspecified, the call might block (if no such child exists). It might be ORed logically with `Process::WUNTRACED` to catch child processes that have been stopped. This second parameter is rather OS sensitive; experiment before relying on its behavior.

The `exit` method can be passed `true`, `false`, or an integer. The UNIX standard is to exit with status 0 for success, and 1 or greater for failure. Thus, passing `true` will exit with a status of 0, and `false` will exit with a status of 1. Passing any integer will exit with a status of that value.

The `exit!` method exits immediately from a process (bypassing any exit handlers). Any given integer will be used as the exit code, but the default is 1 (not 0):

```
pid1 = fork { exit! }     # Return 1 exit code
pid2 = fork { exit! 0 }   # Return 0 exit code
```

The `pid` and `ppid` methods will return the process ID of the current process and the parent process, respectively:

```
proc1 = Process.pid
fork do
  if Process.ppid == proc1
    puts "proc1 is my parent" # Prints this message
  else
    puts "What's going on?"
  end
end
```

The `kill` method can be used to send a UNIX-style signal to a process. The first parameter can be an integer, a POSIX signal name including the `SIG` prefix, or a non-prefixed signal name. The second parameter represents a pid; if it is zero, it refers to the current process:

```
Process.kill(1, pid1)           # Send signal 1 to process pid1
Process.kill("HUP", pid2)       # Send SIGHUP to pid2
Process.kill("SIGHUP", pid2)    # Send SIGHUP to pid3
Process.kill("SIGHUP", 0)       # Send SIGHUP to self
```

The `Kernel.trap` method can be used to handle such signals. It typically takes a signal number or name and a block to be executed:

```
trap(1) do
  puts "OUCH!"
  puts "Caught signal 1"
end


Process.kill(1,0) # Send to self
```

The `trap` method can be used to allow complex control of your process. For more information, consult Ruby and UNIX references on process signals.

The `Process` module also has methods for examining and setting such attributes as userid, effective userid, priority, and others. Consult any Ruby reference for details.

14.1.4 Manipulating Standard Input and Output

You saw how `IO.popen` and `IO.pipe` work in Chapter 10, but there is a little library we haven't looked at that can prove handy at times.

The `Open3` library contains a method called `popen3` that will return an array of three `IO` objects. These objects correspond to the standard input, standard output, and standard error for the process kicked off by the `popen3` call. Here's an example:

```
require "open3"

filenames = %w[ file1 file2 this that another one_more ]
output, errout = [], []

Open3.popen3("xargs", "ls", "-l") do |inp, out, err|
  filenames.each { |f| inp.puts f }   # Write to the process's stdin
  inp.close                           # Close is necessary!

  output = out.readlines              # Read from its stdout
  errout = err.readlines              # Also read from its stderr
end

puts "Sent #{filenames.size} lines of input."
puts "Got back #{output.size} lines from stdout"
puts "and #{errout.size} lines from stderr."
```

This contrived example does an `ls -l` on each of the specified filenames and captures the standard output and standard error separately. Note that closing the input is needed so that the subprocess will be aware that the input is complete. Also note that Open3 uses `fork`, which doesn't exist on Windows; on that platform, you will have to use the `win32-open3` library (written and maintained by Daniel Berger and Park Heesob).

See also Section 14.3, "The `shell` Library."

14.2   Command-Line Options and Arguments

Rumors of the death of the command line are greatly exaggerated. Although we live in the age of the GUI, every day thousands of us use older text-based interfaces for one reason or another.

Ruby has many of its roots in UNIX, as we've said. Yet even in the Windows world, there is such a thing as a command line, and, frankly, we don't see it going away any time soon.

When operating at this level, you use parameters and switches to communicate with the program at the time of its invocation. This section shows how to deal with these parameters (or arguments) and switches (or options).

14.2.1   Working with ARGV

The global constant ARGV represents the list of arguments passed to the Ruby program via the command line. This is essentially just an array:

```
n = ARGV.size
argstr = %{"#{ARGV * ', '}"}
puts "I was given #{n} arguments..."
puts "They are: #{argstr}"
puts "Note that ARGV[0] = #{ARGV[0]}"
```

Assume that we invoke this program with the argument string `red green blue` on the command line. It then produces this output:

```
I was given 3 arguments...
They are: "red, green, blue"
Note that ARGV[0] = red
```

Where ARGV in some languages would also supply a count of arguments, there is no need for that in Ruby because that information is part of the array.

Another thing that might trip up old-timers is the assignment of the zeroth argument to an actual argument (rather than, for example, the script name). The arguments themselves are zero-based rather than one-based as in C and the various shell languages.

14.2.2   Working with ARGF

The special global constant ARGF represents the pseudo-file resulting from a concatenation of every file named on the command line. It behaves like an IO object in most ways.

When you have a "bare" input method (without a receiver), you are typically using a method mixed in from the Kernel module. (Examples are gets and readlines.) The actual source of input will default to STDIN if no files are on the command line. If there are files, however, input will be taken from them. End of file will of course be reached only at the end of the last file.

If you prefer, you can access ARGF explicitly using the following fragment:

```
# Copy named files to stdout, just like 'cat'
puts ARGF.readlines
```

Perhaps contrary to expectations, end of file is set after each file. The previous code fragment will output all the files. This one will output only the first:

```
puts ARGF.gets until ARGF.eof?
```

Whether this is a bug or a feature, we will leave it to you to decide. Of course, other unexpected surprises might actually be pleasant. The input isn't simply a stream of bytes flowing through our program; we can actually perform operations such as seek and rewind on ARGF as though it were a "real file."

There is also a file method associated with ARGF; it returns an IO object corresponding to the file currently being processed. As such, the value it returns will change as the files on the command line are processed in sequence.

What if we don't want command-line arguments to be interpreted as files? The solution is to not use the "bare" (receiverless) call of the input methods. If you want to read standard input, call methods on STDIN, and all will work as expected.

14.2.3   Parsing Command-Line Options

Ruby has had a long and varied history of command-line parsing libraries, and today
it provides the OptionParser library. Essentially, OptionParser gives you a simple
domain-specific language (DSL) for describing just how you want the arguments to
your program parsed.

This is probably best explained with an example. Suppose we have a tool with
these options: -h or –help will print help information; -f or –file will specify a filename argument; -l or –lines will truncate the output after the specified number of
lines (defaulting to 100). We could begin in this way:

```ruby
require 'optparse'

args = {lines: 100}

OptionParser.new do |opts|
  opts.banner = "Usage: tool [options] COMMAND"

  opts.on("-f", "–file FILE") do |file|
    args[:file] = file
  end

  opts.on("-l", "–lines [LINES]", Integer,
    "Number of lines to output (default 100)"
  ) do |lines|
    args[:lines] = lines
  end

  opts.on_tail("-h", "–help", "Show this help") do
    puts opts
    exit
  end
end.parse!

p args
p ARGV.first
```

With this code saved into a file named tool.rb, running it produces the output
that one would (hopefully) expect:

```
$ ruby tool.rb -h
Usage: tool [options] COMMAND
    -f, -file FILE
    -l, -lines [LINES]    Number of lines to output (default 100)
    -h, -help             Show this help

$ ruby tool.rb -file book.txt
{:lines=>100, :file=>"book.txt"}
[]

$ ruby tool.rb -f book.txt -lines 10 print
{:lines=>10, :file=>"book.txt"}
["print"]
```

As you can see from the example, the work involved in using `OptionParser` is mostly about building a new instance, and most of that goes into calls to the on method. The idea is that each call to on describes one option that the parser will recognize.

You need to supply two key bits to the on method: First, you need the name of the option, which can be either short (as in `-f`) or long (as in `-file`). In the second string, surrounding the name of the argument with square brackets indicates to `OptionParser` that the option is, well, optional, and doesn't need to be given.

As you can see in the `lines` parameter, it is possible to give both a type and a description of a particular option. The string from the command-line argument will be converted into the given type, and the description will be printed as part of the help message.

Second, you need to provide a block of code, which will be executed any time `OptionParser` sees that option. The code block can either do something directly, as the `-h` option does in the example, or simply save some data for later, as the `-file` and `-lines` blocks do.

When the `parse!` method is finally called, the parser examines the contents of `ARGV`, removes any entries that it recognizes as options, and runs the blocks for those options. Afterwards, the `args` hash contains the options that were passed, and the `ARGV` array contains only arguments that were not part of an option.

Many gems are available that provide various approaches to parsing command-line flags and arguments. You may find `highline`, `slop`, `cocaine`, `thor`, or some other library more suitable for your use case.

14.3   The `Shell` Library

Ruby isn't necessarily convenient to use as a scripting language in every situation. For example, a bash script can execute external programs simply by naming them, with no extraneous syntax.

The power and flexibility of Ruby has given it a more complex syntax than the average shell language. Additionally, its functionality is segmented into different classes, modules, and libraries.

This situation motivated the creation of the `Shell` library. This library makes it easier to do things such as connecting commands with pipes and redirecting output to files. It also consolidates functionality from several different sources so that they are transparently accessible from a `Shell` object. (It doesn't always work well on Windows.)

14.3.1   Using `Shell` for I/O Redirection

The `Shell` class has two methods—`new` and `cd`—for instantiating a new object. The former creates a shell object associated with the current directory; the latter creates a shell object whose working directory will be the one specified:

```
require "shell"

sh1 = Shell.new                # Work in the current directory
sh2 = Shell.cd("/tmp/hal")     # Work in /tmp/hal
```

The `Shell` library defines a few built-in commands as methods, such as `echo`, `cat`, and `tee`. These always return objects of class `Filter` (as do the user-defined commands that we'll look at shortly).

The nice thing about a `Filter` is that it understands I/O redirection. The methods (or operators) < , > , and | are defined so that they behave more or less as we expect after using them in shell scripts.

If a redirection method has a string as a parameter, that string is taken to be the name of a file. If it has an `IO` object as a parameter, that object is used for the input or output operation. Here are some small examples:

```
sh = Shell.new

# Print the readme.txt file to stdout
sh.cat("readme.txt") > STDOUT
```

```
# Print it again
(sh.cat < "readme.txt") > STDOUT
(sh.echo "This is a test") > "myfile.txt"

# Cat two files to stdout, tee-ing to a third
(sh.cat "myfile.txt",  "readme.txt") | (sh.tee "file3.txt") > STDOUT
```

Note that the > operator binds tightly. The parentheses that you see in the preceding code are necessary in most cases. Here are two correct usages and one incorrect one:

```
# Ruby parser understands this...
sh.cat("readme.txt") > STDOUT

# ...and this also.
(sh.cat "readme.txt") > STDOUT

# But not this: TypeError! (a precedence problem)
sh.cat "readme.txt" > STDOUT
```

Note that it's also possible to add system commands of your own choosing. The method def_system_command will accomplish this. For example, here we define two methods—ls and ll—which will list files in the current directory (short and long listings, respectively):

```
# Method name is identical to command...
# only one parameter necessary
Shell.def_system_command "ls"

# Two parameters needed here
Shell.def_system_command "ll", "ls -l"

sh = Shell.new
sh.ls > STDOUT    # Short listing
sh.ll > STDOUT    # Long listing
```

You will notice that in many cases, we explicitly send output to STDOUT. This is because output from a Shell command doesn't automatically go anywhere. It's simply associated with the Filter object until that object is connected to a file or an IO object.

14.3.2   Other Notes on `Shell`

The `transact` method will execute a block in the context of the `shell` instance. Therefore, we can use the following shorthand:

```
sh = Shell.new
sh.transact do
  echo("A line of data") > "somefile.txt"
  cat("somefile.txt", "otherfile.txt") > "thirdfile"
  cat("thirdfile") | tee("file4") > STDOUT
end
```

The iterator `foreach` will take either a file or a directory as a parameter. If it is a file, it will iterate over the lines of that file; if it is a directory, it will iterate over the filenames in that directory:

```
sh = Shell.new

# List all lines in /tmp/foo
sh.foreach("/tmp/foo") {|l| puts l }

# List all files in /tmp
sh.foreach("/tmp") {|f| puts f }
```

The `pushdir` and `popdir` methods will save and restore the current directory, respectively. Aliases are `pushd` and `popd`. The method `pwd` will determine the current working directory; aliases are `getwd`, `cwd`, and `dir`:

```
sh = Shell.cd "/home"

puts sh.pwd      # /home
sh.pushd "/tmp"
puts sh.pwd      # /tmp

sh.popd
puts sh.pwd      # /home
```

For convenience, numerous methods are imported into `Shell` from various sources, including `File` and `FileUtils`. This saves the trouble of doing requires, includes, creating objects, qualifying method calls, and so on:

```
sh = Shell.new
flag1 = sh.exist? "myfile"  # Test file existence
sh.delete "somefile"        # Delete a file
```

There are other features of the `Shell` library that we don't cover here. See the class documentation for more details.

14.4 Accessing Environment Variables

Occasionally we need to access environment variables as a link between our program and the outer world. An *environment variable* is essentially a label referring to a piece of text (typically a small piece); environment variables can be used to store configuration information such as paths, usernames, and so on.

The notion of an environment variable is common in the UNIX world. The Windows world has borrowed it from UNIX (by way of MS-DOS), so the code we show here should run on variants of both Windows and UNIX.

14.4.1 Getting and Setting Environment Variables

The global constant `ENV` can be used as a hash for the purposes of retrieving and assigning values. In the following code, we retrieve the value of an environment variable. (You would use a semicolon rather than a colon on Windows.)

```
mypath = ENV["PATH"]
# Let's get an array now...
dirs = mypath.split(":")
```

Here's an example of setting a variable. We take the trouble to fork another process to illustrate two facts. First, a child process inherits the environment variables that its parent knows. Second, an environment variable set by a child is *not* propagated back up to the parent:

```
ENV["alpha"] = "123"
ENV["beta"] = "456"
puts "Parent: alpha = #{ENV['alpha']}"
puts "Parent: beta = #{ENV['beta']}"

fork do   # Child code...
  x = ENV["alpha"]
  ENV["beta"] = "789"
```

```
    y = ENV["beta"]
    puts " Child: alpha = #{x}"
    puts " Child: beta = #{y}"
end

Process.wait
a = ENV["alpha"]
b = ENV["beta"]
puts "Parent: alpha = #{a}"
puts "Parent: beta = #{b}"
```

Here is the output:

```
Parent: alpha = 123
Parent: beta = 456
 Child: alpha = 123
 Child: beta = 789
Parent: alpha = 123
Parent: beta = 456
```

There is a consequence of the fact that parent processes don't know about their children's variables. Because a Ruby program is typically run in a subshell, any variables changed during execution will *not* be reflected in the current shell after execution has terminated.

14.4.2   Storing Environment Variables as an Array or Hash

It's important to realize that ENV isn't really a hash; it just looks like one. For example, we can't call the invert method on it; it gives us a NameError because there is no such method. The reason for this implementation is the close tie between the ENV object and the underlying operating system; setting a value has an actual impact on the OS, a behavior that a mere hash can't mimic.

However, we can call the to_hash method to give us a real live hash:

```
envhash = ENV.to_hash
val2var = envhash.invert
```

Of course, after we have a hash, we can convert it to any other form we prefer (for example, an array):

```
envarr = ENV.to_hash.to_a
```

It's not possible to directly reassign a hash to ENV, but we can fake it easily if we need to:

```
envhash = ENV.to_hash
# Manipulate as needed... then assign back.
envhash.each {|k,v| ENV[k] = v }
```

14.5 Working with Files, Directories, and Trees

A broad area of everyday scripting is to work with files and directories, including entire subtrees of files. We mentioned some ways to work with files in Chapter 4, "Internationalization in Ruby," so we will provide more depth here.

Because I/O is a fairly system-dependent thing, many tricks will vary from one operating system to another. When in doubt, check the documentation and always try experimenting.

14.5.1 A Few Words on Text Filters

Many tools we use every day (both vendor supplied and homegrown) are simply *text filters*—that is, they accept textual input, process or transform it in some way, and output it again. Classic examples of text filters in the UNIX world are sort and uniq, among others.

Sometimes a file is small enough to be read into memory. This allows processing that might otherwise be difficult:

```
lines = File.open(filename){|f| f.readlines }
# Manipulate as needed...
lines.each {|x| puts x }
```

Sometimes we'll need to process it a line at a time:

```
File.open(filename) do |file|
  file.each_line do |line|
    # Manipulate as needed...
    puts line
  end
end
```

Finally, don't forget that any filenames on the command line are automatically gathered into ARGF, representing a concatenation of all input (see Section 14.2.2, "Working with ARGF"). In this case, we can use calls such as ARGF.readlines just as if ARGF were an IO object. All output will go to standard output, as usual.

14.5.2   Copying a Directory Tree

Suppose that you want to copy an entire directory structure to a new location. There are various ways of performing this operation, but if the tree has internal symbolic links, it becomes more difficult.

Listing 14.1 shows a recursive solution with a little added user-friendliness. It is smart enough to check the most basic error conditions and also to print a usage message.

Listing 14.1   Copying a Directory Tree

```
require "fileutils"

def recurse(src, dst)
  Dir.mkdir(dst)
  Dir.foreach(src) do |e|
    # Don't bother with . and ..
    next if [".",".."].include? e
    fullname = src + "/" + e
    newname = fullname.sub(Regexp.new(Regexp.escape(src)), dst)
    if File.directory?(fullname)
      recurse(fullname, newname)
    elsif File.symlink?(fullname)
      linkname = 'ls -l #{fullname}'.sub(/.* -> /,"").chomp
      newlink = linkname.dup
      n = newlink.index($oldname)
      next if n == nil
      n2 = n + $oldname.length - 1
      newlink[n..n2] = $newname
      newlink.sub!(/\/\//,"/")
      newlink = linkname.sub(Regexp.new(Regexp.escape(src)), dst)
      File.symlink(newlink, newname)
    elsif File.file?(fullname)
      FileUtils.copy(fullname, newname)
    else
      puts "??? : #{fullname}"
    end
  end
end


# "Main"
```

```
if ARGV.size != 2
  puts "Usage: copytree oldname newname"
  exit
end

oldname = ARGV[0]
newname = ARGV[1]

if !File.directory?(oldname)
  puts "Error: First parameter must be an existing directory."
  exit
end

if File.exist?(newname)
  puts "Error: #{newname} already exists."
  exit
end

oldname = File.expand_path(oldname)
newname = File.expand_path(newname)

$oldname=oldname
$newname=newname

recurse(oldname, newname)
```

Whereas modern UNIX variants such as Mac OS X provide a `cp -R` command that will preserve symlinks, older UNIX variants did not. Listing 14.1 was written to address that need in a real-life situation.

14.5.3 Deleting Files by Age or Other Criteria

Imagine that you want to scan through a directory and delete the oldest files. This directory might be some kind of repository for temporary files, log files, browser cache files, or similar data.

Here, we present a little code fragment that will remove all the files older than a certain timestamp (passed in as a `Time` object):

```
def delete_older(dir, time)
  Dir.chdir(dir) do
    Dir.foreach(".") do |entry|
      # We're not handling directories here
      next if File.stat(entry).directory?
      # Use the modification time
      File.delete(entry) if File.mtime(entry) < time
```

```
      end
    end
  end


delete_older("/tmp", Time.local(2014,1,1,0,0,0))
```

This is nice, but let's generalize it. Let's make a similar method called `delete_if` that takes a block that will evaluate to `true` or `false`. Let's then delete the file only if it fits the given criteria:

```
def delete_if(dir)
  Dir.chdir(dir) do
    Dir.foreach(".") do |entry|
      # We're not handling directories here
      next if File.stat(entry).directory?
      File.delete(entry) if yield entry
    end
  end
end


# Delete all files over 300 megabytes
delete_if("/tmp") { |f| File.size(f) > 300*1024*1024 }


# Delete all files with extensions LOG or BAK
delete_if("/tmp") { |f| f =~ /\.(log|bak)$/i }
```

14.5.4   Determining Free Space on a Disk

Suppose that you want to know how many gigabytes are free on a certain drive. The following code example is a crude way of doing this, by running a system utility:

```
def freespace(device=".")
  lines = %x(df -k #{device}).split("\n")
  n = (lines.last.split[3].to_f / 1024 / 1024).round(2)
end


puts freespace("/")    # 48.7
```

On Windows, there is a somewhat more elegant solution (supplied by Daniel Berger):

```
require 'Win32API'

GetDiskFreeSpaceEx = Win32API.new('kernel32', 'GetDiskFreeSpaceEx',
                                  'PPPP', 'I')

def freespace(dir=".")
  total_bytes = [0].pack('Q')
  total_free = [0].pack('Q')
  GetDiskFreeSpaceEx.call(dir, 0, total_bytes, total_free)

  total_bytes = total_bytes.unpack('Q').first
  total_free = total_free.unpack('Q').first
end

puts freespace("C:")        # 5340389376
```

14.6   Other Scripting Tasks

The remaining tasks did not have a section of their own, so we have grouped them
together here in the uncreatively named "other" section.

14.6.1   Distributing Ruby Programs

There are occasions where you might want to distribute your Ruby program so that
others can use it. If your intended recipients are running Mac OS X, you're in luck,
because Apple includes Ruby with Mac OS X (version 2.0.0 as of this writing).

For Windows users, rubyinstaller.org provides a Ruby installer package, also version 2.0.0. Any Linux user should be able to install Ruby via their distribution's package manager.

Keep in mind, however, that these options limit you to older versions of Ruby
(version 2.1.2 is the latest, and these options mostly only offer 2.0.0). To install Ruby
for development work, refer to Section 21.6, "Ruby Version Managers," in Chapter
21, "Ruby Development Tools."

Besides asking end users to install their own copies of Ruby, there is a tool called
Omnibus (by the creators of the Chef configuration management system) that allows
building an entire self-contained package that includes Ruby itself, and any Rubygems
that are needed as well.

Beyond Omnibus, other options are available on the Web. Each option has various tradeoffs, and I encourage you to investigate before deciding on one for yourself.

14.6.2   Piping into the Ruby Interpreter

Because the Ruby interpreter is a single-pass translator, it is possible to pipe code into it and have it executed. One conceivable purpose for this is to use Ruby for more complex tasks when you are required by circumstance to work in a traditional scripting language such as bash.

Listing 14.2, for example, is a bash script that uses Ruby (via a here-document) to calculate the elapsed time in seconds between two dates. The Ruby program prints a single value to standard output, which is then captured by the shell script.

Listing 14.2   bash Scripts Invoking Ruby

```
# Let bash find the difference in seconds
# between two dates using Ruby...

export time1="2007-04-02 15:56:12"
export time2="2007-12-08 12:03:19"

export time1="2007-04-02 15:56:17"

#cat <<EOF | ruby | read elapsed
cat <<EOF | ruby
require "time"

time1 = ENV["time1"]
time2 = ENV["time2"]

t1 = Time.parse(time1)
t2 = Time.parse(time2)

diff = t2 - t1
puts diff
EOF

echo "Elapsed seconds = " $elapsed
```

Note that the two input values in this case are passed as environment variables (which must be exported). The two lines that retrieve these values could also be coded in this way:

```
time1="$time1" # Embed the shell variable directly
time2="$time2" #   into a string...
```

However, the difficulties are obvious. It could get very confusing whether a certain string represents a bash variable or a Ruby global variable, and there could be a host of problems with quoting and escaping.

It's also possible to use a Ruby "one-liner" with the -e option. Here's a little script that reverses a string using Ruby:

```
#!/usr/bin/bash
string="Francis Bacon"
reversed=$(ruby -e "puts '$string'.reverse")
echo $reversed  # "nocaB sicnarF"
```

In fact, Ruby provides multiple options for one-liners. To automatically run the given code once per line of input, add the -n option. That allows us to reverse each line of input:

```
$ echo -e "Knowledge\nis\npower\n" | ruby -ne 'print $_.reverse'

egdelwonK
si
rewop
```

Simplifying things even further, the -p option acts like -n, but with an added print statement for each line after the code has run:

```
$ echo -e "France\nis\nBacon\n" | ruby -pe '$_.reverse!'

ecnarF
si
nocaB
```

UNIX geeks will note that awk has been used in a similar way since time immemorial.

14.6.3   Testing Whether a Program Is Running Interactively

A good way to determine whether a program is interactive is to test its standard input. The method tty? (historically, a "teletype") will tell us whether the device is an interactive one as opposed to a disk file or socket (though this is not available on Windows):

```
if STDIN.tty?
  puts "Hi! Looks like you're typing at me."
else
  puts "Input is not from a keyboard."
end
```

14.6.4   Determining the Current Platform or Operating System

If a program wants to know what operating system it's running on, it can use the `RbConfig::CONFIG` hash to retrieve the `'host_os'`. This will return a semi-cryptic string (like `darwin13.3.0`, `cygwin`, or `solaris2`) indicating the operating system where this copy of Ruby was built.

Ruby runs primarily on Mac OS X (Darwin), UNIX variants like Linux and Solaris, or Windows (whether XP, Vista, 7, or 8). As a result, it is possible to distinguish between platforms using a very simple regular expression:

```
def os_family
  case RbConfig::CONFIG['host_os']
  when /(mingw|mswin|windows)/i
    "windows"
  when /cygwin/i
    "cygwin"
  when /(darwin|mac os)/i
    "osx"
  when /(linux|bsd|aix|solaris)/i
    "unix"
  end
end
```

Of course, this is only a clumsy way of determining OS-specific information. Even if you correctly determine the OS family, that might not always imply the availability (or absence) of any specific feature.

14.6.5   Using the `Etc` Module

The `Etc` module retrieves useful information from the `/etc/passwd` and `/etc/group` files (which, to be fair, is only useful in a UNIX environment).

The `getlogin` method will return the login name of the user. If it fails, `getp-wuid` might work (taking an optional parameter, which is the uid):

```
require 'etc'

myself = Etc.getlogin                 # That's me!
root_name = Etc.getpwuid(0).name      # Root's name

# Without a parameter, getpwuid calls
# getuid internally...
me2 = Etc.getpwuid.name               # Me again!
```

The getpwnam method returns a passwd struct, which contains relevant entries such as name, dir (home directory), shell (login shell), and others:

```
rootshell = Etc.getpwnam("root").shell   # /sbin/sh
```

At the group level, getgrgid and getgrnam behave similarly. They will return a group struct consisting of group name, group passwd, and so on.

The iterator passwd will iterate over all entries in the /etc/passwd file. Each entry passed into the block is a passwd struct:

```
require 'etc'

all_users = []
Etc.passwd { |entry| all_users << entry.name }
```

There is an analogous iterator group for group entries.

14.7 Conclusion

That ends our discussion of Ruby scripting for everyday automation tasks. We've seen how to get information in and out of a program by way of environment variables and standard I/O. We've seen how to perform many common "glue" operations to get other pieces of software to talk to each other. We've also looked at how to interact with the operating system at various levels.

Because much of this material is operating system dependent, I urge you to experiment on your own. There are differences between Mac OS X, Linux, and Windows, and there are even differences in behavior depending on the particular version involved.

Our next topic is a similarly broad one. We'll look at using Ruby to process various kinds of data formats, from image files to XML.

CHAPTER 15

Ruby and Data Formats

"Your information, sir," the Librarian says.
"Are you smart enough to tie that information into YOU ARE HERE?"
Hiro says. "I'll see what I can do, sir. The formats appear to be reconcilable."

—Snow Crash, *by Neal Stephenson*

In computing, it is a fact of life that when information becomes complex enough, it evolves its own "mini-language" in which that information is best expressed. More often, it evolves *multiple* such mini-languages. We call these *file formats* or *data formats.*

Anyone who has used a computer can name many file formats. There are image formats such as GIF, JPG, and PNG; document formats such as DOC and PDF; "universal" formats such as CSV, JSON, and XML; and countless thousands of proprietary data formats, many of which are variations on the fixed-column data storage so common in the ancient times of the 1960s.

The simplest and most common data format is plain text. Files full of bytes encoded as ASCII (or its supersets, ISO 8859-1 and UTF-8) have proven themselves to be the most enduring and accessible form of data over the decades.

Even files containing only simple text, however, may have a structure (hence the popularity of JSON and XML). Other formats may be pure binary (such as Protocol Buffers) or some mixture of text and binary (such as RTF). The primary tradeoff between text and binary formats is readability versus speed; therefore, one or the other will be better depending on the circumstances.

No matter what format data is stored in, sooner or later we want to read it, parse it, and write it again. This chapter covers a few of the most common file formats, but there is no way to cover even all the common ones in a single book. If you want to parse such a format as vCard, iCal, or one of the hundreds of others, you will have to do a search for the appropriate libraries, or you may have to write your own.

15.1   Parsing JSON

JSON, short for *JavaScript Object Notation*, was designed as a human-readable format allowing arrays, hashes, numbers, and strings to be serialized as plain text to communicate data between programs, no matter what language they are written in. Designed partially as a reaction to the verboseness of XML, JSON is sparse both in the number of characters required and in the number of data types it supports.

We briefly looked at using JSON as a way to store Ruby data in Section 10.2.5, "Persisting Data with JSON" of Chapter 10, "I/O and Data Storage." In this section, we'll look at how to parse and manipulate the type of JSON data that might be provided by a website API. Before we do that, though, let's review how to parse a string or file containing JSON data into a Ruby hash:

```
require 'json'

data = JSON.parse('{"students":[
  {"name":"Alice","grade":4},
  {"name":"Bob","grade":3}
]}')
p data["students"].first.values_at("name", "grade")
# ["Alice", 4]
```

What JSON calls an "object" corresponds almost perfectly to what we in Ruby-land know as a hash. Meanwhile, JSON contains several other easily recognizable types: arrays, strings, and numbers. JSON (including the strings contained inside it) is always encoded as UTF-8, and the only other types it is able to encode are `true`, `false`, and `null` (or `nil` in Ruby).

15.1.1 Navigating JSON Data

Once the JSON has been parsed, the nested hashes and arrays that are returned can be navigated to extract the specific data required. To illustrate this, we'll use some JSON data provided by the GitHub public API:

```ruby
require 'json'
require 'open-uri'
require 'pp'

json = open("https://api.github.com/repos/ruby/ruby/contributors")
users = JSON.parse(json)

pp users.first
# {"login"=>"nobu",
#  "id"=>16700,
#  "url"=>"https://api.github.com/users/nobu",
#  "html_url"=>"https://github.com/nobu",
#  [...other attributes...]
#  "type"=>"User",
#  "site_admin"=>false,
#  "contributions"=>9850}

users.sort_by!{|u| -u["contributions"] }
puts users[0...10].map{|u| u["login"] }.join(", ")
# nobu, akr, nurse, unak, eban, ko1, drbrain, knu, kosaki, mame
```

In the preceding code, we are using the open-uri library for convenience. This is explained in greater detail in Chapter 18, "Network Programming"; for now, just be aware that it enables us to use the open method on a URI much as if it were a simple file.

Using open-uri, we download a string that contains a JSON array of the GitHub accounts of contributors to the main Ruby interpreter. (Many contributors who lack GitHub accounts are not included in this list.) Parsing the JSON gives us an array of hashes, with each hash containing information about one particular contributor, with keys including login, id, url, and contributions, among others.

Then, we use pp, the "prettyprint" library, to print the hash of attributes for the first contributor. (Every attribute is printed by pp, but we've elided some of them here to save space.) Next, we reverse-sort the list by the number of contributions so that the hashes are ordered from most commits to least commits. Finally, we map the sorted hashes of contributor information into just their login (or username) and print them as a comma-separated list.

Most real-world uses of JSON data are similar to this one: Write some code to fetch the data, parse the data into a native Ruby hash or array, and then find the array items or hash keys that contain the data you are interested in.

15.1.2   Handling Non-JSON Data Types

As you saw in Chapter 10, JSON cannot hold Ruby objects. Most of the time, using JSON will mean writing code to convert your objects into a hash of strings and numbers and then back again. Some JSON libraries, such as Oj, provide an automatic form of this object conversion.

Although most objects can be converted into a hash of string or number attributes, some data is not so easily converted. Symbols, instances of `Time` and `Date`, and currency amounts with exact cents are just a few examples of Ruby objects that cannot be directly represented in JSON.

For symbols, that means straightforward conversion into a JSON string. For `Time` objects, it means using the `iso8601` or `to_i` method and then the `parse` or `at` method to reverse the process. For currencies, it means a decimal number stored as a JSON string. (The JSON spec allows any number to be floating point. As a result, numbers cannot be trusted to accurately contain hundredths without adding or subtracting small fractions.)

Ultimately, the way to use JSON to store such data always boils down to this: Convert it into a string or floating point number and then later parse that string or number back into the object you actually want.

15.1.3   Other JSON Libraries

In addition to the `json` standard library, a number of additional libraries provide specialized JSON functionality.

Sometimes JSON documents are so large that they will not fit entirely into memory, and need to be streamed from a file or over a network. In those cases, it is possible to use the `json-stream` gem to parse the JSON document as a stream. With stream parsing, it is possible to run a specific block of code any time a document, array, or object starts or ends, or whenever a key or value is parsed. Refer to the `json-stream` gem's documentation for further information.

Another common use of JSON on the Web is to use a long-running HTTP connection to send a stream of events, with each event encoded as a separate JSON document. The Twitter API is perhaps the most common example of this use case, but many other activity streams offer similar APIs. The `yajl-ruby` gem is specifically optimized to handle this case. It can stream-parse JSON objects from an `IO` object as well as make the entire HTTP request itself, calling the provided block each time a JSON document is finished parsing.

Finally, there is the `oj` gem, which is written in C and is highly optimized for high-speed encoding and parsing. It has sometimes been subtly incompatible with other JSON encoders, so be sure to test the results when using it. That said, its performance is highly impressive, and can be up to two to five times faster than the other JSON gems.

15.2 Parsing XML (and HTML)

XML, the *eXtensible Markup Language*, is a tag-based markup language. HTML, the *HyperText Markup Language*, is very similar (and, in fact, both XML and HTML are based on an earlier tag-based system called SGML). XML and HTML both rose to massive popularity in the 1990s, and are still used heavily today in development tools, program data storage and transfer, and all over the Web.

In XML and HTML, every element is named, and the entire document is hierarchically structured. Although it is highly verbose, everything is written in plain text and can be read by a human being directly, if needed. Another advantage over formats from the 70s and 80s is that XML allows variable-length data, rather than requiring each data field to fit into a specific number of bytes.

Three or four decades ago, memory constraints would have rendered XML largely impractical. However, if it had been used back then, issues such as the infamous "Y2K" problem would never have occurred (although even Y2K turned out to be more of a nuisance than a problem). There was a Y2K issue solely because most of our legacy data was stored and manipulated in fixed-length formats. So, although it has shortcomings, XML also has its uses.

In Ruby, the most common way to read, manipulate, and write XML or HTML is with the Nokogiri gem. The gem provides a Ruby interface (also called *binding*) for the `libXML2` library, which is written in C. Nokogiri has two primary APIs, which could be called *document based* and *stream based*. We'll look at both approaches.

15.2.1 Document Parsing

In a document-based approach, the entire file is parsed into a hierarchical, tree-like structure. This structure can be navigated, similar to the way we navigated hashes parsed from JSON earlier. Unlike hashes, Nokogiri documents also provide a *query language* that can be used to select only a particular subset of the elements in the document. Nokogiri supports two query languages: CSS selectors and XPaths.

Parsing HTML using the Nokogiri library can be done using the `Nokogiri::HTML` class method `parse`. The resulting document can be navigated and manipulated the same way as an XML document can, so we will only give XML examples here.

For our XML code examples, we'll use the same simple XML file (shown in Listing 15.1). It represents part of a private library of books.

Listing 15.1   The `books.xml` File

```
<library shelf="Recent Acquisitions">
  <section name="Ruby">
    <book isbn="0321714636">
      <title>The Ruby Way</title>
      <author>Hal Fulton</author>
      <author>André Arko</author>
      <description>Third edition. The book you are now reading.
                   Ain't recursion grand?
      </description>
    </book>
  </section>
  <section name="Space">
    <book isbn="0684835509">
      <title>The Case for Mars</title>
      <author>Robert Zubrin</author>
      <description>Pushing toward a second home for the human
                   race.
      </description>
    </book>
    <book isbn="074325631X">
      <title>First Man: The Life of Neil A. Armstrong</title>
      <author>James R. Hansen</author>
      <description>Definitive biography of the first man on
                   the moon.
      </description>
    </book>
  </section>
</library>
```

Let's first parse our XML data as a document. We begin by requiring the nokogiri library and then parsing the XML:

```
require 'nokogiri'
doc = Nokogiri::XML.parse File.read("books.xml")

doc.root.name        # library
doc.root["shelf"]    # Recent Acquisitions
```

The `root` method returns an instance of `Nokogiri::XML::Element` that represents the "root" XML tag that contains the rest of the document. Any attributes on a tag (set inside the angle brackets) can be read with the `[]` method, similar to accessing a hash. Next, we navigate the document and select some other elements:

```
books = doc.css("section book")      # a NodeSet, much like an array
books = doc.xpath("//section/book") # the same NodeSet

books.each do |book|
  title = book.elements.first.text
  authors = book.css("author").map(&:text)
  puts "#{title} (ISBN #{book["isbn"]})"
  puts "  by #{authors.join(' and ')}"
end
# Output:
# The Ruby Way (ISBN 0672328844)
#   by Hal Fulton and André Arko
# The Case for Mars (ISBN 0684835509)
#   by Robert Zubrin
# First Man: The Life of Neil A. Armstrong (ISBN 074325631X)
#   by James R. Hansen
```

Using the `css` and `xpath` methods, we are able to select only `book` tags that are also inside `section` tags. For detailed information about CSS selectors or XPath syntax, refer to a documentation website such as `developer.mozilla.org`. The methods both return a `NodeSet`, which acts much like an array. It provides methods such as `each` and `size`, as well as allowing indexed access with `[]`.

Once we have selected the `book` tags, we use them to print the text from the first element (which is the `title` tag), and we then use the `css` method to get the `author` tags inside each individual `book` tag. Finally, we read the `"isbn"` attribute from each book using the `[]` method, and print information about each book. Now let's look at the `section` tags:

```
doc.root.elements.map{|e| e["name"] }  # ["Ruby", "Space"]
```

```
space = doc.at_css("section[name=Space]")       # an Element
space = doc.at_xpath("//section[@name='Space']") # the same Element

books.include?(space.elements.first)  # true
```

Each element has its own `elements` method, returning the list of elements contained inside that element. By reading the `"name"` attribute, we can see the
`section` tag names. Next, we use the `at_css` and `at_xpath` methods to select the
`section` tag whose `"name"` attribute is set to `"Space"`. The `at_` methods only return
the first element selected, if more than one element matches the given selector. Finally,
we show that the elements returned via different methods are all the same Ruby
objects, because the first `book` inside the `section` named `"Space"` is also inside the
books we selected earlier.

There are many different ways to select the same elements, including the
`elements` array and the `css` and `xpath` methods. It is also possible to use any of the
`Enumerable` methods such as `find` or `select` to select elements using a block.

You can also manipulate elements. Each method we've used here, such as `text` or
`[ ]`, has a corresponding setter that can be used to add, delete, or modify attributes and
element contents. Afterward, the new XML or HTML can be written to a string using
the `to_xml` or `to_html`, respectively.

For more information on using Nokogiri to parse XML and HTML documents,
see the full API documentation at nokogiri.org.

15.2.2 Stream Parsing

The stream-style approach is a "parse as you go" technique, useful when your documents are large or you have memory limitations; it parses the file as it reads it from
disk, and the entire file is never stored in memory. Instead, as each element is read,
user-supplied methods or blocks are run as *callbacks*. This allows the entire file to be
processed incrementally.

Let's process the same XML data file in a stream-oriented way. (We probably
wouldn't do that in reality because this file is small.) There are variations on this concept, but Listing 15.2 shows one way. The trick is to define a *listener* class whose methods will be the target of callbacks from the parser. When you're parsing XML, make
your class a subclass of `Nokogiri::XML::SAX::Document`. When you're parsing
HTML, subclass `Nokogiri::HTML::SAX::Document` instead.

Listing 15.2 Stream Parsing

```ruby
require 'nokogiri'
class Listener < Nokogiri::XML::SAX::Document
  def start_element(name, attrs = [])
    case name
    when "book"
      isbn = attrs.find{|k,v| k == "isbn" }.last
      puts "New book with ISBN number #{isbn}"
    when "title", "author", "description"
      print "#{name.capitalize}: "
    else
    end
  end

  def characters(string)
    return unless string =~ /\w/ # ignore all-whitespace
    print string.tr("\n", " ").squeeze(" ")
  end

  def end_element(name)
    print "\n" if %w[book title author description].include?(name)
  end

  def end_document
    puts "The document has ended."
  end
end

xml = File.read("books.xml")
Nokogiri::XML::SAX::Parser.new(Listener.new).parse(xml)
```

The `Nokogiri::XML::SAX::Document` class provides empty callback methods, which we override in our subclass `Listener`. For example, when the parser encounters an opening tag, it calls the `start_element` method with the name of the tag and any attributes set on that tag. Inside that method, we use the name of the tag to decide what to do: If it is a `book` tag, we announce that a new book has been found, and we print its ISBN number. If it is a `title`, `author`, or `description`, we print that name, and for other tags, we do nothing.

In the `characters` method, the guard clause at the beginning of the method returns without printing unless the string contains at least one "word" character. Then, we simply print the text inside any tag, after replacing newlines with spaces and replacing any repeated spaces with a single space.

The `end_element` method prints a newline when each book information tag ends, after we have printed out the text that was contained inside that tag. We check the list of tags because we do not want to print a newline at the end of `section` and `library` tags. The `end_document` method works similarly, but it's only called once.

Although Listing 15.2 is somewhat contrived, using it to process `books.xml` produces the organized (and hopefully useful) output seen in Listing 15.3.

Listing 15.3   Output from the Stream Parsing Example

```
New book with ISBN number 0321714636
Title: The Ruby Way
Author: Hal Fulton
Author: André Arko
Description: Third edition. The book you are now reading.
Ain't recursion grand?

New book with ISBN number 0684835509
Title: The Case for Mars
Author: Robert Zubrin
Description: Pushing toward a second home for the human race.

New book with ISBN number 074325631X
Title: First Man: The Life of Neil A. Armstrong
Author: James R. Hansen
Description: Definitive biography of the first man on the moon.

The document has ended.
```

For more information on using Nokogiri to parse XML and HTML documents, see the full API documentation at nokogiri.org.

15.3   Working with RSS and Atom

As the Web grew, developers noticed a need to announce events, changes, or just content that had been newly added to a particular site. The solution that eventually emerged is typically referred to as a site's *feed*, served as XML structured according to the RSS or Atom feed standard.

RSS (Really Simple Syndication) was standardized early on in the development of the Internet, and different developers extended it with additional features in interesting (and sometimes contradictory) ways. A new standardization effort eventually produced Atom, which is the most capable and widely used feed format today.

RSS is XML based, so you *could* simply parse it as XML. However, the fact that it is slightly higher level makes it appropriate to have a dedicated parser for the format. Furthermore, the messiness of the RSS standard is legendary, and it is not

unusual at all for broken software to produce RSS that a parser may have great difficulty parsing.

This inconvenience is even more true because there are multiple incompatible
versions of the RSS standard; the most common versions are 0.9, 1.0, and 2.0. The
RSS versions, like the manufacturing of hotdogs, are something whose details you
don't want to know unless you must.

15.3.1   Parsing Feeds

Let's look briefly at processing both RSS and Atom using the Ruby standard library
`rss`, which can seamlessly handle not only all three versions of RSS, but Atom as well.
Here, we take the feed from NASA's Astronomy Picture of the Day service and then
print the title of each item in the feed:

```
require 'rss'
require 'open-uri'

xml = open("http://apod.nasa.gov/apod.rss").read
feed = RSS::Parser.parse(xml, false)

puts feed.channel.description
feed.items.each_with_index do |item, i|
  puts "#{i + 1}. #{item.title.strip}"
end
```

Note how the RSS parser retrieves the *channel* for the RSS feed; our code then
prints the title associated with that channel. There is also a list of items (retrieved by
the `items` accessor), which can be thought of as a list of articles. Our code retrieves
the entire list and prints the title of each one.

Of course, the output from this is highly time sensitive, but here are the results
when I ran that code:

```
Astronomy Picture of the Day
1. Star Trails Over Indonesia
2. Jupiter and Venus from Earth
3. No X rays from SN 2014J
4. Perseid in Moonlight
5. Surreal Moon
6. Rings Around the Ring Nebula
7. Collapse in Hebes Chasma on Mars
```

Before going any further, let me talk about courtesy to feed providers. A program like the preceding one should be run with caution because it uses the provider's bandwidth. In any real application, such as an actual feed aggregator, caching should always be done. Here is a naive (but functional) cache:

```ruby
unless File.exist?("apod.rss")
  File.write("apod.rss", open("http://apod.nasa.gov/apod.rss"))
end

xml = File.read("apod.rss")
```

This simple cache just reads the feed from a file and then fetches the feed into that file if it does not exist. More useful caching would check the age of the cached file and refetch the feed if the file is older than some threshold. It would also use the HTTP header `If-Modified-Since` or `If-None-Match`. However, such a system is beyond the scope of this simple example.

Atom feeds can be parsed by the same `RSS::Parser.parse` method. The `rss` library will read the feed contents to determine which parser to use. The only real difference to note is that Atom lacks a `channel` attribute. Instead, look for the `title` and `author` attributes directly on the feed itself.

15.3.2   Generating Feeds

In addition to parsing feeds, it's also possible to generate RSS or Atom using the RSS standard library's `RSS::Maker` class. Here, we create a small Atom feed for a hypothetical website:

```ruby
require 'rss'

feed = RSS::Maker.make("atom") do |f|
  f.channel.title = "Feed Your Head"
  f.channel.id =  "http://nosuchplace.org/home/"
  f.channel.author = "Y.T."
  f.channel.logo = "http://nosuchplace.org/images/headshot.jpg"
  f.channel.updated = Time.now

  f.items.new_item do |i|
    i.title = "Once again, here we are"
    i.link = "http://nosuchplace.org/articles/once_again/"
    i.description = "Don't you feel more like you do now than usual?"
    i.updated = Time.parse("2014-08-17 10:23AM")
  end
```

```
    f.items.new_item do |i|
      i.title = "So long, and thanks for all the fiche"
      i.link = "http://nosuchplace.org/articles/so_long_and_thanks/"
      i.description = "I really miss the days of microfilm..."
      i.updated = Time.parse("2014-08-12 3:52PM")
    end
  end


  puts feed.to_xml
```

The `Maker` is created with a block initializer similar to the one we discussed in Section 11.1.3, "Using More Elaborate Constructors," of Chapter 11, "OOP and Dynamic Features in Ruby." We use the block to set the feed's `title`, `id`, `author`, and `updated` timestamp, because they are all required for the Atom feed to be valid.

Then, we use the `new_item` method, which creates a new feed entry and adds it to the feed's list of entries, again using a block. Each item has a `title`, `description` (or summary), `link` to the URL with the full content, and an `updated` timestamp. The optional `content` attribute provides a place to include the full content in the feed, if desired.

The RSS standard library is fairly well developed, but keep in mind that other libraries exist to both parse and generate RSS and Atom feeds. If your needs aren't well served by the standard library, check ruby-toolbox.com and search around the Web to see if there's something that suits you better.

15.4 Manipulating Image Data with RMagick

As computers, tablets, and phones become the dominant way to consume media, working with images and graphics is becoming a more and more important part of creating programs. Programmers need ways to create and manipulate images across different platforms in many different, complicated formats. In Ruby, the easiest way to do this is with RMagick, a gem created by Tim Hunter.

The RMagick gem is a Ruby binding for the ImageMagick library. It can be installed by running `gem install rmagick`, but you must you have the ImageMagick library installed first. If you are on Linux, you probably already have it; if you are on Mac OS X, you can install it using Homebrew. If you need help installing it, the ImageMagick website at http://imagemagick.org might be a good place to start.

Because RMagick is just a binding, it is able to support all the image formats supported by the underlying library. Those include all the common ones, such as JPG, GIF, PNG, and TIFF, but also dozens of others. The same is true for the operations

RMagick can perform. The gem implements the full ImageMagick API, adapted to Ruby via the use of symbols, blocks, and other features.

The ImageMagick API is really huge, by the way. This chapter would not be enough to cover it in detail, nor would this book. The upcoming sections will give you a good background in RMagick, however, and you can find out anything else you may need from the project website at http://www.imagemagick.org/RMagick/doc/.

15.4.1   Common Graphics Tasks

One of the easiest and most common tasks you might want to perform on an image file is simply to determine its characteristics (width and height in pixels, and so on). Let's look at retrieving a few of these pieces of metadata.

Figure 15.1 shows a pair of simple images that we'll use for this code example (and later examples in the next section). The first one (`smallpic.jpg`) is a simple abstract picture created with a drawing program; it features a few different shades of gray, a few straight lines, and a few curves. The second is a photograph I took in 2002 of a battered automobile in rural Mexico. Both images were converted to grayscale for printing purposes. Listing 15.4 shows how to read these images and extract a few pieces of information.

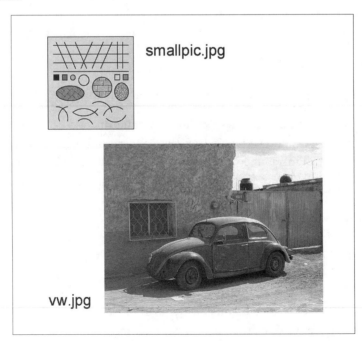

Figure 15.1   Two sample image files

Listing 15.4   Retrieving Information from an Image

```ruby
require 'rmagick'

def show_info(fname)
  img = Magick::Image::read(fname).first
  fmt = img.format
  w,h = img.columns, img.rows
  dep = img.depth
  nc = img.number_colors
  nb = img.filesize
  xr = img.x_resolution
  yr = img.y_resolution
  res = Magick::PixelsPerInchResolution ? "inch" : "cm"

  puts <<-EOF.gsub(/^\s+/, '')
  File:       #{fname}
  Format:     #{fmt}
  Dimensions: #{w}x#{h} pixels
  Colors:     #{nc}
  Image size: #{nb} bytes
  Resolution: #{xr}/#{yr} pixels per #{res}
  EOF
  puts
end

show_info("smallpic.jpg")
show_info("vw.jpg")
```

Here is the output of the Listing 15.4 code:

```
File:       smallpic.jpg
Format:     JPEG
Dimensions: 257x264 pixels
Colors:     248
Image size: 19116 bytes
Resolution: 72.0/72.0 pixels per inch

File:       vw.jpg
Format:     JPEG
Dimensions: 640x480 pixels
Colors:     256
Image size: 55892 bytes
Resolution: 72.0/72.0 pixels per inch
```

Now let's examine the details of how the code in Listing 15.4 gave us that output. Notice how we retrieve all the contents of a file with `Magick::Image::read`. Because a file (such as an animated GIF) can contain more than one image, this operation actually returns an array of images (and we look at the first one by calling `first`). We can also use `Magick::ImageList.new` to read an image file.

The image object has a number of readers such as `format` (the name of the image format), `filesize`, `depth`, and others that are intuitive. It may be less intuitive that the width and height of the object are retrieved by `columns` and `rows`, respectively. (This is because we are supposed to think of an image as a grid of pixels.) It also may not be intuitive that the resolution is stored as two numbers. Images can have rectangular pixels, which produces different horizontal and vertical resolutions.

There are many other properties and pieces of metadata you can retrieve from an image. Refer to the online documentation for RMagick for more details.

One common task we often perform is to convert an image from one format to another. The easy way to do this in RMagick is to read an image in any supported format and then write it to another file. The file extension is used to determine the new format. Needless to say, it does a lot of conversion behind the scenes. Here is a simple example:

```
img = Magick::Image.read("smallpic.jpg")
img.first.write("smallpic.gif")              # Convert to a GIF
```

Frequently, we want to change the size of an image (smaller or larger). The most common methods for this are `thumbnail`, `resize`, and `scale`. These can all accept either a floating point number (representing a scaling factor) or a pair of numbers (representing the actual new dimensions in pixels). Other differences are summarized in Listing 15.5 and its comments.

Listing 15.5 Four Ways to Resize an Image

```
require 'rmagick'

img = Magick::ImageList.new("vw.jpg")

# Thumbnail is designed to shrink a large image to a small
# preview. It is the fastest, especially with small sizes.

pic1 = img.thumbnail(0.2)        # Reduce to 20%
pic2 = img.thumbnail(64,48)      # Reduce to 64x48 pixels

# Resize is medium speed, and makes an image fit inside the
# given dimensions without changing aspect ratio. The
# optional 3rd and 4th parameters are the filter and blur,
```

```
# defaulting to LanczosFilter and 1.0, respectively.

pic3 = img.resize(0.40)        # Reduce to 40%
pic4 = img.resize(320, 240)    # Fit inside 320x240
pic5 = img.resize(300, 200, Magick::LanczosFilter, 0.92)

# Scale is the slowest, as it scales each dimension of the
# image independently (distorting it if necessary).

pic8 = img.scale(0.60)         # Reduce to 60%
pic9 = img.scale(400, 300)     # Reduce to 400x300
```

Many other transformations can be performed on an image. Some of these are simple and easy to understand, whereas others are complex. We'll explore a few interesting transformations and special effects in the next section.

15.4.2   Special Effects and Transformations

Some operations we might want to do on an image are to flip it, reverse it, rotate it, distort it, alter its colors, and so on. RMagick provides literally dozens of methods to perform such operations, and many of these are highly "tunable" by their parameters.

Listing 15.6 demonstrates 12 different effects. To make the code a little more concise, the method `example` simply takes a filename, a symbol corresponding to a method, and a new filename; it basically does a read, a method call, and a write. The individual methods (such as `do_rotate`) are simple for the most part; these are where the image passed in gets an actual instance method called (and then the resulting image is the return value).

Listing 15.6   Twelve Special Effects and Transformations

```
require 'RMagick'

def do_flip(img)
  img.flip
end

def do_rotate(img)
  img.rotate(45)
end

def do_implode(img)
  img = img.implode(0.65)
end

def do_resize(img)
  img.resize(120,240)
```

```ruby
end

def do_text(img)
  text = Magick::Draw.new
  text.annotate(img, 0, 0, 0, 100, "HELLO") do
    self.gravity = Magick::SouthGravity
    self.pointsize = 72
    self.stroke = 'black'
    self.fill = '#FAFAFA'
    self.font_weight = Magick::BoldWeight
    self.font_stretch = Magick::UltraCondensedStretch
  end
  img
end

def do_emboss(img)
  img.emboss
end


def do_spread(img)
  img.spread(10)
end

def do_motion(img)
  img.motion_blur(0,30,170)
end

def do_oil(img)
  img.oil_paint(10)
end

def do_charcoal(img)
  img.charcoal
end

def do_vignette(img)
  img.vignette
end

def do_affine(img)
  spin_xform = Magick::AffineMatrix.new(
    1, Math::PI/6, Math::PI/6, 1, 0, 0)
  img.affine_transform(spin_xform)          # Apply the transform
end


def example(old_file, meth, new_file)
  img = Magick::ImageList.new(old_file)
  new_img = send(meth,img)
  new_img.write(new_file)
end
```

```
example("smallpic.jpg", :do_flip,    "flipped.jpg")
example("smallpic.jpg", :do_rotate, "rotated.jpg")
example("smallpic.jpg", :do_resize, "resized.jpg")
example("smallpic.jpg", :do_implode, "imploded.jpg")
example("smallpic.jpg", :do_text,    "withtext.jpg")
example("smallpic.jpg", :do_emboss, "embossed.jpg")

example("vw.jpg", :do_spread,   "vw_spread.jpg")
example("vw.jpg", :do_motion,   "vw_motion.jpg")
example("vw.jpg", :do_oil,      "vw_oil.jpg")
example("vw.jpg", :do_charcoal, "vw_char.jpg")
example("vw.jpg", :do_vignette, "vw_vig.jpg")
example("vw.jpg", :do_affine,   "vw_spin.jpg")
```

The methods used here are `flip`, `rotate`, `implode`, `resize`, `annotate`, and others. The results are shown in Figure 15.2 in a montage.

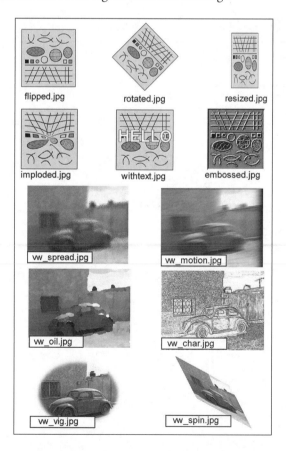

Figure 15.2   Twelve special effects and transformations

Many other transformations can be performed on an image. Consult the online documentation at http://www.imagemagick.org/RMagick/doc/.

15.4.3   The Drawing API

RMagick has an extensive drawing API for drawing lines, polygons, and curves of various kinds. It deals with filling, opacity, colors, text fonts, rotating/skewing, and other issues.

A full treatment of the API is beyond the scope of this book. Let's look at a simple example, however, to understand a few concepts.

Listing 15.7 shows a program that draws a simple grid on the background and draws a few filled shapes on that grid. The image is converted to grayscale, resulting in the image shown in Figure 15.3.

Listing 15.7   A Simple Drawing

```
require 'rmagick'

img = Magick::ImageList.new
img.new_image(500, 500)

purplish = "#ff55ff"
yuck = "#5fff62"
bleah = "#3333ff"

line = Magick::Draw.new
50.step(450, 50) do |n|
  line.line(n, 50, n, 450) # vert line
  line.draw(img)
  line.line(50, n, 450, n) # horiz line
  line.draw(img)
end

# Draw a circle
cir = Magick::Draw.new
cir.fill(purplish)
cir.stroke('black').stroke_width(1)
cir.circle(250, 200, 250, 310)
cir.draw(img)

rect = Magick::Draw.new
rect.stroke('black').stroke_width(1)
rect.fill(yuck)
rect.rectangle(340, 380, 237, 110)
rect.draw(img)

tri = Magick::Draw.new
tri.stroke('black').stroke_width(1)
```

```
tri.fill(bleah)
tri.polygon(90, 320, 160, 370, 390, 120)
tri.draw(img)

img = img.quantize(256, Magick::GRAYColorspace)
img.write("drawing.gif")
```

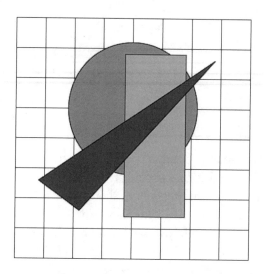

Figure 15.3 A simple drawing

Let's examine Listing 15.7 in detail. We start by creating an "empty" image with `ImageList.new` and then calling `new_image` on the result. Think of this as giving us a "blank canvas" of the specified size (500 by 500 pixels).

For convenience, let's define a few colors (with creative names such as `purplish` and `yuck`). These are strings that specify colors just as we would in HTML. The underlying ImageMagick library is also capable of understanding many color names such as `"red"` and `"black"`; when in doubt, experiment or specify the color in hex.

We then create a drawing object called `line`; this is the Ruby object corresponding to the graphical object we will see on the screen. The variable is sometimes named `gc` or something similar (probably standing for *graphics context*), but a more descriptive name seems natural here.

We then call the method `line` on our drawing object (which admittedly gets a little confusing). In fact, we call it repeatedly, twice in each iteration of a loop. If you spend a moment studying the coordinates, you'll see that each iteration of the loop draws a horizontal line and a vertical one.

After each `line` call, we call `draw` on the same drawing object and pass in the image reference. This is an essential step because it is when the graphical object actually gets added to the canvas.

If you are like me, a call such as `shape.draw(image)` may be a little confusing. In general, my method calls look like this:

```
big_thing.operation(little_thing)
# For example: dog.wag(tail)
```

However, the call in question feels to me more like this:

```
little_thing.operation(big_thing)
# Continuing the analogy: tail.wag(dog)
```

But this idiom is actually common, especially in the realm of drawing programs and GUI frameworks. And it makes perfect sense in a classic OOP way: A shape should know how to draw itself, implying it should have a `draw` method. It needs to know where to draw itself, so it needs the canvas (or whatever) passed in.

If you're not like me, though, you were never bothered by the question of which object should be the receiver. That puts you at a tiny advantage.

So after we draw the grid of lines, we then draw a few shapes. The `circle` method takes the center of the circle and a *point* on the circle as parameters. (Notice we don't draw by specifying the radius!) The `rectangle` method is even simpler; we draw it by specifying the upper-left corner (lower-numbered coordinates) and the lower-right corner (higher-numbered coordinates). Finally, we draw a triangle, which is just a special case of a polygon; we specify each point in order, and the final line (from end point to start point) is added automatically.

Each of these graphical objects has a few methods called that we haven't looked at yet. Look at this "chained" call:

```
shape.stroke('black').stroke_width(1)
```

This gives us a "pen" of sorts; it draws in black ink with a width of 1 pixel. The color of the stroke actually does matter in many cases, especially when we are trying to fill a shape with a color.

That, of course, is the other method we call on our three shapes. We call `fill` to specify what color it should have. (There are other more complex kinds of filling involving hatching, shading, and so on.) The `fill` method replaces the interior color of the shape with the specified color, knowing that the stroke color serves as a boundary between "inside" and "outside" the shape.

Numerous other methods in the drawing API deal with opacity, spatial transformations, and many more things. There are methods that analyze, draw, and manipulate graphical text strings. There is even a special RVG API (Ruby Vector Graphics) that is conformant to the W3C recommendation on SVG (Scalable Vector Graphics).

There is no room here to document these and many other features. For more information, go to http://www.imagemagick.org/RMagick/doc/, as usual.

15.5 Creating PDF Documents with Prawn

The Portable Document Format (PDF), originally popularized by Adobe's Acrobat Reader, has been popular for many years. It has proven useful in distributing "printer-ready" documents in a rich format that is independent of any particular word processing software or operating system.

The most widely adopted library for creating PDFs from Ruby is the Prawn gem, created by Gregory Brown and many other contributors. We'll look at how Prawn works and then use it to create a PDF document.

15.5.1 Basic Concepts and Techniques

The class that "drives" Prawn is `Prawn::Document`. This class enables the creation of PDF documents using two or three coding styles. Here is one example:

```
require "prawn"

doc = Prawn::Document.new        # Start a new document
doc.text "Lorem ipsum dolor..."  # Add some text
doc.render_file "my_first.pdf"   # Write to a file
```

Alternatively, you may call the class method `generate` and pass it the output file name and a block:

```
Prawn::Document.generate("portrait.pdf") do
  text "Once upon a time and a very good time it was "
  text "there was a moocow coming down along the road..."
end
```

If you specify a parameter for the block, the generator object is passed in explicitly:

```
Prawn::Document.generate("ericblair.pdf") do |doc|
  doc.text "It was a bright cold day in April, "
  doc.text "and the clocks were striking thirteen."
end
```

These forms are all basically equivalent. Choosing one is mostly a matter of style and convenience.

Now let's talk about *page coordinates*. The origin of a PDF page is [0,0] (which is at the bottom left of the page, as we're used to in mathematics). A *bounding box* is an imaginary rectangle within the space of a page. There is one default bounding box called the *margin box*, which serves as a container or boundary for all content on the page.

The *cursor* in Prawn naturally starts at the top, even though the coordinate system has its origin at the bottom. Adding text to the document moves the cursor (or the cursor can be moved manually via such methods as move_cursor_to, move_up, and move_down). The method cursor returns the current cursor position.

Prawn uses the "standard" measurement of a *point* (which is 1/72 inch). If you require 'prawn/measurement_extensions' you can use other units as needed.

Prawn also has a large set of text-handling routines as well as graphics primitives for drawing lines, curves, and shapes.

15.5.2   An Example Document

Let's look at a fairly contrived example. This program (see Listing 15.8) divides the page into four rectangles and places different items in each of them. Figure 15.4 shows the result.

Listing 15.8   pdf-demo.rb

```
require 'prawn'

# Adapted from code contributed by Brad Ediger

class DemoDocument
  def initialize
    @pdf = Prawn::Document.new
  end
```

```ruby
  def render_file(file)
    render
    @pdf.render_file(file)
  end

  def render
    side = @pdf.bounds.width / 2.0
    box(0,    0,    side, side) { star }
    box(side, 0,    side, side) { heart }
    box(0,    side, side, side) { ruby }
    box(side, side, side, side) { misc_text }
  end

  private

  # Run the given block in a bounding box inset from the parent by
  # 'padding' PDF points.
  def inset(padding)
    left = @pdf.bounds.left + padding
    top  = @pdf.bounds.top - padding
    @pdf.bounding_box([left, top],
      width: @pdf.bounds.width - 2*padding,
      height: @pdf.bounds.height - 2*padding) { yield }
  end

  # Draw a width-by-heigt box at (x, y), yielding inside a bounding
  # box so content may be drawn inside.
  def box(x, y, w, h)
    @pdf.bounding_box([x, @pdf.bounds.top - y], width: w, height: h) do
      @pdf.stroke_bounds
      inset(10) { yield }
    end
  end

  def star
    reps = 15
    size = 0.24 * @pdf.bounds.width
    radius = 0.26 * @pdf.bounds.width
    center_x = @pdf.bounds.width / 2.0
    center_y = @pdf.bounds.height / 2.0
    reps.times do |i|
      @pdf.rotate i * 360.0 / reps, origin: [center_x, center_y] do
        edge = center_y + radius
        @pdf.draw_text ")", size: size, at: [center_x, edge]
      end
    end
  end

  def ruby
    @pdf.image "ruby.png",
               at: [0, @pdf.cursor],
               width: @pdf.bounds.width,
```

```ruby
          height: @pdf.bounds.height
  end

  def heart
    10.times do |i|
      inset(i*10) do
        box = @pdf.bounds
        center = box.width / 2.0
        cusp_y = 0.6 * box.top

        k = center * Prawn::Graphics::KAPPA
        @pdf.stroke_color(0, 0, 0, 100-(i*10))
        @pdf.stroke do
          # Draw a heart using a Bezier curve with two paths
          paths = [[0, 0.9*center], [box.right, 1.1*center]]
          paths.each do |side, midside|
            @pdf.move_to [center, cusp_y]
            @pdf.curve_to [side, cusp_y],
              bounds: [[center, cusp_y + k], [side, cusp_y + k]]
            @pdf.curve_to [center, box.bottom],
              bounds: [[side, 0.6 * cusp_y], [midside, box.bottom]]
          end
        end
      end
    end

    # reset stroke color
    @pdf.stroke_color 0, 0, 0, 100
  end

  def misc_text
    first_lines = <<-EOF
      Call me Ishmael. Somewhere in la Mancha, in a place whose
      name I do not care to remember, a gentleman lived not long
      ago, one of those who has a lance and ancient shield on a
      shelf and keeps a skinny nag and a greyhound for racing.
      The sky above the port was the color of television, tuned to
      a dead channel. It was a pleasure to burn. Granted: I am an
      inmate of a mental hospital; my keeper is watching me, he
      never lets me out of his sight; there's a peephole in the
      door, and my keeper's eye is the shade of brown that can
      never see through a blue-eyed type like me. Whether I shall
      turn out to be the hero of my own life, or whether that
      station will be held by anybody else, these pages must show.
      I have never begun a novel with more misgiving.
    EOF
    first_lines.gsub!(/\n/, " ")
    first_lines.gsub!(/ +/, " ")
    @pdf.text first_lines
  end
end

DemoDocument.new.render_file("demo.pdf")
```

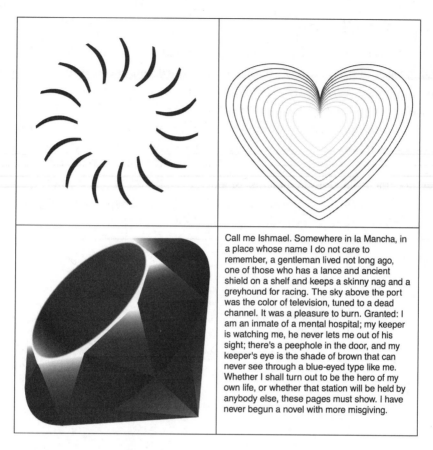

Call me Ishmael. Somewhere in la Mancha, in a place whose name I do not care to remember, a gentleman lived not long ago, one of those who has a lance and ancient shield on a shelf and keeps a skinny nag and a greyhound for racing. The sky above the port was the color of television, tuned to a dead channel. It was a pleasure to burn. Granted: I am an inmate of a mental hospital; my keeper is watching me, he never lets me out of his sight; there's a peephole in the door, and my keeper's eye is the shade of brown that can never see through a blue-eyed type like me. Whether I shall turn out to be the hero of my own life, or whether that station will be held by anybody else, these pages must show. I have never begun a novel with more misgiving.

Figure 15.4   Output of `pdf-demo.rb`

The top two "boxes" illustrate the use of the drawing API. In the upper left, we see an abstract "star" pattern created by drawing a sequence of arcs with the same radius but different centers. In the upper right, a more advanced use of the drawing API uses Bezier curves to produce a heart shape.

In the lower left, we embed a PNG image using the `image` method. Finally, in the lower right, we see simple text wrapping around its bounding box.

This example, however, illustrates only a tiny portion of the Prawn API. Consult the reference documentation at prawnpdf.org for complete information on the rich API.

15.6   Conclusion

In this chapter, we have looked at how to parse and manipulate JSON, and how to use Nokogiri to parse XML in both stream-oriented and document-oriented styles. We've looked at parsing feeds in XML-based formats, and have seen how the rss library handles reading and writing both RSS and Atom.

We've looked at reading and manipulating graphic images in many formats with RMagick; we've also seen its drawing API, which enables us to add arbitrary text and shapes to an image. Finally, we've seen how Prawn can produce complex, high-quality PDF documents in a programmatic fashion.

In the next chapter, we will look at a different topic entirely. The next chapter deals with effective testing and debugging in Ruby.

CHAPTER 16

Testing and Debugging

I've just picked up a fault in the AE35 unit. It's going to go 100% failure in 72 hours.

—HAL 9000, in 2001: A Space Odyssey

Testing is important. All competent programmers know this fact, even if it isn't always at the forefront of their minds.

Of course, true exhaustive testing is usually impossible. A program or system of any significant size is always going to hold a few surprises as it goes through its life cycle. The best we can do is to test carefully and selectively, and get as wide a coverage as we can.

Historically, programmers don't always test as adequately as they should. The typical reasons for this are tests that are difficult to set up and run, require manual intervention, or take too long to run.

In the 1990s, the computing community saw a "culture of testing" reach maturity. The term *extreme programming* is now old-fashioned, but the foundations are still relevant. Concepts such as *test-driven development* (TDD) and *behavior-driven development* (BDD) have gained firm mindshare among developers everywhere.

Whether you are a hard-core "test first" person is not the point. The point is that *everyone* can benefit from tests that are automated, easy to write, and easy to run.

Testing tools are in general easier to write in Ruby because Ruby is dynamic and flexible. In the same way, they are easy to use and (dare I say it?) sometimes even *fun* to use. There is something satisfying about making a software change and then watching every test run to completion and pass.

Besides these testing tools, Ruby also has various other tools and libraries for debugging, profiling, and code coverage. This chapter gives an overview of what is available.

We'll start with the very popular RSpec, and also look at Minitest, which provides the classic style of testing. In addition, we'll look at Cucumber for acceptance testing, and do a quick overview of other tools.

16.1   Testing with RSpec

In recent years, the idea of behavior-driven development (BDD) has become very widespread. This is the idea that a specification of a system's behavior is a natural basis for testing it.

RSpec, the work of David Chelimsky and others, is probably the most common BDD framework for Ruby. It was originally based on JBehave for Java.

For the purposes of illustrating this testing framework as well as others, we'll introduce a small piece of code here. (I hope you don't mind a little flashback to 9th-grade math.)

The method `quadratic` (which we'll store in the file `quadratic.rb`) solves a simple quadratic equation. It takes the three coefficients of a simple polynomial and returns an array of zero, one, or two real roots. For a little extra functionality, the fourth parameter is a Boolean value that tells whether to allow complex values as results:

```ruby
require 'complex'

def quadratic(a, b, c, complex=false)
  raise ArgumentError unless [a, b, c].all? {|x| Numeric === x }
  discr = b*b - 4*a*c
  if (discr > 0) || (complex && discr < 0)
    val = Math.sqrt(discr)
    r1 = (-b + val)/(2*a.to_f)
    r2 = (-b - val)/(2*a.to_f)
    return [r1, r2]
  elsif discr.zero?
    r1 = -b/(2*a.to_f)
    return [r1]
  else # complex is false here
```

```
        return []
    end

end
```

To test this, we'll put together a fairly simple set of RSpec tests to be run using the `rspec` gem. These tests normally live under a `spec` directory and have a base name ending in _spec with an `.rb` extension.

In general, a single spec file tests a "chunk" of related functionality. This chunk usually corresponds to a single class, but may be smaller or larger than a class.

A typical spec file has the following form:

```
# spec/foobar_spec.rb
require 'foobar'

RSpec.describe Foobar do
  describe "some_method" do
    it "returns something when called" do
      # Test code here...
    end
  end
end
```

After installing the `rspec` gem, you can run this spec file with the RSpec runner:

```
$ rspec spec/foobar_spec.rb
```

When `rspec` is run, it reads the `.rspec` file for command-line options. The default `.rspec` file contains —require `spec_helper`. This file, `spec/spec_helper.rb`, is a place to configure RSpec or place shared code that we need during testing. It is optional.

The spec file itself must require whatever class or other code is about to be tested. In our examples, we assume that the code being tested is located in `lib`. RSpec (or the spec helper) should add the `lib` directory to Ruby's `$LOAD_PATH` so that files inside it can be required directly, as in the preceding example.

The `describe` method takes a parameter that is typically a class name but may be a descriptive string. The block contains all the test examples (and may also contain nested describe-blocks).

Now let's look at a test of our quadratic formula method. See Listing 16.1 for the contents of the `quadratic_spec.rb` file.

Listing 16.1 Testing `quadratic.rb` with RSpec

```
require 'quadratic'

describe "Quadratic equation solver" do
  it "can take integers as arguments" do
    expect(quadratic(1, 2, 1)).to eq([-1.0])
  end

  it "can take floats as arguments" do
    expect(quadratic(1.0, 2.0, 1.0)).to eq([-1.0])
  end

  it "returns an empty solution set when appropriate" do
    expect(quadratic(2, 3, 9)).to eq([])
  end

  it "honors the 'complex' Boolean argument" do
    solution = quadratic(1, -2, 2, true)
    expect(solution).to eq([Complex(1.0,1.0), Complex(1.0,-1.0)])
  end

  it "raises ArgumentError when for non-numeric coefficients" do
    expect { quadratic(3, 4, "foo") }.to raise_error(ArgumentError)
  end
end
```

Each test example is a call of the `it` method; this method is named so that we have the illusion of an English-like pseudo-sentence with "it" as the subject. The string parameter completes that illusion, and the block contains code that actually performs the relevant test.

The test may contain arbitrary code, but it always must contain at least one statement that does the "real test" (technically called an *expectation expression*).

A typical expectation expression consists of the `expect` method (called on a subject), an expectation, and a matcher. The expectation methods are `to` and `to_not`.

In arguably its most common form, this expression simply checks to make sure that something equals something else: `expect(result).to eq(value)`.

There are many matches, and you can define your own as well. Some of the most common ones are illustrated here (all testing `true`):

```
expect(5).to eq(5)
expect(5).to_not eq(6)
expect(5).to_not be_nil
expect(5).to be_truthy
expect(5).to_not eq(false)
```

```
expect(nil).to be_nil
expect("").to be_empty # "be_xxx" calls the "xxx?" method
expect([]).to be_empty # on the subject
expect([1,2,3]).to include(2)
expect([1,2]).to be_an(Array)
```

To test exceptions, the code must be placed inside a block that is passed to the expect method:

```
expect { x = 1 / 0 }.to raise_error
```

This raise_error method can take the class of the exception as a parameter as well as a string value. Both parameters are optional; usually the string comparison is considered overkill.

There is much more to RSpec. For advanced testing, you may need the before, after, and let methods (to handle setup, teardown, and so on). For these and other details, consult a complete reference.

Obviously RSpec does a lot of "black magic" under the hood. If it doesn't suit your taste for this or any other reason, consider trying minitest, which is based on the more traditional "test unit" style of testing.

16.2 Testing with Minitest

The minitest gem, created by Ryan Davis, allows testing Ruby code in the "classic" test-unit style. It may be included with your copy of Ruby; if not, you can install it by running gem install minitest.

The Minitest::Test class uses reflection to analyze your test code. When you subclass it, any methods named starting with test are executed as test code:

```
require 'minitest/autorun'

class TestMyThing < Minitest::Test

  def test_that_it_works
    # ...
  end

  def test_it_doesnt_do_the_wrong_thing
    # ...
  end
```

```
  # ...
end
```

It is highly inadvisable, and arguably *incorrect*, for the behavior of the tests to rely on the order in which they are run. Be careful to not write your tests in such a way that they only pass when run in the order they are written. Minitest will deliberately run them in a different random order each time.

It's also not a bad idea to put a one-line comment describing the purpose and meaning of the test, especially if it's complex or subtle. In general, each test should have one, and only one, purpose.

If we need to do some setup for each test, we can create `setup` and `teardown` methods for the class. It might seem counterintuitive, but these methods are called before and after *every* test.

What if we need to do some kind of setup that takes a long time? It's not practical to do this for every single test, and we can't put it inside the first test method (because the tests will be run in a random order). To do some setup only once, before any of the tests, you could put code in the body of the class, before the test methods (or even before the class itself).

But what if we want to do a corresponding teardown after all the tests? The "best" way is to override the class's run method so as to "wrap" its functionality. While we're at it, we add a class method for setup before all tests as well. Look at the example in Listing 16.2.

Listing 16.2 Setup and Teardown

```
require 'minitest/autorun'

class MyTest < Minitest::Test

  def self.setup
    # ...
  end

  def self.teardown
    # ...
  end

  def self.run(*)
    self.setup
    super # run each test method as usual
    self.teardown
  end
```

```
def setup
  # ...
end

def teardown
  # ...
end

def test_it_works
  # ...
end

def test_it_is_not_broken
  # ...
end

# ...
end
```

You probably won't find yourself doing this kind of thing often, but it can be extremely helpful when it's needed.

Once the tests are running, what goes inside each test? We need to have some way of deciding whether a test passed or failed. We use *assertions* for that purpose.

The simplest assertion is just the `assert` method. It takes a parameter to be tested and an optional second parameter (which is a message); if the parameter tests true (that is, anything but `false` or `nil`), all is well. If it doesn't test true, the test fails and the message (if any) is printed out.

Some other assertion methods follow (with comments indicating the meaning). Notice how the "expected" value always comes before the "actual" value; this is significant if you use the default error messages and don't want the results to be stated backward:

```
assert_equal(expected, actual) # assert(expected == actual)
refute_equal(expected, actual) # assert(expected != actual)
assert_match(regex, string)    # assert(regex =~ string)
refute_match(regex, string)    # assert(regex !~ string)
assert_nil(object)             # assert(object.nil?)
refute_nil(object)             # assert(!object.nil?)
```

Some assertions have a more object-oriented flavor (and have paired `refute` versions as well):

```
assert_instance_of(klass, obj) # assert(obj.instance_of? klass)
assert_kind_of(klass, obj)     # assert(obj.kind_of? klass)
assert_respond_to(obj, meth)   # assert(obj.respond_to? meth)
```

Some deal specifically with exceptions and thrown symbols. They do not have refute counterparts, because if throw and raise are not called, the code will simply run as usual. Because calling them stops code from running as usual, they both have to take a block:

```
assert_throws(symbol) { ... }    # checks that symbol was thrown
assert_raises(exception) { ... } # checks exception was raised
```

Collections and other Enumerable objects have a few matchers as well:

```
assert_empty(coll)         # assert(coll.empty?)
assert_includes(coll, obj) # assert(coll.includes?(obj))
```

There are several others, but these form a basic complement that will cover most of what you need. For others, consult the Minitest documentation online.

There is also a flunk method, which always fails. This is more or less just a place-holder for tests that have not been written yet.

Armed with assertions, let's test our quadratic formula. Test files go in the test directory. The naming convention is to mirror the lib directory (like RSpec), ending each filename in _test.rb (see Listing 16.3).

Listing 16.3 Testing quadratic.rb with Minitest::Test

```
require 'minitest/autorun'
require 'quadratic'

class QuadraticTest < MiniTest::Unit::TestCase
  def test_integers
    assert_equal [-1], quadratic(1, 2, 1)
  end

  def test_floats
    assert_equal [-1.0], quadratic(1.0, 2.0, 1.0)
  end

  def test_no_real_solutions
    assert_equal quadratic(2, 3, 9), []
  end

  def test_complex_solutions
```

```
    actual = quadratic(1, -2, 2, true)
    assert_equal actual, [Complex(1.0,1.0), Complex(1.0,-1.0)]
  end

  def test_bad_args
    assert_raises(ArgumentError) { quadratic(3, 4, "foo") }
  end
end
```

When you run a test file and do nothing special, the console test runner is invoked by default. This gives us feedback using good old-fashioned 1970s technology. In this case, Minitest produces the following output when running our tests:

```
Run options: —seed 7759

# Running tests:

.....

Finished tests in 0.000702s, 7122.5071 tests/s,
  7122.5071 assertions/s.

5 tests, 5 assertions, 0 failures, 0 errors, 0 skips
```

If you are a fan of RSpec, Minitest can be used in a similar style. The primary difference is that RSpec uses the `expect(subject).to` something style, Minitest uses the more direct `subject.must_something` style. See Listing 16.4 for an example.

Listing 16.4   Testing `quadratic.rb` with `Minitest::Spec`

```
require 'minitest/autorun'
require 'quadratic'

describe "Quadratic equation solver" do
  it "can take integers as arguments" do
    quadratic(1, 2, 1).must_equal([-1.0])
  end

  it "can take floats as arguments" do
    quadratic(1.0, 2.0, 1.0).must_equal([-1.0])
  end

  it "returns an empty solution set when appropriate" do
    quadratic(2, 3, 9).must_equal([])
  end
```

```
it "honors the 'complex' Boolean argument" do
  actual = quadratic(1, -2, 2, true)
  expected = [Complex(1.0,1.0), Complex(1.0,-1.0)]
  actual.must_equal expected
end

it "raises ArgumentError when for non-numeric coefficients" do
  lambda { quadratic(3, 4, "foo") }.must_raise ArgumentError
end
end
```

Running these spec-style tests produces the same output as running the tests did before.

In addition to what we've seen here, there are dozens of extensions for Minitest that add or change testing features. Some are listed in the Minitest readme, and you can check Rubygems.org and GitHub for more if you're interested.

16.3   Testing with Cucumber

Another very powerful BDD test framework is Cucumber. This uses a very simple, flexible "language" or notation called Gherkin, which is close to plain English.

It is a matter of opinion when it might be appropriate to use Cucumber. It adds overhead and maintenance to test suites, but provides an explanation of what is being tested in language that nontechnical clients or managers can understand. An ideal case might be one where semi-technical or nontechnical stakeholders take part in writing specifications.

In other situations, especially those where everyone involved has a technical background, it can be dramatically less complex to write tests (up to and including integration and acceptance tests) directly in code.

The quadratic formula example is arguably less appropriate here, but let's look at it anyhow. We'll start by creating a structure with a directory called `features` and one under it called `step_definitions`. Under `features` there could be many files; in Listing 16.5, we'll create just one, `first.feature`.

Listing 16.5   A Feature File for `quadratic.rb`

```
Feature: Check all behaviors of the quadratic equation solver

Scenario: Real roots
  Given coefficients that should yield one real root
  Then the solver returns an array of one Float r1
  And r1 is a valid solution.
```

```
    Given coefficients that should yield two real roots
    Then the solver returns an array of two Floats, r1 and r2
    And r1 and r2 are both valid solutions.

  Scenario: No real roots, and complex flag is off
    Given coefficients that should yield no real roots
    And the complex flag is missing or false
    Then the solver returns an empty array.

  Scenario: No real roots, and complex flag is on
    Given coefficients that should yield no real roots
    And the complex flag is true
    Then the solver returns an array of two complex roots, r1 and r2
    And r1 and r2 are both valid solutions.
```

If you run Cucumber at this point, it does a clever and helpful thing—it creates a "skeleton" for you to use in writing *step definitions*, which are merely the Ruby implementations of the tests you described in the English-like spec. You can copy this into a file (in this case, I used step_definitions/first.rb) and modify it as you go along. Tests are already marked pending so that they will not "fail" when there is no code yet written.

Here is an example of that skeleton output:

```
Given(/^coefficients that should yield one real root$/) do
   pending # express the regexp above with the code you wish you had
end

Then(/^the solver returns an array of one Float r(\d+)$/) do |arg1|
   pending # express the regexp above with the code you wish you had
end

Then(/^r(\d+) is a valid solution\.$/) do |arg1|
   pending # express the regexp above with the code you wish you had
end
```

Notice how the regular expression is used to associate the English (Gherkin) expression with the corresponding Ruby code. Here is how I filled out that section (in first.rb):

```
Given(/^coefficients that should yield one real root$/) do
   @result = quadratic(1, 2, 1)
end
```

```
Then(/^the solver returns an array of one Float r(\d+)$/) do |arg1|
  expect(@result.size).to eq(1)
  expect(@result.first).to be_a(Float)
end

Then(/^r(\d+) is a valid solution\.$/) do |arg1|
  expect(@result).to eq([-1.0])
end
```

These three small tests now pass. By filling out the rest of the step definitions in a similar way, it is possible to end up with a specification written in readable English that can still be executed to verify the results of your code.

Cucumber is very powerful and has many useful functions. For a fuller description of its features, check the Cucumber documentation online, or *The Cucumber Book* by Matt Wynne and Aslak Hellesøy.

16.4   Using the `byebug` Debugger

The most popular library for debugging in Ruby is the `byebug` gem. It is implemented using the `TracePoint` functionality that we investigated in Section 11.4.4, "Monitoring Program Execution," of Chapter 11, "OOP and Dynamic Features in Ruby." In versions of Ruby before 2.0, the `debugger` gem provided very similar functionality.

Truthfully, debuggers don't seem to get much standalone use in Ruby. My own use of Byebug is via the `pry` tool, which is examined in the next section. We'll look at how to use the debugger first, and then move on to Pry and the additional features it provides beyond debugging.

To invoke Byebug by itself, simply invoke `byebug` instead of `ruby` on the command line:

```
byebug myfile.rb
```

At the prompt, which looks like (byebug), you can type such commands as `step` to step into a method call, `list` to print any or all of the program, and so on. Here are the most common of these commands:

- **continue** (**c**)—Continue running up to a line.
- **break** (**b**)—List or set a breakpoint.

- **delete**—Delete some or all breakpoints.

- **catch**—List or set a catchpoint.

- **step** (**s**)—Step into a method.

- **next** (**n**)—Got to the next line (step over a method).

- **where** (**w**)—Print the current stacktrace.

- **help** (**h**)—Get help (list all commands).

- **quit** (**q**)—Quit the debugger.

Listing 16.6 presents the code of a simple program (too simple to need debugging, really).

Listing 16.6   A Simple Program for Debugging

```
STDOUT.sync = true

def palindrome?(word)
  word == word.reverse
end

def signature(w)
  w.split("").sort.join
end

def anagrams?(w1,w2)
  signature(w1) == signature(w2)
end

print "Give me a word: "
w1 = gets.chomp

print "Give me another word: "
w2 = gets.chomp

verb = palindrome?(w1) ? "is" : "is not"
puts "'#{w1}' #{verb} a palindrome."

verb = palindrome?(w2) ? "is" : "is not"
puts "'#{w2}' #{verb} a palindrome."

verb = anagrams?(w1,w2) ? "are" : "are not"
puts "'#{w1}' and '#{w2}' #{verb} anagrams."
```

Listing 16.7 shows an entire debugging session, though some lines of the program that were printed have been removed for brevity. While reading it, keep in mind that the console is used for input and output as well as for debugging.

Listing 16.7   A Simple Debugging Session

```
$ byebug simple.rb

[1, 10] in simple.rb
=>  1:      STDOUT.sync = true

(byebug) b Object#palindrome?
Created breakpoint 1 at Object::palindrome?
(byebug) b Object#anagrams?
Created breakpoint 2 at Object::anagrams?
(byebug) info b
Num Enb What
1   y   at Object:palindrome?
2   y   at Object:anagrams?
(byebug) c 16
Give me a word:
Stopped by breakpoint 3 at simple.rb:16

[11, 20] in simple.rb
   15:     print "Give me a word: "
=> 16:     w1 = gets.chomp
   17:

(byebug) c 19
live
Give me another word:
[14, 23] in simple.rb
 . 18:     print "Give me another word: "
=> 19:     w2 = gets.chomp

(byebug) n
evil

[16, 25] in simple.rb
=> 21:     verb = palindrome?(w1) ? "is" : "is not"
   22:     puts "'#{w1}' #{verb} a palindrome."

(byebug) c
Stopped by breakpoint 1 at Object:palindrome?

[1, 10] in simple.rb
=>  3:     def palindrome?(word)
    4:         word == word.reverse
```

```
(byebug)

[1, 10] in simple.rb
    3:      def palindrome?(word)
=>  4:          word == word.reverse
    5:      end

(byebug)
Next went up a frame because previous frame finished

[17, 26] in simple.rb
   21:          verb = palindrome?(w1) ? "is" : "is not"
=> 22:          puts "'#{w1}' #{verb} a palindrome."

(byebug) c
'live' is not a palindrome.
'evil' is not a palindrome.

Stopped by breakpoint 2 at Object:anagrams?

[6, 15] in simple.rb
=> 11:      def anagrams?(w1,w2)
   12:          signature(w1) == signature(w2)
   13:      end

(byebug) c
'live' and 'evil' are anagrams.
```

Note that you can repeat the last command given by simply pressing Return. While using a debugger, be aware that if you require other libraries, you may find yourself stepping over quite a few things at the beginning. I suggest you call `continue` with the line number of a line that interests you to execute to that point.

The debugger recognizes many other commands. You can examine the call stack and move up and down in it. You can "watch" expressions and break automatically when they change. You can add expressions to a "display" list. You can handle multiple threads and switch between them.

All these features are probably not well documented anywhere. If you use the debugger, I suggest you use its online `help` command and proceed by trial and error.

Some other debuggers are graphical. See Chapter 21, "Ruby Development Tools," for a discussion of Ruby IDEs (integrated development environments) if you want this kind of tool.

16.5   Using `pry` for Debugging

Every Rubyist is familiar with irb. But in recent years, the `pry` tool has emerged as something that many people find superior. You can install Pry by adding it to your project's Gemfile or running `gem install pry`.

Like irb, `pry` is a REPL (read-eval-print-loop) tool. However, it includes several more sophisticated features, as well as an extension system so anyone can add more. There are extensions that integrate `pry` with the `byebug` and `debugger` gems to provide all the features of a full debugger as well as the advanced REPL of `pry`.

Let's look at how we can halt a running program and debug its internal behavior. We'll take Listing 16.6 and make a couple of changes, adding `require 'pry'` at the beginning and then adding a call to `binding.pry` sometime later:

```ruby
require 'pry'

# ...
w2 = gets.chomp

binding.pry

 # ...
```

Here are some of the more important commands (excerpted from online help):

```
cd                Move into a new context (object or scope).
find-method       Recursively search for a method within a Class/
                  Module or the current namespace.
ls                Show the list of vars and methods in the current
                  scope.
whereami          Show code surrounding the current context.
wtf?              Show the backtrace of the most recent exception.
show-doc          Show the documentation for a method or class.
show-source       Show the source for a method or class.
reload-code       Reload the source file that contains the
                  specified code object.
```

So let's run this. The following session shows how we enter the `pry` environment and look around:

```
$ ruby myprog.rb
Give me a word: parental
```

```
Give me another word: prenatal

From: /Users/Hal/rubyway/ch16/myprog.rb @ line 23 :

      18:      w1 = gets.chomp
      19:
      20:      print "Give me another word: "
      21:      w2 = gets.chomp
      22:
  => 23:      binding.pry
      24:
      25:      verb = palindrome?(w1) ? "is" : "is not"
      26:      puts "'#{w1}' #{verb} a palindrome."
      27:
      28:      verb = palindrome?(w2) ? "is" : "is not"

[1] pry(main)> w1
=> "parental"
[2] pry(main)> w2
=> "prenatal"
[3] pry(main)> palindrome?(w1)
=> false
[4] pry(main)> anagrams?(w1, w2)
=> true
[5] pry(main)> exit
'parental' is not a palindrome.
'prenatal' is not a palindrome.
'parental' and 'prenatal' are anagrams.
```

Although pry by itself is not a "debugger" in the traditional sense, it can embed a debugger, and has many powerful features that plain debuggers do not have besides. Refer to Chapter 21 for more information on those features (and as always, the most recent documentation online).

16.6   Measuring Performance

I don't like to place too much emphasis on optimizing for speed. The best way to do this in general is to simply select an algorithm that runs in a reasonable amount of time for your use case.

Certainly speed matters. In some cases, it matters greatly. However, it is usually a mistake to worry about speed *too soon* in the development cycle. The saying goes,

"Premature optimization is the root of all evil." (This originated with Hoare and was restated by Knuth.) Or as someone else put it: "Make it right, then make it fast." At the application level, this is generally a good heuristic (though at the level of large systems, it may be of less value).

I would add to this precept: *Don't optimize until you measure.*

That isn't so much to ask. Refrain from refactoring for speed until you actually know two things: First, is it really too slow? And second, exactly which parts are causing the speed problem?

The second question is more important than it appears. Programmers tend to think they have a pretty good idea of where the execution time is going, but in reality, studies have shown conclusively that on the average they are extraordinarily *bad* at making these determinations. "Seat of the pants" optimization is not a viable option for most of us.

We need objective measurements. We need a profiler.

Ruby comes with a profiler called `profile`. Invoking it is as easy as requiring the library:

```
ruby -rprofile myprog.rb
```

Consider the program Listing 16.8. Its purpose is to open the `/usr/share/dict/words` file and look for anagrams. It then looks for which words have the most anagrams and prints them out.

Listing 16.8   Finding Anagrams in the Dictionary

```
words = File.readlines("/usr/share/dict/words")
words.map! {|x| x.chomp }

hash = {}
words.each do |word|
  key = word.split("").sort.join
  hash[key] ||= []
  hash[key] << word
end

sizes = hash.values.map {|v| v.size }
most = sizes.max
list = hash.find_all {|k,v| v.size == most }

puts "No word has more than #{most-1} anagrams."
list.each do |key,val|
```

```
  anagrams = val.sort
  first = anagrams.shift
  puts "The word #{first} has #{most-1} anagrams:"
  anagrams.each {|a| puts "   #{a}" }
end

num = 0
hash.keys.each do |key|
  n = hash[key].size
  num += n if n > 1
end

puts
puts "The dictionary has #{words.size} words,"
puts "of which #{num} have anagrams."
```

I know you are curious about the output. Here it is:

```
No word has more than 14 anagrams.
The word alerts has 14 anagrams:
    alters
    artels
    estral
    laster
    lastre
    rastle
    ratels
    relast
    resalt
    salter
    slater
    staler
    stelar
    talers

The dictionary has 483523 words,
of which 79537 have anagrams.
```

On my systems, that file has more than 483,000 words, and the program runs in a little more than 18 seconds. Where do you think the time is going? Let's find out. The output from the profiler is more than 100 lines long, sorted by decreasing time. We'll look at the first 20 lines:

% time	cumulative seconds	self seconds	calls	self ms/call	total ms/call	name
42.78	190.93	190.93	15	12728.67	23647.33	Array#each
10.78	239.04	48.11	1404333	0.03	0.04	Hash#[]
7.04	270.48	31.44	2	15720.00	25575.00	Hash#each
5.66	295.73	25.25	483523	0.05	0.05	String#split
5.55	320.51	24.78	1311730	0.02	0.02	Array#size
3.64	336.76	16.25	1	16250.00	25710.00	Array#map
3.24	351.23	14.47	483524	0.03	0.03	Array#sort
3.12	365.14	13.91	437243	0.03	0.03	Fixnum#==
3.04	378.72	13.58	483526	0.03	0.03	Array#join
2.97	391.98	13.26	437244	0.03	0.03	Hash#default
2.59	403.53	11.55	437626	0.03	0.03	Hash#[]=
2.43	414.38	10.85	483568	0.02	0.02	Array#<<
2.29	424.59	10.21	1	10210.00	13430.00	Array#map!
1.94	433.23	8.64	437242	0.02	0.02	Fixnum#<=>
1.86	441.54	8.31	437244	0.02	0.02	Fixnum#>
0.72	444.76	3.22	483524	0.01	0.01	String#chomp!
0.11	445.26	0.50	4	125.00	125.00	Hash#keys
0.11	445.73	0.47	1	470.00	470.00	Hash#values
0.06	446.00	0.27	1	270.00	270.00	IO#readlines
0.05	446.22	0.22	33257	0.01	0.01	Fixnum#+

Here we see that the `Array#each` method is taking more time than anything else. That makes sense; we have a loop that runs for each word and does significant work with each iteration. The average is misleading because the first call of `each` takes almost all the time; the other 14 calls (see `anagrams.each`) take a short amount of time.

We also notice that `Hash#[]` is an expensive operation (largely because we do it so often); 1.4 million of these calls take not quite 11 seconds.

Notice where the `readlines` call fell—almost off our list of the top 20. This program is not I/O bound at all; it is compute bound. The read of the entire file took hardly more than a fourth of a second.

The real value of profiling is not seen in this example, however. This program doesn't have any methods or any class structure. In real life, you would see your own methods listed among the core methods. You would then be able to tell which of your methods was among the top 20 "time wasters."

One thing to realize about the Ruby profiler is that (perhaps ironically) the profiler itself is slow. It hooks into the program in many places and monitors execution at a low level (in pure Ruby). So don't be surprised if your program runs an order of magnitude slower. This program when profiled took 7 minutes 40 seconds (or 460 seconds), slowed down by a factor of 25 or more.

Besides the profiler, there is a lower-level tool you should be aware of: The `benchmark` standard library is also useful in measuring performance.

One way to use this little tool is to invoke the `Benchmark.measure` method and pass it a block:

```
require 'benchmark'

file = "/usr/share/dict/words"
result = Benchmark.measure { File.readlines(file) }
puts result

 # Output:     0.350000    0.070000    0.420000 ( 0.418825)
```

The output from this method is as follows:

- User CPU time (in seconds)
- System CPU time
- Sum of user and system times
- Elapsed real time

For comparing several different items, the `Benchmark.bm` method is convenient. Give it a block, and it will pass in a reporting object. Invoke that object with a label and a block, and it will output the label and time the block. Look at the following code:

```
require 'benchmark'

n = 200_000
s1 = ""
s2 = ""
s3 = ""

Benchmark.bm do |rep|
  rep.report("str <<     ") { n.times { s1 << "x" } }
  rep.report("str.insert ") { n.times { s3.insert(-1,"x") } }
  rep.report("str +=     ") { n.times { s2 += "x" } }
end
```

Here, we compare three ways of getting a character into the end of a string; the result is the same in each case. We do each operation 200,000 times so as to measure the effect better. Here is the output:

```
              user       system      total        real
str <<      0.180000    0.000000   0.180000  ( 0.174697)
str.insert  0.200000    0.000000   0.200000  ( 0.200479)
str +=     15.250000   13.120000  28.370000  (28.375998)
```

Notice how time consuming the third case is? It's a full two orders of magnitude slower. Why is this? What lesson can we learn?

You might conclude that the + operator is slow for some reason, but that isn't the case. This is the only one of the three methods that doesn't operate on the same object every time but creates a new object.

The lesson is that object creation is an expensive operation. There may be many such small lessons to be learned by using Benchmark, but I still recommend profiling at a higher level first.

Minitest also has benchmarking capabilities (see the `minitest/benchmark` library), and RSpec has the −`profile` option to print the slowest specs.

16.7 Pretty-Printing Objects

The purpose of the `inspect` method (and the p method that invokes it) is to show objects in human-readable form. In that sense, there is a connection with testing and debugging that justifies covering this here.

The only problem with p is that the object it prints out can be difficult to read. That is why we have the standard library pp, which adds a method of the same name.

Consider the following contrived object called `my_obj`:

```
class MyClass

  attr_accessor :alpha, :beta, :gamma

  def initialize(a,b,c)
    @alpha, @beta, @gamma = a, b, c
  end

end
```

```
x = MyClass.new(2, 3, 4)
y = MyClass.new(5, 6, 7)
z = MyClass.new(7, 8, 9)

my_obj = { x => y, z => [:p, :q] }
p my_obj
```

Running this code produces the following output:

```
{#<MyClass:0xb7eed86c @beta=3, @alpha=2,
 @gamma=4>=>#<MyClass:0xb7eed72c @beta=6, @alpha=5, @gamma=7>,
 #<MyClass:0xb7eed704 @beta=8, @alpha=7, @gamma=9>=>[:p, :q]}
```

It's accurate, and it's technically readable—but it isn't pretty. Now let's require the pp library and use pp instead:

```
require 'pp'

# ...

 pp my_obj
```

In this case, we get the following output:

```
{#<MyClass:0xb7f7a050 @alpha=7, @beta=8, @gamma=9>=>[:p, :q],
 #<MyClass:0xb7f7a1b8 @alpha=2, @beta=3, @gamma=4>=>
  #<MyClass:0xb7f7a078 @alpha=5, @beta=6, @gamma=7>}
```

At least it adds some spacing and line breaks. It's an improvement, but we can do better. Suppose we add the special `pretty_print` method to `MyClass`:

```
class MyClass

  def pretty_print(printer)
    printer.text "MyClass(#@alpha, #@beta, #@gamma)"
  end

end
```

The `printer` argument is passed in by the caller (or ultimately by `pp`). It is a text accumulator of class `PP`; we call its `text` method and give it a textual representation of `self`. The result we get follows:

```
{MyClass(7, 8, 9)=>[:p, :q], MyClass(2, 3, 4)=>MyClass(5, 6, 7)}
```

Of course, we can customize this as much as we want. We could put the instance variables on separate lines and indent them, for instance.

In fact, the `pp` library does have a number of facilities for "pp-enabling" your own classes. Methods such as `object_group`, `seplist`, `breakable`, and others are available for controlling comma separation, line breaks, and similar formatting tasks. For more details, consult the documentation for `pp`.

16.8   Not Covered Here

This book can cover only a portion of the Ruby ecosystem. I'll give passing mention to a few more items. Also see Chapter 21 because that material is related.

I am a great believer in code coverage tools. It is *incredibly* useful to know what parts of your code are not getting exercised. This helps you to know when you have areas that are lacking in unit tests.

In recent years, the most popular code coverage tool has been `simple-cov`; this is a successor to `rcov` and can be installed as a gem. On execution, it creates a directory called `coverage`, where you will find HTML files. The `index.html` has an overview of the results, and it links to all the sources with the lines highlighted according to whether they were executed.

There are several continuous integration tools for Ruby; the most popular self-hosted tool is Jenkins. The most popular hosted service for open-source projects is Travis CI. Hosted options for private projects include Travis CI, Circle CI, Semaphore, and Codeship. Search online for what might work best for you.

Also, many static code analysis tools are available for Ruby. I have used `flog`, which helps find "ugly" or complex code; `flay` helps find code that is structurally similar and can perhaps be refactored (in accordance with the DRY principle, "Don't Repeat Yourself"). The tool `heckle` is particularly useful (and frustrating) because it helps discover weaknesses in your tests (by mutating the code and checking whether a failure results). The hosted service Code Climate automatically runs these quality tools, as well as code coverage and security-auditing tools, to track code quality and test coverage over time.

As far as consistent Ruby style goes, the rubocop tool is fairly useful. However, I specifically disagree with one or two of its default rules.

16.9 Conclusion

In this chapter, we've looked at some of the mechanics of testing (especially unit testing). We looked specifically at Minitest, RSpec, and Cucumber.

We've looked briefly at the Ruby debugger. We also saw how pry can be used to "jump" into an interactive REPL session. And, finally, we've looked at profiling and benchmarking to measure the speed of our Ruby code.

If you're working on software for public consumption, what do you do after testing is complete? It's time then to worry about packaging and distributing the software. This is the topic of the next chapter.

Chapter 17

Packaging and Distributing Code

With aspirin leading the way, more and more products are coming out in fiercely protective packaging designed to prevent consumers from consuming them.

—Dave Barry

This chapter is all about being nice to developers who work on or use your code. If no one (including you) works on your code, or you don't want to be nice to anyone (including yourself), feel free to skip this chapter.

Typical programmers don't want to think about user documentation or installation procedures. I encourage you to think about both. Even if you are the only person who will ever see your code, just a few months is typically enough time to forget all the intricacies and details of the code you wrote. Always make things as easy as possible for other developers, because your future self will be one of them.

Being nice to other developers consists primarily of just a few things: making it easy to use the code, making it easy to work on the code, and making it easy to understand the code. You can use Rubygems, Bundler, and RDoc to do each of these things. We'll look at how to use these tools in this chapter.

17.1   Libraries and Rubygems

Sharing Ruby code with other developers is amazingly easy: just give them a copy of
the file with the code in it. They can `require` your file and start using your code. The
problems arise when you want to update your code, or share it more broadly
with the entire community. Rubygems (and `rubygems.org`) are the solution for those
problems.

Rubygems has been included with Ruby itself since Ruby 1.9, and is central to
Ruby code distribution. It allows Ruby developers to package their code up into a single compressed file, called a "gem." Gems have filenames that end in the `.gem` extension, and they contain both the Ruby code that makes up the library in question and
metadata about the library, including author and version information.

Rubygems.org is the community-funded host for public gems. This site creates
a page for every gem that lists the gem's authors and versions. If the gem's author has
provided them, links to the gem's home page, source code, and online documentation
will also be shown. Anyone can create a gem and host it on `rubygems.org` for
others to use, for free.

17.1.1   Using Rubygems

The Rubygems executable is called `gem`. It has subcommands and options that make
sense for each subcommand. The most basic usage is quite simple. To install the rake
gem, you would run `gem install rake`. Rubygems will look for a `.gem` file in the
current directory, and then check `rubygems.org`. Once found, the gem will be
installed so that any other Ruby code can use it. The latest version of the gem will be
installed by default, but if you wanted to install rake version 10.0.1, you could run
`gem install rake -v 10.0.1`. See `gem help install` for more options while
installing gems.

Sometimes a gem will have dependencies on other gems. In that case, Rubygems
will automatically search for and install those dependencies as well, leaving you with
all the gems you need to use the gem you asked for.

How do you know what to ask for? The `rubygems.org` gem server lists every
gem that has ever been created, and the names of all gems can be found there.
Alternatively, you can look for gems on `rubygems.org` by name with the command
`gem list -r NAME`.

However, neither of those options is helpful if you don't already know the name
of a gem. At `ruby-toolbox.com`, you can find an extremely handy directory of gems
grouped together by what they do, rather than how they are named. The Ruby

Toolbox also provides popularity and recent development information, which can be helpful when deciding between multiple gems with similar functionality.

After installing some gems, you can list all the gems you have installed with gem list. Predictably, you can also uninstall gems with gem uninstall NAME.

Now that you know how to find and install gems, let's look at how to create your own.

17.1.2 Creating Gems

Creating a new gem simply requires creating a single file with the .gemspec extension and putting some specific code inside it. Here is a sample .gemspec file for a gem named drummer:

```
# drummer.gemspec
Gem::Specification.new do |spec|
  spec.name          = "Drummer"
  spec.version       = "1.0.2"
  spec.authors       = ["H. Thoreau"]
  spec.email         = ["cabin@waldenpond.net"]
  spec.description   = %q{A Ruby library for those who march to a
different drummer.}
  spec.summary       = %q{Drum different}
  spec.homepage      = "http://waldenpond.com/drummer"
  spec.license       = "MIT"

  spec.files         = Dir["./**/*"]
  spec.executables   = Dir["./bin/*"]
  spec.test_files    = Dir["./spec/**/*"]
  spec.require_paths = ["lib"]

  spec.add_development_dependency "rake"
  spec.add_runtime_dependency "activerecord", "~> 4.1.0"
end
```

Hopefully this .gemspec is more or less self-explanatory, but you don't need to worry about the exact details just yet. After creating this .gemspec, it is possible to build a gem from it by running the command gem build drummer.gemspec. Then, to upload the gem to rubygems.org, just run gem push drummer-1.0.2.gem.

Covering Rubygems in detail would likely take an entire book, so we'll stop here. For more information about Rubygems, including the gem command and .gemspec files, refer to the Rubygems guides at http://guides.rubygems.org.

17.2   Managing Dependencies with Bundler

Now that it's easy to package and distribute individual libraries as gems, we have a new problem. Gems are designed to be small, focused libraries that are dedicated to a single task. Useful applications will probably need more than one gem. How do we keep track of all the gems needed for our larger project? What if we want to use a newer version of a gem we already use? The answer to these and other problems is Bundler, the Ruby language dependency manager.

Before Bundler, Ruby projects lacked a way to declare what gems they needed. Setting up a project on a new machine meant checking the readme for needed gems, hoping none were missing, and then hoping that those gems hadn't changed to break anything since the readme was written. By keeping track of every gem and version used in your project, Bundler lets you install every gem the project needs with a single command.

It wasn't just tracking gems that was hard before Bundler, though. Upgrading to new versions of gems might break your application if that gem turned out to depend on different versions of other gems that you already use. By analyzing every gem your project depends on at once, Bundler finds a set of versions for every gem that will all work together.

Setting up a new project to use Bundler is very straightforward, and consists of creating a single file named `Gemfile` and listing needed gems inside it. A Gemfile must have at least one `source` call, though it may have more. Following that, there is typically a list of calls to the `gem` method. Here is a Gemfile containing made-up examples, illustrating the most common forms these calls may take:

```
source "https://rubygems.org" # Download gems from rubygems.org

gem 'red'                   # A dependency on a gem called "red"
gem 'green',   '1.2.1'      # Gem "green" - version 1.2.1 exactly
gem 'blue',    '>= 1.0'     # Version 1.0 or greater of gem "blue"
gem 'yellow',  '~> 1.1'     # "yellow" 1.1 or greater, less than 2.0
gem 'purple',  '~> 1.1.1'   # At least 1.1.1, but less than 1.2
```

The `Gemfile` exists to store a list of the gems required by your project, and which versions are allowed. In any project containing a Gemfile, simply run `bundle install` to install all the required gems.

If it did not already exist, the `Gemfile.lock` file will also be created. In contrast to the `Gemfile`, the lock stores the names and exact installed versions of every required gem, including the dependencies of your gems, the dependencies of those dependencies, and so on.

Add both `Gemfile` and `Gemfile.lock` to your project's source code. This allows other developers to install all your project dependencies at once, by running `bundle install`.

Because each project has its own version of each gem, it is often the case that two projects will use different versions of common gems such as `rake` and `rspec`. Bundler can restrict your commands to only use the correct gem version for your current project, but it must load first in order to do that.

To run a gem command using the correct version for a given project, prepend the gem command with `bundle exec`. So, for example, instead of running `rake spec`, you would run `bundle exec rake spec`. This guarantees that the version of `rake` that is used will be the version that the project requires.

Because it quickly gets tedious to type `bundle exec` all the time, it can be helpful to add a shell alias to a shorter command, such as b. Alternatively, Bundler can create project-specific executables in `bin`, such as `bin/rake`. For more information, see Bundler's help about binstubs. Another trick is simply to do `bundle exec bash` to start a new shell with the proper environment set up.

If your application is simply a Ruby file, instead of an executable, it will need to require Bundler before any other gems are required. The most straightforward way to do this is with a single line:

```
require 'bundler/setup'
# other libraries can be required here...
```

Rails applications also run `Bundler.require` inside the `boot.rb` file. That means that every gem listed in the Gemfile will also be required automatically. Requiring many gems can be very slow, and is a common reason for applications to take a long time to start. The authors of Bundler recommend avoiding `Bundler.require` and adding `require` statements only where they are actually needed instead.

For the latest and most detailed information about Bundler, refer to the Bundler documentation website at http://bundler.io.

17.2.1   Semantic Versioning

At this point, you might be wondering why the Gemfile allows you to specify a range of versions, such as `< 2.5` or `>= 3.1.4`. Version requirements, as these are called, allow you to update gems without having to edit your Gemfile. In an application with the Gemfile `gem "drummer", "~> 1.0"`, you can upgrade your application from 1.0.2 to the newly released 1.0.3 by running `bundle update drummer`.

Updating gems can be dangerous, though—what if the new version of the gem works differently? Your application might break. To mitigate that problem, many gem developers adhere to a system for version numbers called "semantic versioning." It sounds a bit complicated, but it boils down to three principles, one for each number in a gem version.

The first number, known as the "major" version, indicates that something fundamental has changed. If the major version increases, don't expect to be able to keep using that gem without changing your own code. Likewise, if you make a change in your own gem that means current uses will break, *always* increment the major version.

The "minor" version is the second number in a gem version, and it indicates that new features have been added, but existing features have not changed. The gem will continue to provide exactly what it did before, and something new is also available that wasn't there before.

Last is the "tiny" version, which comes third in a gem version. Sometimes it is omitted if it is zero, as in a versions such as 2.2. When the tiny version increases, a bug has been fixed. Tiny updates should be the lowest-risk updates because they contain no new code and no breaking changes.

Semantic versioning is generally accepted as the most helpful system for version numbering. Even Ruby itself uses semantic versioning starting with 2.1.0. Keep in mind, however, than not all gems use this versioning scheme.

Although semantic versioning provides a strong indication of how much a gem has changed between versions, it isn't a perfect or complete fix to the problem of upgrading gems. Always write tests for code that needs to work correctly, and always run the tests after updating gems. That said, careful use of version requirements and `bundle update` can make updating gems, well, not exactly painless, but a much smaller hassle.

17.2.2   Dependencies from Git

In addition to managing gems and their versions, Bundler allows you to use gems directly from the git repos containing their source code. Because git allows you to create your own copy of a repo, Bundler makes it trivial to fork a gem repo, fix a bug, and test out your fix. Then, you can use the fixed version from your git repo while waiting for the gem owner to accept your fix and release a new version to rubygems.org.

The following Gemfile tells Bundler that you need the gem named `"rake"` and that you want to use it directly from Jim Weirich's git repository on Github:

```
gem "rake", git: "https://github.com/jimweirich/rake.git",
  branch: "master"
```

Running `bundle install` will clone the git repository from the given URL and check out the given branch or commit.

17.2.3 Creating Gems with Bundler

Although Bundler exists primarily to manage installing gems, it provides a very handy set of shortcuts that build on Rubygems to make creating and releasing gems as easy as possible.

To create our "drummer" gem with Bundler, we can simply run `bundle gem drummer`. This will create a `drummer` directory, with a ruby source file ready for our code, and a `.gemspec` file ready for our name and description. Releasing the gem is likewise made easier. The version of the gem is stored in the file `lib/drummer/version.rb`. After we update that file, releasing the gem to rubygems.org is as simple as running `rake release`.

As you develop your own code, be aware of code that gets reused and be ready to extract it to a gem. It's easy to create a gem this way and to start using it as a private gem (which we'll talk about in the next section). After a while, once those private gems have proven themselves useful, release them to rubygems.org if you can. The number of open-source, freely available gems that exist today is one of the greatest strengths of the Ruby community.

17.2.4 Private Gems

Once a project or company has grown for long enough, it's extremely likely that private, internal gems will emerge. These gems contain code that is shared across applications or services but is not for public consumption. Although it is better to extract reusable libraries from private code and open source them whenever possible, private gems are practically guaranteed on any project that is large enough.

Initially, private gems can be managing using git gems, because git repositories can easily be made private. Only users authorized for access to the repository will be able to install those gems. Once there are more than a few private gems, however, it's time to use a private gem server. Services such as Gemnasium provide private gem servers for a few dollars a month, whereas projects such as Geminabox allow you to install your own gem server wherever you like.

Now that you know how to create and use gems, let's look at how to make them understandable to programmers who look at them later. It's time to talk about documentation.

17.3   Using RDoc

The RDoc tool, created by Dave Thomas and maintained by Eric Hodel, is included with Ruby. It takes Ruby code as input, and it produces a `doc` directory containing HTML that documents the Ruby classes, methods, constants, and so on from the source files.

One great thing about RDoc is that it tries to produce useful output *even if there are no comments in the source*. It does this by parsing the code and organizing information on all the classes, modules, constants, methods, and so on. Therefore, you can get reasonably useful HTML out of a program source that doesn't even have any real internal documentation. If you haven't done this before, I suggest you try it.

But it gets better. RDoc also tries to associate the comments it finds with specific parts of the program. The general rule is that a block comment preceding a definition (such as a class or method) will be taken as the description of that definition.

If you simply invoke RDoc on a Ruby source, it will create a `doc` directory with all the files under it. (The default template looks good, but there are also others.) Browse to `index.html` and take a look.

Listing 17.1 shows a simple (nearly empty) source file. All the methods are empty, and none of it really does anything. But RDoc will still take it and produce a pretty doc page (see Figure 17.1).

Listing 17.1   A Simple Source File

```
require 'foo'

# The outer class, MyClass
class MyClass
  CONST = 237

  # The inner MyClass::Alpha class...
  class Alpha

    # The MyClass::Alpha::Beta class...
    class Beta
      # Beta's mymeth1 method
```

```
        def mymeth1
        end
      end

      # Alpha's mymeth2 method
      def mymeth2
      end
    end

    # Initialize the object
    def initialize(a,b,c)
    end

    # Create an object with default values
    def self.create
    end

    # An instance method
    def do_something
    end
end
```

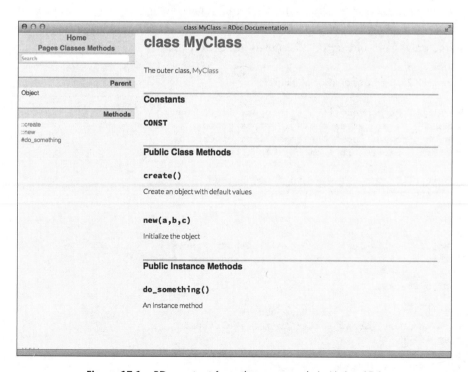

Figure 17.1   RDoc output from the source code in Listing 17.1

We'll discuss two other useful features in this section. The documentation for every method can also display the source code of that method. This is an absolutely invaluable tool in learning a library; the API documentation is linked directly back to the code itself.

Also be aware that when RDoc recognizes a URL, it places a hyperlink in the output. The text of the link defaults to be the same as the URL, but you can change this. If you put descriptive text in braces followed by a URL in brackets (that is, `{descriptive text}[myurl]`), your descriptive text will be used in the link. If the text is a single word, the braces may be omitted.

17.3.1   Simple Markup

If you want to add more elaborate rich-text documentation, RDoc supports a simple markup format that allows formatting the HTML that it will generate. The markup is designed to be straightforward and easily readable when the code is being edited, but translate into HTML formatting in a clear-cut manner.

Listing 17.2 shows a few examples of markup capability; for more examples, consult *Programming Ruby* or the RDoc API documentation online. The output (bottom frame only) from Listing 17.2 is shown in Figure 17.2.

Listing 17.2   Examples of RDoc Markup

```
# This block comment will not appear in the output.
# Rdoc only processes a single block comment before
# each piece of code. The empty line after this
# block separates it from the block below.

# This block comment will be detected and
# included in the rdoc output.
#
# Here are some formatting tricks.
#
# Boldface, italics, and "code" (without spaces):
# This is *bold*, this is _italic_, and this is +code+.
#
# With spaces:
#
# This is a bold phrase. Have you read Intruder
# in the Dust? Don't forget to require thread
# at the top.
#
# = First level heading
# == Second level heading
# === Third level heading
```

```
#
# Here's a horizontal rule:
# ---
#
# Here's a list:
# - item one
# - item two
# - item three

class MarkupDocumentation
  # This block will not appear because the class after
  # it has been marked with a :nodoc: directive.
  class NotDocumented # :nodoc:
  end
end

# This block comment will not show up in in the output.
# Rdoc only processes blocks immediately before code,
# and this comment block is after the only code in this
# listing.
```

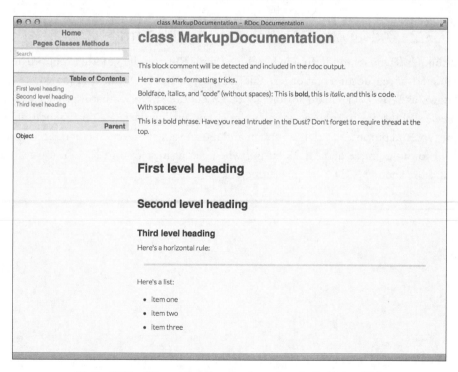

Figure 17.2   RDoc output from markup examples in Listing 17.2

Listing 17.2 outlines some of the rules RDoc uses to parse comments. Not all of these are necessarily intuitive. There is a strong tendency for blank lines to terminate a section of comments, even if the blank line is immediately followed by another block comment.

Note that inside a block comment starting with #, we can "turn off" the copying of text into the output with a #– line (and turn it back on again the same way). Not all comments are intended to go into the user docs, after all.

Finally, some tags can be used inside block comments to alter the RDoc HTML output. Here are most of them:

- `:include:`—Used to include the contents of the specified file in the documentation. Indentation will be adjusted for consistency.

- `:title`:—Used to set the title of the document.

- `:main:`—Used to set the initial page displayed in the output.

17.3.2   Advanced Documentation with Yard

Although RDoc is wonderful (and included with Ruby itself), another tool provides more advanced documentation capabilities: Yay! A Ruby Documentation tool, also known as YARD. The main advantages of YARD over RDoc is that it provides a live preview of the documentation as you write it, and it allows detailed documentation of the type and purpose for each argument and return value for every method. See Figure 17.3 for an example of YARD's output when run against Listing 17.1. You can find out more about YARD at http://yardoc.org.

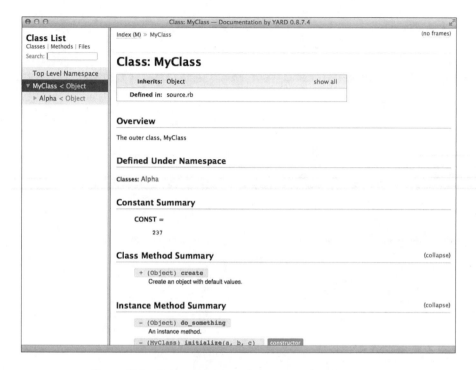

Figure 17.3   YARD output from the source code in Listing 17.1

17.4   Conclusion

In this chapter, we've looked at the Ruby library system, Rubygems, and the Ruby dependency manager, Bundler. We've looked at finding gems, creating gems, and publishing gems for other developers to use. We've also discussed the basics of how to document a project using RDoc or YARD. In the next chapter, we'll shift gears again and talk about an interesting and complex problem domain: network programming.

CHAPTER 18

Network Programming

Never underestimate the bandwidth of a station wagon full of tapes hurtling down the highway.

—*Andrew S. Tanenbaum*

When a marketing type says "networking," he probably means he wants to give you his business card. But when a programmer says it, he's talking about electronic communication between physically separated machines—whether across the room, across the city, or across the world.

In the programmer's world, networking usually implies TCP/IP, the native tongue in which millions of machines whisper back and forth across the Internet. I'll say a few words about this before diving into some concrete examples.

Network communication is conceptualized at different levels (or layers) of abstraction. The lowest level is the *data link layer*, or actual hardware-level communication, which we won't discuss here. Immediately above this is the *network layer*, which is concerned with the actual moving around of packets; this is the realm of IP (Internet Protocol). At a still higher level of abstraction is the *transport layer*, where we find TCP (Transmission Control Protocol) and UDP (User Datagram Protocol). At the level above this, we find the *application layer*; at this point, we finally enter the world of telnet, FTP, email protocols, and much more.

It's possible to communicate directly in IP, but normally you wouldn't do such a thing. Most of the time, we are concerned with TCP or UDP.

TCP provides communication between two hosts with consistent ordering and automatic retries; it is concerned with formatting packet data, acknowledgment of receipt, and so on. Any application using it can know data will be read in the same order it was sent.

UDP is much simpler, merely sending packets (datagrams) to the remote host, like binary postcards. There is no guarantee that these will be received, let alone received in order. It is useful for situations such as video chat and gaming, where only the latest data matters, and missed packets should not be re-sent.

Ruby supports low-level networking (chiefly in TCP and UDP) as well as coding at higher levels. These higher levels include telnet, FTP, SMTP, and so on. Figure 18.1 is a class hierarchy showing the highlights of Ruby's networking support.

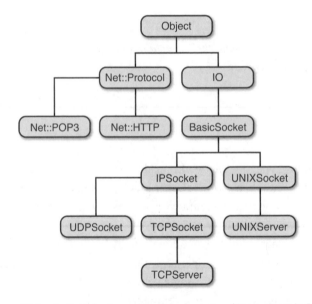

Figure 18.1   Partial inheritance hierarchy for networking support in Ruby.

Note that the bulk of these classes derive from the IO class. This means that we can use the methods of IO that are so familiar to us. In addition to these classes, the standard library includes Net::IMAP, Net::POPMail, Net::SMTP, Net::Telnet, and Net::FTP, all inheriting directly from Object.

Documenting all the features of all these classes would far exceed the space requirements of this book. I'll only present a task-oriented approach to all of this and offer a little explanation. For a comprehensive list of available methods, consult a reference such as rdoc.info.

A few significant areas are not covered here at all, so we'll mention these up front. The Net::Telnet class is mentioned only in connection with NTP servers in Section 18.2.2, "Contacting an Official Timeserver"; this class is not just for implementing your own telnet client but is potentially useful for automating anything that has a telnet interface.

The Net::FTP library is also not covered here. In general, FTP is easy to automate in its everyday form, so there is less motivation to use this class than there might be for some others.

The Net::Protocol class, which is the parent of HTTP and POP3, is not covered in this chapter. Although it would probably prove useful in the development of customized networking protocols, that is beyond the scope of this book.

That ends our broad overview. Let's look at low-level networking in more detail.

18.1 Network Servers

A *server* spends its lifetime waiting for messages and answering them. It may have to do some serious processing to construct those answers, such as accessing a database, but from a networking point of view, it simply receives requests and sends responses.

Having said that, there is still more than one way to accomplish this. A server may respond to only one request at a time, or it may thread its responses. The former is easier to code, but the latter is better if many clients are trying to connect simultaneously.

It's also conceivable that a server may be used to facilitate communication in some way between the clients. The classic examples are chat servers, game servers, and peer-to-peer file sharing.

18.1.1 A Simple Server: Time of Day

Let's look at the simplest server we can think of, which may require a little suspension of disbelief. Let's suppose we have a server whose clock is so accurate that we use it as a standard. There are such servers, of course, but they don't communicate with the simple protocol we show here. (Actually, you can refer to Section 18.2.2, "Contacting an Official Timeserver," for an example of contacting such a server via the `Telnet` interface.)

In this low-level example, a single-threaded server handles requests inline. When the client makes a request of us, we return a string with the time of day. Here's the server code:

```
require "socket"

server = UDPSocket.open # Using UDP here...
server.bind nil, 12321

loop do
  text, sender = server.recvfrom(1)
  server.send("#{Time.now}\n", 0, sender[3], sender[1])
end
```

And here is the client code:

```
require "socket"
require "timeout"

socket = UDPSocket.new
socket.connect("localhost", 12321)

socket.send("", 0)
timeout(10) do
  time = socket.gets
  puts "The time is #{time}"
end
```

Note that the client makes its request simply by sending a null packet. Because network requests are unreliable, we time out after a reasonable length of time.

The following is a similar server implemented with TCP. It listens on port 12321 and can actually be used by telnetting into that port (or by using the client code we show afterward):

```
require "socket"

server = TCPServer.new(12321)

loop do
  session = server.accept
  session.puts Time.new
  session.close
end
```

Note the straightforward use of the `TCPServer` class. The call to `accept` is a blocking one, pausing execution until a client connects. Once a client has connected, the connection socket is returned and can be used in the server code.

Here is the TCP version of the client code:

```
require "socket"

session = TCPSocket.new("localhost", 12321)
puts "The time is #{session.gets.chomp}"
session.close
```

18.1.2 Implementing a Threaded Server

If this server ever gets more than one request at the same time, one request will have to wait (or *queue*) until the first request is finished. To handle multiple requests at the same time, handle each request with a separate thread.

Here is a reimplementation of the time-of-day server in the previous example. It uses TCP and threads all the client requests:

```
require "socket"

server = TCPServer.new(12321)

loop do
  Thread.new(server.accept) do |session|
    session.puts Time.new
    session.close
  end
end
```

Because it uses threads and spawns a new one with every client request, greater parallelism is achieved. No `join` is done because the loop is essentially infinite, running until the server is interrupted manually.

The client code is, of course, unchanged. From the point of view of the client, the server's behavior is unchanged (except that it may appear faster).

18.1.3   Case Study: A Peer-to-Peer Chess Server

It isn't always the server that we're ultimately concerned about communicating with. Sometimes the server is more of a directory service to put clients in touch with each other. One example is a peer-to-peer file-sharing service such as those so popular 10–15 years ago; other examples are chat servers or any number of game servers.

Let's create a skeletal implementation of a chess server. Here, we don't mean a server that will play chess with a client, but simply one that will point clients to each other so that they can then play without the server's involvement.

I'll warn you that for the sake of simplicity, the code really knows nothing about chess. All of the game logic is simulated (stubbed out) so that we can focus on the networking issues.

First, let's use TCP for the initial communication between each client and the server. We could use UDP, but then we would have to handle retries and out-of-order data by ourselves.

We'll let each client provide two pieces of information: his own name (such as a username) and the name of the desired opponent. We'll introduce the notation `user:hostname` to fully identify the opponent; we use a colon instead of the more intuitive @ so that it won't resemble an email address, which it isn't.

When a client contacts the server, the server stores the client's information in a list. When *both* clients have contacted the server, a message is sent back to each of them; each client is given enough information to contact his opponent.

There's also the small issue of white and black. Somehow the roles have to be assigned in such a way that both players agree on what color they are playing. For simplicity, we're letting the server assign this. The first client contacting the server will get to play white (and thus move first); the other player will play the black pieces.

Don't get confused here. The initial clients talk to each other so that effectively one of them is really a server by this point. This is a semantic distinction that I won't bother with.

Because the clients will be talking to each other in alternation and there is more than just a single brief exchange, we'll use TCP for their communication. This means that the client that is "really" a server will instantiate a TCPServer, and the other will instantiate a TCPSocket at the other end. We're assuming a well-known port for peer-to-peer communication as we did with the initial client-server handshaking. (The two ports are different, of course.)

What we're really describing here is a simple application-level protocol. It could certainly be made more sophisticated.

Let's look first at the server (see Listing 18.1). For the convenience of running it at a command line, we start a thread that terminates the server when a carriage return is pressed. The main server logic is threaded; we can handle multiple clients connecting at once. For safety's sake, we use a mutex to protect access to the user data; without it, two clients connecting at once would mean multiple threads might try to add users to the list at the same time.

Listing 18.1   The Chess Server

```
require "thread"
require "socket"

PORT = 12000

# Exit if user presses Enter
waiter = Thread.new do
  puts "Press Enter to exit the server."
  gets
  exit
end

@mutex = Mutex.new
@list = {}

def match?(p1, p2)
  return false unless @list[p1] && @list[p2]
  @list[p1][0] == p2 && @list[p2][0] == p1
end

def handle_client(sess, msg, addr, port, ipname)
  cmd, player1, player2 = msg.split

  # Note: We get user:hostname on the command line,
  # but we store it in the form user:address
  player1 << ":#{addr}"            # Append user's IP addr

  user2, host2 = player2.split(":")
  host2 = ipname if host2 == nil
```

```
    player2 = user2 + ":" + IPSocket.getaddress(host2)

    if cmd != "login"
      puts "Protocol error: client msg was #{msg}"
    end

    @mutex.synchronize do
      @list[player1] = [player2, addr, port, ipname, sess]
    end

    if match?(player1, player2)
      notify_clients(player1, player2)
    end
  end

  def notify_clients(player1, player2)
    # Note these names are "backwards" now: player2
    # logged in first, if we got here.
    p1, p2 = @mutex.synchronize do
      [@list.delete(player1), @list.delete(player2)]
    end

    p1name = player1.split(":")[0]
    p2name = player2.split(":")[0]

    # Player ID = name:ip:color
    # Color: 0=white, 1=black
    p1id = "#{p1name}:#{p1[3]}:1"
    p2id = "#{p2name}:#{p2[3]}:0"

    sess2 = p2[4]
    sess2.puts p1id
    sess2.close

    sleep 0.2 # let the player-server start up
    sess1 = p1[4]
    sess1.puts p2id
    sess1.close
  end

  # Abort in this short example, skipping threaded error-handling
  Thread.abort_on_exception = true

  server = TCPServer.new("0.0.0.0", PORT)
  loop do
    Thread.new(server.accept) do |sess|
      text = sess.gets
      print "Received: #{text}" # So we know server gets it
      domain, port, ipname, ipaddr = sess.peeraddr
      handle_client sess, text, ipaddr, port, ipname
    end
  end
```

The `handle_client` method stores information for the client. If the correspon-ding client is already stored, each client is sent a message telling the whereabouts of the other client. As we've defined this simple problem, the server's responsibility ends at this point.

The client code (see Listing 18.2) is naturally written so that there is only a sin-gle program; the first invocation will become the TCP server, and the second will become the TCP client. To be fair, we should point out that our choice to make the server white and the client black is arbitrary. There's no particular reason we couldn't implement the application so that the color issue was independent of such considera-tions.

Listing 18.2   The Chess Client

```
require "socket"
require "timeout"

ChessServer     = "10.0.1.7" # Replace this IP address
ChessServerPort = 12000
PeerPort        = 12001
White, Black    = 0, 1

def draw_board(board)
  puts <<-EOF

    +-------------------------------+
    | Stub! Drawing the board here... |
    +-------------------------------+

  EOF
end

def analyze_move(who, move, num, board)
  # Stub - black always wins on 4th move
  if who == Black and num == 4
    move << " Checkmate!"
  end
  true # Stub again - always say it's legal.
end

def get_move(who, move, num, board)
  ok = false
  until ok do
    print "\nYour move: "
    move = STDIN.gets.chomp
    ok = analyze_move(who, move, num, board)
    puts "Illegal move" unless ok
  end
  move
end
```

```ruby
def my_move(who, lastmove, num, board, opponent, sock)
  move = get_move(who, lastmove, num, board)
  sock.puts move
  draw_board(board)

  case move
  when "resign"
    puts "\nYou've resigned. #{opponent} wins."
    true
  when /Checkmate/
    puts "\nYou have checkmated #{opponent}!"
    true
  else
    false
  end
end

def other_move(who, move, num, board, opponent, sock)
  move = sock.gets.chomp
  puts "\nOpponent: #{move}"
  draw_board(board)

  case move
  when "resign"
    puts "\n#{opponent} has resigned... you win!"
    true
  when /Checkmate/
    puts "\n#{opponent} has checkmated you."
    true
  else
    false
  end
end

if ARGV[0]
  myself = ARGV[0]
else
  print "Your name? "
  myself = STDIN.gets.chomp
end

if ARGV[1]
  opponent_id = ARGV[1]
else
  print "Your opponent? "
  opponent_id = STDIN.gets.chomp
end

opponent = opponent_id.split(":")[0]   # Remove hostname

# Contact the server
```

```ruby
socket = TCPSocket.new(ChessServer, ChessServerPort)

socket.puts "login #{myself} #{opponent_id}"
socket.flush
response = socket.gets.chomp
name, ipname, color = response.split ":"
color = color.to_i

if color == Black            # Other player's color
  puts "\nConnecting..."

  server = TCPServer.new(PeerPort)
  session = server.accept

  begin
    timeout(30) do
      str = session.gets.chomp
      if str != "ready"
        raise "Protocol error: ready-message was #{str}"
      end
    end
  rescue Timeout::Error
    raise "Did not get ready-message from opponent."
  end

  puts "Playing #{opponent}... you are white.\n"

  who = White
  move = nil
  board = nil        # Not really used in this dummy example
  num = 0
  draw_board(board) # Draw the board initially for white

  loop do
    num += 1
    won = my_move(who, move, num, board, opponent, session)
    break if won
    lost = other_move(who, move, num, board, opponent, session)
    break if lost
  end
else                           # We're black
  puts "\nConnecting..."

  socket = TCPSocket.new(ipname, PeerPort)
  socket.puts "ready"

  puts "Playing #{opponent}... you are black.\n"

  who = Black
  move = nil
  board = nil        # Not really used in this dummy example
  num = 0
```

```
draw_board(board) # Draw board initially

loop do
  num += 1
  lost = other_move(who, move, num, board, opponent, socket)
  break if lost
  won = my_move(who, move, num, board, opponent, socket)
  break if won
end

socket.close
end
```

I've defined this little protocol so that the black client sends a "ready" message to the white client to let it know it's prepared to begin the game. The white player then moves first. The move is sent to the black client so that it can draw its own board in sync with the other player's board.

Again, there's no real knowledge of chess built in to this application. There's a stub in place to check the validity of each player's move; this check is done on the local side in each case. However, this is only a stub that always says that the move is legal. At the same time, it does a bit of hocus-pocus; we want this simulated game to end after only a few moves, so we fix the game so that black always wins on the fourth move. This win is indicated by appending the string `"Checkmate!"` to the move; this prints on the opponent's screen and also serves to terminate the loop.

Besides the "traditional" notation (for example, "P-K4"), there is also an "algebraic" notation preferred by most people. However, the code is stubbed so heavily that it doesn't even know which notation we're using.

Because it's easy to do, we allow a player to resign at any time. This is simply a win for the opponent. The drawing of the board is also a stub. Those wanting to do so can easily design some bad ASCII art to output here.

The `my_move` method always refers to the local side. Likewise, `other_move` refers to the remote side. Listing 18.3 shows some sample output.

Listing 18.3   Sample Chess Client Execution

```
$ ruby chess.rb Hal                    $ ruby chess.rb Capablanca
  Capablanca:deepthought.org             Hal:deepdoodoo.org

Connecting...                          Connecting...
Playing Capablanca...you are white.    Playing Hal... you are black.
+-------------------------------+      +-------------------------------+
| Stub! Drawing the board here... |    | Stub! Drawing the board here... |
+-------------------------------+      +-------------------------------+

Your move: N-QB3                       Opponent: N-QB3
+-------------------------------+      +-------------------------------+
| Stub! Drawing the board here... |    | Stub! Drawing the board here... |
+-------------------------------+      +-------------------------------+

Opponent: P-K4                         Your move: P-K4
+-------------------------------+      +-------------------------------+
| Stub! Drawing the board here... |    | Stub! Drawing the board here... |
+-------------------------------+      +-------------------------------+

Your move: P-K4                        Opponent: P-K4
+-------------------------------+      +-------------------------------+
| Stub! Drawing the board here... |    | Stub! Drawing the board here... |
+-------------------------------+      +-------------------------------+

Opponent: B-QB4                        Your move: B-QB4
+-------------------------------+      +-------------------------------+
| Stub! Drawing the board here... |    | Stub! Drawing the board here... |
+-------------------------------+      +-------------------------------+

Your move: B-QB4                       Opponent: B-QB4
+-------------------------------+      +-------------------------------+
| Stub! Drawing the board here... |    | Stub! Drawing the board here... |
+-------------------------------+      +-------------------------------+

Opponent: Q-KR5                        Your move: Q-KR5
+-------------------------------+      +-------------------------------+
| Stub! Drawing the board here... |    | Stub! Drawing the board here... |
+-------------------------------+      +-------------------------------+

Your move: N-KB3                       Opponent: N-KB3
+-------------------------------+      +-------------------------------+
| Stub! Drawing the board here... |    | Stub! Drawing the board here... |
+-------------------------------+      +-------------------------------+

Opponent: QxP Checkmate!               Your move: QxP
+-------------------------------+      +-------------------------------+
| Stub! Drawing the board here... |    | Stub! Drawing the board here... |
+-------------------------------+      +-------------------------------+

Capablanca has checkmated you.         You have checkmated Hal!
```

18.2   Network Clients

Sometimes the server is a well-known entity or is using a well-established protocol. In this case, we need simply to design a client that will talk to this server in the way it expects.

This can be done with TCP or UDP, as you saw in Section 18.1, "Network Servers." However, it is common to use other higher-level protocols such as HTTP and SNMP. We'll look at a few examples here.

18.2.1   Retrieving Truly Random Numbers from the Web

Anyone who attempts to generate random numbers by deterministic means is, of course, living in a state of sin.

—John von Neumann

The rand function in Kernel returns a random number, but there is a fundamental problem with it: It isn't really random. If you are a mathematician, cryptographer, or other nitpicker, you will refer to this as a *pseudorandom* number generator because it uses algebraic methods to generate numbers in a deterministic fashion. These numbers "look" random to the casual observer, and may even have the correct statistical properties, but the sequences do repeat eventually, and we can even repeat a sequence purposely (or accidentally) by using the same seed.

However, processes in nature are considered to be truly random. That is why in state lotteries, winners of millions of dollars are picked based on the chaotic motions of little white balls. Other sources of randomness are radioactive emissions and atmospheric noise.

You can find sources of random numbers on the Web. One of these is www.random.org, which we use in this example.

The sample code in Listing 18.4 simulates the throwing of five ordinary (six-sided) dice. Of course, gaming fans could extend this to 10-sided or 20-sided dice, but the ASCII art would get tedious.

Listing 18.4 Casting Dice at Random

```
require 'net/http'

URL = "http://www.random.org/integers/"

def get_random_numbers(count=1, min=0, max=99)
  uri = URI.parse(URL)
  uri.query = URI.encode_www_form(
    col: 1, base: 10, format: "plain", rnd: "new",
    num: count, min: min, max: max
  )
  response = Net::HTTP.get_response(uri)
  case response
  when Net::HTTPOK
    response.body.lines.map(&:to_i)
  else
    []
  end
end

DICE_LINES = [
  "+-----+ +-----+ +-----+ +-----+ +-----+ +-----+ ",
  "|     | |  *  | |*    | | * * | | * * | | * * | ",
  "|  *  | |     | |  *  | |     | |  *  | | * * | ",
  "|     | |  *  | |    *| | * * | | * * | | * * | ",
  "+-----+ +-----+ +-----+ +-----+ +-----+ +-----+ ",
]

DIE_WIDTH = DICE_LINES[0].length/6

def draw_dice(values)
  DICE_LINES.each do |line|
    for v in values
      print line[(v-1)*DIE_WIDTH, DIE_WIDTH]
      print " "
    end
    puts
  end
end

draw_dice(get_random_numbers(5, 1, 6))
```

In this code, we're using the Net::HTTP class to communicate directly with a web server. Think of it as a highly special-purpose web browser. We form the URL and try to connect; when we make a connection, we get a response; if the response indicates that all is well, we can parse the response body that we got back. Exceptions are assumed to be handled by the caller.

Let's look at a variation on the same basic idea. What if we really wanted to use these random numbers in an application? Because the CGI at the server end allows us to specify how many numbers we want returned, it's logical to buffer them. It's a fact of life that a delay is usually involved when accessing a remote site. We want to fill a buffer so that we are not making frequent web accesses and incurring delays.

In Listing 18.5, we implement this variation. The buffer is filled by a separate thread, and it is shared among all the instances of the class. The buffer size and the "low water mark" (@slack) are both tunable; appropriate real-world values for them would be dependent on the reachability (ping time) of the server and on how often the application requested a random number from the buffer.

Listing 18.5   A Buffered Random Number Generator

```ruby
require "net/http"
require "thread"

class TrueRandom

  URL = "http://www.random.org/integers/"

  def initialize(min = 0, max = 1, buffsize = 1000, slack = 300)
    @buffer = SizedQueue.new(buffsize)
    @min, @max, @slack = min, max, slack
    @thread = Thread.new { fillbuffer }
  end

  def fillbuffer
    count = @buffer.max - @buffer.size

    uri = URI.parse(URL)
    uri.query = URI.encode_www_form(
      col: 1, base: 10, format: "plain", rnd: "new",
      num: count, min: @min, max: @max
    )

    Net::HTTP.get(uri).lines.each do |line|
      @buffer.push line.to_i
    end
  end

  def rand
    if @buffer.size < @slack && !@thread.alive?
      @thread = Thread.new { fillbuffer }
    end

    @buffer.pop
  end
```

```
end

t = TrueRandom.new(1, 6, 1000, 300)
count = Hash.new(0)

10000.times do |n|
  count[t.rand] += 1
end

p count

# In one run:
# {4=>1692, 5=>1677, 1=>1678, 6=>1635, 2=>1626, 3=>1692}
```

18.2.2   Contacting an Official Timeserver

As we promised, here's a bit of code to contact a Network Time Protocol (NTP) server on the Net, using TCPSocket to connect to a public time server and read the time:

```
require "socket"

resp = TCPSocket.new("time.nist.gov", 13).read
time = ts.split(" ")[2] + " UTC"
remote = Time.parse(time)

puts "Local : #{Time.now.utc.strftime("%H:%M:%S")}"
puts "Remote: #{remote.strftime("%H:%M:%S")}"
```

We establish a connection and read from the socket. The server response includes the Julian date, the date in YY-MM-DD format, the time in HH:MM:SS format, days left until a change to or from Daylight Saving Time, and some other informational flags. We read the entire response, parse only the time, and then print the time on the local machine for comparison.

Note that this example does not use the NTP protocol, which is a more complex format that contains additional data (such as the latency of responses with the time). Instead, we used the much simpler DAYTIME protocol. A full implementation of NTP is too long to reproduce here (although it is only about three pages of code). To see a full NTP implementation, read the source of the net-ntp gem online.

18.2.3   Interacting with a POP Server

The Post Office Protocol (POP) is commonly used by mail servers. Ruby's POP3 class enables you to examine the headers and bodies of all messages waiting on a server and process them as you see fit. After processing, you can easily delete one or all of them.

The Net::POP3 class must be instantiated with the name or IP address of the server; the port number defaults to 110. No connection is established until the method start is invoked (with the appropriate username and password).

Invoking the method mails on this object will return an array of objects of class POPMail. (There is also an iterator each that will run through these one at a time.)

A POPMail object corresponds to a single email message. The header method will retrieve the message's headers; the method all will retrieve the header and the body. (There are also other usages of all, as you'll see shortly.)

A code fragment is worth a thousand words. Here's a little example that will log on to the server and print the subject line for each email:

```
require "net/pop"

pop = Net::POP3.new("pop.fakedomain.org")
pop.start("gandalf", "mellon")      # user, password
pop.mails.each do |msg|
  puts msg.header.lines.grep /^Subject: /
end
```

The delete method will delete a message from the server. (Some servers require that finish be called to close the POP connection before such an operation becomes final.) Here is the world's most trivial spam filter:

```
require "net/pop"

pop = Net::POP3.new("pop.fakedomain.org")
pop.start("gandalf", "mellon")      # user, password
pop.mails.each do |msg|
  if msg.all =~ /.*make money fast.*/
    msg.delete
  end
end
pop.finish
```

We'll mention that start can be called with a block. By analogy with File.open, it opens the connection, executes the block, and closes the connection.

The all method can also be called with a block. This will simply iterate over the lines in the email message; it is equivalent to calling each_line on the string resulting from all:

```
# Print each line backwards... how useful!
msg.all { |line| print line.reverse }
# Same thing...
msg.all.each_line { |line| print line.reverse }
```

We can also pass an object into the all method. In this case, it will call the append operator (<<) repeatedly for each line in the string. Because this operator is defined differently for different objects, the behavior may be radically different, as shown here:

```
arr = []            # Empty array
str = "Mail: "      # String
out = $stdout        # IO object

msg.all(arr)        # Build an array of lines
msg.all(str)        # Concatenate onto str
msg.all(out)        # Write to standard output
```

Finally, we'll give you a way to return only the body of the message, ignoring all headers:

```
module Net
  class POPMail
    def body
      # Skip header bytes
      self.all[self.header.size..-1]
    end
  end
end
```

This doesn't have all the properties that all has, but it could be extended. We'll leave that to you.

For those who prefer IMAP to POP3, see Section 18.2.5, "Interacting with an IMAP Server."

18.2.4   Sending Mail with SMTP

A child of five could understand this. Fetch me a child of five.

—*Groucho Marx*

The Simple Mail Transfer Protocol (SMTP) may seem like a misnomer. If it is "simple," it is only by comparison with more complex protocols.

Of course, the smtp library shields the programmer from most of the details of the protocol. However, we have found that the design of this library is not entirely intuitive and perhaps overly complex (and we hope it will change in the future). In this section, we try to present a few examples to you in easily digested pieces.

The Net::SMTP class has two class methods, new and start. The new method takes two parameters—the name of the server (defaulting to localhost) and the port number (defaulting to the well-known port 25).

The start method takes these parameters:

- *server* is the IP name of the SMTP server, defaulting to "localhost".

- *port* is the port number, defaulting to 25.

- *domain* is the domain of the mail sender, defaulting to ENV["HOSTNAME"].

- *account* is the username; the default is nil.

- *password* is the user password, defaulting to nil.

- *authtype* is the authorization type, defaulting to :cram_md5.

Many or most of these parameters may be omitted under normal circumstances.

If start is called "normally" (without a block), it returns an object of class SMTP. If it is called with a block, that object is passed into the block as a convenience.

An SMTP object has an instance method called sendmail, which will typically be used to do the work of mailing a message. It takes three parameters:

- *source* is a string or array (or anything with an each iterator returning one string at a time).

- *sender* is a string that will appear in the "from" field of the email.

- *recipients* is a string or an array of strings representing the addressee(s).

Here is an example of using the class methods to send an email:

```
require 'net/smtp'

msg = <<EOF
Subject: Many things
"The time has come," the Walrus said,
"To talk of many things —
Of shoes, and ships, and sealing wax,
Of cabbages and kings;
And why the sea is boiling hot,
And whether pigs have wings."
EOF

Net::SMTP.start("smtp-server.fake.com") do |smtp|
   smtp.sendmail msg, 'walrus@fake1.com', 'alice@fake2.com'
end
```

Because the string Subject: was specified at the beginning of the string, Many things will appear as the subject line when the message is received.

There is also an instance method named start, which behaves much the same as the class method. Because new specifies the server, start doesn't have to specify it. This parameter is omitted, and the others are the same as for the class method. This gives us a similar example using an SMTP object:

```
require 'net/smtp'

msg = <<EOF
Subject: Logic
"Contrariwise," continued Tweedledee,
"if it was so, it might be, and if it
were so, it would be; but as it isn't,
it ain't. That's logic."
EOF

smtp = Net::SMTP.new("smtp-server.fake.com")
smtp.start
smtp.sendmail msg, 'tweedledee@fake1.com', 'alice@fake2.com'
```

In case you are not confused yet, the instance method can also take a block:

```
require 'net/smtp'

msg = <<EOF
Subject: Moby-Dick
Call me Ishmael.
EOF

addressees = ['reader1@fake2.com', 'reader2@fake3.com']

smtp = Net::SMTP.new("smtp-server.fake.com")
smtp.start do |obj|
  obj.sendmail msg, 'narrator@fake1.com', addressees
end
```

As the example shows, the object passed into the block (obj) certainly need not be named the same as the receiver (smtp). I'll also take this opportunity to emphasize that the recipient can be an array of strings.

There is also an oddly named instance method called ready. This is much the same as sendmail, with some crucial differences. Only the sender and recipients are specified; the body of the message is constructed using an adapter—an object of class Net::NetPrivate::WriteAdapter—which has a write method as well as an append method. This adapter is passed into the block and can be written to in an arbitrary way:

```
require "net/smtp"

smtp = Net::SMTP.new("smtp-server.fake1.com")

smtp.start

smtp.ready("t.s.eliot@fake1.com", "reader@fake2.com") do |obj|
  obj.write "Let us go then, you and I,\r\n"
  obj.write "When the evening is spread out against the sky\r\n"
  obj.write "Like a patient etherised upon a table...\r\n"
end
```

Note here that the carriage-return linefeed pairs are necessary (if we actually want line breaks in the message). Those who are familiar with the actual details of the protocol should note that the message is "finalized" (with "dot" and "QUIT") without any action on our part.

We can append instead of calling `write` if we want:

```
smtp.ready("t.s.eliot@fake1.com", "reader@fake2.com") do |obj|
  obj << "In the room the women come and go\r\n"
  obj << "Talking of Michelangelo.\r\n"
end
```

Finally, we offer a minor improvement. We add a `puts` method that will tack on the newline for us:

```
class Net::NetPrivate::WriteAdapter
  def puts(args)
    args << "\r\n"
    self.write(*args)
  end
end
```

This new method enables us to write this way:

```
smtp.ready("t.s.eliot@fake1.com", "reader@fake2.com") do |obj|
  obj.puts "We have lingered in the chambers of the sea"
  obj.puts "By sea-girls wreathed with seaweed red and brown"
  obj.puts "Till human voices wake us, and we drown."
end
```

If your needs are more specific than what we've detailed here, we suggest you do your own experimentation. And if you decide to write a new interface for SMTP, please feel free.

18.2.5   Interacting with an IMAP Server

The IMAP protocol is not the prettiest in the world, but it is superior to POP3 in many ways. Messages may be stored on the server indefinitely (individually marked as read or unread). Messages may be stored in hierarchical folders. These two facts alone are enough to establish IMAP as more powerful than POP3.

The standard library `net/imap` enables us to interact with an IMAP server. As you would expect, you connect to the server and then log in to an account with a username and password, as shown in the following code:

```
require 'net/imap'

host = "imap.hogwarts.edu"
user, pass = "lupin", "riddikulus"

imap = Net::IMAP.new(host)
begin
  imap.login(user, pass)
  # Or alternately:
  # imap.authenticate("LOGIN", user, pass)
rescue Net::IMAP::NoResponseError
  abort "Could not login as #{user}"
end

# Process as needed...
imap.logout    # break the connection
```

After you have a connection, you can do an examine on a mailbox; the default mailbox in IMAP is called INBOX. The responses method retrieves information about the mailbox, returning a hash of arrays (with the interesting data in the last element of each array). The following code finds the total number of messages in the mailbox ("EXISTS") and the number of unread messages ("RECENT"):

```
imap.examine("INBOX")
total = imap.responses["EXISTS"].last    # total messages
recent = imap.responses["RECENT"].last   # unread messages
imap.close                               # close the mailbox
```

Note that examine gives you read-only access to the mailbox. If, for example, you want to delete messages or make other changes, you should use select instead.

IMAP mailboxes are hierarchical and look similar to UNIX pathnames. You can use the create, delete, and rename methods to manipulate mailboxes:

```
imap.create("lists")
imap.create("lists/ruby")
imap.create("lists/rails")
imap.create("lists/foobar")

# Oops, kill that last one:
imap.delete("lists/foobar")
```

There are also methods named `list` (to list all the available mailboxes) and `lsub` (to list all the "active" or "subscribed" mailboxes). The `status` method will return information about the mailbox.

The `search` method will find messages according to specified criteria, and `fetch` will fetch a given message. Here is an example:

```
msgs = imap.search("TO","lupin")
msgs.each do |mid|
  env = imap.fetch(mid, "ENVELOPE")[0].attr["ENVELOPE"]
  puts "From #{env.from[0].name}     #{env.subject}"
end
```

The `fetch` command in the preceding code appears convoluted because it returns an array of hashes. The envelope itself is similarly complex; some of its accessors are arrays of complex objects, and some are simply strings.

IMAP has the concept of unique IDs (UIDs) and sequence numbers for messages. Typically, methods such as `fetch` deal with sequence numbers and have counterparts such as `uid_fetch` that deal with UIDs. There is no room here to explain why both numbering systems are appropriate; if you are doing any significant programming with IMAP, however, you will need to know the difference (and never get them mixed up).

The `net/imap` library has extensive support for handling mailboxes, messages, attachments, and so on. For more details, refer to the API reference documentation.

18.2.6   Encoding/Decoding Attachments

Files are usually attached to email or news messages in a special encoded form. More often than not, the encoding is `base64`, which can be encoded or decoded with the `Base64` class:

```
bin = File.read("new.gif")
str = Base64.encode64(bin)    # str is now encoded
orig = Base64.decode64(str)   # orig == bin
```

Older mail clients may prefer to work with uuencode and uudecode; in a case like this, an attachment is more a state of mind than anything else. The attachment is simply appended to the end of the email text, bracketed inside `begin` and `end` lines, with the `begin` line also specifying file permissions (which may be ignored) and filename. The pack directive `u` serves to encode a uuencoded string. The following code shows an example:

```
# Assume mailtext holds the text of the email

filename = "new.gif"
bin = File.read(filename)
encoded = [bin].pack("u")

mailtext << "begin 644 #{filename}"
mailtext << encoded
mailtext << "end"
# ...
```

On the receiving end, we would extract the encoded information and use `unpack` to decode it:

```
# ...
# Assume 'attached' has the encoded data (including the
# begin and end lines)

lines = attached.lines
filename = /begin \d\d\d (.*)/.scan(lines[0]).first.first
encoded = lines[1..-2].join("\n")
decoded = encoded.unpack("u")       # Ready to write to filename
```

More modern mail readers usually use MIME format for email; even the text part of the email is wrapped (although the client strips all the header information before the user sees it).

A complete treatment of MIME would be lengthy and off topic here. However, the following code shows a simple example of encoding and sending an email with a text portion and a binary attachment. The encoding for binaries is usually `base64`, as shown here:

```
require 'net/smtp'

def text_plus_attachment(subject,body,filename)
  marker = "MIME_boundary"
  middle = "-#{marker}\n"
  ending = "-#{middle}-\n"
  content = "Content-Type: Multipart/Related; " +
            "boundary=#{marker}; " +
            "typw=text/plain"
  head1 = <<-EOF
MIME-Version: 1.0
```

```
#{content}
Subject: #{subject}
  EOF
  binary = File.read(filename)
  encoded = [binary].pack("m")    # base64
  head2 = <<EOF
Content-Description: "#{filename}"
Content-Type: image/gif; name="#{filename}"
Content-Transfer-Encoding: Base64
Content-Disposition: attachment; filename="#{filename}"

EOF

  # Return...
  head1 + middle + body + middle + head2 + encoded + ending
end


domain = "someserver.com"
smtp    = "smtp.#{domain}"
user, pass = "elgar","enigma"


body = <<EOF
This is my email. There isn't
much to say. I attached a
very small GIF file here.


        — Bob
EOF

mailtext = text_plus_attachment("Hi there...",body,"new.gif")

Net::SMTP.start(smtp, 25, domain, user, pass, :plain) do |mailer|
  mailer.sendmail(mailtext, 'fromthisguy@wherever.com',
                  ['destination@elsewhere.com'])
end
```

18.2.7   Case Study: A Mail-News Gateway

Online communities keep in touch with each other in many ways. Two of the most traditional of these are mailing lists and newsgroups.

Not everyone wants to be on a mailing list that may generate dozens of messages per day; some would rather read a newsgroup and pick through the information at random intervals. On the other hand, some people are impatient with Usenet and want to get the messages before the electrons have time to cool off.

Therefore, we get situations in which a fairly small, private mailing list deals with the same subject matter as an unmoderated newsgroup open to the whole world. Eventually someone gets the idea for a mirror—a gateway between the two.

Such a gateway isn't appropriate in every situation, but in the case of the Ruby mailing list, there was such a gateway from 2001 to 2011. The newsgroup messages were copied to the list, and the list emails were posted on the newsgroup.

This task was accomplished by Dave Thomas (in Ruby, of course), and we present the code with his kind permission in Listings 18.6 and 18.7.

But let's look at a little background first. We've taken a quick look at how email is sent and received, but how do we handle Usenet? As it turns out, we can access the newsgroups via a protocol called the Network News Transfer Protocol (NNTP). This creation, incidentally, was the work of Larry Wall, who later on gave us Perl.

Ruby doesn't have a "standard" library to handle NNTP, but there are several gems available that provide NNTP functionality. These examples depend on the NNTP library written by a Japanese developer (known to us only as "greentea").

The nntp.rb library defines a module NNTP containing a class called NNTPIO; it has instance methods connect, get_head, get_body, and post (among others). To retrieve messages, you connect to the server and call get_head and get_body, repetitively. (We're oversimplifying this.) Likewise, to post a message, you basically construct the headers, connect to the server, and call the post method.

These programs use the smtp library, which we've looked at previously. The original code also does some logging to track progress and record errors; we've removed this logging for greater simplicity.

The file params.rb is used by both programs. This file contains the parameters that drive the whole mirroring process—the names of the servers, account names, and so on. The following is a sample file that you will need to reconfigure for your own purposes. (The domain names used in the code, which all contain the word *fake*, are obviously intended to be fictitious.)

```
# These are various parameters used by the mail-news gateway
module Params
  NEWS_SERVER   = "usenet.fake1.org"      # name of the news server
  NEWSGROUP     = "comp.lang.ruby"        # mirrored newsgroup
  LOOP_FLAG     = "X-rubymirror: yes"     # avoid loops
  LAST_NEWS_FILE = "/tmp/m2n/last_news"   # last msg num read
  SMTP_SERVER   = "localhost"            # host for outgoing mail
```

```
    MAIL_SENDER = "myself@fake2.org"        # Name used to send mail
    # (On a subscription-based list, this
    # name must be a list member.)

    MAILING_LIST = "list@fake3.org"         # Mailing list address
  end
```

The module `Params` merely contains constants that are accessed by the two programs. Most are self-explanatory; we'll only point out a couple of items here. First, the `LAST_NEWS_FILE` constant identifies a file where the most recent newsgroup message ID is stored; this is "state information," so that work is not duplicated or lost.

Perhaps even more important, the `LOOP_FLAG` constant defines a string that marks a message as having already passed through the gateway. This avoids infinite recursion and prevents the programmer from being mobbed by hordes of angry netizens who have received thousands of copies of the same message.

You might be wondering, how do we actually get the mail into the `mail2news` program? After all, it appears to read standard input. Well, the author recommends a setup like this: The `sendmail` program's `.forward` file first forwards all incoming mail to `procmail`. The `.procmail` file is set up to scan for messages from the mailing list and pipe them into the `mail2news` program. For the exact details of this, see the documentation associated with RubyMirror (found in the Ruby Application Archive). Of course, if you are on a non-UNIX system, you will likely have to come up with your own scheme for handling this situation.

Aside from what we've already said, we'll let the code stand on its own, as shown in Listings 18.6 and 18.7.

Listing 18.6 Mail-to-News

```
# mail2news: Take a mail message and post it
# as a news article

require "nntp"
include NNTP

require "params"

# Read in the message, splitting it into a
# heading and a body. Only allow certain
# headers through in the heading

HEADERS = %w{From Subject References Message-ID
             Content-Type Content-Transfer-Encoding Date}
```

```
allowed_headers = Regexp.new(%{^(#{HEADERS.join("|")}):})

# Read in the header. Only allow certain
# ones. Add a newsgroups line and an
# X-rubymirror line.

head = "Newsgroups: #{Params::NEWSGROUP}\n"
subject = "unknown"

while line = gets
  exit if line =~ /^#{Params::LOOP_FLAG}/o # shouldn't happen
  break if line =~ /^\s*$/
  next if line =~ /^\s/
  next unless line =~ allowed_headers

  # strip off the [ruby-talk:nnnn] prefix on the subject before
  # posting back to the news group
  if line =~ /^Subject:\s*(.*)/
    subject = $1

    # The following strips off the special ruby-talk number
    # from the front of mailing list messages before
    # forwarding them on to the news server.

    line.sub!(/\[ruby-talk:(\d+)\]\s*/, '')
    subject = "[#$1] #{line}"
    head << "X-ruby-talk: #$1\n"
  end
  head << line
end

head << "#{Params::LOOP_FLAG}\n"

body = ""
while line = gets
  body << line
end

msg = head + "\n" + body
msg.gsub!(/\r?\n/, "\r\n")

nntp = NNTPIO.new(Params::NEWS_SERVER)
raise "Failed to connect" unless nntp.connect
nntp.post(msg)
```

Listing 18.7   News-to-Mail

```
##
# Simple script to help mirror the comp.lang.ruby
# traffic on to the ruby-talk mailing list.
```

```
#
# We are called periodically (say once every 20 minutes).
# We look on the news server for any articles that have a
# higher message ID than the last message we'd sent
# previously. If we find any, we read those articles,
# send them on to the mailing list, and record the
# new hightest message id.

require 'nntp'
require 'net/smtp'
require 'params'

include NNTP

##
# Send mail to the mailing-list. The mail must be
# from a list participant, although the From: line
# can contain any valid address
#

def send_mail(head, body)
  smtp = Net::SMTP.new
  smtp.start(Params::SMTP_SERVER)
  smtp.ready(Params::MAIL_SENDER, Params::MAILING_LIST) do |a|
    a.write head
    a.write "#{Params::LOOP_FLAG}\r\n"
    a.write "\r\n"
    a.write body
  end
end

##
# We store the message ID of the last news we received.

begin
  last_news = File.open(Params::LAST_NEWS_FILE) {|f| f.read} .to_i
rescue
  last_news = nil
end

##
# Connect to the news server, and get the current
# message numbers for the comp.lang.ruby group
#
nntp = NNTPIO.new(Params::NEWS_SERVER)
raise "Failed to connect" unless nntp.connect
count, first, last = nntp.set_group(Params::NEWSGROUP)

##
# If we didn't previously have a number for the highest
# message number, we do now
```

```
if not last_news
  last_news = last
end

##
# Go to the last one read last time, and then try to get more.
# This may raise an exception if the number is for a
# nonexistent article, but we don't care.

begin
  nntp.set_stat(last_news)
rescue
end

##
# Finally read articles until there aren't any more,
# sending each to the mailing list.

new_last = last_news

begin
  loop do
    nntp.set_next
    head = ""
    body = ""
    new_last, = nntp.get_head do |line|
      head << line
    end

    # Don't sent on articles that the mail2news program has
    # previously forwarded to the newsgroup (or we'd loop)
    next if head =~ %r{^X-rubymirror:}

    nntp.get_body do |line|
      body << line
    end

    send_mail(head, body)
  end
rescue
end

##
# And record the new high water mark

File.open(Params::LAST_NEWS_FILE, "w") do |f|
  f.puts new_last
end unless new_last == last_news
```

18.2.8   Retrieving a Web Page from a URL

Suppose that, for whatever reason, we want to retrieve an HTML document from where it lives on the Web. Maybe our intent is to do a checksum and find whether it has changed so that our software can inform us of this automatically. Maybe our intent is to write our own web browser; this would be the proverbial first step on a journey of a thousand miles.

Here's the code:

```ruby
require "net/http"

begin
  # Space as in space travel
  uri = URI(http://www.space.com/index.html)
  res = Net::HTTP.get(uri)
rescue => err
  puts "Error: #{err.class}: #{err.message}"
  exit
end

puts "Retrieved #{res.body.lines.size} lines " \
     "and#{res.body.size} bytes"
# Process as desired...
```

We begin by creating a `URI` object with the complete protocol, domain name, and path. (The port is implied by the protocol to be 80, but can be added with a colon after the domain.) We then call the `Net::HTTP.get` method, which returns a `Net::HTTP` response object. Here, we don't actually test the response, but if there is some kind of error, we'll catch it and exit.

If we skip the `rescue` clause as we normally would, we can expect to have an entire web page stored in the `res.body` string. We can then process it however we want.

What could go wrong here—what kind of errors do we catch? Actually, there are several. The domain name could be nonexistent or unreachable; there could be a time-out error, an IO error, a socket error, or any of several system errors.

In addition, the response might not have succeeded: There could be a redirect to another page (which we don't handle here), or we might get the dreaded 404 error (meaning that the document was not found). We'll leave handling these errors and responses to you.

The next section will also be useful to you. It shows a slightly simpler way of handling this kind of task.

18.2.9   Using the Open-URI Library

The Open-URI library is the work of Tanaka Akira. Its purpose is to "unify" the programmatic treatment of net resources so that they are all intuitive and easy to handle.

This code is essentially a wrapper for the `net/http`, `net/https`, and `net/ftp` libraries, making available an `open` method that will handle an arbitrary URI. The example from the preceding section can be written this way:

```
require 'open-uri'
site = open("http://www.marsdrive.com/")
data = site.read
puts "Retrieved #{data.split.size} lines, #{data.size} bytes"
```

The file returned by `open` (`site` in the previous case) is not just a file. This object also has the methods of the `OpenURI::Meta` module so that we can access metadata:

```
# ...
uri = f.base_uri            # a URI object with its own readers
ct = f.content_type         # "text/html"
cs = f.charset              # "utf-8"
ce = f.content_encoding     # []
```

The library allows the specifying of additional header fields by using a hash with the `open` command. It also handles proxy servers and has several other useful features. There are cases where this library may be insufficient; for example, you may need to parse HTTP headers, buffer extremely large downloads, send cookies, and other such tasks. In those cases, you can use the `net/http` library or a gem for making HTTP requests, such the `http`, `curb`, or `httparty` gem. As always, API documentation for these libraries and gems is available online at rdoc.info.

18.3   Conclusion

In this chapter, we've had a good introduction to lower-level networking, including simple servers and clients. We've seen how to write a client for an existing server that we didn't create.

We've looked at higher-level protocols such as POP and IMAP for receiving mail. Likewise, we've looked at SMTP for sending mail. In connection with these, we've seen how to encode and decode file attachments. We've also had an exposure to NNTP through the mail-news gateway code.

Now it's time to look more closely at a subset of this topic. One of the most important types of network programming today is web development, which is the topic of the next chapter.

CHAPTER 19

Ruby and Web Applications

O, what a tangled web we weave…!

—*Sir Walter Scott,* The Lay of the Last Minstrel

Ruby rose to extreme (and some might even say overhyped) popularity over the last decade or so. Although Ruby is a general-purpose language, and can be used for any programming task, the majority of Ruby's rise to fame is the result of a single Ruby library, Ruby on Rails. Created by David Heinemeier Hansson and first released in 2004, Rails (as it is popularly known) allows developers to produce rich, interactive web applications with previously unprecedented speed.

In this chapter, we'll examine how to respond to HTTP requests from a web browser or API client (such as a mobile application or another web service). We'll give an overview of the advantages provided by Ruby web frameworks such as Rails and Sinatra, and examine the many tools that integrate with those frameworks to ease working with data stores, HTML, CSS, and JavaScript. Finally, we'll look briefly at how to produce and consume HTTP APIs from Ruby, and how to generate complex static sites easily.

To start off, we'll look at HTTP servers.

19.1   HTTP Servers

HTTP servers make up a huge proportion of the programs in service today. They provide interfaces to our communications, documents, finances, travel plans, and nearly every other aspect of life. As complex as those web apps can be, though, they are all served over HTTP, which is a very simple protocol. In essence, HTTP is just a few lines of plain text describing each request and response, all sent over a TCP socket.

19.1.1   A Simple HTTP Server

To demonstrate exactly how simple HTTP is, we will begin by writing an HTTP server in Ruby that can be accessed using any web browser. Try running Listing 19.1 and then opening the URL `http://localhost:3000` in your web browser.

Listing 19.1   A Simple HTTP Server

```
require 'socket'
server = TCPServer.new 3000

loop do
  # Accept the connection
  socket = server.accept

  # Print the request, which ends in a blank line
  puts line = socket.readline until line == "\r\n"

  # Tell the browser we are an HTTP server
  socket.write "HTTP/1.1 200 OK\r\n"
  # Tell the browser the body is 52 bytes
  socket.write "Content-Length: 51\r\n"
  # Empty line to separate headers from body
  socket.write "\r\n"
  # Write the HTML that makes up the body
  socket.write "<html><body>"
  socket.write "<h1>Hello from Ruby!</h1>"
  socket.write "</body></html>\n"
  # Close the connection
  socket.close
end
```

In this server, we accept incoming requests for a TCP connection. Then, we print each line of text sent by the web browser until there is an empty line. Next, we send an *HTTP Response*, which is just text in a specific format that the browser can understand.

The response consists of a status code, headers, and body. In our response, we send the status code 200, which indicates a successful request and response. There are many other status codes, including redirection to a different location (301 and 302), no item at that address (404), or even an error on the server (500). For a complete list, refer to a reference online such as Wikipedia or httpstatus.es.

After the status code, we send a single header, indicating to the browser how many bytes there will be in the body we are about to send. Additional headers are optional, and can be used to indicate things such as what we are sending in the body (HTML, JSON, XML, or even a video or audio file), whether the body will be compressed, and other information.

Last, we send an empty line that indicates the headers are over and the body will follow. As you may have noticed, the line breaks are not simple \n linefeed characters, but are \r\n (the carriage return character followed by the linefeed character). A single linefeed is the standard line break on UNIX and Mac OS X machines, whereas the combined carriage return and linefeed is the standard line break on Windows machines and some other systems, as well as HTTP requests and responses.

At this point, if you have run the server and opened localhost:3000 in your browser, you should be able to see a large, bold "Hello from Ruby!" in your web browser. In your terminal, you will be able to see the exact text that the browser sent to your server. For me, the terminal output looked like this:

```
GET / HTTP/1.1
Host: localhost:3000
Accept: text/html,application/xhtml+xml,application/xml;q=0.9,
   */*;q=0.8
Accept-Encoding: gzip, deflate
Accept-Language: en-us
User-Agent: Mozilla/5.0 (Macintosh; Intel Mac OS X 10_9_4)
   AppleWebKit/537.78.2 (KHTML, like Gecko)
   Version/7.0.6 Safari/537.78.2
Cache-Control: max-age=0
Connection: keep-alive
```

This output is the contents of an HTTP request. As you can see, it is very similar to the HTTP response we created in Listing 19.1. The request opens with a line declaring the request: in this case, a GET request for the path /. The Host header indicates the domain name for the request, which is localhost. The various Accept headers indicate that the browser would like a response in HTML, XHTML, or XML, the response may be compressed, and the response should be in English. The User-Agent header indicates the request is coming from the Safari browser (version 7.0.6).

19.1.2   Rack and Web Servers

Every HTTP server accepts requests like the one we just looked at, and sends responses like the one we constructed earlier. In 2007, Christian Neukirchen created a library called Rack. Rack provides a single API for all Ruby HTTP servers and web applications to share.

Bear in mind that Rack is not for high-level development so much as for the creation of tools, libraries, and frameworks. So it is more for use by expert developers, and framework or library users do not usually see its API. Once you grasp its purpose and usage, it becomes very powerful.

In my opinion, Rack is pure genius. Since its introduction several years ago, Rack-based software has processed many trillions of requests in Ruby-based applications.

Let's look at some details of how this works. An HTTP request consists at minimum of a hash-like set of parameters. The response that comes back comprises three parts: A status code, a set of headers, and a body.

Imagine that an object has a `call` method that returns an array of data in this format. Any class that follows these rules is a Rack application. Here is the simplest possible example of such a class:

```
class MyRackApp
  def call(env)
    [200, {'Content-type' => 'text/plain'}, ["Welcome to Rack!"]]
  end
end
```

Notice that the body itself is an array rather than just a string. This is because of a convention that the body should respond to the `each` method. (Actually, a simple string would also work here if it responded to `each` as in older versions of Ruby.)

So how do we run this application? There is more than one way. Rack comes with a utility called rackup which is part of the Rack gem. Basically this is just an app runner that works with a .ru file. Here is such a file, where we just invoke the app by passing the object as a parameter to the run method.

```
# Assumes previous definition
app = MyRackApp.new
run app
```

By convention, a Rack application is set up in a Ruby file named `config.ru`. Using Rack's simple API, we can rewrite our HTTP server much more simply. In this code fragment, we return the same HTTP response via Rack. Note the use of a simple "stabby lambda" rather than a more verbose solution.

```
run -> (env) { [
  200, {"Content-Type" => "text/html"}, ["<html><body>",
    "<h1>Hello from Ruby!</h1>", "</body></html>"]
] }
```

Every Rack application must respond to the `call` method, which is invoked once per request. The `env` argument that is passed to the `call` method contains information about that request, including the HTTP verb, requested path, request headers, client IP address, and more.

Because `Proc` objects all respond to `call`, the simplest Rack app is just a lambda, as in our example. Every Rack application must return a Rack response: one three-element array, consisting of the status code (as a number), the response headers (as a hash), and the body (as an object that responds to `each`, in this case an array).

An important concept making Rack useful is the idea of *middleware*. Think of a piece of middleware as an entity that sits between the browser (or client) and the server. This entity will process requests from the client to the server, and will also process responses from the server to the client.

In this way, middleware can be "chained" more or less arbitrarily. Each successive middleware component transforms the stream of information in some way. Think of the UNIX "pipe" (|) as an analogy.

There are conventions and techniques for writing your own middleware, but we won't cover that here. We'll just mention that there are numerous components already out there, either part of Rack or written by third parties. These enable functionality such as HTTP caching, spam traps, heartbeat checking, Google analytics, and more.

If you use Rack seriously, you may want to know the details of `Rack::Builder`; this is a DSL for building up a Rack application incrementally and "gluing" the various pieces into a single application. The rackup utility transforms your `.ru` file into a builder instance "behind the scenes"; but for more power and flexibility, you can do these operations yourself.

To run a Rack application, we can use one of the many Rack-compatible HTTP servers written in Ruby. Using a Ruby web server saves the trouble of writing and maintaining code to create a TCP server and correctly parse HTTP requests and format HTTP responses. If no servers are installed, Rack will use the Webrick server from the Ruby standard library, but it is not suitable for production applications. The most popular Ruby web server is Unicorn, which is optimized for single-threaded applications running on MRI. For more information about Unicorn, refer to the Unicorn documentation, hosted at `unicorn.bogomips.org`. With support for multi-threaded applications, as well as MRI, JRuby, and Rubinius, Puma is my Ruby web server of choice. For more on Puma, see the Puma website at `puma.io`.

Notice also the terminal output, which is now generated by the combination of Puma and Rack. This server generates just a single line of output for each request, but that line includes the IP address the request came from, the date and time, the HTTP verb, the path, the HTTP version, the status code that was returned, and the amount of time that it took to generate the response. Here is the output after starting Puma and making a single request:

```
Puma starting in single mode...
* Version 2.9.0 (ruby 2.1.2-p95), codename: Team High Five
* Min threads: 0, max threads: 16
* Environment: development
* Listening on tcp://0.0.0.0:9292
Use Ctrl-C to stop
127.0.0.1 - - [02/Sep/2014 16:32:26] "GET / HTTP/1.1" 200 - 0.0001
```

When we are using Rack, it is possible to access all the same information that we had access to when we accepted a TCP connection and read the request ourselves, but we don't have to do anywhere near as much work. We can simply access various keys on the env hash to get the data directly. Building on top of Rack and the unified cross-server API it provides are various application frameworks such as Rails.

19.2 Application Frameworks

As you can probably imagine, web applications can quickly become complex and unwieldy, even with the abstractions provided by Rack. That is where web application frameworks like Rails and Sinatra step in. A web framework provides (at a minimum) an additional layer of abstraction, making it possible to call different methods depending on the HTTP verb, the path, or any other conditional.

Ruby on Rails is the "batteries included" framework of the Ruby world. It includes a command-line tool to create and run Rails applications, and many individual libraries that manage responsibilities such as data storage, HTML template rendering, CSS and JavaScript management, and much more.

Sinatra is much more minimal, and provides barely more than a mapping between a particular URL and some Ruby code. Any additional facilities must be provided by other libraries (and in fact many Sinatra applications also use some parts of Rails). We'll give some examples from both Rails and Sinatra in this section, and then look at additional tools and libraries that integrate with Rails (and may be usable from Sinatra) for the remainder of this chapter.

There are other Ruby web application frameworks, including the venerable Ramaze, the brand-new Lotus, and others. If you're interested in different ways to build a web application framework, definitely check out the other options as well. If you're only interested in building your own web application, I recommend that you just use Rails. It has the widest adoption, the most users, and the most examples, solutions, and tutorials out there on the Web for times when more help is needed.

When a request is made, the first thing a Ruby application framework needs to do is decide what code should be run to respond to the request. This is usually called *routing,* and is provided by both Rails and Sinatra, albeit in different ways. We'll look at Sinatra first, then Rails.

The examples in this chapter were tested against Sinatra version 1.4.5 and Rails 4.1.5, on Ruby 2.1.2. If newer versions are now available, your mileage may vary. If necessary, you can install those exact versions in order to try out these examples.

19.2.1   Routing in Sinatra

Building on top of Rack, the Sinatra gem provides just a little bit more functionality. Sinatra applications map HTTP verbs and paths to code blocks that will be executed if the request matches. In Listing 19.2, we create a Sinatra application that provides the same functionality as our previous example.

We even go beyond our previous example and add an additional path to our application. Without Sinatra, we would have to examine the path of the request ourselves, and call different code based on what the requested path is. Sinatra provides that ability automatically, allowing us to map any HTTP verb and path to some specific Ruby code.

Listing 19.2   A Sinatra Application

```
require 'sinatra'

get "/" do
  <<-HTML
    <html>
      <body>
        <h1>Hello from Ruby!</h1>
      </body>
    </html>
  HTML
end

get "/world" do
  <<-HTML
    <html>
      <body>
        <h1>Hello, World!</h1>
      </body>
    </html>
  HTML
end
```

To run this example, save Listing 19.2 into a file named `sinatra.rb`. If necessary, install the Sinatra gem by running `gem install sinatra`, and then run the server with `ruby sinatra.rb`. At that point, you will be able to browse to `http://localhost:4567` to see our original example, and you will also be able to browse to `http://localhost:4567/world` to see the "Hello, World!" message.

The terminal output when running a Sinatra app is nearly identical to the output when running the Rack app. The only significant difference is that there is now a second log line, for the request to the `"/world"` URL.

```
Puma 2.9.0 starting...
* Min threads: 0, max threads: 16
* Environment: development
* Listening on tcp://localhost:4567
== Sinatra/1.4.5 has taken the stage on 4567 for development with
  backup from Puma
127.0.0.1 - - [02/Sep/2014 17:36:33] "GET / HTTP/1.1" 200 51 0.0047
127.0.0.1 - - [02/Sep/2014 17:36:38] "GET /world HTTP/1.1" 200 48
  0.0004
```

19.2.2 Routing in Rails

Next, we will look at the same example in Rails. The Rails gem itself contains very little code—instead, Rails combines other libraries that handle individual functions. The `ActionController` class, which is part of the `action_pack` gem, approaches the problem of routing somewhat differently from Sinatra. In Rails, the code that will be called is written inside a *controller*, and the `routes.rb` file specifies that a particular path should call a particular controller method.

Let's build our example again as a small Rails application. To start with, install Rails and all its components by running `gem install rails` if you have not already. Then, run the command `rails new hello`. This will create a directory named `hello` containing the entire skeleton of a Rails application. For right now, we don't care about most of those files, but to learn more about each one, you can read the "Getting Started with Rails" guide at `guides.rubyonrails.org`.

Next, `cd hello` to change directories into our new Rails application and then run `bin/rails generate controller hello`. Several files will be created, but the important one for our example is `app/controllers/hello_controller.rb`. Open that file in your editor and change it to match this code:

```
class HelloController < ApplicationController
  def index
    render inline: "<h1>Hello from Ruby!</h1>"
  end

  def world
    render inline: "<h1>Hello, World!</h1>"
  end
end
```

Here, we are defining two methods in the `HelloController`, both `index` and `world`. The names are arbitrary and can be connected to any path by the routing configuration. To add those routes, we need to edit the `config/routes.rb` file. This file is generated containing a lot of explanation about different kinds of routes, but for our example, we only need these four lines:

```
Rails.application.routes.draw do
  get "/" => "hello#index"
  get "/world" => "hello#world"
end
```

The syntax for declaring routes in Rails consists of calling a method with the name of the HTTP verb that will be routed and then passing a hash with the path as a key as well as the controller name and method in the form `name#index`. As you might now guess, this routes file means that a request to `"/"` will be served by the `index` method, and a request to `"/world"` will be served by the `world` method.

To run this example, execute the command `bin/rails server`. As you may have noticed by now, the `rails` command acts as a shortcut to common tasks that you may perform while building a web application using Rails. After the server has started up, browse to `http://localhost:3000` to see the output from our example. To see the alternate output, browse to the `http://localhost:3000/world` URL.

This time, the terminal output is different yet again, and includes several lines per request. These lines include the elements that we can expect from the previous examples: HTTP verb, requested path, requester IP address, timestamp, the HTTP status code returned, and the amount of time it took to generate the response:

```
=> Booting WEBrick
=> Rails 4.1.5 application starting in development on
   http://0.0.0.0:3000
=> Run `rails server -h` for more startup options
=> Ctrl-C to shutdown server
```

```
[2014-09-02 17:29:32] INFO  WEBrick 1.3.1
[2014-09-02 17:29:32] INFO  ruby 2.1.2 (2014-05-08)
  [x86_64-darwin13.0]
[2014-09-02 17:29:32] INFO  WEBrick::HTTPServer#start:
  pid=20372 port=3000

Started GET "/" for 127.0.0.1 at 2014-09-02 17:29:32 -0700
Processing by HelloController#index as HTML
  Rendered inline template (0.6ms)
Completed 200 OK in 10ms (Views: 3.2ms | ActiveRecord: 0.0ms)


Started GET "/world" for 127.0.0.1 at 2014-09-02 17:29:39 -0700
Processing by HelloController#world as HTML
  Rendered inline template (0.2ms)
Completed 200 OK in 1ms (Views: 0.4ms | ActiveRecord: 0.0ms)
```

In the middle two lines, however, we see new information: the name of the controller and method that were called to handle the response, `HelloController` `#index` and `#world`. We also see that the response was generated by rendering an *inline template*. We'll examine templates further in Section 19.4, "Generating HTML."

In addition to a path, HTTP requests can include *parameters*, which are sets of keys and values provided by the browser making the request, usually from input given by the browser's user. In both Sinatra and Rails, parameters can be accessed as a hash, named `params`. Entries in `params` can come from the URL or can be sent as part of the *request body* if the request uses the HTTP verb `POST`. Using request parameters, we can add *dynamic* output to our examples (meaning the output changes depending on the inputs given by the client).

19.2.3   Parameters in Sinatra

We can add another example to our Sinatra application that uses one parameter from the URL and one parameter from the *query string*, which is the part of the URL that comes after a ? symbol. Open the file `sinatra.rb`, saved from Listing 19.3, and add this code to the end of the file:

```
get "/hello/:name" do
  body = "<html><body><h1>Hello"
  body << " from " << CGI.h(params[:from]) if params[:from]
  body << ", " << CGI.h(params[:name])
  body << "!</h1></html></body>"
end
```

Here, we declare a parameter in the URL by using a colon, somewhat like a symbol in Ruby. Sinatra knows to parse the URL, looking for a path such as `/hello/Julia` or `/hello/Tim`. The part of the path that is in the location where `:name` is will be placed into the `params` hash, under the key `:name`. The other parameter we use, `from`, is not part of the path. That means it will have to be provided as part of the query string, in a path that looks something like `/hello/Julia?from=Ruby`.

When we insert either parameter into the HTML that will be returned in the response body, we escape it using the `CGI.h` method. The `h` method is an alias for `escape_html`. The method takes a string as input and returns a string with HTML-specific characters escaped. This escaping is critical for security, and must always be done when a web application will be returning input taken from a user inside an HTML response.

After adding to the file, fire up the server with `ruby sinatra.rb` and try it out! Experiment with different URLs, changing the `name` and `from`, and observing the result. Note that if the `from` key is absent, the response does not say where the hello is from, and if the name is absent (for example, at the path `/hello/`), an error message is returned.

19.2.4   Parameters in Rails

Parameters in Rails are very similar to parameters in Sinatra. We add one additional method to `app/controllers/hello_controller.rb`, named `hello`. (Make sure the method definition is inside the `class`/`end` block.)

```
def name
  response = "<h1>Hello"
  response << " from " << h(params[:from]) if params[:from]
  response << ", " << h(params[:name])
  response << "!</h1>"
  render inline: response
end
```

Then, open the `config/routes.rb` file and add this line, one line above the final end:

```
get "/hello/:name" => "hello#name"
```

As before, the method name `name` is arbitrary, but it is (hopefully) easy to remember that the path `/hello/:name` goes to the controller `Hello` and the method `name`. Start the server again using `bin/rails server` and browse to `http://localhost:3000/hello/Zelda?from=Ruby` to see the same response.

Note that there is a new line of terminal output this time, containing the parameters for the request. Sinatra does not log this information for every request, and instead shows only the path. Rails logs both the path and the parameters of the request, with lines like these:

```
Parameters: {"name"=>"Zelda"}
Parameters: {"from"=>"Ruby", "name"=>"Zelda"}
```

Although there is a great deal of depth available using either Sinatra or Rails, we do not have room here to explore it. For additional information about Sinatra, refer to the Sinatra website at `sinatrarb.com` or read *Sinatra: Up and Running*, by Alan Harris and Konstantin Haase.

We will elaborate slightly on the Rails example in the following sections, but comprehensive documentation is also available on the Web at `rubyonrails.org/documentation` and in print in *The Rails 4 Way*, by Obie Fernandez and Kevin Faustino.

Now that you have learned the basics of routing and parameters in Sinatra and Rails, let's look at storing persistent data across requests using ActiveRecord with Rails.

19.3   Storing Data

In web applications, storing data becomes more difficult than storing data in other Ruby programs. HTTP, as defined, is a *stateless* protocol. That means that an HTTP server is not required to store information between requests. The reasons for that are technical, but they primarily boil down to the idea that it should be possible to have multiple machines running the same application, and clients should be able to get the same response from any of them.

This makes it possible to handle many more requests at a time (since any server can handle the next request, sharing the work), but it means that each individual server cannot save any information (such as user accounts) into variables or files. Variables are only available inside a single Ruby process, and files are available only on a single machine, which rules both of them out.

The solution to this problem is to use a *database* or *data store*. We looked at PostgreSQL, MySQL, and Redis in Section 10.3, "Connecting to External Data Stores," of Chapter 10, "I/O and Data Storage." Rather than reiterate that section here, we will use the ActiveRecord library to create, read, update, and delete data from the database using objects instead of direct SQL queries.

19.3.1   Databases

The ActiveRecord library is able to connect to many kinds of SQL databases, including PostgreSQL, MySQL, Sqlite3, and even Oracle and Microsoft SQL databases. Each table in your database is represented by a class named after that table that inherits from the `ActiveRecord::Base` class. Each row in your table is represented as an instance of that class, with reader and writer methods for each of the column names.

In this section, we'll expand our example Rails application to remember the name of every person it has ever said hello to, and also record where that hello was said from if that parameter was present. In the upcoming section "Generating HTML," we'll add a form with text fields for who the hello will be said to and where it is being said from.

The first thing we'll do is generate a *model* named `Greeting`. Model classes inherit from `ActiveRecord::Base` and operate on a database table that shares their name. To create the model (and a file that will add a table with the same name to the database when it is run), run the command `bin/rails generate resource greeting to:string from:string`. This will generate a few files, but we only care about two of them right now.

The first file is in `db/migrations` and has a name that starts with a timestamp and ends in `create_greetings.rb`. Here's what should be inside that file:

```
class CreateGreetings < ActiveRecord::Migration
  def change
    create_table :greetings do |t|
      t.string :to
      t.string :from
      t.timestamps
    end
  end
end
```

Now, let's run the command `bin/rake db:migrate`. This will create a SQL database for your application as well as run the migration file, which creates a table named greetings with columns named `to` and `from`. Both columns will store strings. After the migration command has run, we can rewrite the `name` method inside `app/controllers/hello_controller.rb`. Change it to look like this:

```
def name
  greeting = Greeting.create!(to: params[:name],
                              from: params[:from])
  render inline: "<h1>" << CGI.h(greeting.to_s) << "!</h1>"
end
```

In this method, we use the `Greeting` class to create a new database row with the values of the `to` and `from` columns set by the corresponding values in the `params` hash. Then, we use the `to_s` method on the instance to create the response.

Normally, it is not a good idea to create (and especially not to delete!) database entries while responding to a `GET` request. Search engine robots that scrape the Internet will repeatedly activate any `GET` URLs they know about, as many as hundreds of times per day. In any real application, you should change data only in response to the HTTP verbs `POST`, `PUT`, `PATCH`, and `DELETE`. We create a database entry in a `GET` request here purely to simplify the example.

After saving the changes to that file, if you run `bin/rails server` and browse to one of the URLs that you tried before, you'll see a strange response that looks something like `#<Greeting:0x007fead16c1df8>!`. That's not what we want to see, so we're going to create our own `to_s` method on the `Greeting` class that returns the greeting we expect. To do that, edit the file `app/models/greeting.rb` and change it to this:

```
class Greeting < ActiveRecord::Base
  def to_s
    s = "Hello"
    s << " from #{from}" if from
    s << ", #{to}"
  end
end
```

This method simply reimplements the same logic we were using before, but in the model instead of in the controller. Because the controller handles HTML escaping the string, we no longer need to escape the string as we build it. After changing `greeting.rb`, run `bin/rails server` again and you will see the familiar greeting that we have been seeing this whole time.

Now that we are saving each greeting that is displayed, we will create a new controller that will display every greeting that has been sent. Note that this list will persist even when the Rails server is stopped and then started again, because it is saved in an external Sqlite3 database.

To create the new controller that will display past greetings, run `bin/rails generate controller greetings index`. This will add the line `get 'greetings/index'` to the routes file, and create the file `app/controllers/greetings_controller.rb`. The route `get 'greetings/index'` is a shorthand for the route `get 'greetings' => 'greetings#index'`. Now, let's edit the controller file to return a response that includes each greeting:

```
class GreetingsController < ApplicationController
  def index
    greetings = Greeting.all
    body = "<h1>Greetings</h1>\n<ol>\n"
    greetings.each do |greeting|
      body << "<li>" << CGI.h(greeting.to_s) << "</li>\n"
    end
    body << "</ol>"
    render inline: body
  end
end
```

In this action, the `all` method loads every row stored in the database in the `greetings` table, converts each row into an instance of `Greeting`, and then returns an array of those instances. We use the `each` method to iterate through that array, adding each greeting to the response. After saving this file, run the server again using `bin/rails server` and browse to `http://localhost:3000/greetings`.

Depending on how much experimentation you did after we added the Greeting model, you might see a long or short list of greetings. Either way, be sure to get a new greeting and then visit the list of greetings again to see that the new greeting has been added to the list.

This concludes our brief look at storing data using ActiveRecord. It is far more complex of a topic than we have room to cover here, and entire books could be (and have been) written about using it. For additional information about using ActiveRecord, refer to the ActiveRecord guides at `guides.rubyonrails.org` and in *The Rails 4 Way*.

19.3.2 Data Stores

ActiveRecord is merely one of many *object-relational mappers* (ORMs) written in Ruby. An ORM is simply a library that contains code to map stored data into Ruby objects, allow the objects to be changed, and then map those objects back into data that can be stored. There are ORMs for many non-SQL data stores, including Mongoid for MongoDB, Couchrest for CouchDB, redis-objects for Redis, among others.

In the vast majority of cases, web applications are best served by the widely used open-source SQL databases PostgreSQL and MySQL. Therefore, in the interest of space, we will not give example usages for any non-SQL data stores. However, we encourage you to research and investigate the different capabilities offered by other data stores.

19.4 Generating HTML

It's possible that you have noticed, especially in the previous examples of this chapter, that creating HTML responses by concatenating strings can be awkward. (If you're not yet familiar with how HTML works, the rest of this section will probably make more sense if you read about it first. The Mozilla Developer Network reference on HTML, located at `developer.mozilla.org/docs/Web/HTML`, is probably a good place to start.)

The more HTML there is present in a response body, the more awkward it is to construct that HTML using strings. Rather than make everyone add strings together, most web frameworks (including Rails) allow the use of *templates*.

Templates are files written in a templating language that can be converted into HTML on demand. Often, they contain Ruby code that inserts the contents of variables into the HTML. Templates can be nested, with the output from one template being inserted into another template.

Usually, using templates means creating one (or sometimes more) *layouts*, which contain the HTML making up the header and footer of your site. The layout will be used for every page, while the template that is rendered by the controller will go inside the layout. Finally, small template fragments (such as those used inside a loop) can be extracted into *partials*. Each individual template uses a single templating language, but layouts, regular templates, and partials do not need to share a templating language to be used together.

The most common templating language, and the default with Rails, is ERB. ERB is part of the Ruby standard library. It looks an awful lot like HTML (or maybe more accurately, like PHP), and it is ultimately a tool for inserting Ruby strings into HTML as easily as possible.

19.4.1   ERB

Using ERB by itself is very, very easy. Here's a simple example that prints the solution
to a math problem:

```
require 'erb'
puts ERB.new("two plus two is <%= 2 + 2 %>").result
# Output: Two plus two is 4
```

ERB consists of text containing *erb tags*, which can look like `<%= code %>` or like
`<% code %>`. With the equals sign, the value of the expression is interpolated into the
file. Without the equals sign, the expression is evaluated, but nothing is inserted into
the file. The tags without equals are mainly used with `if` or `each` and their corresponding `end` statements.

Using ERB from Rails is also very easy. In fact, it is the default. If a controller
action does not render anything, Rails will look for a template with the name of the
action in a directory named after the controller, and return the results of rendering
that template.

To demonstrate this simple example of templates, let's re-create our first example
using a template instead of using the controller. First, we'll need to delete the contents
of the `HelloController` method named `index`, leaving just the empty method definition:

```
def index
end
```

Next, we'll need to create the template that we want Rails to use. Create the file
`app/views/hello/index.html.erb` and then put our usual message into it:

```
<h1>Hello from Ruby!</h1>
```

Once that file is saved, you can start the application with `bin/rails server` and
browse to `http://localhost:3000` to see the message. If you view the terminal output, you will be able to see that Rails has rendered the template named `hello/index`:

```
Rendered hello/index.html.erb within layouts/application (0.7ms)
```

Next, let's convert the list of greetings that we created in the last section to use a
template instead. Edit the `index` method in `app/controllers/greetings_`
`controller.rb` to contain this code:

```
def index
  @greetings = Greeting.all
end
```

In Rails, instance variables that are set in controller methods will be available as instance variables inside the template when it is rendered. To take advantage of this fact, edit the template we generated earlier at `app/views/greetings/index.html.erb`. Change the template to contain this ERB code:

```
<h1>Greetings</h1>
<ol>
<% @greetings.each do |greeting| %>
  <li><%= h(greeting.to_s) %></li>
<% end %>
</ol>
```

This template is nearly identical to the code we had previously written inside the `index` method. The main difference is that we are able to write HTML directly into the file, without having to put it into a string variable. ERB takes care of replacing the ERB tags with the results of running the Ruby code inside them.

Templates in Rails are given some additional helper methods, including the `h` method, which does the same thing as the `CGI.h` method we were using earlier. Note that even inside a template, we still need to HTML-escape the greeting text because part of it came from user inputs.

After changing the controller and template, restart the Rails server and visit `http://localhost:3000/greetings` in your browser. You'll be able to see the same list of greetings as you were seeing before, but the controller method has been reduced to a single line of code.

This example now includes all three parts of the MVC (Model View Controller) paradigm that Rails espouses. Data storage is handled by interacting with the model class, per-request logic is executed by the controller, which then hands of data to the view, which is used to render HTML. The rendered HTML is then returned in the HTTP response body, and the request is complete.

The tooling available for using templates in Rails is far more complex than we have room to cover here. Although we must continue to Haml, another popular templating system, be sure to investigate the powerful rendering system of layouts, templates, and partials that Rails makes available. For more information, refer to the template guides at `guides.rubyonrails.org` and, of course, in *The Rails 4 Way*.

19.4.2   Haml

The Haml library is a templating language very different from ERB. Instead of being HTML with tags inserted, Haml is a terse language that declares HTML tags primarily using punctuation. It avoids the need for closing tags by making indentation meaningful, and does not require any angle brackets.

To use Haml in our Rails example, edit `Gemfile` and add the line `gem "haml"`. Then, run `bundle install` to add Haml to the bundle of gems that will be loaded when the Rails app starts. For more information about Bundler and how it works, refer to the Bundler website at bundler.io.

To illustrate how Haml is different from ERB, we'll convert the list of greetings from ERB to Haml. The first step is to rename the template file in `app/views/greetings` from `index.html.erb` to `index.html.haml`. The first extension indicates to Rails what type of file will be produced, and the second extension indicates what templating system to use to produce that output.

Edit the template at `app/view/greetings/index.html.haml` and change it to contain this Haml code instead:

```
%h1 Greetings
%ol
  - @greetings.each do |greeting|
    %li= h(greeting.to_s)
```

As you can see in this example, neither HTML closing tags or Ruby end lines are necessary. The `%` symbol at the start of a line indicates an HTML tag, and the rest of the line indicates the contents of that tag. An = symbol indicates that the line contains Ruby code and that the tag should contain the results of running that Ruby code, rather than the literal contents of the line. Putting == after the name of the tag indicates that the line contains a Ruby string and should allow string interpolation as usual via #{}.

Many Ruby web developers find Haml more aesthetically pleasing, less repetitive, and dramatically faster to write than ERB. As useful as it can be for writing a large number of tags, though, Haml can make it very difficult to write a large amount of text. For text-heavy pages, ERB is usually easier.

Haml provides a rich API with many options, and it offers a compelling alternative to ERB. For more information about Haml, see the Haml website at haml.info.

19.4.3   Other Templating Systems

ERB and Haml are definitely the most popular templating systems in Ruby, but they aren't the only ones. Other systems take different approaches to building HTML. Slim tries to require as little input as possible. Writing a template in Slim requires even fewer characters than the same template written in Haml.

The Liquid engine, developed for the Shopify online store generator, only allows certain bits of code to run inside it, such as `if` statements and `each` loops. This makes it safe for Liquid templates to be supplied to users because the lack of code prevents security exploits.

The Mustache library takes things even further, and doesn't allow templates to contain any logic at all. Any code must be executed before the template is rendered, in an object that prepares the data for the template.

If neither ERB nor Haml strike your fancy, take a look around! Chances are good that there is a templating engine that meets your wants or needs. And if you don't find one, be assured that writing a templating engine is a time-honored tradition among Rubyists, so feel free to write one of your own.

19.5   The Asset Pipeline

If you spend much time browsing the Web, it's possible that by now you have noticed two things that are missing from our example application that are present on nearly every website today: Cascading Style Sheets (usually just called CSS) for visual styling and JavaScript for user interaction.

Rails provides a unified system for managing CSS and JavaScript. In development, it is very useful to have access to each CSS and JavaScript file for experimentation, debugging, and the like. In production, however, it is far more efficient to combine everything into one CSS file and one JavaScript file. This reduces the number of HTTP requests needed, and speeds up loading each page.

Tooling to automate this process is included with Rails, and is referred to as *the asset pipeline*. Every file in `app/assets` is processed by the asset pipeline and made available as separate files in development and combined in development. The combined files are also stripped of comments, whitespace, and everything else that can be removed, to make them as small as possible.

Similar to the way templates are rendered, assets can be written in one language but output in another language. Our first example of this is the SCSS language, which is processed into CSS.

19.5.1   CSS and Sass

Sass, which its creators have sometimes claimed stands for "Syntactically Awesome Style Sheets," is the processor for the SCSS language. SCSS is a superset of CSS. (If you are not yet familiar with CSS, this section will probably not be terribly helpful. The Mozilla Developer Network also offers reference and tutorial material on CSS, which can be found at `https://developer.mozilla.org/docs/Web/CSS`.)

SCSS being a superset of CSS means that all CSS is valid SCSS, but there is significant additional functionality available as well. The biggest additions made by SCSS include variables, nesting, partials, inheritance, and mathematical operators.

The `sass-rails` gem was included automatically in our `hello` application, so we can alter the visual display of our example application right away by adding to an existing SCSS file. Open the file `app/assets/stylesheets/greetings.css.scss`. At the bottom of that file, add these lines to change how our list of greetings looks:

```
body {
  font-family: "Avenir", "Helvetia Neue", Arial;
}

h1 {
  text-shadow: 2px 2px 5px rgba(150, 150, 150, 1);
}

ol {
  margin-left: 15px;
  li {
    margin-bottom: 10px;
  }
}
```

After saving that file, make sure that the Rails server is still running and then reload the page at `http://localhost:3000`. The list of greetings should look different. The title "Greetings" should appear to have a subtle shadow behind it, and each greeting in the list should now be separated from the edge of the page and from the other items by some white space.

SCSS code is, like CSS, composed of *selectors* and *rules*. Selectors identify specific HTML tags that should be affected by the rules, whereas the rules specify what visual changes should be made. In the preceding SCSS, we change the font that will be used inside the `body` tag (which is all visible text on the page). Then, the `h1` header tag is given a gray background shadow that highlights it and "lifts" it from the page. In the last set of rules, each ordered list (the `ol` tag) is given a left margin of 15 pixels, and every list item (`li` tag) inside of an `ol` is given a bottom margin of 10 pixels.

These changes are simple but demonstrate the entire workflow for stylesheet assets. Files located in `app/assets/stylesheets` are converted into CSS if necessary (using the same file extension scheme as templates use). Then, the resulting CSS is served to the client web browser, which uses it to change the visual display of the HTML that was in the HTTP response body.

Chris Eppstein, one of the authors of Sass, has also created Compass, which is a library of prewritten rules that can be imported and included into SCSS files. Compass collects a large number of commonly used rules that provide cross-browser compatibility, layout management, and typography, as well as rules that will be part of the CSS3 standard but are not yet supported by all browsers. For more information on Compass, see its website at `compass-style.org`.

Even without Compass, Sass is a useful and powerful tool for any developer who needs to write and manage CSS. For more information about Sass, start with the Sass website at sass-lang.com. Also note that there are other CSS preprocessors besides Sass, including Less and Stylus. If Sass doesn't seem that great to you, perhaps one of the other options will.

Now that we've seen how Rails handles stylesheets, let's take a look at how Rails handles JavaScript.

19.5.2   JavaScript and CoffeeScript

Over the years, web applications have become more complex, richer, and more interactive. Well-known examples of so-called "rich client" applications include Google's Gmail and Google Docs, Microsoft's Office 365, and Apple's iWork for iCloud. Each of these web applications uses a vast amount of JavaScript to produce a website that, inside a web browser, closely mimics the appearance and functionality of a complex Windows or Mac OS X application.

For some websites, this type of rich interaction is a requirement. Therefore, in response to this trend, JavaScript frameworks have risen to assist with building richer and more interactive applications. Different JavaScript frameworks target different points on the richness-versus-simplicity spectrum, including Ember, Angular, React, Backbone, and even Batman.js. There are dozens of JavaScript frameworks, with what seems like a new one every week.

Using the asset pipeline, it is possible to add one or more of these JavaScript frameworks to your Rails application. For some frameworks (such as Ember and Angular), the Rails app acts primarily as a JSON API, providing data that is used by a JavaScript application running in a web browser. For other frameworks (such as React and Backbone), the Rails application can serve HTML, JSON, or a combination of the two depending on how the Ruby and JavaScript code is written. For more discussion of JSON APIs, see the next section of this chapter.

Similar to how SCSS can be processed into CSS, JavaScript has a popular language that can be compiled down into JavaScript that browsers can run. CoffeeScript adds many things that its creators felt JavaScript was lacking, including adding iterators, removing almost all parentheses, adding syntax for creating functions, and others.

To demonstrate how using CoffeeScript works in a Rails application, we're going to add some code that adds a new greeting to the list of greetings every time the "Greetings" header is clicked. Edit the file `app/assets/javascripts/greetings.js.coffee` and then add these lines to the end of the file:

```
$('body').ready ->
  $('h1').click () ->
    $.ajax "/hello/Hilda?from=Rails",
      success: (data) ->
        item = $.parseHTML('<li>' + $(data).text() + '</li>')
        $('ol').append item
```

The JavaScript code that results from this CoffeeScript can be viewed in your browser by navigating to the URL `http://localhost:3000/assets/greetings.js`—and we also reproduce it here:

```
(function() {
  $('body').ready(function() {
    return $('h1').click(function(e) {
      return $.ajax("/hello/Hilda?from=Rails", {
        success: function(data) {
          var item;
          item = $.parseHTML('<li>' + $(data).text() + '</li>');
          return $('ol').append(item);
        }
      });
    });
  });
}).call(this);
```

In this example, we use the jQuery JavaScript library (accessible via the variable $) to find the `body` tag and then supply a function that will be run once the browser has finished rendering and the body is "ready." Inside that function, we find the `h1` tag and pass a function that will then be called any time the `h1` tag is clicked. Inside that function, we use jQuery's `ajax` method to request a specific greeting from the `/hello` URL that we set up earlier in our example. Finally, if the request was a success, we create a new `li` tag that contains the text from the response body, and add it to the end of the `ol` list on the page. It is not indicated explicitly, but if the Ajax HTTP request were to fail, nothing would happen. To handle failures, another function must be provided under the key `failure`.

Although this is an extremely simple example of both CoffeeScript and jQuery, it provides a taste of the kinds of things that can be done from within a Rails application by using asset pipeline. Many web applications have expanded from beginnings as humble as these into gigantic, monolithic Rails applications that result in thousands or even millions of dollars worth of revenue.

As this very small example demonstrates, CoffeeScript is arguably shorter, cleaner, and easier to understand than the equivalent JavaScript. This difference can be compounded in larger and larger codebases, making equivalent JavaScript code significantly longer. CoffeeScript comes with some downsides, though. The biggest downside is that CoffeeScript adds its own for-loop and class-based inheritance system on top of JavaScript.

Why is that a downside, you ask? Well, JavaScript will be gaining its own for-loop and class-based inheritance system in the next major revision the language, which is known as ECMAScript 6. ES6 (as it is abbreviated) strives to address many of the shortcomings that motivated the creation of CoffeeScript, but in a way that is similar to existing JavaScript, rather than significantly different.

As is usual with these sorts of programming conundrums, there are tradeoffs in both directions. I, for one, have stopped using CoffeeScript, knowing that it will not be compatible with the next version of JavaScript. For others, the increase in speed (or perhaps the decrease in parentheses) is more valuable, and CoffeeScript is completely worthwhile for them.

In order to learn more about CoffeeScript, refer to its website at `coffee-script.org`. To learn more about JavaScript, I recommend the Mozilla Developer Network's reference and tutorials, which are located at `developer.mozilla.org/docs/Web/JavaScript`.

19.6   Web Services via HTTP

Finally, it's time to mention the ways that programs on the Internet talk to each other, rather than directly to a human being. API stands for *application programming interface*, but is usually just used as shorthand to refer to an interface that one program can use to interact with another.

In the bad old days of networked programming, network APIs might mean writing your own socket client and server programs, as in Chapter 18, "Network Programming." More recently, it has grown to most commonly mean making HTTP requests from your program to an HTTP server that provides a documented set of URLs.

The Ruby standard library's HTTP library, `Net::HTTP`, is a functional client for interacting with these HTTP APIs. Using it can sometimes be baroque or tedious, so other gems exist to provide a smoother API, including http, excon, and typhoeus.

Interacting with HTTP APIs can be quite straightforward, though, even without one of those libraries, especially when using Ruby's built-in `open-uri`:

```
require 'open-uri'
response = open("http://mywebstore.com/products?page=5")
```

After this code has run, the `response.read` method call will return the HTTP response body as a string. Headers can be accessed using the `[]` method, as in `response["Content-Type"]`, which will return the value of the Content-Type header as a string.

Using these HTTP libraries, you'll find it quite straightforward to interact with other websites from your own Ruby programs.

19.6.1   JSON for APIs

During the 1990s and early 2000s, it was most common to use XML (eXtensible Markup Language) to encode the data sent in API requests and responses. Primarily due to XML's complexity and verbosity, it has fallen out of favor. Replacing it is the terse, minimal JSON serialization standard.

JSON stands for *JavaScript Object Notation*, but it has become an ISO standard that is widely used to transmit data between programs in nearly any programming language. Developing web applications will very likely include interacting with HTTP APIs that provide JSON responses.

The Ruby standard library includes a `JSON` library, which can parse JSON into Ruby hashes as well as dump Ruby hashes into JSON. Other libraries exist to provide specific additional features, such as Yajil's JSON stream parsing, or Oj's faster parsing core written in C instead of Ruby.

If the response we fetched in the last example contained an array of products encoded as a JSON object, we could parse the JSON into a Ruby hash and access the array of products with code like this:

```ruby
require 'json'
products = JSON.parse(response.body)["products"]
# products is now an array of hashes, parsed from
#   the JSON string returned by the API
```

The hash of results can be used as input for any task, allowing your program to act based on data provided the other server. For a real-world example of interacting with a JSON API, see Section 15.2, "Working with JSON," in Chapter 15, "Ruby and Data Formats."

19.6.2   REST (and REST-ish) APIs

REST (REpresentational State Transfer), first defined in 2000 by Roy Fielding, is a style of designing software so that it can be interacted with in a predictable way. The ideas behind REST were strong influences on the design of HTTP version 1.1, and provided HTTP with abilities that were largely unused by web developers or browsers. Many years later, parts of the REST philosophy have been adopted by Rails to provide conventional URLs and standard ways to execute Create, Read, Update, and Delete (CRUD) actions in a Rails application.

Rails maps the CRUD operations to different HTTP "verbs," or actions that are allowed by the HTTP standard. Create is done using HTTP's POST, Read using GET, Update using PATCH, and Delete using DELETE.

A hypothetical RESTful API for interacting with a catalog of books might look something like this:

```
GET     /books      # Lists all of the books
POST    /books      # Creates a new book
GET     /books/1    # Lists information about book 1
PATCH   /books/1    # Updates information about book 1
DELETE  /books/1    # Deletes book 1 from the list
```

APIs designed according to these principles are standardized enough that there are Ruby libraries for interacting with REST APIs easily, such as rest-client, httparty, and faraday.

Although Rails dramatically increased the usage of HTTP verbs in web development, what Rails calls "REST" is something simpler but much less powerful than Fielding's original idea. Developers working toward the original idea of REST have taken to calling it "Hypermedia," as a way to distinguish it from the watered-down version that is built in to Rails and other frameworks.

I encourage any developer who needs to (or is simply interested in) creating HTTP services to learn more about REST, both in its initial form and the form that Rails provides. For further development of the concepts in Fielding's original conception of REST, search for discussions of "hypermedia" online.

19.7   Generating Static Sites

While Ruby has gained popularity for building dynamic web applications, it has become a popular language for tools that generate static sites. In a static site, there is no web application running code to handle each incoming request. Instead, a web server simply finds a file on disk whose name matches the request path, and returns the contents of the file in the response body.

The web server in question might even be one written in Ruby, such as Puma or Unicorn. However, it is far more likely that a static site will be served by one of the well-known servers that are heavily optimized for serving static files and serve most of the sites on the Internet, such as Apache or Nginx (which is pronounced "engine x"). Strictly speaking, a so-called "static site" may contain interactive or dynamic elements, implemented with JavaScript. The significant factor is that the site consists of unchanging HTML, CSS, and JavaScript.

In this section, we'll build a static site that is similar to our Rails "Hello" example. Because static sites can't run code for every request, we'll have to settle for a few specific greetings, rather than dynamically generating a new greeting for every request.

19.7.1   Middleman

The Ruby static site generator Middleman provides an environment that is extremely similar to a Rails application, but the resulting site is a set of files that can be served by any HTTP server. To use Middleman to create a static site, start by installing the gem with `gem install middleman`. The gem includes the `middleman` command, which provides several subcommands to assist with creating static sites. To see a list of all the available commands, run `middleman help`.

Once Middleman is installed, let's create a new project by running `middleman init hello_world`. This creates the directory `hello_world`, and fills it with a (mostly empty) site. To see what the site looks like, `cd` into the directory and then run `bundle exec middleman server` to start the preview server, and then browse to `http://localhost:4567`. Much like the Rails server, the Middleman server allows you to quickly see changes that are made to your site while you are developing it.

When you are finished working on your site, you can stop the Middleman server and instead run `middleman build`. The `build` command creates the final static site, placing it in the `public` directory inside the Middleman project. After the static site has been generated, it can be deployed to production by simply copying the files in the `public` directory to the HTTP server that will be serving it.

Because we want our site to show a greeting, edit the file `source/indexhtml.erb` to contain this text instead:

```
title: Hello from Middleman!
<h1>Hello from Middleman!</h1>
```

After saving the file, you can reload the page at `http://localhost:4567` to see the results of your changes. Because Middleman creates static sites, the only URL paths we can use are those that correspond to files. To add a greeting located at `/world`, we'll need to add a file. First, create a new directory by running `mkdir source/world`. Then, create a new file named `source/world/index.html.erb` and add our message to it:

```
<h1>Hello, World!</h1>
```

Now, you can browse to `http://localhost:4567/world` and see that greeting. At this point, you may be wondering why we had to create a directory named `world` and put our `index.html.erb` template inside it. The reason ultimately comes down to prettier URLs.

Static site servers look file files by their exact name, including extension. Request paths that do not include an extension, like `/world`, will fall back on searching for a directory. If the directory contains an *index file*, that file is served automatically. Thus, by creating an index file for the directory `world`, we can view our greeting at the path `/world`. If we had merely created the file `world.html.erb`, we would only have been able to view our greeting at the path `/world.html`.

Static sites generated by Middleman provide most of the same utilities and helpers provided by Rails applications, including helper functions in templates, a full asset pipeline with Sass, Compass, and CoffeeScript integration, and more. For a complete rundown of the features available in Middleman sites, read the Middleman documentation located at `middlemanapp.com`.

19.7.2   Other Static Site Generators

Another popular static site generator written in Ruby is Jekyll. Jekyll uses the Liquid templating language for its templates, but uses Markdown for the contents of each page or post. Jekyll was created by one of the co-founders of GitHub, and it is used at GitHub to generate static sites for projects hosted there. Because GitHub provides hosting for open-source projects, many gem documentation websites are located on GitHub, generated with Jekyll. To read more about Jekyll, start with the Jekyll website at `jekyll.com`. For more about GitHub's free static site hosting, see `pages.github.com`.

Built on top of Jekyll, Octopress is a set of extensions and tools specifically designed to make it easy to create a blog that is published as a static site. Octopress uses Jekyll underneath, but supplies everything that is needed to start writing blog posts right away. It includes a blog template, stylesheets, support for Disqus comments, syntax highlighting for code snippets included in posts, and a huge number of Octopress-specific plug-ins that add additional features. To learn more about Octopress, visit `octopress.org`.

Although not as popular as either Middleman or Jekyll, the Nanoc static site generator is the oldest static site generator written in Ruby. First released in 2007, Nanoc is still actively maintained in 2014. It offers its own take on static site generation, billing itself as "fit for building anything from a small personal blog to a large corporate website." Take a look at Nanoc if you're looking for another option, or are just interested in an open-source project that has continued to thrive for many years. Nanoc's website is located at `nanoc.ws`.

19.8   Conclusion

In this chapter, we looked at low-level details of HTTP, and implemented our own minimal HTTP server. We reviewed frameworks and tools that make creating web applications easier, including Puma, Rails, Sinatra, ActiveRecord, ERB, Haml, Sass, and Less. Finally, we examined ways to communicate between web applications and services via HTTP APIs, and looked at Middleman and Jekyll for generating static site content.

Now let's look at network programming in a much simpler but more abstract way. The next chapter deals with distributed Ruby.

CHAPTER 20

Distributed Ruby

Less is more.

—Robert Browning, "Andrea del Sarto"

In the last 25 years, many technologies enabling distributed computing have been devised. These technologies include various flavors of RPC as well as such things as COM, CORBA, DCE, and Java's RMI.

These all vary in complexity, but they do essentially the same thing. They provide relatively transparent communication between objects in a networking context so that remote objects can be used as though they were local.

Why would we want to do something like this in the first place? There might be many reasons. One excellent reason is to share the burden of a computing problem between many processors at once. An example would be the SETI@home program, which uses your PC to process small data sets in the "search for extraterrestrial intelligence." (SETI@home is not a project of the SETI Institute, by the way.) Another example would be the grassroots effort to decode the RSA129 encryption challenge (which succeeded several years ago). There are countless other areas where it is possible to split a problem into individual parts for a distributed solution.

It's also conceivable that you might want to expose an interface to a service without making the code itself available. This is frequently done via a web application, but the inherently stateless nature of the Web makes this a little unwieldy (in addition to other disadvantages). A distributed programming mechanism makes this kind of thing possible in a more direct way.

In the Ruby world, one answer to this challenge is `drb` or "distributed Ruby," by Masatoshi Seki. (The name is also written DRb.) There are other ways of doing distributed coding with Ruby, but `drb` is arguably the easiest. It doesn't have such advanced facilities as CORBA's naming service, but it is a simple and usable library with all the most basic functionality you would need. In this chapter, we'll look at the basics of using distributed Ruby (along with Rinda, which is built on top of it).

20.1   An Overview: Using `drb`

A `drb` application has two basic components—a server and a client. A rough breakdown of their responsibilities follows.

The server has the following responsibilities:

- Starts a `TCPServer` and listens on a port.

- Binds an object to the `drb` server instance.

- Accepts connections from clients and responds to their messages.

- May optionally provide access control (security).

And the client has these responsibilities:

- Establishes a connection to the server process.

- Binds a local object to the remote server object.

- Sends messages to the server object and gets responses.

The class method `start_service` takes care of starting a TCP server that listens on a specified port; it takes two parameters. The first is a URI (Universal Resource Identifier) specifying a port (if it is `nil`, a port will be chosen dynamically). The second is an object to which we want to bind. This object will be remotely accessible by the client, invoking its methods as though it were local:

```
require "drb"

myobj = MyServer.new
DRb.start_service("druby://:1234", myobj)    # Port 1234

# ...
```

If the port is chosen dynamically, the class method `uri` can be used to retrieve the full URI, including the port number:

```
DRb.start_service(nil, myobj)
myURI = DRb.uri                        # "druby://hal9000:2001"
```

Because `drb` is threaded, any server application will need to do a join on the server thread (to prevent the application from exiting prematurely and killing the thread):

```
# Prevent premature exit
DRb.thread.join
```

On the client side, we can invoke `start_service` with no parameters and use `DRbObject` to create a local object that corresponds to the remote one. We typically use `nil` as the first parameter in creating a new `DRbObject`:

```
require "drb"

DRb.start_service
obj = DRbObject.new(nil, "druby://hal9000:2001")

# Messages passed to obj will get forwarded to the
# remote object on the server side...
```

We should point out that on the server side, when we bind to an object, we really are binding to a single object, which will answer all requests that it receives. If there is more than one client, we will have to make our code thread-safe to avoid that object somehow getting into an inconsistent state. (For really simple or specialized applications, this may not be necessary.)

We can't go into great detail here. Just be aware that if a client both reads and writes the internal state of the remote object, then two or more clients have the potential to interfere with each other. To avoid this, we recommend a straightforward solution using a synchronization mechanism such as a `Mutex`. (Refer to Chapter 13, "Threads and Concurrency," for more on threads and synchronization issues.)

Let's look at security at least a little. After all, you may not want just any old client to connect to your server. You can't prevent clients from trying, but you can prevent their succeeding.

Distributed Ruby has the concept of an access control list (or ACL, often pronounced to rhyme with "crackle"). These are simply lists of clients (or categories of clients) that are specifically allowed (or not allowed) to connect.

Here is an example: We use the ACL class to create a new ACL, passing in one or two parameters. The second (optional) parameter to ACL.new answers the question, "Do we deny all clients except certain ones, or allow all clients except certain ones?" The default is DENY_ALLOW, represented by a 0, whereas ALLOW_DENY is represented by a 1.

The first parameter for ACL.new is simply an array of strings; these strings are taken in pairs, where the first in the pair is "deny" or "allow," and the second represents a client or category of clients (by name or address). The following is an example:

```ruby
require "drb/acl"
acl = ACL.new( %w[ deny all
                   allow 192.168.0.*
                   allow 210.251.121.214
                   allow localhost] )
```

The first entry, deny all, is arguably redundant, but it does make the meaning more explicit.

Now how do we use an ACL? The install_acl method will put an ACL into effect for us. Note that this has to be done before the call to the start_service method, or it will have no effect:

```ruby
# Continuing the above example...

DRb.install_acl(acl)
DRb.start_service(nil, some_object)
# ...
```

When the service then starts, any unauthorized client connection will result in a RuntimeError being thrown by the server.

There is somewhat more to drb than we cover here, but this is enough for a good overview. In the next section, we'll look at a simple drb server and client that are almost real-world code. We'll also look at Rinda and Ring before we close the chapter.

20.2 Case Study: A Stock Ticker Simulation

In this example, we assume that we have a server application that is making stock prices available to the network. Any client wanting to check the value of his or her thousand shares of Gizmonic Institute can contact this server.

We've added a twist to this, however. We don't just want to watch every little fluctuation in the stock price. We've implemented an `Observer` module that will let us subscribe to the stock feed; the client then watches the feed and warns us only when the price goes above or below a certain value.

First, let's look at the `DrbObservable` module. This is a straightforward implementation of the Observer pattern from the excellent book *Design Patterns*, published by Addison-Wesley and authored by the so-called "Gang of Four" (Gamma, Helm, Johnson, and Vlissides). This is also known as the Publish-Subscribe pattern.

Listing 20.1 defines an observer as an object that responds to the `update` method call. Observers are added (by the server) at their own request and are sent information via the `notify_observers` call.

Listing 20.1   The `drb` Observer Module

```ruby
module DrbObservable

  def observer_peers
    @observer_peers ||= []
  end

  def add_observer(observer)
    unless observer.respond_to? :update
      raise NameError, "observer needs to respond to 'update'"
    end
    observer_peers.push observer
  end

  def delete_observer(observer)
    observer_peers.delete(observer)
  end

  def notify_observers(*arg)
    observer_peers.dup.each do |peer|
      peer.update(*arg) rescue delete_observer(i)
    end if observer_peers.any?
  end
end
```

The server (or feed) in Listing 20.2 simulates the stock price by a sequence of pseudorandom numbers. (This is as good a simulation of the market as I have ever seen, if you will pardon me for saying so.) The stock symbol identifying the company is used only for cosmetics in the simulation and has no actual purpose in the code. Every time the price changes, the observers are all notified.

Listing 20.2   The drb Stock Price Feed (Server)

```ruby
require "drb"
require "drb_observer"

# Generate random prices
class MockPrice

  MIN = 75
  RANGE = 50

  def initialize(symbol)
    @price = RANGE / 2
  end

  def price
    @price += (rand() - 0.5)*RANGE
    if @price < 0
      @price = -@price
    elsif @price >= RANGE
      @price = 2*RANGE - @price
    end
    MIN + @price
  end
end

class Ticker # Periodically fetch a stock price
  include DRbObservable

  def initialize(price_feed)
    @feed = price_feed
    Thread.new { run }
  end

  def run
    lastPrice = nil
    loop do
      price = @feed.price
      print "Current price: #{price}\n"
      if price != lastPrice
        lastPrice = price
        notify_observers(Time.now, price)
```

```
        end
        sleep 1
      end
    end
  end
end

ticker = Ticker.new(MockPrice.new("MSFT"))

DRb.start_service('druby://localhost:9001', ticker)
puts 'Press Control-C to exit.'
DRb.thread.join
```

Not surprisingly, the client (in Listing 20.3) begins by contacting the server. It gets a reference to the stock ticker object and sets its own desired values for the high and low marks. Then the client will print a message for the user every time the stock price goes above the high end or below the low end.

Listing 20.3   The drb Stock Price Watcher (Client)

```
require "drb"

class Warner
  include DRbUndumped

  def initialize(ticker, limit)
    @limit = limit
    ticker.add_observer(self)    # all warners are observers
  end
end

class WarnLow < Warner
  def update(time, price)        # callback for observer
    if price < @limit
      print "-- #{time.to_s}: Price below #@limit: #{price}\n"
    end
  end
end

class WarnHigh < Warner
  def update(time, price)        # callback for observer
    if price > @limit
      print "+++ #{time.to_s}: Price above #@limit: #{price}\n"
    end
  end
end

DRb.start_service
ticker = DRbObject.new(nil, "druby://localhost:9001")
```

```
WarnLow.new(ticker, 90)
WarnHigh.new(ticker, 110)

puts "Press [return] to exit."
gets
```

You may wonder about the DRbUndumped module referenced in Listing 20.3. This is included in any object that is not intended to be marshalled. Basically, the mere presence of this module among the ancestors of an object is sufficient to tell drb not to marshal that object. In fact, I recommend you look at the code of this module. Here it is in its entirety:

```
module DRbUndumped
  def _dump(dummy)
    raise TypeError, "can't dump"
  end
end
```

The stock watcher application we saw in this section is long enough to be meaningful but short enough to understand. There are other ways to approach such a problem, but this is a good solution that demonstrates the simplicity and elegance of distributed Ruby.

20.3   Rinda: A Ruby Tuplespace

The term *tuplespace* dates back as far as 1985, and the concept itself is even older than that. A tuple, of course, is simply an array or vector of data items (much like a database row); a tuplespace is a large object space full of tuples, like a kind of "data soup."

So far, a tuplespace implementation sounds boring. It becomes more interesting when you realize that it is accessible in a synchronized way by multiple clients. In short, it is inherently a distributed entity; any client can read from or write to the tuplespace, so they can all use it as a large shared storage or even as a way to communicate.

The original tuplespace implementation was the Linda project, an experiment in parallel programming at Yale University in the 1980s. The Ruby implementation based on drb is naturally called *Rinda*.

A Rinda tuple can actually be an array or a hash. If it is a hash, it has the additional restriction that all its keys must be strings. Here are some simple tuples:

```
t1 = [:add, 5, 9]
t2 = [:name, :add_service, Adder.new, nil]
t3 = { 'type' => 'add', 'value_1' => 5, 'value_2' => 9 }
```

There can be any number of items in a tuple. Each item in a tuple can be an arbitrary object; this works because drb can marshal and unmarshal Ruby objects. (Of course, you may need to use DRbUndumped or make the class definitions available on the server side.)

We create a tuplespace with a simple new call:

```
require 'rinda/tuplespace'

ts = Rinda::TupleSpace.new
# ...
```

Therefore, a server would simply look like this:

```
require 'rinda/tuplespace'

ts = Rinda::TupleSpace.new
DRb.start_service("druby://somehost:9000", ts)
DRb.thread.join # Control-C to kill the server
```

And a client would look like this:

```
require 'rinda/tuplespace'

DRb.start_service
ts = DRbObject.new(nil, "druby://somehost:9000")
# ...
```

We can perform five basic operations on a Rinda tuplespace: read, read_all, write, take, and notify. A read operation is exactly what it sounds like: You are retrieving a tuple from tuplespace. However, identifying the tuple to read may be a little unintuitive; we do it by specifying a tuple that will match the one we want to read. A nil value is in effect a wildcard that will match any value.

```
t1 = ts.read [:sum, nil]      # will retrieve [:sum, 14] for example
```

Normally a read operation will block (as a way of providing synchronization). If you want to do a quick test for the existence of a tuple, you can do a nonblocking read by specifying a timeout value of zero:

```
t2 = ts.read [:result, nil], 0   # raises an exception if nonexistent
```

If we know or expect that more than one tuple will match the pattern, we can use read_all and get an array back:

```
tuples = ts.read_all [:foo, nil, nil]
tuples.each do |t|
  # ...
end
```

The read_all method doesn't take a second parameter. It will always block if no matching tuple is found.

A take operation is basically a read followed by an implicit delete. The take actually removes a tuple from the tuplespace and returns it:

```
t = ts.take [:sum, nil]    # tuple is now removed from tuplespace
```

You might ask why there isn't an explicit method to perform a delete. Obviously, the take method will serve that purpose.

The write method, of course, stores a tuple in tuplespace. Its second parameter tells how long, in seconds, the tuple should be kept before it expires. (The default expiration value is nil, or never expiring.)

```
ts.write [:add, 5, 9]         # Keep this "forever"
ts.write [:foo, "Bar"], 10    # Keep this ten seconds
```

A few words on synchronization are appropriate here. Suppose two clients attempt to take the same tuple at (approximately) the same time. One will succeed, and the other will block. If the first (successful) client then modifies the tuple and writes it back into tuplespace, the second (blocked) client will then retrieve the new modified version of the tuple. So you can think of an "update" operation as being a take followed by a write, and there will be no data loss (as long as the tuplespace only provides the tuple to one client take at a time).

A `notify` method, not surprisingly, enables you to "watch" the tuplespace and be informed when a matching tuple has some operation performed on it. This method (which returns a `NotifyTemplateEntry` object) watches for four kinds of operations:

- `write` operations

- `take` operations

- `delete` operations (when a tuple has expired)

- `close` operations (when the `NotifyTemplateEntry` object has expired)

Because `read` operations are nondestructive, the system does not support notification of reads. Listing 20.4 shows an example of using `notify`.

Listing 20.4   Rinda's Notification Feature

```
require 'rinda/tuplespace'

ts = Rinda::TupleSpace.new

alberts = ts.notify "write", ["Albert", nil]
martins = ts.notify "take",  ["Martin", nil]

Thread.new do
  alberts.each {|op,t| puts "#{op}: #{t.join(' ')}" }
end

Thread.new do
  martins.each {|op,t| puts "#{op}: #{t.join(' ')}" }
end

sleep 1

ts.write ["Martin", "Luther"]
ts.write ["Albert", "Einstein"]
ts.write ["Martin", "Fowler"]
ts.write ["Albert", "Schweitzer"]
ts.write ["Martin", "Scorsese"]
ts.take  ["Martin", "Luther"]

# Output:
# write: Albert Einstein
# write: Albert Schweitzer
# take: Martin Luther
```

We've seen how `read` and other operations use templates that match tuples (conceptually much as a regular expression works). A `nil` value can be a wildcard, as we've seen, but a class can also be specified to match any instance of that class.

```
tem1 = ["X", Integer]     # matches ["X",5] but not ["X","Files"]
tem2 = ["X", NilClass]    # matches a literal nil in the tuple
```

In addition, you can define your own case equality (===) operator if you want a class to match a value in some special way. Otherwise, of course, the class will match based on the default === operator.

Bear in mind that the lifetime of a tuple can be specified upon writing. This ties in with the timeout values on the various tuple operations, ensuring that it's possible to restrict any simple or complex operation to a finite length of time.

The fact that tuples can expire also means that they can be renewed after they expire, often with a custom renewer object. The library comes with a `SimpleRenewer` that simply contacts the tuple's originating `drb` server every 180 seconds; if the server is down, the tuple is allowed to expire. However, don't bother with renewer objects until you are competent in the tuplespace paradigm.

Rounding out our Rinda examples, Listing 20.5 shows a version of the producer/consumer example from Chapter 13 using a `TupleSpace`.

Listing 20.5   The Producer-Consumer Problem Revisited

```
require 'rinda/tuplespace'

ts = Rinda::TupleSpace.new

producer = Thread.new do
  item = 0
  loop do
    sleep rand(0)
    puts "Producer makes item ##{item}"
    ts.write ["Item",item]
    item += 1
  end
end

consumer = Thread.new do
  loop do
    sleep rand(0)
    tuple = ts.take ["Item", nil]
    word, item = tuple
    puts "Consumer retrieves item ##{item}"
```

```
      end
end

sleep 60   # Run a minute, then die and kill threads
```

20.4 Service Discovery with Distributed Ruby

If you have many services running locally, service discovery might be a useful concept to you; it allows services to be located by name. However, if you have few services at well-known locations, this may not be particularly useful.

The Rinda library provides a service discovery facility (naturally based on Rinda) called `Rinda::Ring`. Think of it as providing DNS-like features; it is a central registration service storing information (in a tuplespace) about `drb` processes. The `drb` services can use UDP (datagrams) to find a nearby registration server to advertise themselves and/or to find other services in the neighborhood.

The `Rinda::RingServer` class implements the registration server. It keeps a tuplespace for storing locations of other `drb` services (although, actually, any service may be advertised). When it comes up, the `RingServer` listens for UDP broadcast packets requesting the location of the server. It responds to each of these by connecting back (via `drb`) to the requesting service. The following is an example of running a `RingServer`:

```
require 'rinda/ring'
require 'rinda/tuplespace'

DRb.start_service
Rinda::RingServer.new(Rinda::TupleSpace.new)
DRb.thread.join
```

The `Rinda::RingProvider` class is used to register (or advertise) a service with a `RingServer`. A service is identified by a service type, a front-end object providing the service, and a piece of descriptive text. In the following example, we create a simple `Adder` service that adds two numbers; then we advertise it to the world:

```
require 'rinda/ring'

class Adder
  include DRbUndumped
```

```
    def add(val1, val2)
      return val1 + val2
    end
  end

  adder = Adder.new
  DRb.start_service(nil, adder)
  Rinda::RingProvider.new(:adder, adder, 'Simple Adder')
  DRb.thread.join
```

The `Rinda::RingFinger` class (presumably named for the classic UNIX `finger` command) can be used to locate a `RingServer`. It sends a UDP broadcast packet and waits for the `RingServer` to respond. The tuplespace of the first `RingServer` to respond becomes available via the `primary` method. Any other discovered servers are available via the `to_a` method. The returned tuplespace can then be used to look up advertised services:

```
  require 'rinda/ring'

  DRb.start_service
  rs = Rinda::RingFinger.primary
  every_space = [rs] + Rinda::RingFinger.to_a
  svc = every_space.find_all do |ts|
    ts.read([:name, :adder, nil, nil], 0) rescue nil
  end
```

20.5   Conclusion

This chapter presented a good introduction to distributed Ruby. We saw the basics of starting a service and communicating with clients, and we looked at security issues.

In addition, we saw how Rinda can act as a simple object store that is both distributed and synchronized. Finally, we looked at how `Rinda::Ring` can be used for drb service discovery.

That ends our look at distributed Ruby. Let's move on to a new topic: using development tools associated with Ruby, such as `rake`, `irb`, and others.

CHAPTER 21

Ruby Development Tools

Man is a tool-making animal.

—Benjamin Franklin

A development environment consists of more than just an interpreter. Every good developer is surrounded by a selection of tools that make life easier. Some of these may be language specific, and others may not.

The most important of these is the editor. Because much of what programmers do day-to-day is manipulate text, the choice of editor (or your proficiency with it) has a significant impact on productivity. The language-specific features or the customization capabilities also have an impact. We'll look very briefly at the most common editors here.

Other tools may assist in documentation, library installation, debugging, and similar tasks. We've already looked at the Byebug debugging library (which is not a real standalone application) in Chapter 16, "Testing and Debugging," and we've looked at Rubygems, Bundler, and RDoc in Chapter 17, "Packaging and Distributing Code." These are not covered further here.

This chapter starts off with `rake`, the Ruby version of the UNIX `make` tool. It also covers `irb` and `pry`, both interactive Ruby shells, and `ri` (the command-line documentation tool). Finally, we wrap up with discussion of Ruby version managers.

21.1   Using Rake

The `rake` utility is like a Rubyesque version of the UNIX `make` utility. Instead of the complex and difficult Makefile syntax (which you may know and hate), it uses only pure Ruby code. This utility is the work of Jim Weirich and may be the first formal instance of a DSL (domain-specific language) in Ruby.

You may see the name spelled "Rake" or "rake." The former is the name of the tool, and the latter is the actual name of the executable itself. It's not worth nitpicking, in my opinion.

Rake (which is definitely inspired by `make`) allows you to define tasks, declare dependencies between tasks, and then run a task and all of its dependencies at once. The terminology used is much the same as that of `make`. We still talk about targets, actions, dependencies, and rules.

The uses of Rake are numerous. If you are working with C, C++, or Java code, you can use it to build your projects. (It will work for other languages, too, of course.) You can also use it for generating documentation with RDoc, deploying software, updating a RubyForge project, and many other such tasks.

Like `make` and the Makefile, Rake operates on a file of instructions called the Rakefile. If you want to give the file a different name, you can tell Rake that name using the -f or —`rakefile` option:

```
$ rake             # look for 'Rakefile'
$ rake -f myfile   # use 'myfile' instead
```

The basic "unit of work" in Rake is the task; these are named with Ruby symbols. Every Rakefile is understood to have a default task called `:default`, which will be run if you don't specify a task name:

```
$ rake             # execute the default task
$ rake mytask      # execute 'mytask'
```

Inside a Rakefile, we declare and create a task using the `task` method, passing it a symbol and a block:

```
task :mytask do
  # ...
end
```

The "stuff" that goes inside the block, which we refer to as an *action*, will be run whenever the task is run by name. An action can be anything and can involve arbitrary Ruby code. Some convenience methods are available for common operations. The `sh` method (meant to remind us of the UNIX `sh` executable) will run a system command. The methods `cp`, `mv`, and `rm` are respectively for copying, moving, and deleting files. (Like the `make` utility itself, Rake has an unabashed UNIX flavor about it.) For a complete list of Rake's helper commands, consult the Rake API documentation at rdoc.info or ruby-doc.org.

If you prefer to use braces to delimit a block, you can, but the Ruby parser will typically force you to use parentheses around the parameter in that case:

```
task(:mytask) { do_something }
```

Now, let's take a more concrete example. Imagine we have a C program named `myprog.c` with two other C files associated with it (each with its own header file). In other words, we have these five source files:

```
myprog.c
sub1.c
sub1.h
sub2.c
sub2.h
```

We want to compile all this together into the executable `myprog`. This is a multistep process: First, we will compile all the `.c` files; then we will link the resulting `.o` files together.

Rake provides a shortcut for declaring that a file can only be created if another file already exists. Let's begin by using that shortcut, the `file` method, to specify file dependencies:

```
file "myprog.o" => ["myprog.c"]
file "sub1.o" => ["sub1.c", "sub1.h"]
file "sub2.o" => ["sub2.c", "sub2.h"]
file "myprog" => ["sub1.o", "sub2.o"]
```

Notice how the file method just takes a hash. It associates a filename with an array of dependent filenames.

Now let's look at building the binary files. We'll take the code we just wrote and extend it a little. If we put a block on the file call, we can declare the actions that will produce that file:

```
file "myprog.o" => ["myprog.c"] do
  sh "cc -c -o myprog.o myprog.c"
end

file "sub1.o" => ["sub1.c", "sub1.h"] do
  sh "cc -c -o sub1.o sub1.c"
end

file "sub2.o" => ["sub2.c", "sub2.h"] do
  sh "cc -c -o sub2.o sub2.c"
end

file "myprog" => ["sub1.o", "sub2.o"] do
  sh "cc -o myprog myprog.o sub1.o sub2.o"
end
```

There is some duplication here, but we can get rid of it. As it turns out, Rake has a special facility called a `FileList`; it understands wildcards (glob patterns) and allows us to work with multiple files at once. Here, we find all the `.c` files. This `FileList` acts much like an array:

```
FileList["*.c"]
```

Therefore, we could use `each` to set our file actions; we do so in the following code fragment. (And note that the dependencies are not specified here; Rake is smart enough to combine the dependencies and actions internally if we specify the dependencies elsewhere.)

```
FileList["*.c"].each do |src|
  obj = src.sub(/.c$/,".o")
  file(obj) { sh "cc -c -o #{obj} #{src}" }
end
```

However, it's simpler to use rules, which are another Rake feature (naturally lifted from make):

```
rule '.o' => '.c' do |target|
  sh "cc -c -o #{target.name} #{target.source}"
end
```

A small bit of magic happens here. The `source` attribute gets set internally, and automatically replaces the file extension from the hash key with the extension from the hash value (changing `.o` to `.c`, in this case).

Now let's do a little more magic. If we require the `rake/clean` library, the constants `CLEAN` and `CLOBBER` (initially empty) and tasks `:clean` and `:clobber` are defined for us. These are traditionally named targets; `clean` will remove any temporary files, and `clobber` will remove all these and the final results as well.

These array-like constants have an `include` method that takes a file glob. This is like an implicit use of `FileList`.

Therefore, our Rakefile now looks like this:

```
require 'rake/clean'

CLEAN.include("*.o")
CLOBBER.include("myprog")

SRC = FileList['*.c']
OBJ = SRC.ext('o')

rule '.o' => '.c' do |t|
  sh "cc -c -o #{t.name} #{t.source}"
end

file "hello" => OBJ do
  sh "cc -o hello #{OBJ}"
end

file "myprog.o" => ["myprog.c"]
file "sub1.o" => ["sub1.c", "sub1.h"]
file "sub2.o" => ["sub2.c", "sub2.h"]

task :default => ["myprog"]
```

Notice how we don't have to specify "clean" and "clobber" tasks explicitly. Also note that a "clobber" implicitly includes a "clean" operation. Finally, note that we specified a default task for the convenience of the person running the Rakefile; it's now unnecessary to specify a task in order to compile.

Rake has several useful command-line options. Sometimes you want to test a Rakefile without actually doing any (potentially dangerous) operations; the -n and --dry-run options will allow this. The -T option will list all the targets in a Rakefile. There are also options controlling library path searching, tracing and logging, and more.

Rake is more complex than I've hinted at here (especially the rules). The popular deployment tool Capistrano is based on Rake. In addition, most Rubygems use Rake to some extent to help automate repetitive tasks. Read the Rake documentation (available at rdoc.info or ruby-doc.org) for more details, and search online for posts and tutorials about how to accomplish specific tasks you are interested in.

21.2   Using `irb`

The `irb` utility (interactive Ruby) has been distributed with Ruby for many years. It can be thought of as a "testbed" or "playground" where you try out quick hacks and new ideas.

Basic usage of `irb` is simple. When you start it, you get a prompt where you can type Ruby expressions; each expression is evaluated, and the result is printed for you. Here's a small example of a session:

```
$ irb
irb(main):001:0> "cell" + "o"
=> "cello"
irb(main):002:0> 3*79
=> 237
irb(main):003:0> Dir.entries(".").size
=> 17
irb(main):004:0> rand
=> 0.850757389880155
irb(main):005:0> rand
=> 0.679879756672551
irb(main):006:0> defined? foo
=> nil
irb(main):007:0> defined? Object
=> "constant"
irb(main):008:0> quit
$
```

Of course, it's more than just a calculator. You can type in arbitrary Ruby code if you want:

```
[hal@localhost ch21]$ irb
irb(main):001:0> require 'mathn'
=> true
irb(main):002:0> gen = Prime.instance
=> #<Prime:0x000001019e62e8>
```

The -r option will do a require so that you can include code from a file. Suppose we have the following source file:

```
# File: foo.rb
class MyClass

  attr_accessor :alpha, :beta

  def initialize(a, b)
    @alpha, @beta = a, b
  end

end

obj1 = MyClass.new(23,34)
obj2 = MyClass.new("abc","xyz")
```

Then we can do this:

```
$ irb -rfoo
irb(main):001:0> obj = MyClass.new(88,99)
=> #<MyClass:0x00000102830c90 @a=88, @b=89>
```

But notice that although we can get at the contents of the file (for example, the constant MyClass), that doesn't include the local variables. The local variables for a file are accessible only within that file; a require (inside or outside irb) won't allow you to see them.

Newbies are sometimes confused by output printed in irb:

```
$ irb -rfoo
irb(main):001:0> puts "hello"
hello
=> nil
```

What is the `nil` doing there? It is the return value from the `puts` method, dutifully printed out by `irb` once the method has run.

Be aware that `irb` is highly customizable. When you start it up, it reads whatever initialization data it finds first, looking for an existing file from this list, in order:

- `~/.irbrc`

- `.irbrc`

- `irb.rc`

- `_irbrc`

The initialization file is pure Ruby. It enables customization of prompts and much more. For a complete discussion of this file, the best source is *Programming Ruby* by Dave Thomas and Andy Hunt (also called "the pickaxe book" after the cover illustration). This section will only mention a few highlights.

If your Ruby installation is built with GNU readline support (as is usually the case), you can use the up and down arrow keys to navigate back and forth in the command history. More importantly, you can get Ruby tab completion. This works in a predictable way: When you type a partial identifier and then press the Tab key, `irb` tries to complete the rest of the identifier name for you.

To enable tab completion, add this fragment to your `.irbrc` file:

```
IRB.conf[:AUTO_INDENT] = true
IRB.conf[:USE_READLINE] = true
IRB.conf[:LOAD_MODULES] ||= []
IRB.conf[:LOAD_MODULES] |= ['irb/completion']
```

Bear in mind it's possible to put arbitrary code in your `.irbrc` file. For example, here is a method I find useful sometimes. It is named `sm` for brevity ("show methods"); its purpose is to list (in alphabetical order) all the methods that can be called on an object, excluding the ones it gets from its ancestors:

```
def sm(obj)
  list = obj.methods
  anc = obj.class.ancestors - [obj.class]
  anc.each {|a| list -= a.instance_methods }
  list.sort
end
```

The following is an example of its usage:

```
irb(main):001:0> str = "hello"
=> "hello"
irb(main):002:0> sm str
=> [:%, :*, :+, :<<, :[], :[]=, :ascii_only?, :b, :bytes,
    :bytesize, :byteslice, :capitalize, :capitalize!, :casecmp,
    :center, :chars, :chomp, :chomp!, :chop, :chop!, :chr, :clear,
    :codepoints, :concat, :count, :crypt, :delete, :delete!,
    :downcase, :downcase!, :dump, :each_byte, :each_char,
    :each_codepoint, :each_line, :empty?, :encode, :encode!,
    :encoding, :end_with?, :force_encoding, :getbyte, :gsub,
    :gsub!, :hex, :include?, :index, :insert, :intern, :length,
    :lines, :ljust, :lstrip, :lstrip!, :match, :next, :next!, :oct,
    :ord, :partition, :prepend, :replace, :reverse, :reverse!,
    :rindex, :rjust, :rpartition, :rstrip, :rstrip!, :scan, :scrub,
    :scrub!, :setbyte, :size, :slice, :slice!, :split, :squeeze,
    :squeeze!, :start_with?, :strip, :strip!, :sub, :sub!, :succ,
    :succ!, :sum, :swapcase, :swapcase!, :to_c, :to_f, :to_i,
    :to_r, :to_str, :to_sym, :tr, :tr!, :tr_s, :tr_s!, :unpack,
    :upcase, :upcase!, :upto, :valid_encoding?]
irb(main):003:0> sm String
=> [:allocate, :new, :superclass, :try_convert]
irb(main):004:0> sm 123
=> [:&, :*, :**, :+, :-, :/, :<<, :>>, :[], :^, :bit_length, :size,
    :to_f, :|, :~]
```

It's not seen much, but irb makes it possible to run subsessions within a session. It's possible to run multiple sessions and switch back and forth between them; each one maintains a separate binding.

That may not necessarily seem useful, but one trick that makes it more useful is to specify an object along with the irb subcommand. Then the context of the subsession is that object; self is set as you would expect, the scope is that of the object, and so on:

```
$ irb
irb(main):001:0> t0 = Time.now
=> 2014-08-29 19:01:42 -0700
irb(main):002:0> irb t0
irb#1(2014-08-29 19:01:42 -0700):001:0> strftime("%a %b %c")
=> "Fri Aug Fri Aug 29 19:01:42 2014"
irb#1(2014-08-29 19:01:42 -0700):002:0> to_i
```

```
=> 1409364102
irb#1(2014-08-29 19:01:42 -0700):003:0> self + 1000
=> 2014-08-29 19:18:22 -0700
irb#1(2014-08-29 19:01:42 -0700):004:0> wday
=> 5
irb#1(2014-08-29 19:01:42 -0700):005:0> class
SyntaxError: (irb#1):5: syntax error, unexpected end-of-input

irb#1(2014-08-29 19:01:42 -0700):006:0> self.class
=> Time
irb#1(2014-08-29 19:01:42 -0700):007:0> quit
=> #<IRB::Irb: @context=#<IRB::Context:0x007ff9430437d0>,
  @signal_status=:IN_EVAL, @scanner=#<RubyLex:0x007ff94303b238>>
irb(main):003:0> quit
$
```

Another library that can be helpful for examining the results of Ruby code is the
xmpfilter, which is part of the rcodetools gem. It takes Ruby statements, evaluates them, and places the return value in comments.

There is another "goodie" associated with irb that you might like to know about.
Naturally irb is capable of analyzing Ruby code; the lexer is easily used by other applications as well. Here is a simple example of a program that opens its own file to analyze itself; it produces a sorted list of all identifiers and constants used in the program:

```
require 'irb/ruby-lex'

file = File.new(__FILE__)

parse = RubyLex.new # (file)
parse.set_input(file)

idents = []

loop do
  token =  parse.token
  break if token.nil?
  if token.is_a? RubyToken::TkIDENTIFIER or
     token.is_a? RubyToken::TkCONSTANT
    idents << token.name
  end
end
```

```
p idents.uniq.sort

# Output:
# ["File", "RubyLex", "RubyToken", "TkCONSTANT", "TkIDENTIFIER",
#  "file", "idents", "loop", "name", "new", "p", "parse",
#  "require", "set_input", "sort", "token", "uniq"]
```

So far as I am aware, this is not documented anywhere in English. But if you need a Ruby lexer, you can probably read the source and adapt this one for your needs.

21.3 The Basics of pry

The pry tool is not a standard part of Ruby, but it has gained great popularity. You can think of it as an "enhanced irb" if you like.

Its use as a debugging tool is covered in Chapter 16. Here, we'll look a little further, at ways that pry can assist with interactive development.

Because pry is a complex and powerful tool, we can only scratch the surface here. As always, consult the documentation for additional detail.

Keyboard input in pry is fairly flexible. You can, of course, use the cursor keys to scroll through the command history, but there are also various commands that allow you to view and edit the input buffer in ways that irb does not support.

Some of the relevant commands are shown here:

```
show-input             Display the entire input buffer
amend-line n newtext   Replace line n with newtext
!                      Break out of read loop and empty input buffer
hist —tail k           Show line k of the history
hist —replay m..n      Replay lines m through n of the history
edit                   Open the input buffer in an external editor
```

The edit command can also be used to edit a class, method, or even just the file containing the code that is currently executing (with edit -c). When the editor is closed, pry will reload the edited file, overwriting existing class and method definitions with new ones from the file.

As in irb, you can use an underscore (_) to retrieve the value of the last expression evaluated. To evaluate an expression without displaying this value, you can end an expression with an ampersand; this is useful, for example, when you evaluate an expression with a very lengthy result. Finally, the input and output are stored, respectively, in "variables" called _in_ and _out_:

```
_                       Value of last expression evaluated
expr;                   Evaluate expr, but do not print its value
_in_                    Console input
_out_                   Console output
```

To send a command to the operating system, you can preface it with a dot. You can also interpolate Ruby code as needed:

```
.ps aux                 Run the command "ps aux"
.ps aux | grep #{prog}  Run ps aux and grep for (the value of) prog
```

There is also a shell-mode feature. This basically adds the current directory to the pry prompt and enables (some) filename completion.

The show-source command is for viewing source code, including the source of pry itself, of C extensions, and so on. There are options to modify its behavior.

The show-doc command displays documentation. It can give information on classes, methods, parts of the Ruby core, and so on. Related commands are stat and ri (which invokes the ri tool, examined in the next section).

Finally, the help command displays information on pry features and usage. Other than online references and tutorials, this is your best source of knowledge for this powerful tool.

21.4 The ri Utility

The ri tool is named from "Ruby index" or some such mnemonic. It is a command-line documentation tool, offering information on Ruby classes, methods, modules, and so on. Here is an example:

```
(from ruby core)
Implementation from Enumerator
  e.with_index(offset = 0) {|(*args), idx| ... }
  e.with_index(offset = 0)


Iterates the given block for each element with an index, which
starts from offset. If no block is given, returns a new Enumerator
that includes the index, starting from offset

offset
  the starting index to use
```

By default, installing gems with Rubygems will also generate `ri` format documentation, making it available via the `ri` command.

21.5 Editor Support

Any modern editor should be programmer friendly. With memories of the twentieth century growing dim, we take it for granted that our editors will reconfigure themselves based on the kind of file we are editing. We expect syntax highlighting, auto-indent, and other such features as a matter of course.

The Ruby coder will not be disappointed by the tools and features out there. Many of these are now standard with an editor's distribution; others are not. Let's take a quick look at what's available.

Two excellent graphical text editors are SublimeText 3 ($30, available for Windows, Mac OS X, and Linux), and TextMate 2 (free, Mac OS X only). Both have good Ruby support and can be extended with additional commands and text snippets to increase coding efficiency. TextMate's popularity has decreased in recent years, largely due to several years without a release between version 1 and 2, but is still quite popular. SublimeText has a significant following and continues to gain in popularity.

A third is RubyMine, which is based on Java's Eclipse IDE. Developers coming from Ruby to Java may find it more familiar than other options. This is not just an editor but an IDE in itself—arguably the best (and last surviving) of the IDEs. It is a commercial product, but it is worth having if you want powerful editing features as well as integration with tools and documentation.

Although graphical editors have gained popularity in recent decades, the most common editors in the programmers' world are still Vim and Emacs. Let's look at these briefly.

21.5.1 Vim

Vim users are provided Ruby features by the plug-in named `vim-ruby`. This set of config files offers syntax highlighting, auto-indent, and code completion. It also enables such things as invoking the Ruby interpreter from within the editor (compiler plug-ins).

`vim-ruby` is included in most Vim distributions starting with version 7. However, you may find that these features are disabled (probably for backward compatibility). Turn them on by adding the following to your `.vimrc` file:

```
set nocompatible
syntax on
filetype on
filetype indent on
filetype plugin on
```

In addition, several excellent Vim plug-ins written by Tim Pope are probably worth installing. They can be found on his GitHub profile at https://github.com/ tpope:

- **pathogen**—A Vim plug-in manager.

- **unimpaired**—Handy bracket mappings.

- **surround**—Used to manage parentheses, quotes, XML tags, and more.

- **fugitive**—Git integration for Vim.

- **rails**—Better Rails file navigation and syntax highlighting.

- **dispatch**—A build and test dispatcher.

If you are using Vim to edit Ruby code, I recommend familiarizing yourself with these and other Ruby plug-ins.

Arguably there are many reasons to dislike Vim; one of the greatest reasons is surely vimscript. The good news is it's possible to script Vim's behavior using Ruby. The bad news is this is not well documented. If you want to learn about this, I recommend using `:help ruby` in Vim as a starting point. You can also look at `VimRubyInterface` for more information. Finally, do a search of http://vim.org to see what recent information you can find.

21.5.2   Emacs

The other most popular editor in the world is Emacs. Actually, to call it an editor is a bit misleading; it is more like a miniature operating system that happens to do text editing on the side. One of the great advantages of Emacs is that it is highly extensible; the user can program its behavior in a Lisp variant called elisp. The elisp language is more powerful than vimscript; however, it is just as difficult to read (but in a different way).

Emacs has shipped with built-in Ruby support, in the form of Ruby Mode, since version 23. Newer versions of Ruby Mode are included with Ruby itself. I am not an Emacs user—though I have great respect for those who are—and therefore cannot comment further. For more, see the Emacs Wiki or search the Web for "emacs ruby."

21.6 Ruby Version Managers

In recent years, more tools have been developed to help us install Ruby versions and switch between them. Gem management also falls into this realm because gem versions may change as Ruby versions do (and even more often).

The Ruby Version Manager (rvm) has been a valuable tool in our toolbox since 2010 or earlier. This tool, along with Bundler, has been my habitual choice. But we'll also look briefly at rbenv and chruby as well.

21.6.1 Using rvm

The first version manager is simply named Ruby Version Manager, or RVM. It provides tools to install multiple versions of Ruby, switch between versions, and change the default Ruby version for a machine or just a single project. You can learn more how to install and use it at http://rvm.io.

The first thing to understand about rvm is that it does *not* interact with the "system Ruby installation" at all. It only manages versions that it installs itself.

Here are some common commands:

```
rvm install ruby-2.0.0     Install/compile Ruby 2.0.0 and manage it
rvm uninstall ruby-1.9.2   Uninstall the 1.9.2 version
rvm use ruby-1.9.4         Switch the "current" Ruby to 1.9.4
rvm use system            Switch to the (non-managed) system Ruby
rvm list                  Show a list of all Ruby installations
rvm current               Show current Ruby environment information
```

Note that rvm has the concept of a *gemset*, which is a grouping of related gems relevant to the current project or environment. Much of this functionality is arguably handled as well or better by Bundler, which is described later in this chapter.

The "usual" Ruby (MRI, "Matz's Ruby Interpreter") is the default. Other Ruby interpreters are supported, including JRuby, Rubinius, REE, and MacRuby. For more information, visit the RVM website (http://rvm.io).

RVM's approach is all-encompassing, and it makes changes to the way your shell, Rubygems, and Bundler work. Many argue it is overly complex, error prone, and intrusive in the OS environment. Simpler alternatives have been created. The most popular of those alternatives are rbenv and chruby. We'll take a look at them now.

21.6.2   Using rbenv

The rbenv tool provides support for using multiple Ruby versions. Its philosophy is "Do one thing, do it simply, do it well." Therefore, it does not handle Ruby installation, has no gemset management features, and is not particularly shell sensitive.

Those who use rbenv often use ruby-build for installation. Likewise, they may use bundler for gem management. These tools work essentially independently of each other.

rbenv determines which Ruby interpreter to use by checking these three sources: the RBENV_VERSION environment variable, a local .ruby-version file, and the global ~/.rbenv/version file. The .ruby-version file may be in a directory relative to the application itself or relative to the current directory.

If you have ruby-build on your system, then rbenv install will invoke it in order to install a Ruby version. These are separate packages that work together.

Here are some other rbenv commands:

```
rbenv versions            List all Ruby versions
rbenv local ruby-2.0.0    Set the Ruby version for this directory
rbenv global ruby-1.8.7   Set the global Ruby version
rbenv shell jruby-1.7.1   Set the shell-specific Ruby version
rbenv rehash              Run after installing gems or rubies
                          to enable their commands
rbenv which rake          Display the full path to a command
rbenv whence rackup       List all rubies having the given command
```

Note that the shell-specific version overrides the directory-specific local version, and both of these override the global version. When the global or local version is set, rbenv writes the version to a local or global dot file. When a shell-specific version is set, rbenv sets an environment variable.

The rehash command serves to "refresh" the shell's knowledge of installed Ruby versions and installed gems. Use it any time you install a new version of Ruby or a new Rubygem via gem install.

Note that rbenv is incompatible with rvm. If you have rvm installed, you will have to uninstall it before using rbenv.

21.6.3 Using chruby

The most minimal of all the version management tools is chruby. At the time of this writing, the "guts" of the tool comprise fewer than 100 lines of bash code. It can install Ruby versions using either the ruby-install tool (by the same author) or the ruby-build tool (by the author of rbenv).

Chruby may be installed directly from GitHub, or via a tool such as homebrew or rpm. Refer to the chruby repository on GitHub for detailed setup instructions.

Its general behavior is mostly simple and strives to be intuitive. It sets environment variables including PATH, GEM_HOME, GEM_PATH, and RUBY_ROOT. It defaults to the system Ruby, and it supports fuzzy matching of version names. It can optionally support automatic switching of the active Ruby version via the .ruby-version files that are also respected by rvm and rbenv.

The chruby tool does not overwrite the cd command with a shell function (as rvm does), and it does not replace the ruby command and all gem commands with shell script shims (as rbenv does). It also doesn't require write access to your Ruby installation in order to install gems, and it doesn't require that Ruby versions be installed into your home directory.

Chruby usage is as follows:

```
chruby                       List all installed Ruby versions
chruby 2.1.0                 Switch to Ruby 2.1.0
chruby system                Switch to the system Ruby
```

chruby understands both bash and zsh. It permits migration from rvm or rbenv via the RUBIES variable. It also offers some support for interaction with tools such as capistrano, chef, puppet, and others.

For more information, refer to the chruby documentation online. The chruby repository on GitHub (github.com/postmodern/chruby) contains a readme and wiki that serve as a good starting point.

21.7 Conclusion

We've seen several tools in this chapter that make life easier for the Ruby developer. Common tools are `irb`, `rvm`, and others. We've also looked at editor and IDE support for Ruby.

However, the most important tool of all is not a piece of software. It is "peopleware"—the Ruby community itself. I urge you to seek out groups both online and offline, whether on the Web via Google and Stack Overflow, on IRC (especially on Freenode), or at a Ruby conference (whether international or local). We'll all be there to help you.

CHAPTER 22
The Ruby Community

He who is unable to live in society, or who has no need because he is sufficient for himself, must be either a beast or a god.

—*Aristotle,* Politics

It has been said that one of the best things about Ruby is its community. That's a matter of opinion, of course, and you'll have to judge for yourself. My purpose in this brief chapter is to bring a few of the "watering holes" to your attention—news and learning sources, forums both online and off, and places where Rubyists meet in cyberspace and in real life.

This chapter is intentionally short. Much of the information here is stable, but things will always be in flux. Obviously, when you are in doubt, do a web search.

22.1 Web Resources

The main Ruby site is `ruby-lang.org`, and the latest version of Ruby, as well as news about Ruby releases, can always be found there.

For documentation, don't miss `ruby-doc.org`, maintained by James Britt. It hosts a wealth of RDoc API output for Ruby's core and standard libraries. The site `rdoc.info` provides Yard API documentation not only for Ruby itself, but also for every gem and any Ruby repository on GitHub.

The straightforwardly named site `iwanttolearnruby.com`, created by Amanda Wagener, provides an extensive list of Ruby resources, and it's sortable by type or level of resource. It should be useful to a Ruby developer at any level of expertise.

Many other Ruby resources also exist at various places on the Web and can be found with a search for Ruby books, tutorials, articles, and the like.

22.2   Mailing Lists, Podcasts, and Forums

The `ruby-talk` mailing list is probably the oldest English-language forum for Ruby programmers. The history of the list is searchable online at ruby-talk.org (along with some other related lists such as ruby-core and ruby-math).

The Ruby Weekly mailing list (`rubyweekly.com`) offers one email per week summarizing interesting posts, videos, events, and job offers in the Ruby community.

Ruby Rogues (`rubyrogues.com`) is a long-running weekly podcast with regular panelists and special guests. Each episode is offered as an audio recording or as a transcript posted to their website, and their archives cover many topics of interest to Rubyists over the last few years.

In addition, Ruby Rogues runs a popular and helpful forum called Parley. It costs $10 per year to participate, but that fee seems to ensure that participants are truly interested, and the quality of discussions is usually quite high.

22.3   Ruby Bug Reports and Feature Requests

Ruby continues to evolve. Part of its beauty is that it changes slowly and deliberately.

However, Ruby is definitely not perfect. In order to collect feedback, feature requests, and bug reports, the Ruby core team uses a public issue tracker at bugs.ruby-lang.org, using the open-source issue-tracking system Redmine (which is written in Ruby, naturally).

Before creating a new issue, first make sure that one like it does not exist. Ruby is used by so many people around the world that chances are high your issue has already been reported, and may even be fixed already. Then, if your issue is a new one, read the bug-reporting guide located at bugs.ruby-lang.org/projects/ruby/wiki/ HowToReport.

No one can guarantee that your bug will be fixed or your feature request will be accepted. Most of the developers on the Ruby core team donate their time, and decisions about features ultimately rest in Matz's capable hands. But the more homework you do in advance, the better chance you have of being taken seriously. The ruby-talk mailing list may also be a good place to get feedback on issues or ideas that you have.

22.4 IRC Channels

At any given time of day, chances are that dozens of Rubyists are talking or lurking in IRC (Internet Relay Chat). The servers are owned by freenode.net—visit them on the Web to find the right one for you. A web search will also find a good IRC client for you, whatever your platform may be.

The `#ruby-lang` and `#ruby-on-rails` channels have fairly heavy traffic. It is an international forum, so you may find people there at all hours. The de facto international language is English, but you may find people there who can direct you to channels in your own language.

Observe all normal IRC etiquette. In particular, do not "flood" by pasting sections of code; one or two lines is about the maximum. Instead, use a pasting service such as `gist.github.com` or something similar.

22.5 Ruby Conferences

The first International Ruby Conference (RubyConf) was held in Florida in 2001, and it has rotated cities every year. To see when and where the next RubyConf will be, visit rubyconf.org. Usually Matz himself attends, along with a few other Japanese Rubyists; we have also had attendees from six of the seven continents. (If you work at an Antarctic research station, please feel free to take time off for the next conference.)

Ruby Central (rubycentral.com), the U.S.-based non-profit organization that organizes RubyConf, has also organized the somewhat larger yearly RailsConf since the first one was held in Chicago in 2006. You can visit railsconf.org to find information about the next conference, apply to give a talk, and register online.

Regional and national conferences are held in many other locations around the world. The European Ruby Conference (EuRuKo) was first held in Karlsruhe, Germany in 2003. It is usually a little smaller in terms of attendance, but if you are in Europe, it may be more convenient for you. In 2013, I (Hal) spoke at RubyConf Brasil in Sao Paulo, and found it to be a high-energy event with hundreds of attendees. Tokyo, Japan hosts a national RubyKaigi conference each year, and I (André) spoke there in 2014.

The popularity of Ruby has spawned talks at OOPSLA and OSCON, among others. Expect more of this in the future.

The popularity of the web framework "Ruby on Rails" has led to conferences devoted to Rails, and others are forthcoming. Go to railsconf.org for current information.

In April 2006, the Silicon Valley Ruby Conference in Santa Clara was the first regional Ruby conference in the United States, and there have been many more regional conferences since. The Lone Star Ruby Conference in Austin, Texas, has been held since 2007. Some other popular regional conferences include Madison+Ruby (madisonpl.us/ruby), Gotham RubyConf (goruco.com), Golden Gate RubyConf (gogaruco.com), and MountainWest RubyConf (mtnwestrubyconf.org), but there are many others.

22.6   Local Ruby Groups

Numerous users' groups are springing up all over the United States and the rest of the world. These are typically named with a label such as Cityname.rb, which resembles a Ruby program's filename (with the .rb also standing for Ruby Brigade). Some are informal; others are more structured. Among the larger, more active groups are the ones in Seattle, Washington; Austin, Texas; Asakusa, Tokyo, Japan; Amsterdam, The Netherlands; and New York City. Many groups organize meetings via meetup.com, so check there, or simply do an Internet search to find an active group in your area.

22.7   Conclusion

You have now reached the end of this sizable volume. Contrary to my expectations, readers have told me that they did in fact read the first edition cover to cover; some have also told me that they learned Ruby from this book (though I spent very little time teaching the basics).

It doesn't matter to me whether you have read this whole book sequentially or have just stumbled across this paragraph. In any case, you've reached the end, and I congratulate you.

However, we don't really learn programming from books. We learn it by applying what we learn in those books. Therefore, I urge you to do what programmers do: Go and program. That's the real learning experience. And when you can't learn from experience or from books, turn to the rest of the community. You will find people there who can help you (and people you can help).

Who is a member of the "Ruby community"? Well, if you are reading this, you probably are a member yourself. On behalf of the others, I welcome you and encourage your participation.

Index